Algorithms

THIRD EDITION

in C++

PART 5

GRAPH ALGORITHMS

Robert Sedgewick

Princeton University

Addison-Wesley

Boston • San Francisco • New York • Toronto • Montreal
London • Munich • Paris • Madrid
Capetown • Sydney • Tokyo • Singapore • Mexico City

Many of the designations used by manufacturers and sellers to distinguish their products are claimed as trademarks. Where those designations appear in this book and Addison-Wesley was aware of a trademark claim, the designations have been printed in initial capital letters or all capitals.

The author and publisher have taken care in the preparation of this book, but make no expressed or implied warranty of any kind and assume no responsibility for errors or omissions. No liability is assumed for incidental or consequential damages in connection with or arising out of the use of the information or programs contained herein.

The publisher offers discounts on this book when ordered in quantity for special sales. For more information, please contact: Pearson Education Corporate Sales Division, 201 W. 103rd Street, Indianapolis, IN 46290, (800) 428-5331, corpsales@pearsontechgroup.com.

Visit AW on the Web at www.awl.com/cseng/ .

Library of Congress Cataloging-in-Publication Data

Sedgewick, Robert, 1946 –
    Algorithms in C++ / Robert Sedgewick. — 3d ed.
       p.   cm.
    Includes bibliographical references and index.
    Contents: v. 2, pt. 5. Graph algorithms
    1. C++ (Computer program language) 2. Computer algorithms.
      I. Title.
  QA76.73.C15S38   2002
  005.13'3—dc20   92-901
                                        CIP

ISBN 0-201-36118-3

Text printed on recycled paper
1 2 3 4 5 6 7 8 9 10 – **CRS** – 0504030201
First printing, December 2001

Preface

G RAPHS AND GRAPH algorithms are pervasive in modern computing applications. This book describes the most important known methods for solving the graph-processing problems that arise in practice. Its primary aim is to make these methods and the basic principles behind them accessible to the growing number of people in need of knowing them. The material is developed from first principles, starting with basic information and working through classical methods up through modern techniques that are still under development. Carefully chosen examples, detailed figures, and complete implementations supplement thorough descriptions of algorithms and applications.

Algorithms

This book is the second of three volumes that are intended to survey the most important computer algorithms in use today. The first volume (Parts 1–4) covers fundamental concepts (Part 1), data structures (Part 2), sorting algorithms (Part 3), and searching algorithms (Part 4); this volume (Part 5) covers graphs and graph algorithms; and the (yet to be published) third volume (Parts 6–8) covers strings (Part 6), computational geometry (Part 7), and advanced algorithms and applications (Part 8).

The books are useful as texts early in the computer science curriculum, after students have acquired basic programming skills and familiarity with computer systems, but before they have taken specialized courses in advanced areas of computer science or computer applications. The books also are useful for self-study or as a reference for people engaged in the development of computer systems or applications programs because they contain implementations of useful algorithms and detailed information on these algorithms' performance characteristics. The broad perspective taken makes the series an appropriate introduction to the field.

Together the three volumes comprise the *Third Edition* of a book that has been widely used by students and programmers around the world for many years. I have completely rewritten the text for this edition, and I have added thousands of new exercises, hundreds of new figures, dozens of new programs, and detailed commentary on all the figures and programs. This new material provides both coverage of new topics and fuller explanations of many of the classic algorithms. A new emphasis on abstract data types throughout the books makes the programs more broadly useful and relevant in modern object-oriented programming environments. People who have read previous editions will find a wealth of new information throughout; all readers will find a wealth of pedagogical material that provides effective access to essential concepts.

These books are not just for programmers and computer science students. Everyone who uses a computer wants it to run faster or to solve larger problems. The algorithms that we consider represent a body of knowledge developed during the last 50 years that is the basis for the efficient use of the computer for a broad variety of applications. From N-body simulation problems in physics to genetic-sequencing problems in molecular biology, the basic methods described here have become essential in scientific research; and from database systems to Internet search engines, they have become essential parts of modern software systems. As the scope of computer applications becomes more widespread, so grows the impact of basic algorithms, particularly the fundamental graph algorithms covered in this volume. The goal of this book is to serve as a resource so that students and professionals can know and make intelligent use of graph algorithms as the need arises in whatever computer application they might undertake.

Scope

This book, *Algorithms in C++, Third Edition, Part 5: Graph Algorithms*, contains six chapters that cover graph properties and types, graph search, directed graphs, minimal spanning trees, shortest paths, and networks. The descriptions here are intended to give readers an understanding of the basic properties of as broad a range of fundamental graph algorithms as possible.

You will most appreciate the material here if you have had a course covering basic principles of algorithm design and analysis and programming experience in a high-level language such as C++, Java, or C. *Algorithms in C++, Third Edition, Parts 1–4* is certainly adequate preparation. This volume assumes basic knowledge about arrays, linked lists, and ADT design, and makes use of priority-queue, symbol-table, and union-find ADTs—all of which are described in detail in Parts 1–4 (and in many other introductory texts on algorithms and data structures).

Basic properties of graphs and graph algorithms are developed from first principles, but full understanding often can lead to deep and difficult mathematics. Although the discussion of advanced mathematical concepts is brief, general, and descriptive, you certainly need a higher level of mathematical maturity to appreciate graph algorithms than you do for the topics in Parts 1–4. Still, readers at various levels of mathematical maturity will be able to profit from this book. The topic dictates this approach: some elementary graph algorithms that should be understood and used by everyone differ only slightly from some advanced algorithms that are not understood by anyone. The primary intent here is to place important algorithms in context with other methods throughout the book, not to teach all of the mathematical material. But the rigorous treatment demanded by good mathematics often leads us to good programs, so I have tried to provide a balance between the formal treatment favored by theoreticians and the coverage needed by practitioners, without sacrificing rigor.

Use in the Curriculum

There is a great deal of flexibility in how the material here can be taught, depending on the taste of the instructor and the preparation of the students. The algorithms described have found widespread use for years, and represent an essential body of knowledge for both the practicing programmer and the computer science student. There is sufficient coverage of basic material for the book to be used in a course on data structures and algorithms, and there is sufficient detail and coverage of advanced material for the book to be used for a course on graph algorithms. Some instructors may wish to emphasize implementations and practical concerns; others may wish to emphasize analysis and theoretical concepts.

For a more comprehensive course, this book is also available in a special bundle with Parts 1–4; thereby instructors can cover fundamentals, data structures, sorting, searching, and graph algorithms in one consistent style. A set of slide masters for use in lectures, sample programming assignments, interactive exercises for students, and other course materials may be found by accessing the book's home page.

The exercises—nearly all of which are new to this edition—fall into several types. Some are intended to test understanding of material in the text, and simply ask readers to work through an example or to apply concepts described in the text. Others involve implementing and putting together the algorithms, or running empirical studies to compare variants of the algorithms and to learn their properties. Still other exercises are a repository for important information at a level of detail that is not appropriate for the text. Reading and thinking about the exercises will pay dividends for every reader.

Algorithms of Practical Use

Anyone wanting to use a computer more effectively can use this book for reference or for self-study. People with programming experience can find information on specific topics throughout the book. To a large extent, you can read the individual chapters in the book independently of the others, although, in some cases, algorithms in one chapter make use of methods from a previous chapter.

The orientation of the book is to study algorithms likely to be of practical use. The book provides information about the tools of the trade to the point that readers can confidently implement, debug, and put to work algorithms to solve a problem or to provide functionality in an application. Full implementations of the methods discussed are included, as are descriptions of the operations of these programs on a consistent set of examples. Because we work with real code, rather than write pseudo-code, the programs can be put to practical use quickly. Program listings are available from the book's home page.

Indeed, one practical application of the algorithms has been to produce the hundreds of figures throughout the book. Many algorithms are brought to light on an intuitive level through the visual dimension provided by these figures.

Characteristics of the algorithms and of the situations in which they might be useful are discussed in detail. Connections to the analysis of algorithms and theoretical computer science are developed in context. When appropriate, empirical and analytic results are presented to illustrate why certain algorithms are preferred. When interesting, the relationship of the practical algorithms being discussed to purely theoretical results is described. Specific information on performance characteristics of algorithms and implementations is synthesized, encapsulated, and discussed throughout the book.

Programming Language

The programming language used for all of the implementations is C++. The programs use a wide range of standard C++ idioms, and the text includes concise descriptions of each construct.

Chris Van Wyk and I developed a style of C++ programming based on classes, templates, and overloaded operators that we feel is an effective way to present the algorithms and data structures as real programs. We have striven for elegant, compact, efficient, and portable implementations. The style is consistent whenever possible, so that programs that are similar look similar.

A goal of this book is to present the algorithms in as simple and direct a form as possible. For many of the algorithms, the similarities remain regardless of which language is used: Dijkstra's algorithm (to pick one prominent example) is Dijkstra's algorithm, whether expressed in Algol-60, Basic, Fortran, Smalltalk, Ada, Pascal, C, C++, Modula-3, PostScript, Java, or any of the countless other programming languages and environments in which it has proved to be an effective graph-processing method. On the one hand, our code is informed by experience with implementing algorithms in these and numerous other languages (a C version of this book is also available, and a Java version will appear soon); on the other hand, some of the properties of some of these languages are informed by their designers' experience with some of the algorithms and data structures that we consider in this book. In the end, we feel that the code presented in the book both precisely defines the algorithms and is useful in practice.

Acknowledgments

Many people gave me helpful feedback on earlier versions of this book. In particular, thousands of students at Princeton and Brown have suffered through preliminary drafts over the years. Special thanks are due to Trina Avery and Tom Freeman for their help in producing the first edition; to Janet Incerpi for her creativity and ingenuity in persuading our early and primitive digital computerized typesetting hardware and software to produce the first edition; to Marc Brown for his part in the algorithm visualization research that was the genesis of the figures in the book; to Dave Hanson and Andrew Appel for their willingness to answer my questions about programming languages; and to Kevin Wayne, for patiently answering my basic questions about networks. Kevin urged me to include the network simplex algorithm in this book, but I was not persuaded that it would be possible to do so until I saw a presentation by Ulrich Lauther at Dagstuhl of the ideas on which the implementations in Chapter 22 are based. I would also like to thank the many readers who have provided me with detailed comments about various editions, including Guy Almes, Jon Bentley, Marc Brown, Jay Gischer, Allan Heydon, Kennedy Lemke, Udi Manber, Dana Richards, John Reif, M. Rosenfeld, Stephen Seidman, Michael Quinn, and William Ward.

To produce this new edition, I have had the pleasure of working with Peter Gordon and Helen Goldstein at Addison-Wesley, who patiently shepherded this project as it has evolved from a standard update to a massive rewrite. It has also been my pleasure to work with several other members of the professional staff at Addison-Wesley. The nature of this project made the book a somewhat unusual challenge for many of them, and I much appreciate their forbearance. In particular, Marilyn Rash did an outstanding job managing the book's production within a very tightly compressed schedule.

I have gained three new mentors in writing this book, and particularly want to express my appreciation to them. First, Steve Summit carefully checked early versions of the manuscript on a technical level, and provided me with literally thousands of detailed comments, particularly on the programs. Steve clearly understood my goal of providing elegant, efficient, and effective implementations, and his comments not only helped me to provide a measure of consistency across the implementations, but also helped me to improve many of them substantially. Second, Lyn Dupré also provided me with thousands of detailed comments on the manuscript, which were invaluable in helping me not only to correct and avoid grammatical errors, but also—more important— to find a consistent and coherent writing style that helps bind together the daunting mass of technical material here. Third, Chris Van Wyk implemented and debugged all my algorithms in C++, answered numerous questions about C++, helped to develop an appropriate C++ programming style, and carefully read the manuscript twice. Chris also patiently stood by as I took apart many of his C++ programs and then, as I learned more and more about C++ from him, had to put them back together much as he had written them. I am extremely grateful for the opportunity to learn from Steve, Lyn, and Chris—their input was vital in the development of this book.

Much of what I have written here I have learned from the teaching and writings of Don Knuth, my advisor at Stanford. Although Don had no direct influence on this work, his presence may be felt in the book, for it was he who put the study of algorithms on the scientific footing that makes a work such as this possible. My friend and colleague Philippe Flajolet, who has been a major force in the development of the analysis of algorithms as a mature research area, has had a similar influence on this work.

I am deeply thankful for the support of Princeton University, Brown University, and the Institut National de Recherce en Informatique et Automatique (INRIA), where I did most of the work on the books; and of the Institute for Defense Analyses and the Xerox Palo Alto Research Center, where I did some work on the books while visiting. Many parts of these books are dependent on research that has been generously supported by the National Science Foundation and the Office of Naval Research. Finally, I thank Bill Bowen, Aaron Lemonick, and Neil Rudenstine for their support in building an academic environment at Princeton in which I was able to prepare this book, despite my numerous other responsibilities.

Robert Sedgewick
Marly-le-Roi, France, 1983
Princeton, New Jersey, 1990
Jamestown, Rhode Island, 2001

C++ Consultant's Preface

Bob Sedgewick and I wrote many versions of most of these programs in our quest to implement graph algorithms in clear and natural programs. Because there are so many kinds of graphs and so many different questions to ask about them, we agreed early on not to pursue a single class scheme that would work across the whole book. Remarkably, we ended up using only two schemes: a simple one in Chapters 17 through 19, where the edges of a graph are either present or absent; and an approach similar to STL containers in Chapters 20 through 22, where more information is associated with edges.

C++ classes offer many advantages for presenting graph algorithms. We use classes to collect useful generic functions on graphs (like input/output). In Chapter 18, we use classes to factor out the operations common to several different graph-search methods. Throughout the book, we use an iterator class on the edges emanating from a vertex so that the programs work no matter how the graph is stored. Most important, we package graph algorithms in classes whose constructor processes the graph and whose member functions give us access to the answers discovered. This organization allows graph algorithms to readily use other graph algorithms as subroutines—see, for example, Program 19.13 (transitive closure via strong components), Program 20.8 (Kruskal's algorithm for minimum spanning tree), Program 21.4 (all shortest paths via Dijkstra's algorithm), Program 21.6 (longest path in a directed acyclic graph). This trend culminates in Chapter 22, where most of the programs are built at a higher level of abstraction, using classes that are defined earlier in the book.

For consistency with *Algorithms in C++, Third Edition, Parts 1–4* our programs rely on the stack and queue classes defined there, and we write explicit pointer operations on singly-linked lists in two low-level implementations. We have adopted two stylistic changes from *Parts 1–4*: Constructors use initialization rather than assignment and we use STL vectors instead of arrays. Here is a summary of the STL vector functions we use in our programs:

- The default constructor creates an empty vector.
- The constructor vec(n) creates a vector of n elements.
- The constructor vec(n, x) creates a vector of n elements each initialized to the value x.

- Member function `vec.assign(n, x)` makes vec a vector of n elements each initialized to the value x.
- Member function `vec.resize(n)` grows or shrinks vec to have capacity n.
- Member function `vec.resize(n, x)` grows or shrinks vec to have capacity n and initializes any new elements to the value x.

The STL also defines the assignment operator, copy constructor, and destructor needed to make vectors first-class objects.

Before I started working on these programs, I had read informal descriptions and pseudocode for many of the algorithms, but had only implemented a few of them. I have found it very instructive to work out the details needed to turn algorithms into working programs, and fun to watch them in action. I hope that reading and running the programs in this book will also help you to understand the algorithms better.

Thanks: to Jon Bentley, Brian Kernighan, and Tom Szymanski, from whom I learned much of what I know about programming; to Debbie Lafferty, who asked whether I would be interested in this project; and to Drew University, Lucent Technologies, and Princeton University, for institutional support.

Christopher Van Wyk
Chatham, New Jersey, 2001

To Adam, Andrew, Brett, Robbie,
and especially Linda

Notes on Exercises

Classifying exercises is an activity fraught with peril, because readers of a book such as this come to the material with various levels of knowledge and experience. Nonetheless, guidance is appropriate, so many of the exercises carry one of four annotations, to help you decide how to approach them.

Exercises that *test your understanding* of the material are marked with an open triangle, as follows:

> ▷ **18.34** Consider the graph
>
> 3-7 1-4 7-8 0-5 5-2 3-8 2-9 0-6 4-9 2-6 6-4.
>
> Draw its DFS tree and use the tree to find the graph's bridges and edge-connected components.

Most often, such exercises relate directly to examples in the text. They should present no special difficulty, but working them might teach you a fact or concept that may have eluded you when you read the text.

Exercises that *add new and thought-provoking* information to the material are marked with an open circle, as follows:

> ○ **19.106** Write a program that counts the number of different possible results of topologically sorting a given DAG.

Such exercises encourage you to think about an important concept that is related to the material in the text, or to answer a question that may have occurred to you when you read the text. You may find it worthwhile to read these exercises, even if you do not have the time to work them through.

Exercises that are intended to *challenge you* are marked with a black dot, as follows:

> ● **20.73** Describe how you would find the MST of a graph so large that only V edges can fit into main memory at once.

Such exercises may require a substantial amount of time to complete, depending on your experience. Generally, the most productive approach is to work on them in a few different sittings.

A few exercises that are *extremely difficult* (by comparison with most others) are marked with two black dots, as follows:

> ●● **20.37** Develop a reasonable generator for random graphs with V vertices and E edges such that the running time of the heap-based PFS implementation of Dijkstra's algorithm is superlinear.

These exercises are similar to questions that might be addressed in the research literature, but the material in the book may prepare you to enjoy trying to solve them (and perhaps succeeding).

The annotations are intended to be neutral with respect to your programming and mathematical ability. Those exercises that require expertise in programming or in mathematical analysis are self-evident. All readers are encouraged to test their understanding of the algorithms by implementing them. Still, an exercise such as this one is straightforward for a practicing programmer or a student in a programming course, but may require substantial work for someone who has not recently programmed:

> • **17.74** Write a program that generates V random points in the plane, then builds a network with edges (in both directions) connecting all pairs of points within a given distance d of one another (see Program 3.20), setting each edge's weight to the distance between the two points that it connects. Determine how to set d so that the expected number of edges is E.

In a similar vein, all readers are encouraged to strive to appreciate the analytic underpinnings of our knowledge about properties of algorithms. Still, an exercise such as this one is straightforward for a scientist or a student in a discrete mathematics course, but may require substantial work for someone who has not recently done mathematical analysis:

> ○ **19.5** How many digraphs correspond to each undirected graph with V vertices and E edges?

There are far too many exercises for you to read and assimilate them all; my hope is that there are enough exercises here to stimulate you to strive to come to a broader understanding of the topics that interest you than you could glean by simply reading the text.

Contents

Graph Algorithms

Graph Algorithms

CHAPTER SEVENTEEN

Graph Properties and Types

MANY COMPUTATIONAL APPLICATIONS naturally involve not just a set of *items,* but also a set of *connections* between pairs of those items. The relationships implied by these connections lead immediately to a host of natural questions: Is there a way to get from one item to another by following the connections? How many other items can be reached from a given item? What is the best way to get from this item to this other item?

To model such situations, we use abstract objects called *graphs.* In this chapter, we examine basic properties of graphs in detail, setting the stage for us to study a variety of algorithms that are useful for answering questions of the type just posed. These algorithms make effective use of many of the computational tools that we considered in Parts 1 through 4. They also serve as the basis for attacking problems in important applications whose solution we could not even contemplate without good algorithmic technology.

Graph theory, a major branch of combinatorial mathematics, has been studied intensively for hundreds of years. Many important and useful properties of graphs have been proved, yet many difficult problems remain unresolved. In this book, while recognizing that there is much still to be learned, we draw from this vast body of knowledge about graphs what we need to understand and use a broad variety of useful and fundamental algorithms.

Like so many of the other problem domains that we have studied, the algorithmic investigation of graphs is relatively recent. Although a few of the fundamental algorithms are old, the majority of the interesting ones have been discovered within the last few decades. Even the simplest graph algorithms lead to useful computer programs, and the nontrivial algorithms that we examine are among the most elegant and interesting algorithms known.

To illustrate the diversity of applications that involve graph processing, we begin our exploration of algorithms in this fertile area by considering several examples.

Maps   A person who is planning a trip may need to answer questions such as, "What is the *least expensive* way to get from Princeton to San Jose?" A person more interested in time than in money may need to know the answer to the question "What is the *fastest* way to get from Princeton to San Jose?" To answer such questions, we process information about *connections* (travel routes) between *items* (towns and cities).

Hypertexts   When we browse the Web, we encounter documents that contain references (links) to other documents, and we move from document to document by clicking on the links. The entire web is a graph, where the items are documents and the connections are links. Graph-processing algorithms are essential components of the search engines that help us locate information on the web.

Circuits   An electric circuit comprises elements such as transistors, resistors, and capacitors that are intricately wired together. We use computers to control machines that make circuits, and to check that the circuits perform desired functions. We need to answer simple questions such as, "Is a short-circuit present?" as well as complicated questions such as, "Can we lay out this circuit on a chip without making any wires cross?" In this case, the answer to the first question depends on only the properties of the connections (wires), whereas the answer to the second question requires detailed information about the wires, the items that those wires connect, and the physical constraints of the chip.

Schedules   A manufacturing process requires a variety of tasks to be performed, under a set of constraints that specifies that certain tasks cannot be started until certain other tasks have been completed. We represent the constraints as connections between the tasks (items), and we are faced with a classical *scheduling* problem: How do we schedule the tasks such that we both respect the given constraints and complete the whole process in the least amount of time?

Transactions   A telephone company maintains a database of telephone-call traffic. Here the connections represent telephone calls. We are interested in knowing about the nature of the interconnection structure because we want to lay wires and build switches that can handle the traffic efficiently. As another example, a financial institution tracks buy/sell orders in a market. A connection in this situation represents the transfer of cash between two customers. Knowledge of the nature of the connection structure in this instance may enhance our understanding of the nature of the market.

Matching   Students apply for positions in selective institutions such as social clubs, universities, or medical schools. Items correspond to the students and the institutions; connections correspond to the applications. We want to discover methods for matching interested students with available positions.

Networks   A computer network consists of interconnected sites that send, forward, and receive messages of various types. We are interested not just in knowing that it is possible to get a message from every site to every other site, but also in maintaining this connectivity for all pairs of sites as the network changes. For example, we might wish to check a given network to be sure that no small set of sites or connections is so critical that losing it would disconnect any remaining pair of sites.

Program structure   A compiler builds graphs to represent the call structure of a large software system. The items are the various functions or modules that comprise the system; connections are associated either with the possibility that one function might call another (static analysis) or with actual calls while the system is in operation (dynamic analysis). We need to analyze the graph to determine how best to allocate resources to the program most efficiently.

These examples indicate the range of applications for which graphs are the appropriate abstraction and also the range of computational problems that we might encounter when we work with graphs. Such problems will be our focus in this book. In many of these applications as they are encountered in practice, the volume of data involved is truly huge, and efficient algorithms make the difference between whether or not a solution is at all feasible.

We have already encountered graphs, briefly, in Part 1. Indeed, the first algorithms that we considered in detail, the union-find algorithms in Chapter 1, are prime examples of graph algorithms. We also used graphs in Chapter 3 as an illustration of applications of two-dimensional arrays and linked lists, and in Chapter 5 to illustrate the relationship between recursive programs and fundamental data structures. Any linked data structure is a representation of a graph, and some familiar algorithms for processing trees and other linked structures are special cases of graph algorithms. The purpose of this chapter is to provide a context for developing an understanding of graph algorithms ranging from the simple ones in Part 1 to the sophisticated ones in Chapters 18 through 22.

As always, we are interested in knowing which are the most efficient algorithms that solve a particular problem. The study of the performance characteristics of graph algorithms is challenging because

- The cost of an algorithm depends not just on properties of the set of items, but also on numerous properties of the set of connections (and global properties of the graph that are implied by the connections).
- Accurate models of the types of graphs that we might face are difficult to develop.

We often work with worst-case performance bounds on graph algorithms, even though they may represent pessimistic estimates on actual performance in many instances. Fortunately, as we shall see, a number of algorithms are *optimal* and involve little unnecessary work. Other algorithms consume the same resources on all graphs of a given size. We can predict accurately how such algorithms will perform in specific situations. When we cannot make such accurate predictions, we need to pay particular attention to properties of the various types of graphs that we might expect in practical applications and must assess how these properties might affect the performance of our algorithms.

We begin by working through the basic definitions of graphs and the properties of graphs, examining the standard nomenclature that is used to describe them. Following that, we define the basic ADT (abstract data type) interfaces that we use to study graph algorithms and the two most important data structures for representing graphs—the *adjacency-matrix* representation and the *adjacency-lists* representation, and various approaches to implementing basic ADT functions. Then, we consider client programs that can generate random graphs, which we can use to test our algorithms and to learn properties of graphs. All this material provides a basis for us to introduce graph-processing algorithms that solve three classical problems related to finding paths in graphs, which illustrate that the difficulty of graph problems can differ dramatically even when they might seem similar. We conclude the chapter with a review of the most important graph-processing problems that we consider in this book, placing them in context according to the difficulty of solving them.

17.1 Glossary

A substantial amount of nomenclature is associated with graphs. Most of the terms have straightforward definitions, and, for reference, it is convenient to consider them in one place: here. We have already used some of these concepts when considering basic algorithms in Part 1; others of them will not become relevant until we address associated advanced algorithms in Chapters 18 through 22.

Definition 17.1 *A **graph** is a set of **vertices** and a set of **edges** that connect pairs of distinct vertices (with at most one edge connecting any pair of vertices).*

We use the names 0 through V–1 for the vertices in a V-vertex graph. The main reason that we choose this system is that we can access quickly information corresponding to each vertex, using vector indexing. In Section 17.6, we consider a program that uses a symbol table to establish a 1–1 mapping to associate V arbitrary vertex names with the V integers between 0 and $V - 1$. With that program in hand, we can use indices as vertex names (for notational convenience) without loss of generality. We sometimes assume that the set of vertices is defined implicitly, by taking the set of edges to define the graph and considering only those vertices that are included in at least one edge. To avoid cumbersome usage such as "the ten-vertex graph with the following set of edges," we do not explicitly mention the number of vertices when that number is clear from the context. By convention, we always denote the number of vertices in a given graph by V, and denote the number of edges by E.

We adopt as standard this definition of a graph (which we first encountered in Chapter 5), but note that it embodies two technical simplifications. First, it disallows duplicate edges (mathematicians sometimes refer to such edges as *parallel* edges, and a graph that can contain them as a *multigraph*). Second, it disallows edges that connect vertices to themselves; such edges are called *self-loops*. Graphs that have no parallel edges or self-loops are sometimes referred to as *simple graphs*.

We use simple graphs in our formal definitions because it is easier to express their basic properties and because parallel edges and self-loops are not needed in many applications. For example, we can bound the number of edges in a simple graph with a given number of vertices.

Property 17.1 *A graph with V vertices has at most $V(V-1)/2$ edges.*

Proof: The total of V^2 possible pairs of vertices includes V self-loops and accounts twice for each edge between distinct vertices, so the number of edges is at most $(V^2 - V)/2 = V(V - 1)/2$. ∎

No such bound holds if we allow parallel edges: a graph that is not simple might consist of two vertices and billions of edges connecting them (or even a single vertex and billions of self-loops).

For some applications, we might consider the elimination of parallel edges and self-loops to be a data-processing problem that our implementations must address. For other applications, ensuring that a given set of edges represents a simple graph may not be worth the trouble. Throughout the book, whenever it is more convenient to address an application or to develop an algorithm by using an extended definition that includes parallel edges or self-loops, we shall do so. For example, self-loops play a critical role in a classical algorithm that we will examine in Section 17.4; and parallel edges are common in the applications that we address in Chapter 22. Generally, it is clear from the context whether we intend the term "graph" to mean "simple graph" or "multigraph" or "multigraph with self-loops."

Mathematicians use the words *vertex* and *node* interchangeably, but we generally use *vertex* when discussing graphs and *node* when discussing representations—for example, in C++ data structures. We normally assume that a vertex can have a name and can carry other associated information. Similarly, the words *arc*, *edge*, and *link* are all widely used by mathematicians to describe the abstraction embodying a connection between two vertices, but we consistently use *edge* when discussing graphs and *link* when discussing C++ data structures.

When there is an edge connecting two vertices, we say that the vertices are *adjacent to* one another and that the edge is *incident on* both vertices. The *degree* of a vertex is the number of edges incident on it. We use the notation v–w to represent an edge that connects v and w; the notation w–v is an alternative way to represent the same edge.

A *subgraph* is a subset of a graph's edges (and associated vertices) that constitutes a graph. Many computational tasks involve identifying subgraphs of various types. If we identify a subset of a graph's vertices, we call that subset, together with all edges that connect two of its members, the *induced subgraph* associated with those vertices.

We can draw a graph by marking points for the vertices and drawing lines connecting them for the edges. A drawing gives us intuition about the structure of the graph; but this intuition can be misleading, because the graph is defined independently of the representation. For example, the two drawings in Figure 17.1 and the list of edges represent the same graph, because the graph is only its (unordered) set of vertices and its (unordered) set of edges (pairs of vertices)—nothing more. Although it suffices to consider a graph simply as a set of edges, we examine other representations that are particularly suitable as the basis for graph data structures in Section 17.4.

Placing the vertices of a given graph on the plane and drawing them and the edges that connect them is known as *graph drawing*. The possible vertex placements, edge-drawing styles, and aesthetic constraints on the drawing are limitless. Graph-drawing algorithms that respect various natural constraints have been studied heavily and have many successful applications (*see reference section*). For example, one of the simplest constraints is to insist that edges do not intersect. A *planar graph* is one that can be drawn in the plane without any edges crossing. Determining whether or not a graph is planar is a fascinating algorithmic problem that we discuss briefly in Section 17.8. Being able to produce a helpful visual representation is a useful goal, and graph drawing is a fascinating field of study, but successful drawings are often difficult to realize. Many graphs that have huge numbers of vertices and edges are abstract objects for which no suitable drawing is feasible.

For some applications, such as graphs that represent maps or circuits, a graph drawing can carry considerable information because

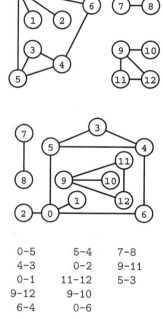

0–5	5–4	7–8
4–3	0–2	9–11
0–1	11–12	5–3
9–12	9–10	
6–4	0–6	

Figure 17.1
Three different representations of the same graph

A graph is defined by its vertices and its edges, not by the way that we choose to draw it. These two drawings depict the same graph, as does the list of edges (bottom), given the additional information that the graph has 13 vertices labeled 0 through 12.

the vertices correspond to points in the plane and the distances between them are relevant. We refer to such graphs as *Euclidean graphs*. For many other applications, such as graphs that represent relationships or schedules, the graphs simply embody connectivity information, and no particular geometric placement of vertices is ever implied. We consider examples of algorithms that exploit the geometric information in Euclidean graphs in Chapters 20 and 21, but we primarily work with algorithms that make no use of any geometric information, and stress that graphs are generally independent of any particular representation in a drawing or in a computer.

Focusing solely on the connections themselves, we might wish to view the vertex labels as merely a notational convenience, and to regard two graphs as being the same if they differ in only the vertex labels. Two graphs are *isomorphic* if we can change the vertex labels on one to make its set of edges identical to the other. Determining whether or not two graphs are isomorphic is a difficult computational problem (see Figure 17.2 and Exercise 17.5). It is challenging because there are $V!$ possible ways to label the vertices—far too many for us to try all the possibilities. Therefore, despite the potential appeal of reducing the number of different graph structures that we have to consider by treating isomorphic graphs as identical structures, we rarely do so.

As we saw with trees in Chapter 5, we are often interested in basic structural properties that we can deduce by considering specific sequences of edges in a graph.

Definition 17.2   *A **path** in a graph is a sequence of vertices in which each successive vertex (after the first) is adjacent to its predecessor in the path. In a **simple path**, the vertices and edges are distinct. A **cycle** is a path that is simple except that the first and final vertices are the same.*

We sometimes use the term *cyclic path* to refer to a path whose first and final vertices are the same (and is otherwise not necessarily simple); and we use the term *tour* to refer to a cyclic path that includes every vertex. An equivalent way to define a path is as the sequence of *edges* that connect the successive vertices. We emphasize this in our notation by connecting vertex names in a path in the same way as we connect them in an edge. For example, the simple paths in Figure 17.1 include 3-4-6-0-2, and 9-12-11, and the cycles in the graph include

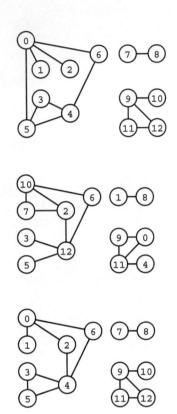

Figure 17.2
Graph isomorphism examples

The top two graphs are isomorphic because we can relabel the vertices to make the two sets of edges identical (to make the middle graph the same as the top graph, change 10 to 4, 7 to 3, 2 to 5, 3 to 1, 12 to 0, 5 to 2, 9 to 11, 0 to 12, 11 to 9, 1 to 7, and 4 to 10). The bottom graph is not isomorphic to the others because there is no way to relabel the vertices to make its set of edges identical to either.

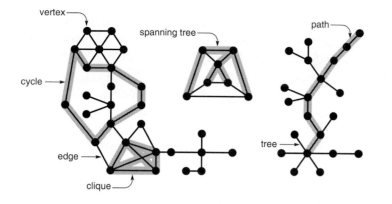

Figure 17.3
Graph terminology

This graph has 55 vertices, 70 edges, and 3 connected components. One of the connected components is a tree (right). *The graph has many cycles, one of which is highlighted in the large connected component* (left). *The diagram also depicts a spanning tree in the small connected component* (center). *The graph as a whole does not have a spanning tree, because it is not connected.*

0-6-4-3-5-0 and 5-4-3-5. We define the *length* of a path or a cycle to be its number of edges.

We adopt the convention that each single vertex is a path of length 0 (a path from the vertex to itself with no edges on it, which is different from a self-loop). Apart from this convention, in a graph with no parallel edges and no self-loops, a pair of vertices uniquely determines an edge, paths must have on them at least two distinct vertices, and cycles must have on them at least three distinct edges and three distinct vertices.

We say that two simple paths are *disjoint* if they have no vertices in common other than, possibly, their endpoints. Placing this condition is slightly weaker than insisting that the paths have no vertices at all in common, and is useful because we can combine simple disjoint paths from s to t and t to u to get a simple disjoint path from s to u if s and u are different (and to get a cycle if s and u are the same). The term *vertex disjoint* is sometimes used to distinguish this condition from the stronger condition of *edge disjoint*, where we require that the paths have no *edge* in common.

Definition 17.3 *A graph is a **connected graph** if there is a path from every vertex to every other vertex in the graph. A graph that is not connected consists of a set of **connected components**, which are maximal connected subgraphs.*

The term *maximal connected subgraph* means that there is no path from a subgraph vertex to any vertex in the graph that is not in the subgraph. Intuitively, if the vertices were physical objects, such as

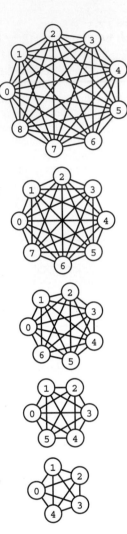

Figure 17.4
Complete graphs

These complete graphs, with every vertex connected to every other vertex, have 10, 15, 21, 28, and 36 edges (bottom to top). *Every graph with between 5 and 9 vertices (there are more than 68 billion such graphs) is a subgraph of one of these graphs.*

knots or beads, and the edges were physical connections, such as strings or wires, a connected graph would stay in one piece if picked up by any vertex, and a graph that is not connected comprises two or more such pieces.

Definition 17.4   *An acyclic connected graph is called a* **tree** *(see Chapter 4). A set of trees is called a* **forest**. *A* **spanning tree** *of a connected graph is a subgraph that contains all of that graph's vertices and is a single tree. A* **spanning forest** *of a graph is a subgraph that contains all of that graph's vertices and is a forest.*

For example, the graph illustrated in Figure 17.1 has three connected components, and is spanned by the forest 7-8 9-10 9-11 9-12 0-1 0-2 0-5 5-3 5-4 4-6 (there are many other spanning forests). Figure 17.3 highlights these and other features in a larger graph.

We explore further details about trees in Chapter 4, and look at various equivalent definitions. For example, a graph G with V vertices is a tree if and only if it satisfies *any* of the following four conditions:

- G has $V - 1$ edges and no cycles.
- G has $V - 1$ edges and is connected.
- Exactly one simple path connects each pair of vertices in G.
- G is connected, but removing any edge disconnects it.

Any one of these conditions is necessary and sufficient to prove the other three, and we can develop other combinations of facts about trees from them (see Exercise 17.1). Formally, we should choose one condition to serve as a definition; informally, we let them collectively serve as the definition, and freely engage in usage such as the "acyclic connected graph" choice in Definition 17.4.

Graphs with all edges present are called *complete graphs* (see Figure 17.4). We define the *complement* of a graph G by starting with a complete graph that has the same set of vertices as the original graph and then removing the edges of G. The *union* of two graphs is the graph induced by the union of their sets of edges. The union of a graph and its complement is a complete graph. All graphs that have V vertices are subgraphs of the complete graph that has V vertices. The total number of different graphs that have V vertices is $2^{V(V-1)/2}$ (the number of different ways to choose a subset from the $V(V-1)/2$ possible edges). A complete subgraph is called a *clique*.

Most graphs that we encounter in practice have relatively few of the possible edges present. To quantify this concept, we define the *density* of a graph to be the average vertex degree, or $2E/V$. A *dense graph* is a graph whose average vertex degree is proportional to V; a *sparse graph* is a graph whose complement is dense. In other words, we consider a graph to be dense if E is proportional to V^2 and sparse otherwise. This asymptotic definition is not necessarily meaningful for a particular graph, but the distinction is generally clear: A graph that has millions of vertices and tens of millions of edges is certainly sparse, and a graph that has thousands of vertices and millions of edges is certainly dense. We might contemplate processing a sparse graph with billions of vertices, but a dense graph with billions of vertices would have an overwhelming number of edges.

Knowing whether a graph is sparse or dense is generally a key factor in selecting an efficient algorithm to process the graph. For example, for a given problem, we might develop one algorithm that takes about V^2 steps and another that takes about $E \lg E$ steps. These formulas tell us that the second algorithm would be better for sparse graphs, whereas the first would be preferred for dense graphs. For example, a dense graph with millions of edges might have only thousands of vertices: in this case V^2 and E would be comparable in value, and the V^2 algorithm would be 20 times faster than the $E \lg E$ algorithm. On the other hand, a sparse graph with millions of edges also has millions of vertices, so the $E \lg E$ algorithm could be *millions* of times faster than the V^2 algorithm. We could make specific tradeoffs on the basis of analyzing these formulas in more detail, but it generally suffices in practice to use the terms *sparse* and *dense* informally to help us understand fundamental performance characteristics.

When analyzing graph algorithms, we assume that V/E is bounded above by a small constant, so that we can abbreviate expressions such as $V(V + E)$ to VE. This assumption comes into play only when the number of edges is tiny in comparison to the number of vertices—a rare situation. Typically, the number of edges far exceeds the number of vertices (V/E is much less than 1).

A *bipartite graph* is a graph whose vertices we can divide into two sets such that all edges connect a vertex in one set with a vertex in the other set. Figure 17.5 gives an example of a bipartite graph. Bipartite graphs arise in a natural way in many situations, such as the matching problems described at the beginning of this chapter. Any subgraph of a bipartite graph is bipartite.

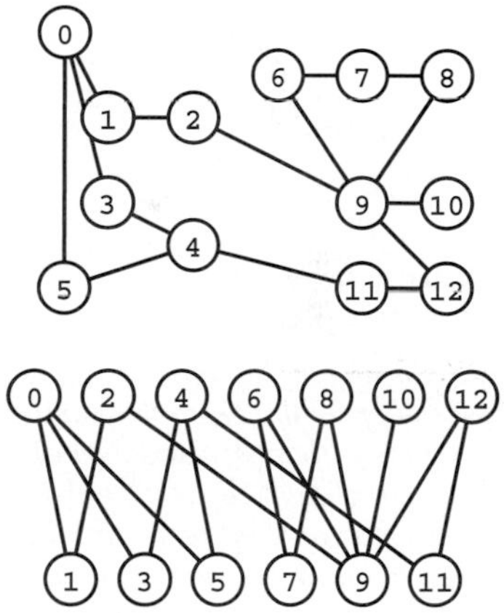

Figure 17.5
A bipartite graph

All edges in this graph connect odd-numbered vertices with even-numbered ones, so it is bipartite. The bottom diagram makes the property obvious.

Graphs as defined to this point are called *undirected graphs*. In *directed graphs*, also known as *digraphs*, edges are one-way: we consider the pair of vertices that defines each edge to be an *ordered* pair that specifies a one-way adjacency where we think about having the ability to get from the first vertex to the second but not from the second vertex to the first. Many applications (for example, graphs that represent the Web, scheduling constraints, or telephone-call transactions) are naturally expressed in terms of digraphs.

We refer to edges in digraphs as *directed edges*, though that distinction is generally obvious in context (some authors reserve the term *arc* for directed edges). The first vertex in a directed edge is called the *source*; the second vertex is called the *destination*. (Some authors use the terms *tail* and *head*, respectively, to distinguish the vertices in directed edges, but we avoid this usage because of overlap with our use of the same terms in data-structure implementations.) We draw directed edges as arrows pointing from source to destination, and often say that the edge *points to* the destination. When we use the notation v–w in a digraph, we mean it to represent an edge that points from v to w; it is different from w–v, which represents an edge that points from w to v. We speak of the *indegree* and *outdegree* of a vertex (the number of edges where it is the destination and the number of edges where it is the source, respectively).

Sometimes, we are justified in thinking of an undirected graph as a digraph that has two directed edges (one in each direction); other times, it is useful to think of undirected graphs simply in terms of connections. Normally, as discussed in detail in Section 17.4, we use the same representation for directed and undirected graphs (see Figure 17.6). That is, we generally maintain two representations of each edge for undirected graphs, one pointing in each direction, so that we can immediately answer questions such as, "Which vertices are connected to vertex v?"

Chapter 19 is devoted to exploring the structural properties of digraphs; they are generally more complicated than the corresponding properties for undirected graphs. A *directed cycle* in a digraph is a cycle in which all adjacent vertex pairs appear in the order indicated by (directed) graph edges. A *directed acyclic graph (DAG)* is a digraph that has no directed cycles. A DAG (an acyclic digraph) is not the same as a tree (an acyclic undirected graph). Occasionally, we refer to the

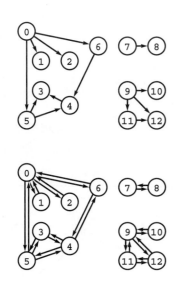

Figure 17.6
Two digraphs

The drawing at the top is a representation of the example graph in Figure 17.1 interpreted as a directed graph, where we take the edges to be ordered pairs and represent them by drawing an arrow from the first vertex to the second. It is also a DAG. The drawing at the bottom is a representation of the undirected graph from Figure 17.1 that indicates the way that we usually represent undirected graphs: as digraphs with two edges corresponding to each connection (one in each direction).

underlying undirected graph of a digraph, meaning the undirected graph defined by the same set of edges, but where these edges are not interpreted as directed.

Chapters 20 through 22 are generally concerned with algorithms for solving various computational problems associated with graphs in which other information is associated with the vertices and edges. In *weighted graphs*, we associate numbers (*weights*) with each edge, which generally represents a distance or cost. We also might associate a weight with each vertex, or multiple weights with each vertex and edge. In Chapter 20 we work with weighted undirected graphs; in Chapters 21 and 22 we study weighted digraphs, which we also refer to as *networks*. The algorithms in Chapter 22 solve classic problems that arise from a particular interpretation of networks known as *flow networks*.

As was evident even in Chapter 1, the combinatorial structure of graphs is extensive. This extent of this structure is all the more remarkable because it springs forth from a simple mathematical abstraction. This underlying simplicity will be reflected in much of the code that we develop for basic graph processing. However, this simplicity sometimes masks complicated dynamic properties that require deep understanding of the combinatorial properties of graphs themselves. It is often far more difficult to convince ourselves that a graph algorithm works as intended than the compact nature of the code might suggest.

Exercises

17.1 Prove that any acyclic connected graph that has V vertices has $V - 1$ edges.

▷ **17.2** Give all the connected subgraphs of the graph

0-1 0-2 0-3 1-3 2-3.

▷ **17.3** Write down a list of the nonisomorphic cycles of the graph in Figure 17.1. For example, if your list contains 3-4-5-3, it should not contain 3-5-4-3, 4-5-3-4, 4-3-5-4, 5-3-4-5, or 5-4-3-5.

17.4 Consider the graph

3-7 1-4 7-8 0-5 5-2 3-8 2-9 0-6 4-9 2-6 6-4.

Determine the number of connected components, give a spanning forest, list all the simple paths with at least three vertices, and list all the nonisomorphic cycles (see Exercise 17.3).

○ **17.5**   Consider the graphs defined by the following four sets of edges:

    0-1 0-2 0-3 1-3 1-4 2-5 2-9 3-6 4-7 4-8 5-8 5-9 6-7 6-9 7-8
    0-1 0-2 0-3 0-3 1-4 2-5 2-9 3-6 4-7 4-8 5-8 5-9 6-7 6-9 7-8
    0-1 1-2 1-3 0-3 0-4 2-5 2-9 3-6 4-7 4-8 5-8 5-9 6-7 6-9 7-8
    4-1 7-9 6-2 7-3 5-0 0-2 0-8 1-6 3-9 6-3 2-8 1-5 9-8 4-5 4-7.

Which of these graphs are isomorphic to one another? Which of them are planar?

17.6   Consider the more than 68 billion graphs referred to in the caption to Figure 17.4. What percentage of them has fewer than nine vertices?

▷ **17.7**   How many different subgraphs are there in a given graph with V vertices and E edges?

● **17.8**   Give tight upper and lower bounds on the number of connected components in graphs that have V vertices and E edges.

○ **17.9**   How many different undirected graphs are there that have V vertices and E edges?

●●● **17.10** If we consider two graphs to be different only if they are not isomorphic, how many different graphs are there that have V vertices and E edges?

17.11 How many V-vertex graphs are bipartite?

17.2 Graph ADT

We develop our graph-processing algorithms using an ADT that defines the fundamental tasks, using the standard mechanisms introduced in Chapter 4. Program 17.1 is the ADT interface that we use for this purpose. Basic graph representations and implementations for this ADT are the topic of Sections 17.3 through 17.5. Later in the book, whenever we consider a new graph-processing problem, we consider the algorithms that solve it and their implementations in the context of client programs and ADTs that access graphs through this interface. This scheme allows us to address graph-processing tasks ranging from elementary maintenance functions to sophisticated solutions of difficult problems.

The interface is based on our standard mechanism that hides representations and implementations from client programs (see Section 4.8). It also includes a simple structure type definition that allows our programs to manipulate edges in a uniform way. The interface provides the basic mechanisms that allow clients to build graphs (by constructing the graph and then adding the edges), to maintain the

Program 17.1 Graph ADT interface

This interface is a starting point for implementing and testing graph algorithms. It defines two data types: a trivial Edge data type, including a constructor function that creates an Edge from two given vertices; and a GRAPH data type, which is defined with the standard representation-independent ADT interface methodology from Chapter 4.

The GRAPH constructor takes two arguments: an integer giving the number of vertices and a boolean that tells whether the graph is undirected or directed (a digraph), with undirected the default.

The basic operations that we use to process graphs and digraphs are ADT functions to create and destroy them; to report the number of vertices and edges; and to add and delete edges. The iterator class adjIterator allows clients to process each of the vertices adjacent to any given vertex. Programs 17.2 and 17.3 illustrate its use.

```
struct Edge
  { int v, w;
    Edge(int v = -1, int w = -1) : v(v), w(w) { }
  };
class GRAPH
  { private:
      // Implementation-dependent code
    public:
      GRAPH(int, bool);
      ~GRAPH();
      int V() const;
      int E() const;
      bool directed() const;
      int insert(Edge);
      int remove(Edge);
      bool edge(int, int);
      class adjIterator
        {
          public:
            adjIterator(const GRAPH &, int);
            int beg();
            int nxt();
            bool end();
        };
  };
```

graphs (by removing some edges and adding others), and to examine the graphs (using an iterator for processing the vertices adjacent to any given vertex).

The ADT in Program 17.1 is primarily a vehicle to allow us to develop and test algorithms; it is not a general-purpose interface. As usual, we work with the simplest interface that supports the basic graph-processing operations that we wish to consider. Defining such an interface for use in practical applications involves making numerous tradeoffs among simplicity, efficiency, and generality. We consider a few of these tradeoffs next; we address many others in the context of implementations and applications throughout this book.

The graph constructor takes the maximum possible number of vertices in the graph as an argument, so that implementations can allocate memory accordingly. We adopt this convention solely to make the code compact and readable. A more general graph ADT might include in its interface the capability to add and remove vertices as well as edges; this would impose more demanding requirements on the data structures used to implement the ADT. We might also choose to work at an intermediate level of abstraction, and consider the design of interfaces that support higher-level abstract operations on graphs that we can use in implementations. We revisit this idea briefly in Section 17.5, after we consider several concrete representations and implementations.

A general graph ADT needs to take into account parallel edges and self-loops, because nothing prevents a client program from calling insert with an edge that is already present in the graph (parallel edge) or with an edge whose two vertex indices are the same (self-loop). It might be necessary to disallow such edges in some applications, desirable to include them in other applications, and possible to ignore them in still other applications. Self-loops are trivial to handle, but parallel edges can be costly to handle, depending on the graph representation. In certain situations, including a *remove parallel edges* ADT function might be appropriate; then, implementations can let parallel edges collect, and clients can remove or otherwise process parallel edges when warranted. We will revisit these issues when we examine graph representations in Sections 17.3 and 17.4.

Program 17.2 is a function that illustrates the use of the iterator class in the graph ADT. It is a function that extracts a graph's

Program 17.2 Example of a graph-processing client function

This function shows one way to use the graph ADT to implement a basic graph-processing operation in a manner independent of the representation. It returns all the graph's edges in a vector.

This implementation illustrates the basis for most of the programs that we consider: we process each edge in the graph by checking all the vertices adjacent to each vertex. We generally do not call beg, end, and nxt *except* as illustrated here, so that we can better understand the performance characteristics of our implementations (see Section 17.5).

```
template <class Graph>
vector <Edge> edges(Graph &G)
  { int E = 0;
    vector <Edge> a(G.E());
    for (int v = 0; v < G.V(); v++)
      {
        typename Graph::adjIterator A(G, v);
        for (int w = A.beg(); !A.end(); w = A.nxt())
          if (G.directed() || v < w)
            a[E++] = Edge(v, w);
      }
    return a;
  }
```

set of edges and returns it in a C++ Standard Template Library (STL) vector. Λ graph is nothing more nor less than its set of edges, and we often need a way to retrieve a graph in this form, regardless of its internal representation. The order in which the edges appear in the vector is immaterial and will differ from implementation to implementation. We use a template for such functions to allow for using multiple implementations of the graph ADT.

Program 17.3 is another example of the use of the iterator class in the graph ADT, to print out a table of the vertices adjacent to each vertex, as shown in Figure 17.7. The code in these two examples is quite similar and is similar to the code in numerous graph-processing algorithms. Remarkably, we can build all of the algorithms that we consider in this book on this basic abstraction of processing all the vertices adjacent to each vertex (which is equivalent to processing all the edges in the graph), as in these functions.

Program 17.3 A client function that prints a graph

This implementation of the show function from the io class of Program 17.4 uses the graph ADT to print a table of the vertices adjacent to each graph vertex. The order in which the vertices appear depends upon the graph representation and the ADT implementation (see Figure 17.7).

```
template <class Graph>
void IO<Graph>::show(const Graph &G)
  {
    for (int s = 0; s < G.V(); s++)
      {
        cout.width(2); cout << s << ":";
        typename Graph::adjIterator A(G, s);
        for (int t = A.beg(); !A.end(); t = A.nxt())
          { cout.width(2); cout << t << " "; }
        cout << endl;
      }
  }
```

```
 0:  1 2 5 6
 1:  0
 2:  0
 3:  4 5
 4:  3 5 6
 5:  0 3 4
 6:  0 4
 7:  8
 8:  7
 9:  10 11 12
10:  9
11:  9 12
12:  9 11
```

**Figure 17.7
Adjacency lists format**

This table illustrates yet another way to represent the graph in Figure 17.1: we associate each vertex with its set of adjacent vertices (those connected to it by a single edge). Each edge affects two sets: for every edge u-v in the graph, u appears in v's set and v appears in u's set.

As discussed in Section 17.5, we often package related graph-processing functions into a single class. Program 17.4 is an interface for such a class. It defines the show function of Program 17.3 and two functions for inserting into a graph edges taken from standard input (see Exercise 17.12 and Program 17.14 for implementations of these functions).

Generally, the graph-processing tasks that we consider in this book fall into one of three broad categories:

- Compute the value of some measure of the graph.
- Compute some subset of the edges of the graph.
- Answer queries about some property of the graph.

Examples of the first are the number of connected components and the length of the shortest path between two given vertices in the graph; examples of the second are a spanning tree and the longest cycle containing a given vertex; examples of the third are whether two given vertices are in the same connected component. Indeed, the terms that we defined in Section 17.1 immediately bring to mind a host of computational problems.

Program 17.4 Graph-processing input/output interface

This class illustrates how we might package related graph-processing functions together in a single class. It defines functions for printing a graph (see Program 17.3); inserting edges defined by pairs of integers on standard input (see Exercise 17.12); and inserting edges defined by pairs of symbols on standard input (see Program 17.14).

```
template <class Graph>
class IO
  {
    public:
      static void show(const Graph &);
      static void scanEZ(Graph &);
      static void scan(Graph &);
  };
```

Our convention for addressing such tasks will be to build ADTs that are clients of the basic ADT in Program 17.1, but that, in turn, allow us to separate client programs that need to solve the problem from implementations. For example, Program 17.5 is an interface for a graph-connectivity ADT. We can write client programs that use this ADT to create objects that can provide the number of connected components in the graph and that can test whether or not any two vertices are in the same connected component. We describe implementations of this ADT and their performance characteristics in Section 18.5, and we develop similar ADTs throughout the book. Typically, such ADTs include a *preprocessing* public member function (usually the constructor), private data members that keep information learned during the preprocessing, and *query* public member functions that use this information to provide clients with information about the graph.

In this book, we generally work with *static* graphs, which have a fixed number of vertices V and edges E. Generally, we build the graphs by executing E calls to insert, then process them either by calling some ADT function that takes a graph as argument and returns some information about that graph, or by using objects of the kind just described to preprocess the graph so as to be able to efficiently answer queries about it. In either case, changing the graph by calling insert or remove necessitates reprocessing the graph. *Dynamic* problems,

---

Program 17.5 Connectivity interface

This ADT interface illustrates a typical paradigm that we use for implementing graph-processing algorithms. It allows a client to construct an object that processes a graph so that it can answer queries about the graph's connectivity. The count member function returns the number of connected components and the connect member function tests whether two given vertices are connected. Program 18.4 is an implementation of this interface.

```
template <class Graph>
class CC
  {
    private:
      // implementation-dependent code
    public:
      CC(const Graph &);
      int count();
      bool connect(int, int);
  };
```

---

where we want to intermix graph processing with edge and vertex insertion and removal, take us into the realm of *online algorithms* (also known as *dynamic algorithms*), which present a different set of challenges. For example, the connectivity problem that we solved with union-find algorithms in Chapter 1 is an example of an online algorithm, because we can get information about the connectivity of a graph as we insert edges. The ADT in Program 17.1 supports *insert edge* and *remove edge* operations, so clients are free to use them to make changes in graphs, but there may be performance penalties for certain sequences of operations. For example, union-find algorithms may require reprocessing the whole graph if a client uses *remove edge*. For most of the graph-processing problems that we consider, adding or deleting a few edges can dramatically change the nature of the graph and thus necessitate reprocessing it.

One of our most important challenges in graph processing is to have a clear understanding of performance characteristics of implementations and to make sure that client programs make appropriate use of them. As with the simpler problems that we considered in

---

Program 17.6 Example of a graph-processing client program

This program illustrates the use of the graph-processing ADTs described in this section, using the ADT conventions described in Section 4.5. It constructs a graph with V vertices, inserts edges taken from standard input, prints the resulting graph if it is small, and computes (and prints) the number of connected components. It assumes that Program 17.1, Program 17.4, and Program 17.5 (with implementations) are in the files GRAPH.cc, IO.cc, and CC.cc (respectively).

```
#include <iostream.h>
#include <stdlib.h>
#include "GRAPH.cc"
#include "IO.cc"
#include "CC.cc"
main(int argc, char *argv[])
  { int V = atoi(argv[1]);
    GRAPH G(V);
    IO<GRAPH>::scan(G);
    if (V < 20) IO<GRAPH>::show(G);
    cout << G.E() << " edges ";
    CC<GRAPH> Gcc(G);
    cout << Gcc.count() << " components" << endl;
  }
```

Parts 1 through 4, our use of ADTs makes it possible to address such issues in a coherent manner.

Program 17.6 is an example of a graph-processing client program. It uses the basic ADT of Program 17.1, the input-output class of Program 17.4 to read the graph from standard input and print it to standard output, and the connectivity class of Program 17.5 to find its number of connected components. We use similar but more sophisticated clients to generate other types of graphs, to test algorithms, to learn other properties of graphs, and to use graphs to solve other problems. The basic scheme is amenable for use in any graph-processing application.

In Sections 17.3 through 17.5, we examine the primary classical graph representations and implementations of the ADT functions in Program 17.1. These implementations provide a basis for us to expand the interface to include the graph-processing tasks that are our focus for the next several chapters.

The first decision that we face in developing an ADT implementation is which graph representation to use. We have three basic requirements. First, we must be able to accommodate the types of graphs that we are likely to encounter in applications (and we also would prefer not to waste space). Second, we should be able to construct the requisite data structures efficiently. Third, we want to develop efficient algorithms to solve our graph-processing problems without being unduly hampered by any restrictions imposed by the representation. Such requirements are standard ones for any domain that we consider—we emphasize them again them here because, as we shall see, different representations give rise to huge performance differences for even the simplest of problems.

For example, we might consider a *vector of edges* representation as the basis for an ADT implementation (see Exercise 17.16). That direct representation is simple, but it does not allow us to perform efficiently the basic graph-processing operations that we shall be studying. As we will see, most graph-processing applications can be handled reasonably with one of two straightforward classical representations that are only slightly more complicated than the vector-of-edges representation: the *adjacency-matrix* or the *adjacency-lists* representation. These representations, which we consider in detail in Sections 17.3 and 17.4, are based on elementary data structures (indeed, we discussed them both in Chapters 3 and 5 as example applications of sequential and linked allocation). The choice between the two depends primarily on whether the graph is dense or sparse, although, as usual, the nature of the operations to be performed also plays an important role in the decision on which to use.

Exercises

▷ **17.12** Implement the `scanEZ` function from Program 17.4: write a function that builds a graph by reading edges (pairs of integers between 0 and $V - 1$) from standard input.

▷ **17.13** Write an ADT client that adds all the edges in a given vector to a given graph.

▷ **17.14** Write a function that calls `edges` and prints out all the edges in the graph, in the format used in this text (vertex numbers separated by a hyphen).

○ **17.15** Develop an implementation for the connectivity ADT of Program 17.5, using a union-find algorithm (see Chapter 1).

• **17.16** Provide an implementation of the ADT functions in Program 17.1 that uses a vector of edges to represent the graph. Use a brute-force implementation of `remove` that removes an edge v-w by scanning the vector to find v-w or w-v and then exchanges the edge found with the final one in the vector. Use a similar scan to implement the iterator. *Note*: Reading Section 17.3 first might make this exercise easier.

17.3 Adjacency-Matrix Representation

An *adjacency-matrix* representation of a graph is a *V*-by-*V* matrix of Boolean values, with the entry in row v and column w defined to be 1 if there is an edge connecting vertex v and vertex w in the graph, and to be 0 otherwise. Figure 17.8 depicts an example.

Program 17.7 is an implementation of the graph ADT interface that uses a direct representation of this matrix, built as a `vector` of `vectors`, as depicted in Figure 17.9. It is a two-dimensional existence table with the entry `adj[v][w]` set to `true` if there is an edge connecting v and w in the graph, and set to `false` otherwise. Note that maintaining this property in an undirected graph requires that each edge be represented by *two* entries: the edge v-w is represented by `true` values in *both* `adj[v][w]` and `adj[w][v]`, as is the edge w-v.

The name `DenseGRAPH` in Program 17.7 emphasizes that the implementation is more suited for dense graphs than for sparse ones, and distinguishes it from other implementations. Clients may use `typedef` to make this type equivalent to `GRAPH` or use `DenseGRAPH` explicitly.

In the adjacency matrix that represents a graph G, row v is a vector that is an existence table whose `i`th entry is `true` if vertex `i` is adjacent to v (the edge v-i is in G). Thus, to provide clients with the capability to process the vertices adjacent to v, we need only provide code that scans through this vector to find `true` entries, as shown in Program 17.8. We need to be mindful that, with this implementation, processing all of the vertices adjacent to a given vertex requires (at least) time proportional to *V*, no matter how many such vertices exist.

As mentioned in Section 17.2, our interface requires that the number of vertices is known to the client when the graph is initialized. If desired, we could allow for inserting and deleting vertices (see Exercise 17.21). A key feature of the constructor in Program 17.7 is

	0	1	2	3	4	5	6	7	8	9	10	11	12
0	0	1	1	0	0	1	1	0	0	0	0	0	0
1	1	0	0	0	0	0	0	0	0	0	0	0	0
2	1	0	0	0	0	0	0	0	0	0	0	0	0
3	0	0	0	0	1	1	0	0	0	0	0	0	0
4	0	0	0	1	0	1	1	0	0	0	0	0	0
5	1	0	0	1	1	0	0	0	0	0	0	0	0
6	1	0	0	0	1	0	0	0	0	0	0	0	0
7	0	0	0	0	0	0	0	0	1	0	0	0	0
8	0	0	0	0	0	0	0	1	0	0	0	0	0
9	0	0	0	0	0	0	0	0	0	0	1	1	1
10	0	0	0	0	0	0	0	0	0	1	0	0	0
11	0	0	0	0	0	0	0	0	0	1	0	0	1
12	0	0	0	0	0	0	0	0	0	1	0	1	0

**Figure 17.8
Adjacency-matrix graph representation**

*This Boolean matrix is another representation of the graph depicted in Figure 17.1. It has a 1 (*true*) in row v and column w if there is an edge connecting vertex v and vertex w and a 0 (*false*) in row v and column w if there is no such edge. The matrix is symmetric about the diagonal. For example, the sixth row (and the sixth column) says that vertex 6 is connected to vertices 0 and 4. For some applications, we will adopt the convention that each vertex is connected to itself, and assign 1s on the main diagonal. The large blocks of 0s in the upper right and lower left corners are artifacts of the way we assigned vertex numbers for this example, not characteristic of the graph (except that they do indicate the graph to be sparse).*

Program 17.7 Graph ADT implementation (adjacency matrix)

This class is a straightforward implementation of the interface in Program 17.1 that is based on representing the graph with a vector of boolean vectors (see Figure 17.9). Edges are inserted and removed in constant time. Duplicate edge `insert` requests are silently ignored, but clients can use `edge` to test whether an edge exists. Constructing the graph takes time proportional to V^2.

```
class DenseGRAPH
{ int Vcnt, Ecnt; bool digraph;
  vector <vector <bool> > adj;
public:
  DenseGRAPH(int V, bool digraph = false) :
    adj(V), Vcnt(V), Ecnt(0), digraph(digraph)
    {
      for (int i = 0; i < V; i++)
        adj[i].assign(V, false);
    }
  int V() const { return Vcnt; }
  int E() const { return Ecnt; }
  bool directed() const { return digraph; }
  void insert(Edge e)
    { int v = e.v, w = e.w;
      if (adj[v][w] == false) Ecnt++;
      adj[v][w] = true;
      if (!digraph) adj[w][v] = true;
    }
  void remove(Edge e)
    { int v = e.v, w = e.w;
      if (adj[v][w] == true) Ecnt--;
      adj[v][w] = false;
      if (!digraph) adj[w][v] = false;
    }
  bool edge(int v, int w) const
    { return adj[v][w]; }
  class adjIterator;
  friend class adjIterator;
};
```

Program 17.8 Iterator for adjacency-matrix representation

This implementation of the iterator for Program 17.7 uses an index i to scan past false entries in row v of the adjacency matrix (adj[v]). A call to beg() followed by a sequence of calls to nxt() (checking that end() is false before each call) gives a sequence of the vertices adjacent to v in G in order of their vertex index.

```
class DenseGRAPH::adjIterator
{ const DenseGRAPH &G;
  int i, v;
public:
  adjIterator(const DenseGRAPH &G, int v) :
    G(G), v(v), i(-1) { }
  int beg()
    { i = -1; return nxt(); }
  int nxt()
    {
      for (i++; i < G.V(); i++)
        if (G.adj[v][i] == true) return i;
      return -1;
    }
  bool end()
    { return i >= G.V(); }
};
```

---

that it initializes the graph by setting the matrix entries all to false. We need to be mindful that this operation takes time proportional to V^2, no matter how many edges are in the graph. Error checks for insufficient memory are not included in Program 17.7 for brevity—it is prudent programming practice to add them before using this code (see Exercise 17.24).

To add an edge, we set the indicated matrix entries to true (one for digraphs, two for undirected graphs). This representation does not allow parallel edges: If an edge is to be inserted for which the matrix entries are already 1, the code has no effect. In some ADT designs, it might be preferable to inform the client of the attempt to insert a parallel edge, perhaps using a return code from insert. This

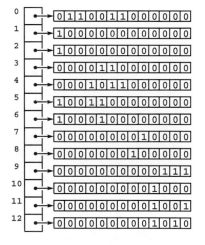

**Figure 17.9
Adjacency matrix data structure**

This figure depicts the C++ representation of the graph in Figure 17.1, as an vector of vectors.

representation does allow self-loops: An edge v–v is represented by a nonzero entry in a[v][v].

To remove an edge, we set the indicated matrix entries to `false`. If a nonexistent edge (one for which the matrix entries are already `false`) is to be removed, the code has no effect. Again, in some ADT designs, we might wish to arrange to inform the client of such conditions.

If we are processing huge graphs or huge numbers of small graphs, or space is otherwise tight, there are several ways to save space. For example, adjacency matrices that represent undirected graphs are symmetric: a[v][w] is always equal to a[w][v]. Thus, we could save space by storing only one-half of this symmetric matrix (see Exercise 17.22). Another way to save a signigicant amount of space is to use a matrix of bits (assuming that `vector<bool>` does not do so). In this way, for instance, we could represent graphs of up to about 64,000 vertices in about 64 million 64-bit words (see Exercise 17.23). These implementations have the slight complication that we need to add an ADT operation to test for the existence of an edge (see Exercise 17.20). (We do not use such an operation in our implementations because we can test for the existence of an edge v–w by simply testing a[v][w].) Such space-saving techniques are effective, but come at the cost of extra overhead that may fall in the inner loop in time-critical applications.

Many applications involve associating other information with each edge—in such cases, we can generalize the adjacency matrix to hold any information whatever, not just `bool`s. Whatever data type that we use for the matrix elements, we need to include an indication whether the indicated edge is present or absent. In Chapters 20 and 21, we explore such representations.

Use of adjacency matrices depends on associating vertex names with integers between 0 and $V-1$. This assignment might be done in one of many ways—for example, we consider a program that does so in Section 17.6). Therefore, the specific matrix of 0–1 values that we represent with a vector of vectors in C++ is but one possible representation of any given graph as an adjacency matrix, because another program might assign different vertex names to the indices we use to specify rows and columns. Two matrices that appear to be markedly different could represent the same graph (see Exercise 17.17). This observation is a restatement of the graph isomorphism problem: Although we might like to determine whether or not two different matrices represent the same graph, no one has devised an algorithm that can always do so efficiently. This difficulty is fundamental. For example, our ability to find an efficient solution to various important graph-processing problems depends completely on the way in which the vertices are numbered (see, for example, Exercise 17.26).

Program 17.3, which we considered in Section 17.2, prints out a table with the vertices adjacent to each vertex. When used with the implementation in Program 17.7, it prints the vertices in order of their vertex index, as in Figure 17.7. Notice, though, that it is not part of the definition of adjIterator that it visits vertices in index order, so developing an ADT client that prints out the adjacency-matrix representation of a graph is not a trivial task (see Exercise 17.18). The output produced by these programs are themselves graph representations that clearly illustrate a basic performance tradeoff. To print out the matrix, we need room on the page for all V^2 entries; to print out the lists, we need room for just $V + E$ numbers. For sparse graphs, when V^2 is huge compared to $V + E$, we prefer the lists; for dense graphs, when E and V^2 are comparable, we prefer the matrix. As we shall soon see, we make the same basic tradeoff when we compare the adjacency-matrix representation with its primary alternative: an explicit representation of the lists.

The adjacency-matrix representation is not satisfactory for huge sparse graphs: We need at least V^2 bits of storage and V^2 steps just to construct the representation. In a dense graph, when the number of edges (the number of 1 bits in the matrix) is proportional to V^2, this cost may be acceptable, because time proportional to V^2 is required to process the edges no matter what representation we use. In a sparse graph, however, just initializing the matrix could be the dominant factor in the running time of an algorithm. Moreover, we may not even have enough space for the matrix. For example, we may be faced with graphs with millions of vertices and tens of millions of edges, but we may not want—or be able—to pay the price of reserving space for *trillions* of 0 entries in the adjacency matrix.

On the other hand, when we do need to process a huge dense graph, then the 0-entries that represent absent edges increase our space needs by only a constant factor and provide us with the ability to determine whether any particular edge is present in constant time. For example, disallowing parallel edges is automatic in an adjacency matrix but is costly in some other representations. If we do have space available to hold an adjacency matrix, and either V^2 is so small as to represent a negligible amount of time or we will be running a complex algorithm that requires more than V^2 steps to complete, the adjacency-matrix representation may be the method of choice, no matter how dense the graph.

Exercises

▷ **17.17** Give the adjacency-matrix representations of the three graphs depicted in Figure 17.2.

○ **17.18** Give an implementation of show for the representation-independent io package of Program 17.4 that prints out a two-dimensional matrix of 0s and 1s like the one illustrated in Figure 17.8. *Note*: You cannot depend upon the iterator producing vertices in order of their indices.

17.19 Given a graph, consider another graph that is identical to the first, except that the names of (integers corresponding to) two vertices are interchanged. How are the adjacency matrices of these two graphs related?

▷ **17.20** Add a function edge to the graph ADT that allows clients to test whether there is an edge connecting two given vertices, and provide an implementation for the adjacency-matrix representation.

○ **17.21** Add functions to the graph ADT that allow clients to insert and delete vertices, and provide implementations for the adjacency-matrix representation.

▷ **17.22** Modify Program 17.7, augmented as described in Exercise 17.20, to cut its space requirements about in half by not including array entries a[v][w] for w greater than v.

17.23 Modify Program 17.7, augmented as described in Exercise 17.20, to ensure that, if your computer has B bits per word, a graph with V vertices is represented in about V^2/B words (as opposed to V^2). Do empirical tests to assess the effect of packing bits into words on the time required for the ADT operations.

17.24 Describe what happens if there is insufficient memory available to represent the matrix when the constructor in Program 17.7 is invoked, and suggest appropriate modifications to the code to handle this situation.

17.25 Develop a version of Program 17.7 that uses a single vector with V^2 entries.

○ **17.26** Suppose that all k vertices in a group have consecutive indices. How can you determine from the adjacency matrix whether or not that group of vertices constitutes a clique? Write a client ADT function that finds, in time proportional to V^2, the largest group of vertices with consecutive indices that constitutes a clique.

17.4 Adjacency-Lists Representation

The standard representation that is preferred for graphs that are not dense is called the *adjacency-lists* representation, where we keep track of all the vertices connected to each vertex on a linked list that is associated with that vertex. We maintain a vector of lists so that, given a vertex, we can immediately access its list; we use linked lists so that we can add new edges in constant time.

Program 17.9 is an implementation of the ADT interface in Program 17.1 that is based on this approach, and Figure 17.10 depicts an example. To add an edge connecting v and w to this representation of the graph, we add w to v's adjacency list and v to w's adjacency list. In this way, we still can add new edges in constant time, but the total amount of space that we use is proportional to the number of vertices plus the number of edges (as opposed to the number of vertices squared, for the adjacency-matrix representation). For undirected graphs, we again represent each edge in two different places: an edge connecting v and w is represented as nodes on both adjacency lists. It is important to include both; otherwise, we could not answer efficiently simple questions such as, "Which vertices are adjacent to vertex v?" Program 17.10 implements the iterator that answers this question for clients, in time proportional to the number of such vertices.

The implementation in Programs 17.9 and 17.10 is a low-level one. An alternative is to use the STL `list` to implement each linked list (see Exercise 17.30). The disadvantage of doing so is that STL `list` implementations need to support many more operations than we need and therefore typically carry extra overhead that might affect the performance of all of our algorithms (see Exercise 17.31). Indeed, all of our graph algorithms use the `Graph` ADT interface, so this implementation is an appropriate place to encapsulate all the low-level operations and concentrate on efficiency without affecting our other code. Another advantage of using the linked-list representation is that it provides a concrete basis for understanding the performance characteristics of our implementations.

But an important factor to consider is that the linked-list–based implementation in Programs 17.9 and 17.10 is incomplete, because it lacks a destructor and a copy constructor. For many applications, this defect could lead to unexpected results or severe performance prob-

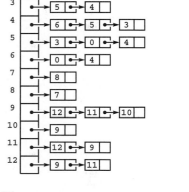

**Figure 17.10
Adjacency-lists data structure**

This figure depicts a representation of the graph in Figure 17.1 as an array of linked lists. The space used is proportional to the number of nodes plus the number of edges. To find the indices of the vertices connected to a given vertex v, we look at the vth position in an array, which contains a pointer to a linked list containing one node for each vertex connected to v. The order in which the nodes appear on the lists depends on the method that we use to construct the lists.

Program 17.9 Graph ADT implementation (adjacency lists)

This implementation of the interface in Program 17.1 uses a vector of linked lists, one corresponding to each vertex. It is equivalent to the representation of Program 3.15, where an edge v-w is represented by a node for w on list v and a node for v on list w.

Implementations of remove and edge are left for exercises, as are the copy constructor and the destructor. The insert code keeps insertion time constant by not checking for duplicate edges, and the total amount of space used is proportional to $V+E$; hence, this representation is most suitable for sparse multigraphs.

Clients may use typedef to make this type equivalent to GRAPH or use SparseMultiGRAPH explicitly.

```
class SparseMultiGRAPH
{ int Vcnt, Ecnt; bool digraph;
  struct node
    { int v; node* next;
      node(int x, node* t) { v = x; next = t; }
    };
  typedef node* link;
  vector <link> adj;
public:
  SparseMultiGRAPH(int V, bool digraph = false) :
    adj(V), Vcnt(V), Ecnt(0), digraph(digraph)
    { adj.assign(V, 0); }
  int V() const { return Vcnt; }
  int E() const { return Ecnt; }
  bool directed() const { return digraph; }
  void insert(Edge e)
    { int v = e.v, w = e.w;
      adj[v] = new node(w, adj[v]);
      if (!digraph) adj[w] = new node(v, adj[w]);
      Ecnt++;
    }
  void remove(Edge e);
  bool edge(int v, int w) const;
  class adjIterator;
  friend class adjIterator;
};
```

Program 17.10 Iterator for adjacency-lists representation

This implementation of the iterator for Program 17.9 maintains a link
t to traverse the linked list associated with vertex v. A call to beg()
followed by a sequence of calls to nxt() (checking that end() is false
before each call) gives a sequence of the vertices adjacent to v in G.

```
class SparseMultiGRAPH::adjIterator
{ const SparseMultiGRAPH &G;
  int v;
  link t;
public:
  adjIterator(const SparseMultiGRAPH &G, int v) :
    G(G), v(v) { t = 0; }
  int beg()
    { t = G.adj[v]; return t ? t->v : -1; }
  int nxt()
    { if (t) t = t->next; return t ? t->v : -1; }
  bool end()
    { return t == 0; }
};
```

---

lems. These functions are direct extensions of those in the first-class
queue implementation of Program 4.22 (see Exercise 17.29). We assume throughout the book that SparseMultiGRAPH objects have them.
Using the STL list instead of low-level singly-linked lists has the distinct advantage that this extra code is unnecessary because a proper
destructor and copy constructor are automatically defined. For example, DenseGRAPH objects built by Program 17.7 are properly destroyed
and copied in client programs that manipulate them, because they are
built from STL objects.

By contrast to Program 17.7, Program 17.9 builds multigraphs,
because it does not remove parallel edges. Checking for duplicate edges
in the adjacency-lists structure would necessitate searching through the
lists and could take time proportional to V. Similarly, Program 17.9
does not include an implementation of the *remove edge* operation or
the edge existence test. Adding implementations for these functions is
an easy exercise (see Exercise 17.28), but each operation might take
time proportional to V, to search through the lists for the nodes that

represent the edges. These costs make the basic adjacency-lists representation unsuitable for applications involving huge graphs where parallel edges cannot be tolerated, or applications involving heavy use of *remove edge* or of edge existence tests. In Section 17.5, we discuss adjacency-list implementations that support constant-time *remove edge* and *edge existence* operations.

When a graph's vertex names are not integers, then (as with adjacency matrices) two different programs might associate vertex names with the integers from 0 to $V - 1$ in two different ways, leading to two different adjacency-list structures (see, for example, Program 17.15). We cannot expect to be able to tell whether two different structures represent the same graph because of the difficulty of the graph isomorphism problem.

Moreover, with adjacency lists, there are numerous representations of a given graph even for a given vertex numbering. No matter in what order the edges appear on the adjacency lists, the adjacency-list structure represents the same graph (see Exercise 17.33). This characteristic of adjacency lists is important to know because the order in which edges appear on the adjacency lists affects, in turn, the order in which edges are processed by algorithms. That is, the adjacency-list structure determines how our various algorithms see the graph. Although an algorithm should produce a correct answer no matter how the edges are ordered on the adjacency lists, it might get to that answer by different sequences of computations for different orderings. If an algorithm does not need to examine all the graph's edges, this effect might affect the time that it takes. And, if there is more than one correct answer, different input orderings might lead to different output results.

The primary advantage of the adjacency-lists representation over the adjacency-matrix representation is that it always uses space proportional to $E + V$, as opposed to V^2 in the adjacency matrix. The primary disadvantage is that testing for the existence of specific edges can take time proportional to V, as opposed to constant time in the adjacency matrix. These differences trace, essentially, to the difference between using linked lists and vectors to represent the set of vertices incident on each vertex.

Thus, we see again that an understanding of the basic properties of linked data structures and vectors is critical if we are to develop efficient graph ADT implementations. Our interest in these performance differences is that we want to avoid implementations that are inappropriately inefficient under unexpected circumstances when a wide range of operations is to be demanded of the ADT. In Section 17.5, we discuss the application of basic data structures to realize many of the theoretical benefits of both structures. Nonetheless, Program 17.9 is a simple implementation with the essential characteristics that we need to learn efficient algorithms for processing sparse graphs.

Exercises

▷ **17.27** Show, in the style of Figure 17.10, the adjacency-lists structure produced when you use Program 17.9 to insert the edges in the graph

$$3\text{-}7 \quad 1\text{-}4 \quad 7\text{-}8 \quad 0\text{-}5 \quad 5\text{-}2 \quad 3\text{-}8 \quad 2\text{-}9 \quad 0\text{-}6 \quad 4\text{-}9 \quad 2\text{-}6 \quad 6\text{-}4$$

(in that order) into an initially empty graph.

17.28 Provide implementations of remove and edge for the adjacency-lists graph class (Program 17.9). *Note*: Duplicates may be present, but it suffices to remove *any* edge connecting the specified vertices.

17.29 Add a copy constructor and a destructor to the adjacency-lists graph class (Program 17.9). *Hint*: See Program 4.22.

○ **17.30** Modify the implementation of SparseMultiGRAPH Programs 17.9 and 17.10 to use an STL list instead of a linked list for each adjacency list.

17.31 Run empirical tests to compare your SparseMultiGRAPH implementation of Exercise 17.30 with the implementation in the text. For a well-chosen set of values for V, compare running times for a client program that builds complete graphs with V vertices, then extracts the edges using Program 17.2.

○ **17.32** Give a simple example of an adjacency-lists graph representation that could not have been built by repeated insertion of edges by Program 17.9.

17.33 How many different adjacency-lists representations represent the same graph as the one depicted in Figure 17.10?

○ **17.34** Add a public member function declaration to the graph ADT (Program 17.1) that removes self-loops and parallel edges. Provide the trivial implementation of this function for the adjacency-matrix–based class (Program 17.7), and provide an implementation of the function for the adjacency-list–based class (Program 17.9) that uses time proportional to E and extra space proportional to V.

17.35 Write a version of Program 17.9 that disallows parallel edges (by scanning through the adjacency list to avoid adding a duplicate entry on each edge

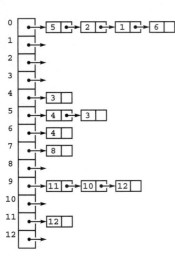

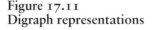

Figure 17.11
Digraph representations

The adjacency-matrix and adjacency-lists representations of a digraph have only one representation of each edge, as illustrated in the adjacency-matrix (top) and adjacency-lists (bottom) representation of the set of edges in Figure 17.1 interpreted as a digraph (see Figure 17.6, top).

insertion) and self-loops. Compare your implementation with the implementation described in Exercise 17.34. Which is better for static graphs? *Note*: See Exercise 17.49 for an efficient implementation.

17.36 Write a client of the graph ADT that returns the result of removing self-loops, parallel edges, and degree-0 (isolated) vertices from a given graph. *Note*: The running time of your program should be linear in the size of the graph representation.

• **17.37** Write a client of the graph ADT that returns the result of removing self-loops, collapsing paths that consist solely of degree-2 vertices from a given graph. Specifically, every degree-2 vertex in a graph with no parallel edges appears on some path u–...–w where u and w are either equal or not of degree 2. Replace any such path with u-w, and then remove all unused degree-2 vertices as in Exercise 17.36. *Note*: This operation may introduce self-loops and parallel edges, but it preserves the degrees of vertices that are not removed.

▷ **17.38** Give a (multi)graph that could result from applying the transformation described in Exercise 17.37 on the sample graph in Figure 17.1.

17.5 Variations, Extensions, and Costs

In this section, we describe a number of options for improving the graph representations discussed in Sections 17.3 and 17.4. The topics fall into one of three categories. First, the basic adjacency-matrix and adjacency-lists mechanisms extend readily to allow us to represent other types of graphs. In the relevant chapters, we consider these extensions in detail and give examples; here, we look at them briefly. Second, we discuss graph ADT designs with more features than our basic one and implementations that use more advanced data structures to efficiently implement them. Third, we discuss our general approach to addressing graph-processing tasks, by developing task-specific classes that use the basic graph ADT.

Our implementations in Programs 17.7 and 17.9 build digraphs if the call to the constructor includes a second argument with value true. We represent each edge just once, as illustrated in Figure 17.11. An edge v–w in a digraph is represented by a 1 in the entry in row v and column w in the adjacency matrix or by the appearance of w on v's adjacency list in the adjacency-lists representation. These representations are simpler than the corresponding representations that we have been considering for undirected graphs, but the asymmetry makes digraphs more complicated combinatorial objects than undirected graphs, as we see in Chapter 19. For example, the standard adjacency-lists representation gives no direct way to find all edges coming into a vertex in a digraph, so we would need to choose a different representation if that operation needs to be supported.

For *weighted graphs* and *networks*, we fill the adjacency matrix with structures containing information about edges (including their presence or absence) instead of Boolean values; in the adjacency-lists representation, we include this information in adjacency-list elements.

It is often necessary to associate still more information with the vertices or edges of a graph, to allow that graph to model more complicated objects. We can associate extra information with each edge by extending the Edge type in Program 17.1 as appropriate, then using instances of that type in the adjacency matrix, or in the list nodes in the adjacency lists. Or, since vertex names are integers between 0 and $V-1$, we can use vertex-indexed vectors to associate extra information for vertices, perhaps using an appropriate ADT. We consider ADTs of this sort in Chapters 20 through 22. Alternatively, we could use a separate symbol-table ADT to associate extra information with each vertex and edge (see Exercise 17.48 and Program 17.15).

To handle various specialized graph-processing problems, we often define classes that contain specialized auxiliary data structures related to the graph. The most common such data structure is a vertex-indexed vector, as we saw already in Chapter 1, where we used vertex-indexed vectors to answer connectivity queries. We use vertex-indexed vectors in numerous implementations throughout the book.

As an example, suppose that we wish to know whether a vertex v in a graph is isolated. Is v of degree 0? For the adjacency-lists representation, we can find this information immediately, simply by checking whether adj[v] is null. But for the adjacency-matrix representation, we need to check all V entries in the row or column corresponding to v to know that each one is not connected to any other vertex; and for the vector-of-edges representation, we have no better approach than to check all E edges to see whether there are any that involve v. We need to enable clients to avoid these potentially time-consuming computations. As discussed in Section 17.2 one way to do so is to define a client ADT for the problem, such as the example in Program 17.11. This implementation, after preprocessing the graph in time proportional to the size of its representation, allows clients to find the degree of any

Program 17.11 Vertex-degrees class implementation

This class provides a way for clients to learn the degree of any given vertex in a GRAPH in constant time, after linear-time preprocessing in the constructor. The implementation is based on maintaining a vertex-indexed vector of vertex degrees as a private data member and overloading [] as a public function member. We initialize all entries to 0, then process all edges in the graph, incrementing the appropriate entry for each edge.

We use classes like this one throughout the book to develop object-oriented implementations of graph-processing functions as clients of class GRAPH.

```
template <class Graph> class DEGREE
{ const Graph &G;
  vector <int> degree;
public:
  DEGREE(const Graph &G) : G(G), degree(G.V(), 0)
    {
      for (int v = 0; v < G.V(); v++)
      { typename Graph::adjIterator A(G, v);
        for (int w = A.beg(); !A.end(); w = A.nxt())
          degree[v]++;
      }
    }
  int operator[](int v) const
    { return degree[v]; }
};
```

vertex in constant time. That is no improvement if the client needs the degree of just one vertex, but it represents a substantial savings for clients that need to know the degrees of many vertices. Such a substantial performance differential for such a simple problem is typical in graph processing.

For each of the graph-processing tasks that we consider in this book, we encapsulate solutions in classes like this one, with private data and function members and public function members specific to the task. Clients create objects whose member functions do the graph processing. This approach amounts to extending the graph ADT interface by defining a cooperating set of classes. Any set of such classes defines a graph-processing interface, but each encapsulates its own private data and function members.

There are many other ways to build upon an interface in C++. One way to proceed is to simply add public function members (and whatever private data and function members we might need) to the basic GRAPH ADT definition. While this approach has all of the virtues extolled in Chapter 4, it also has some serious drawbacks, because the world of graph-processing is significantly more expansive than the kinds of basic data structures that are the subject of Chapter 4. Chief among these drawbacks are the following:

- There are many more graph-processing functions to implement than we can accurately define in a single interface.
- Simple graph-processing tasks have to use the same interface needed by complicated tasks.
- One member function can access a data member intended for use by another member function, contrary to encapsulation principles that we would like to follow.

Interfaces of this kind have come to be known as *fat* interfaces. In a book filled with graph-processing algorithms, an interface of this sort would be fat indeed.

Another approach is to use inheritance to define various types of graphs that provide clients with various sets of graph-processing tasks. Comparing the intricacies of this approach with the simpler approach that we use is a worthwhile exercise in the study of software engineering, but would take us still further afield from the subject of graph-processing algorithms, our main focus.

Table 17.1 shows the dependence of the cost of various simple graph-processing operations on the representation that we use. This table is worth examining before we consider the implementation of more complicated operations; it will help you to develop an intuition for the difficulty of various primitive operations. Most of the costs listed follow immediately from inspecting the code, with the exception of the bottom row, which we consider in detail at the end of this section.

In several cases, we can modify the representation to make simple operations more efficient, although we have to take care that doing so does not increase costs for other simple operations. For example, the entry for adjacency-matrix *destroy* is an artifact of our vector-

Table 17.1 Worst-case cost of graph-processing operations

The performance characteristics of basic graph-processing ADT operations for different graph representations vary widely, even for simple tasks, as indicated in this table of the worst-case costs (all within a constant factor for large V and E). These costs are for the simple implementations we have described in previous sections; various modifications that affect the costs are described in the text of this section.

	array of edges	adjacency matrix	adjacency lists
space	E	V^2	$V + E$
initialize empty	1	V^2	V
copy	E	V^2	E
destroy	1	V	E
insert edge	1	1	1
Ændremove edge	E	1	V
is v isolated?	E	V	1
path from u to v?	$E \lg^* V$	V^2	$V + E$

of-vectors allocation scheme for two-dimensional matrices (see Section 3.7). It is not difficult to reduce this cost to be constant (see Exercise 17.25). On the other hand, if graph edges are sufficiently complex structures that the matrix entries are pointers, then to *destroy* an adjacency matrix would take time proportional to V^2.

Because of their frequent use in typical applications, we consider the *find edge* and *remove edge* operations in detail. In particular, we need a *find edge* operation to be able to remove or disallow parallel edges. As we saw in Section 17.3, these operations are trivial if we are using an adjacency-matrix representation—we need only to check or set a matrix entry that we can index directly. But how can we implement these operations efficiently in the adjacency-lists representation? In C++, we could use the STL; here we describe underlying mechanisms, to gain perspective on efficiency issues. One approach is described next, and another is described in Exercise 17.50. Both approaches are based on symbol-table implementations. If we use, for example, dynamic hash table implementations (see Section 14.5), both approaches take space proportional to E and allow us to perform either operation in constant time (on the average, amortized).

Specifically, to implement *find edge* when we are using adjacency lists, we could use an auxiliary symbol table for the edges. We can assign an edge v–w the integer key v*V+w and use an STL map or any of the symbol-table implementations from Part 4. (For undirected graphs, we might assign the same key to v–w and w–v.) We can insert each edge into the symbol table, after first checking whether it has already been inserted. We can choose either to disallow parallel edges (see Exercise 17.49) or to maintain duplicate records in the symbol table for parallel edges (see Exercise 17.50). In the present context, our main interest in this technique is that it provides a constant-time *find edge* implementation for adjacency lists.

To be able to remove edges, we need a pointer in the symbol-table record for each edge that refers to its representation in the adjacency-lists structure. But even this information is not sufficient to allow us to remove the edge in constant time unless the lists are doubly linked (see Section 3.4). Furthermore, in undirected graphs, it is not sufficient to remove the node from the adjacency list, because each edge appears on two different adjacency lists. One solution to this difficulty is to put both pointers in the symbol table; another is to link together the two list nodes that correspond to a particular edge (see Exercise 17.46). With either of these solutions, we can remove an edge in constant time.

Removing vertices is more expensive. In the adjacency-matrix representation, we essentially need to remove a row and a column from the matrix, which is not much less expensive than starting over again with a smaller matrix (although that cost can be amortized using the same mechanism as for dynamic hash tables). If we are using an adjacency-lists representation, we see immediately that it is not sufficient to remove nodes from the vertex's adjacency list, because each node on the adjacency list specifies another vertex whose adjacency list we must search to remove the other node that represents the same edge. We need the extra links to support constant-time edge removal as described in the previous paragraph if we are to remove a vertex in time proportional to V.

We omit implementations of these operations here because they are straightforward programming exercises using basic techniques from Part 1, because the STL provides implementations that we could use, because maintaining complex structures with multiple pointers per node is not justified in typical applications that involve static graphs, and because we wish to avoid getting bogged down in layers of abstraction or in low-level details of maintaining multiple pointers when implementing graph-processing algorithms that do not otherwise use them. In Chapter 22, we do consider implementations of a similar structure that play an essential role in the powerful general algorithms that we consider in that chapter.

For clarity in describing and developing implementations of algorithms of interest, we use the simplest appropriate representation. Generally, we strive to use data structures that are directly relevant to the task at hand. Many programmers practice this kind of minimalism as a matter of course, knowing that maintaining the integrity of a data structure with multiple disparate components can be a challenging task, indeed.

We might also consider alternate implementations that modify the basic data structures in a performance-tuning process to save space or time, particularly when processing huge graphs (or huge numbers of small graphs). For example, we can dramatically improve the performance of algorithms that process huge static graphs represented with adjacency lists by stripping down the representation to use vectors of varying length instead of linked lists to represent the set of vertices incident on each vertex. With this technique, we can ultimately represent a graph with just $2E$ integers less than V and V integers less than V^2 (see Exercises 17.52 and 17.54). Such representations are attractive for processing huge static graphs.

The algorithms that we consider adapt readily to all the variations that we have discussed in this section, because they are based on a few high-level abstract operations such as "perform the following operation for each edge adjacent to vertex v" that are supported by our basic ADT.

In some instances, our algorithm-design decisions depend on certain properties of the representation. Working at a higher level of abstraction might obscure our knowledge of that dependence. If we *know* that one representation would lead to poor performance but another would not, we would be taking an unnecessary risk were we to consider the algorithm at the wrong level of abstraction. As usual, our goal is to craft implementations such that we can make precise statements about performance. For this reason, though both implement the basic graph ADT, we retain separate `DenseGRAPH` and `SparseMultiGRAPH` types for the adjacency-matrix and adjacency-lists representations, respectively, to emphasize that clients can use these implementations as appropriate to suit the task at hand.

All of the operations that we have considered so far are simple, albeit necessary, data-processing functions; and the bottom line of the discussion in this section is that basic algorithms and data structures from Parts 1 through 3 are effective for handling them. As we develop more sophisticated graph-processing algorithms, we face more difficult challenges in finding the best implementations for specific practical problems. To illustrate this point, we consider the last row in Table 17.1, which gives the costs of determining whether there is a path connecting two given vertices.

In the worst case, the simple path-finding algorithm in Section 17.7 examines all E edges in the graph (as do several other methods that we consider in Chapter 18). The entries in the center and right column on the bottom row in Table 17.1 indicate, respectively, that the algorithm may examine all V^2 entries in an adjacency-matrix representation, and all V list heads and all E nodes on the lists in an adjacency-lists representation. These facts imply that the algorithm's running time is linear in the size of the graph representation, but they also exhibit two anomalies: The worst-case running time is *not* linear in the number of edges in the graph if we are using an adjacency-matrix representation for a sparse graph or either representation for an extremely sparse graph (one with a huge number of isolated vertices). To avoid repeatedly considering these anomalies, we assume throughout that *the size of the representation that we use is proportional to the number of edges in the graph*. This point is moot in the majority of applications because they involve huge sparse graphs and thus require an adjacency-lists representation.

The left column on the bottom row in Table 17.1 derives from the use of the union-find algorithms in Chapter 1 (see Exercise 17.15). This method is attractive because it only requires space proportional to V, but has the drawback that it cannot exhibit the path. This entry highlights the importance of completely and precisely specifying graph-processing problems.

Even after taking all of these factors into consideration, one of the most significant challenges that we face when developing practical graph-processing algorithms is assessing the extent to which the results of worst-case performance analyses, such as those in Table 17.1, over-estimate time and space needs for processing graphs that we encounter in practice. Most of the literature on graph algorithms describes performance in terms of such worst-case guarantees, and, while this information is helpful in identifying algorithms that can have unacceptably poor performance, it may not shed much light on which of several simple, direct programs may be most suitable for a given application. This situation is exacerbated by the difficulty of developing useful models of average-case performance for graph algorithms, leaving us with (perhaps unreliable) benchmark testing and (perhaps overly conservative) worst-case performance guarantees to work with. For example, the graph-search methods that we discuss in Chapter 18 are all effective linear-time algorithms for finding a path between two given vertices, but their performance characteristics differ markedly, depending both upon the graph being processed and its representation. When using graph-processing algorithms in practice, we constantly fight this disparity between the worst-case performance guarantees that we can prove and the actual performance characteristics that we can expect. This theme will recur throughout the book.

Exercises

17.39 Develop an adjacency-matrix representation for dense multigraphs, and provide an ADT implementation for Program 17.1 that uses it.

○ **17.40** Why not use a direct representation for graphs (a data structure that models the graph exactly, with vertex objects that contain adjacency lists with references to the vertices)?

▷ **17.41** Why does Program 17.11 not increment *both* deg[v] and deg[w] when it discovers that w is adjacent to v?

▷ **17.42** Add to the graph class that uses adjacency matrices (Program 17.7) a vertex-indexed vector that holds the degree of each vertex. Add a public member function degree that returns the degree of a given vertex.

17.43 Do Exercise 17.42 for the adjacency-lists representation.

▷ **17.44** Add a row to Table 17.1 for the problem of determining the number of isolated vertices in a graph. Support your answer with function implementations for each of the three representations.

○ **17.45** Give a row to add to Table 17.1 for the problem of determining whether a given digraph has a vertex with indegree V and outdegree 0. Support your answer with function implementations for each of the three representations. *Note*: Your entry for the adjacency-matrix representation should be V.

17.46 Use doubly-linked adjacency lists with cross links as described in the text to implement a constant-time *remove edge* function `remove` for the graph ADT implementation that uses adjacency lists (Program 17.9).

17.47 Add a *remove vertex* function `remove` to the doubly-linked adjacency-lists graph class described in the previous exercise.

○ **17.48** Modify your solution to Exercise 17.16 to use a dynamic hash table, as described in the text, such that *insert edge* and *remove edge* take constant amortized time.

17.49 Add to the graph class that uses adjacency lists (Program 17.9) a symbol table to ignore duplicate edges, so that it represents graphs instead of multigraphs. Use dynamic hashing for your symbol-table implementation so that your implementation uses space proportional to E and can insert, find, and remove edges in constant time (on the average, amortized).

17.50 Develop a multigraph class based on a vector-of-symbol-tables representation (with one symbol table for each vertex, which contains its list of adjacent edges). Use dynamic hashing for your symbol-table implementation so that your implementation uses space proportional to E and can insert, find, and remove edges in constant time (on the average, amortized).

17.51 Develop a graph ADT intended for static graphs, based upon a constructor that takes a vector of edges as an argument and uses the basic graph ADT to build a graph. (Such an implementation might be useful for performance comparisons with the implementations described in Exercises 17.52 through 17.55.)

17.52 Develop an implementation for the constructor described in Exercise 17.51 that uses a compact representation based on the following data structures:

```
struct node { int cnt; vector <int> edges; };
struct graph { int V; int E; vector <node> adj; };
```

A graph is a vertex count, an edge count, and a vector of vertices. A vertex contains an edge count and a vector with one vertex index corresponding to each adjacent edge.

● **17.53** Add to your solution to Exercise 17.52 a function that eliminates self-loops and parallel edges, as in Exercise 17.34.

○ **17.54** Develop an implementation for the static-graph ADT described in Exercise 17.51 that uses just two vectors to represent the graph: one vector of E vertices, and another of V indices or pointers into the first vector. Implement `io::show` for this representation.

● **17.55** Add to your solution to Exercise 17.54 a function that eliminates self-loops and parallel edges, as in Exercise 17.34.

17.56 Develop a graph ADT interface that associates (x, y) coordinates with each vertex, so that you can work with graph drawings. Include functions drawV and drawE to draw a vertex and to draw an edge, respectively.

17.57 Write a client program that uses your interface from Exercise 17.56 to produce drawings of edges that are being added to a small graph.

17.58 Develop an implementation of your interface from Exercise 17.56 that produces a PostScript program with drawings as output (see Section 4.3).

17.59 Find an appropriate graphics interface that allows you to develop an implementation of your interface from Exercise 17.56 that directly draws graphs in a window on your display.

● **17.60** Extend your solution to Exercises 17.56 and 17.59 to include functions to erase vertices and edges and to draw them in different styles, so that you can write client programs that provide dynamic graphical animations of graph algorithms in operation.

17.6 Graph Generators

To develop further appreciation for the diverse nature of graphs as combinatorial structures, we now consider detailed examples of the types of graphs that we use later to test the algorithms that we study. Some of these examples are drawn from applications. Others are drawn from mathematical models that are intended both to have properties that we might find in real graphs and to expand the range of input trials available for testing our algorithms.

To make the examples concrete, we present them as client functions of Program 17.1, so that we can put them to immediate use when we test implementations of the graph algorithms that we consider. In addition, we consider the implementation of io::scan from Program 17.4, which reads a sequence of pairs of arbitrary names from standard input and builds a graph with vertices corresponding to the names and edges corresponding to the pairs.

The implementations that we consider in this section are based upon the interface of Program 17.1, so they function properly, in theory, for any graph representation. In practice, however, some combinations of interface and representation can have unacceptably poor performance, as we shall see.

Program 17.12 Random graph generator (random edges)

This function adds random edges to a graph by generating E random pairs of integers, interpreting the integers as vertex labels and the pairs of vertex labels as edges. It leaves the decision about the treatment of parallel edges and self-loops to the implementation of the `insert` member function of `Graph`. This method is generally not suitable for generating huge dense graphs because of the number of parallel edges that it generates.

```
static void randE(Graph &G, int E)
  {
    for (int i = 0; i < E; i++)
      {
        int v = int(G.V()*rand()/(1.0+RAND_MAX));
        int w = int(G.V()*rand()/(1.0+RAND_MAX));
        G.insert(Edge(v,w));
      }
  }
```

As usual, we are interested in having "random problem instances," both to exercise our programs with arbitrary inputs and to get an idea of how the programs might perform in real applications. For graphs, the latter goal is more elusive than for other domains that we have considered, although it is still a worthwhile objective. We shall encounter various different models of randomness, starting with these two.

Random edges This model is simple to implement, as indicated by the generator given in Program 17.12. For a given number of vertices V, we generate random edges by generating pairs of numbers between 0 and $V - 1$. The result is likely to be a random multigraph with self-loops. A given pair could have two identical numbers (hence, self-loops could occur); and any pair could be repeated multiple times (hence, parallel edges could occur). Program 17.12 generates edges until the graph is known to have E edges, leaving to the implementation the decision of whether to eliminate parallel edges. If parallel edges are eliminated, the number of edges generated is substantially higher than then number of edges used (E) for dense graphs (see Exercise 17.62); so this method is normally used for sparse graphs.

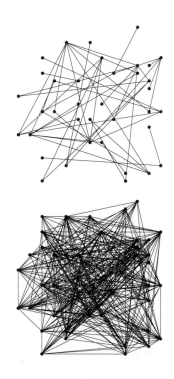

Figure 17.12
Two random graphs

Both of these random graphs have 50 vertices. The sparse graph at the top has 50 edges, while the dense graph at the bottom has 500 edges. The sparse graph is not connected, with each vertex connected only to a few others; the dense graph is certainly connected, with each vertex connected to 20 others, on the average. These diagrams also indicate the difficulty of developing algorithms that can draw arbitrary graphs (the vertices here are placed in random position).

Program 17.13　Random graph generator (random graph)

Like Program 17.12, this function generates random pairs of integers between 0 and V-1 to add random edges to a graph, but it uses a different probabilistic model where each possible edge occurs independently with some probability p. The value of p is calculated such that the expected number of edges $(pV(V-1)/2)$ is equal to E. The number of edges in any particular graph generated by this code will be close to E but is unlikely to be precisely equal to E. This method is primarily suitable for dense graphs, because its running time is proportional to V^2.

```
static void randG(Graph &G, int E)
  { double p = 2.0*E/G.V()/(G.V()-1);
    for (int i = 0; i < G.V(); i++)
      for (int j = 0; j < i; j++)
        if (rand() < p*RAND_MAX)
          G.insert(Edge(i, j));
  }
```

Random graph　　The classic mathematical model for random graphs is to consider all possible edges and to include each in the graph with a fixed probability p. If we want the expected number of edges in the graph to be E, we can choose $p = 2E/V(V-1)$. Program 17.13 is a function that uses this model to generate random graphs. This model precludes duplicate edges, but the number of edges in the graph is only equal to E *on the average*. This implementation is well-suited for dense graphs, but not for sparse graphs, since it runs in time proportional to $V(V-1)/2$ to generate just $E = pV(V-1)/2$ edges. That is, for sparse graphs, the running time of Program 17.13 is quadratic in the size of the graph (see Exercise 17.68).

These models are well-studied and are not difficult to implement, but they do not necessarily generate graphs with properties similar to the ones that we see in practice. In particular, graphs that model maps, circuits, schedules, transactions, networks, and other practical situations are usually not only sparse but also exhibit a *locality* property—edges are much more likely to connect a given vertex to vertices in a particular set than to vertices that are not in the set. We might consider many different ways of modeling locality, as illustrated in the following examples.

k-**neighbor graph**   The graph depicted at the top in Figure 17.13 is drawn from a simple modification to a random-edges graph generator, where we randomly pick the first vertex v, then randomly pick the second from among those whose indices are within a fixed constant k of v (wrapping around from $V - 1$ to 0, when the vertices are arranged in a circle as depicted). Such graphs are easy to generate and certainly exhibit locality not found in random graphs.

Euclidean neighbor graph   The graph depicted at the bottom in Figure 17.13 is drawn from a generator that generates V points in the plane with random coordinates between 0 and 1, and then generates edges connecting any two points within distance d of one another. If d is small, the graph is sparse; if d is large, the graph is dense (see Exercise 17.74). This graph models the types of graphs that we might expect when we process graphs from maps, circuits, or other applications where vertices are associated with geometric locations. They are easy to visualize, exhibit properties of algorithms in an intuitive manner, and exhibit many of the structural properties that we find in such applications.

One possible defect in this model is that the graphs are not likely to be connected when they are sparse; other difficulties are that the graphs are unlikely to have high-degree vertices and that they do not have any long edges. We can change the models to handle such situations, if desired, or we can consider numerous similar examples to try to model other situations (see, for example, Exercises 17.72 and 17.73).

Or, we can test our algorithms on real graphs. In many applications, there is no shortage of problem instances drawn from actual data that we can use to test our algorithms. For example, huge graphs drawn from actual geographic data are easy to find; two more examples are listed in the next two paragraphs. The advantage of working with real data instead of a random graph model is that we can see solutions to real problems as algorithms evolve. The disadvantage is that we may lose the benefit of being able to predict the performance of our algorithms through mathematical analysis. We return to this topic when we are ready to compare several algorithms for the same task, at the end of Chapter 18.

Transaction graph   Figure 17.14 illustrates a tiny piece of a graph that we might find in a telephone company's computers. It has a

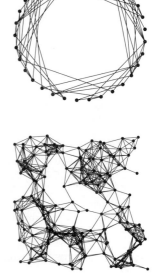

Figure 17.13
Random neighbor graphs

These figures illustrate two models of sparse graphs. The neighbor graph at the top has 33 vertices and 99 edges, with each edge restricted to connect vertices whose indices differ by less than 10 (modulo V). The Euclidean neighbor graph at the bottom models the types of graphs that we might find in applications where vertices are tied to geometric locations. Vertices are random points in the plane; edges connect any pair of vertices within a specified distance d of each other. This graph is sparse (177 vertices and 1001 edges); by adjusting d, we can generate graphs of any desired density.

900–435–5100	201–332–4562
415–345–3030	757–995–5030
757–310–4313	201–332–4562
747–511–4562	609–445–3260
900–332–3162	212–435–3562
617–945–2152	408–310–4150
757–995–5030	757–310–4313
212–435–3562	803–568–8358
913–410–3262	212–435–3562
401–212–4152	907–618–9999
201–232–2422	415–345–3120
913–495–1030	802–935–5112
609–445–3260	415–345–3120
201–310–3100	415–345–3120
408–310–4150	802–935–5113
708–332–4353	803–777–5834
413–332–3562	905–828–8089
815–895–8155	208–971–0020
802–935–5115	408–310–4150
708–410–5032	212–435–3562
201–332–4562	408–310–4150
815–511–3032	201–332–4562
301–292–3162	505–709–8080
617–833–2425	208–907–9098
800–934–5030	408–310–4150
408–982–3100	201–332–4562
415–345–3120	905–569–1313
413–435–4313	415–345–3120
747–232–8323	408–310–4150
802–995–1115	908–922–2239

Figure 17.14
Transaction graph

A sequence of pairs of numbers like this one might represent a list of telephone calls in a local exchange, or financial transfers between accounts, or any similar situation involving transactions between entities with unique identifiers. The graphs are hardly random—some phones are far more heavily used than others and some accounts are far more active than others.

Program 17.14 Building a graph from pairs of symbols

This implementation of the scan function from Program 17.4 uses a symbol table to build a graph by reading pairs of symbols from standard input. The symbol-table ADT function index associates an integer with each symbol: on unsuccessful search in a table of size N it adds the symbol to the table with associated integer N+1; on successful search, it simply returns the integer previously associated with the symbol. Any of the symbol-table methods in Part 4 can be adapted for this use; for example, see Program 17.15.

```
#include "ST.cc"
template <class Graph>
void IO<Graph>::scan(Graph &G)
  { string v, w;
    ST st;
    while (cin >> v >> w)
      G.insert(Edge(st.index(v), st.index(w)));
  }
```

vertex defined for each phone number, and an edge for each pair i and j with the property that i made a telephone call to j within some fixed period. This set of edges represents a huge multigraph. It is certainly sparse, since each person places calls to only a tiny fraction of the available telephones. It is representative of many other applications. For example, a financial institution's credit card and merchant account records might have similar information.

Function call graph We can associate a graph with any computer program with functions as vertices and an edge connecting X and Y whenever function X calls function Y. We can instrument the program to create such a graph (or have a compiler do it). Two completely different graphs are of interest: the static version, where we create edges at compile time corresponding to the function calls that appear in the program text of each function; and a dynamic version, where we create edges at run time when the calls actually happen. We use static function call graphs to study program structure and dynamic ones to study program behavior. These graphs are typically huge and sparse.

In applications such as these, we face massive amounts of data, so we might prefer to study the performance of algorithms on real

Program 17.15 Symbol indexing for vertex names

This implementation of symbol-table indexing for string keys (which is described in the commentary for Program 17.14) accomplishes the task by adding an index field to each node in an existence-table TST (see Program 15.8). The index associated with each key is kept in the index field in the node corresponding to its end-of-string character.

　　We use the characters in the search key to move down the TST, as usual. When we reach the end of the key, we set its index if necessary and also set the private data member val, which is returned to the caller after all recursive calls to the function have returned.

```
#include <string>
class ST
{ int N, val;
  struct node
    { int v, d; node* l, *m, *r;
      node(int d) : v(-1), d(d), l(0), m(0), r(0) {}
    };
  typedef node* link;
  link head;
  link indexR(link h, const string &s, int w)
    { int i = s[w];
      if (h == 0) h = new node(i);
      if (i == 0)
        {
          if (h->v == -1) h->v = N++;
          val = h->v;
          return h;
        }
      if (i < h->d) h->l = indexR(h->l, s, w);
      if (i == h->d) h->m = indexR(h->m, s, w+1);
      if (i > h->d) h->r = indexR(h->r, s, w);
      return h;
    }
public:
  ST() : head(0), N(0) { }
  int index(const string &key)
    { head = indexR(head, key, 0); return val; }
};
```

sample data rather than on random models. We might choose to try to avoid degenerate situations by randomly ordering the edges or by introducing randomness in the decision making in our algorithms, but that is a different matter from generating a random graph. Indeed, in many applications, learning the properties of the graph structure is a goal in itself.

In several of these examples, vertices are natural named objects, and edges appear as pairs of named objects. For example, a transaction graph might be built from a sequence of pairs of telephone numbers, and a Euclidean graph might be built from a sequence of pairs of cities or towns. Program 17.14 is an implementation of the scan function in Program 17.4, which we can use to build a graph in this common situation. For the client's convenience, it takes the set of edges as defining the graph and deduces the set of vertex names from their use in edges. Specifically, the program reads a sequence of pairs of symbols from standard input, uses a symbol table to associate the vertex numbers 0 to $V - 1$ to the symbols (where V is the number of different symbols in the input), and builds a graph by inserting the edges, as in Programs 17.12 and 17.13. We could adapt any symbol-table implementation to support the needs of Program 17.14; Program 17.15 is an example that uses ternary search trees (TSTs) (see Chapter 14). These programs make it easy for us to test our algorithms on real graphs that may not be characterized accurately by any probabilistic model.

Program 17.14 is also significant because it validates the assumption we have made in all of our algorithms that the vertex names are integers between 0 and $V - 1$. If we have a graph that has some other set of vertex names, then the first step in representing the graph is to use Program 17.15 to map the vertex names to integers between 0 and $V - 1$.

Some graphs are based on implicit connections among items. We do not focus on such graphs, but we note their existence in the next few examples and devote a few exercises to them. When faced with processing such a graph, we can certainly write a program to construct explicit graphs by enumerating all the edges; but there also may be solutions to specific problems that do not require that we enumerate all the edges and therefore can run in sublinear time.

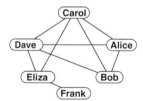

Figure 17.15
Degrees-of-separation graph

The graph at the bottom is defined by the groups at the top, with one vertex for each person and an edge connecting a pair of people whenever they are in the same group. Shortest path lengths in the graph correspond to degrees of separation. For example, Frank is three degrees of separation from Alice and Bob.

Degrees-of-separation graph Consider a collection of subsets drawn from V items. We define a graph with one vertex corresponding to each element in the union of the subsets and edges between two vertices if both vertices appear in some subset (see Figure 17.15). If desired, the graph might be a multigraph, with edge labels naming the appropriate subsets. All items incident on a given item v are said to be 1 *degree of separation* from v. Otherwise, all items incident on any item that is i degrees of separation from v (that are not already known to be i or fewer degrees of separation from v) are $(i+1)$ degrees of separation from v. This construction has amused people ranging from mathematicians (Erdös number) to movie buffs (separation from Kevin Bacon).

Interval graph Consider a collection of V intervals on the real line (pairs of real numbers). We define a graph with one vertex corresponding to each interval, with edges between vertices if the corresponding intervals intersect (have any points in common).

de Bruijn graph Suppose that V is a power of 2. We define a digraph with one vertex corresponding to each nonnegative integer less than V, with edges from each vertex i to $2i$ and $(2i+1)$ mod $\lg V$. These graphs are useful in the study of the sequence of values that can occur in a fixed-length shift register for a sequence of operations where we repeatedly shift all the bits one position to the left, throw away the leftmost bit, and fill the rightmost bit with 0 or 1. Figure 17.16 depicts the de Bruijn graphs with 8, 16, 32, and 64 vertices.

The various types of graphs that we have considered in this section have a wide variety of different characteristics. However, they all look the same to our programs: They are simply collections of edges. As we saw in Chapter 1, learning even the simplest facts about them can be a computational challenge. In this book, we consider numerous ingenious algorithms that have been developed for solving practical problems related to many types of graphs.

Based just on the few examples presented in this section, we can see that graphs are complex combinatorial objects, far more complex than those underlying other algorithms that we studied in Parts 1 through 4. In many instances, the graphs that we need to consider in applications are difficult or impossible to characterize. Algorithms that perform well on random graphs are often of limited applicability because it is often difficult to be persuaded that random graphs have structural characteristics the same as those of the graphs that arise in applications. The usual approach to overcome this objection is to design algorithms that perform well in the worst case. While this approach is successful in some instances, it falls short (by being too conservative) in others.

While we are often not justified in assuming that performance studies on graphs generated from one of the random graph models that we have discussed will give information sufficiently accurate to allow us to predict performance on real graphs, the graph generators that we have considered in this section are useful in helping us to test implementations and to understand our algorithms' performance. Before we even attempt to predict performance for applications, we must at least verify any assumptions that we might have made about the relationship between the application's data and whatever models or sample data we may have used. While such verfication is wise when we are working in any applications domain, it is particularly important when we are processing graphs, because of the broad variety of types of graphs that we encounter.

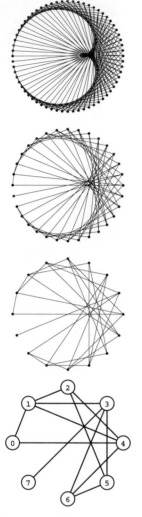

Figure 17.16
de Bruijn graphs

A de Bruijn digraph of order n has 2^n vertices with edges from i to $2i$ mod n and $(2i+1)$ mod 2^n, for all i. Pictured here are the underlying undirected de Bruijn graphs of order 6, 5, 4, and 3 (top to bottom).

Exercises

▷ **17.61** When we use Program 17.12 to generate random graphs of density αV, what fraction of edges produced are self-loops?

● **17.62** Calculate the expected number of parallel edges produced when we use Program 17.12 to generate random graphs with V vertices of density α. Use the result of your calculation to draw plots showing the fraction of parallel edges produced as a function of α, for $V = 10$, 100, and 1000.

17.63 Use an STL map to develop an alternate implementation of the ST class of Program 17.15.

● **17.64** Find a large undirected graph somewhere online—perhaps based on network-connectivity information, or a separation graph defined by coauthors in a set of bibliographic lists or by actors in movies.

▷ **17.65** Write a program that generates sparse random graphs for a well-chosen set of values of V and E, and prints the amount of space that it used for the graph representation and the amount of time that it took to build it. Test your program with a sparse-graph class (Program 17.9) and with the random-graph generator (Program 17.12), so that you can do meaningful empirical tests on graphs drawn from this model.

▷ **17.66** Write a program that generates dense random graphs for a well-chosen set of values of V and E, and prints the amount of space that it used for the graph representation and the amount of time that it took to build it. Test your program with a dense-graph class (Program 17.7) and with the random-graph generator (Program 17.13), so that you can do meaningful empirical tests on graphs drawn from this model.

• **17.67** Give the standard deviation of the number of edges produced by Program 17.13.

• **17.68** Write a program that produces each possible graph with precisely the same probability as does Program 17.13, but uses time and space proportional to only $V + E$, not V^2. Test your program as described in Exercise 17.65.

○ **17.69** Write a program that produces each possible graph with precisely the same probability as does Program 17.12, but uses time proportional to E, even when the density is close to 1. Test your program as described in Exercise 17.66.

• **17.70** Write a program that produces, with equal likelihood, each of the possible graphs with V vertices and E edges (see Exercise 17.9). Test your program as described in Exercise 17.65 (for low densities) and as described in Exercise 17.66 (for high densities).

○ **17.71** Write a program that generates random graphs by connecting vertices arranged in a $\sqrt{V}$-by-$\sqrt{V}$ grid to their neighbors (see Figure 1.2), with k extra edges connecting each vertex to a randomly chosen destination vertex (each destination vertex equally likely). Determine how to set k such that the expected number of edges is E. Test your program as described in Exercise 17.65.

○ **17.72** Write a program that generates random digraphs by randomly connecting vertices arranged in a $\sqrt{V}$-by-$\sqrt{V}$ grid to their neighbors, with each of the possible edges occurring with probability p (see Figure 1.2). Determine how to set p such that the expected number of edges is E. Test your program as described in Exercise 17.65.

○ **17.73** Augment your program from Exercise 17.72 to add R extra random edges, computed as in Program 17.12. For large R, shrink the grid so that the total number of edges remains about V.

• **17.74** Write a program that generates V random points in the plane, then builds a graph consisting of edges connecting all pairs of points within a given distance d of one another (see Figure 17.13 and Program 3.20). Determine how to set d such that the expected number of edges is E. Test your program as described in Exercise 17.65 (for low densities) and as described in Exercise 17.66 (for high densities).

• **17.75** Write a program that generates V random intervals in the unit interval, all of length d, then builds the corresponding interval graph. Determine how to set d such that the expected number of edges is E. Test your program as described in Exercise 17.65 (for low densities) and as described in Exercise 17.66 (for high densities). *Hint*: Use a BST.

• **17.76** Write a program that chooses V vertices and E edges at random from the real graph that you found for Exercise 17.64. Test your program as described in Exercise 17.65 (for low densities) and as described in Exercise 17.66 (for high densities).

○ **17.77** One way to define a transportation system is with a set of sequences of vertices, each sequence defining a path connecting the vertices. For example, the sequence 0-9-3-2 defines the edges 0-9, 9-3, and 3-2. Write a program that builds a graph from an input file consisting of one sequence per line, using symbolic names. Develop input suitable to allow you to use your program to build a graph corresponding to the Paris metro system.

17.78 Extend your solution to Exercise 17.77 to include vertex coordinates, along the lines of Exercise 17.60, so that you can work with graphical representations.

○ **17.79** Apply the transformations described in Exercises 17.34 through 17.37 to various graphs (see Exercises 17.63–76), and tabulate the number of vertices and edges removed by each transformation.

○ **17.80** Implement a constructor for Program 17.1 that allows clients to build separation graphs without having to call a function for each implied edge. That is, the number of function calls required for a client to build a graph should be proportional to the sum of the sizes of the groups. Develop an efficient implementation of this modified ADT (based on data structures involving groups, not implied edges).

17.81 Give a tight upper bound on the number of edges in any separation graph with N different groups of k people.

▷ **17.82** Draw graphs in the style of Figure 17.16 that, for $V = 8$, 16, and 32, have V vertices numbered from 0 to $V - 1$ and an edge connecting each vertex i with $\lfloor i/2 \rfloor$.

17.83 Modify the ADT interface in Program 17.1 to allow clients to use symbolic vertex names and edges to be pairs of instances of a generic `Vertex` type. Hide the vertex-index representation and the symbol-table ADT usage completely from clients.

17.84 Add a function to the ADT interface from Exercise 17.83 that supports a *join* operation for graphs, and provide implementations for the adjacency-matrix and adjacency-lists representations. *Note:* Any vertex or edge in either graph should be in the *join*, but vertices that are in both graphs appear only once in the *join*, and you should remove parallel edges.

17.7 Simple, Euler, and Hamilton Paths

Our first nontrivial graph-processing algorithms solve fundamental problems concerning paths in graphs. They introduce the general recursive paradigm that we use throughout the book, and they illustrate

Program 17.16 Simple path search

This class uses a recursive depth-first search function `searchR` to find a simple path connecting two given vertices in a graph and provides a member function `exists` to allow clients to check path existence. Given two vertices `v` and `w`, `searchR` checks each edge `v-t` adjacent to `v` to see whether it could be the first edge on a path to `w`. The vertex-indexed vector `visited` keeps the function from revisiting any vertex, so only simple paths are traversed.

```
template <class Graph> class sPATH
{ const Graph &G;
  vector <bool> visited;
  bool found;
  bool searchR(int v, int w)
    {
      if (v == w) return true;
      visited[v] = true;
      typename Graph::adjIterator A(G, v);
      for (int t = A.beg(); !A.end(); t = A.nxt())
        if (!visited[t])
          if (searchR(t, w)) return true;
      return false;
    }
public:
  sPATH(const Graph &G, int v, int w) :
    G(G), visited(G.V(), false)
    { found = searchR(v, w); }
  bool exists() const
    { return found; }
};
```

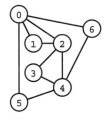

```
2-0 searchR(G, 0, 6)
  0-1 searchR(G, 1, 6)
    1-0
    1-2
  0-2
  0-5 searchR(G, 5, 6)
    5-0
    5-4 searchR(G, 4, 6)
      4-2
      4-3 searchR(G, 3, 6)
        3-2
        3-4
      4-6 searchR(G, 6, 6)
```

Figure 17.17
Trace for simple path search

This trace shows the operation of the recursive function in Program 17.16 for the call `searchR(G, 2, 6)` *to find a simple path from 2 to 6 in the graph shown at the top. There is a line in the trace for each edge considered, indented one level for each recursive call. To check 2-0, we call* `searchR(G, 0, 6)`. *This call causes us to check 0-1, 0-2, and 0-5. To check 0-1, we call* `searchR(G, 1, 6)`, *which causes us to check 1-0 and 1-2, which do not lead to recursive calls because 0 and 2 are marked. For this example, the function discovers the path 2-0-5-4-6.*

that apparently similar graph-processing problems can range widely in difficulty.

These problems take us from local properties such as the existence of edges or the degrees of vertices to global properties that tell us about a graph's structure. The most basic such property is whether two vertices are connected. If they are, we are interested in finding a simple path that connects them.

Simple path   Given two vertices, is there a simple path in the graph that connects them? In some applications, we might be satisfied to know merely whether or not such a path exists, but we are concerned here with the problem of finding a specific path.

Program 17.16 is a direct solution that finds a path. It is based on *depth-first search*, a fundamental graph-processing paradigm that we considered briefly in Chapters 3 and 5 and shall study in detail in Chapter 18. The algorithm is based on a recursive private function member that determines whether there is a simple path from v to w by checking, for each edge v-t incident on v, whether there is a simple path from t to w that does not go through v. It uses a vertex-indexed vector to mark v so that no path through v will be checked in any recursive call.

The code in Program 17.16 simply tests for the existence of a path. How can we augment it to print the path's edges? Thinking recursively suggests an easy solution:

- Add a statement to print t-v just after the recursive call in searchR finds a path from t to w.
- Switch w and v in the call on searchR in the constructor.

Alone, the first change would cause the path from v to w to be printed in reverse order: If the call to searchR(t, w) finds a path from t to w (and prints that path's edges in reverse order), then printing t-v completes the job for the path from v to w. The second change reverses the order: To print the edges on the path from v to w, we print the edges on the path from w to v in reverse order. (This trick only works for undirected graphs.) We could use this same strategy to implement an ADT function that calls a client-supplied function for each of the path's edges (see Exercise 17.88).

Figure 17.17 gives an example of the dynamics of the recursion. As with any recursive program (indeed, any program with function calls at all), such a trace is easy to produce: To modify Program 17.16 to produce one, we can add a variable depth that is incremented on entry and decremented on exit to keep track of the depth of the recursion, then add code at the beginning of the recursive function to print out depth spaces followed by the appropriate information (see Exercises 17.86 and 17.87).

Property 17.2   *We can find a path connecting two given vertices in a graph in linear time.*

The recursive depth-first search function in Program 17.16 immediately implies a proof by induction that the ADT function determines whether or not a path exists. Such a proof is easily extended to establish that, in the worst case, Program 17.16 checks all the entries in the adjacency matrix exactly once. Similarly, we can show that the analogous program for adjacency lists checks all of the graph edges exactly twice (once in each direction), in the worst case. ∎

We use the phrase *linear* in the context of graph algorithms to mean a quantity whose value is within a constant factor of $V + E$, the size of the graph. As discussed at the end of Section 17.5, such a value is also normally within a constant factor of the size of the graph representation. Property 17.2 is worded so as to allow for the use of the adjacency-lists representation for sparse graphs and the adjacency-matrix representation for dense graphs, our general practice. It is not appropriate to use the term "linear" to describe an algorithm that uses an adjacency matrix and runs in time proportional to V^2 (even though it is linear in the size of the graph representation) *unless* the graph is dense. Indeed, if we use the adjacency-matrix representation for a sparse graph, we cannot have a linear-time algorithm for *any* graph-processing problem that could require examination of all the edges.

We study depth-first search in detail in a more general setting in the next chapter, and we consider several other connectivity algorithms there. For example, a slightly more general version of Program 17.16 gives us a way to pass through all the edges in the graph, building a vertex-indexed vector that allows a client to test in constant time whether there exists a path connecting any two vertices.

Property 17.2 can substantially overestimate the actual running time of Program 17.16, because it might find a path after examining only a few edges. For the moment, our interest is in knowing a method that is guaranteed to find in linear time a path connecting any two vertices in any graph. By contrast, other problems that appear similar are much more difficult to solve. For example, consider the following problem, where we seek paths connecting pairs of vertices, but add the restriction that they visit all the other vertices in the graph, as well.

Hamilton path Given two vertices, is there a simple path connecting them that visits every vertex in the graph exactly once? If the path is from a vertex back to itself, this problem is known as the

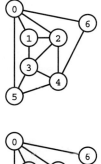

**Figure 17.18
Hamilton tour**

The graph at the top has the Hamilton tour 0–6–4–2–1–3–5–0, which visits each vertex exactly once and returns to the start vertex, but the graph at the bottom has no such tour.

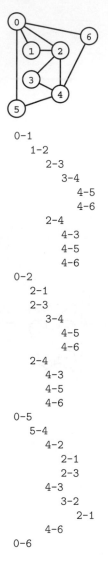

```
0-1
  1-2
    2-3
      3-4
          4-5
          4-6
    2-4
      4-3
      4-5
      4-6
0-2
  2-1
  2-3
    3-4
      4-5
      4-6
  2-4
    4-3
    4-5
    4-6
0-5
  5-4
    4-2
      2-1
      2-3
    4-3
      3-2
        2-1
    4-6
0-6
```

Figure 17.19
Hamilton-tour–search trace

This trace shows the edges checked by Program 17.17 when discovering that the graph shown at the top has no Hamilton tour. For brevity, edges to marked vertices are omitted.

Program 17.17 Hamilton path

This recursive function differs from the one in Program 17.16 in just two respects: First, it takes the length of the path sought as its third argument and returns successfully only if it finds a path of length V; second, it resets the visited marker before returning unsuccessfully.

If we replace the recursive function in Program 17.16 by this one, and add a third argument G.V()-1 to the searchR call in search, then search looks for a Hamilton path. *But do not expect the search to end except in tiny graphs* (*see text*).

```
bool searchR(int v, int w, int d)
  {
    if (v == w) return (d == 0);
    visited[v] = true;
    typename Graph::adjIterator A(G, v);
    for (int t = A.beg(); !A.end(); t = A.nxt())
      if (!visited[t])
        if (searchR(t, w, d-1)) return true;
    visited[v] = false;
    return false;
  }
```

Hamilton tour problem. Is there a cycle that visits every vertex in the graph exactly once?

At first blush, this problem seems to admit a simple solution: We can use the simple modification to the recursive part of the path-finding class that is shown in Program 17.17. But this program is not likely to be useful for many graphs, because its worst-case running time is *exponential* in the number of vertices in the graph.

Property 17.3 *A recursive search for a Hamilton tour could take exponential time.*

Proof: Consider a graph where vertex V-1 is isolated and the edges, with the other $V - 1$ vertices, constitute a complete graph. Program 17.17 will never find a Hamilton path, but it is easy to see by induction that it will examine all of the $(V - 1)!$ paths in the complete graph, all of which involve $V - 1$ recursive calls. The total number of recursive calls is therefore about $V!$, or about $(V/e)^V$, which is higher than any constant to the Vth power. ∎

Our implementations Program 17.16 for finding simple paths and Program 17.17 for finding Hamilton paths are extremely similar. If no path exists, both programs terminate when all the elements of the visited vector are set to true. Why are the running times so dramatically different? Program 17.16 is guaranteed to finish quickly because it sets at least one element of the visited vector to 1 each time searchR is called. Program 17.17, on the other hand, can set visited elements back to 0, so we cannot guarantee that it will finish quickly.

When searching for simple paths, in Program 17.16, we know that, if there is a path from v to w, we will find it by taking one of the edges v–t from v, and the same is true for Hamilton paths. But there this similarity ends. If we cannot find a simple path from t to w, then we can conclude that there is no simple path from v to w that goes through t; but the analogous situation for Hamilton paths does not hold. It could be the case that there is no Hamilton path to w that starts with v–t, but there is one that starts with v–x–t for some other vertex x. We have to make a recursive call from t corresponding to every path that leads to it from v. In short, we may have to check every path in the graph.

It is worthwhile to reflect on just how slow a factorial-time algorithm is. If we could process a graph with 15 vertices in 1 second, it would take 1 day to process a graph with 19 vertices, over 1 year for 21 vertices, and over 6 centuries for 23 vertices. Faster computers do not help much, either. A computer that is 200,000 times faster than our original one would still take more than a day to solve that 23-vertex problem. The cost to process graphs with 100 or 1000 vertices is too high to contemplate, let alone graphs of the size that we might encounter in practice. It would take millions of pages in this book just to write down the number of centuries required to process a graph that contained millions of vertices.

In Chapter 5, we examined a number of simple recursive programs that are similar in character to Program 17.17 but that could be drastically improved with top-down dynamic programming. This recursive program is entirely different in character: The number of intermediate results that would have to be saved is exponential. Despite many people doing an extensive amount of work on the problem, no one has been able to find any algorithm that can promise reasonable performance for large (or even medium-sized) graphs.

Now, suppose that we change the restriction from having to visit all the *vertices* to having to visit all the *edges*. Is this problem easy, like finding a simple path, or hopelessly difficult, like finding a Hamilton path?

Euler path   Is there a path connecting two given vertices that uses each *edge* in the graph exactly once? The path need not be simple—vertices may be visited multiple times. If the path is from a vertex back to itself, we have the *Euler tour* problem. Is there a cyclic path that uses each edge in the graph exactly once? We prove in the corollary to Property 17.4 that the path problem is equivalent to the tour problem in a graph formed by adding an edge connecting the two vertices. Figure 17.20 gives two small examples.

This classical problem was first studied by L. Euler in 1736. Indeed, some people trace the origin of the study of graphs and graph theory to Euler's work on this problem, starting with a special case known as the *bridges of Königsberg* problem (see Figure 17.21). The Swiss town of Königsberg had seven bridges connecting riverbanks and islands, and people in the town found that they could not seem to cross all the bridges without crossing one of them twice. Their problem amounts to the Euler tour problem.

These problems are familiar to puzzle enthusiasts. They are commonly seen in the form of puzzles where you are to draw a given figure without lifting your pencil from the paper, perhaps under the constraint that you must start and end at particular points. It is natural for us to consider Euler paths when developing graph-processing algorithms, because an Euler path is an efficient representation of the graph (putting the edges in a particular order) that we might consider as the basis for developing efficient algorithms.

Euler showed that it is easy to determine whether or not a path exists, because all that we need to do is to check the degree of each of the vertices. The property is easy to state and apply, but the proof is a tricky exercise in graph theory.

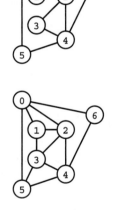

Figure 17.20
Euler tour and path examples

The graph at the top has the Euler tour 0-1-2-0-6-4-3-2-4-5-0, which uses all the edges exactly once. The graph at the bottom no such tour, but it has the Euler path 1-2-0-1-3-4-2-3-5-4-6-0-5.

Property 17.4   *A graph has an Euler tour if and only if it is connected and all its vertices are of even degree.*

Proof: To simplify the proof, we allow self-loops and parallel edges, though it is not difficult to modify the proof to show that this property also holds for simple graphs (see Exercise 17.94).

If a graph has an Euler tour, then it must be connected because the tour defines a path connecting each pair of vertices. Also, any given vertex v must be of even degree because when we traverse the tour (starting anywhere else), we enter v on one edge and leave on a different edge (neither of which appear again on the tour); so the number of edges incident upon v must be twice the number of times we visit v when traversing the tour, an even number.

To prove the converse, we use induction on the number of edges. The claim is certainly true for graphs with no edges. Consider any connected graph that has more than one edge, with all vertices of even degree. Suppose that, starting at any vertex v, we follow and remove any edge, and we continue doing so until arriving at a vertex that has no more edges. This process certainly must terminate, since we delete an edge at every step, but what are the possible outcomes? Figure 17.22 illustrates examples. Immediately, we see that we must end up back at v, because we end at a vertex other than v if and only if that vertex had an odd degree when we started.

One possibility is that we trace the full tour; if so, we are done. Otherwise, all the vertices in the graph that remains have even degree, but it may not be connected. Still, each connected component has an Euler tour by the inductive hypothesis. Moreover, the cyclic path just removed connects those tours together into an Euler tour for the original graph: traverse the cyclic path, taking detours to do the Euler tours for the connected components. Each detour is a proper Euler tour that takes us back to the vertex on the cyclic path where it started. Note that a detour may touch the cyclic path multiple times (see Exercise 17.98). In such a case, we take the detour only once (say, when we first encounter it). ∎

Corollary *A graph has an Euler path if and only if it is connected and exactly two of its vertices are of odd degree.*

Proof: This statement is equivalent to Property 17.4 in the graph formed by adding an edge connecting the two vertices of odd degree (the ends of the path). ∎

Therefore, for example, there is no way for anyone to traverse all the bridges of Königsberg in a continuous path without retracing their steps, since all four vertices in the corresponding graph have odd degree (see Figure 17.21).

**Figure 17.21
Bridges of Königsberg**

A well-known problem studied by Euler has to do with the town of Königsberg, in which there is an island at the point where the river Pregel forks. There are seven bridges connecting the island with the two banks of the river and the land between the forks, as shown in the diagram at top. Is there a way to cross the seven bridges in a continuous walk through the town, without recrossing any of them? If we label the island 0, the banks 1 and 2, and the land between the forks 3 and define an edge corresponding to each bridge, we get the multigraph shown at the bottom. The problem is to find a path through this graph that uses each edge exactly once.

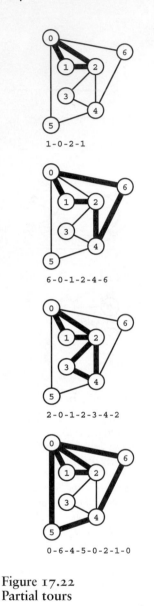

Figure 17.22
Partial tours

Following edges from any vertex in a graph that has an Euler tour always takes us back to that vertex, as shown in these examples. The cycle does not necessarily use all the edges in the graph.

As discussed in Section 17.5, we can find all the vertex degrees in time proportional to E for the adjacency-lists or set-of-edges representation and in time proportional to V^2 for the adjacency-matrix representation, or we can maintain a vertex-indexed vector with vertex degrees as part of the graph representation (see Exercise 17.42). Given the vector, we can check whether Property 17.4 is satisfied in time proportional to V. Program 17.18 implements this strategy and demonstrates that determining whether a given graph has an Euler path is an easy computational problem. This fact is significant because we have little intuition to suggest that the problem should be easier than determining whether a given graph has a Hamilton path.

Now, suppose that we actually wish to find an Euler path. We are treading on thin ice because a direct recursive implementation (find a path by trying an edge and then making a recursive call to find a path for the rest of the graph) will have the same kind of factorial-time performance as Program 17.17. We expect not to have to live with such performance because it is so easy to test whether a path exists, so we seek a better algorithm. It is possible to avoid factorial-time blowup with a fixed-cost test for determining whether or not to use an edge (rather than unknown costs from the recursive call), but we leave this approach as an exercise (see Exercises 17.96 and 17.97).

Another approach is suggested by the proof of Property 17.4. Traverse a cyclic path, deleting the edges encountered and pushing onto a stack the vertices that it encounters, so that (*i*) we can trace back along that path, printing out its edges, and (*ii*) we can check each vertex for additional side paths (which can be spliced into the main path). This process is illustrated in Figure 17.23.

Program 17.19 is an implementation along these lines. It assumes that an Euler path exists, and it destroys its local copy of the graph; thus, it is important that the `Graph` class that this program uses have a copy constructor that creates a completely separate copy of the graph. The code is tricky—novices may wish to postpone trying to understand it until gaining more experience with graph-processing algorithms in the next few chapters. Our purpose in including it here is to illustrate that good algorithms and clever implementations can be very effective for solving some graph-processing problems.

Property 17.5 *We can find an Euler tour in a graph, if one exists, in linear time.*

Program 17.18 Euler path existence

With this class, clients can test for the existence of an Euler path in a graph. It keeps v and w as private data members so that clients can use the function member show (which uses the private function member tour) to print the path (see Program 17.19).

The test is based upon the corollary to Property 17.4 and uses Program 17.11. It takes time proportional to V, not including preprocessing time to check connectivity and to build the vertex-degree table in DEGREE.

```
template <class Graph> class ePATH
  { Graph G;
    int v, w;
    bool found;
    STACK <int> S;
    int tour(int v);
public:
    ePATH(const Graph &G, int v, int w) :
      G(G), v(v), w(w)
      { DEGREE<Graph> deg(G);
        int t = deg[v] + deg[w];
        if ((t % 2) != 0) { found = false; return; }
        for (t = 0; t < G.V(); t++)
          if ((t != v) && (t != w))
            if ((deg[t] % 2) != 0)
              { found = false; return; }
        found = true;
      }
    bool exists() const
      { return found; }
    void show();
  };
```

We leave a full induction proof as an exercise (see Exercise 17.100). Informally, after the first call on path, the stack contains a path from v to w, and the graph that remains (after removal of isolated vertices) consists of the smaller connected components (sharing at least one vertex with the path so far found) that also have Euler tours. We pop isolated vertices from the stack and use path to find Euler tours that

Program 17.19 Linear-time Euler path

This implementation of show for the class in Program 17.18 prints an Euler path between two given vertices, if one exists. Unlike most of our other implementations, this code relies on the Graph ADT implementation having a proper copy constructor, because it makes a copy of the graph and destroys the copy by removing edges from it while printing the path. With a constant-time implementation of remove (see Exercise 17.46), show runs in linear time. The private function member tour follows and removes edges on a cyclic path and pushes vertices onto a stack, to be checked for side loops (*see text*). The main loop calls tour as long as there are vertices with side loops to traverse.

```
template <class Graph>
int ePATH<Graph>::tour(int v)
  {
    while (true)
      { typename Graph::adjIterator A(G, v);
        int w = A.beg(); if (A.end()) break;
        S.push(v);
        G.remove(Edge(v, w));
        v = w;
      }
    return v;
  }
template <class Graph>
void ePATH<Graph>::show()
    {
      if (!found) return;
      while (tour(v) == v && !S.empty())
        { v = S.pop(); cout << "-" << v; }
      cout << endl;
    }
```

contain the nonisolated vertices, in the same manner. Each edge in the graph is pushed onto (and popped from) the stack exactly once, so the total running time is proportional to E. ∎

Despite their appeal as a systematic way to traverse all the edges and vertices, we rarely use Euler tours in practice because few graphs have them. Instead, we typically use depth-first search to explore

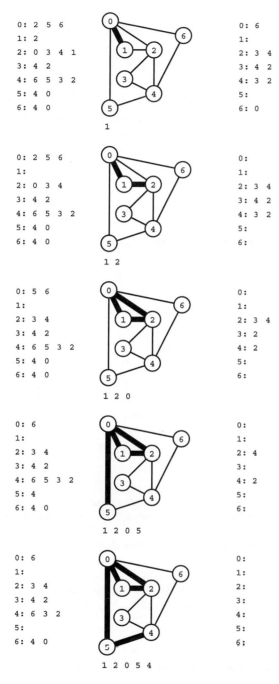

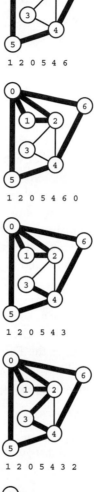

Figure 17.23
Euler tour by removing cycles

This figure shows how Program 17.19 discovers an Euler tour from 0 back to 0 in a sample graph. Thick black edges are those on the tour, the stack contents are listed below each diagram, and adjacency lists for the non-tour edges are shown at left.

First, the program adds the edge 0–1 to the tour and removes it from the adjacency lists (in two places) (top left, lists at left). Second, it adds 1–2 to the tour in the same way (left, second from top). Next, it winds up back at 0 but continues to do another cycle 0–5–4–6–0, winding up back at 0 with no more edges incident upon 0 (right, second from top). Then it pops the isolated vertices 0 and 6 from the stack until 4 is at the top and starts a tour from 4 (right, third from from top), which takes it to 3, 2, and back to 4, whereupon it pops all the now-isolated vertices 4, 2, 3, and so forth. The sequence of vertices popped from the stack defines the Euler tour 0–6–4–2–3–4–5–0–2–1–0 of the whole graph.

graphs, as described in detail in Chapter 18. Indeed, as we shall see, doing depth-first search in an undirected graph amounts to computing a *two-way Euler tour*: a path that traverses each edge exactly *twice*, once in each direction.

In summary, we have seen in this section that it is easy to find simple paths in graphs, that it is even easier to know whether we can tour all the *edges* of a large graph without revisiting any of them (by just checking that all vertex degrees are even), and that there is even a clever algorithm to find such a tour; but that it is practically impossible to know whether we can tour all the graph's *vertices* without revisiting any. We have simple recursive solutions to all these problems, but the potential for exponential growth in the running time renders some of the solutions useless in practice. Others provide insights that lead to fast practical algorithms.

This range of difficulty among apparently similar problems that is illustrated by these examples is typical in graph processing, and is fundamental to the theory of computing. As discussed briefly in Section 17.8 and in detail in Part 8, we must acknowledge what seems to be an insurmountable barrier between problems that seem to require exponential time (such as the Hamilton tour problem and many other commonly encountered problems) and problems for which we know algorithms that can guarantee to find a solution in polynomial time (such as the Euler tour problem and many other commonly encountered problems). In this book, our primary objective is to develop efficient algorithms for problems in the latter class.

Exercises

▷ **17.85** Show, in the style of Figure 17.17, the trace of recursive calls (and vertices that are skipped) when Program 17.16 finds a path from 0 to 5 in the graph

    3-7 1-4 7-8 0-5 5-2 3-8 2-9 0-6 4-9 2-6 6-4.

17.86 Modify the recursive function in Program 17.16 to print out a trace like Figure 17.17, using a global variable as described in the text.

17.87 Do Exercise 17.86 by adding an argument to the recursive function to keep track of the depth.

○ **17.88** Using the method described in the text, give an implementation of sPATH that provides a public member function that calls a client-supplied function for each edge on a path from v to w, if any such path exists.

○ **17.89** Modify Program 17.16 such that it takes a third argument d and tests the existence of a path connecting u and v of length greater than d. In particular, search(v, v, 2) should be nonzero if and only if v is on a cycle.

● **17.90** Run experiments to determine empirically the probability that Program 17.16 finds a path between two randomly chosen vertices for various graphs (see Exercises 17.63–76)and to calculate the average length of the paths found for each type of graph.

○ **17.91** Consider the graphs defined by the following four sets of edges:

```
0-1 0-2 0-3 1-3 1-4 2-5 2-9 3-6 4-7 4-8 5-8 5-9 6-7 6-9 7-8
0-1 0-2 0-3 1-3 0-3 2-5 5-6 3-6 4-7 4-8 5-8 5-9 6-7 6-9 8-8
0-1 1-2 1-3 0-3 0-4 2-5 2-9 3-6 4-7 4-8 5-8 5-9 6-7 6-9 7-8
4-1 7-9 6-2 7-3 5-0 0-2 0-8 1-6 3-9 6-3 2-8 1-5 9-8 4-5 4-7.
```

Which of these graphs have Euler tours? Which of them have Hamilton tours?

○ **17.92** Give necessary and sufficient conditions for a *directed* graph to have a (directed) Euler tour.

17.93 Prove that every connected undirected graph has a two-way Euler tour.

17.94 Modify the proof of Property 17.4 to make it work for graphs with parallel edges and self-loops.

▷ **17.95** Show that adding one more bridge could give a solution to the bridges-of-Königsberg problem.

● **17.96** Prove that a connected graph has an Euler path from v to w only if it has an edge incident on v whose removal does not disconnect the graph (except possibly by isolating v).

● **17.97** Use Exercise 17.96 to develop an efficient recursive method for finding an Euler tour in a graph that has one. Beyond the basic graph ADT functions, you may use the classes from this chapter that can give vertex degrees (see Program 17.11) and test whether a path exists between two given vertices (see Program 17.16). Implement and test your program for both sparse and dense graphs.

▷ **17.98** Give an example where the graph remaining after the first call to path in Program 17.19 is not connected (in a graph that has an Euler tour).

▷ **17.99** Describe how to modify Program 17.19 so that it can be used to detect whether or not a given graph has an Euler tour, in linear time.

17.100 Give a complete proof by induction that the linear-time Euler tour algorithm described in the text and implemented in Program 17.19 properly finds an Euler tour.

○ **17.101** Find the number of V-vertex graphs that have an Euler tour, for as large a value of V as you can feasibly afford to do the computation.

• **17.102** Run experiments to determine empirically the average length of the path found by the first call to `path` in Program 17.19 for various graphs (see Exercises 17.63–76). Calculate the probability that this path is cyclic.

○ **17.103** Write a program that computes a sequence of $2^n + n - 1$ bits in which no two pairs of n consecutive bits match. (For example, for $n = 3$, the sequence 0001110100 has this property.) *Hint*: Find a Euler tour in a de Bruijn digraph.

▷ **17.104** Show, in the style of Figure 17.19, the trace of recursive calls (and vertices that are skipped), when Program 17.16 finds a Hamilton tour in the graph

3-7 1-4 7-8 0-5 5-2 3-8 2-9 0-6 4-9 2-6 6-4.

○ **17.105** Modify Program 17.17 to print out the Hamilton tour if it finds one.

• **17.106** Find a Hamilton tour of the graph

1-2 5-2 4-2 2-6 0-8 3-0 1-3 3-6 1-0 1-4 4-0 4-6 6-5 2-6
6-9 9-0 3-1 4-3 9-2 4-9 6-9 7-9 5-0 9-7 7-3 4-5 0-5 7-8

or show that none exists.

•• **17.107** Determine how many V-vertex graphs have a Hamilton tour, for as large a value of V as you can feasibly afford to do the computation.

17.8 Graph-Processing Problems

Armed with the basic tools developed in this chapter, we consider in Chapters 18 through 22 a broad variety of algorithms for solving graph-processing problems. These algorithms are fundamental ones and are useful in many applications, but they serve as only an introduction to the subject of graph algorithms. Many interesting and useful algorithms have been developed that are beyond the scope of this book, and many interesting problems have been studied for which good algorithms have still not yet been invented.

As is true in any domain, the first challenge that we face in addressing a new graph-processing problem is determining how difficult it is to solve. For graph processing, this decision can be far more difficult than we might imagine, even for problems that appear to be simple to solve. Moreover, our intuition is not always helpful in distinguishing easy problems from difficult or hitherto unsolved ones. In this section, we describe briefly important classical problems and the state of our knowledge of them.

Given a new graph-processing problem, what type of challenge do we face in developing an implementation to solve it? The unfortunate truth is that there is no good method to answer this question for any problem that we might encounter, but we can provide a general description of the difficulty of solving various classical graph-processing problems. To this end, we will roughly categorize the problems according to the difficulty of solving them, as follows:

- Easy
- Tractable
- Intractable
- Unknown

These terms are intended to convey information relative to one another and to the current state of knowledge about graph algorithms.

As indicated by the terminology, our primary reason for categorizing problems in this way is that there are many graph problems, such as the Hamilton tour problem, that no one knows how to solve efficiently. We will eventually see (in Part 8) how to make that statement meaningful in a precise technical sense; at this point, we can at least be warned that we face significant obstacles to writing an efficient program to solve these problems.

We defer full context on many of the graph-processing problems until later in the book. Here, we present brief statements that are easily understood, in order to introduce the general issue of classifying the difficulty of graph-processing problems.

An *easy* graph processing problem is one that can be solved by the kind of elegant and efficient short programs to which we have grown accustomed in Parts 1 through 4. We often find the running time to be linear in the worst case, or bounded by a small-degree polynomial in the number of vertices or the number of edges. Generally, as we have done in many other domains, we can establish that a problem is easy by developing a brute-force solution that, although it may be too slow for huge graphs, is useful for small and even intermediate-sized problems. Then, once we know that the problem is easy, we look for efficient solutions that we might use in practice and try to identify the best among those. The Euler tour problem that we considered in Section 17.7 is a prime example of such a problem, and we shall see many others in Chapters 18 through 22 including, most notably, the following.

Simple connectivity   Is a given graph connected? That is, is there a path connecting every pair of vertices? Is there a cycle in the graph, or is it a forest? Given two vertices, are they on a cycle? We first considered these basic graph-processing question in Chapter 1. We consider numerous solutions to such problems in Chapter 18. Some are trivial to implement in linear time; others have rather sophisticated linear-time solutions that bear careful study.

Strong connectivity in digraphs   Is there a *directed* path connecting every pair of vertices in a digraph? Given two vertices, are they connected by directed paths in both directions (are they on a directed cycle)? Implementing efficient solutions to these problems is a much more challenging task than for the corresponding simple-connectivity problem in undirected graphs, and much of Chapter 19 is devoted to studying them. Despite the clever intricacies involved in solving them, we classify the problems as easy because we can write a compact, efficient, and useful implementation.

Transitive closure   What set of vertices can be reached by following directed edges from each vertex in a digraph? This problem is closely related to strong connectivity and to other fundamental computational problems. We study classical solutions that amount to a few lines of code in Chapter 19.

Minimum spanning tree   In a weighted graph, find a minimum-weight set of edges that connects all the vertices. This is one of the oldest and best-studied graph-processing problems; Chapter 20 is devoted to the study of various classical algorithms to solve it. Researchers still seek faster algorithms for this problem.

Single-source shortest paths   What are the shortest paths connecting a given vertex v with each other vertex in a weighted digraph (network)? Chapter 21 is devoted to the study of this problem, which is extremely important in numerous applications. The problem is decidedly *not* easy if edge weights can be negative.

A *tractable* graph-processing problem is one for which an algorithm is known whose time and space requirements are guaranteed to be bounded by a polynomial function of the size of the graph $(V + E)$. All easy problems are tractable, but we make a distinction because many tractable problems have the property that developing an efficient practical program to solve is an extremely challenging, if not impossible, task. Solutions may be too complicated to present in this book, because implementations might require hundreds or even thousands of lines of code. The following examples are two of the most important problems in this class.

Planarity   Can we draw a given graph without any of the lines that represent edges intersecting? We have the freedom to place the vertices anywhere, so we can solve this problem for many graphs, but it is impossible to solve for many other graphs. A remarkable classical result known as *Kuratowski's theorem* provides an easy test for determining whether a graph is planar: it says that the only graphs that cannot be drawn with no edge intersections are those that contain some subgraph that, after removing vertices of degree 2, is isomorphic to one of the graphs in Figure 17.24. A straightforward implementation of that test, even without taking the vertices of degree 2 into consideration, would be too slow for large graphs (see Exercise 17.110), but in 1974 R. Tarjan developed an ingenious (but intricate) algorithm for solving the problem in *linear* time, using a depth-first search scheme that extends those that we consider in Chapter 18. Tarjan's algorithm does not necessarily give a practical layout; it just certifies that a layout exists. As discussed in Section 17.1, developing a visually pleasing layout in applications where vertices do not necessarily relate directly to the physical world has turned out to be a challenging research problem.

Matching   Given a graph, what is the largest subset of its edges with the property that no two are connected to the same vertex? This classical problem is known to be solvable in time proportional to a polynomial function of V and E, but a fast algorithm that is suitable for huge graphs is still an elusive research goal. The problem is easier to solve when restricted in various ways. For example, the problem of matching students to available positions in selective institutions is an example of *bipartite matching*: We have two different types of vertices (students and institutions) and we are concerned with only those edges that connect a vertex of one type with a vertex of the other type. We see a solution to this problem in Chapter 22.

The solutions to some tractable problems have never been written down as programs, or have running times so high that we could not contemplate using them in practice. The following example is in this class. It also demonstrates the capricious nature of the mathematical reality of the difficulty of graph processing.

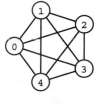

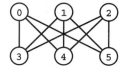

**Figure 17.24
Forbidden subgraphs in planar graphs**

Neither of these graphs can be drawn in the plane without intersecting edges, nor can any graph that contains either of these graphs as a subgraph (after we remove vertices of degree two); but all other graphs can be so drawn.

Even cycles in digraphs   Does a given digraph have a cycle of even length? This question would seem simple to resolve because the corresponding question for undirected graphs is easy to solve (see Section 18.4), as is the question of whether a digraph has a cycle of odd length. However, for many years, the problem was not sufficiently well understood for us even to know whether or not there exists an efficient algorithm for solving it (*see reference section*). A theorem establishing the existence of an efficient algorithm was proved in 1999, but the method is so complicated that no mathematician or programmer would attempt to implement it.

One of the important themes of Chapter 22 is that many tractable graph problems are best handled by algorithms that can solve a whole class of problems in a general setting. The *shortest-paths* algorithms of Chapter 21, the *network-flow* algorithms of Chapter 22, and the powerful *network-simplex* algorithm of Chapter 22 are capable of solving many graph problems that otherwise might present a significant challenge. Examples of such problems include the following.

Assignment   This problem, also known as *bipartite weighted matching*, is to find a perfect matching of minimum weight in a bipartite graph. It is easily solved with network-flow algorithms. Specific methods that attack the problem directly are known, but they have been shown to be essentially equivalent to network-flow solutions.

General connectivity   What is the minimum number of edges whose removal will separate a graph into two disjoint parts (edge connectivity)? What is the minimum number of vertices whose removal will separate a graph into two disjoint parts (vertex connectivity)? As we see in Chapter 22, these problems, although difficult to solve directly, can both be solved with network-flow algorithms.

Mail carrier   Given a graph, find a tour with a minimal number of edges that uses every edge in the graph *at least* once (but is allowed to use edges multiple times). This problem is much more difficult than the Euler tour problem but much less difficult than the Hamilton tour problem.

The step from convincing yourself that a problem is tractable to providing software that can be used in practical situations can be a large step, indeed. On the one hand, when proving that a problem is tractable, researchers tend to brush past numerous details that have to be dealt with in an implementation; on the other hand, they have to account for numerous potential situations even though they may not arise in practice. This gap between theory and practice is particularly acute when investigators are considering graph algorithms, both because mathematical research is filled with deep results describing a bewildering variety of structural properties that we may need to take into account when processing graphs, and because the relationships between those results and the properties of graphs that arise in practice are little understood. The development of general schemes such as the network-simplex algorithm has been an extremely effective approach to dealing with such problems.

An *intractable* graph-processing problem is one for which there is no known algorithm that is guaranteed to solve the problem in a reasonable amount of time. Many such problems have the characteristic that we can use a brute-force method where we can try all possibilities to compute the solution—we consider them to be intractable because there are far too many possibilities to consider. This class of problems is extensive and includes many important problems that we would like to know how to solve. The term *NP-hard* describes the problems in this class. Most experts believe that no efficient algorithms exist for these problems. We consider the bases for this terminology and this belief in more detail in Part 8. The Hamilton path problem that we discussed in Section 17.7 is a prime example of an NP-hard graph-processing problem, as are those on the following list.

Longest path   What is the longest simple path connecting two given vertices in a graph? Despite its apparent similarity to shortest-paths problems, this problem is a version of the Hamilton tour problem, and is NP-hard.

Colorability   Is there a way to assign one of k colors to each of the vertices of a graph such that no edge connects two vertices of the same color? This classical problem is easy for $k = 2$ (see Section 18.4), but it is NP-hard for $k = 3$.

Independent set   What is the size of the largest subset of the vertices of a graph with the property that no two are connected by an edge? Just as we saw when contrasting the Euler and Hamilton tour problems, this problem is NP-hard, despite its apparent similarity to the matching problem, which is solvable in polynomial time.

Clique   What is size of the largest clique (complete subgraph) in a given graph? This problem generalizes part of the planarity problem, because if the largest clique has more than four nodes, the graph is not planar.

These problems are formulated as *existence* problems—we are asked to determine whether or not a particular subgraph exists. Some of the problems ask for the size of the largest subgraph of a particular type, which we can do by framing an existence problem where we test for the existence of a subgraph of size k that satisfies the property of interest, then use binary search to find the largest. In practice, we actually often want to find a complete solution, which is potentially much harder to do. Four example, the famous *four-color theorem* tells us that it is possible use just four colors to color all the vertices of a planar graph such that no edge connects two vertices of the same color. But the theorem does not tell us how to do so for a particular planar graph: knowing that a coloring exists does not help us find a complete solution to the problem. Another famous example is the *traveling salesperson* problem, which asks us to find the minimum-length tour through all the vertices of a weighted graph. This problem is related to the Hamilton path problem, but it is certainly no easier: if we cannot find an efficient solution to the Hamilton path problem, we cannot expect to find one for the traveling salesperson problem. As a rule, when faced with difficult problems, we work with the simplest version that we cannot solve. Existence problems are within the spirit of this rule, but they also play an essential role in the theory, as we shall see in Part 8.

The problems just listed are but a few of the thousands of NP-hard problems that have been identified. They arise in all types of computational applications, as we shall discuss in Part 8; they are particularly prevalent in graph processing, so we have to be aware of their existence throughout this book.

Note that we are insisting that our algorithms *guarantee* efficiency, in the worst case. Perhaps we should instead settle for algorithms that are efficient for typical inputs (but not necessarily in the worst case). Similarly, many of the problems involve *optimization*. Perhaps we should instead settle for a long path (not necessarily the longest) or a large clique (not necessarily the maximum). For graph processing, it might be easy to find a good answer for graphs that arise in practice, and we may not even be interested in looking for an algorithm that could find an optimal solution in fictional graphs that we will never see. Indeed, intractable problems can often be attacked with straightforward or general-purpose algorithms similar to Program 17.17 that, although they have exponential running time in the worst case, can quickly find a solution (or a good approximation) for specific problem instances that arise in practice. We would be reluctant to use a program that will crash or produce a bad answer for certain inputs, but we do sometimes find ourselves using programs that run in exponential time for certain inputs. We consider this situation in Part 8.

There are also many research results proving that various intractable problems remain intractable even when we relax various restrictions. Moreover, there are many specific practical problems that we cannot solve because no one knows a sufficiently fast algorithm. In this part of the book, we will label problems NP-hard when we encounter them and interpret this label as meaning, at the very least, that we are not going to expect to find efficient algorithms to solve them and that we are not going to attack them without using advanced techniques of the type discussed in Part 8 (except perhaps to use brute-force methods to solve tiny problems).

There are some graph-processing problems whose difficulty is *unknown*. Neither is there an efficient algorithm known for them, nor are they known to be NP-hard. It is possible, as our knowledge of graph-processing algorithms and properties of graphs expands, that some of these problems will turn out to be tractable, or even easy. The following important natural problem, which we have already encountered (see Figure 17.2), is the best-known problem in this class.

Graph isomorphism Can we make two given graphs identical by renaming vertices? Efficient algorithms are known for this problem for many special types of graphs, but the difficulty of the general problem remains open.

The number of significant problems whose intrinsic difficulty is unknown is very small in comparison to the other categories that we have considered, because of intense research in this field over the past several decades. Certain problems in this class, such as graph isomorphism, are of immense practical interest; other problems in this class are of significance primarily by virtue of having resisted classification.

Table 17.2 Difficulty of classical graph-processing problems

This table summarizes the discussion in the text about the relative difficulty of various classical graph-processing problems, comparing them in
rough subjective terms. These examples indicate not only the range of
difficulty of the problems but also that classifying a given problem can
be a challenging task.

	E	T	I	?
undirected graphs				
connectivity	*			
general connectivity		*		
Euler tour	*			
Hamilton tour			*	
bipartite matching	*			
maximum matching		*		
planarity		*		
maximum clique			*	
2-colorability	*			
3-colorability			*	
shortest paths	*			
longest paths			*	
vertex cover			*	
isomorphism				*
digraphs				
transitive closure	*			
strong connectivity	*			
odd-length cycle	*			
even-length cycle		*		
weighted graphs				
minimum spanning tree	*			
traveling salesperson			*	
networks				
shortest paths (nonnegative weights)	*			
shortest paths (negative weights)			*	
maximum flow	*			
assignment		*		
minimum-cost flow		*		

Key:
E   Easy—efficient classical algorithm known (see reference)
T   Tractable—solution exists (implementation difficult)
I   Intractable—no efficient solution known (NP-hard)
?   Unknown

For the class of easy algorithms, we are used to the idea of comparing algorithms with different worst-case performance characteristics and trying to predict performance through analysis and empirical tests. For graph processing, these tasks are particularly challenging because of the difficulty of characterizing the types of graphs that might arise in practice. Fortunately, many of the important classical algorithms have optimal or near-optimal worst-case performance, or have a running time that depends on only the number of vertices and edges, rather than on the graph structure; we thus can concentrate on streamlining implementations and still can predict performance with confidence.

In summary, there is a wide spectrum of problems and algorithms known for graph processing. Table 17.2 summarizes some of the information that we have discussed. Every problem comes in different versions for different types of graphs (directed, weighted, bipartite, planar, sparse, dense), and there are thousands of problems and algorithms to consider. We certainly cannot expect to solve every problem that we might encounter, and some problems that appear to be simple are still baffling the experts. Despite a natural a priori expectation that we should have no problem distinguishing easy problems from intractable ones, the many examples that we have discussed illustrate that placing a problem even into these rough categories can turn into a significant research challenge.

As our knowledge about graphs and graph algorithms expands, given problems may move among these categories. Despite a flurry of research activity in the 1970s and intensive work by many researchers since then, the possibility still remains that all the problems that we are discussing will someday be categorized as "easy" (solvable by an algorithm that is compact, efficient, and possibly ingenious).

Having developed this context, we shall press on to consider numerous useful graph-processing algorithms. Problems that we can solve do arise often, the graph algorithms that we study serve well in a great variety of applications, and these algorithms serve as the basis for attacking numerous other problems that we need to handle even if we cannot guarantee efficient solutions.

Exercises

● **17.108** Prove that neither of the two graphs depicted in Figure 17.24 is planar.

17.109 Write a graph ADT client that determines whether or not a graph contains one of the graphs depicted in Figure 17.24, using a brute-force algorithm where you test all possible subsets of five vertices for the clique and all possible subsets of six vertices for the complete bipartite graph. *Note:* This test does not suffice to show whether the graph is planar, because it ignores the condition that removing vertices of degree 2 in some subgraph might give one of the two forbidden subgraphs.

17.110 Give a drawing of the graph

```
3-7 1-4 7-8 0-5 5-2 3-0 2-9 0-6 4-9 2-6
6-4 1-5 8-2 9-0 8-3 4-5 2-3 1-6 3-5 7-6
```

that has no intersecting edges, or prove that no such drawing exists.

17.111 Find a way to assign three colors to the vertices of the graph

```
3-7 1-4 7-8 0-5 5-2 3-0 2-9 0-6 4-9 2-6
6-4 1-5 8-2 9-0 8-3 4-5 2-3 1-6 3-5 7-6
```

such that no edge connects two vertices of the same color, or show that it is not possible to do so.

17.112 Solve the independent-set problem for the graph

```
3-7 1-4 7-8 0-5 5-2 3-0 2-9 0-6 4-9 2-6
6-4 1-5 8-2 9-0 8-3 4-5 2-3 1-6 3-5 7-6.
```

17.113 What is the size of the largest clique in a de Bruijn graph of order n?

CHAPTER EIGHTEEN

Graph Search

WE OFTEN LEARN properties of a graph by systematically examining each of its vertices and each of its edges. Determining some simple graph properties—for example, computing the degrees of all the vertices—is easy if we just examine each edge (in any order whatever). Many other graph properties are related to paths, so a natural way to learn them is to move from vertex to vertex along the graph's edges. Nearly all the graph-processing algorithms that we consider use this basic abstract model. In this chapter, we consider the fundamental *graph-search* algorithms that we use to move through graphs, learning their structural properties as we go.

Graph searching in this way is equivalent to exploring a maze. Specifically, passages in the maze correspond to edges in the graph, and points where passages intersect in the maze correspond to vertices in the graph. When a program changes the value of a variable from vertex v to vertex w because of an edge v-w, we view it as equivalent to a person in a maze moving from point v to point w. We begin this chapter by examining a systematic exploration of a maze. By correspondence with this process, we see precisely how the basic graph-search algorithms proceed through every edge and every vertex in a graph.

In particular, the recursive *depth-first search* (DFS) algorithm corresponds precisely to the particular maze-exploration strategy of Section 18.1. DFS is a classic and versatile algorithm that we use to solve connectivity and numerous other graph-processing problems. The basic algorithm admits two simple implementations: one that is recursive, and another that uses an explicit stack. Replacing the stack with a FIFO queue leads to another classic algorithm, *breadth-first search* (BFS), which we use to solve another class of graph-processing problems related to shortest paths.

The main topics of this chapter are DFS, BFS, their related algorithms, and their application to graph processing. We briefly considered DFS and BFS in Chapter 5; we treat them from first principles here, in the context of search-based graph-processing classes, and use them to demonstrate relationships among various graph algorithms. In particular, we consider a general approach to searching graphs that encompasses a number of classical graph-processing algorithms, including both DFS and BFS.

As illustrations of the application of these basic graph-searching methods to solve more complicated problems, we consider algorithms for finding connected components, biconnected components, spanning trees, and shortest paths, and for solving numerous other graph-processing problems. These implementations exemplify the approach that we shall use to solve more difficult problems in Chapters 19 through 22.

We conclude the chapter by considering the basic issues involved in the analysis of graph algorithms, in the context of a case study comparing several different algorithms for finding the number of connected components in a graph.

18.1 Exploring a Maze

It is instructive to think about the process of searching through a graph in terms of an equivalent problem that has a long and distinguished history (*see reference section*)—finding our way through a maze that consists of passages connected by intersections. This section presents a detailed study of a basic method for exploring every passage in any given maze. Some mazes can be handled with a simple rule, but most mazes require a more sophisticated strategy (see Figure 18.1). Using the terminology *maze* instead of *graph*, *passage* instead of *edge*, and *intersection* instead of *vertex* is making mere semantic distinctions, but, for the moment, doing so will help to give us an intuitive feel for the problem.

One trick for exploring a maze without getting lost that has been known since antiquity (dating back at least to the legend of Theseus and the Minotaur) is to unroll a ball of string behind us. The string

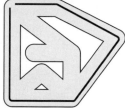

Figure 18.1
Exploring a maze

We can explore every passageway in a simple maze by following a simple rule such as "keep your right hand on the wall." Following this rule in the maze at the top, we explore the whole maze, going through each passage once in each direction. But if we follow this rule in a maze with a cycle, we return to the starting point without exploring the whole maze, as illustrated in the maze at the bottom.

guarantees that we can always find a way out, but we are also interested in being sure that we have explored every part of the maze, and we do not want to retrace our steps unless we have to. To accomplish these goals, we need some way to mark places that we have been. We could use the string for this purpose as well, but we use an alternative approach that models a computer implementation more closely.

We assume that there are lights, initially off, in every intersection, and doors, initially closed, at both ends of every passage. We further assume that the doors have windows and that the lights are sufficiently strong and the passages sufficiently straight that we can determine, by opening the door at one end of a passage, whether or not the intersection at the other end is lit (even if the door at the other end is closed). Our goals are to turn on all the lights and to open all the doors. To reach them, we need a set of rules to follow, systematically. The following maze-exploration strategy, which we refer to as *Trémaux exploration*, has been known at least since the nineteenth century (*see reference section*):

(*i*) If there are no closed doors at the current intersection, go to step (*iii*). Otherwise, open any closed door to any passage leading out of the current intersection (and leave it open).

(*ii*) If you can see that the intersection at the other end of that passage is already lighted, try another door at the current intersection (step (*i*)). Otherwise (if you can see that the intersection at the other end of the passage is dark), follow the passage to that intersection, unrolling the string as you go, turn on the light, and go to step (*i*).

(*iii*) If all the doors at the current intersection are open, check whether you are back at the start point. If so, stop. If not, use the string to go back down the passage that brought you to this intersection for the first time, rolling the string back up as you go, and look for another closed door there (that is, return to step (*i*)).

Figures 18.2 and 18.3 depict a traversal of a sample graph and show that, indeed, every light is lit and every door is opened for that example. The figures depict just one of many possible outcomes of the exploration, because we are free to open the doors in any order at each intersection. Convincing ourselves that this method is always effective is an interesting exercise in mathematical induction.

Figure 18.2
Trémaux maze exploration
example

In this diagram, places that we have not visited are shaded (dark) and places that we have visited are white (light). We assume that there are lights in the intersections, and that, when we have opened doors into lighted intersections on both ends of a passage, the passage is lighted. To explore the maze, we begin at 0 and take the passage to 2 (left, top). Then we proceed to 6, 4, 3, and 5, opening the doors to the passages, lighting the intersections as we proceed through them, and leaving a string trailing behind us (left). When we open the door that leads to 0 from 5, we can see that 0 is lighted, so we skip that passage (top right). Similarly, we skip the passage from 5 to 4 (right, second from top), leaving us with nowhere to go from 5 except back to 3 and then back to 4, rolling up our ball of string. When we open the doorway from the passage from 4 to 5, we can see that 5 is lighted through the open door at the other end, and we therefore skip that passage (right, bottom). We never walked down the passage connecting 4 and 5, but we lighted it by opening the doors at both ends.

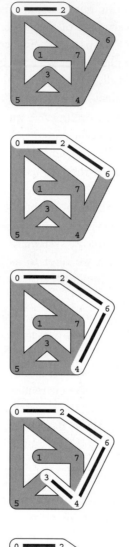

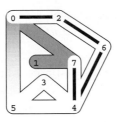

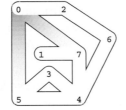

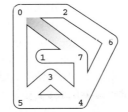

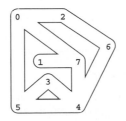

**Figure 18.3
Trémaux maze exploration
example (continued)**

*Next, we proceed to 7 (top left),
open the door to see that 0 is
lighted (left, second from top),
and then proceed to 1 (left, third
from top). At this point, most of
the maze is traversed, and we use
our string to take us back to the
beginning, moving from 1 to 7 to 4
to 6 to 2 to 0. Back at 0, we complete our exploration by checking
the passages to 5 (right, second
from bottom) and 7 (bottom right),
leaving all passages and intersections lighted. Again, the passages
connecting 0 to 5 and 0 to 7 are
both lighted because we opened
the doors at both ends, but we did
not walk through them.*

Property 18.1 *When we use Trémaux maze exploration, we light all lights and open all doors in the maze and end up back where we started.*

Proof: To prove this assertion by induction, we first note that it holds, trivially, for a maze that contains one intersection and no passages—we just turn on the light. For any maze that contains more than one intersection, we assume the property to be true for all mazes with fewer intersections. It suffices to show that we visit all intersections, since we open all the doors at every intersection that we visit. Now, consider the first passage that we take from the first intersection, and divide the intersections into two subsets: (*i*) those that we can reach by taking that passage without returning to the start, and (*ii*) those that we *cannot* reach from that passage without returning to the start. Applying the inductive hypothesis, we know that we visit all intersections in (*i*) (ignoring any passages back to the start intersection, which is lit) and end up back at the start intersection. Then, applying the the inductive hypothesis again, we know that we visit all intersections in (*ii*) (ignoring the passages from the start to intersections in (*i*), which are lit). ∎

From the detailed example in Figures 18.2 and 18.3, we see that there are four different possible situations that arise for each passage that we consider taking:

(*i*) The passage is dark, so we take it.

(*ii*) The passage is the one that we used to enter (it has our string in it), so we use it to exit (and we roll up the string).

(*iii*) The door at the other end of the passage is closed (but the intersection is lit), so we skip the passage.

(*iv*) The door at the other end of the passage is open (and the intersection is lit), so we skip it.

The first and second situations apply to any passage that we traverse, first at one end and then at the other end. The third and fourth situations apply to any passage that we skip, first at one end and then at the other end. Next, we see how this perspective on maze exploration translates directly to graph search.

Exercises

▷ **18.1** Assume that intersections 6 and 7 (and all the hallways connected to them) are removed from the maze in Figures 18.2 and 18.3, and a hallway is added that connects 1 and 2. Show a Trémaux exploration of the resulting maze, in the style of Figures 18.2 and 18.3.

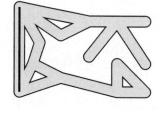
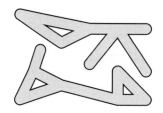

Figure 18.4
Decomposing a maze

To prove by induction that Trémaux exploration takes us everywhere in a maze (top), we break it into two smaller pieces, by removing all edges connecting the first intersection with any intersection that can be reached from the first passage without going back through the first intersection (bottom).

○ **18.2** Which of the following could *not* be the order in which lights are turned on at the intersections during a Trémaux exploration of the maze depicted in Figures 18.2 and 18.3?

                    0-7-4-5-3-1-6-2
                    0-2-6-4-3-7-1-5
                    0-5-3-4-7-1-6-2
                    0-7-4-6-2-1-3-5

● **18.3** How many different ways are there to traverse the maze depicted in Figures 18.2 and 18.3 with a Trémaux exploration?

18.2 Depth-First Search

Our interest in Trémaux exploration is that this technique leads us immediately to the classic recursive function for traversing graphs: To visit a vertex, we mark it as having been visited, then (recursively) visit all the vertices that are adjacent to it and that have not yet been marked. This method, which we considered briefly in Chapters 3 and 5 and used to solve path problems in Section 17.7, is called *depth-first search (DFS)*. It is one of the most important algorithms that we shall encounter. DFS is deceptively simple because it is based on a familiar concept and is easy to implement; in fact, it is a subtle and powerful algorithm that we put to use for numerous difficult graph-processing tasks.

Program 18.1 is a DFS class that visits all the vertices and examines all the edges in a connected graph. Like the simple path-search functions that we considered in Section 17.7, it is based on a recursive function that keeps a private vector to mark vertices as having been visited. In this implementation, ord is a vector of integers that records the order in which vertices are visited. Figure 18.5 is a trace that shows the order in which Program 18.1 visits the edges and vertices for the example depicted in Figures 18.2 and 18.3 (see also Figure 18.17), when the adjacency-matrix graph implementation DenseGRAPH of Section 17.3 is used. Figure 18.6 depicts the maze-exploration process using standard graph drawings.

These figures illustrate the dynamics of a recursive DFS and show the correspondence with Trémaux exploration of a maze. First, the vertex-indexed vector corresponds to the lights in the intersections: When we encounter an edge to a vertex that we have already visited (see a light at the end of the passage), we do not make a recursive

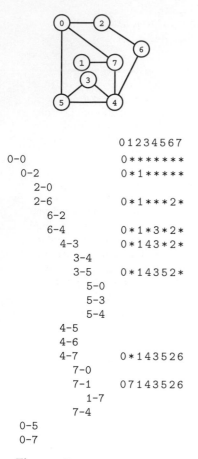

	01234567
0-0	0*******
0-2	0*1*****
2-0	
2-6	0*1***2*
6-2	
6-4	0*1*3*2*
4-3	0*143*2*
3-4	
3-5	0*14352*
5-0	
5-3	
5-4	
4-5	
4-6	
4-7	0*143526
7-0	
7-1	07143526
1-7	
7-4	
0-5	
0-7	

Figure 18.5
DFS trace

This trace shows the order in which DFS checks the edges and vertices for the adjacency-matrix representation of the graph corresponding to the example in Figures 18.2 and 18.3 (top) and traces the contents of the ord *vector (right) as the search progresses (asterisks represent* -1, *for unseen vertices). There are two lines in the trace for every graph edge (once for each orientation). Indentation indicates the level of recursion.*

Program 18.1 Depth-first search of a connected component

This DFS class corresponds to Trémaux exploration. The constructor marks as visited all vertices in the same connected component as v by calling the recursive searchC, which visits all the vertices adjacent to v by checking them all and calling itself for each edge that leads from v to an unmarked vertex. Clients can use the count function to learn the number of vertices encountered and the overloaded [] operator to learn the order in which the search visited the vertices.

```cpp
#include <vector>
template <class Graph> class cDFS
{ int cnt;
  const Graph &G;
  vector <int> ord;
  void searchC(int v)
    {
      ord[v] = cnt++;
      typename Graph::adjIterator A(G, v);
      for (int t = A.beg(); !A.end(); t = A.nxt())
        if (ord[t] == -1) searchC(t);
    }
public:
  cDFS(const Graph &G, int v = 0) :
    G(G), cnt(0), ord(G.V(), -1)
    { searchC(v); }
  int count() const { return cnt; }
  int operator[](int v) const { return ord[v]; }
};
```

call to follow that edge (go down that passage). Second, the function call–return mechanism in the program corresponds to the string in the maze: When we have processed all the edges adjacent to a vertex (explored all the passages leaving an intersection), we "return" (in both senses of the word).

In the same way that we encounter each passage in the maze twice (once at each end), we encounter each edge in the graph twice (once at each of its vertices). In Trémaux exploration, we open the doors at each end of each passage; in DFS of an undirected graph, we

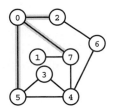 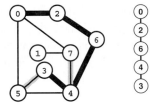

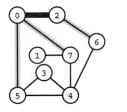

Figure 18.6
Depth-first search

These diagrams are a graphical view of the process depicted in Figure 18.5, showing the DFS recursive-call tree as it evolves. Thick black edges in the graph correspond to edges in the DFS tree shown to the right of each graph diagram. Shaded edges are the candidates to be added to the tree next. In the early stages (left) the tree grows down in a straight line, as we make recursive calls for 0, 2, 6, and 4 (left). Then we make recursive calls for 3, then 5 (right, top two diagrams); and return from those calls to make a recursive call for 7 from 4 (right, second from bottom) and to 1 from 7 (right, bottom).

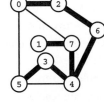 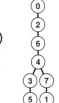

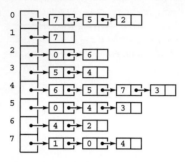

```
              01234567
0-0           0*******
  0-7         0******1
    7-1       02*****1
      1-7
    7-0
    7-4       02**3**1
      4-6     02**3*41
        6-4
        6-2   025*3*41
          2-0
          2-6
        4-5   025*3641
          5-0
          5-4
          5-3 02573641
            3-5
            3-4
      4-7
      4-3
  0-5
  0-2
```

Figure 18.7
DFS trace (adjacency lists)

This trace shows the order in which DFS checks the edges and vertices for the adjacency-lists representation of the same graph as in Figure 18.5.

check each of the two representations of each edge. If we encounter an edge v–w, we either do a recursive call (if w is not marked) or skip the edge (if w is marked). The second time that we encounter the edge, in the opposite orientation w–v, we always ignore it, because the destination vertex v has certainly already been visited (the first time that we encountered the edge).

One difference between DFS as implemented in Program 18.1 and Trémaux exploration as depicted in Figures 18.2 and 18.3, although it is inconsequential in many contexts, is worth taking the time to understand. When we move from vertex v to vertex w, we have not examined any of the entries in the adjacency matrix that correspond to edges from w to other vertices in the graph. In particular, we know that there is an edge from w to v and that we will ignore that edge when we get to it (because v is marked as visited). That decision happens at a time different from in the Trémaux exploration, where we open the doors corresponding to the edge from v to w when we go to w for the first time, from v. If we were to *close* those doors on the way in and open them on the way out (having identified the passage with the string), then we would have a precise correspondence between DFS and Trémaux exploration.

Figure 18.6 also depicts the tree corresponding to the recursive calls as it evolves, in correspondence with Figure 18.5. This recursive-call tree, which is known as the *DFS tree*, is a structural description of the search process. As we see in Section 18.4, the DFS tree, properly augmented, can provide a full description of the search dynamics, in addition to just the call structure.

The order in which vertices are visited depends not just on the graph, but on its representation and ADT implementation. For example, Figure 18.7 shows the search dynamic when the SparseMultiGRAPH adjacency-lists implementation of Section 17.4 is used. For the adjacency-matrix representation, we examine the edges incident on each vertex in numerical order; for the adjacency-lists representation, we examine them in the order that they appear on the lists. This difference leads to a completely different recursive search dynamic, as would differences in the order in which edges appear on the lists (which occur, for example, when the same graph is constructed by inserting edges in a different order). Note also that the existence of parallel edges is inconsequential for DFS because any edge that is parallel to an edge that has already been traversed is ignored, since its destination vertex has been visited.

Despite all of these possibilities, the critical fact remains that DFS visits all the edges and all the vertices connected to the start vertex, *regardless of in what order* it examines the edges incident on each vertex. This fact is a direct consequence of Property 18.1, since the proof of that property does not depend on the order in which the doors are opened at any given intersection. All the DFS-based algorithms that we examine have this same essential property. Although the dynamics of their operation might vary substantially depending on the graph representation and details of the implementation of the search, the recursive structure gives us a way to make relevant inferences about the graph itself, no matter how it is represented and no matter which order we choose to examine the edges incident upon each vertex.

Exercises

▷ **18.4** Add a public member function to Program 18.1 that returns the size of the connected component searched by the constructor.

18.5 Write a client program like Program 17.6 that scans a graph from standard input, uses Program 18.1 to run a search starting at each vertex, and prints out the parent-link representation of each spanning forest. Use the DenseGRAPH graph ADT implementation from Section 17.3.

▷ **18.6** Show, in the style of Figure 18.5, a trace of the recursive function calls made when a cDFS<DenseGRAPH> object is constructed for the graph

    0-2 0-5 1-2 3-4 4-5 3-5.

Draw the corresponding DFS recursive-call tree.

18.7 Show, in the style of Figure 18.6, the progress of the search for the example in Exercise 18.6.

18.3 Graph-Search ADT Functions

DFS and the other graph-search methods that we consider later in this chapter all involve following graph edges from vertex to vertex, with the goal of systematically visiting every vertex and every edge in the graph. But following graph edges from vertex to vertex can lead us to all the vertices in only the same connected component as the starting vertex. In general, of course, graphs might not be connected, so we need one call on a search function for each connected component. We

Program 18.2 Graph search

This base class is for processing graphs that may not be connected.
Derived classes must define a function searchC that, when called with a
self-loop to v as its second argument, sets ord[t] to cnt++ for each vertex
t in the same connected component as v. Typically, constructors in
derived classes call search, which calls searchC once for each connected
component in the graph.

```
template <class Graph> class SEARCH
{
  protected:
    const Graph &G;
    int cnt;
    vector <int> ord;
    virtual void searchC(Edge) = 0;
    void search()
      { for (int v = 0; v < G.V(); v++)
          if (ord[v] == -1) searchC(Edge(v, v)); }
  public:
    SEARCH (const Graph &G) : G(G),
      ord(G.V(), -1), cnt(0) { }
    int operator[](int v) const { return ord[v]; }
};
```

will typically use graph-search functions that perform the following
steps until all of the vertices of the graph have been marked as having
been visited:

- Find an unmarked vertex (a *start* vertex).
- Visit (and mark as visited) all the vertices in the connected component that contains the start vertex.

The method for marking vertices is not specified in this description,
but we most often use the same method that we used for the DFS
implementations in Section 18.2: We initialize all entries in a private vertex-indexed vector to a negative integer, and mark vertices by
setting their corresponding entry to a nonnegative value. Using this
procedure amounts to using a single bit (the sign bit) for the mark;
most implementations are also concerned with keeping other information associated with marked vertices in the vector (such as, for the

DFS implementation in Section 18.2, the order in which vertices are marked). The method for looking for a vertex in the next connected component is also not specified, but we most often use a scan through the vector in order of increasing index.

We pass an *edge* to the search function (using a dummy self-loop in the first call for each connected component), instead of passing its destination vertex, because the edge tells us how we reached the vertex. Knowing the edge corresponds to knowing which passage led to a particular intersection in a maze. This information is useful in many DFS classes. When we are simply keeping track of which vertices we have visited, this information is of little consequence; but more interesting problems require that we always know from whence we came.

Program 18.2 is an implementation that illustrates these choices. Figure 18.8 gives an example that illustrates how every vertex is visited, by the effect on the ord vector of any derived class. Typically, the derived classes that we consider also examine all edges incident upon each vertex visited. In such cases, knowing that we visit all vertices tells us that we visit all edges as well, as in Trémaux traversal.

Program 18.3 is an example that shows how we derive a DFS-based class for computing a spanning forest from the SEARCH base class of Program 18.2. We include a private vector st in the derived class to hold a parent-link representation of the tree that we initialize in the constructor; define a searchC that is similar to searchC from Program 18.1, except that it takes an edge v-w as argument and to set st[w] to v; and add a public member function that allows clients to learn the parent of any vertex. Spanning forests are of interest in many applications, but our primary interest in them in this chapter is their relevance in understanding the dynamic behavior of the DFS, the topic of Section 18.4.

In a connected graph, the constructor in Program 18.2 calls searchC once for 0-0 and then finds that all the other vertices are marked. In a graph with more than one connected component, the constructor checks all the connected components in a straightforward manner. DFS is the first of several methods that we consider for searching a connected component. No matter which method (and no matter what graph representation) we use, Program 18.2 is an effective method for visiting all the graph vertices.

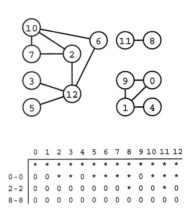

	0	1	2	3	4	5	6	7	8	9	10	11	12
	*	*	*	*	*	*	*	*	*	*	*	*	*
0-0	0	0	*	0	0	*	*	*	*	0	*	*	*
2-2	0	0	0	0	0	0	0	0	*	0	0	*	0
8-8	0	0	0	0	0	0	0	0	0	0	0	0	0

Figure 18.8
Graph search

The table at the bottom shows vertex marks (contents of the ord *vector) during a typical search of the graph at the top. Initially, the function* GRAPHsearch *in Program 18.2 unmarks all vertices by setting the marks all to* -1 *(indicated by an asterisk). Then it calls* search *for the dummy edge 0-0, which marks all of the vertices in the same connected component as 0 (second row) by setting them to a non-negative values (indicated by 0s). In this example, it marks 0, 1, 4, and 9 with the values 0 through 3 in that order. Next, it scans from left to right to find the unmarked vertex 2 and calls* search *for the dummy edge 2-2 (third row), which marks the seven vertices in the same connected component as 2. Continuing the left-to-right scan, it calls* search *for 8-8 to mark 8 and 11 (bottom row). Finally,* GRAPHsearch *completes the search by discovering that 9 through 12 are all marked.*

Program 18.3 Derived class for depth-first search

This code shows how we derive a spanning-forest DFS class from the base class defined in Program 18.2. The constructor builds a representation of the forest in st (parent links) along with ord (from the base class). Clients can use a DFS object to find any given vertex's parent in the forest (ST), or any given vertex's position in a preorder walk of the forest (overloaded [] operator). Properties of these forests and representations are the topic of Section 18.4.

```
template <class Graph>
class DFS : public SEARCH<Graph>
{ vector<int> st;
  void searchC(Edge e)
    { int w = e.w;
      ord[w] = cnt++; st[e.w] = e.v;
      typename Graph::adjIterator A(G, w);
      for (int t = A.beg(); !A.end(); t = A.nxt())
        if (ord[t] == -1) searchC(Edge(w, t));
    }
public:
  DFS(const Graph &G) : SEARCH<Graph>(G),
    st(G.V(), -1) { search(); }
  int ST(int v) const { return st[v]; }
};
```

Property 18.2 *A graph-search function checks each edge and marks each vertex in a graph if and only if the search function that it uses marks each vertex and checks each edge in the connected component that contains the start vertex.*

Proof: By induction on the number of connected components. ■

Graph-search functions provide a systematic way of processing each vertex and each edge in a graph. Generally, our implementations are designed to run in linear or near-linear time, by doing a fixed amount of processing per edge. We prove this fact now for DFS, noting that the same proof technique works for several other search strategies.

Property 18.3 *DFS of a graph represented with an adjacency matrix requires time proportional to V^2.*

Proof: An argument similar to the proof of Property 18.1 shows that searchC not only marks all vertices connected to the start vertex but also calls itself exactly once for each such vertex (to mark that vertex). An argument similar to the proof of Property 18.2 shows that a call to search leads to exactly one call to searchC for each graph vertex. In searchC, the iterator checks every entry in the vertex's row in the adjacency matrix. In other words, the search checks each entry in the adjacency matrix precisely once. ∎

Property 18.4 *DFS of a graph represented with adjacency lists requires time proportional to $V + E$.*

Proof: From the argument just outlined, it follows that we call the recursive function precisely V times (hence the V term), and we examine each entry on each adjacency list (hence the E term). ∎

The primary implication of Properties 18.3 and 18.4 is that they establish the running time of DFS to be *linear* in the size of the data structure used to represent the graph. In most situations, we are also justified in thinking of the running time of DFS as being linear in the size of the graph, as well: If we have a dense graph (with the number of edges proportional to V^2) then either representation gives this result; if we have a sparse graph, then we assume use of an adjacency-lists representation. Indeed, we normally think of the running time of DFS as being linear in E. That statement is technically not true if we are using adjacency matrices for sparse graphs or for extremely sparse graphs with $E << V$ and most vertices isolated, but we can usually avoid the former situation, and we can remove isolated vertices (see Exercise 17.34) in the latter situation.

As we shall see, these arguments all apply to any algorithm that has a few of the same essential features of DFS. If the algorithm marks each vertex and examines all the latter's incident vertices (and does any other work that takes time per vertex bounded by a constant), then these properties apply. More generally, if the time per vertex is bounded by some function $f(V, E)$, then the time for the search is guaranteed to be proportional to $E + V f(V, E)$. In Section 18.8, we see that DFS is one of a family of algorithms that has just these characteristics; in Chapters 19 through 22, we see that algorithms from this family serve as the basis for a substantial fraction of the code that we consider in this book.

Much of the graph-processing code that we examine is ADT-implementation code for some particular task, where we develop a class that does a basic search to compute structural information in other vertex-indexed vectors. We can derive the class from Program 18.2 or, in simple cases, just reimplement the search. Many of our graph-processing classes are of this nature because we typically can uncover a graph's structure by searching it. We normally add code to the search function that is executed when each vertex is marked, instead of working with a more generic search (for example, one that calls a specified function each time a vertex is visited), solely to keep the code compact and self-contained. Providing a more general ADT mechanism for clients to process all the vertices with a client-supplied function is a worthwhile exercise (see Exercises 18.13 and 18.14).

In Sections 18.5 and 18.6, we examine numerous graph-processing functions that are based on DFS. In Sections 18.7 and 18.8, we look at other implementations of search and at some graph-processing functions that are based on them. Although we do not build this layer of abstraction into our code, we take care to identify the basic graph-search strategy underlying each algorithm that we develop. For example, we use the term *DFS class* to refer to any implementation that is based on the recursive DFS scheme. The simple-path–search class Program 17.11 and the spanning-forest class Program 18.3 are examples of DFS classes.

Many graph-processing functions are based on the use of vertex-indexed vectors. We typically include such vectors as private data members in class implementations, to hold information about the structure of graphs (which is discovered during the search) that helps us solve the problem at hand. Examples of such vectors are the deg vector in Program 17.11 and the ord vector in Program 18.1. Some implementations that we will examine use multiple vectors to learn complicated structural properties.

Our convention in graph-search functions is to initialize all entries in vertex-indexed vectors to -1, and to set the entries corresponding to each vertex visited to nonnegative values in the search function. Any such vector can play the role of the ord vector (marking vertices as visited) in Programs 18.2 through 18.3. When a graph-search function is based on using or computing a vertex-indexed vector, we often just implement the search and use that vector to mark vertices, rather than deriving the class from SEARCH or maintaining the ord vector.

The specific outcome of a graph search depends not just on the nature of the search function but also on the graph representation and even the order in which search examines the vertices. For specificity in the examples and exercises in this book, we use the term *standard adjacency-lists DFS* to refer to the process of inserting a sequence of edges into a graph ADT implemented with an adjacency-lists representation (Program 17.9), then doing a DFS with, for example, Program 18.3. For the adjacency-matrix representation, the order of edge insertion does not affect search dynamics, but we use the parallel term *standard adjacency-matrix DFS* to refer to the process of inserting a sequence of edges into a graph ADT implemented with an adjacency-matrix representation (Program 17.7), then doing a DFS with, for example, Program 18.3.

Exercises

18.8 Show, in the style of Figure 18.5, a trace of the recursive function calls made for a standard adjacency-matrix DFS of the graph

       3-7 1-4 7-8 0-5 5-2 3-8 2-9 0-6 4-9 2-6 6-4.

18.9 Show, in the style of Figure 18.7, a trace of the recursive function calls made for a standard adjacency-lists DFS of the graph

       3-7 1-4 7-8 0-5 5-2 3-8 2-9 0-6 4-9 2-6 6-4.

18.10 Modify the adjacency-matrix graph ADT implementation in Program 17.7 to use a dummy vertex that is connected to all the other vertices. Then, provide a simplified DFS implementation that takes advantage of this change.

18.11 Do Exercise 18.10 for the adjacency-lists ADT implementation in Program 17.9.

• **18.12** There are 13! different permutations of the vertices in the graph depicted in Figure 18.8. How many of these permutations could specify the order in which vertices are visited by Program 18.2?

18.13 Implement a graph ADT client function that calls a client-supplied function for each vertex in the graph.

18.14 Implement a graph ADT client that calls a client-supplied function for each *edge* in the graph. Such a function might be a reasonable alternative to GRAPHedges (see Program 17.2).

Figure 18.9
DFS tree representations

If we augment the DFS recursive-call tree to represent edges that are checked but not followed, we get a complete description of the DFS process (left). Each tree node has a child representing each of the nodes adjacent to it, in the order they were considered by the DFS, and a preorder traversal gives the same information as Figure 18.5: first we follow 0-0, then 0-2, then we skip 2-0, then we follow 2-6, then we skip 6-2, then we follow 6-4, then 4-3, and so forth. The ord *vector specifies the order in which we visit tree vertices during this preorder walk, which is the same as the order in which we visit graph vertices in the DFS. The* st *vector is a parent-link representation of the DFS recursive-call tree (see Figure 18.6).*

There are two links in the tree for every edge in the graph, one for each of the two times it encounters the edge. The first is to an unshaded node and either corresponds to making a recursive call (if it is to an internal node) or to skipping a recursive call because it goes to an ancestor for which a recursive call is in progress (if it is to an external node). The second is to a shaded external node and always corresponds to skipping a recursive call, either because it goes back to the parent (circles) or because it goes to a descendent of the parent for which a recursive call is in progress (squares). If we eliminate shaded nodes (center), then replace the external nodes with edges, we get another drawing of the graph (right).

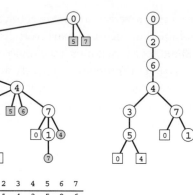
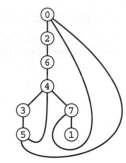

	0	1	2	3	4	5	6	7
ord	0	7	1	4	3	5	2	6
st	0	7	0	4	6	3	2	4

18.4 Properties of DFS Forests

As noted in Section 18.2, the trees that describe the recursive structure of DFS function calls give us the key to understanding how DFS operates. In this section, we examine properties of the algorithm by examining properties of DFS trees.

If we add external nodes to the DFS tree to record the moments when we skipped recursive calls for vertices that had already been visited, we get the compact representation of the dynamics of DFS illustrated in Figure 18.9. This representation is worthy of careful study. The tree is a representation of the graph, with a vertex corresponding to each graph vertex and an edge corresponding to each graph edge. We can choose to show the two representations of the edge that we process (one in each direction), as shown in the left part of the figure, or just one representation of each edge, as shown in the center and right parts of the figure. The former is useful in understanding that the algorithm processes each and every edge; the latter is useful in understanding that the DFS tree is simply another graph representation. Traversing the internal nodes of the tree in preorder gives the vertices in the order in which DFS visits them; moreover, the order in which we visit the *edges* of the tree as we traverse it in preorder is the same as the order in which DFS examines the *edges* of the graph.

Indeed, the DFS tree in Figure 18.9 contains the same information as the trace in Figure 18.5 or the step-by-step illustration of Trémaux traversal in Figures 18.2 and 18.3. Edges to internal nodes represent edges (passages) to unvisited vertices (intersections), edges to external nodes represent occasions where DFS checks edges that lead to previously visited vertices (intersections), and shaded nodes represent edges to vertices for which a recursive DFS is in progress (when we open a door to a passage where the door at the other end is already open). With these interpretations, a preorder traversal of the tree tells the same story as that of the detailed maze-traversal scenario.

To study more intricate graph properties, we classify the edges in a graph according to the role that they play in the search. We have two distinct edge classes:

- Edges representing a recursive call (*tree* edges)
- Edges connecting a vertex with an ancestor in its DFS tree that is not its parent (*back* edges)

When we study DFS trees for digraphs in Chapter 19, we examine other types of edges, not just to take the direction into account, but also because we can have edges that go across the tree, connecting nodes that are neither ancestors nor descendants in the tree.

Since there are two representations of each graph edge that each correspond to a link in the DFS tree, we divide the tree links into four classes, using the *preorder numbers* and the parent links (in the `ord` and `st` arrays, respectively) that our DFS code computes. We refer to a link from v to w in a DFS tree that represents a tree edge as

- A *tree* link if w is unmarked
- A *parent* link if `st[w]` is v

and a link from v to w that represents a back edge as

- A *back* link if `ord[w]` < `ord[v]`
- A *down* link if `ord[w]` > `ord[v]`

Each tree edge in the graph corresponds to a tree link and a parent link in the DFS tree, and each back edge in the graph corresponds to a back link and a down link in the DFS tree.

In the graphical DFS representation illustrated in Figure 18.9, tree links point to unshaded circles, parent links point to shaded circles, back links point to unshaded squares, and down links point to shaded squares. Each graph edge is represented either as one tree link and one parent link or as one down link and one back link. These classifications are tricky and worthy of study. For example, note that even though parent links and back links both point to ancestors in the tree, they are quite different: A parent link is just the other representation of a tree link, but a back link gives us new information about the structure of the graph.

The definitions just given provide sufficient information to distinguish among tree, parent, back, and down links in a DFS class implementation. Note that parent links and back links both have ord[w] < ord[v], so we have also to know that st[w] is not v to know that v-w is a back link. Figure 18.10 depicts the result of printing out the classification of the DFS tree link for each graph edge as that edge is encountered during a sample DFS. It is yet another complete representation of the basic search process that is an intermediate step between Figure 18.5 and Figure 18.9.

The four types of tree links correspond to the four different ways in which we treat edges during a DFS, as described (in maze-exploration terms) at the end of Section 18.1. A tree link corresponds to DFS encountering the first of the two representations of a tree edge, leading to a recursive call (to as-yet-unseen vertices); a parent link corresponds to DFS encountering the other representation of the tree edge (when going through the adjacency list on that first recursive call) and ignoring it. A back link corresponds to DFS encountering the first of the two representations of a back edge, which points to a vertex for which the recursive search function has not yet completed; a down link corresponds to DFS encountering a vertex for which the recursive search *has* completed at the time that the edge is encountered. In Figure 18.9, tree links and back links connect unshaded nodes, represent the first encounter with the corresponding edge, and constitute a representation of the graph; parent links and down links go to shaded nodes and represent the second encounter with the corresponding edge.

We have considered this tree representation of the dynamic characteristics of recursive DFS in detail not just because it provides a complete and compact description of both the graph and the operation of the algorithm, but also because it gives us a basis for understanding numerous important graph-processing algorithms. In the remainder of this chapter, and in the next several chapters, we consider a number of examples of graph-processing problems that draw conclusions about a graph's structure from the DFS tree.

Search in a graph is a generalization of tree traversal. When invoked on a tree, DFS is precisely equivalent to recursive tree traversal; for graphs, using it corresponds to traversing a tree that spans the graph

```
0-0 tree
  0-2 tree
    2-0 parent
    2-6 tree
      6-2 parent
      6-4 tree
        4-3 tree
          3-4 parent
          3-5 tree
            5-0 back
            5-3 parent
            5-4 back
        4-5 down
        4-6 parent
        4-7 tree
          7-0 back
          7-1 tree
            1-7 parent
          7-4 parent
  0-5 down
  0-7 down
```

Figure 18.10
DFS trace (tree link classifications)

This version of Figure 18.5 shows the classification of the DFS tree link corresponding to each graph edge representation encountered. Tree edges (which correspond to recursive calls) are represented as tree links on the first encounter and parent links on the second encounter. Back edges are back links on the first encounter and down links on the second encounter.

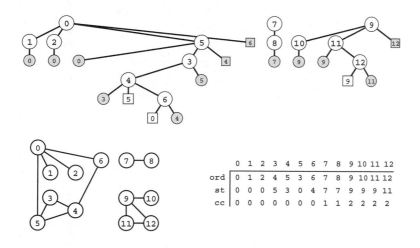

and that is discovered as the search proceeds. As we have seen, the particular tree traversed depends on how the graph is represented. DFS corresponds to preorder tree traversal. In Section 18.6, we examine the graph-searching analog to level-order tree traversal and explore its relationship to DFS; in Section 18.7, we examine a general schema that encompasses any traversal method.

When traversing graphs with DFS, we have been using the ord vector to assign preorder numbers to the vertices in the order that we start processing them. We can also assign *postorder numbers* to vertices, in the order that we *finish* processing them (just before returning from the recursive search function). When processing a graph, we do more than simply traverse the vertices—as we shall see, the preorder and postorder numbering give us knowledge about global graph properties that helps us to accomplish the task at hand. Preorder numbering suffices for the algorithms that we consider in this chapter, but we use postorder numbering in later chapters.

We describe the dynamics of DFS for a general undirected graph with a *DFS forest* that has one DFS tree for each connected component. An example of a DFS forest is illustrated in Figure 18.11.

With an adjacency-lists representation, we visit the edges connected to each vertex in an order different from that for the adjacency-matrix representation, so we get a different DFS forest, as illustrated in Figure 18.12. DFS trees and forests are graph representations that describe not only the dynamics of DFS but also the internal representa-

**Figure 18.11
DFS forest**

The DFS forest at the top represents a DFS of an adjacency-matrix representation of the graph at the bottom right. The graph has three connected components, so the forest has three trees. The ord vector is a preorder numbering of the nodes in the tree (the order in which they are examined by the DFS) and the st vector is a parent-link representation of the forest. The cc vector associates each vertex with a connected-component index (see Program 18.4). As in Figure 18.9, edges to circles are tree edges; edges that go to squares are back edges; and shaded nodes indicate that the incident edge was encountered earlier in the search, in the other direction.

Figure 18.12
Another DFS forest

This forest describes depth-first search of the same graph as Figure 18.11, but using an adjacency-list representation, so the search order is different because it is determined by the order that nodes appear in adjacency lists. Indeed, the forest itself tells us that order: it is the order in which children are listed for each node in the tree. For instance, the nodes on 0's adjacency list were found in the order **5 2 1 6**, *the nodes on 4's list are in the order* **6 5 3**, *and so forth. As before, all vertices and edges in the graph are examined during the search, in a manner that is precisely described by a preorder walk of the tree. The* ord *and* st *vectors depend upon the graph representation and the search dynamics and are different from Figure 18.11, but the vector* cc *depends on graph properties and is the same.*

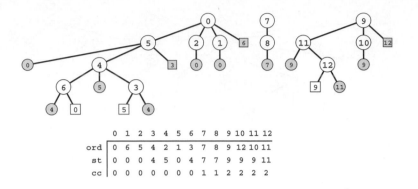

	0	1	2	3	4	5	6	7	8	9	10	11	12
ord	0	6	5	4	2	1	3	7	8	9	12	10	11
st	0	0	0	4	5	0	4	7	7	9	9	9	11
cc	0	0	0	0	0	0	0	1	1	2	2	2	2

tion of the graph. For example, by reading the children of any node in Figure 18.12 from left to right, we see the order in which they appear on the adjacency list of the vertex corresponding to that node. We can have many different DFS forests for the same graph—each ordering of nodes on adjacency lists leads to a different forest.

Details of the structure of a particular forest inform our understanding of how DFS operates for particular graphs, but most of the important DFS properties that we consider depend on graph properties that are independent of the structure of the forest. For example, the forests in Figures 18.11 and 18.12 both have three trees (as would any other DFS forest for the same graph) because they are just different representations of the same graph, which has three connected components. Indeed, a direct consequence of the basic proof that DFS visits all the nodes and edges of a graph (see Properties 18.2 through 18.4) is that the number of connected components in the graph is equal to the number of trees in the DFS forest. This example illustrates the basis for our use of graph search throughout the book: A broad variety of graph-processing class implementations are based on learning graph properties by processing a particular graph representation (a forest corresponding to the search).

Potentially, we could analyze DFS tree structures with the goal of improving algorithm performance. For example, should we attempt to speed up an algorithm by rearranging the adjacency lists before starting the search? For many of the important classical DFS-based algorithms, the answer to this question is no, because they are optimal—their worst-case running time depends on *neither* the graph structure *nor* the order in which edges appear on the adjacency lists (they essentially process each edge exactly once). Still, DFS forests have a characteristic structure that is worth understanding because it distinguishes them from other fundamental search schema that we consider later in this chapter.

Figure 18.13 shows a DFS tree for a larger graph that illustrates the basic characteristics of DFS search dynamics. The tree is tall and thin, and it demonstrates several characteristics of the graph being searched and of the DFS process.

- There exists at least one long path that connects a substantial fraction of the nodes.
- During the search, most vertices have at least one adjacent vertex that we have not yet seen.
- We rarely make more than one recursive call from any node.
- The depth of the recursion is proportional to the number of vertices in the graph.

This behavior is typical for DFS, though these characteristics are not guaranteed for all graphs. Verifying facts of this kind for graph models of interest and various types of graphs that arise in practice requires detailed study. Still, this example gives an intuitive feel for DFS-based algorithms that is often borne out in practice. Figure 18.13 and similar figures for other graph-search algorithms (see Figures 18.24 and 18.29) help us understand differences in their behavior.

Exercises

18.15 Draw the DFS forest that results from a standard adjacency-matrix DFS of the graph

    3-7 1-4 7-8 0-5 5-2 3-8 2-9 0-6 4-9 2-6 6-4.

18.16 Draw the DFS forest that results from a standard adjacency-lists DFS of the graph

    3-7 1-4 7-8 0-5 5-2 3-8 2-9 0-6 4-9 2-6 6-4.

18.17 Write a DFS trace program to produce output that classifies each of the two representations of each graph edge as corresponding to a tree, parent, back, or down link in the DFS tree, in the style of Figure 18.10.

○ **18.18** Write a program that computes a parent-link representation of the full DFS tree (including the external nodes), using an vector of E integers between 0 and $V - 1$. *Hint*: The first V entries in the vector should be the same as those in the st vector described in the text.

Figure 18.13
Depth-first search

This figure illustrates the progress of DFS in a random Euclidean near-neighbor graph (left). The figures show the DFS tree vertices and edges in the graph as the search progresses through 1/4, 1/2, 3/4, and all of the vertices (top to bottom). The DFS tree (tree edges only) is shown at the right. As is evident from this example, the search tree for DFS tends to be quite tall and thin for this type of graph (as it is for many other types of graphs commonly encountered in practice). We normally find a vertex nearby that we have not seen before.

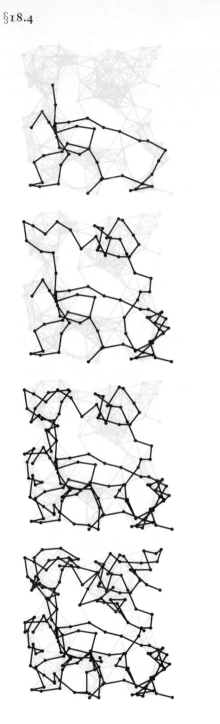

○ **18.19** Instrument the spanning-forest DFS class (Program 18.3) by adding member functions (and appropriate private data members) that return the height of the tallest tree in the forest, the number of back edges, and the percentage of edges processed to see every vertex.

• **18.20** Run experiments to determine empirically the average values of the quantities described in Exercise 18.19 for graphs of various sizes, drawn from various graph models (see Exercises 17.64–76).

• **18.21** Write a function that builds a graph by inserting edges from a given vector into an initially empty graph, in random order. Using this function with an adjacency-lists implementation of the graph ADT, run experiments to determine empirically properties of the *distribution* of the quantities described in Exercise 18.19 for all the adjacency-lists representations of large sample graphs of various sizes, drawn from various graph models (see Exercises 17.64–76).

18.5 DFS Algorithms

Regardless of the graph structure or the representation, any DFS forest allows us to identify edges as tree or back edges and gives us dependable insights into graph structure that allow us to use DFS as a basis for solving numerous graph-processing problems. We have already seen, in Section 17.7, basic examples related to finding paths. In this section, we consider DFS-based ADT function implementations for these and other typical problems; in the remainder of this chapter and in the next several chapters, we look at numerous solutions to much more difficult problems.

Cycle detection Does a given graph have any cycles? (Is the graph a forest?) This problem is easy to solve with DFS because any back edge in a DFS tree belongs to a cycle consisting of the edge plus the tree path connecting the two nodes (see Figure 18.9). Thus, we can use DFS immediately to check for cycles: A graph is acyclic if and only if we encounter no back (or down!) edges during a DFS. For example, to test this condition in Program 18.1, we simply add an `else` clause to the `if` statement to test whether `t` is equal to `v`. If it is, we have just encountered the parent link `w-v` (the second representation of the edge `v-w` that led us to `w`). If it is not, `w-t` completes a cycle with the edges from `t` down to `w` in the DFS tree. Moreover, we do not need to examine all the edges: We know that we must find a cycle or finish the search without finding one before examining V edges, because any graph with V or more edges must have a cycle. Thus, we can test whether a graph is acyclic in time proportional to V with the adjacency-lists representation, although we may need time proportional to V^2 (to find the edges) with the adjacency-matrix representation.

Simple path   Given two vertices, is there a path in the graph that connects them? We saw in Section 17.7 that a DFS class that can solve this problem in linear time is easy to devise.

Simple connectivity   As discussed in Section 18.3, we determine whether or not a graph is connected whenever we use DFS, in linear time. Indeed, our graph-search strategy is based upon calling a search function for each connected component. In a DFS, the graph is connected if and only if the graph-search function calls the recursive DFS function just once (see Program 18.2). The number of connected components in the graph is precisely the number of times that the recursive function is called from GRAPHsearch, so we can find the number of connected components by simply keeping track of the number of such calls.

More generally, Program 18.4 illustrates a DFS class that supports constant-time connectivity queries after a linear-time preprocessing step in the constructor. It visits vertices in the same order as does Program 18.3. The recursive function uses a vertex as its second argument instead of an edge, since it does not need to know the identity of the parent. Each tree in the DFS forest identifies a connected component, so we arrange to decide quickly whether two vertices are in the same component by including a vertex-indexed vector in the graph representation, to be filled in by a DFS and accessed for connectivity queries. In the recursive DFS function, we assign the current value of the component counter to the entry corresponding to each vertex visited. Then, we know that two vertices are in the same component if and only if their entries in this vector are equal. Again, note that this vector reflects structural properties of the graph, rather than artifacts of the graph representation or of the search dynamics.

Program 18.4 typifies the basic approach that we shall use in addressing numerous graph-processing tasks. We develop a task-specific class so that clients can create objects to perform the task. Typically, we invest preprocessing time in the constructor to compute private data about relevant structural graph properties that help us to provide efficient implementations of public query functions. In this case, the con-

Program 18.4 Graph connectivity

The CC constructor computes, in linear time, the number of connected components in a graph and stores a component index associated with each vertex in the private vertex-indexed vector id. Clients can use a CC object to find the number of connected components (count) or test whether any pair of vertices are connected (connect), in constant time.

```
template <class Graph> class CC
{ const Graph &G;
  int ccnt;
  vector <int> id;
  void ccR(int w)
    {
      id[w] = ccnt;
      typename Graph::adjIterator A(G, w);
      for (int v = A.beg(); !A.end(); v = A.nxt())
        if (id[v] == -1) ccR(v);
    }
public:
  CC(const Graph &G) : G(G), ccnt(0), id(G.V(), -1)
    {
      for (int v = 0; v < G.V(); v++)
        if (id[v] == -1) { ccR(v); ccnt++; }
    }
  int count() const { return ccnt; }
  bool connect(int s, int t) const
    { return id[s] == id[t]; }
};
```

structor preprocesses with a (linear-time) DFS and keeps a private data member (the vertex-indexed vector id) that allows it to answer connectivity queries in constant time. For other graph-processing problems, our constructors might use more space, preprocessing time, or query time. As usual, our focus is on minimizing such costs, although doing so is often challenging. For example, much of Chapter 19 is devoted to solving the connectivity problem for digraphs, where achieving linear time preprocessing and constant query time, as in Program 18.4, is an elusive goal.

Program 18.5 Two-way Euler tour

This DFS class prints each edge twice, once in each orientation, in a two-way–Euler-tour order. We go back and forth on back edges and ignore down edges (*see text*). It is derived from the SEARCH base class in Program 18.2.

```
template <class Graph>
class EULER : public SEARCH<Graph>
{
  void searchC(Edge e)
  { int v = e.v, w = e.w;
    ord[w] = cnt++;
    cout << "-" << w;
    typename Graph::adjIterator A(G, w);
    for (int t = A.beg(); !A.end(); t = A.nxt())
      if (ord[t] == -1) searchC(Edge(w, t));
      else if (ord[t] < ord[v])
        cout << "-" << t << "-" << w;
    if (v != w) cout << "-" << v; else cout << endl;
  }
public:
  EULER(const Graph &G) : SEARCH<Graph>(G)
    { search(); }
};
```

How does the DFS-based solution for graph connectivity in Program 18.4 compare with the union-find approach that we considered in Chapter 1 for the problem of determining whether a graph is connected, given an edge list? In theory, DFS is faster than union-find because it provides a constant-time guarantee, which union- find does not; in practice, this difference is negligible, and union-find is faster because it does not have to build a full representation of the graph. More important, union-find is an online algorithm (we can check whether two vertices are connected in near-constant time at any point), whereas the DFS solution preprocesses the graph to answer connectivity queries in constant time. Therefore, for example, we prefer union-find when determining connectivity is our only task or when we have a large num-

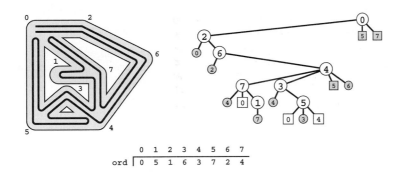

Figure 18.14
A two-way Euler tour

Depth-first search gives us a way to explore any maze, traversing both passages in each direction. We modify Trémaux exploration to take the string with us wherever we go and take a back-and-forth trip on passages without any string in them that go to intersections that we have already visited. This figure shows a different traversal order than shown in Figures 18.2 and 18.3, primarily so that we can draw the tour without crossing itself. This ordering might result, for example, if the edges were processed in some different order when building an adjacency-lists representation of the graph; or, we might explicitly modify DFS to take the geometric placement of the nodes into account (see Exercise 18.26). Moving along the lower track leading out of 0, we move from 0 to 2 to 6 to 4 to 7, then take a trip from 7 to 0 and back because ord[0] is less than ord[7]. Then we go to 1, back to 7, back to 4, to 3, to 5, from 5 to 0 and back, from 5 to 4 and back, back to 3, back to 4, back to 6, back to 2, and back to 0. This path may be obtained by a recursive pre- and postorder walk of the DFS tree (ignoring the shaded vertices that represent the second time we encounter the edges) where we print out the vertex name, recursively visit the subtrees, then print out the vertex name again.

ber of queries intermixed with edge insertions but may find the DFS solution more appropriate for use in a graph ADT because it makes efficient use of existing infrastructure. Neither approach handles efficiently huge numbers of intermixed edge insertions, edge deletions, and connectivity queries; both require a separate DFS to compute the path. These considerations illustrate the complications that we face when analyzing graph algorithms; we explore them in detail in Section 18.9.

Two-way Euler tour Program 18.5 is a DFS-based class for finding a path that uses all the edges in a graph exactly twice—once in each direction (see Section 17.7). The path corresponds to a Trémaux exploration in which we take our string with us everywhere that we go, check for the string instead of using lights (so we have to go down the passages that lead to intersections that we have already visited), and first arrange to go back and forth on each back link (the first time that we encounter each back edge), then ignore down links (the second time that we encounter each back edge). We might also choose to ignore the back links (first encounter) and to go back and forth on down links (second encounter) (see Exercise 18.25).

Spanning forest Given a connected graph with V vertices, find a set of $V - 1$ edges that connects the vertices. If the graph has C connected components, find a spanning forest (with $V - C$ edges). We have already seen a DFS class that solves this problem: Program 18.3.

Vertex search How many vertices are in the same connected component as a given vertex? We can solve this problem easily by starting a DFS at the vertex and counting the number of vertices marked. In a dense graph, we can speed up the process considerably by stopping the DFS after we have marked V vertices—at that point, we know that

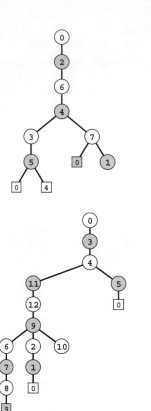

Figure 18.15
Two-coloring a DFS tree

To two-color a graph, we alternate colors as we move down the DFS tree, then check the back edges for inconsistencies. In the tree at the top, a DFS tree for the sample graph illustrated in Figure 18.9, the back edges 5-4 and 7-0 prove that the graph is not two-colorable because of the odd-length cycles 4-3-5-4 and 0-2-6-4-7-0, respectively. In the tree at the bottom, a DFS tree for the bipartite graph illustrated in Figure 17.5, there are no such inconsistencies, and the indicated shading is a two-coloring of the graph.

Program 18.6 Two-colorability (bipartiteness)

The constructor in this DFS class sets OK to true if and only if it is able to assign the values 0 or 1 to the vertex-indexed vector vc such that, for each graph edge v-w, vc[v] and vc[w] are different.

```
template <class Graph> class BI
  { const Graph &G;
    bool OK;
    vector <int> vc;
    bool dfsR(int v, int c)
      {
        vc[v] = (c+1) %2;
        typename Graph::adjIterator A(G, v);
        for (int t = A.beg(); !A.end(); t = A.nxt())
          if (vc[t] == -1)
            { if (!dfsR(t, vc[v])) return false; }
          else if (vc[t] != c) return false;
        return true;
      }
  public:
    BI(const Graph &G) : G(G), OK(true), vc(G.V(),-1)
      {
        for (int v = 0; v < G.V(); v++)
          if (vc[v] == -1)
            if (!dfsR(v, 0)) { OK = false; return; }
      }
    bool bipartite() const { return OK; }
    int color(int v) const { return vc[v]; }
};
```

no edge will take us to a vertex that we have not yet seen, so we will be ignoring all the rest of the edges. This improvement is likely to allow us to visit all vertices in time proportional to $V \log V$, not E (see Section 18.8).

Two-colorability, bipartiteness, odd cycle   Is there a way to assign one of two colors to each vertex of a graph such that no edge connects two vertices of the same color? Is a given graph bipartite (see Section 17.1)? Does a given graph have a cycle of odd length?

These three problems are all equivalent: The first two are different nomenclature for the same problem; any graph with an odd cycle is clearly not two-colorable, and Program 18.6 demonstrates that any graph that is free of odd cycles can be two-colored. The program is a DFS-based ADT function implementation that tests whether a graph is bipartite, two-colorable, and free of odd cycles. The recursive function is an outline for a proof by induction that the program two-colors any graph with no odd cycles (or finds an odd cycle as evidence that a graph that is not free of odd cycles cannot be two-colored). To two-color a graph with a given color assigned to a vertex v, two-color the remaining graph, assigning the other color to each vertex adjacent to v. This process is equivalent to assigning alternate colors on levels as we proceed down the DFS tree, checking back edges for consistency in the coloring, as illustrated in Figure 18.15. Any back edge connecting two vertices of the same color is evidence of an odd cycle.

These basic examples illustrate ways in which DFS can give us insight into the structure of a graph. They also demonstrate that we can learn various important graph properties in a single linear-time sweep through the graph, where we examine every edge twice, once in each direction. Next, we consider an example that shows the utility of DFS in discovering more intricate details about the graph structure, still in linear time.

Exercises

○ **18.22** Implement a DFS-based cycle-testing class that preprocesses a graph in time proportional to V in the constructor to support public member functions for detecting whether a graph has any cycles and for printing a cycle if one exists.

18.23 Describe a family of graphs with V vertices for which a standard adjacency-matrix DFS requires time proportional to V^2 for cycle detection.

▷ **18.24** Implement the graph-connectivity class of Program 18.4 as a derived graph-search class, like Program 18.3.

▷ **18.25** Specify a modification to Program 18.5 that will produce a two-way Euler tour that does the back-and-forth traversal on down edges instead of back edges.

● **18.26** Modify Program 18.5 such that it always produces a two-way Euler tour that, like the one in Figure 18.14, can be drawn such that it does not cross itself at any vertex. For example, if the search in Figure 18.14 were to take the edge 4–3 before the edge 4–7, then the tour would have to cross itself; your task is to ensure that the algorithm avoids such situations.

18.27 Develop a version of Program 18.5 that sorts the edges of a graph in order of a two-way Euler tour. Your program should return a vector of edges that corresponds to a two-way Euler tour.

18.28 Prove that a graph is two-colorable if and only if it contains no odd cycle. *Hint*: Prove by induction that Program 18.6 determines whether or not any given graph is two-colorable.

○ **18.29** Explain why the approach taken in Program 18.6 does not generalize to give an efficient method for determining whether a graph is three-colorable.

18.30 Most graphs are not two-colorable, and DFS tends to discover that fact quickly. Run empirical tests to study the number of edges examined by Program 18.6, for graphs of various sizes, drawn from various graph models (see Exercises 17.64–76).

○ **18.31** Prove that every connected graph has a vertex whose removal will not disconnect the graph, and write a DFS function that finds such a vertex. *Hint*: Consider the leaves of the DFS tree.

18.32 Prove that every graph with more than one vertex has at least two vertices whose removal will not increase the number of connected components.

18.6 Separability and Biconnectivity

To illustrate the power of DFS as the basis for graph-processing algorithms, we turn to problems related to generalized notions of connectivity in graphs. We study questions such as the following: Given two vertices, are there two different paths connecting them?

If it is important that a graph *be* connected in some situation, it might also be important that it *stay* connected when an edge or a vertex is removed. That is, we may want to have more than one route between each pair of vertices in a graph, so as to handle possible failures. For example, we can fly from New York to San Francisco even if Chicago is snowed in by going through Denver instead. Or, we might imagine a wartime situation where we want to arrange our railroad network such that an enemy must destroy at least two stations to cut our rail lines. Similarly, we might expect the main communications lines in an integrated circuit or a communications network to be connected such that the rest of the circuit still can function if one wire is broken or one link is down.

These examples illustrate two distinct concepts: In the circuit and in the communications network, we are interested in staying connected if an *edge* is removed; in the air or train routes, we are interested in

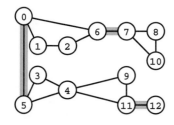

Figure 18.16
An edge-separable graph

This graph is not edge connected. The edges 0–5, 6–7, and 11–12 (shaded) are separating edges (bridges). The graph has 4 edge-connected components: one comprising vertices 0, 1, 2, and 6; another comprising vertices 3, 4, 9, and 11; another comprising vertices 7, 8, and 10; and the single vertex 12.

staying connected if a *vertex* is removed. We begin by examining the former in detail.

Definition 18.1 *A* **bridge** *in a graph is an edge that, if removed, would separate a connected graph into two disjoint subgraphs. A graph that has no bridges is said to be* **edge-connected**.

When we speak of *removing* an edge, we mean to delete that edge from the set of edges that define the graph, even when that action might leave one or both of the edge's vertices isolated. An edge-connected graph remains connected when we remove any single edge. In some contexts, it is more natural to emphasize our ability to disconnect the graph rather than the graph's ability to stay connected, so we freely use alternate terminology that provides this emphasis: We refer to a graph that is not edge-connected as an *edge-separable* graph, and we call bridges *separation edges*. If we remove all the bridges in an edge-separable graph, we divide it into *edge-connected components* or *bridge-connected components*: maximal subgraphs with no bridges. Figure 18.16 is a small example that illustrates these concepts.

Finding the bridges in a graph seems, at first blush, to be a nontrivial graph-processing problem, but it actually is an application of DFS where we can exploit basic properties of the DFS tree that we have already noted. Specifically, back edges cannot be bridges because we know that the two nodes they connect are also connected by a path in the DFS tree. Moreover, we can add a simple test to our recursive DFS function to test whether or not tree edges are bridges. The basic idea, stated formally next, is illustrated in Figure 18.17.

Property 18.5 *In any DFS tree, a tree edge* v-w *is a bridge if and only if there are no back edges that connect a descendant of* w *to an ancestor of* w.

Proof: If there is such an edge, v-w cannot be a bridge. Conversely, if v-w is not a bridge, then there has to be some path from w to v in the graph other than w-v itself. Every such path has to have some such edge. ∎

Asserting this property is equivalent to saying that the only link in the subtree rooted at w that points to a node not in the subtree is the parent link from w back to v. This condition holds if and only if every path connecting any of the nodes in w's subtree to any node that

Figure 18.17
DFS tree for finding bridges

Nodes 5, 7, and 12 in this DFS tree for the graph in Figure 18.16 all have the property that no back edge connects a descendant with an ancestor, and no other nodes have that property. Therefore, as indicated, breaking the edge between one of these nodes and its parent would disconnect the sub-tree rooted at that node from the rest of the graph. That is, the edges 0-5, 11-12, and 6-7 are bridges. We use the vertex-indexed array `low` *to keep track of the lowest preorder number (*`ord`* value) referenced by any back edge in the subtree rooted at the vertex. For example, the value of* `low[9]` *is 2 because one of the back edges in the subtree rooted at 9 points to 4 (the vertex with preorder number 2), and no other back edge points higher in the tree. Nodes 5, 7, and 12 are the ones for which the* `low` *value is equal to the* `ord` *value.*

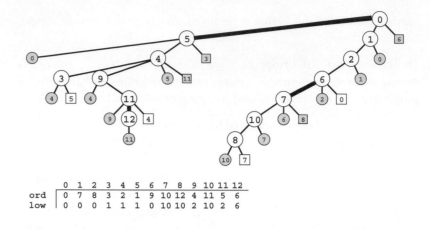

	0	1	2	3	4	5	6	7	8	9	10	11	12
ord	0	7	8	3	2	1	9	10	12	4	11	5	6
low	0	0	0	1	1	1	0	10	10	2	10	2	6

is not in w's subtree includes v-w. In other words, removing v-w would disconnect from the rest of the graph the subgraph corresponding to w's subtree.

Program 18.7 shows how we can augment DFS to identify bridges in a graph, using Property 18.5. For every vertex v, we use the recursive function to compute the lowest preorder number that can be reached by a sequence of zero or more tree edges followed by a single back edge from any node in the subtree rooted at v. If the computed number is equal to v's preorder number, then there is no edge connecting a descendant with an ancestor, and we have identified a bridge. The computation for each vertex is straightforward: We proceed through the adjacency list, keeping track of the minimum of the numbers that we can reach by following each edge. For tree edges, we do the computation recursively; for back edges, we use the preorder number of the adjacent vertex. If the call to the recursive function for an edge w-t does not uncover a path to a node with a preorder number less than t's preorder number, then w-t is a bridge.

Property 18.6 *We can find a graph's bridges in linear time.*

Proof: Program 18.7 is a minor modification to DFS that involves adding a few constant-time tests, so it follows directly from Properties 18.3 and 18.4 that finding the bridges in a graph requires time proportional to V^2 for the adjacency-matrix representation and to $V + E$ for the adjacency-lists representation. ∎

Program 18.7 Edge connectivity

This DFS class counts the bridges in a graph. Clients can use an EC object to find the number of edge-connected components; adding a member function for testing whether two vertices are in the same edge-connected component is left as an exercise (see Exercise 18.36). The low vector keeps track of the lowest preorder number that can be reached from each vertex by a sequence of tree edges followed by one back edge.

```
template <class Graph>
class EC : public SEARCH<Graph>
{ int bcnt;
  vector <int> low;
  void searchC(Edge e)
  { int w = e.w;
    ord[w] = cnt++; low[w] = ord[w];
    typename Graph::adjIterator A(G, w);
    for (int t = A.beg(); !A.end(); t = A.nxt())
      if (ord[t] == -1)
        {
          searchC(Edge(w, t));
          if (low[w] > low[t]) low[w] = low[t];
          if (low[t] == ord[t])
            bcnt++; // w-t is a bridge
        }
      else if (t != e.v)
        if (low[w] > ord[t]) low[w] = ord[t];
  }
public:
  EC(const Graph &G) : SEARCH<Graph>(G),
    bcnt(0), low(G.V(), -1)
    { search(); }
  int count() const { return bcnt+1; }
};
```

In Program 18.7, we use DFS to discover properties of the graph. The graph representation certainly affects the order of the search, but it does not affect the results because bridges are a characteristic of the graph rather than of the way that we choose to represent or search

Figure 18.18
Another DFS tree for finding bridges

This diagram shows a different DFS tree than the one in Figure 18.17 for the graph in Figure 18.16, where we start the search at a different node. Although we visit the nodes and edges in a completely different order, we still find the same bridges (of course). In this tree, 0, 7, and 11 are the ones for which the low value is equal to the ord value, so the edges connecting each of them to their parents (12–11, 5–0, and 6–7, respectively) are bridges.

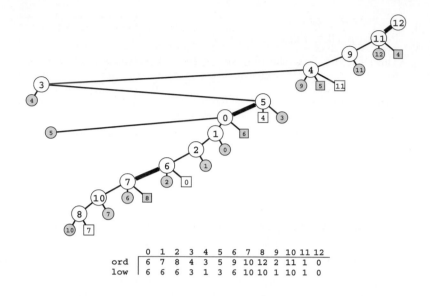

	0	1	2	3	4	5	6	7	8	9	10	11	12
ord	6	7	8	4	3	5	9	10	12	2	11	1	0
low	6	6	6	3	1	3	6	10	10	1	10	1	0

the graph. As usual, any DFS tree is simply another representation of the graph, so all DFS trees have the same connectivity properties. The correctness of the algorithm depends on this fundamental fact. For example, Figure 18.18 illustrates a different search of the graph, starting from a different vertex, that (of course) finds the same bridges. Despite Property 18.6, when we examine different DFS trees for the same graph, we see that some search costs may depend not just on properties of the graph but also on properties of the DFS tree. For example, the amount of space needed for the stack to support the recursive calls is larger for the example in Figure 18.18 than for the example in Figure 18.17.

As we did for regular connectivity in Program 18.4, we may wish to use Program 18.7 to build a class for testing whether a graph is edge-connected or to count the number of edge-connected components. If desired, we can proceed as for Program 18.4 to gives clients the ability to create (in linear time) objects that can respond in constant time to queries that ask whether two vertices are in the same edge-connected component (see Exercise 18.36).

We conclude this section by considering other generalizations of connectivity, including the problem of determining which *vertices* are critical to keeping a graph connected. By including this material here, we keep in one place the basic background material for the more complex algorithms that we consider in Chapter 22. If you are new to connectivity problems, you may wish to skip to Section 18.7 and return here when you study Chapter 22.

When we speak of *removing a vertex*, we also mean that we remove all its incident edges. As illustrated in Figure 18.19, removing either of the vertices on a bridge would disconnect a graph (unless the bridge were the only edge incident on one or both of the vertices), but there are also other vertices, not associated with bridges, that have the same property.

Definition 18.2 *An **articulation point** in a graph is a vertex that, if removed, would separate a connected graph into at least two disjoint subgraphs.*

We also refer to articulation points as *separation vertices* or *cut vertices*. We might use the term "vertex connected" to describe a graph that has no separation vertices, but we use different terminology based on a related characterization that turns out to be equivalent.

Definition 18.3 *A graph is said to be **biconnected** if every pair of vertices is connected by two disjoint paths.*

The requirement that the paths be *disjoint* is what distinguishes biconnectivity from edge connectivity. An alternate definition of edge connectivity is that every pair of vertices is connected by two *edge-disjoint* paths—these paths can have a vertex (but no edge) in common. Biconnectivity is a stronger condition: An edge-connected graph remains connected if we remove any edge, but a biconnected graph remains connected if we remove any vertex (and all that vertex's incident edges). Every biconnected graph is edge-connected, but an edge-connected graph need not be biconnected. We also use the term *separable* to refer to graphs that are not biconnected, because they can be separated into two pieces by removal of just one vertex. The separation vertices are the key to biconnectivity.

Property 18.7 *A graph is biconnected if and only if it has no separation vertices (articulation points).*

Proof: Assume that a graph has a separation vertex. Let s and t be vertices that would be in two different pieces if the separation vertex were removed. All paths between s and t must contain the

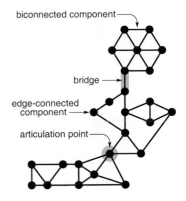

**Figure 18.19
Graph separability terminology**

This graph has two edge-connected components and one bridge. The edge-connected component above the bridge is also biconnected; the one below the bridge consists of two biconnected components that are joined at an articulation point.

separation vertex, therefore the graph is not biconnected. The proof in the other direction is more difficult and is a worthwhile exercise for the mathematically inclined reader (see Exercise 18.40). ∎

We have seen that we can partition the edges of a graph that is not connected into a set of connected subgraphs, and that we can partition the edges of a graph that is not edge-connected into a set of bridges and edge-connected subgraphs (which are connected by bridges). Similarly, we can divide any graph that is not biconnected into a set of bridges and *biconnected components*, which are each biconnected subgraphs. The biconnected components and bridges are not a proper partition of the graph because articulation points may appear on multiple biconnected components (see, for example, Figure 18.20). The biconnected components are connected at articulation points, perhaps by bridges.

A connected component of a graph has the property that there exists a path between any two vertices in the graph. Analogously, a biconnected component has the property that there exist *two* disjoint paths between any pair of vertices.

We can use the same DFS-based approach that we used in Program 18.7 to determine whether or not a graph is biconnected and to identify the articulation points. We omit the code because it is very similar to Program 18.7, with an extra test to check whether the root of the DFS tree is an articulation point (see Exercise 18.43). Developing code to print out the biconnected components is also a worthwhile exercise that is only slightly more difficult than the corresponding code for edge connectivity (see Exercise 18.44).

Property 18.8 *We can find a graph's articulation points and biconnected components in linear time.*

Proof: As for Property 18.7, this fact follows from the observation that the solutions to Exercises 18.43 and 18.44 involve minor modifications to DFS that amount to adding a few constant-time tests per edge. ∎

Biconnectivity generalizes simple connectivity. Further generalizations have been the subjects of extensive studies in classical graph theory and in the design of graph algorithms. These generalizations indicate the scope of graph-processing problems that we might face, many of which are easily posed but less easily solved.

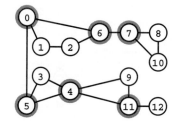

Figure 18.20
Articulation points (separation vertices)

This graph is not biconnected. The vertices 0, 4, 5, 6, 7, and 11 (shaded) are articulation points. The graph has five biconnected components: one comprising edges 4-9, 9-11, and 4-11; another comprising edges 7-8, 8-10, and 7-10; another comprising edges 0-1, 1-2, 2-6, and 6-0; another comprising edges 3-5, 4-5, and 3-4; and the single vertex 12. Adding an edge connecting 12 to 7, 8, or 10 would biconnect the graph.

Definition 18.4 *A graph is* **k-connected** *if there are at least k vertex-disjoint paths connecting every pair of vertices in the graph. The* **vertex connectivity** *of a graph is the minimum number of vertices that need to be removed to separate it into two pieces.*

In this terminology, "1-connected" is the same as "connected" and "2-connected" is the same as "biconnected." A graph with an articulation point has vertex connectivity 1 (or 0), so Property 18.7 says that a graph is 2-connected if and only if its vertex connectivity is not less than 2. It is a special case of a classical result from graph theory, known as *Whitney's theorem*, which says that a graph is k-connected if and only if its vertex connectivity is not less than k. Whitney's theorem follows directly from *Menger's theorem* (see Section 22.7), which says that the minimum number of vertices whose removal disconnects two vertices in a graph is equal to the maximum number of vertex-disjoint paths between the two vertices (to prove Whitney's theorem, apply Menger's theorem to every pair of vertices).

Definition 18.5 *A graph is* **k–edge-connected** *if there are at least k edge-disjoint paths connecting every pair of vertices in the graph. The* **edge connectivity** *of a graph is the minimum number of edges that need to be removed to separate it into two pieces.*

In this terminology, "2–edge-connected" is the same as "edge-connected" (that is, an edge-connected graph has edge connectivity greater than 1, and a graph with at least one bridge has edge connectivity 1). Another version of Menger's theorem says that the minimum number of vertices whose removal disconnects two vertices in a graph is equal to the maximum number of vertex-disjoint paths between the two vertices, which implies that a graph is k–edge-connected if and only if its edge connectivity is k.

With these definitions, we are led to generalize the connectivity problems that we considered at the beginning of this section.

st-connectivity What is the minimum number of edges whose removal will separate two given vertices s and t in a given graph? What is the minimum number of vertices whose removal will separate two given vertices s and t in a given graph?

General connectivity Is a given graph k-connected? Is a given graph k–edge-connected? What is the edge connectivity and the vertex connectivity of a given graph?

Although these problems are much more difficult to solve than are the simple connectivity problems that we have considered in this section, they are members of a large class of graph-processing problems that we can solve using the general algorithmic tools that we consider in Chapter 22 (with DFS playing an important role); we consider specific solutions in Section 22.7.

Exercises

▷ **18.33** If a graph is a forest, all its edges are separation edges; but which vertices are separation vertices?

▷ **18.34** Consider the graph

3-7 1-4 7-8 0-5 5-2 3-8 2-9 0-6 4-9 2-6 6-4.

Draw the standard adjacency-lists DFS tree. Use it to find the bridges and the edge-connected components.

18.35 Prove that every vertex in any graph belongs to exactly one edge-connected component.

○ **18.36** Add a public member function to Program 18.7 that allows clients to test whether two vertices are in the same edge-connected component.

▷ **18.37** Consider the graph

3-7 1-4 7-8 0-5 5-2 3-8 2-9 0-6 4-9 2-6 6-4.

Draw the standard adjacency-lists DFS tree. Use it to find the articulation points and the biconnected components.

▷ **18.38** Do the previous exercise using the standard adjacency-matrix DFS tree.

18.39 Prove that every edge in a graph either is a bridge or belongs to exactly one biconnected component.

● **18.40** Prove that any graph with no articulation points is biconnected. *Hint*: Given a pair of vertices s and t and a path connecting them, use the fact that none of the vertices on the path are articulation points to construct two disjoint paths connecting s and t.

18.41 Derive a class from Program 18.2 for determining whether a graph is biconnected, using a brute-force algorithm that runs in time proportional to $V(V + E)$. *Hint*: If you mark a vertex as having been seen before you start the search, you effectively remove it from the graph.

○ **18.42** Extend your solution to Exercise 18.41 to derive a class that determines whether a graph is 3-connected. Give a formula describing the approximate number of times your program examines a graph edge, as a function of V and E.

18.43 Prove that the root of a DFS tree is an articulation point if and only if it has two or more (internal) children.

• **18.44** Derive a class from Program 18.2 that prints the biconnected components of the graph.

18.45 What is the minimum number of edges that must be present in any biconnected graph with V vertices?

18.46 Modify Program 18.7 to simply determine whether or not the graph is edge-connected (returning as soon as it identifies a bridge if the graph is not) and instrument it to keep track of the number of edges examined. Run empirical tests to study this cost, for graphs of various sizes, drawn from various graph models (see Exercises 17.64–76).

○ **18.47** Derive a class from Program 18.2 that allows clients to create objects that know the number of articulation points, bridges, and biconnected components in a graph.

• **18.48** Run experiments to determine empirically the average values of the quantities described in Exercise 18.47 for graphs of various sizes, drawn from various graph models (see Exercises 17.64–76).

18.49 Give the edge connectivity and the vertex connectivity of the graph

0-1 0-2 0-8 2-1 2-8 8-1 3-8 3-7 3-6 3-5 3-4 4-6 4-5 5-6 6-7 7-8.

18.7 Breadth-First Search

Suppose that we want to find a *shortest path* between two specific vertices in a graph—a path connecting the vertices with the property that no other path connecting those vertices has fewer edges. The classical method for accomplishing this task, called *breadth-first search (BFS)*, is also the basis of numerous algorithms for processing graphs, so we consider it in detail in this section. DFS offers us little assistance in solving this problem, because the order in which it takes us through the graph has no relationship to the goal of finding shortest paths. In contrast, BFS is based on this goal. To find a shortest path from v to w, we start at v and check for w among all the vertices that we can reach by following one edge, then we check all the vertices that we can reach by following two edges, and so forth.

When we come to a point during a graph search where we have more than one edge to traverse, we choose one and save the others to be explored later. In DFS, we use a pushdown stack (that is managed by the system to support the recursive search function) for this purpose. Using the LIFO rule that characterizes the pushdown stack corresponds to exploring passages that are close by in a maze: We

Figure 18.21
Breadth-first search

This figure traces the operation of BFS on our sample graph. We begin with all the edges adjacent to the start vertex on the queue (top left). Next, we move edge 0-2 from the queue to the tree and process its incident edges 2-0 and 2-6 (second from top, left). We do not put 2-0 on the queue because 0 is already on the tree. Third, we move edge 0-5 from the queue to the tree; again 5's incident edge (to 0) leads nowhere new, but we add 5-3 and 5-4 to the queue (third from top, left). Next, we add 0-7 to the tree and put 7-1 on the queue (bottom left).

The edge 7-4 is printed in gray because we could also avoid putting it on the queue, since there is another edge that will take us to 4 that is already on the queue. To complete the search, we take the remaining edges off the queue, completely ignoring the gray edges when they come to the front of the queue (right). Edges enter and leave the queue in order of their distance from 0.

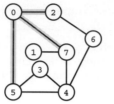
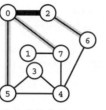
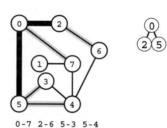
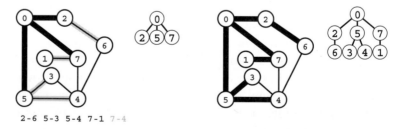
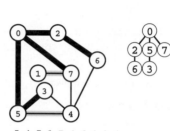
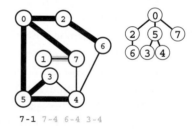

0-2 0-5 0-7

0-5 0-7 2-6

0-7 2-6 5-3 5-4

2-6 5-3 5-4 7-1 7-4

5-3 5-4 7-1 7-4 6-4

5-4 7-1 7-4 6-4 3-4

7-1 7-4 6-4 3-4

choose, of the passages yet to be explored, the one that was most recently encountered. In BFS, we want to explore the vertices in order of their distance from the start. For a maze, doing the search in this order might require a search team; within a computer program, however, it is easily arranged: We simply use a *FIFO queue* instead of a stack.

Program 18.8 is an implementation of BFS. It is based on maintaining a queue of all edges that connect a visited vertex with an unvisited vertex. We put a dummy self-loop to the start vertex on the queue, then perform the following steps until the queue is empty:

- Take edges from the queue until finding one that points to an unvisited vertex.
- Visit that vertex; put onto the queue all edges that go from that vertex to unvisited vertices.

Figure 18.21 shows the step-by-step development of BFS on a sample graph.

As we saw in Section 18.4, DFS is analogous to one person exploring a maze. BFS is analogous to a group of people exploring by fanning out in all directions. Although DFS and BFS are different in many respects, there is an essential underlying relationship between the two methods—one that we noted when we briefly considered the methods in Chapter 5. In Section 18.8, we consider a generalized graph-searching method that we can specialize to include these two algorithms and a host of others. Each algorithm has particular dynamic characteristics that we use to solve associated graph-processing problems. For BFS, the distance from each vertex to the start vertex (the length of a shortest path connecting the two) is the key property of interest.

Property 18.9 *During BFS, vertices enter and leave the FIFO queue in order of their distance from the start vertex.*

Proof: A stronger property holds: The queue always consists of zero or more vertices of distance k from the start, followed by zero or more vertices of distance $k + 1$ from the start, for some integer k. This stronger property is easy to prove by induction. ∎

For DFS, we understood the dynamic characteristics of the algorithm with the aid of the DFS search forest that describes the recursive-call structure of the algorithm. An essential property of that forest is that the forest represents the paths from each vertex back to the place

Program 18.8 Breadth-first search

This graph-search class visits a vertex by scanning through its incident edges, putting any edges to unvisited vertices onto the queue of vertices to be visited. Vertices are marked in the visit order given by the vector ord. The search function that is called by the constructor builds an explicit parent-link representation of the BFS tree (the edges that first take us to each node) in another vector st, which can be used to solve basic shortest-paths problems (*see text*).

```
#include "QUEUE.cc"
template <class Graph>
class BFS : public SEARCH<Graph>
{ vector<int> st;
  void searchC(Edge e)
  { QUEUE<Edge> Q;
    Q.put(e);
    while (!Q.empty())
      if (ord[(e = Q.get()).w] == -1)
      { int v = e.v, w = e.w;
        ord[w] = cnt++; st[w] = v;
        typename Graph::adjIterator A(G, w);
        for (int t = A.beg(); !A.end(); t = A.nxt())
          if (ord[t] == -1) Q.put(Edge(w, t));
      }
  }
public:
  BFS(Graph &G) : SEARCH<Graph>(G), st(G.V(), -1)
    { search(); }
  int ST(int v) const { return st[v]; }
};
```

that the search started for its connected component. As indicated in the implementation and shown in Figure 18.22, such a spanning tree also helps us to understand BFS. As with DFS, we have a forest that characterizes the dynamics of the search, one tree for each connected component, one tree node for each graph vertex, and one tree edge for each graph edge. BFS corresponds to traversing each of the trees in this forest in level order. As with DFS, we use a vertex-indexed vector

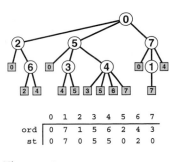

> **Program 18.9 Improved BFS**
>
> To guarantee that the queue that we use during BFS has at most V entries, we mark the vertices as we put them on the queue.
>
> ```
> void searchC(Edge e)
> { QUEUE<Edge> Q;
>   Q.put(e); ord[e.w] = cnt++;
>   while (!Q.empty())
>     {
>       e = Q.get(); st[e.w] = e.v;
>       typename Graph::adjIterator A(G, e.w);
>       for (int t = A.beg(); !A.end(); t = A.nxt())
>         if (ord[t] == -1)
>           { Q.put(Edge(e.w, t)); ord[t] = cnt++; }
>     }
> }
> ```

Figure 18.22
BFS tree

This tree provides a compact description of the dynamic properties of BFS, in a manner similar to the tree depicted in Figure 18.9. Traversing the tree in level order tells us how the search proceeds, step by step: first we visit 0; then we visit 2, 5, and 7; then we check from 2 that 0 was visited and visit 6; and so forth. Each tree node has a child representing each of the nodes adjacent to it, in the order they were considered by the BFS. As in Figure 18.9, links in the BFS tree correspond to edges in the graph: if we replace edges to external nodes by lines to the indicated node, we have a drawing of the graph. Links to external nodes represent edges that were not put onto the queue because they led to marked nodes: they are either parent links or cross links that point to a node either on the same level or one level closer to the root.

The st *vector is a parent-link representation of the tree, which we can use to find a shortest path from any node to the root. For example, 3–5–0 is a path in the graph from 3 to 0, since* st[3] *is 5 and* st[5] *is 0. No other path from 3 to 0 is shorter.*

to represent explicitly the forest with parent links. For BFS, this forest carries essential information about the graph structure:

Property 18.10 *For any node w in the BFS tree rooted at v, the tree path from v to w corresponds to a shortest path from v to w in the corresponding graph.*

Proof: The tree-path lengths from nodes coming off the queue to the root are nondecreasing, and all nodes closer to the root than w are on the queue; so no shorter path to w was found *before* it comes off the queue, and no path to w that is discovered *after* it comes off the queue can be shorter than w's tree path length. ∎

As indicated in Figure 18.21 and noted in Chapter 5, there is no need to put an edge on the queue with the same destination vertex as any edge already on the queue, since the FIFO policy ensures that we will process the old queue edge (and visit the vertex) before we get to the new edge. One way to implement this policy is to use a queue ADT implementation where such duplication is disallowed by an ignore-the-new-item policy (see Section 4.7). Another choice is to use the global vertex-marking vector for this purpose: Instead of marking a vertex as having been visited when we take it *off* the queue, we do so when we put it *on* the queue. Testing whether a vertex is marked (whether its entry has changed from its initial sentinel value) then stops us from putting any other edges that point to the same vertex on the queue. This change, shown in Program 18.9, gives a BFS implementation where there are never more than V edges on the queue (one edge pointing to each vertex, at most).

Property 18.11   *BFS visits all the vertices and edges in a graph in time proportional to V^2 for the adjacency-matrix representation and to $V + E$ for the adjacency-lists representation.*

Proof: As we did in proving the analogous DFS properties, we note by inspecting the code that we check each entry in the adjacency-matrix row or in the adjacency list precisely once for every vertex that we visit, so it suffices to show that we visit each vertex. Now, for each connected component, the algorithm preserves the following invariant: All vertices that can be reached from the start vertex (*i*) are on the BFS tree, (*ii*) are on the queue, or (*iii*) can be reached from a vertex on the queue. Each vertex moves from (*iii*) to (*ii*) to (*i*), and the number of vertices in (*i*) increases on each iteration of the loop, so that the BFS tree eventually contains all the vertices that can be reached from the start vertex. Thus, as we did for DFS, we consider BFS to be a linear-time algorithm. ∎

With BFS, we can solve the spanning tree, connected components, vertex search, and several other basic connectivity problems that we described in Section 18.4, since the solutions that we considered depend on only the ability of the search to examine every node and edge connected to the starting point. As we shall see, BFS and DFS are representative of numerouus algorithms that have this property. Our primary interest in BFS, as mentioned at the outset of this section, is that it is the natural graph-search algorithm for applications where we want to know a shortest path between two specified vertices. Next, we consider a specific solution to this problem and its extension to solve two related problems.

Shortest path   Find a shortest path in the graph from v to w. We can accomplish this task by starting a BFS that maintains the parent-link representation st of the search tree at v, then stopping when we reach w. The path up the tree from w to v is a shortest path. For example, after construction a BFS<Graph> object bfs a client could use the following code to print the path connecting w to v:

```
for (t = w; t !=v; t = bfs.ST(t)) cout << t << "-";
cout << v << endl;
```

To get the path from v to w, replace the cout operations in this code by stack pushes, then go into a loop that prints the vertex indices after popping them from the stack. Or, start the search at w and stop at v in the first place.

Single-source shortest paths   Find shortest paths connecting a given vertex v with each other vertex in the graph. The full BFS tree rooted at v provides a way to accomplish this task: The path from each vertex to the root is a shortest path to the root. Therefore, to solve the problem, we run BFS to completion starting at v. The st vector that results from this computation is a parent-link representation of the BFS tree, and the code in the previous paragraph will give the shortest path to any other vertex w.

All-pairs shortest paths   Find shortest paths connecting each pair of vertices in the graph. The way to accomplish this task is to use a BFS class that solves the single-source problem for each vertex in the graph and supports member functions that can handle huge numbers of shortest-path queries efficiently by storing the path lengths and parent-link tree representations for each vertex (see Figure 18.23). This preprocessing requires time proportional to VE and space proportional to V^2, a potentially prohibitive cost for huge sparse graphs. However, it allows us to build an ADT with optimal performance: After investing in the preprocessing (and the space to hold the results), we can return shortest-path lengths in constant time and the paths themselves in time proportional to their length (see Exercise 18.55).

These BFS-based solutions are effective, but we do not consider implementations in any further detail here, because they are special cases of algorithms that we consider in detail in Chapter 21. The term *shortest paths* in graphs is generally taken to describe the corresponding problems for digraphs and networks. Chapter 21 is devoted to this topic. The solutions that we examine there are strict generalizations of the BFS-based solutions described here.

The basic characteristics of BFS search dynamics contrast sharply with those for DFS search, as illustrated in the large graph depicted in Figure 18.24, which you should compare with Figure 18.13. The tree

Figure 18.23
All-pairs shortest paths example

These figures depict the result of doing BFS from each vertex, thus computing the shortest paths connecting all pairs of vertices. Each search gives a BFS tree that defines the shortest paths connecting all graph vertices to the vertex at the root. The results of all the searches are summarized in the two matrices at the bottom. In the left matrix, the entry in row v and column w gives the length of the shortest path from v to w (the depth of v in w's tree). Each row of the right matrix contains the st array for the corresponding search. For example, the shortest path from 3 to 2 has three edges, as indicated by the entry in row 3 and column 2 of the left matrix. The third BFS tree from the top on the left tells us that the path is 3-4-6-2, and this information is encoded in row 2 in the right matrix. The matrix is not necessarily symmetric when there is more than one shortest path, because the paths found depend on the BFS search order. For example, the BFS tree at the bottom on the left and row 3 of the right matrix tell us that the shortest path from 2 to 3 is 2-0-5-3.

	0	1	2	3	4	5	6	7
0	0	2	1	2	2	1	2	1
1	2	0	3	3	2	3	3	1
2	1	3	0	3	2	2	1	2
3	2	3	3	0	1	1	2	2
4	2	2	2	1	0	1	1	1
5	1	3	2	1	1	0	2	2
6	2	3	1	2	1	2	0	2
7	1	1	2	2	1	2	2	0

	0	1	2	3	4	5	6	7
0	0	7	0	5	7	0	2	0
1	7	1	0	4	7	4	4	1
2	2	7	2	4	6	0	2	0
3	5	7	0	3	3	3	4	4
4	7	7	6	4	4	4	4	4
5	5	7	0	5	5	5	4	4
6	2	7	6	4	6	4	6	4
7	7	7	0	4	7	4	4	7

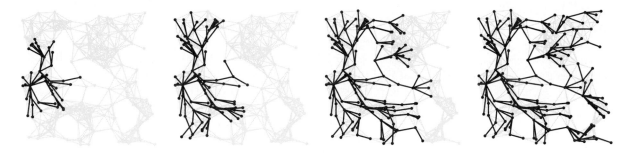

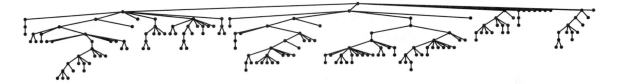

is shallow and broad, and demonstrates a set of facts about the graph being searched different from those shown by DFS. For example,

- There exists a relatively short path connecting each pair of vertices in the graph.
- During the search, most vertices are adjacent to numerous unvisited vertices.

Again, this example is typical of the behavior that we expect from BFS, but verifying facts of this kind for graph models of interest and graphs that arise in practice requires detailed analysis.

DFS wends its way through the graph, storing on the stack the points where other paths branch off; BFS sweeps through the graph, using a queue to remember the frontier of visited places. DFS explores the graph by looking for new vertices far away from the start point, taking closer vertices only when dead ends are encountered; BFS completely covers the area close to the starting point, moving farther away only when everything nearby has been examined. The order in which the vertices are visited depends on the graph structure and representation, but these global properties of the search trees are more informed by the algorithms than by the graphs or their representations.

The key to understanding graph-processing algorithms is to realize not only that various different search strategies are effective ways

Figure 18.24
Breadth-first search

This figure illustrates the progress of BFS in random Euclidean near-neighbor graph (left), in the same style as Figure 18.13. As is evident from this example, the search tree for BFS tends to be quite short and wide for this type of graph (and many other types of graphs commonly encountered in practice). That is, vertices tend to be connected to one another by rather short paths. The contrast between the shapes of the DFS and BFS trees is striking testimony to the differing dynamic properties of the algorithms.

to learn various different graph properties, but also that we can implement many of them uniformly. For example, the DFS illustrated in Figure 18.13 tells us that the graph has a long path, and the BFS illustrated in Figure 18.24 tells us that it has many short paths. Despite these marked dynamic differences, DFS and BFS are similar, essentially differing in only the data structure that we use to save edges that are not yet explored (and the fortuitous circumstance that we can use a recursive implementation for DFS with the system maintaining an implicit stack for us). Indeed, we turn next to a generalized graph-search algorithm that encompasses DFS, BFS, and a host of other useful strategies and will serve as the basis for solutions to numerous classic graph-processing problems.

Exercises

18.50 Draw the BFS forest that results from a standard adjacency-lists BFS of the graph

$$3\text{-}7 \ 1\text{-}4 \ 7\text{-}8 \ 0\text{-}5 \ 5\text{-}2 \ 3\text{-}8 \ 2\text{-}9 \ 0\text{-}6 \ 4\text{-}9 \ 2\text{-}6 \ 6\text{-}4.$$

18.51 Draw the BFS forest that results from a standard adjacency-matrix BFS of the graph

$$3\text{-}7 \ 1\text{-}4 \ 7\text{-}8 \ 0\text{-}5 \ 5\text{-}2 \ 3\text{-}8 \ 2\text{-}9 \ 0\text{-}6 \ 4\text{-}9 \ 2\text{-}6 \ 6\text{-}4.$$

▷ **18.52** Modify Programs 18.8 and 18.9 to use an STL `queue` instead of the ADT from Section 4.8.

○ **18.53** Give a BFS implementation (a version of Program 18.9) that uses a queue of vertices (see Program 5.22). Include a test in the BFS search code to ensure that no duplicates go on the queue.

18.54 Give the all-shortest-path matrices (in the style of Figure 18.23) for the graph

$$3\text{-}7 \ 1\text{-}4 \ 7\text{-}8 \ 0\text{-}5 \ 5\text{-}2 \ 3\text{-}8 \ 2\text{-}9 \ 0\text{-}6 \ 4\text{-}9 \ 2\text{-}6 \ 6\text{-}4,$$

assuming that you use the adjacency-matrix representation.

18.55 Develop a shortest-paths class, which supports shortest-path queries after preprocessing to compute all shortest paths. Specifically, define a two-dimensional matrix as a private data member, and write a constructor that assigns values to all its entries as illustrated in Figure 18.23. Then, implement two query functions `length(v, w)` (that returns the shortest-path length between v and w) and `path(v, w)` (that returns the vertex adjacent to v that is on a shortest path between v and w).

▷ **18.56** What does the BFS tree tell us about the distance from v to w when neither is at the root?

18.57 Develop a class whose objects know the path length that suffices to connect any pair of vertices in a graph. (This quantity is known as the graph's *diameter*). *Note*: You need to define a convention for the return value in the case that the graph is not connected.

18.58 Give a simple optimal recursive algorithm for finding the diameter of a *tree* (see Exercise 18.57).

○ **18.59** Instrument the BFS class Program 18.9 by adding member functions (and appropriate private data members) that return the the height of the BFS tree and the percentage of edges that must be processed for every vertex to be seen.

● **18.60** Run experiments to determine empirically the average values of the quantities described in Exercise 18.59 for graphs of various sizes, drawn from various graph models (see Exercises 17.64–76).

18.8 Generalized Graph Search

DFS and BFS are fundamental and essential graph-traversal methods that lie at the heart of numerous graph-processing algorithms. Knowing their essential properties, we now move to a higher level of abstraction, where we see that both methods are special cases of a generalized strategy for moving through a graph, one that is suggested by our BFS implementation (Program 18.9).

The basic idea is simple: We revisit our description of BFS from Section 18.6, but we use the term generic term *fringe*, instead of *queue*, to describe the set of edges that are possible candidates for being next added to the tree. We are led immediately to a general strategy for searching a connected component of a graph. Starting with a self-loop to a start vertex on the fringe and an empty tree, perform the following operation until the fringe is empty:

> *Move an edge from the fringe to the tree. If the vertex to which it leads is unvisited, visit that vertex, and put onto the fringe all edges that lead from that vertex to unvisited vertices.*

This strategy describes a family of search algorithms that will visit all the vertices and edges of a connected graph, *no matter what* type of generalized queue we use to hold the fringe edges.

When we use a queue to implement the fringe, we get BFS, the topic of Section 18.6. When we use a stack to implement the fringe, we get DFS. Figure 18.25, which you should compare with Figures 18.6

Figure 18.25
Stack-based DFS

Together with Figure 18.21, this figure illustrates that BFS and DFS differ only in the underlying data structure. For BFS, we used a queue; for DFS we use a stack. We begin with all the edges adjacent to the start vertex on the stack (top left). Second, we move edge 0-7 from the stack to the tree and push onto the stack its incident edges that go to vertices not yet on the tree 7-1, 7-4, and 7-6 (second from top, left). The LIFO stack discipline implies that, when we put an edge on the stack, any edges that point to the same vertex are obsolete and will be ignored when they reach the top of the stack. Such edges are printed in gray. Third, we move edge 7-6 from the stack to the tree and push its incident edges on the stack (third from top, left). Next, we pop edge 4-6 and push its incident edges on the stack, two of which will take us to new vertices (bottom left). To complete the search, we take the remaining edges off the stack, completely ignoring the gray edges when they come to the top of the stack (right).

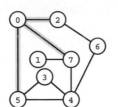
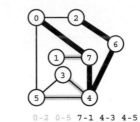

0-2 0-5 0-7

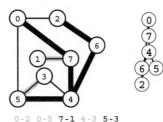

0-2 0-5 7-1 4-3 4-5

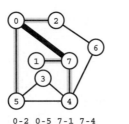

0-2 0-5 7-1 7-4

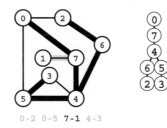

0-2 0-5 7-1 4-3 5-3

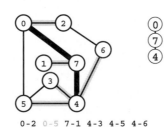

0-2 0-5 7-1 4-3 4-5 4-6

0-2 0-5 7-1 4-3

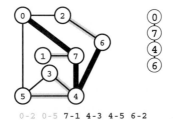

0-2 0-5 7-1 4-3 4-5 6-2

and 18.21, illustrates this phenomenon in detail. Proving this equivalence between recursive and stack-based DFS is an interesting exercise in recursion removal, where we essentially transform the stack underlying the recursive program into the stack implementing the fringe (see Exercise 18.63). The search order for the DFS depicted in Figure 18.25 differs from the one depicted in Figure 18.6 only because the stack discipline implies that we check the edges incident on each vertex in reverse of the order that we encounter them in the adjacency matrix (or the adjacency lists). The basic fact remains that, if we change the data structure used by Program 18.8 to be a stack instead of a queue (which is trivial to do because the ADT interfaces of the two data structures differ in only the function names), then we change that program from BFS to DFS.

Now, as we discussed in Section 18.7, this general method may not be as efficient as we would like, because the fringe becomes cluttered up with edges that point to vertices that are moved to the tree during the time that the edge is on the fringe. For FIFO queues, we avoid this situation by marking destination vertices when we put edges on the queue. We ignore edges to fringe vertices because we know that they will never be used: The old one will come off the queue (and the vertex visited) before the new one does (see Program 18.9). For a stack implementation, we want the opposite: When an edge is to be added to the fringe that has the same destination vertex as the one already there, we know that the *old* edge will never be used, because the new one will come off the stack (and the vertex visited) before the old one. To encompass these two extremes and to allow for fringe implementations that can use some other policy to disallow edges on the fringe that point to the same vertex, we modify our general scheme as follows:

> Move an edge from the fringe to the tree. Visit the vertex that it leads to, and put all edges that lead from that vertex to unvisited vertices onto the fringe, using a replacement policy on the fringe that ensures that no two edges on the fringe point to the same vertex.

The no-duplicate-destination-vertex policy on the fringe guarantees that we do not need to test whether the destination vertex of the edge coming off the queue has been visited. For BFS, we use a queue implementation with an ignore-the-new-item policy; for DFS, we need

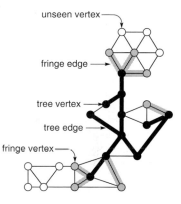

**Figure 18.26
Graph search terminology**

During a graph search, we maintain a search tree (black) and a fringe (gray) of edges that are candidates to be next added to the tree. Each vertex is either on the tree (black), the fringe (gray), or not yet seen (white). Tree vertices are connected by tree edges, and each fringe vertex is connected by a fringe edge to a tree vertex.

Figure 18.27
Graph search strategies

This figure illustrates different possibilities when we take a next step in the search illustrated in Figure 18.26. We move a vertex from the fringe to the tree (in the center of the wheel at the top right) *and check all its edges, putting those to unseen vertices on the fringe and using an algorithm-specific replacement rule to decide whether those to fringe vertices should be skipped or should replace the fringe edge to the same vertex. In DFS, we always replace the old edges; in BFS, we always skip the new edges; and in other strategies, we might replace some and skip others.*

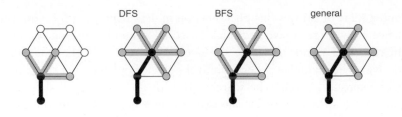

a stack with a forget-the-old-item policy; but any generalized queue and any replacement policy at all will still yield an effective method for visiting all the vertices and edges of the graph in linear time and extra space proportional to V. Figure 18.27 is a schematic illustration of these differences. We have a family of graph-searching strategies that includes both DFS and BFS and whose members differ only in the generalized-queue implementation that they use. As we shall see, this family encompasses numerous other classical graph-processing algorithms.

Program 18.10 is an implementation based on these ideas for graphs represented with adjacency lists. It puts fringe edges on a generalized queue and uses the usual vertex-indexed vectors to identify fringe vertices so that it can use an explicit *update* ADT operation whenever it encounters another edge to a fringe vertex. The ADT implementation can choose to ignore the new edge or to replace the old one.

Property 18.12 *Generalized graph searching visits all the vertices and edges in a graph in time proportional to V^2 for the adjacency-matrix representation and to $V + E$ for the adjacency-lists representation plus, in the worst case, the time required for V insert, V remove, and E update operations in a generalized queue of size V.*

Proof: The proof of Property 18.12 does not depend on the queue implementation, and therefore applies. The stated extra time requirements for the generalized-queue operations follow immediately from the implementation. ∎

There are many other effective ADT designs for the fringe that we might consider. For example, as with our first BFS implementation, we could stick with our first general scheme and simply put all the edges on the fringe, then ignore those that go to tree vertices when

---

Program 18.10 Generalized graph search

This graph-search class generalizes BFS and DFS and supports numerous graph-processing algorithms (see Section 21.2 for a discussion of these algorithms and alternate implementations). It maintains a generalized queue of edges called the *fringe*. We initialize the fringe with a self-loop to the start vertex; then, while the fringe is not empty, we move an edge e from the fringe to the tree (attached at e.v) and scan e.w's adjacency list, moving unseen vertices to the fringe and calling update for new edges to fringe vertices.

This code makes judicious use of ord and st to guarantee that no two edges on the fringe point to the same vertex. A vertex v is the destination vertex of a fringe edge if and only if it is marked (ord[v] is not -1) but it is not yet on the tree (st[v] is -1).

```cpp
#include "GQ.cc"
template <class Graph>
class PFS : public SEARCH<Graph>
{ vector<int> st;
  void searchC(Edge e)
  { GQ<Edge> Q(G.V());
    Q.put(e); ord[e.w] = cnt++;
    while (!Q.empty())
      {
        e = Q.get(); st[e.w] = e.v;
        typename Graph::adjIterator A(G, e.w);
        for (int t = A.beg(); !A.end(); t = A.nxt())
          if (ord[t] == -1)
            { Q.put(Edge(e.w, t)); ord[t] = cnt++; }
          else
            if (st[t] == -1) Q.update(Edge(e.w, t));
      }
  }
public:
  PFS(Graph &G) : SEARCH<Graph>(G), st(G.V(), -1)
    { search(); }
  int ST(int v) const { return st[v]; }
};
```

Program 18.11 Random queue implementation

When we remove an item from this data structure, it is equally likely to be any one of the items currently in the data structure. We can use this code to implement the generalized-queue ADT for graph searching to search a graph in a "random" fashion (*see text*).

```
template <class Item>
class GQ
  {
    private:
      vector<Item> s; int N;
    public:
      GQ(int maxN) : s(maxN+1), N(0) { }
      int empty() const
        { return N == 0; }
      void put(Item item)
        { s[N++] = item; }
      void update(Item x) { }
      Item get()
        { int i = int(N*rand()/(1.0+RAND_MAX));
          Item t = s[i];
          s[i] = s[N-1];
          s[N-1] = t;
          return s[--N]; }
  };
```

---

we take them off. The disadvantage of this approach, as with BFS, is that the maximum queue size has to be E instead of V. Or, we could handle updates implicitly in the ADT implementation, just by specifying that no two edges with the same destination vertex can be on the queue. But the simplest way for the ADT implementation to do so is essentially equivalent to using a vertex-indexed vector (see Exercises 4.51 and 4.54), so the test fits more comfortably into the client graph-search program.

The combination of Program 18.10 and the generalized-queue abstraction gives us a general and flexible graph-search mechanism. To illustrate this point, we now consider briefly two interesting and useful alternatives to BFS and DFS.

The first alternative strategy is based on *randomized queues* (see Section 4.6). In a randomized queue, we *remove* items randomly: Each item on the data structure is equally likely to be the one removed. Program 18.11 is an implementation that provides this functionality. If we use this code to implement the generalized queue ADT for Program 18.10, then we get a randomized graph-searching algorithm, where each vertex on the fringe is equally likely to be the next one added to the tree. The edge (to that vertex) that is added to the tree depends on the implementation of the *update* operation. The implementation in Program 18.11 does no updates, so each fringe vertex is added to the tree with the edge that caused it to be moved to the fringe. Alternatively, we might choose to always do updates (which results in the most recently encountered edge to each fringe vertex being added to the tree), or to make a random choice.

Another strategy, which is critical in the study of graph-processing algorithms because it serves as the basis for a number of the classical algorithms that we address in Chapters 20 through 22, is to use a *priority-queue* ADT (see Chapter 9) for the fringe: We assign priority values to each edge on the fringe, update them as appropriate, and choose the highest-priority edge as the one to be added next to the tree. We consider this formulation in detail in Chapter 20. The queue-maintenance operations for priority queues are more costly than are those for stacks and queues because they involve implicit comparisons among items on the queue, but they can support a much broader class of graph-search algorithms. As we shall see, several critical graph-processing problems can be addressed simply with judicious choice of priority assignments in a priority-queue–based generalized graph search.

All generalized graph-searching algorithms examine each edge just once and take extra space proportional to V in the worst case; they do differ, however, in some performance measures. For example, Figure 18.28 shows the size of the fringe as the search progresses for DFS, BFS, and randomized search; Figure 18.29 shows the tree computed by randomized search for the same example as Figure 18.13 and Figure 18.24. Randomized search has neither the long paths of DFS nor the high-degree nodes of BFS. The shapes of these trees and the fringe plots depend on the structure of the particular graph being searched, but they also characterize the different algorithms.

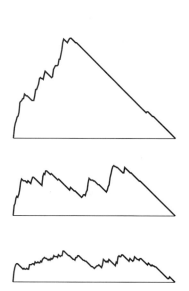

Figure 18.28
Fringe sizes for DFS, randomized graph search, and BFS

These plots of the fringe size during the searches illustrated in Figures 18.13, 18.24, and 18.29 indicate the dramatic effects that the choice of data structure for the fringe can have on graph searching. When we use a stack, in DFS (top), we fill up the fringe early in the search as we find new nodes at every step, then we end the search by removing everything. When we use a randomized queue (center), the maximum queue size is much lower. When we use a FIFO queue in BFS (bottom), the maximum queue size is still lower, and we discover new nodes throughout the search.

Figure 18.29
Randomized graph search

This figure illustrates the progress of randomized graph searching (left), in the same style as Figures 18.13 and 18.24. The search tree shape falls somewhere between the BFS and DFS shapes. The dynamics of these three algorithms, which differ only in the data structure for work to be completed, could hardly be more different.

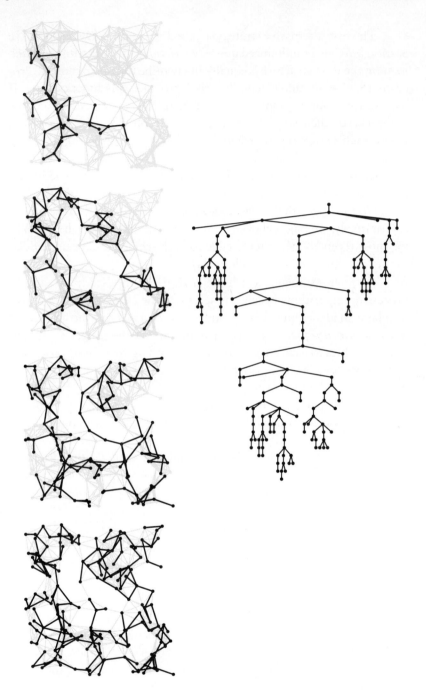

We could generalize graph searching still further by working with a forest (not necessarily a tree) during the search. Although we stop short of working at this level of generality throughout, we consider a few algorithms of this sort in Chapter 20.

Exercises

○ **18.61** Discuss the advantages and disadvantages of a generalized graph-searching implementation that is based on the following policy: "Move an edge from the fringe to the tree. If the vertex that it leads to is unvisited, visit that vertex and put all its incident edges onto the fringe."

18.62 Develop an adjacency-lists ADT implementation that keeps edges (not just destination vertices) on the lists, then implement a graph search based on the strategy described in Exercise 18.61 that visits every edge but destroys the graph, taking advantage of the fact that you can move all of a vertex's edges to the fringe with a single link change.

• **18.63** Prove that recursive DFS (Program 18.3) is equivalent to generalized graph search using a stack (Program 18.10), in the sense that both programs will visit all vertices in precisely the same order for all graphs if and only if the programs scan the adjacency lists in opposite orders.

18.64 Give three different possible traversal orders for randomized search through the graph

$$3\text{-}7 \ \ 1\text{-}4 \ \ 7\text{-}8 \ \ 0\text{-}5 \ \ 5\text{-}2 \ \ 3\text{-}8 \ \ 2\text{-}9 \ \ 0\text{-}6 \ \ 4\text{-}9 \ \ 2\text{-}6 \ \ 6\text{-}4.$$

18.65 Could randomized search visit the vertices in the graph

$$3\text{-}7 \ \ 1\text{-}4 \ \ 7\text{-}8 \ \ 0\text{-}5 \ \ 5\text{-}2 \ \ 3\text{-}8 \ \ 2\text{-}9 \ \ 0\text{-}6 \ \ 4\text{-}9 \ \ 2\text{-}6 \ \ 6\text{-}4$$

in numerical order of their indices? Prove your answer.

18.66 Use the STL to build a generalized-queue implementation for graph edges that disallows edges with duplicate vertices on the queue, using an ignore-the-new-item policy.

○ **18.67** Develop a randomized graph search that chooses each *edge* on the fringe with equal likelihood. *Hint*: See Program 18.8.

○ **18.68** Describe a maze-traversal strategy that corresponds to using a standard pushdown stack for generalized graph searching (see Section 18.1).

○ **18.69** Instrument generalized graph searching (see Program 18.10) to print out the height of the tree and the percentage of edges processed for every vertex to be seen.

• **18.70** Run experiments to determine empirically the average values of the quantities described in Exercise 18.69 for generalized graph search with a random queue in graphs of various sizes, drawn from various graph models (see Exercises 17.64–76).

• **18.71** Implement a derived class that does dynamic graphical animations of generalized graph search for graphs that have (x, y) coordinates associated with each vertex (see Exercises 17.55 through 17.59). Test your program on random Euclidean neighbor graphs, using as many points as you can process in a reasonable amount of time. Your program should produce images like the snapshots shown in Figures 18.13, 18.24, and 18.29, although you should feel free to use colors instead of shades of gray to denote tree, fringe, and unseen vertices and edges.

18.9 Analysis of Graph Algorithms

We have for our consideration a broad variety of graph-processing problems and methods for solving them, so we do not always compare numerous different algorithms for the same problem, as we have in other domains. Still, it is always valuable to gain experience with our algorithms by testing them on real data, or on artificial data that we understand and that have relevant characteristics that we might expect to find in actual applications.

As we discussed briefly in Chapter 2, we seek—ideally—natural input models that have three critical properties:

• They reflect reality to a sufficient extent that we can use them to predict performance.
• They are sufficiently simple that they are amenable to mathematical analysis.
• We can write generators that provide problem instances that we can use to test our algorithms.

With these three components, we can enter into a design-analysis-implementation-test scenario that leads to efficient algorithms for solving practical problems.

For domains such as sorting and searching, we have seen spectacular success along these lines in Parts 3 and 4. We can analyze algorithms, generate random problem instances, and refine implementations to provide extremely efficient programs for use in a host of practical situations. For some other domains that we study, various difficulties can arise. For example, mathematical analysis at the level that we would like is beyond our reach for many geometric problems, and developing an accurate model of the input is a significant challenge for many string-processing algorithms (indeed, doing so is an essential part of the computation). Similarly, graph algorithms take us to a situation where, for many applications, we are on thin ice with respect to all three properties listed in the previous paragraph:

- The mathematical analysis is challenging, and many basic analytic questions remain unanswered.
- There is a huge number of different types of graphs, and we cannot reasonably test our algorithms on all of them.
- Characterizing the types of graphs that arise in practical problems is, for the most part, a poorly understood problem.

Graphs are sufficiently complicated that we often do not fully understand the essential properties of the ones that we see in practice *or* of the artificial ones that we can perhaps generate and analyze.

The situation is perhaps not as bleak as just described for one primary reason: Many of the graph algorithms that we consider are *optimal* in the worst case, so predicting performance is a trivial exercise. For example, Program 18.7 finds the bridges after examining each edge and each vertex just once. This cost is the same as the cost of building the graph data structure, and we can confidently predict, for example, that doubling the number of edges will double the running time, no matter what kind of graphs we are processing.

When the running time of an algorithm depends on the structure of the input graph, predictions are much harder to come by. Still, when we need to process huge numbers of huge graphs, we want efficient algorithms for the same reasons that we want them for any other problem domain, and we will continue to pursue the goals of understanding the essential properties of algorithms and applications, striving to identify those methods that can best handle the graphs that might arise in practice.

To illustrate some of these issues, we revisit the study of graph connectivity, a problem that we considered already in Chapter 1 (!). Connectivity in random graphs has fascinated mathematicians for years, and it has been the subject of an extensive literature. That literature is beyond the scope of this book, but it provides a backdrop that validates our use of the problem as the basis for some experimental studies that help us understand the basic algorithms that we use and the types of graphs that we are considering.

For example, growing a graph by adding random edges to a set of initially isolated vertices (essentially, the process behind Program 17.12) is a well-studied process that has served as the basis for

Table 18.1 Connectivity in two random graph models

This table shows the number of connected components and the size of the largest connected component for 100000-vertex graphs drawn from two different distributions. For the random graph model, these experiments support the well-known fact that the graph is highly likely to consist primarily of one giant component if the average vertex degree is larger than a small constant. The right two columns give experimental results when we restrict the edges to be chosen from those that connect each vertex to just one of 10 specified neighbors.

	random edges		random 10-neighbors	
E	C	L	C	L
1000	99000	5	99003	3
2000	98000	4	98010	4
5000	95000	6	95075	5
10000	90000	8	90300	7
20000	80002	16	81381	9
50000	50003	1701	57986	27
100000	16236	79633	28721	151
200000	1887	98049	3818	6797
500000	4	99997	19	99979
1000000	1	100000	1	100000

Key:
C number of connected components
L size of largest connected component

classical random graph theory. It is well known that, as the number of edges grows, the graph coalesces into just one giant component. The literature on random graphs gives extensive information about the nature of this process. For example,

Property 18.13 *If $E > \frac{1}{2}V \ln V + \mu V$ (with μ positive), a random graph with V vertices and E edges consists of a single connected component and an average of less than $e^{-2\mu}$ isolated vertices, with probability approaching 1 as V approaches infinity.*

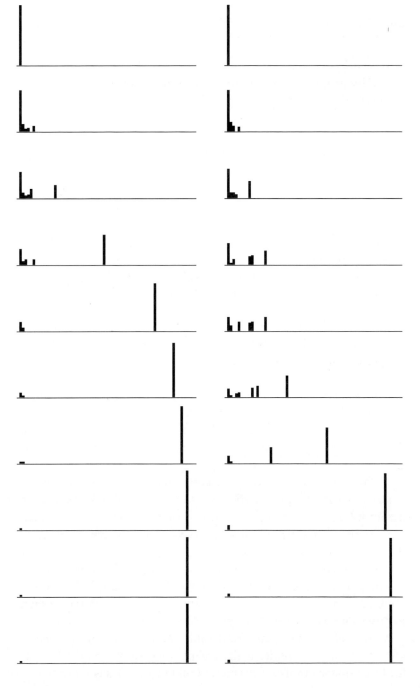

Figure 18.30
Connectivity in random graphs

This figures show the evolution of two types of random graphs at 10 equal increments as a total of $2E$ edges are added to initially empty graphs. Each plot is a histogram of the number of vertices in components of size 1 through $V-1$ (left to right). We start out with all vertices in components of size 1 and end with nearly all vertices in a giant component. The plot at left is for a standard random graph: the giant component forms quickly, and all other components are small. The plot at right is for a random neighbor graph: components of various sizes persist for a longer time.

Proof: This fact was established by seminal work of Erdös and Renyi in 1960. The proof is beyond the scope of this book (*see reference section*). ∎

This property tells us that we can expect large nonsparse random graphs to be connected. For example, if $V > 1000$ and $E > 10V$, then $\mu > 10 - \frac{1}{2}\ln 1000 > 6.5$ and the average number of vertices not in the giant component is (almost surely) less than $e^{-13} < .000003$. If we generate a million random 1000-vertex graphs of density greater than 10, we might get a few with a single isolated vertex, but the rest will all be connected.

Figure 18.30 compares random graphs with random neighbor graphs, where we allow only edges that connect vertices whose indices are within a small constant of one another. The neighbor-graph model yields graphs that are evidently substantially different in character from random graphs. We eventually get a giant component, but it appears suddenly, when two large components merge.

Table 18.2 shows that these structural differences between random graphs and neighbor graphs persist for V and E in ranges of practical interest. Such structural differences certainly may be reflected in the performance of our algorithms.

Table 18.3 gives empirical results for the cost of finding the number of connected components in a random graph, using various algorithms. Although the algorithms perhaps are not subject to direct comparison for this specific task because they are designed to handle different tasks, these experiments do validate a subset of the general conclusions that we have drawn.

First, it is plain from the table that we should not use the adjacency-matrix representation for large sparse graphs (and cannot use it for huge ones), not just because the cost of initializing the matrix is prohibitive, but also because the algorithm inspects every entry in the matrix, so its running time is proportional to the size (V^2) of the matrix rather than to the number of 1s in it (E). The table shows, for example, that it takes about as long to process a graph that contains 1000 edges as it does to process one that contains 100000 edges when we are using an adjacency matrix.

Second, it is also plain from Table 18.3 that the cost of allocating memory for the list nodes is significant when we build adjacency lists for large sparse graphs. The cost of building the lists is more than five

Table 18.2 Empirical study of graph-search algorithms

This table shows relative timings for various algorithms for the task of determining the number of connected components (and the size of the largest one) for graphs with various numbers of vertices and edges. As expected, algorithms that use the adjacency-matrix representation are slow for sparse graphs but competitive for dense graphs. For this specialized task, the union-find algorithms that we considered in Chapter 1 are the fastest, because they build a data structure tailored to solve the problem and do not need otherwise to represent the graph. Once the data structure representing the graph has been built, however, DFS and BFS are faster and more flexible. Adding a test to stop when the graph is known to consist of a single connected component significantly speeds up DFS and union-find (but not BFS) for dense graphs.

E	U	U*	adjacency matrix			adjacency lists				
			I	D	D*	I	D	D*	B	B*
5000 vertices										
500	1	0	255	312	356	1	0	0	0	1
1000	0	1	255	311	354	1	0	0	0	1
5000	1	2	258	312	353	2	2	1	2	1
10000	3	3	258	314	358	5	2	1	2	1
50000	12	6	270	315	202	25	6	4	5	6
100000	23	7	286	314	181	52	9	2	10	11
500000	117	5	478	248	111	267	54	16	56	47
100000 vertices										
5000	5	3				3	8	7	24	24
10000	4	5				6	7	7	24	24
50000	18	18				26	12	12	28	28
100000	34	35				51	28	24	34	34
500000	133	137				259			88	89

Key:

- U weighted quick union with halving (Program 1.4)
- I initial construction of the graph representation
- D recursive DFS (Program 18.3)
- B BFS (Program 18.9)
- * exit when graph is found to be fully connected

times the cost of traversing them. In the typical situation where we are going to perform numerous searches of various types after building the graph, this cost is acceptable. Otherwise, we might consider alternate implementations to reduce this cost.

Third, the absence of numbers in the DFS columns for large sparse graphs is significant. These graphs cause excessive recursion depth, which (eventually) cause the program to crash. If we want to use DFS on such graphs, we need to use the nonrecursive version that we discussed in Section 18.7.

Fourth, the table shows that the union-find–based method from Chapter 1 is faster than DFS or BFS, primarily because it does not have to represent the entire graph. Without such a representation, however, we cannot answer simple queries such as "Is there an edge connecting v and w?" so union-find–based methods are not suitable if we want to do more than what they are designed to do (answer "Is there a path between v and w?" queries intermixed with adding edges). Once the internal representation of the graph has been built, it is not worthwhile to implement a union-find algorithm just to determine whether it is connected, because DFS or BFS can provide the answer about as quickly.

When we run empirical tests that lead to tables of this sort, various anomalies might require further explanation. For example, on many computers, the cache architecture and other features of the memory system might have dramatic impact on performance for large graphs. Improving performance in critical applications may require detailed knowledge of the machine architecture in addition to all the factors that we are considering.

Careful study of these tables will reveal more properties of these algorithms than we are able to address. Our aim is not to do an exhaustive comparison but to illustrate that, despite the many challenges that we face when we compare graph algorithms, we can and should run empirical studies and make use of any available analytic results, both to get a feeling for the algorithms' important characteristics and to predict performance.

Exercises

○ **18.72** Do an empirical study culminating in a table like Table 18.2 for the problem of determining whether or not a graph is bipartite (two-colorable).

18.73 Do an empirical study culminating in a table like Table 18.2 for the problem of determining whether or not a graph is biconnected.

○ **18.74** Do an empirical study to find the expected size of the second largest connected component in sparse graphs of various sizes, drawn from various graph models (see Exercises 17.64–76).

18.75 Write a program that produces plots like those in Figure 18.30, and test it on graphs of various sizes, drawn from various graph models (see Exercises 17.64–76).

○ **18.76** Modify your program from Exercise 18.75 to produce similar histograms for the sizes of edge-connected components.

•• **18.77** The numbers in the tables in this section are results for only one sample. We might wish to prepare a similar table where we run 1000 experiments for each entry and give the sample mean and standard deviation, but we probably could not include nearly as many entries. Would this approach be a better use of computer time? Defend your answer.

Digraphs and DAGs

WHEN WE ATTACH significance to the order in which the two vertices are specified in each edge of a graph, we have an entirely different combinatorial object known as a *digraph*, or *directed graph*. Figure 19.1 shows a sample digraph. In a digraph, the notation s-t describes an edge that goes from s to t but provides no information about whether or not there is an edge from t to s. There are four different ways in which two vertices might be related in a digraph: no edge; an edge s-t from s to t; an edge t-s from t to s; or two edges s-t and t-s, which indicate connections in both directions. The one-way restriction is natural in many applications, easy to enforce in our implementations, and seems innocuous; but it implies added combinatorial structure that has profound implications for our algorithms and makes working with digraphs quite different from working with undirected graphs. Processing digraphs is akin to traveling around in a city where *all* the streets are one-way, with the directions not necessarily assigned in any uniform pattern. We can imagine that getting from one point to another in such a situation could be a challenge indeed.

We interpret edge directions in digraphs in many ways. For example, in a telephone-call graph, we might consider an edge to be directed from the caller to the person receiving the call. In a transaction graph, we might have a similar relationship where we interpret an edge as representing cash, goods, or information flowing from one entity to another. We find a modern situation that fits this classic model on the Internet, with vertices representing Web pages and edges the links between the pages. In Section 19.4, we examine other examples, many of which model situations that are more abstract.

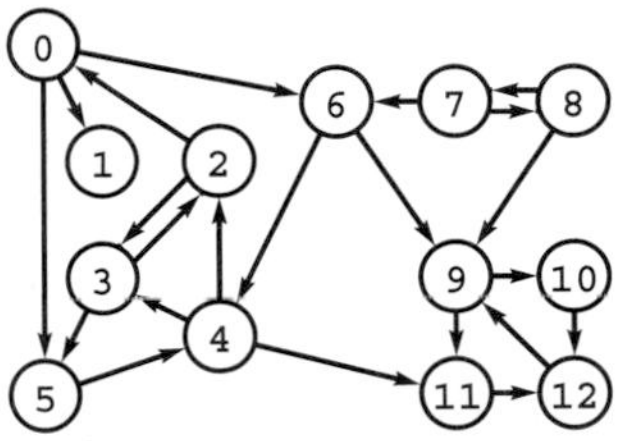

4-2	11-12	4-11	5-4
2-3	12-9	4-3	0-5
3-2	9-10	3-5	6-4
0-6	9-11	7-8	6-9
0-1	8-9	8-7	7-6
2-0	10-12		

Figure 19.1
A directed graph (digraph)

A digraph is defined by a list of nodes and edges (bottom), with the order that we list the nodes when specifying an edge implying that the edge is directed from the first node to the second. When drawing a digraph, we use arrows to depict directed edges (top).

One common situation is for the edge direction to reflect a precedence relationship. For example, a digraph might model a manufacturing line: Vertices correspond to jobs to be done, and an edge exists from vertex s to vertex t if the job corresponding to vertex s must be done before the job corresponding to vertex t. Another way to model the same situation is to use a *PERT chart*: edges represent jobs and vertices implicitly specify the precedence relationships (at each vertex, all incoming jobs must complete before any outgoing jobs can begin). How do we decide when to perform each of the jobs so that none of the precedence relationships are violated? This is known as a *scheduling* problem. It makes no sense if the digraph has a cycle so, in such situations, we are working with *directed acyclic graphs (DAGs)*. We shall consider basic properties of DAGs and algorithms for this simple scheduling problem, which is known as *topological sorting*, in Sections 19.5 through 19.7. In practice, scheduling problems generally involve weights on the vertices or edges that model the time or cost of each job. We consider such problems in Chapters 21 and 22.

The number of possible digraphs is truly huge. Each of the V^2 possible directed edges (including self-loops) could be present or not, so the total number of different digraphs is 2^{V^2}. As illustrated in Figure 19.2, this number grows very quickly, even by comparison with the number of different undirected graphs and even when V is small. As with undirected graphs, there is a much smaller number of classes of digraphs that are isomorphic to each other (the vertices of one can be relabeled to make it identical to the other), but we cannot take advantage of this reduction because we do not know an efficient algorithm for digraph isomorphism.

Certainly, any program will have to process only a tiny fraction of the possible digraphs; indeed, the numbers are so large that we can be certain that virtually all digraphs will not be among those processed by any given program. Generally, it is difficult to characterize the digraphs that we might encounter in practice, so we design our algorithms such that they can handle any possible digraph as input. On the one hand, this situation is not new to us (for example, virtually none of the 1000! permutations of 1000 elements have ever been processed by any sorting program). On the other hand, it is perhaps unsettling to know that, for example, even if all the electrons in the universe could run supercomputers capable of processing 10^{10} graphs per second for the

V	undirected graphs	digraphs
2	8	16
3	64	512
4	1024	65536
5	32768	33554432
6	2097152	68719476736
7	268435456	562949953421312

Figure 19.2
Graph enumeration

While the number of different undirected graphs with V vertices is huge, even when V is small, the number of different digraphs with V vertices is much larger. For undirected graphs, the number is given by the formula $2^{V(V+1)/2}$; for digraphs, the formula is 2^{V^2}.

estimated lifetime of the universe, those supercomputers would see far fewer than 10^{-100} percent of the 10-vertex digraphs (see Exercise 19.9).

This brief digression on graph enumeration perhaps underscores several points that we cover whenever we consider the analysis of algorithms and indicates their particular relevance to the study of digraphs. Is it important to design our algorithms to perform well in the worst case, when we are so unlikely to see any particular worst-case digraph? Is it useful to choose algorithms on the basis of average-case analysis, or is that a mathematical fiction? If our intent is to have implementations that perform efficiently on digraphs that we see in practice, we are immediately faced with the problem of characterizing those digraphs. Mathematical models that can convincingly describe the digraphs that we might expect in applications are even more difficult to develop than are models for undirected graphs.

In this chapter, we revisit, in the context of digraphs, a subset of the basic graph-processing problems that we considered in Chapter 17, and we examine several problems that are specific to digraphs. In particular, we look at DFS and several of its applications, including *cycle detection* (to determine whether a digraph is a DAG); *topological sort* (to solve, for example, the scheduling problem for DAGs that was just described); and computation of the *transitive closure* and the *strong components* (which have to do with the basic problem of determining whether or not there is a directed path between two given vertices). As in other graph-processing domains, these algorithms range from the trivial to the ingenious; they are both informed by and give us insight into the complex combinatorial structure of digraphs.

Exercises

● **19.1** Find a large digraph somewhere online—perhaps a transaction graph in some online system, or a digraph defined by links on Web pages.

● **19.2** Find a large DAG somewhere online—perhaps one defined by function-definition dependencies in a large software system, or by directory links in a large file system.

19.3 Make a table like Figure 19.2, but exclude from the counts graphs and digraphs with self-loops.

19.4 How many digraphs are there that contain V vertices and E edges?

○ **19.5** How many digraphs correspond to each undirected graph that contains V vertices and E edges?

▷ **19.6** How many digits do we need to express the number of digraphs that have V vertices as a base-10 number?

○ **19.7** Draw the nonisomorphic digraphs that contain three vertices.

••• **19.8** How many different digraphs are there with V vertices and E edges if we consider two digraphs to be different only if they are not isomorphic?

○ **19.9** Compute an upper bound on the percentage of 10-vertex digraphs that could ever be examined by any computer, under the assumptions described in the text and the additional ones that the universe has less than 10^{80} electrons and that the age of the universe will be less than 10^{20} years.

19.1 Glossary and Rules of the Game

Our definitions for digraphs are nearly identical to those in Chapter 17 for undirected graphs (as are some of the algorithms and programs that we use), but they are worth restating. The slight differences in the wording to account for edge directions imply structural properties that will be the focus of this chapter.

Definition 19.1 *A* **digraph** *(or* **directed graph***) is a set of* **vertices** *plus a set of* **directed edges** *that connect ordered pairs of vertices (with no duplicate edges). We say that an edge goes* **from** *its first vertex* **to** *its second vertex.*

As we did with undirected graphs, we disallow duplicate edges in this definition but reserve the option of allowing them when convenient for various applications and implementations. We explicitly allow self-loops in digraphs (and usually adopt the convention that every vertex has one) because they play a critical role in the basic algorithms.

Definition 19.2 *A* **directed path** *in a digraph is a list of vertices in which there is a (directed) digraph edge connecting each vertex in the list to its successor in the list. We say that a vertex* t *is* **reachable** *from a vertex* s *if there is a directed path from* s *to* t*.*

We adopt the convention that each vertex is reachable from itself and normally implement that assumption by ensuring that self-loops are present in our digraph representations.

Understanding many of the algorithms in this chapter requires understanding the connectivity properties of digraphs and the effect of these properties on the basic process of moving from one vertex

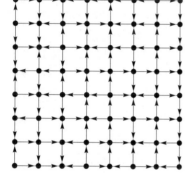

Figure 19.3
A grid digraph

This small digraph is similar to the large grid network that we first considered in Chapter 1, except that it has a directed edge on every grid line, with the direction randomly chosen. Even though the graph has relatively few nodes, its connectivity properties are not readily apparent. Is there a directed path from the upper left corner to the lower right corner?

to another along digraph edges. Developing such an understanding is more complicated for digraphs than for undirected graphs. For example, we might be able to tell at a glance whether a small undirected graph is connected or contains a cycle; these properties are not as easy to spot in digraphs, as indicated in the typical example illustrated in Figure 19.3.

While examples like this highlight differences, it is important to note that what a human considers difficult may or may not be relevant to what a program considers difficult—for instance, writing a DFS class to find cycles in digraphs is no more difficult than for undirected graphs. More important, digraphs and graphs have essential structural differences. For example, the fact that t is reachable from s in a digraph indicates nothing about whether s is reachable from t. This distinction is obvious, but critical, as we shall see.

As mentioned in Section 17.3, the representations that we use for digraphs are essentially the same as those that we use for undirected graphs. Indeed, they are more straightforward because we represent each edge just once, as illustrated in Figure 19.4. In the adjacency-lists representation, an edge s-t is represented as a list node containing t in the linked list corresponding to s. In the adjacency-matrix representation, we need to maintain a full V-by-V matrix and to represent an edge s-t by a 1 bit in row s and column t. We do not put a 1 bit in row t and column s unless there is also an edge t-s. In general, the adjacency matrix for a digraph is not symmetric about the diagonal.

There is no difference in these representations between an undirected graph and a directed graph with self-loops at every vertex and two directed edges for each edge connecting distinct vertices in the undirected graph (one in each direction). Thus, we can use the algorithms that we develop in this chapter for digraphs to process undirected graphs, provided that we interpret the results appropriately. In addition, we use the programs that we considered in Chapter 17 as the basis for our digraph programs: Our DenseGRAPH and SparseMultiGRAPH class implementations Programs 17.7 through 17.10 build digraphs when the constructor has true as a second argument.

The *indegree* of a vertex in a digraph is the number of directed edges that lead to that vertex. The *outdegree* of a vertex in a digraph is the number of directed edges that emanate from that vertex. No

	0	1	2	3	4	5	6	7	8	9	10	11	12
0	1	1	0	0	0	1	1	0	0	0	0	0	0
1	0	1	0	0	0	0	0	0	0	0	0	0	0
2	1	0	1	1	0	0	0	0	0	0	0	0	0
3	0	0	1	1	0	1	0	0	0	0	0	0	0
4	0	0	1	1	1	0	0	0	0	0	0	1	0
5	0	0	0	0	1	1	0	0	0	0	0	0	0
6	0	0	0	0	1	0	1	0	0	1	0	0	0
7	0	0	0	0	0	0	1	1	1	0	0	0	0
8	0	0	0	0	0	0	0	1	1	1	0	0	0
9	0	0	0	0	0	0	0	0	0	1	1	1	0
10	0	0	0	0	0	0	0	0	0	0	1	0	1
11	0	0	0	0	0	0	0	0	0	0	0	1	1
12	0	0	0	0	0	0	0	0	0	1	0	0	1

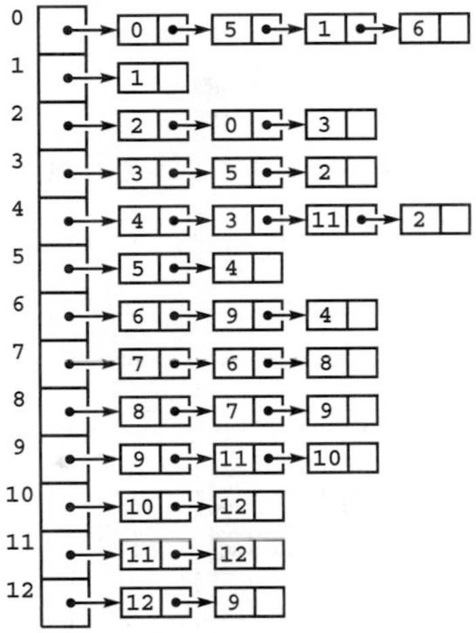

```
0   → 0 → 5 → 1 → 6
1   → 1
2   → 2 → 0 → 3
3   → 3 → 5 → 2
4   → 4 → 3 → 11 → 2
5   → 5 → 4
6   → 6 → 9 → 4
7   → 7 → 6 → 8
8   → 8 → 7 → 9
9   → 9 → 11 → 10
10  → 10 → 12
11  → 11 → 12
12  → 12 → 9
```

Figure 19.4
Digraph representations

The adjacency-matrix and adjacency-lists representations of a digraph have only one representation of each edge, as illustrated in the adjacency-matrix (top) and adjacency-lists (bottom) representation of the graph depicted in Figure 19.1. These representations both include self-loops at every vertex, which is typical in digraph processing.

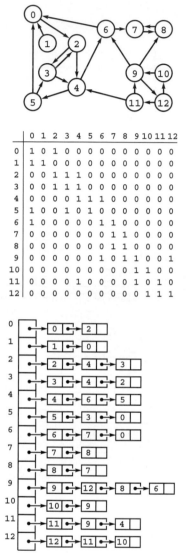

	0	1	2	3	4	5	6	7	8	9	10	11	12
0	1	0	1	0	0	0	0	0	0	0	0	0	0
1	1	1	0	0	0	0	0	0	0	0	0	0	0
2	0	0	1	1	1	0	0	0	0	0	0	0	0
3	0	0	1	1	1	0	0	0	0	0	0	0	0
4	0	0	0	0	1	1	1	0	0	0	0	0	0
5	1	0	0	1	0	1	0	0	0	0	0	0	0
6	1	0	0	0	0	0	1	1	0	0	0	0	0
7	0	0	0	0	0	0	0	1	1	0	0	0	0
8	0	0	0	0	0	0	0	1	1	0	0	0	0
9	0	0	0	0	0	0	1	0	1	1	0	0	1
10	0	0	0	0	0	0	0	0	0	1	1	0	0
11	0	0	0	0	1	0	0	0	0	1	0	1	0
12	0	0	0	0	0	0	0	0	0	0	1	1	1

Figure 19.5
Digraph reversal

Reversing the edges of a digraph corresponds to transposing the adjacency matrix but requires rebuilding the adjacency lists (see Figures 19.1 and 19.4).

Program 19.1 Reversing a digraph

This function adds the edges of the digraph in its first argument to the digraph in its second argument, with their directions reversed. It uses two template parameters, so that the graphs can have different representations.

```
template <class inGraph, class outGraph>
void reverse(const inGraph &G, outGraph &R)
  {
    for (int v = 0; v < G.V(); v++)
      { typename inGraph::adjIterator A(G, v);
        for (int w = A.beg(); !A.end(); w = A.nxt())
          R.insert(Edge(w, v));
      }
  }
```

vertex is reachable from a vertex of outdegree 0, which is called a *sink*; a vertex of indegree 0, which is called a *source*, is not reachable from any other vertex. A digraph where self-loops are allowed and every vertex has outdegree 1 is called a *map* (a function from the set of integers from 0 to $V - 1$ onto itself). We can easily compute the indegree and outdegree of each vertex, and find sources and sinks, in linear time and space proportional to V, using vertex-indexed vectors (see Exercise 19.19).

The *reverse* of a digraph is the digraph that we obtain by switching the direction of all the edges. Figure 19.5 shows the reverse and its representations for the digraph of Figure 19.1. We use the reverse in digraph algorithms when we need to know from where edges come because our standard representations tell us only where the edges go. For example, indegree and outdegree change roles when we reverse a digraph.

For an adjacency-matrix representation, we could compute the reverse by making a copy of the matrix and transposing it (interchanging its rows and columns). If we know that the graph is not going to be modified, we can actually use the reverse without any extra computation by simply interchanging the vertices in our *references* to edges when we want to refer to the reverse. For example, an edge s-t in a digraph G is indicated by a 1 in adj[s][t]. Thus, if we were to compute the reverse R of G, it would have a 1 in adj[t][s]. We do not need to do so, however, if we base our client implementations on the edge test edge(s, t), because to switch to the reverse we just replace every such reference by edge(t, s). This opportunity may seem obvious, but it is often overlooked. For an adjacency-lists representation, the reverse is a completely different data structure, and we need to take time proportional to the number of edges to build it, as shown in Program 19.1.

Yet another option, which we shall address in Chapter 22, is to maintain two representations of each edge, in the same manner as we do for undirected graphs (see Section 17.3) but with an extra bit that indicates edge direction. For example, to use this method in an adjacency-lists representation we would represent an edge s-t by a node for t on the adjacency list for s (with the direction bit set to indicate that to move from s to t is a forward traversal of the edge) and a node for s on the adjacency list for t (with the direction bit set to indicate that to move from t to s is a backward traversal of the edge). This representation supports algorithms that need to traverse edges in digraphs in both directions. It is also generally convenient to include pointers connecting the two representations of each edge in such cases. We defer considering this representation in detail to Chapter 22, where it plays an essential role.

In digraphs, by analogy to undirected graphs, we speak of directed cycles, which are directed paths from a vertex back to itself, and simple directed paths and cycles, where the vertices and edges are distinct. Note that s-t-s is a cycle of length 2 in a digraph but that cycles in undirected graphs must have at least three distinct vertices.

In many applications of digraphs, we do not expect to see any cycles, and we work with yet another type of combinatorial object.

Definition 19.3 *A **directed acyclic graph** (DAG) is a digraph with no directed cycles.*

We expect DAGs, for example, in applications where we are using digraphs to model precedence relationships. DAGs not only arise naturally in these and other important applications, but also, as we shall see, in the study of the structure of general digraphs. A sample DAG is illustrated in Figure 19.6.

Directed cycles are therefore the key to understanding connectivity in digraphs that are not DAGs. An undirected graph is connected

2-3	11-12	3-5	6-4
0-6	9-12	8-7	6-9
0-1	9-10	5-4	7-6
2-0	9-11	0-5	

Figure 19.6
A directed acyclic graph (DAG)

This digraph has no cycles, a property that is not immediately apparent from the edge list or even from examining its drawing.

if there is a path from every vertex to every other vertex; for digraphs, we modify the definition as follows:

Definition 19.4 *A digraph is* **strongly connected** *if every vertex is reachable from every vertex.*

The graph in Figure 19.1 is not strongly connected because, for example, there are no directed paths from vertices 9 through 12 to any of the other vertices in the graph.

As indicated by *strongly*, this definition implies a relationship between each pair of vertices stronger than reachability. In any digraph, we say that a pair of vertices s and t are *strongly connected* or *mutually reachable* if there is a directed path from s to t *and* a directed path from t to s. (Our convention that each vertex is reachable from itself implies that each vertex is strongly connected to itself.) A digraph is strongly connected if and only if all pairs of vertices are strongly connected. The defining property of strongly connected digraphs is one that we take for granted in connected undirected graphs: If there is a path from s to t, then there is a path from t to s. In the case of undirected graphs, we know this fact because the *same* path fits the bill, traversed in the other direction; in digraphs, it must be a different path.

Another way of saying that a pair of vertices is strongly connected is that they lie on some directed cyclic path. Recall that we use the term *cyclic path* instead of *cycle* to indicate that the path does not need to be simple. For example, in Figure 19.1, 5 and 6 are strongly connected because 6 is reachable from 5 via the directed path 5-4-2-0-6 and 5 is reachable from 6 via the directed path 6-4-3-5; and these paths imply that 5 and 6 lie on the directed cyclic path 5-4-2-0-6-4-3-5, but they do not lie on any (simple) directed cycle. Note that no DAG that contains more than one vertex is strongly connected.

Like simple connectivity in undirected graphs, this relation is transitive: If s is strongly connected to t, and t is strongly connected to u, then s is strongly connected to u. Strong connectivity is an equivalence relation that divides the vertices into equivalence classes containing vertices that are strongly connected to each other. (See Section 19.4 for a detailed discussion of equivalence relations.) Again, strong connectivity provides a property for digraphs that we take for granted with respect to connectivity in undirected graphs.

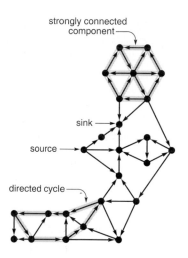

Figure 19.7
Digraph terminology

Sources (vertices with no edges coming in) and sinks (vertices with no edges going out) are easy to identify in digraph drawings like this one, but directed cycles and strongly connected components are more difficult to identify. What is the longest directed cycle in this digraph? How many strongly connected components with more than one vertex are there?

Property 19.1 *A digraph that is not strongly connected comprises a set of* **strongly connected components** *(***strong components,** *for short), which are maximal strongly connected subgraphs, and a set of directed edges that go from one component to another.*

Proof: Like components in undirected graphs, strong components in digraphs are induced subgraphs of subsets of vertices: Each vertex is in exactly one strong component. To prove this fact, we first note that every vertex belongs to at least one strong component, which contains (at least) the vertex itself. Then we note that every vertex belongs to at most one strong component: If a vertex were to belong to two different components, then there would be paths through that vertex connecting vertices in those components to each other, in both directions, which contradicts the maximality of both components. ∎

For example, a digraph that consists of a single directed cycle has just one strong component. At the other extreme, each vertex in a DAG is a strong component, so each edge in a DAG goes from one component to another. In general, not all edges in a digraph are in the strong components. This situation is in contrast to the analogous situation for connected components in undirected graphs, where every vertex *and* every edge belongs to some connected component, but similar to the analogous situation for edge-connected components in undirected graphs. The strong components in a digraph are connected by edges that go from a vertex in one component to a vertex in another but do not go back again.

Property 19.2 *Given a digraph D, define another digraph $K(D)$ with one vertex corresponding to each strong component of D and one edge in $K(D)$ corresponding to each edge in D that connects vertices in different strong components (connecting the vertices in K that correspond to the strong components that it connects in D). Then, $K(D)$ is a DAG (which we call the* **kernel DAG** *of D).*

Proof: If $K(D)$ were to have a directed cycle, then vertices in two different strong components of D would fall on a directed cycle, and that would be a contradiction. ∎

Figure 19.8 shows the strong components and the kernel DAG for a sample digraph. We look at algorithms for finding strong components and building kernel DAGs in Section 19.6.

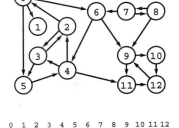

Figure 19.8
Strong components and kernel DAG

This digraph (top) *consists of four strong components, as identified (with arbitrary integer labels) by the vertex-indexed array* id *(center). Component 0 consists of the vertices 9, 10, 11 and 12; component 1 consists of the single vertex 1; component 2 consists of the vertices 0, 2, 3, 4, 5, and 6; and component 3 consists of the vertices 7 and 8. If we draw the graph defined by the edges between different components, we get a DAG (bottom).*

From these definitions, properties, and examples, it is clear that we need to be precise when referring to paths in digraphs. We need to consider at least the following three situations:

Connectivity   We reserve the term *connected* for undirected graphs. In digraphs, we might say that two vertices are connected if they are connected in the undirected graph defined by ignoring edge directions, but we generally avoid such usage.

Reachability   In digraphs, we say that vertex t is reachable from vertex s if there is a directed path from s to t. We generally avoid the term *reachable* when referring to undirected graphs, although we might consider it to be equivalent to *connected* because the idea of one vertex being reachable from another is intuitive in certain undirected graphs (for example, those that represent mazes).

Strong connectivity   Two vertices in a digraph are strongly connected if they are mutually reachable; in undirected graphs, two connected vertices imply the existence of paths from each to the other. Strong connectivity in digraphs is similar in certain ways to edge connectivity in undirected graphs.

We wish to support digraph ADT operations that take two vertices s and t as arguments and allow us to test whether

- t is reachable from s
- s and t are strongly connected (mutually reachable)

What resource requirements are we willing to expend for these operations? As we saw in Section 17.5, DFS provides a simple solution for connectivity in undirected graphs that takes time proportional to V, but if we are willing to invest preprocessing time proportional to $V + E$ and space proportional to V, we can answer connectivity queries in constant time. Later in this chapter, we examine algorithms for strong connectivity that have these same performance characteristics.

But our primary aim is to address the fact that *reachability* queries in digraphs are more difficult to handle than connectivity or strong connectivity queries. In this chapter, we examine classical algorithms that require preprocessing time proportional to VE and space proportional to V^2, develop implementations that can achieve constant-time reachability queries with linear space and preprocessing time for some digraphs, and study the difficulty of achieving this optimal performance for all digraphs.

Exercises

▷ **19.10** Give the adjacency-lists structure that is built by Program 17.9 for the digraph

$$3\text{-}7\ 1\text{-}4\ 7\text{-}8\ 0\text{-}5\ 5\text{-}2\ 3\text{-}8\ 2\text{-}9\ 0\text{-}6\ 4\text{-}9\ 2\text{-}6\ 6\text{-}4.$$

▷ **19.11** Write a program to generate random sparse digraphs for a well-chosen set of values of V and E such that you can use it to run meaningful empirical tests on digraphs drawn from the random-edges model.

▷ **19.12** Write a program to generate random sparse graphs for a well-chosen set of values of V and E such that you can use it to run meaningful empirical tests on graphs drawn from the random-graph model.

○ **19.13** Write a program that generates random digraphs by connecting vertices arranged in a $\sqrt{V}$-by-$\sqrt{V}$ grid to their neighbors, with edge directions randomly chosen (see Figure 19.3).

○ **19.14** Augment your program from Exercise 19.13 to add R extra random edges (all possible edges equally likely). For large R, shrink the grid so that the total number of edges remains about V. Test your program as described in Exercise 19.11.

○ **19.15** Modify your program from Exercise 19.14 such that an extra edge goes from a vertex s to a vertex t with probability inversely proportional to the Euclidean distance between s and t.

○ **19.16** Write a program that generates V random intervals in the unit interval, all of length d, then builds a digraph with an edge from interval s to interval t if and only if at least one of the endpoints of s falls within t (see Exercise 17.75). Determine how to set d so that the expected number of edges is E. Test your program as described in Exercise 19.11 (for low densities) and as described in Exercise 19.12 (for high densities).

● **19.17** Write a program that chooses V vertices and E edges from the real digraph that you found for Exercise 19.1. Test your program as described in Exercise 19.11 (for low densities) and as described in Exercise 19.12 (for high densities).

● **19.18** Write a program that produces each of the possible digraphs with V vertices and E edges with equal likelihood (see Exercise 17.70). Test your program as described in Exercise 19.11 (for low densities) and as described in Exercise 19.12 (for high densities).

▷ **19.19** Implement a class that provides clients with the capability to learn the indegree and outdegree of any given vertex in a digraph, in constant time, after linear-time preprocessing in the constructor. Then add member functions that return the number of sources and sinks, in constant time.

○ **19.20** Use your program from Exercise 19.19 to find the average number of sources and sinks in various types of digraphs (see Exercises 19.11–18).

▷ **19.21** Show the adjacency-lists structure that is produced when you use Program 19.1 to find the reverse of the digraph

3-7 1-4 7-8 0-5 5-2 3-8 2-9 0-6 4-9 2-6 6-4.

○ **19.22** Characterize the reverse of a map.

19.23 Design a digraph class that explicitly provides clients with the capability to refer to both a digraph and its reverse, and provide an implementation, for any representation that supports `edge` queries.

19.24 Provide an alternate implementation for your class in Exercise 19.23 that maintains both orientations of edges on adjacency lists.

▷ **19.25** Describe a family of strongly connected digraphs with V vertices and no (simple) directed cycles of length greater than 2.

○ **19.26** Give the strong components and a kernel DAG of the digraph

3-7 1-4 7-8 0-5 5-2 3-8 2-9 0-6 4-9 2-6 6-4.

• **19.27** Give a kernel DAG of the grid digraph shown in Figure 19.3.

19.28 How many digraphs have V vertices, all of outdegree k?

• **19.29** What is the expected number of different adjacency-lists representations of a random digraph? *Hint*: Divide the total number of possible representations by the total number of digraphs.

19.2 Anatomy of DFS in Digraphs

We can use our DFS code for undirected graphs from Chapter 18 to visit each edge and each vertex in a digraph. The basic principle behind the recursive algorithm holds: To visit every vertex that can be reached from a given vertex, we mark the vertex as having been visited, then (recursively) visit all the vertices that can be reached from each of the vertices on its adjacency list.

In an undirected graph, we have two representations of each edge, but the second representation that is encountered in a DFS always leads to a marked vertex and is ignored (see Section 18.2). In a digraph, we have just one representation of each edge, so we might expect DFS algorithms to be more straightforward. But digraphs themselves are more complicated combinatorial objects than undirected graphs, so this expectation is not justified. For example, the search trees that we use to understand the operation of the algorithm have a more complicated structure for digraphs than for undirected graphs. This complication makes digraph-processing algorithms more difficult to devise. For example, as we will see, it is more difficult to make inferences about directed paths in digraphs than it is to make inferences about paths in graphs.

As we did in Chapter 18, we use the term *standard adjacency-lists DFS* to refer to the process of inserting a sequence of edges into a digraph ADT implemented with an adjacency-lists representation (Program 17.9, invoked with `true` as the constructor's second argument), then doing a DFS with, for example, Program 18.3 and the parallel term *standard adjacency-matrix DFS* to refer to the process of inserting a sequence of edges into a digraph ADT implemented with an adjacency-matrix representation (Program 17.7, invoked with `true` as the constructor's second argument), then doing a DFS with, for example, Program 18.3.

For example, Figure 19.9 shows the recursive-call tree that describes the operation of a standard adjacency-lists DFS on the sample digraph in Figure 19.1. Just as for undirected graphs, such trees have internal nodes that correspond to calls on the recursive DFS function for each vertex, with links to external nodes that correspond to edges that take us to vertices that have already been seen. Classifying the nodes and links gives us information about the search (and the digraph), but the classification for digraphs is quite different from the classification for undirected graphs.

In undirected graphs, we assigned each link in the DFS tree to one of four classes according to whether it corresponded to a graph edge that led to a recursive call and to whether it corresponded to the first or second representation of the edge encountered by the DFS. In digraphs, there is a one-to-one correspondence between tree links and graph edges, and they fall into four distinct classes:

- Those representing a recursive call (*tree* edges)
- Those from a vertex to an ancestor in its DFS tree (*back* edges)
- Those from a vertex to a descendant in its DFS tree (*down* edges)
- Those from a vertex to another vertex that is neither an ancestor nor a descendant in its DFS tree (*cross* edges)

A tree edge is an edge to an unvisited vertex, corresponding to a recursive call in the DFS. Back, cross, and down edges go to visited vertices. To identify the type of a given edge, we use preorder and

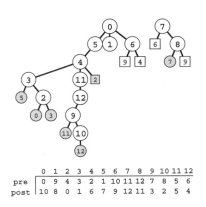

	0	1	2	3	4	5	6	7	8	9	10	11	12
pre	0	9	4	3	2	1	10	11	12	7	8	5	6
post	10	8	0	1	6	7	9	12	11	3	2	5	4

Figure 19.9
DFS forest for a digraph

This forest describes a standard adjacency-lists DFS of the sample digraph in Figure 19.1. External nodes represent previously visited internal nodes with the same label; otherwise the forest is a representation of the digraph, with all edges pointing down. There are four types of edges: tree edges, to internal nodes; back edges, to external nodes representing ancestors (shaded circles); down edges, to external nodes representing descendants (shaded squares); and cross edges, to external nodes representing nodes that are neither ancestors nor descendants (white squares). We can determine the type of edges to visited nodes, by comparing the preorder and postorder numbers (bottom) of their source and destination:

pre	post	example	type
<	>	4–2	down
>	<	2–0	back
>	>	7–6	cross

For example, 7–6 is a cross edge because 7's preorder and postorder numbers are both larger than 6's.

postorder numbering (the order in which nodes are visited in preorder and postorder walks of the forest, respectively).

Property 19.3 *In a DFS forest corresponding to a digraph, an edge to a visited node is a back edge if it leads to a node with a higher postorder number; otherwise, it is a cross edge if it leads to a node with a lower preorder number and a down edge if it leads to a node with a higher preorder number.*

Proof: These facts follow from the definitions. A node's ancestors in a DFS tree have lower preorder numbers and higher postorder numbers; its descendants have higher preorder numbers and lower postorder numbers. It is also true that both numbers are lower in previously visited nodes in other DFS trees, and both numbers are higher in yet-to-be-visited nodes in other DFS trees, but we do not need code that tests for these cases. ∎

Program 19.2 is a DFS class that identifies the type of each edge in the digraph. Figure 19.10 illustrates its operation on the example digraph of Figure 19.1. During the search, testing to see whether an edge leads to a node with a higher postorder number is equivalent to testing whether a postorder number has yet been assigned. Any node for which a preorder number has been assigned but for which a postorder number has not yet been assigned is an ancestor in the DFS tree and will therefore have a postorder number higher than that of the current node.

As we saw in Chapter 17 for undirected graphs, the edge types are properties of the dynamics of the search, rather than of only the graph. Indeed, different DFS forests of the same graph can differ remarkably in character, as illustrated in Figure 19.11. For example, even the number of trees in the DFS forest depends upon the start vertex.

Despite these differences, several classical digraph-processing algorithms are able to determine digraph properties by taking appropriate action when they encounter the various types of edges during a DFS. For example, consider the following basic problem:

Directed cycle detection   Does a given digraph have any directed cycles? (Is the digraph a DAG?) In undirected graphs, any edge to a visited vertex indicates a cycle in the graph; in digraphs, we must restrict our attention to back edges.

```
0-0 tree
  0-5 tree
    5-4 tree
      4-3 tree
        3-5 back
        3-2 tree
          2-0 back
          2-3 back
      4-11 tree
        11-12 tree
          12-9 tree
            9-11 back
            9-10 tree
              10-12 back
      4-2 down
  0-1 tree
  0-6 tree
    6-9 cross
    6-4 cross
7-7 tree
  7-6 cross
  7-8 tree
    8-7 back
    8-9 cross
```

Figure 19.10
Digraph DFS trace

This DFS trace is the output of Program 19.2 for the example digraph in Figure 19.1. It corresponds precisely to a preorder walk of the DFS tree depicted in Figure 19.9.

Program 19.2 DFS of a digraph

This DFS class uses preorder and postorder numberings to show the role
that each edge in the graph plays in the DFS (see Figure 19.10).

```
template <class Graph> class DFS
{ const Graph &G;
  int depth, cnt, cntP;
  vector<int> pre, post;
  void show(char *s, Edge e)
    { for (int i = 0; i < depth; i++) cout << "  ";
      cout << e.v << "-" << e.w << s << endl; }
  void dfsR(Edge e)
    { int w = e.w; show(" tree", e);
      pre[w] = cnt++; depth++;
      typename Graph::adjIterator A(G, w);
      for (int t = A.beg(); !A.end(); t = A.nxt())
      { Edge x(w, t);
        if (pre[t] == -1) dfsR(x);
        else if (post[t] == -1) show(" back", x);
        else if (pre[t] > pre[w]) show(" down", x);
        else show(" cross", x);
      }
      post[w] = cntP++; depth--;
    }
public:
  DFS(const Graph &G) : G(G), cnt(0), cntP(0),
    pre(G.V(), -1), post(G.V(), -1)
    { for (int v = 0; v < G.V(); v++)
        if (pre[v] == -1) dfsR(Edge(v, v)); }
};
```

Property 19.4 *A digraph is a DAG if and only if we encounter no
back edges when we use DFS to examine every edge.*

Proof: Any back edge belongs to a directed cycle that consists of the
edge plus the tree path connecting the two nodes, so we will find no
back edges when using DFS on a DAG. To prove the converse, we
show that if the digraph has a cycle, then the DFS encounters a back

Figure 19.11
DFS forests for a digraph

These forests describes depth-first search of the same graph as Figure 19.9, when the graph search function checks the vertices (and calls the recursive function for the unvisited ones) in the order s, s+1, ..., V-1, 0, 1, ..., s-1 for each s. The forest structure is determined both by the search dynamics and the graph structure. Each node has the same children (the nodes on its adjacency list, in order) in every forest. The leftmost tree in each forest contains all the nodes reachable from its root, but reachability inferences about other nodes are complicated because of back, cross, and down edges. Even the number of trees in the forest depends on the starting node, so we do not necessarily have a direct correspondence between trees in the forest and strong components, the way that we did for components in undirected graphs. For example, we see that all vertices are reachable from 8 only when we start the DFS at 8.

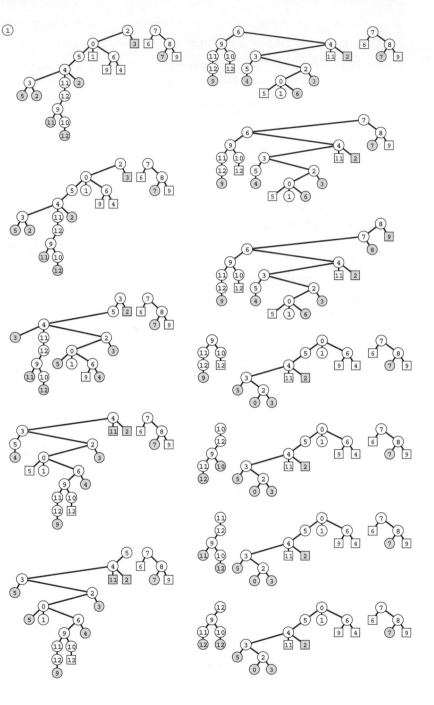

edge. Suppose that v is the first of the vertices on the cycle that is visited by the DFS. That vertex has the lowest preorder number of all the vertices on the cycle. The edge that points to it will therefore be a back edge: It will be encountered during the recursive call for v (for a proof that it must be, see Property 19.5), and it points from some node on the cycle to v, a node with a lower preorder number (see Property 19.3). ∎

We can convert any digraph into a DAG by doing a DFS and removing any graph edges that correspond to back edges in the DFS. For example, Figure 19.9 tells us that removing the edges 2-0, 3-5, 2-3, 9-11, 10-12, 4-2, and 8-7 makes the digraph in Figure 19.1 a DAG. The specific DAG that we get in this way depends on the graph representation and the associated implications for the dynamics of the DFS (see Exercise 19.37). This method is a useful way to generate large arbitrary DAGs randomly (see Exercise 19.76) for use in testing DAG-processing algorithms.

Directed cycle detection is a simple problem, but contrasting the solution just described with the solution that we considered in Chapter 18 for undirected graphs gives insight into the necessity of considering the two types of graphs as different combinatorial objects, even though their representations are similar and the same programs work on both types for some applications. By our definitions, we seem to be using the same method to solve this problem as for cycle detection in undirected graphs (look for back edges), but the implementation that we used for undirected graphs would not work for digraphs. For example, in Section 18.5 we were careful to distinguish between parent links and back links since the existence of a parent link does not indicate a cycle (cycles in undirected graphs must involve at least three vertices). But to ignore links back to a node's parents in digraphs would be incorrect; we do consider a doubly-connected pair of vertices in a digraph to be a cycle. Theoretically, we could have defined back edges in undirected graphs in the same way as we have done here, but then we would have needed an explicit exception for the two-vertex case. More important, we can detect cycles in undirected graphs in time proportional to V (see Section 18.5), but we may need time proportional to E to find a cycle in a digraph (see Exercise 19.32).

The essential purpose of DFS is to provide a systematic way to visit all the vertices and all the edges of a graph. It therefore gives

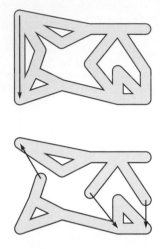

Figure 19.12
Decomposing a digraph

To prove by induction that DFS takes us everywhere reachable from a given node in a digraph, we use essentially the same proof as for Trémaux exploration. The key step is depicted here as a maze (top), for comparison with Figure 18.4. We break the graph into two smaller pieces (bottom), induced by two sets of vertices: Those vertices that can be reached by following the first edge from the start vertex without revisiting it (bottom piece), and those vertices that cannot be reached by following the first edge without going back through the start vertex (top piece). Any edge that goes from a vertex in the first set to the start vertex is skipped during the search of the first set because of the mark on the start vertex. Any edge that goes from a vertex in the second set to a vertex in the first set is skipped because all vertices in the first set are marked before the search of the second subgraph begins.

us a basic approach for solving reachability problems in digraphs, although, again, the situation is more complicated than for undirected graphs.

Single-source reachability   Which vertices in a given digraph can be reached from a given start vertex s? How many such vertices are there?

Property 19.5   *With a recursive DFS starting at s, we can solve the single-source reachability problem for a vertex s in time proportional to the number of edges in the subgraph induced by the reachable vertices.*

Proof: This proof is essentially the same as the proof of Property 18.1, but it is worth restating to underline the distinction between reachability in digraphs and connectivity in undirected graphs. The property is certainly true for a digraph that has one vertex and no edges. For any digraph that has more than one vertex, we assume the property to be true for all digraphs that have fewer vertices. Now, the first edge that we take from s divides the digraph into the subgraphs induced by two subsets of vertices (see Figure 19.12): (*i*) the vertices that we can reach by directed paths that begin with that edge and do not otherwise include s; and (*ii*) the vertices that we cannot reach with a directed path that begins with that edge without returning to s. We apply the inductive hypothesis to these subgraphs, noting that there are no directed edges from a vertex in the first subgraph to any vertex other than s in the second subgraph (such an edge would be a contradiction because its destination vertex should be in the first subgraph), that directed edges to s will be ignored because it has the lowest preorder number, and that all the vertices in the first subgraph have lower preorder numbers than any vertex in the second subgraph, so all directed edges from a vertex in the second subgraph to a vertex in the first subgraph will be ignored. ∎

By contrast with undirected graphs, a DFS on a digraph does *not* give full information about reachability from any vertex other than the start node, because tree edges are directed and because the search structures have cross edges. When we leave a vertex to travel down a tree edge, we cannot assume that there is a way to get back to that vertex via digraph edges; indeed, there is not, in general. For example, there is no way to get back to 4 after we take the tree edge 4–11 in Figure 19.9. Moreover, when we ignore cross and forward edges (because they lead to vertices that have been visited and are no longer active), we are ignoring information that they imply (the set of vertices that are reachable from the destination). For example, following the cross edge 6–9 in Figure 19.9 is the only way for us to find out that 10, 11, and 12 are reachable from 6.

To determine which vertices are reachable from another vertex, we apparently need to start over with a new DFS from that vertex (see Figure 19.11). Can we make use of information from previous searches to make the process more efficient for later ones? We consider such reachability questions in Section 19.7.

To determine connectivity in undirected graphs, we rely on knowing that vertices are connected to their ancestors in the DFS tree, through (at least) the path in the tree. By contrast, the tree path goes in the wrong direction in a digraph: There is a directed path from a vertex in a digraph to an ancestor only if there is a back edge from a descendant to that or a more distant ancestor. Moreover, connectivity in undirected graphs for each vertex is restricted to the DFS tree rooted at that vertex; in contrast, in digraphs, cross edges can take us to any previously visited part of the search structure, even one in another tree in the DFS forest. For undirected graphs, we were able to take advantage of these properties of connectivity to identify each vertex with a connected component in a single DFS, then to use that information as the basis for a constant-time ADT operation to determine whether any two vertices are connected. For digraphs, as we see in this chapter, this goal is elusive.

We have emphasized throughout this and the previous chapter that different ways of choosing unvisited vertices lead to different search dynamics for DFS. For digraphs, the structural complexity of the DFS trees leads to differences in search dynamics that are even more pronounced than those we saw for undirected graphs. For example, Figure 19.11 illustrates that we get marked differences for digraphs even when we simply vary the order in which the vertices are examined in the top-level search function. Only a tiny fraction of even these possibilities is shown in the figure—in principle, each of the $V!$ different orders of examining vertices might lead to different results. In Section 19.7, we shall examine an important algorithm that specifically takes advantage of this flexibility, processing the unvisited vertices at the top level (the roots of the DFS trees) in a particular order that immediately exposes the strong components.

Exercises

19.30 Draw the DFS forest that results from a standard adjacency-lists DFS of the digraph

$$3\text{-}7 \quad 1\text{-}4 \quad 7\text{-}8 \quad 0\text{-}5 \quad 5\text{-}2 \quad 3\text{-}8 \quad 2\text{-}9 \quad 0\text{-}6 \quad 4\text{-}9 \quad 2\text{-}6 \quad 6\text{-}4.$$

19.31 Draw the DFS forest that results from a standard adjacency-matrix DFS of the digraph

$$3\text{-}7 \quad 1\text{-}4 \quad 7\text{-}8 \quad 0\text{-}5 \quad 5\text{-}2 \quad 3\text{-}8 \quad 2\text{-}9 \quad 0\text{-}6 \quad 4\text{-}9 \quad 2\text{-}6 \quad 6\text{-}4.$$

○ **19.32** Describe a family of digraphs with V vertices and E edges for which a standard adjacency-lists DFS requires time proportional to E for cycle detection.

▷ **19.33** Show that, during a DFS in a digraph, no edge connects a node to another node whose preorder and postorder numbers are both smaller.

○ **19.34** Show all possible DFS forests for the digraph

$$0\text{-}1 \quad 0\text{-}2 \quad 0\text{-}3 \quad 1\text{-}3 \quad 2\text{-}3.$$

Tabulate the number of tree, back, cross, and down edges for each forest.

19.35 If we denote the number of tree, back, cross, and down edges by t, b, c, and d, respectively, then we have $t + b + c + d = E$ and $t < V$ for any DFS of any digraph with V vertices and E edges. What other relationships among these variables can you infer? Which of the values are dependent solely on graph properties, and which are dependent on dynamic properties of the DFS?

▷ **19.36** Prove that every source in a digraph must be a root of some tree in the forest corresponding to any DFS of that digraph.

○ **19.37** Construct a connected DAG that is a subgraph of Figure 19.1 by removing five edges (see Figure 19.11).

19.38 Implement a digraph class that provides the capability for a client to check that a digraph is indeed a DAG, and provide a DFS-based implementation.

19.39 Use your solution to Exercise 19.38 to estimate (empirically) the probability that a random digraph with V vertices and E edges is a DAG for various types of digraphs (see Exercises 19.11–18).

19.40 Run empirical studies to determine the relative percentages of tree, back, cross, and down edges when we run DFS on various types of digraphs (see Exercises 19.11–18).

19.41 Describe how to construct a sequence of directed edges on V vertices for which there will be no cross or down edges and for which the number of back edges will be proportional to V^2 in a standard adjacency-lists DFS.

○ **19.42** Describe how to construct a sequence of directed edges on V vertices for which there will be no back or down edges and for which the number of cross edges will be proportional to V^2 in a standard adjacency-lists DFS.

19.43 Describe how to construct a sequence of directed edges on V vertices for which there will be no back or cross edges and for which the number of down edges will be proportional to V^2 in a standard adjacency-lists DFS.

○ **19.44** Give rules corresponding to Trémaux traversal for a maze where all the passages are one-way.

● **19.45** Extend your solutions to Exercises 17.56 through 17.60 to include arrows on edges (see the figures in this chapter for examples).

19.3 Reachability and Transitive Closure

To develop efficient solutions to reachability problems in digraphs, we begin with the following fundamental definition.

Definition 19.5 *The **transitive closure** of a digraph is a digraph with the same vertices but with an edge from s to t in the transitive closure if and only if there is a directed path from s to t in the given digraph.*

In other words, the transitive closure has an edge from each vertex to all the vertices reachable from that vertex in the digraph. Clearly, the transitive closure embodies all the requisite information for solving reachability problems. Figure 19.13 illustrates a small example.

One appealing way to understand the transitive closure is based on adjacency-matrix digraph representations, and on the following basic computational problem.

Boolean matrix multiplication A *Boolean matrix* is a matrix whose entries are all binary values, either 0 or 1. Given two Boolean matrices A and B, compute a Boolean product matrix C, using the logical *and* and *or* operations instead of the arithmetic operations $*$ and $+$, respectively.

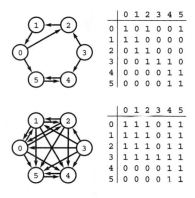

**Figure 19.13
Transitive closure**

This digraph (top) has just eight directed edges, but its transitive closure (bottom) shows that there are directed paths connecting 19 of the 30 pairs of vertices. Structural properties of the digraph are reflected in the transitive closure. For example, rows 0, 1, and 2 in the adjacency matrix for the transitive closure are identical (as are columns 0, 1, and 2) because those vertices are on a directed cycle in the digraph.

The textbook algorithm for computing the product of two V-by-V matrices computes, for each s and t, the dot product of row s in the first matrix and row t in the second matrix, as follows:

```
for (s = 0; s < V; s++)
  for (t = 0; t < V; t++)
    for (i = 0, C[s][t] = 0; i < V; i++)
      C[s][t] += A[s][i]*B[i][t];
```

In matrix notation, we write this operation simply as $C = A * B$. This operation is defined for matrices comprising any type of entry for which 0, +, and * are defined. In particular, if we interpret a+b to be the logical *or* operation and a*b to be the logical *and* operation, then we have Boolean matrix multiplication. In C++, we can use the following version:

```
for (s = 0; s < V; s++)
  for (t = 0; t < V; t++)
    for (i = 0, C[s][t] = 0; i < V; i++)
      if (A[s][i] && B[i][t]) C[s][t] = 1;
```

To compute C[s][t] in the product, we initialize it to 0, then set it to 1 if we find some value i for which both A[s][i] and B[i][t] are both 1. Running this computation is equivalent to setting C[s][t] to 1 if and only if the result of a bitwise logical *and* of row s in A with column t in B has a nonzero entry.

Now suppose that A is the adjacency matrix of a digraph A and that we use the preceding code to compute $C = A * A \equiv A^2$ (simply by changing the reference to B in the code into a reference to A). Reading the code in terms of the interpretation of the adjacency-matrix entries immediately tells us what it computes: For each pair of vertices s and t, we put an edge from s to t in C if and only if there is some vertex i for which there is both a path from s to i and a path from i to t in A. In other words, directed edges in A^2 correspond precisely to directed paths of length 2 in A. If we include self-loops at every vertex in A, then A^2 also has the edges of A; otherwise, it does not. This relationship between Boolean matrix multiplication and paths in digraphs is illustrated in Figure 19.14. It leads immediately to an elegant method for computing the transitive closure of any digraph.

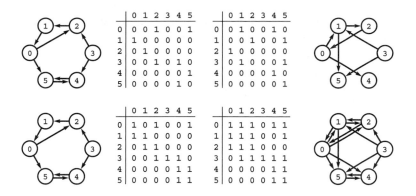

Figure 19.14
Squaring an adjacency matrix

If we put 0s on the diagonal of a digraph's adjacency matrix, the square of the matrix represents a graph with an edge corresponding to each path of length 2 (top). If we put 1s on the diagonal, the square of the matrix represents a graph with an edge corresponding to each path of length 1 or 2 (bottom).

Property 19.6 *We can compute the transitive closure of a digraph by constructing the latter's adjacency matrix A, adding self-loops for every vertex, and computing A^V.*

Proof: Continuing the argument in the previous paragraph, A^3 has an edge for every path of length less than or equal to 3 in the digraph, A^4 has an edge for every path of length less than or equal to 4 in the digraph, and so forth. We do not need to consider paths of length greater than V because of the pigeonhole principle: Any such path must revisit some vertex (since there are only V of them) and therefore adds no information to the transitive closure because the same two vertices are connected by a directed path of length less than V (which we could obtain by removing the cycle to the revisited vertex). ■

Figure 19.15 shows the adjacency-matrix powers for a sample digraph converging to transitive closure. This method takes V matrix multiplications, each of which takes time proportional to V^3, for a grand total of V^4. We can actually compute the transitive closure for any digraph with just $\lceil \lg V \rceil$ Boolean matrix-multiplication operations: We compute A^2, A^4, A^8, ... until we reach an exponent greater than or equal to V. As shown in the proof of Property 19.6, $A^t = A^V$ for any $t > V$; so the result of this computation, which requires time proportional to $V^3 \lg V$, is A^V—the transitive closure.

Although the approach just described is appealing in its simplicity, an even simpler method is available. We can compute the transitive

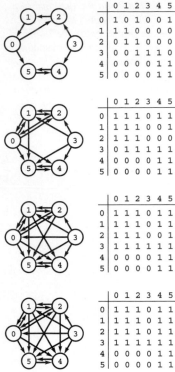

	0	1	2	3	4	5
0	1	0	1	0	0	1
1	1	1	0	0	0	0
2	0	1	1	0	0	0
3	0	0	1	1	1	0
4	0	0	0	0	1	1
5	0	0	0	0	1	1

	0	1	2	3	4	5
0	1	1	1	0	1	1
1	1	1	1	0	0	1
2	1	1	1	0	0	0
3	0	1	1	1	1	1
4	0	0	0	0	1	1
5	0	0	0	0	1	1

	0	1	2	3	4	5
0	1	1	1	0	1	1
1	1	1	1	0	1	1
2	1	1	1	0	0	1
3	1	1	1	1	1	1
4	0	0	0	0	1	1
5	0	0	0	0	1	1

	0	1	2	3	4	5
0	1	1	1	0	1	1
1	1	1	1	0	1	1
2	1	1	1	0	1	1
3	1	1	1	1	1	1
4	0	0	0	0	1	1
5	0	0	0	0	1	1

Figure 19.15
Adjacency matrix powers and directed paths

This sequence shows the first, second, third, and fourth powers (right, top to bottom) of the adjacency matrix at the top right, which gives graphs with edges for each of the paths of lengths less than 1, 2, 3, and 4, respectively, (left, top to bottom) in the graph that the matrix represents. The bottom graph is the transitive closure for this example, since there are no paths of length greater than 4 that connect vertices not connected by shorter paths.

closure with just *one* operation of this kind, building up the transitive closure from the adjacency matrix in place, as follows:

```
for (i = 0; i < V; i++)
  for (s = 0; s < V; s++)
    for (t = 0; t < V; t++)
      if (A[s][i] && A[i][t]) A[s][t] = 1;
```

This classical method, invented by S. Warshall in 1962, is the method of choice for computing the transitive closure of dense digraphs. The code is similar to the code that we might try to use to square a Boolean matrix in place: The difference (which is significant!) lies in the order of the `for` loops.

Property 19.7 *With Warshall's algorithm, we can compute the transitive closure of a digraph in time proportional to V^3.*

Proof: The running time is immediately evident from the structure of the code. We prove that it computes the transitive closure by induction on i. After the first iteration of the loop, the matrix has a 1 in row s and column t if and only if we have either the paths s-t or s-0-t. The second iteration checks all the paths between s and t that include 1 and perhaps 0, such as s-1-t, s-1-0-t, and s-0-1-t. We are led to the following inductive hypothesis: The ith iteration of the loop sets the bit in row s and column t in the matrix to 1 if and only if there is a directed path from s to t in the digraph that does not include any vertices with indices greater than i (except possibly the endpoints s and t). As just argued, the condition is true when i is 0, after the first iteration of the loop. Assuming that it is true for the ith iteration of the loop, there is a path from s to t that does not include any vertices with indices greater than i+1 if and only if (*i*) there is a path from s to t that does not include any vertices with indices greater than i, in which case A[s][t] was set on a previous iteration of the loop (by the inductive hypothesis); or (*ii*) there is a path from s to i+1 and a path from i+1 to t, neither of which includes any vertices with indices greater than i (except endpoints), in which case A[s][i+1] and A[i+1][t] were previously set to 1 (by hypothesis), so the inner loop sets A[s][t]. ∎

We can improve the performance of Warshall's algorithm with a simple transformation of the code: We move the test of A[s][i] out of the inner loop because its value does not change as t varies. This move allows us to avoid executing the t loop entirely when A[s][i] is

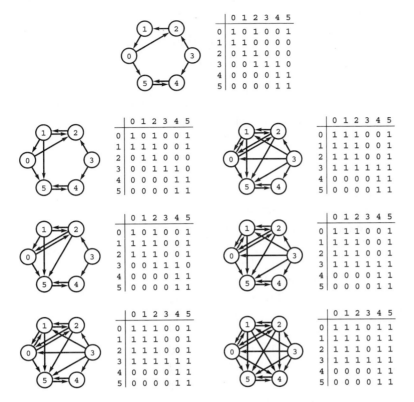

**Figure 19.16
Warshall's algorithm**

This sequence shows the development of the transitive closure (bottom) of an example digraph (top) as computed with Warshall's algorithm. The first iteration of the loop (left column, top) adds the edges 1-2 and 1-5 because of the paths 1-0-2 and 1-0-5, which include vertex 0 (but no vertex with a higher number); the second iteration of the loop (left column, second from top) adds the edges 2-0 and 2-5 because of the paths 2-1-0 and 2-1-0-5, which include vertex 1 (but no vertex with a higher number); and the third iteration of the loop (left column, bottom) adds the edges 0-1, 3-0, 3-1, and 3-5 because of the paths 0-2-1, 3-2-1-0, 3-2-1, and 3-2-1-0-5, which include vertex 2 (but no vertex with a higher number). The right column shows the edges added when paths through 3, 4, and 5 are considered. The last iteration of the loop (right column, bottom) adds the edges from 0, 1, and 2, to 4, because the only directed paths from those nodes to 4 include 5, the highest-numbered vertex.

zero. The savings that we achieve from this improvement depends on the digraph and is substantial for many digraphs (see Exercises 19.53 and 19.54). Program 19.3 implements this improvement and packages Warshall's method such that clients can preprocess a digraph (compute the transitive closure), then compute the answer to any reachability query in constant time.

We are interested in pursuing more efficient solutions, particularly for sparse digraphs. We would like to reduce both the preprocessing time and the space because both make the use of Warshall's method prohibitively costly for huge sparse digraphs.

In modern applications, abstract data types provide us with the ability to separate out the idea of an operation from any particular implementation so that we can focus on efficient implementations. For the transitive closure, this point of view leads to a recognition that we do not necessarily need to compute the entire matrix to provide clients

---

Program 19.3 Warshall's algorithm

The constructor for class TC computes the transitive closure of G in the private data member T, so that clients can use TC objects to test whether any given vertex in a digraph is reachable from any other given vertex. The constructor initializes T with a copy of G, adds self-loops, then uses Warshall's algorithm to complete the computation. The tcGraph class must include an implementation of the edge existence test.

```
template <class tcGraph, class Graph> class TC
{ tcGraph T;
public:
  TC(const Graph &G) : T(G)
    {
      for (int s = 0; s < T.V(); s++)
        T.insert(Edge(s, s));
      for (int i = 0; i < T.V(); i++)
        for (int s = 0; s < T.V(); s++)
          if (T.edge(s, i))
            for (int t = 0; t < T.V(); t++)
              if (T.edge(i, t))
                T.insert(Edge(s, t));
    }
  bool reachable(int s, int t) const
    { return T.edge(s, t); }
};
```

---

with the transitive-closure abstraction. One possibility might be that the transitive closure is a huge sparse matrix, so an adjacency-lists representation is called for because we cannot store the matrix representation. Even when the transitive closure is dense, client programs might test only a tiny fraction of possible pairs of edges, so computing the whole matrix is wasteful.

We use the term *abstract transitive closure* to refer to an ADT that provides clients with the ability to test reachability after preprocessing a digraph, like Program 19.3. In this context, we need to measure an algorithm not just by its cost to compute the transitive closure (preprocessing cost) but also by the space required and the query time achieved. That is, we rephrase Property 19.7 as follows:

Property 19.8 *We can support constant-time reachability testing (abstract transitive closure) for a digraph, using space proportional to V^2 and time proportional to V^3 for preprocessing.*

This property follows immediately from the basic performance characteristics of Warshall's algorithm. ∎

For most applications, our goal is not just to compute the transitive closure of a digraph quickly but also to support constant query time for the abstract transitive closure using far less space and far less preprocessing time than specified in Property 19.8. Can we find an implementation that will allow us to build clients that can afford to handle such digraphs? We return to this question in Section 19.8.

There is an intimate relationship between the problem of computing the transitive closure of a digraph and a number of other fundamental computational problems, and that relationship can help us to understand this problem's difficulty. We conclude this section by considering two examples of such problems.

First, we consider the relationship between the transitive closure and the *all-pairs shortest-paths* problem (see Section 18.7). For digraphs, the problem is to find, for each pair of vertices, a directed path with a minimal number of edges.

Given a digraph, we initialize a *V*-by-*V* integer matrix A by setting A[s][t] to 1 if there is an edge from s to t and to the sentinel value V if there is no such edge. Our goal is to set A[s][t] equal to the length of (the number of edges on) a shortest directed path from s to t, using the sentinel value V to indicate that there is no such path. The following code accomplishes this objective:

```
for (i = 0; i < V; i++)
  for (s = 0; s < V; s++)
    for (t = 0; t < V; t++)
      if (A[s][i] + A[i][t] < A[s][t])
        A[s][t] = A[s][i] + A[i][t];
```

This code differs from the version of Warshall's algorithm that we saw just before Property 19.7 in only the `if` statement in the inner loop. Indeed, in the proper abstract setting, the computations are precisely the same (see Exercises 19.55 and 19.56). Converting the proof of Property 19.7 into a direct proof that this method accomplishes the desired objective is straightforward. This method is a special case of *Floyd's algorithm* for finding shortest paths in weighted graphs (see Chapter 21). The BFS-based solution for undirected graphs that we considered in Section 18.7 also finds shortest paths in digraphs (appropriately modified). Shortest paths are the subject of Chapter 21, so we defer considering detailed performance comparisons until then.

Second, as we have seen, the transitive-closure problem is also closely related to the Boolean matrix-multiplication problem. The basic algorithms that we have seen for both problems require time proportional to V^3, using similar computational schema. Boolean matrix multiplication is known to be a difficult computational problem: Algorithms that are asymptotically faster than the straightforward method are known, but it is debatable whether the savings are sufficiently large to justify the effort of implementing any of them. This fact is significant in the present context because we could use a fast algorithm for Boolean matrix multiplication to develop a fast transitive-closure algorithm (slower by just a factor of $\lg V$) using the repeated-squaring method illustrated in Figure 19.15. Conversely, we have a lower bound on the difficulty of computing the transitive closure:

Property 19.9 *We can use any transitive-closure algorithm to compute the product of two Boolean matrices with at most a constant-factor difference in running time.*

Proof: Given two V-by-V Boolean matrices A and B, we construct the following $3V$-by-$3V$ matrix:

$$\begin{pmatrix} I & A & 0 \\ 0 & I & B \\ 0 & 0 & I \end{pmatrix}$$

Here, 0 denotes the V-by-V matrix with all entries equal to 0, and I denotes the V-by-V identity matrix with all entries equal to 0 except those on the diagonal, which are equal to 1. Now, we consider this matrix to be the adjacency matrix for a digraph and compute its transitive closure by repeated squaring. But we only need one step:

$$\begin{pmatrix} I & A & 0 \\ 0 & I & B \\ 0 & 0 & I \end{pmatrix}^2 = \begin{pmatrix} I & A & A*B \\ 0 & I & B \\ 0 & 0 & I \end{pmatrix}$$

The matrix on the right-hand side of this equation is the transitive closure because further multiplications give back the same matrix. But this matrix has the V-by-V product $A * B$ in its upper-right corner. Whatever algorithm we use to solve the transitive-closure problem, we can use it to solve the Boolean matrix-multiplication problem at the same cost (to within a constant factor). ∎

The significance of this property depends on the conviction of experts that Boolean matrix multiplication is difficult: Mathematicians have been working for decades to try to learn precisely how difficult it is, and the question is unresolved; the best known results say that the running time should be proportional to about $V^{2.5}$ (*see reference section*). Now, if we could find a linear-time (proportional to V^2) solution to the transitive-closure problem, then we would have a linear-time solution to the Boolean matrix-multiplication problem as well. This relationship between problems is known as *reduction*: We say that the Boolean matrix-multiplication problem *reduces to* the transitive-closure problem (see Section 21.6 and Part 8). Indeed, the proof actually shows that Boolean matrix multiplication reduces to finding the paths of length 2 in a digraph.

Despite a great deal of research by many people, no one has been able to find a linear-time Boolean matrix-multiplication algorithm, so we cannot present a simple linear-time transitive-closure algorithm. On the other hand, no one has proved that no such algorithm exists, so we hold open that possibility for the future. In short, we take Property 19.9 to mean that, barring a research breakthrough, we cannot expect the worst-case running time of any transitive-closure algorithm that we can concoct to be proportional to V^2. Despite this conclusion, we can develop fast algorithms for certain classes of digraphs. For example, we have already touched on a simple method for computing the transitive closure that is much faster than Warshall's algorithm for sparse digraphs.

Property 19.10 *With DFS, we can support constant query time for the abstract transitive closure of a digraph, with space proportional to V^2 and time proportional to $V(E + V)$ for preprocessing (computing the transitive closure).*

Proof: As we observed in the previous section, DFS gives us all the vertices reachable from the start vertex in time proportional to E, if we use the adjacency-lists representation (see Property 19.5 and Figure 19.11). Therefore, if we run DFS V times, once with each vertex as

---

Program 19.4 DFS-based transitive closure

This DFS class implements the same interface as does Program 19.3. It computes the transitive closure T by doing a separate DFS starting at each vertex of G to compute its set of reachable nodes. Each call on the recursive function adds an edge from the start vertex and makes recursive calls to fill the corresponding row in the transitive-closure matrix. The matrix also serves to mark the visited vertices during the DFS, so it requires that the Graph class support the edge existence test.

```
template <class Graph> class tc
{ Graph T; const Graph &G;
  void tcR(int v, int w)
  {
    T.insert(Edge(v, w));
    typename Graph::adjIterator A(G, w);
    for (int t = A.beg(); !A.end(); t = A.nxt())
      if (!T.edge(v, t)) tcR(v, t);
  }
public:
  tc(const Graph &G) : G(G), T(G.V(), true)
    { for (int v = 0; v < G.V(); v++) tcR(v, v); }
  bool reachable(int v, int w)
    { return T.edge(v, w); }
};
```

---

the start vertex, then we can compute the set of vertices reachable from each vertex—the transitive closure—in time proportional to $V(E+V)$. The same argument holds for any linear-time generalized search (see Section 18.8 and Exercise 19.66). ∎

Program 19.4 is an implementation of this search-based transitive-closure algorithm. This class implements the same interface as does Program 19.3. The result of running this program on the sample digraph in Figure 19.1 is illustrated in the first tree in each forest in Figure 19.11.

For sparse digraphs, this search-based approach is the method of choice. For example, if E is proportional to V, then Program 19.4 computes the transitive closure in time proportional to V^2. How can it do so, given the reduction to Boolean matrix multiplication that we just considered? The answer is that this transitive-closure algorithm does indeed give an optimal way to multiply *certain types* of Boolean matrices (those with $O(V)$ nonzero entries). The lower bound tells us that we should not expect to find a transitive-closure algorithm that runs in time proportional to V^2 for *all* digraphs, but it does not preclude the possibility that we might find algorithms, like this one, that are faster for *certain classes* of digraphs. If such graphs are the ones that we need to process, the relationship between transitive closure and Boolean matrix multiplication may not be relevant to us.

It is easy to extend the methods that we have described in this section to provide clients with the ability to find a specific path connecting two vertices by keeping track of the search tree, as described in Section 17.8. We consider specific ADT implementations of this sort in the context of the more general shortest-paths problems in Chapter 21.

Table 19.1 shows empirical results comparing the elementary transitive-closure algorithms described in this section. The adjacency-lists implementation of the search-based solution is by far the fastest method for sparse digraphs. The implementations all compute an adjacency matrix (of size V^2), so none of them are suitable for huge sparse digraphs.

For sparse digraphs whose transitive closure is also sparse, we might use an adjacency-lists implementation for the closure so that the size of the output is proportional to the number of edges in the transitive closure. This number certainly is a lower bound on the cost of computing the transitive closure, which we can achieve for certain types of digraphs using various algorithmic techniques (see Exercises 19.64 and 19.65). Despite this possibility, we generally view the objective of a transitive-closure computation to be dense, so we can use a representation like DenseGRAPH that can easily answer reachability queries, and we regard transitive-closure algorithms that compute the matrix in time proportional to V^2 as being optimal since they take time proportional to the size of their output.

If the adjacency matrix is symmetric, it is equivalent to an undirected graph, and finding the transitive closure is the same as finding the connected components—the transitive closure is the union of complete graphs on the vertices in the connected components (see Exercise 19.48). Our connectivity algorithms in Section 18.5 amount to an abstract–transitive-closure computation for symmetric digraphs

Table 19.1 Empirical study of transitive-closure algorithms

This table shows running times that exhibit dramatic performance differences for various algorithms for computing the transitive closure of random digraphs, both dense and sparse. For all but the adjacency-lists DFS, the running time goes up by a factor of 8 when we double V, which supports the conclusion that it is essentially proportional to V^3. The adjacency-lists DFS takes time proportional to VE, which explains the running time roughly increasing by a factor of 4 when we double both V and E (sparse graphs) and by a factor of about 2 when we double E (dense graphs), except that list-traversal overhead degrades performance for high-density graphs.

sparse (10V edges)					dense (250 vertices)				
V	W	W*	A	L	E	W	W*	A	L
25	0	0	1	0	5000	289	203	177	23
50	3	1	2	1	10000	300	214	184	38
125	35	24	23	4	25000	309	226	200	97
250	275	181	178	13	50000	315	232	218	337
500	2222	1438	1481	54	100000	326	246	235	784

Key:

  W   Warshall's algorithm (Section 19.3)
  W* Improved Warshall's algorithm (Program 19.3)
  A   DFS, adjacency-matrix representation (Programs 19.4 and 17.7)
  L   DFS, adjacency-lists representation (Program 19.417.9)

(undirected graphs) that uses space proportional to V and still supports constant-time reachability queries. Can we do as well in general digraphs? Can we reduce the preprocessing time still further? For what types of graphs can we compute the transitive closure in linear time? To answer these questions, we need to study the structure of digraphs in more detail, including, specifically, that of DAGs.

Exercises

▷ **19.46** What is the transitive closure of a digraph that consists solely of a directed cycle with V vertices?

19.47 How many edges are there in the transitive closure of a digraph that consists solely of a simple directed path with V vertices?

▷ **19.48** Give the transitive closure of the undirected graph

3-7 1-4 7-8 0-5 5-2 3-8 2-9 0-6 4-9 2-6 6-4.

• **19.49** Show how to construct a digraph with V vertices and E edges with the property that the number of edges in the transitive closure is proportional to t, for any t between E and V^2. As usual, assume that $E > V$.

19.50 Give a formula for the number of edges in the transitive closure of a digraph that is a directed forest as a function of structural properties of the forest.

19.51 Show, in the style of Figure 19.15, the process of computing the transitive closure of the digraph

3-7 1-4 7-8 0-5 5-2 3-8 2-9 0-6 4-9 2-6 6-4

through repeated squaring.

19.52 Show, in the style of Figure 19.16, the process of computing the transitive closure of the digraph

3-7 1-4 7-8 0-5 5-2 3-8 2-9 0-6 4-9 2-6 6-4

with Warshall's algorithm.

○ **19.53** Give a family of sparse digraphs for which the improved version of Warshall's algorithm for computing the transitive closure (Program 19.3) runs in time proportional to VE.

○ **19.54** Find a sparse digraph for which the improved version of Warshall's algorithm for computing the transitive closure (Program 19.3) runs in time proportional to V^3.

○ **19.55** Develop a base class from which you can derive classes that implement both Warshall's algorithm and Floyd's algorithm. (This exercise is a version of Exercise 19.56 for people who are more familiar with abstract data types than with abstract algebra.)

• **19.56** Use abstract algebra to develop a generic algorithm that encompasses both Warshall's algorithm and Floyd's algorithm. (This exercise is a version of Exercise 19.55 for people who are more familiar with abstract algebra than with abstract data types.)

○ **19.57** Show, in the style of Figure 19.16, the development of the all-shortest paths matrix for the example graph in the figure as computed with Floyd's algorithm.

19.58 Is the Boolean product of two symmetric matrices symmetric? Explain your answer.

19.59 Add a public function member to Programs 19.3 and 19.4 to allow clients to use tc objects to find the number of edges in the transitive closure.

19.60 Design a way to maintain the count of the number of edges in the transitive closure by modifying it when edges are added and removed. Give the cost of adding and removing edges with your scheme.

▷ **19.61** Add a public member function for use with Programs 19.3 and 19.4 that returns a vertex-indexed vector that indicates which vertices are reachable from a given vertex.

○ **19.62** Run empirical studies to determine the number of edges in the transitive closure, for various types of digraphs (see Exercises 19.11–18).

● **19.63** Consider the bit-matrix graph representation that is described in Exercise 17.23. Which method can you speed up by a factor of B (where B is the number of bits per word on your computer): Warshall's algorithm or the DFS-based algorithm? Justify your answer by developing an implementation that does so.

○ **19.64** Give a program that computes the transitive closure of a digraph that is a directed forest in time proportional to the number of edges in the transitive closure.

○ **19.65** Implement an abstract–transitive-closure algorithm for sparse graphs that uses space proportional to T and can answer reachability requests in constant time after preprocessing time proportional to $VE + T$, where T is the number of edges in the transitive closure. *Hint*: Use dynamic hashing.

▷ **19.66** Provide a version of Program 19.4 that is based on generalized graph search (see Section 18.8), and run empirical studies to see whether the choice of graph-search algorithm has any effect on performance.

19.4 Equivalence Relations and Partial Orders

This section is concerned with basic concepts in set theory and their relationship to abstract–transitive-closure algorithms. Its purposes are to put the ideas that we are studying into a larger context and to demonstrate the wide applicability of the algorithms that we are considering. Mathematically inclined readers who are familiar with set theory may wish to skip to Section 19.5 because the material that we cover is elementary (although our brief review of terminology may be helpful); readers who are not familiar with set theory may wish to consult an elementary text on discrete mathematics because our treatment is rather succinct. The connections between digraphs and these fundamental mathematical concepts are too important for us to ignore.

Given a set, a *relation* among its objects is defined to be a set of ordered pairs of the objects. Except possibly for details relating to parallel edges and self-loops, this definition is the same as our definition of a digraph: Relations and digraphs are different representations of the same abstraction. The mathematical concept is somewhat more powerful because the sets may be infinite, whereas our computer programs all work with finite sets, but we ignore this difference for the moment.

Typically, we choose a symbol R and use the notation sRt as shorthand for the statement "the ordered pair (s, t) is in the relation R." For example, we use the symbol "$<$" to represent the "less than" relation among numbers. Using this terminology, we can characterize various properties of relations. For example, a relation R is said to be *symmetric* if sRt implies that tRs for all s and t; it is said to be *reflexive* if sRs for all s. Symmetric relations are the same as undirected graphs. Reflexive relations correspond to graphs in which all vertices have self-loops; relations that correspond to graphs where no vertices have self-loops are said to be *irreflexive*.

A relation R is said to be *transitive* when sRt and tRu implies that sRu for all s, t, and u. The *transitive closure* of a relation is a well-defined concept; but instead of redefining it in set-theoretic terms, we appeal to the definition that we gave for digraphs in Section 19.3. Any relation is equivalent to a digraph, and the transitive closure of the relation is equivalent to the transitive closure of the digraph. The transitive closure of any relation is transitive.

In the context of graph algorithms, we are particularly interested in two particular transitive relations that are defined by further constraints. These two types, which are widely applicable, are known as *equivalence relations* and *partial orders*.

An *equivalence relation* $\equiv$ is a transitive relation that is also reflexive and symmetric. Note that a symmetric, transitive relation that includes each object in some ordered pair must be an equivalence relation: If $s \equiv t$, then $t \equiv s$ (by symmetry) and $s \equiv s$ (by transitivity). Equivalence relations divide the objects in a set into subsets known as *equivalence classes*. Two objects s and t are in the same equivalence class if and only if $s \equiv t$. The following examples are typical equivalence relations:

Modular arithmetic   Any positive integer k defines an equivalence relation on the set of integers, with $s \equiv t \pmod{k}$ if and only if the remainder that results when we divide s by k is equal to the the remainder that results when we divide t by k. The relation is obviously symmetric; a short proof establishes that it is also transitive (see Exercise 19.67) and therefore is an equivalence relation.

Connectivity in graphs   The relation "is in the same connected component as" among vertices is an equivalence relation because it is symmetric and transitive. The equivalence classes correspond to the connected components in the graph.

When we build a graph ADT that gives clients the ability to test whether two vertices are in the same connected component, we are implementing an equivalence-relation ADT that provides clients with the ability to test whether two objects are equivalent. In practice, this correspondence is significant because the graph is a succinct representation of the equivalence relation (see Exercise 19.71). In fact, as we saw in Chapters 1 and 18, to build such an ADT we need to maintain only a single vertex-indexed vector.

A *partial order* $\prec$ is a transitive relation that is also irreflexive. As a direct consequence of transitivity and irreflexivity, it is trivial to prove that partial orders are also *asymmetric*: If $s \prec t$ and $t \prec s$, then $s \prec s$ (by transitivity), which contradicts irreflexivity, so we cannot have both $s \prec t$ and $t \prec s$. Moreover, extending the same argument shows that a partial order cannot have a cycle, such as $s \prec t$, $t \prec u$, and $u \prec s$. The following examples are typical partial orders:

Subset inclusion   The relation "includes but is not equal to" ($\subset$) among subsets of a given set is a partial order—it is certainly irreflexive, and if $s \subset t$ and $t \subset u$, then certainly $s \subset u$.

Paths in DAGs   The relation "can be reached by a nonempty directed path from" is a partial order on vertices in DAGs with no self-loops because it is transitive and irreflexive. Like equivalence relations and undirected graphs, this particular partial order is significant for many applications because a DAG provides a succinct implicit representation of the partial order. For example, Figure 19.17 illustrates DAGs for subset containment partial orders whose number of edges is only a fraction of the cardinality of the partial order (see Exercise 19.73).

Indeed, we rarely define partial orders by enumerating all their ordered pairs, because there are too many of such pairs. Instead, we generally specify an irreflexive relation (a DAG) and consider its transitive closure. This usage is a primary reason for considering

0	000	ϕ
1	001	$\{c\}$
2	010	$\{b\}$
3	011	$\{b,c\}$
4	100	$\{a\}$
5	101	$\{a,c\}$
6	110	$\{a,b\}$
7	111	$\{a,b,c\}$

Figure 19.17
Set-inclusion DAG

In the DAG at the top, we interpret vertex indices to represent subsets of a set of 3 elements, as shown in the table at the bottom. The transitive closure of this DAG represents the subset inclusion partial order: There is a directed path between two nodes if and only if the subset represented by the first is included in the subset represented by the second.

abstract–transitive-closure ADT implementations for DAGs. Using DAGs, we consider examples of partial orders in Section 19.5.

A *total order* T is a partial order where either sTt or tTs for all $s \neq t$. Familiar examples of total orders are the "less than" relation among integers or real numbers and lexicographic ordering among strings of characters. Our study of sorting and searching algorithms in Parts 3 and 4 was based on a total-order ADT implementation for sets. In a total order, there is one and only one way to arrange the elements in the set such that sTt whenever s is before t in the arrangement; in a partial order that is not total, there are many ways to do so. In Section 19.5, we examine algorithms for this task.

In summary, the following correspondences between sets and graph models help us to understand the importance and wide applicability of fundamental graph algorithms.

- Relations and digraphs
- Symmetric relations and undirected graphs
- Transitive relations and paths in graphs
- Equivalence relations and paths in undirected graphs
- Partial orders and paths in DAGs

This context places in perspective the types of graphs and algorithms that we are considering and provides one motivation for us to move on to consider basic properties of DAGs and algorithms for processing those DAGs.

Exercises

19.67 Show that "has the same remainder after dividing by k" is a transitive relation (and therefore is an equivalence relation) on the set of integers.

19.68 Show that "is in the same edge-connected component as" is an equivalence relation among vertices in any graph.

19.69 Show that "is in the same biconnected component as" is not an equivalence relation among vertices in all graphs.

19.70 Prove that the transitive closure of an equivalence relation is an equivalence relation and that the transitive closure of a partial order is a partial order.

▷ **19.71** The cardinality of a relation is its number of ordered pairs. Prove that the cardinality of an equivalence relation is equal to the sum of the squares of the cardinalities of that relation's equivalence classes.

○ **19.72** Using an online dictionary, build a graph that represents the equivalence relation "has k letters in common with" among words. Determine the number of equivalence classes for $k = 1$ through 5.

19.73 The cardinality of a partial order is its number of ordered pairs. What is the cardinality of the subset containment partial order for an n-element set?

▷ **19.74** Show that "is a factor of" is a partial order among integers.

19.5 DAGs

In this section, we consider various applications of directed acyclic graphs (DAGs). We have two reasons to do so. First, because they serve as implicit models for partial orders, we work directly with DAGs in many applications and need efficient algorithms to process them. Second, these various applications give us insight into the nature of DAGs, and understanding DAGs is essential to understanding general digraphs.

Since DAGs are a special type of digraph, all DAG-processing problems trivially reduce to digraph-processing problems. Although we expect processing DAGs to be easier than processing general digraphs, we know when we encounter a problem that is difficult to solve on DAGs we should not expect to do any better solving the same problem on general digraphs. As we shall see, the problem of computing the transitive closure lies in this category. Conversely, understanding the difficulty of processing DAGs is important because every digraph has a kernel DAG (see Property 19.2), so we encounter DAGs even when we work with digraphs that are not DAGs.

The prototypical application where DAGs arise directly is called *scheduling*. Generally, solving scheduling problems has to do with arranging for the completion of a set of *tasks*, under a set of *constraints*, by specifying when and how the tasks are to be performed. Constraints might involve functions of the time taken or other resources consumed by the tasks. The most important type of constraints are *precedence constraints*, which specify that certain tasks must be performed before certain others, thus comprising a partial order among the tasks. Different types of additional constraints lead to many different types of scheduling problems, of varying difficulty. Literally thousands of different problems have been studied, and researchers still seek better algorithms for many of them. Perhaps the simplest nontrivial scheduling problem may be stated as follows:

Scheduling Given a set of tasks to be completed, with a partial order that specifies that certain tasks have to be completed before certain other tasks are begun, how can we schedule the tasks such that they are all completed while still respecting the partial order?

In this basic form, the scheduling problem is called *topological sorting*; it is not difficult to solve, as we shall see in the next section by examining two algorithms that do so. In more complicated practical applications, we might need to add other constraints on how the tasks might be scheduled, and the problem can become much more difficult. For example, the tasks might correspond to courses in a student's schedule, with the partial order specifying prerequisites. Topological sorting gives a feasible course schedule that meets the prerequisite requirements, but perhaps not one that respects other constraints that need to be added to the model, such as course conflicts, limitations on enrollments, and so forth. As another example, the tasks might be part of a manufacturing process, with the partial order specifying sequential requirements of the particular process. Topological sorting gives us a way to schedule the tasks, but perhaps there is another way to do so that uses less time, money, or some other resources not included in the model. We examine versions of the scheduling problem that capture more general situations such as these in Chapters 21 and 22.

Often, our first task is to check whether or not a given DAG indeed has no directed cycles. As we saw in Section 19.2, we can easily implement a class that allows clients to test whether a general digraph is a DAG in linear time, by running a standard DFS and checking that the DFS forest has no back edges (see Exercise 19.75). To implement DAG-specific algorithms, we implement task-specific client classes of our standard GRAPH ADT that assume they are processing digraphs with no cycles, leaving the client the responsibility of checking for cycles. This arrangement allows for the possibility that a DAG-processing algorithm produces useful results even when run on a digraph with cycles, which is sometimes the case. Sections 19.6 and 19.7 are devoted to implementations of classes for topological sorting (DAGts) and reachability in DAGs (DAGtc and DAGreach); Program 19.13 is an example of a client of such a class.

In a sense, DAGs are part tree, part graph. We can certainly take advantage of their special structure when we process them. For example, we can view a DAG almost as we view a tree, if we wish. Suppose that we want to traverse the vertices of the DAG D as though it were a tree rooted at w, so that, for example, the result of traversing the two DAGs in Figure 19.18 with this program would be the same. The following simple program accomplishes this task in the same manner as would a recursive tree traversal:

```
void traverseR(Dag D, int v)
  {
    visit(v);
    typename Dag::adjIterator A(D, v);
     for (int t = A.beg(); !A.end(); t = A.nxt())
       traverseR(D, t);
  }
```

We rarely use a full traversal of this kind, however, because we normally want to take advantage of the same economies that save space in a DAG to save time in traversing it (for example, by marking visited nodes in a normal DFS). The same idea applies to a *search*, where we make a recursive call for only one link incident on each vertex. In such an algorithm, the search cost will be the same for the DAG and the tree, but the DAG uses far less space.

Because they provide a compact way to represent trees that have identical subtrees, we often use DAGs instead of trees when we represent computational abstractions. In the context of algorithm design, the distinction between the DAG representation and the tree representation of a program in execution is the essential distinction behind dynamic programming (see, for example, Figure 19.18 and Exercise 19.78). DAGs are also widely used in compilers as intermediate representations of arithmetic expressions and programs (see, for example, Figure 19.19) and in circuit-design systems as intermediate representations of combinational circuits.

Along these lines, an important example that has many applications arises when we consider binary trees. We can apply the same restriction to DAGs that we applied to trees to define binary trees.

Definition 19.6 *A **binary DAG** is a directed acyclic graph with two edges leaving each node, identified as the left edge and the right edge, either or both of which may be null.*

The distinction between a binary DAG and a binary tree is that in the binary DAG we can have more than one link pointing to a node. As did our definition for binary trees, this definition models a natural representation, where each node is a structure with a left link and a right

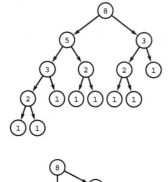

**Figure 19.18
DAG model of Fibonacci
computation**

The tree at the top shows the dependence of computing each Fibonacci number on computing its two predecessors. The DAG at the bottom shows the same dependence with only a fraction of the nodes.

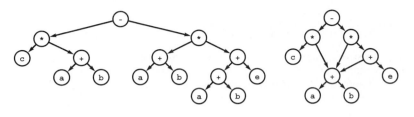

Figure 19.19
DAG representation of an arithmetic expression

Both of these DAGs are representations of the arithmetic expression
(c*(a+b))-((a+b))*((a+b)+e)).
In the binary parse tree at left, leaf nodes represent operands and internal nodes each represent operators to be applied to the expressions represented by their two subtrees (see Figure 5.31). The DAG at right is a more compact representation of the same tree. More important, we can compute the value of the expression in time proportional to the size of the DAG, which is typically significantly less than the size of the tree (see Exercises 19.112 and 19.113).

link that point to other nodes (or are null), subject to only the global restriction that no directed cycles are allowed. Binary DAGs are significant because they provide a compact way to represent binary trees in certain applications. For example, we can compress an existence trie into a binary DAG without changing the search implementation, as shown Figure 19.20 and Program 19.5.

An equivalent application is to view the trie keys as corresponding to rows in the truth table of a Boolean function for which the function is true (see Exercises 19.84 through 19.87). The binary DAG is a model for an economical circuit that computes the function. In this application, binary DAGs are known as *binary decision diagrams (BDD)s.*

Motivated by these applications, we turn, in the next two sections, to the study of DAG-processing algorithms. Not only do these algorithms lead to efficient and useful DAG ADT function implementations, but also they provide insight into the difficulty of processing digraphs. As we shall see, even though DAGs would seem to be substantially simpler structures than general digraphs, some basic problems are apparently no easier to solve.

Exercises

▷ **19.75** Implement a DFS class for use by clients for verifying that a DAG has no cycles.

○ **19.76** Write a program that generates random DAGs by generating random digraphs, doing a DFS from a random starting point, and throwing out the back edges (see Exercise 19.40). Run experiments to decide how to set parameters in your program to expect DAGs with E edges, given V.

▷ **19.77** How many nodes are there in the tree and in the DAG corresponding to Figure 19.18 for F_N, the Nth Fibonacci number?

19.78 Give the DAG corresponding to the dynamic-programming example for the knapsack model from Chapter 5 (see Figure 5.17).

○ **19.79** Develop an ADT for binary DAGs.

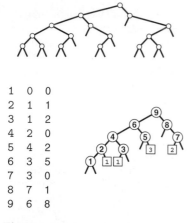

1	0	0
2	1	1
3	1	2
4	2	0
5	4	2
6	3	5
7	3	0
8	7	1
9	6	8

Figure 19.20
Binary tree compression

The table of nine pairs of integers at the bottom left is a compact representation of a binary DAG (bottom right) that is a compressed version of the binary tree structure at top. Node labels are not explicitly stored in the data structure: The table represents the eighteen edges 1–0, 1–0, 2–1, 2–1, 3–1, 3–2, and so forth, but designates a left edge and a right edge leaving each node (as in a binary tree) and leaves the source vertex for each edge implicit in the table index.

An algorithm that depends only upon the tree shape will work effectively on the DAG. For example, suppose that the tree is an existence trie for binary keys corresponding to the leaf nodes, so it represents the keys 0000, 0001, 0010, 0110, 1100, and 1101. A successful search for the key 1101 in the trie moves right, right, left, and right to end at a leaf node. In the DAG, the same search goes from 9 to 8 to 7 to 2 to 1.

Program 19.5 Representing a binary tree with a binary DAG

This code snippet is a postorder walk that constructs a compact representation of a binary DAG corresponding to a binary tree structure (see Chapter 12) by identifying common subtrees. It uses an indexing class like ST in Program 17.15 (modified to accept pairs of integer instead of string keys) to assign a unique integer to each distinct tree structure for use in representing the DAG as an vector of 2-integer structures (see Figure 19.20). The empty tree (null link) is assigned index 0, the single-node tree (node with two null links) is assigned index 1, and so forth.

The index corresponding to each subtree is computed recursively. Then a key is created such that any node with the same subtrees will have the same index and that index returned after the DAG's edge (subtree) links are filled.

```
int compressR(link h)
  { STx st;
    if (h == NULL) return 0;
    l = compressR(h->l);
    r = compressR(h->r);
    t = st.index(l, r);
    adj[t].l = l; adj[t].r = r;
    return t;
  }
```

• **19.80** Can every DAG be represented as a binary DAG (see Property 5.4)?

○ **19.81** Write a function that performs an inorder traversal of a single-source binary DAG. That is, the function should visit all vertices that can be reached via the left edge, then visit the source, then visit all the vertices that can be reached via the right edge.

▷ **19.82** In the style of Figure 19.20, give the existence trie and corresponding binary DAG for the keys 01001010 10010101 00100001 11101100 01010001 00100001 00000111 01010011 .

19.83 Implement an ADT based on building an existence trie from a set of 32-bit keys, compressing it as a binary DAG, then using that data structure to support existence queries.

○ **19.84** Draw the BDD for the truth table for the odd parity function of four variables, which is 1 if and only if the number of variables that have the value 1 is odd.

19.85 Write a function that takes a 2^n-bit truth table as argument and returns the corresponding BDD. For example, given the input 1110001000001100, your program should return a representation of the binary DAG in Figure 19.20.

19.86 Write a function that takes a 2^n-bit truth table as argument, computes every permutation of its argument variables, and, using your solution to Exercise 19.85, finds the permutation that leads to the smallest BDD.

• **19.87** Run empirical studies to determine the effectiveness of the strategy of Exercise 19.87 for various Boolean functions, both standard and randomly generated.

19.88 Write a program like Program 19.5 that supports common subexpression removal: Given a binary tree that represents an arithmetic expression, compute a binary DAG that represents the same expression with common subexpressions removed.

○ **19.89** Draw all the nonisomorphic DAGs with two, three, four, and five vertices.

•• **19.90** How many different DAGs are there with V vertices and E edges?

••• **19.91** How many different DAGs are there with V vertices and E edges, if we consider two DAGs to be different only if they are not isomorphic?

19.6 Topological Sorting

The goal of topological sorting is to be able to process the vertices of a DAG such that every vertex is processed before all the vertices to which it points. There are two natural ways to define this basic operation; they are essentially equivalent. Both tasks call for a permutation of the integers 0 through V-1, which we put in vertex-indexed vectors, as usual.

    Topological sort (relabel)   Given a DAG, relabel its vertices such that every directed edge points from a lower-numbered vertex to a higher-numbered one (see Figure 19.21).

    Topological sort (rearrange)   Given a DAG, rearrange its vertices on a horizontal line such that all the directed edges point from left to right (see Figure 19.22).

    As indicated in Figure 19.22, it is easy to establish that the relabeling and rearrangement permutations are inverses of one another: Given a rearrangement, we can obtain a relabeling by assigning the label 0 to the first vertex on the list, 1 to the second label on the list, and

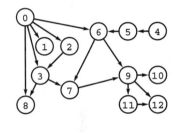

Figure 19.21
Topological sort (relabeling)

Given any DAG (top), topological sorting allows us to relabel its vertices so that every edge points from a lower-numbered vertex to a higher-numbered one (bottom). In this example, we relabel 4, 5, 7, and 8 to 7, 8, 5, and 4, respectively, as indicated in the array tsI. *There are many possible labelings that achieve the desired result.*

Figure 19.22
**Topological sorting (rear-
rangement)**

*This diagram shows another way to
look at the topological sort in Figure 19.21, where we specify a way
to rearrange the vertices, rather
than relabel them. When we place
the vertices in the order specified
in the array* ts, *from left to right,
then all directed edges point from
left to right. The inverse of the permutation* ts *is the permutation* tsI
*that specifies the relabeling de-
scribed in Figure 19.21.*

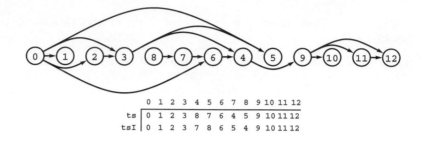

so forth. For example, if a vector ts has the vertices in topologically
sorted order, then the loop

```
for (i = 0; i < V; i++) tsI[ts[i]] = i;
```

defines a relabeling in the vertex-indexed vector tsI. Conversely, we
can get the rearrangement from the relabeling with the loop

```
for (i = 0; i < V; i++) ts[tsI[i]] = i;
```

which puts the vertex that would have label 0 first in the list, the vertex
that would have label 1 second in the list, and so forth. Most often,
we use the term *topological sort* to refer to the rearrangement version
of the problem. Note that ts is *not* a vertex-indexed vector.

In general, the vertex order produced by a topological sort is not
unique. For example,

8	7	0	1	2	3	6	4	9	10	11	12	5
0	1	2	3	8	6	4	9	10	11	12	5	7
0	2	3	8	6	4	7	5	9	10	1	11	12
8	0	7	6	2	3	4	9	5	1	11	12	10

are all topological sorts of the example DAG in Figure 19.6 (and there
are many others). In a scheduling application, this situation arises
whenever one task has no direct or indirect dependence on another and
thus they can be performed either before or after the other (or even in
parallel). The number of possible schedules grows exponentially with
the number of such pairs of tasks.

As we have noted, it is sometimes useful to interpret the edges in
a digraph the other way around: We say that an edge directed from
s to t means that vertex s "depends" on vertex t. For example, the
vertices might represent terms to be defined in a book, with an edge
from s to t if the definition of s uses t. In this case, it would be

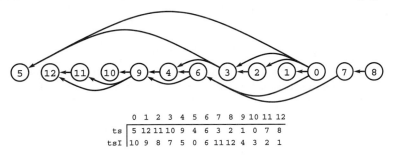

Figure 19.23
Reverse topological sort

In this reverse topological sort of our sample digraph, the edges all point from right to left. Numbering the vertices as specified by the inverse permutation tsI gives a graph where every edge points from a higher-numbered vertex to a lower-numbered vertex.

useful to find an ordering with the property that every term is defined before it is used in another definition. Using this ordering corresponds to positioning the vertices in a line such that edges all go from right to left—a *reverse topological sort*. Figure 19.23 illustrates a reverse topological sort of our sample DAG.

Now, it turns out that we have already seen an algorithm for reverse topological sorting: our standard recursive DFS! When the input graph is a DAG, a *postorder numbering* puts the vertices in reverse topological order. That is, we number each vertex as the final action of the recursive DFS function, as in the post vector in the DFS implementation in Program 19.2. As illustrated in Figure 19.24, using this numbering is equivalent to numbering the nodes in the DFS forest in postorder, and gives a topological sort: The vertex-indexed vector post gives the relabeling and its inverse the rearrangement depicted in Figure 19.23—a reverse topological sort of the DAG.

Property 19.11 *Postorder numbering in DFS yields a reverse topological sort for any DAG.*

Proof: Suppose that s and t are two vertices such that s appears before t in the postorder numbering even though there is a directed edge s-t in the graph. Since we are finished with the recursive DFS for s at the time that we assign s its number, we have examined, in particular, the edge s-t. But if s-t were a tree, down, or cross edge, the recursive DFS for t would be complete, and t would have a lower number; however, s-t cannot be a back edge because that would imply a cycle. This contradiction implies that such an edge s-t cannot exist. ∎

Thus, we can easily adapt a standard DFS to do a topological sort, as shown in Program 19.6. This implementation does a reverse

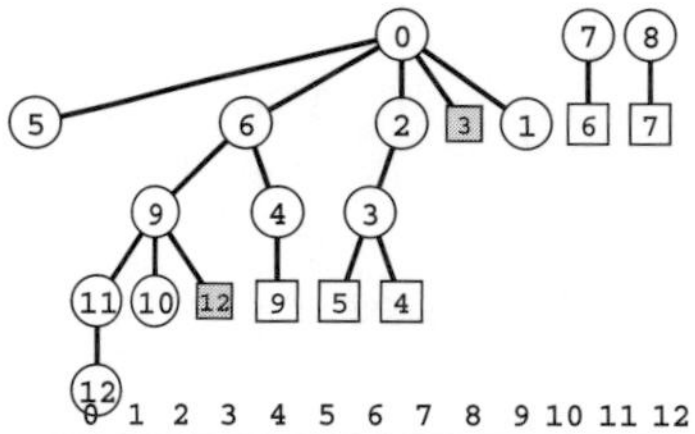

Program 19.6 Reverse topological sort

This DFS class computes postorder numbering of the DFS forest (a reverse topological sort). Clients can use a TS object to relabel a DAG's vertices so that every edge points from a higher-numbered vertex to a lower-numbered one or to arrange vertices such that the source vertex of every edge appears after the destination vertex (see Figure 19.23).

```
template <class Dag> class dagTS
  { const Dag &D;
    int cnt, tcnt;
    vector<int> pre, post, postI;
    void tsR(int v)
      {
        pre[v] = cnt++;
        typename Dag::adjIterator A(D, v);
        for (int t = A.beg(); !A.end(); t = A.nxt())
          if (pre[t] == -1) tsR(t);
        post[v] = tcnt; postI[tcnt++] = v;
      }
  public:
    dagTS(const Dag &D) : D(D), tcnt(0), cnt(0),
      pre(D.V(), -1), post(D.V(), -1), postI(D.V(), -1)
      { for (int v = 0; v < D.V(); v++)
          if (pre[v] == -1) tsR(v); }
    int operator[](int v) const { return postI[v]; }
    int relabel(int v) const { return post[v]; }
};
```

	1	2	3	4	5	6	7	8	9	10	11	12
post	10	9	8	7	5	0	6	11	12| 4	3	2	1
postI	5	12	11	10	9	4	6	3	2	1	0	7	8

Figure 19.24
DFS forest for a DAG

A DFS forest of a digraph has no back edges (edges to nodes with a higher postorder number) if and only if the digraph is a DAG. The non-tree edges in this DFS forest for the DAG of Figure 19.21 are either down edges (shaded squares) or cross edges (unshaded squares). The order in which vertices are encountered in a postorder walk of the forest, shown at the bottom, is a reverse topological sort (see Figure 19.23).

topological sort: It computes the postorder numbering permutation and its inverse, so that clients can relabel or rearrange vertices.

Computationally, the distinction between topological sort and reverse topological sort is not crucial. We can simply change the [] operator to return postI[G.V()-1 - v], or we can modify the implementation in one of the following ways:

- Do a reverse topological sort on the reverse of the given DAG.
- Rather than using it as an index for postorder numbering, push the vertex number on a stack as the final act of the recursive

---

Program 19.7 Topological sort

If we use this implementation of `tsR` in Program 19.6, the constructor computes a topological sort, not the reverse (for any DAG implementation that supports edge), because it replaces the reference to `edge(v, w)` in the DFS by `edge(w, v)`, thus processing the reverse graph (*see text*).

```
    void tsR(int v)
      {
        pre[v] = cnt++;
        for (int w = 0; w < D.V(); w++)
          if (D.edge(w, v))
            if (pre[w] == -1) tsR(w);
        post[v] = tcnt; postI[tcnt++] = v;
      }
```

---

procedure. After the search is complete, pop the vertices from the stack. They come off the stack in topological order.

- Number the vertices in reverse order (start at $V - 1$ and count down to 0). If desired, compute the inverse of the vertex numbering to get the topological order.

The proofs that these changes give a proper topological ordering are left for you to do as an exercise (see Exercise 19.97).

To implement the first of the options listed in the previous paragraph for sparse graphs (represented with adjacency lists), we would need to use Program 19.1 to compute the reverse graph. Doing so essentially doubles our space usage, which may thus become onerous for huge graphs. For dense graphs (represented with an adjacency matrix), as noted in Section 19.1, we can do DFS on the reverse without using any extra space or doing any extra work, simply by exchanging rows and columns when referring to the matrix, as illustrated in Program 19.7.

Next, we consider an alternative classical method for topological sorting that is more like breadth-first search (BFS) (see Section 18.7). It is based on the following property of DAGs.

Property 19.12 *Every DAG has at least one source and at least one sink.*

Figure 19.25
Topologically sorting a DAG by removing sources

Since it is a source (no edges point to it), 0 can appear first in a topological sort of this example graph (left, top). If we remove 0 (and all the edges that point from it to other vertices), then 1 and 2 become sources in the resulting DAG (left, second from top), *which we can then sort using the same algorithm.* This figure illustrates the operation of Program 19.8, which picks from among the sources (the shaded nodes in each diagram) using the FIFO discipline, though any of the sources could be chosen at each step. See Figure 19.26 for the contents of the data structures that control the specific choices that the algorithm makes. The result of the topological sort illustrated here is the node order 0 8 2 1 7 3 6 5 4 9 11 10 12.

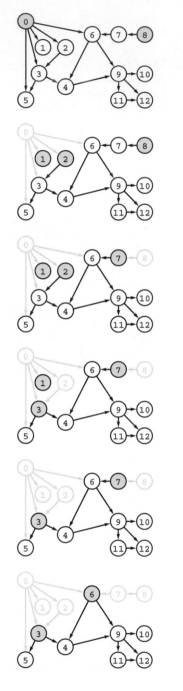

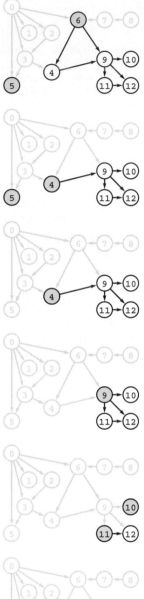

Proof: Suppose that we have a DAG that has no sinks. Then, starting at any vertex, we can build an arbitrarily long directed path by following any edge from that vertex to any other vertex (there is at least one edge, since there are no sinks), then following another edge from that vertex, and so on. But once we have been to $V + 1$ vertices, we must have seen a directed cycle, by the pigeonhole principle (see Property 19.6), which contradicts the assumption that we have a DAG. Therefore, every DAG has at least one sink. It follows that every DAG also has at least one source: its reverse's sink. ■

From this fact, we can derive a topological-sort algorithm: Label any source with the smallest unused label, then remove it and label the rest of the DAG, using the same algorithm. Figure 19.25 is a trace of this algorithm in operation for our sample DAG.

Implementing this algorithm efficiently is a classic exercise in data-structure design (*see reference section*). First, there may be multiple sources, so we need to maintain a queue to keep track of them (any generalized queue will do). Second, we need to identify the sources in the DAG that remains when we remove a source. We can accomplish this task by maintaining a vertex-indexed vector that keeps track of the indegree of each vertex. Vertices with indegree 0 are sources, so we can initialize the queue with one scan through the DAG (using DFS or any other method that examines all of the edges). Then, we perform the following operations until the source queue is empty:

- Remove a source from the queue and label it.
- Decrement the entries in the indegree vector corresponding to the destination vertex of each of the removed vertex's edges.
- If decrementing any entry causes it to become 0, insert the corresponding vertex onto the source queue.

Program 19.8 is an implementation of this method, using a FIFO queue, and Figure 19.26 illustrates its operation on our sample DAG, providing the details behind the dynamics of the example in Figure 19.25.

The source queue does not empty until every vertex in the DAG is labeled, because the subgraph induced by the vertices not yet labeled is always a DAG, and every DAG has at least one source. Indeed, we can use the algorithm to test whether a graph is a DAG by inferring that there must be a cycle in the subgraph induced by the vertices not

0	1	2	3	4	5	6	7	8	9	10	11	12			
0	1	1	2	2	2	2	1	0	2	1	1	2	0	8	
0	0	0	1	2	1	1	1	0	2	1	1	2	8	2	1
0	0	0	1	2	1	1	0	0	2	1	1	2	2	1	7
0	0	0	0	2	1	1	0	0	2	1	1	2	1	7	3
0	0	0	0	2	1	1	0	0	2	1	1	2	7	3	
0	0	0	0	2	1	0	0	0	2	1	1	2	3	6	
0	0	0	0	1	0	0	0	0	2	1	1	2	6	5	
0	0	0	0	0	0	0	0	0	1	1	1	2	5	4	
0	0	0	0	0	0	0	0	0	1	1	1	2	4		
0	0	0	0	0	0	0	0	0	0	1	1	2	9		
0	0	0	0	0	0	0	0	0	0	0	0	1	11	10	
0	0	0	0	0	0	0	0	0	0	0	0	0	10	12	
0	0	0	0	0	0	0	0	0	0	0	0	0	12		

Figure 19.26
Indegree table and queue contents

This sequence depicts the contents of the indegree table (left) *and the source queue* (right) *during the execution of Program 19.8 on the sample DAG corresponding to Figure 19.25. At any given point in time, the source queue contains the nodes with indegree 0. Reading from top to bottom, we remove the leftmost node from the source queue, decrement the indegree entry corresponding to every edge leaving that node, and add any vertices whose entries become 0 to the source queue. For example, the second line of the table reflects the result of removing 0 from the source queue, then (because the DAG has the edges 0–1, 0–2, 0–3, 0–5, and 0–6) decrementing the indegree entries corresponding to 1, 2, 3, 5, and 6 and adding 2 and 1 to the source queue (because decrementing made their indegree entries 0). Reading the leftmost entries in the source queue from top to bottom gives a topological ordering for the graph.*

Program 19.8 Source-queue–based topological sort

This class implements the same interface as does Programs 19.6 and 19.7. It maintains a queue of sources and uses a table that keeps track of the indegree of each vertex in the DAG induced by the vertices that have not been removed from the queue.

When we remove a source from the queue, we decrement the indegree entries corresponding to each of the vertices on its adjacency list (and put on the queue any vertices corresponding to entries that become 0). Vertices come off the queue in topologically sorted order.

```cpp
#include "QUEUE.cc"
template <class Dag> class dagTS
{ const Dag &D;
  vector<int> in, ts, tsI;
public:
  dagTS(const Dag &D) : D(D),
    in(D.V(), 0), ts(D.V(), -1), tsI(D.V(), -1)
  { QUEUE<int> Q;
    for (int v = 0; v < D.V(); v++)
      {
        typename Dag::adjIterator A(D, v);
        for (int t = A.beg(); !A.end(); t = A.nxt())
          in[t]++;
      }
    for (int v = 0; v < D.V(); v++)
      if (in[v] == 0) Q.put(v);
    for (int j = 0; !Q.empty(); j++)
      {
        ts[j] = Q.get(); tsI[ts[j]] = j;
        typename Dag::adjIterator A(D, ts[j]);
        for (int t = A.beg(); !A.end(); t = A.nxt())
          if (--in[t] == 0) Q.put(t);
      }
  }
  int operator[](int v) const { return ts[v]; }
  int relabel(int v) const { return tsI[v]; }
};
```

yet labeled if the queue empties before all the vertices are labeled (see Exercise 19.104).

Processing vertices in topologically sorted order is a basic technique in processing DAGs. A classic example is the problem of finding the length of the longest path in a DAG. Considering the vertices in reverse topologically sorted order, the length of the longest path originating at each vertex v is easy to compute: Add one to the maximum of the lengths of the longest paths originating at each of the vertices reachable by a single edge from v. The topological sort ensures that all those lengths are known when v is processed, and that no other paths from v will be found afterwards. For example, taking a left-to-right scan of the reverse topological sort shown in Figure 19.23, we can quickly compute the following table of lengths of the longest paths originating at each vertex in the sample graph in Figure 19.21.

```
5  12  11  10  9  4  6  3  2  1  0  7  8
0   0   1   0  2  3  4  4  5  0  6  5  6
```

For example, the 6 corresponding to 0 (third column from the right) says that there is a path of length 6 originating at 0, which we know because there is an edge 0-2, we previously found the length of the longest path from 2 to be 5, and no other edge from 0 leads to a node having a longer path.

Whenever we use topological sorting for such an application, we have several choices in developing an implementation:

- Use `DAGts` in a DAG ADT, then proceed through the vector it computes to process the vertices.
- Process the vertices after the recursive calls in a DFS.
- Process the vertices as they come off the queue in a source-queue–based topological sort.

All of these methods are used in DAG-processing implementations in the literature, and it is important to know that they are all equivalent. We will consider other topological-sort applications in Exercises 19.111 and 19.114 and in Sections 19.7 and 21.4.

Exercises

▷ **19.92** Write a function that checks whether or not a given permutation of a DAG's vertices is a proper topological sort of that DAG.

19.93 How many different topological sorts are there of the DAG that is depicted in Figure 19.6?

▷ **19.94**   Give the DFS forest and the reverse topological sort that results from doing a standard adjacency-lists DFS (with postorder numbering) of the DAG

3-7 1-4 7-8 0-5 5-2 3-8 2-9 0-6 4-9 2-6 6-4 4-3 2-3.

○ **19.95**   Give the DFS forest and the topological sort that results from building a standard adjacency-lists representation of the DAG

3-7 1-4 7-8 0-5 5-2 3-8 2-9 0-6 4-9 2-6 6-4 4-3 2-3,

then using Program 19.1 to build the reverse, then doing a standard adjacency-lists DFS with postorder numbering.

▷ **19.96**   Program 19.6 uses postorder numbering to do a reverse topological sort—why not use preorder numbering to do a topological sort? Give a three-vertex example that illustrates the reason.

● **19.97**   Prove the correctness of each of the three suggestions given in the text for modifying DFS with postorder numbering such that it computes a topological sort instead of a reverse topological sort.

▷ **19.98**   Give the DFS forest and the topological sort that results from doing a standard adjacency-matrix DFS with implicit reversal (and postorder numbering) of the DAG

3-7 1-4 7-8 0-5 5-2 3-8 2-9 0-6 4-9 2-6 6-4 4-3 2-3

(see Program 19.7).

● **19.99**   Given a DAG, does there exist a topological sort that cannot result from applying a DFS-based algorithm, no matter what order the vertices adjacent to each vertex are chosen? Prove your answer.

▷ **19.100**   Show, in the style of Figure 19.26, the process of topologically sorting the DAG

3-7 1-4 7-8 0-5 5-2 3-8 2-9 0-6 4-9 2-6 6-4 4-3 2-3

with the source-queue algorithm (Program 19.8).

▷ **19.101**   Give the topological sort that results if the data structure used in the example depicted in Figure 19.25 is a stack rather than a queue.

● **19.102**   Given a DAG, does there exist a topological sort that cannot result from applying the source-queue algorithm, no matter what queue discipline is used? Prove your answer.

19.103   Modify the source-queue topological-sort algorithm to use a generalized queue. Use your modified algorithm with a LIFO queue, a stack, and a randomized queue.

▷ **19.104**   Use Program 19.8 to provide an implementation for a class for verifying that a DAG has no cycles (see Exercise 19.75).

○ **19.105** Convert the source-queue topological-sort algorithm into a sink-queue algorithm for reverse topological sorting.

19.106 Write a program that generates all possible topological orderings of a given DAG, or, if the number of such orderings exceeds a bound taken as an argument, prints that number.

19.107 Write a program that converts any digraph with V vertices and E edges into a DAG by doing a DFS-based topological sort and changing the orientation of any back edge encountered. Prove that this strategy always produces a DAG.

●● **19.108** Write a program that produces each of the possible DAGs with V vertices and E edges with equal likelihood (see Exercise 17.70).

19.109 Give necessary and sufficient conditions for a DAG to have just one possible topologically sorted ordering of its vertices.

19.110 Run empirical tests to compare the topological-sort algorithms given in this section for various DAGs (see Exercise 19.2, Exercise 19.76, Exercise 19.107, and Exercise 19.108). Test your program as described in Exercise 19.11 (for low densities) and as described in Exercise 19.12 (for high densities).

▷ **19.111** Modify Program 19.8 so that it computes the number of different simple paths from any source to each vertex in a DAG.

○ **19.112** Write a class that evaluates DAGs that represent arithmetic expressions (see Figure 19.19). Use a vertex-indexed vector to hold values corresponding to each vertex. Assume that values corresponding to leaves have been established.

○ **19.113** Describe a family of arithmetic expressions with the property that the size of the expression tree is exponentially larger than the size of the corresponding DAG (so the running time of your program from Exercise 19.112 for the DAG is proportional to the logarithm of the running time for the tree).

○ **19.114** Develop a method for finding the longest simple directed path in a DAG, in time proportional to V. Use your method to implement a class for printing a Hamilton path in a given DAG, if one exists.

19.7 Reachability in DAGs

To conclude our study of DAGs, we consider the problem of computing the transitive closure of a DAG. Can we develop algorithms for DAGs that are more efficient than the algorithms for general digraphs that we considered in Section 19.3?

Any method for topological sorting can serve as the basis for a transitive-closure algorithm for DAGs, as follows: We proceed through

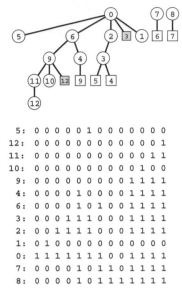

```
 5:  0 0 0 0 0 1 0 0 0 0 0 0 0
12:  0 0 0 0 0 0 0 0 0 0 0 0 1
11:  0 0 0 0 0 0 0 0 0 0 0 1 1
10:  0 0 0 0 0 0 0 0 0 0 1 0 0
 9:  0 0 0 0 0 0 0 0 0 1 1 1 1
 4:  0 0 0 0 1 0 0 0 0 0 1 1 1
 6:  0 0 0 0 1 0 1 0 0 1 1 1 1
 3:  0 0 0 1 1 1 0 0 0 1 1 1 1
 2:  0 0 1 1 1 1 0 0 0 1 1 1 1
 1:  0 1 0 0 0 0 0 0 0 0 0 0 0
 0:  1 1 1 1 1 1 1 0 0 1 1 1 1
 7:  0 0 0 0 1 0 1 1 0 1 1 1 1
 8:  0 0 0 0 1 0 1 1 1 1 1 1 1
```

Figure 19.27
Transitive closure of a DAG

This sequence of row vectors is the transitive closure of the DAG in Figure 19.21, with rows created in reverse topological order, computed as the last action in a recursive DFS function (see Program 19.9). Each row is the logical or *of the rows for adjacent vertices, which appear earlier in the list. For example, to compute the row for* 0 *we take the logical* or *of the rows for* 5, 2, 1, *and* 6 *(and put a 1 corresponding to* 0 *itself) because the edges* 0–5, 0–2, 0–1, *and* 0–6 *take us from* 0 *to any vertex that is reachable from any of those vertices. We can ignore down edges because they add no new information. For example, we ignore the edge from* 0 *to* 3 *because the vertices reachable from* 3 *are already accounted for in the row corresponding to* 2.

the vertices in reverse topological order, computing the reachability vector for each vertex (its row in the transitive-closure matrix) from the rows corresponding to its adjacent vertices. The reverse topological sort ensures that all those rows have already been computed. In total, we check each of the V entries in the vector corresponding to the destination vertex of each of the E edges, for a total running time proportional to VE. Although it is simple to implement, this method is no more efficient for DAGs than for general digraphs.

When we use a standard DFS for the topological sort (see Program 19.7), we can improve performance for some DAGs, as shown in Program 19.9. Since there are no cycles in a DAG, there are no back edges in any DFS. More important, both cross edges and down edges point to nodes for which the DFS has completed. To take advantage of this fact, we develop a recursive function to compute all vertices reachable from a given start vertex, but (as usual in DFS) we make no recursive calls for vertices for which the reachable set has already been computed. In this case, the reachable vertices are represented by a row in the transitive closure, and the recursive function takes the logical *or* of all the rows associated with its adjacent edges. For tree edges, we do a recursive call to compute the row; for cross edges, we can skip the recursive call because we know that the row has been computed by a previous recursive call; for down edges, we can skip the whole computation because any reachable nodes that it would add have already been accounted for in the set of reachable nodes for the destination vertex (lower and earlier in the DFS tree).

Using this version of DFS might be characterized as using dynamic programming to compute the transitive closure because we make use of results that have already been computed (and saved in the adjacency matrix rows corresponding to previously-processed vertices) to avoid making unnecessary recursive calls. Figure 19.27 illustrates the computation of the transitive closure for the sample DAG in Figure 19.6.

Property 19.13 *With dynamic programming and DFS, we can support constant query time for the abstract transitive closure of a DAG with space proportional to V^2 and time proportional to $V^2 + VX$ for preprocessing (computing the transitive closure), where X is the number of cross edges in the DFS forest.*

Program 19.9 Transitive closure of a DAG

The constructor in this class computes the transitive closure of a DAG with a single DFS. It recursively computes the reachable vertices from each vertex from the reachable vertices of its children in the DFS tree.

```
template <class tcDag, class Dag> class dagTC
{ tcDag T; const Dag &D;
  int cnt;
  vector<int> pre;
  void tcR(int w)
  {
    pre[w] = cnt++;
    typename Dag::adjIterator A(D, w);
    for (int t = A.beg(); !A.end(); t = A.nxt())
      {
        T.insert(Edge(w, t));
        if (pre[t] > pre[w]) continue;
        if (pre[t] == -1) tcR(t);
        for (int i = 0; i < T.V(); i++)
          if (T.edge(t, i)) T.insert(Edge(w, i));
      }
  }
  public:
    dagTC(const Dag &D) : D(D), cnt(0),
      pre(D.V(), -1), T(D.V(), true)
      { for (int v = 0; v < D.V(); v++)
          if (pre[v] == -1) tcR(v); }
    bool reachable(int v, int w) const
      { return T.edge(v, w); }
};
```

Proof: The proof is immediate by induction from the recursive function in Program 19.9. We visit the vertices in reverse topological order. Every edge points to a vertex for which we have already computed all reachable vertices, and we can therefore compute the set of reachable vertices of any vertex by merging together the sets of reachable vertices associated with the destination vertex of each edge. Taking the logical *or* of the specified rows in the adjacency matrix accomplishes this merge. We access a row of size V for each tree edge and each cross edge. There are no back edges, and we can ignore down edges because we accounted for any vertices they reach when we processed any ancestors of both nodes earlier in the search. ■

If our DAG has no down edges (see Exercise 19.42), the running time of Program 19.9 is proportional to VE and represents no improvement over the transitive-closure algorithms that we examined for general digraphs in Section 19.3 (such as, for example, Program 19.4) or the approach based on topological sorting that is described at the beginning of this section. On the other hand, if the number of down edges is large (or, equivalently, the number of cross edges is small), Program 19.9 will be significantly faster than these methods.

The problem of finding an optimal algorithm (one that is guaranteed to finish in time proportional to V^2) for computing the transitive closure of dense DAGs is still unsolved. The best known worst-case performance bound is VE. However, we are certainly better off using an algorithm that runs faster for a large class of DAGs, such as Program 19.9, than we are using one that always runs in time proportional to VE, such as Program 19.4. As we see in Section 19.9, this performance improvement for DAGs has direct implications for our ability to compute the transitive closure of general digraphs as well.

Exercises

○ **19.115** Show, in the style of Figure 19.27, the reachability vectors that result when we use Program 19.9 to compute the transitive closure of the DAG

    3-7 1-4 7-8 0-5 5-2 3-8 2-9 0-6 4-9 2-6 6-4 4-3 2-3.

○ **19.116** Develop a version of Program 19.9 that uses a representation of the transitive closure that does not support edge testing and that runs in time proportional to $V^2 + \sum_e v(e)$, where the sum is over all edges in the DAG and $v(e)$ is the number of vertices reachable from the destination vertex of edge e. This cost will be significantly less than VE for some sparse DAGs (see Exercise 19.65).

○ **19.117** Implement an abstract–transitive-closure class for DAGs that uses extra space at most proportional to V (and is suitable for huge DAGs). Use topological sorting to provide quick response when the vertices are not connected, and use a source-queue implementation to return the length of the path when they are connected.

○ **19.118** Develop a transitive-closure implementation based on a sink-queue–based reverse topological sort (see Exercise 19.105).

○ **19.119** Does your solution to Exercise 19.118 require that you examine all edges in the DAG, or are there edges that can be ignored, such as the down edges in DFS? Give an example that requires examination of all edges, or characterize the edges that can be skipped.

19.8 Strong Components in Digraphs

Undirected graphs and DAGs are both simpler structures than general digraphs because of the structural symmetry that characterizes the reachability relationships among the vertices: In an undirected graph, if there is a path from s to t, then we know that there is also a path from t to s; in a DAG, if there is a directed path from s to t, then we know that there is *no* directed path from t to s. For general digraphs, knowing that t is reachable from s gives no information about whether s is reachable from t.

To understand the structure of digraphs, we consider *strong connectivity*, which has the symmetry that we seek. If s and t are strongly connected (each reachable from the other), then, by definition, so are t and s. As discussed in Section 19.1, this symmetry implies that the vertices of the digraph divide into *strong components*, which consist of mutually reachable vertices. In this section, we discuss three algorithms for finding the strong components in a digraph.

We use the same interface as for connectivity in our general graph-searching algorithms for undirected graphs (see Program 18.4). The goal of our algorithms is to assign component numbers to each vertex in a vertex-indexed vector, using the labels 0, 1, ..., for the strong components. The highest number assigned is one less than the number of strong components, and we can use the component numbers to provide a constant-time test of whether two vertices are in the same strong component.

A brute-force algorithm to solve the problem is simple to develop. Using an abstract–transitive-closure ADT, check every pair of vertices s and t to see whether t is reachable from s and s is reachable from t. Define an undirected graph with an edge for each such pair: The connected components of that graph are the strong components of the digraph. This algorithm is simple to describe and to implement, and its running time is dominated by the costs of the abstract–transitive-closure implementation, as described by, say, Property 19.10.

The algorithms that we consider in this section are triumphs of modern algorithm design that can find the strong components of any graph in *linear* time, a factor of V faster than the brute-force algorithm. For 100 vertices, these algorithms will be 100 times faster than the brute-force algorithm; for 1000 vertices, they will be 1000 times faster; and we can contemplate addressing problems involving billions of vertices. This problem is a prime example of the power of good algorithm design, one which has motivated many people to study graph algorithms closely. Where else might we contemplate reducing resource usage by a factor of 1 billion or more with an elegant solution to an important practical problem?

The history of this problem is instructive (*see reference section*). In the 1950s and 1960s, mathematicians and computer scientists began to study graph algorithms in earnest in a context where the analysis of algorithms itself was under development as a field of study. The broad variety of graph algorithms to be considered—coupled with ongoing developments in computer systems, languages, and our understanding of performing computations efficiently—left many difficult problems unsolved. As computer scientists began to understand many of the basic principles of the analysis of algorithms, they began to understand which graph problems could be solved efficiently and which could not and then to develop increasingly efficient algorithms for the former set of problems. Indeed, R. Tarjan introduced linear-time algorithms for strong connectivity and other graph problems in 1972, the same year that R. Karp documented the intractability of the traveling-salesperson problem and many other graph problems. Tarjan's algorithm has been a staple of advanced courses in the analysis of algorithms for many years because it solves an important practical problem using simple data structures. In the 1980s, R. Kosaraju took a fresh look at the problem and developed a new solution; people later realized that a paper that describes essentially the same method appeared in the Russian scientific literature in 1972. Then, in 1999, H. Gabow found a simple implementation of one of the first approaches tried in the 1960s, giving a third linear-time algorithm for this problem.

The point of this story is not just that difficult graph-processing problems can have simple solutions, but also that the abstractions that we are using (DFS and adjacency lists) are more powerful than we might realize. As we become more accustomed to using these and

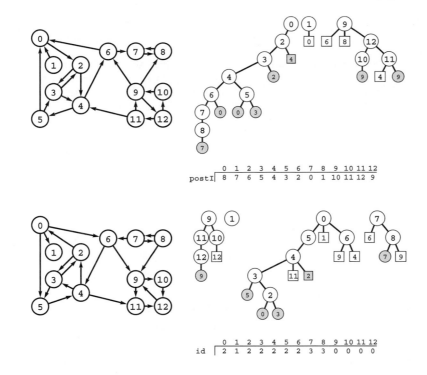

Figure 19.28
Computing strong compo-
nents (Kosaraju's algo-
rithm)

*To compute the strong components
of the digraph at the lower left, we
first do a DFS of its reverse (top
left), computing a postorder vector that gives the vertex indices in
the order in which the recursive
DFS completed (top). This order
is equivalent to a postorder walk
of the DFS forest (top right). Then
we use the reverse of that order to
do a DFS of the original digraph
(bottom). First we check all nodes
reachable from 9, then we scan
from right to left through the vector to find that 1 is the rightmost
unvisited vertex, so we do the recursive call for 1, and so forth. The
trees in the DFS forest that results
from this process define the strong
components: All vertices in each
tree have the same value in the
vertex-indexed* id *vector (bottom).*

similar tools, we should not be surprised to discover simple solutions
to other important graph problems as well. Researchers still seek concise implementations like these for numerous other important graph
algorithms; many such algorithms remain to be discovered.

Kosaraju's method is simple to explain and implement. To find
the strong components of a graph, first run DFS on its reverse, computing the permutation of vertices defined by the postorder numbering.
(This process constitutes a topological sort if the digraph is a DAG.)
Then, run DFS again on the graph, but to find the next vertex to search
(when calling the recursive search function, both at the outset and each
time that the recursive search function returns to the top-level search
function), *use the unvisited vertex with the highest postorder number.*

The magic of the algorithm is that, when the unvisited vertices
are checked according to the topological sort in this way, the trees in
the DFS forest define the strong components just as trees in a DFS
forest define the connected components in undirected graphs—two
vertices are in the same strong component if and only if they belong

Program 19.10 Strong components (Kosaraju's algorithm)

Clients can use objects of this class to find the number of strong components of a digraph (count) and to do strong-connectivity tests (stronglyconnected). The SC constructor first builds the reverse digraph and does a DFS to compute a postorder numbering. Next, it does a DFS of the original digraph, using the reverse of the postorder from the first DFS in the search loop that calls the recursive function. Each recursive call in the second DFS visits all the vertices in a strong component.

```
template <class Graph> class SC
{ const Graph &G;
  int cnt, scnt;
  vector<int> postI, postR, id;
  void dfsR(const Graph &G, int w)
  {
    id[w] = scnt;
    typename Graph::adjIterator A(G, w);
    for (int t = A.beg(); !A.end(); t = A.nxt())
      if (id[t] == -1) dfsR(G, t);
    postI[cnt++] = w;
  }
public:
  SC(const Graph &G) : G(G), cnt(0), scnt(0),
    postI(G.V()), postR(G.V()), id(G.V(), -1)
    { Graph R(G.V(), true);
      reverse(G, R);
      for (int v = 0; v < R.V(); v++)
        if (id[v] == -1) dfsR(R, v);
      postR = postI; cnt = scnt = 0;
      id.assign(G.V(), -1);
      for (int v = G.V()-1; v >= 0; v--)
        if (id[postR[v]] == -1)
          { dfsR(G, postR[v]); scnt++; }
    }
  int count() const { return scnt; }
  bool stronglyreachable(int v, int w) const
    { return id[v] == id[w]; }
};
```

to the same tree in this forest. Figure 19.28 illustrates this fact for our example, and we will prove it in a moment. Therefore, we can assign component numbers as we did for undirected graphs, incrementing the component number each time that the recursive function returns to the top-level search function. Program 19.10 is a full implementation of the method.

Property 19.14 *Kosaraju's method finds the strong components of a graph in linear time and space.*

Proof: The method consists of minor modifications to two DFS procedures, so the running time is certainly proportional to V^2 for dense graphs and $V + E$ for sparse graphs (using an adjacency-lists representation), as usual. To prove that it computes the strong components properly, we have to prove that two vertices s and t are in the same tree in the DFS forest for the second search if and only if they are mutually reachable.

If s and t are mutually reachable, they certainly will be in the same DFS tree because when the first of the two is visited, the second is unvisited and is reachable from the first and so will be visited before the recursive call for the root terminates.

To prove the converse, we assume that s and t are in the same tree, and let r be the root of the tree. The fact that s is reachable from r (through a directed path of tree edges) implies that there is a directed path from s to r in the reverse digraph. Now, the key to the proof is that there must also be a path from r to s in the reverse digraph because r has a higher postorder number than s (since r was chosen first in the second DFS at a time when both were unvisited) and there is a path from s to r: If there were no path from r to s, then the path from s to r in the reverse would leave s with a higher postorder number. Therefore, there are directed paths from s to r and from r to s in the digraph and its reverse: s and r are strongly connected. The same argument proves that t and r are strongly connected, and therefore s and t are strongly connected. ∎

The implementation for Kosaraju's algorithm for the adjacency-matrix digraph representation is even simpler than Program 19.10 because we do not need to compute the reverse explicitly; that problem is left as an exercise (see Exercise 19.125).

Program 19.11 Strong components (Tarjan's algorithm)

This DFS class is another implementation of the same interface as Program 19.10. It uses a stack S to hold each vertex until determining that all the vertices down to a certain point at the top of the stack belong to the same strong component. The vertex-indexed vector low keeps track of the lowest preorder number reachable via a series of down links followed by one up link from each node (*see text*).

```
#include "STACK.cc"
template <class Graph> class SC
{ const Graph &G;
  STACK<int> S;
  int cnt, scnt;
  vector<int> pre, low, id;
  void scR(int w)
  { int t;
    int min = low[w] = pre[w] = cnt++;
    S.push(w);
    typename Graph::adjIterator A(G, w);
    for (t = A.beg(); !A.end(); t = A.nxt())
      {
        if (pre[t] == -1) scR(t);
        if (low[t] < min) min = low[t];
      }
    if (min < low[w]) { low[w] = min; return; }
    do
      { id[t = S.pop()] = scnt; low[t] = G.V(); }
    while (t != w);
    scnt++;
  }
public:
  SC(const Graph &G) : G(G), cnt(0), scnt(0),
    pre(G.V(), -1), low(G.V()), id(G.V())
    { for (int v = 0; v < G.V(); v++)
        if (pre[v] == -1) scR(v); }
  int count() const { return scnt; }
  bool stronglyreachable(int v, int w) const
    { return id[v] == id[w]; }
};
```

Program 19.10 represents an optimal solution to the strong-connectivity problem that is analogous to our solutions for connectivity in Chapter 18. In Section 19.9, we examine the task of extending this solution to compute the transitive closure and to solve the reachability (abstract–transitive-closure) problem for digraphs.

First, however, we consider Tarjan's algorithm and Gabow's algorithm—ingenious methods that require only a few simple modifications to our basic DFS procedure. They are preferable to Kosaraju's algorithm because they use only one pass through the graph and because they do not require computation of the reverse for sparse graphs.

Tarjan's algorithm is similar to the program that we studied in Chapter 17 for finding bridges in undirected graphs (see Program 18.7). The method is based on two observations that we have already made in other contexts. First, we consider the vertices in reverse topological order so that when we reach the end of the recursive function for a vertex we know we will not encounter any more vertices in the same strong component (because all the vertices that can be reached from that vertex have been processed). Second, the back links in the tree provide a second path from one vertex to another and bind together the strong components.

The recursive DFS function uses the same computation as Program 18.7 to find the highest vertex reachable (via a back edge) from any descendant of each vertex. It also uses a vertex-indexed vector to keep track of the strong components and a stack to keep track of the current search path. It pushes the vertex names onto a stack on entry to the recursive function, then pops them and assigns component numbers after visiting the final member of each strong component. The algorithm is based on our ability to identify this moment with a simple test (based on keeping track of the highest ancestor reachable via one up link from all descendants of each node) at the end of the recursive procedure that tells us that all vertices encountered since entry (except those already assigned to a component) belong to the same strong component.

The implementation in Program 19.11 is a succinct and complete description of the algorithm that fills in the details missing from the brief sketch just given. Figure 19.29 illustrates the operation of the algorithm for our sample digraph from Figure 19.1.

Figure 19.29
Computing strong components (Tarjan and Gabow algorithms)

Tarjan's algorithm is based on a recursive DFS, augmented to push vertices on a stack. It computes a component index for each vertex in a vertex-indexed vector id, *using auxiliary vectors* pre *and* low *(center). The DFS tree for our sample graph is shown at the top and an edge trace at the bottom left. In the center at the bottom is the main stack: We push vertices reached by tree edges. Using a DFS to consider the vertices in reverse topological order, we compute, for each* v, *the highest point reachable via a back link from an ancestor (*low[v]*). When a vertex* v *has* pre[v] = low[v] *(vertices 11, 1, 0, and 7 here) we pop it and all the vertices above it (shaded) and assign them all the next component number.*

In Gabow's algorithm, we push vertices on the main stack, just as in Tarjan's algorithm, but we also keep a second stack (bottom right) with vertices on the search path that are known to be in different strong components, by popping all vertices after the destination of each back edge. When we complete a vertex v *with* v *at the top of this second stack (shaded), we know that all vertices above* v *on the main stack are in the same strong component.*

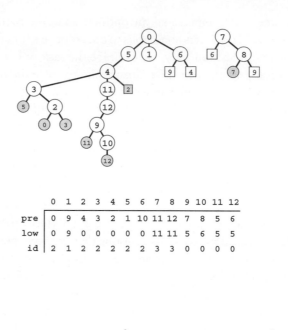

	0	1	2	3	4	5	6	7	8	9	10	11	12
pre	0	9	4	3	2	1	10	11	12	7	8	5	6
low	0	9	0	0	0	0	0	11	11	5	6	5	5
id	2	1	2	2	2	2	2	3	3	0	0	0	0

```
0-0                         0                        0
  0-5                       0 5                      0 5
    5-4                     0 5 4                    0 5 4
      4-3                   0 5 4 3                  0 5 4 3
        3-5                 0 5 4 3                  0 5
        3-2                 0 5 4 3 2                0 5 2
          2-0               0 5 4 3 2                0
          2-3               0 5 4 3 2                0
      4-11                  0 5 4 3 2 11             0 11
        11-12               0 5 4 3 2 11 12          0 11 12
          12-9              0 5 4 3 2 11 12 9        0 11 12 9
            9-11            0 5 4 3 2 11 12 9        0 11
            9-10            0 5 4 3 2 11 12 9 10     0 11 10
              10-12         0 5 4 3 2 11 12 9 10     0 11
        11                  0 5 4 3 2                0
      4-2                   0 5 4 3 2                0
    0-1                     0 5 4 3 2 1              0 1
    1                       0 5 4 3 2                0
  0-6                       0 5 4 3 2 6              0 6
    6-9                     0 5 4 3 2 6              0 9
    6-4                     0 5 4 3 2 6              0
0
7-7                         7                        7
  7-6                       7                        7
  7-8                       7 8                      7 8
    8-7                     7 8                      7
    8-9                     7 8                      7
7
```

Property 19.15 *Tarjan's algorithm finds the strong components of a digraph in linear time.*

Proof sketch: If a vertex s has no descendants or up links in the DFS tree, or if it has a descendant in the DFS tree with an up link that points to s and no descendants with up links that point higher up in the tree, then it and all its descendants (except those vertices that satisfy the same property and their descendants) constitute a strong component. To establish this fact, we note that every descendant t of s that does not satisfy the stated property has some descendant that has an up link pointing higher than t in the tree. There is a path from s to t down through the tree and we can find a path from t to s as follows: Go down from t to the vertex with the up link that reaches past t, then continue the same process from that vertex until reaching s.

As usual, the method is linear time because it consists of adding a few constant-time operations to a standard DFS. ∎

In 1999 Gabow discovered the version of Tarjan's algorithm in Program 19.12. The algorithm maintains the same stack of vertices in the same way as does Tarjan's algorithm, but it uses a second stack (instead of a vertex-indexed vector of preorder numbers) to decide when to pop all the vertices in each strong component from the main stack. The second stack contains vertices on the search path. When a back edge shows that a sequence of such vertices all belong to the same strong component, we pop that stack to leave only the destination vertex of the back edge, which is nearer the root of the tree than are any of the other vertices. After processing all the edges for each vertex (making recursive calls for the tree edges, popping the path stack for the back edges, and ignoring the down edges), we check to see whether the current vertex is at the top of the path stack. If it is, it and all the vertices above it on the main stack make a strong component, and we pop them and assign the next strong component number to them, as we did in Tarjan's algorithm.

The example in Figure 19.29 also shows the contents of this second stack. Thus, this figure also illustrates the operation of Gabow's algorithm.

Property 19.16 *Gabow's algorithm finds the strong components of a digraph in linear time.*

> ### Program 19.12 Strong components (Gabow's algorithm)
>
> This alternate implementation of the recursive member function in Program 19.11 uses a second stack path instead of the vertex-indexed vector low to decide when to pop the vertices in each strong component from the main stack (*see text*).
>
> ```cpp
> void scR(int w)
> { int v;
>   pre[w] = cnt++;
>   S.push(w); path.push(w);
>   typename Graph::adjIterator A(G, w);
>   for (int t = A.beg(); !A.end(); t = A.nxt())
>     if (pre[t] == -1) scR(t);
>     else if (id[t] == -1)
>       while (pre[path.top()] > pre[t]) path.pop();
>   if (path.top() == w) path.pop(); else return;
>   do { id[v = S.pop()] = scnt; } while (v != w);
>   scnt++;
> }
> ```

Formalizing the argument just outlined and proving the relationship between the stack contents that it depends upon is an instructive exercise for mathematically inclined readers (see Exercise 19.132). As usual, the method is linear time because it consists of adding a few constant-time operations to a standard DFS. ∎

The strong-components algorithms that we have considered in this section are all ingenious and are deceptively simple. We have considered all three because they are testimony to the power of fundamental data structures and carefully crafted recursive programs. From a practical standpoint, the running time of all the algorithms is proportional to the number of edges in the digraph, and performance differences are likely to be dependent upon implementation details. For example, pushdown-stack ADT operations constitute the inner loop of Tarjan's and Gabow's algorithm. Our implementations use the bare-bones stack class implementations of Chapter 4; implementations that use STL stacks, which do error-checking and carry other overhead, may be slower. The implementation of Kosaraju's algorithm is perhaps the simplest of the three, but it suffers the slight disadvantage (for sparse digraphs) of requiring three passes through the edges (one to make the reverse and two DFS passes).

Next, we consider a key application of computing strong components: building an efficient reachability (abstract–transitive-closure) ADT for digraphs.

Exercises

▷ **19.120** Describe what happens when you use Kosaraju's algorithm to find the strong components of a DAG.

▷ **19.121** Describe what happens when you use Kosaraju's algorithm to find the strong components of a digraph that consists of a single cycle.

•• **19.122** Can we avoid computing the reverse of the digraph in the adjacency-lists version of Kosaraju's method (Program 19.10) by using one of the three techniques mentioned in Section 19.4 for avoiding the reverse computation when doing a topological sort? For each technique, give either a proof that it works or a counterexample that shows that it does not work.

○ **19.123** Show, in the style of Figure 19.28, the DFS forests and the contents of the auxiliary vertex-indexed vectors that result when you use Kosaraju's algorithm to compute the strong components of the reverse of the digraph in Figure 19.5. (You should have the same strong components.)

19.124 Show, in the style of Figure 19.28, the DFS forests and the contents of the auxiliary vertex-indexed vectors that result when you use Kosaraju's algorithm to compute the strong components of the digraph

3-7 1-4 7-8 0-5 5-2 3-8 2-9 0-6 4-9 2-6 6-4.

○ **19.125** Implement Kosaraju's algorithm for finding the strong components of a digraph for a digraph representation that suports `edge` existence testing. Do not explicitly compute the reverse. *Hint*: Consider using two different recursive DFS functions.

▷ **19.126** Describe what happens when you use Tarjan's algorithm to find the strong components of a DAG.

▷ **19.127** Describe what happens when you use Tarjan's algorithm to find the strong components of a digraph that consists of a single cycle.

○ **19.128** Show, in the style of Figure 19.29, the DFS forest, stack contents during the execution of the algorithm, and the final contents of the auxiliary vertex-indexed vectors that result when you use Tarjan's algorithm to compute the strong components of the reverse of the digraph in Figure 19.5. (You should have the same strong components.)

19.129 Show, in the style of Figure 19.29, the DFS forest, stack contents during the execution of the algorithm, and the final contents of the auxiliary vertex-indexed vectors that result when you use Tarjan's algorithm to compute the strong components of the digraph

        3-7 1-4 7-8 0-5 5-2 3-8 2-9 0-6 4-9 2-6 6-4.

○ **19.130** Modify the implementations of Tarjan's algorithm in Program 19.11 and of Gabow's algorithm in Program 19.12 such that they use sentinel values to avoid the need to check explicitly for cross links.

19.131 Show, in the style of Figure 19.29, the DFS forest, contents of both stacks during the execution of the algorithm, and the final contents of the auxiliary vertex-indexed vectors that result when you use Gabow's algorithm to compute the strong components of the digraph

        3-7 1-4 7-8 0-5 5-2 3-8 2-9 0-6 4-9 2-6 6-4.

● **19.132** Give a full proof of Property 19.16.

○ **19.133** Develop a version of Gabow's algorithm that finds bridges and edge-connected components in undirected graphs.

● **19.134** Develop a version of Gabow's algorithm that finds articulation points and biconnected components in undirected graphs.

19.135 Develop a table in the spirit of Table 18.1 to study strong connectivity in random digraphs (see Table 19.2). Let S be the set of vertices in the largest strong component. Keep track of the size of S and study the percentages of edges in the following four classes: those connecting two vertices in S, those pointing out of S, those pointing in to S, those connecting two vertices not in S.

19.136 Run empirical tests to compare the brute-force method for computing strong components described at the beginning of this section, Kosaraju's algorithm, Tarjan's algorithm, and Gabow's algorithm, for various types of digraphs (see Exercises 19.11–18).

●●● **19.137** Develop a linear-time algorithm for *strong 2-connectivity*: Determine whether a strongly connected digraph has the property that it remains strongly connected after removing any vertex (and all its incident edges).

19.9 Transitive Closure Revisited

By putting together the results of the previous two sections, we can develop an algorithm to solve the abstract–transitive-closure problem for digraphs that—although it offers no improvement over a DFS-based solution in the worst case—will provide an optimal solution in many situations.

The algorithm is based on preprocessing the digraph to build the latter's kernel DAG (see Property 19.2). The algorithm is efficient if the kernel DAG is small relative to the size of the original digraph. If the digraph is a DAG (and therefore is identical to its kernel DAG) or if it has just a few small cycles, we will not see any significant cost savings; however, if the digraph has large cycles or large strong components (and therefore a small kernel DAG), we can develop optimal or near-optimal algorithms. For clarity, we assume the kernel DAG to be sufficiently small that we can afford an adjacency-matrix representation, although the basic idea is still effective for larger kernel DAGs.

To implement the abstract transitive closure, we preprocess the digraph as follows:

- Find its strong components
- Build its kernel DAG
- Compute the transitive closure of the kernel DAG

We can use Kosaraju's, Tarjan's, or Gabow's algorithm to find the strong components; a single pass through the edges to build the kernel DAG (as described in the next paragraph); and DFS (Program 19.9) to compute its transitive closure. After this preprocessing, we can immediately access the information necessary to determine reachability.

Once we have a vertex-indexed vector with the strong components of a digraph, building an adjacency-matrix representation of its kernel DAG is a simple matter. The vertices of the DAG are the component numbers in the digraph. For each edge s-t in the original digraph, we simply set `D->adj[sc[s]][sc[t]]` to 1. We would have to cope with duplicate edges in the kernel DAG if we were using an adjacency-lists representation—in an adjacency matrix, duplicate edges simply correspond to setting to 1 a matrix entry that has already been set to 1. This small point is significant because the number of duplicate edges is potentially huge (relative to the size of the kernel DAG) in this application.

Property 19.17 *Given two vertices s and t in a digraph D, let $sc(s)$ and $sc(t)$, respectively, be their corresponding vertices in D's kernel DAG K. Then, t is reachable from s in D if and only if $sc(t)$ is reachable from $sc(s)$ in K.*

This simple fact follows from the definitions. In particular, this property assumes the convention that a vertex is reachable from itself (all

Program 19.13 Strong-component–based transitive closure

This class implements the (abstract) transitive closure interface for digraphs by computing the strong components (using, say Program 19.11), kernel DAG, and the transitive closure of the kernel DAG (using Program 19.9). It assumes that class SC has a public member function ID that returns the strong component index (from the id array) for any given vertex. These numbers are the vertex indices in the kernel DAG. A vertex t is reachable from a vertex s in the digraph if and only if ID(t) is reachable from ID(s) in the kernel DAG.

```
template <class Graph> class TC
{ const Graph &G; DenseGRAPH *K;
  dagTC<DenseGRAPH, Graph> *Ktc;
  SC<Graph> *Gsc;
public:
  TC(const Graph &G) : G(G)
    {
      Gsc = new SC<Graph>(G);
      K = new DenseGRAPH(Gsc->count(), true);
      for (int v = 0; v < G.V(); v++)
      { typename Graph::adjIterator A(G, v);
        for (int t = A.beg(); !A.end(); t = A.nxt())
          K->insert(Edge(Gsc->ID(v), Gsc->ID(t))); }
      Ktc = new dagTC<DenseGRAPH, Graph>(*K);
    }
  ~TC() { delete K; delete Ktc; delete Gsc; }
  bool reachable(int v, int w)
  { return Ktc->reachable(Gsc->ID(v), Gsc->ID(w));}
};
```

vertices have self-loops). If the vertices are in the same strong component ($sc(s) = sc(t)$), then they are mutually reachable. ∎

We determine whether a given vertex t is reachable from a given vertex s in the same way as we built the kernel DAG: We use the vertex-indexed vector computed by the strong-components algorithm to get the component numbers $sc(s)$ and $sc(t)$ (in constant time), which we interpret as *abstract vertex* indices for the kernel DAG. Using them as vertex indices for the transitive closure of the kernel DAG tells us the result.

Program 19.13 is an implementation of the abstract–transitive-closure ADT that embodies these ideas. We use an *abstract*–transitive-closure interface for the kernel DAG as well. The running time of this implementation depends not just on the number of vertices and edges in the digraph but also on properties of its kernel DAG. For purposes of analysis, we suppose that we use an adjacency-matrix representation for the kernel DAG because we expect the kernel DAG to be small, if not also dense.

Property 19.18 *We can support constant query time for the abstract transitive closure of a digraph with space proportional to $V + v^2$ and time proportional to $E + v^2 + vx$ for preprocessing (computing the transitive closure), where v is the number of vertices in the kernel DAG and x is the number of cross edges in its DFS forest.*

Proof: Immediate from Property 19.13. ∎

If the digraph is a DAG, then the strong-components computation provides no new information, and this algorithm is the same as Program 19.9; in general digraphs that have cycles, however, this algorithm is likely to be significantly faster than Warshall's algorithm or the DFS-based solution. For example, Property 19.18 immediately implies the following result.

Property 19.19 *We can support constant query time for the abstract transitive closure of any digraph whose kernel DAG has less than $\sqrt[3]{V}$ vertices with space proportional to V and time proportional to $E + V$ for preprocessing.*

Proof: Take $v < \sqrt[3]{V}$ in Property 19.18 and note that $x < v^2$. ∎

We might consider other variations on these bounds. For example, if we are willing to use space proportional to E, we can achieve the same time bounds when the kernel DAG has up to $\sqrt[3]{E}$ vertices. Moreover, these time bounds are conservative because they assume that the kernel DAG is dense with cross edges—and certainly it need not be so.

The primary limiting factor in the applicability of this method is the size of the kernel DAG. The more similar our digraph is to a DAG (the larger its kernel DAG), the more difficulty we face in computing its

Table 19.2 Properties of random digraphs

This table shows the numbers of edges and vertices in the kernel DAGs for random digraphs generated from two different models (the directed versions of the models in Table 18.1). In both cases, the kernel DAG becomes small (and is sparse) as the density increases.

	E	random edges		random 10-neighbors	
		v	e	v	e
1000 vertices					
	1000	983	981	916	755
	2000	424	621	713	1039
	5000	13	13	156	313
	10000	1	1	8	17
	20000	1	1	1	1
10000 vertices					
	50000	144	150	1324	150
	100000	1	1	61	123
	200000	1	1	1	1

Key:
  v Number of vertices in kernel DAG
  e Number of edges in kernel DAG

transitive closure. Note that (of course) we still have not violated the lower bound implicit in Property 19.9, since the algorithm runs in time proportional to V^3 for dense DAGs; we have, however, significantly broadened the class of graphs for which we can avoid this worst-case performance. Indeed, constructing a random-digraph model that produces digraphs for which the algorithm is slow is a challenge (see Exercise 19.142).

Table 19.2 displays the results of an empirical study; it shows that random digraphs have small kernel DAGs even for moderate densities and even in models with severe restrictions on edge placement. Although there can be no guarantees in the worst case, we can expect to see huge digraphs with small kernel DAGs in practice. When we do have such a digraph, we can provide an efficient implementation of the abstract–transitive-closure ADT.

Exercises

• **19.138** Develop a version of the implementation of the abstract transitive closure for digraphs based on using a sparse-graph representation of the kernel DAG. Your challenge is to eliminate duplicates on the list without using an excessive amount of time or space (see Exercise 19.65).

▷ **19.139** Show the kernel DAG computed by Program 19.13 and its transitive closure for the digraph

$$\text{3-7 1-4 7-8 0-5 5-2 3-8 2-9 0-6 4-9 2-6 6-4.}$$

○ **19.140** Convert the strong-component–based abstract–transitive-closure implementation (Program 19.13) into an efficient program that computes the adjacency matrix of the transitive closure for a digraph represented with an adjacency matrix, using Gabow's algorithm to compute the strong components and the improved Warshall's algorithm to compute the transitive closure of the DAG.

19.141 Do empirical studies to estimate the expected size of the kernel DAG for various types of digraphs (see Exercises 19.11–18).

•• **19.142** Develop a random-digraph model that generates digraphs that have large kernel DAGs. Your generator must generate edges one at a time, but it must not make use of any structural properties of the resulting graph.

19.143 Develop an implementation of the abstract transitive closure in a digraph by finding the strong components and building the kernel DAG, then answering reachability queries in the affirmative if the two vertices are in the same strong component, and doing a DFS in the DAG to determine reachability otherwise.

19.10 Perspective

In this chapter, we have considered algorithms for solving the topological-sorting, transitive-closure, and shortest-paths problems for digraphs and for DAGs, including fundamental algorithms for finding cycles and strong components in digraphs. These algorithms have numerous important applications in their own right and also serve as the basis for the more difficult problems involving weighted graphs that we consider in the next two chapters. Worst-case running times of these algorithms are summarized in Table 19.3.

In particular, a common theme through the chapter has been the solution of the abstract–transitive-closure problem, where we wish

Table 19.3 Worst-case cost of digraph-processing operations

This table summarizes the cost (worst-case running time) of algorithms for various digraph-processing problems considered in this chapter, for random graphs and graphs where edges randomly connect each vertex to one of 10 specified neighbors. All costs assume use of the adjacency-list representation; for the adjacency-matrix representation the E entries become V^2 entries, so, for example, the cost of computing all shortest paths is V^3. The linear-time algorithms are optimal, so the costs will reliably predict the running time on any input; the others may be overly conservative estimates of cost, so the running time may be lower for certain types of graphs. Performance characteristics of the fastest algorithms for computing the transitive closure of a digraph depend on the digraph's structure, particularly the size of its kernel DAG.

	problem	cost	algorithm
digraphs			
	cycle detect	E	DFS
	transitive closure	V(E+V)	DFS from each vertex
	single-source shortest paths	E	DFS
	all shortest paths	V(E+V)	DFS from each vertex
	strong components	E	Kosaraju, Tarjan, or Gabow
	transitive closure	E + v(v + x)	kernel DAG
DAGs			
	acyclic verify	E	DFS or source queue
	topological sort	E	DFS or source queue
	transitive closure	V(V+E)	DFS
	transitive closure	V(V+X)	DFS/dynamic programming

to support an ADT that can determine quickly, after preprocessing, whether there is a directed path from one given vertex to another. Despite a lower bound that implies that our worst-case preprocessing costs are significantly higher than V^2, the method discussed in Section 19.7 melds the basic methods from throughout the chapter into a simple solution that provides optimal performance for many types of digraphs—the significant exception being dense DAGs. The lower bound suggests that better guaranteed performance on all graphs will be difficult to achieve, but we can use these methods to get good performance on practical graphs.

The goal of developing an algorithm with performance characteristics similar to the union-find algorithms of Chapter 1 for dense digraphs remains elusive. Ideally, we would like to define an ADT where we can add directed edges or test whether one vertex is reachable from another and to develop an implementation where we can support all the operations in constant time (see Exercises 19.153 through 19.155). As discussed in Chapter 1, we can come close to that goal for undirected graphs, but comparable solutions for digraphs or DAGs are still not known. (Note that removing edges presents a challenge even for undirected graphs.) Not only does this *dynamic reachability* problem have both fundamental appeal and direct application in practice, but also it plays a critical role in the development of algorithms at a higher level of abstraction. For example, reachability lies at the heart of the problem of implementing the network simplex algorithm for the min-cost flow problem, a problem-solving model of wide applicability that we consider in Chapter 22.

Many other algorithms for processing digraphs and DAGs have important practical applications and have been studied in detail, and many digraph-processing problems still call for the development of efficient algorithms. The following list is representative.

Dominators Given a DAG with all vertices reachable from a single source r, a vertex s *dominates* a vertex t if every path from r to t contains s. (In particular, each vertex dominates itself.) Every vertex v other than the source has an *immediate dominator* that dominates v but does not dominate any dominator of v but v and itself. The set of immediate dominators is a tree that spans all vertices reachable from the source. This structure is important in compiler implementations. The dominator tree can be computed in linear time with a DFS-based approach that uses several ancillary data structures, although a slightly slower version is typically used in practice.

Transitive reduction Given a digraph, find a digraph that has the same transitive closure and the smallest number of edges among all such digraphs. This problem is tractable (see Exercise 19.150); but if we restrict it to insist that the result be a subgraph of the original graph, it is NP-hard.

Directed Euler path   Given a digraph, is there a directed path connecting two given vertices that uses each edge in the digraph exactly once? This problem is easy by essentially the same arguments as for the corresponding problem for undirected graphs, which we considered in Section 17.7 (see Exercise 17.92).

Directed mail carrier   Given a digraph, find a directed tour with a minimal number of edges that uses every edge in the graph at least once (but is allowed to use edges multiple times). As we shall see in Section 22.7, this problem reduces to the mincost-flow problem and is therefore tractable.

Directed Hamilton path   Find the longest simple directed path in a digraph. This problem is NP-hard, but it is easy if the digraph is a DAG (see Exercise 19.114).

Uniconnected subgraph   A digraph is said to be *uniconnected* if there is at most one directed path between any pair of vertices. Given a digraph and an integer k, determine whether there is a uniconnected subgraph with at least k edges. This problem is known to be NP-hard for general k.

Feedback vertex set   Decide whether a given digraph has a subset of at most k vertices that contains at least one vertex from every directed cycle in G. This problem is known to be NP-hard.

Even cycle   Decide whether a given digraph has a cycle of even length. As mentioned in Section 17.8, this problem, while not intractable, is so difficult to solve that no one has yet devised an algorithm that is useful in practice.

Just as for undirected graphs, myriad digraph-processing problems have been studied, and knowing whether a problem is easy or intractable is often a challenge (see Section 17.8). As indicated throughout this chapter, some of the facts that we have discovered about digraphs are expressions of more general mathematical phenomena, and many of our algorithms have applicability at levels of abstraction different from that at which we have been working. On the one hand, the concept of intractability tells us that we might encounter fundamental roadblocks in our quest for efficient algorithms that can guarantee efficient solutions to some problems. On the other hand, the classic algorithms described in this chapter are of fundamental importance and have broad applicability, as they provide efficient solutions to problems that arise frequently in practice and would otherwise be difficult to solve.

Exercises

19.144 Adapt Programs 17.18 and 17.19 to implement an ADT function for printing an Euler path in a digraph, if one exists. Explain the purpose of any additions or changes that you need to make in the code.

▷ **19.145** Draw the dominator tree of the digraph

> 3-7 1-4 7-8 0-5 5-2 3-0 2-9 0-6 4-9 2-6
>
> 6-4 1-5 8-2 9-0 8-3 4-5 2-3 1-6 3-5 7-6.

•• **19.146** Write class that uses DFS to create a parent-link representation of the dominator tree of a given digraph (*see reference section*).

○ **19.147** Find a transitive reduction of the digraph

> 3-7 1-4 7-8 0-5 5-2 3-0 2-9 0-6 4-9 2-6
>
> 6-4 1-5 8-2 9-0 8-3 4-5 2-3 1-6 3-5 7-6.

• **19.148** Find a subgraph of the digraph

> 3-7 1-4 7-8 0-5 5-2 3-0 2-9 0-6 4-9 2-6
>
> 6-4 1-5 8-2 9-0 8-3 4-5 2-3 1-6 3-5 7-6

that has the same transitive closure and the smallest number of edges among all such subgraphs.

○ **19.149** Prove that every DAG has a unique transitive reduction, and give an efficient ADT function implementation for computing the transitive reduction of a DAG.

• **19.150** Write an efficient ADT function for digraphs that computes a transitive reduction.

19.151 Give an algorithm that determines whether or not a given digraph is uniconnected. Your algorithm should have a worst-case running time proportional to VE.

19.152 Find the largest uniconnected subgraph in the digraph

> 3-7 1-4 7-8 0-5 5-2 3-0 2-9 0-6 4-9 2-6
>
> 6-4 1-5 8-2 9-0 8-3 4-5 2-3 1-6 3-5 7-6.

▷ **19.153** Develop a digraph class implemention that supports inserting an edge, removing an edge, and testing whether two vertices are in the same strong component, such that construction, edge insertion, and edge removal all take linear time and strong-connectivity queries take constant time, in the worst case.

○ **19.154** Solve Exercise 19.153, in such a way that edge insertion, edge removal, and strong-connectivity queries all take time proportional to log V in the worst case.

●●● **19.155** Solve Exercise 19.153, in such a way that edge insertion, edge removal, and strong-connectivity queries all take near-constant time (as they do for the union-find algorithms for connectivity in undirected graphs).

CHAPTER TWENTY

Minimum Spanning Trees

GRAPH MODELS WHERE we associate *weights* or *costs* with each edge are called for in many applications. In an airline map where edges represent flight routes, these weights might represent distances or fares. In an electric circuit where edges represent wires, the weights might represent the length of the wire, its cost, or the time that it takes a signal to propagate through it. In a job-scheduling problem, weights might represent time or the cost of performing tasks or of waiting for tasks to be performed.

Questions that entail cost minimization naturally arise for such situations. We examine algorithms for two such problems: (*i*) find the lowest-cost way to connect all of the points, and (*ii*) find the lowest-cost path between two given points. The first type of algorithm, which is useful for undirected graphs that represent objects such as electric circuits, finds a *minimum spanning tree*; it is the subject of this chapter. The second type of algorithm, which is useful for digraphs that represent objects such as an airline route map, finds the *shortest paths*; it is the subject of Chapter 21. These algorithms have broad applicability beyond circuit and map applications, extending to a variety of problems that arise on weighted graphs.

When we study algorithms that process weighted graphs, our intuition is often supported by thinking of the weights as distances: We speak of "the vertex closest to x," and so forth. Indeed, the term "shortest path" embraces this bias. Despite numerous applications where we actually do work with distance and despite the benefits of geometric intuition in understanding the basic algorithms, it is important to remember that the weights do not need to be proportional to a distance at all; they might represent time or cost or an entirely different variable. Indeed, as we see in Chapter 21, weights in shortest-paths problems can even be *negative*.

To appeal to intuition in describing algorithms and examples while still retaining general applicability, we use ambiguous terminology where we refer interchangeably to edge lengths and weights. When we refer to a "short" edge, we mean a "low-weight" edge, and so forth. For most of the examples in this chapter, we use weights that are proportional to the distances between the vertices, as shown in Figure 20.1. Such graphs are more convenient for examples, because we do not need to carry the edge labels and can still tell at a glance that longer edges have weights higher than those of shorter edges. When the weights do represent distances, we can consider algorithms that gain efficiency by taking into account geometric properties (Sections 20.7 and 21.5). With that exception, the algorithms that we consider simply process the edges and do not take advantage of any implied geometric information (see Figure 20.2).

The problem of finding the minimum spanning tree of an arbitrary weighted undirected graph has numerous important applications, and algorithms to solve it have been known since at least the 1920s; but the efficiency of implementations varies widely, and researchers still seek better methods. In this section, we examine three classical algorithms that are easily understood at a conceptual level; in Sections 20.3 through 20.5, we examine implementations of each in detail; and in Section 20.6, we consider comparisons of and improvements on these basic approaches.

Definition 20.1 *A **minimum spanning tree** (MST) of a weighted graph is a spanning tree whose weight (the sum of the weights of its edges) is no larger than the weight of any other spanning tree.*

If the edge weights are all positive, it suffices to define the MST as the set of edges with minimal total weight that connects all the vertices, as such a set of edges must form a spanning tree. The spanning-tree condition in the definition is included so that it applies for graphs that may have negative edge weights (see Exercises 20.2 and 20.3).

If edges can have equal weights, the minimum spanning tree may not be unique. For example, Figure 20.2 shows a graph that has two different MSTs. The possibility of equal weights also complicates the

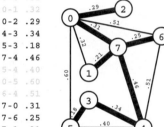

```
0-6  .51
0-1  .32
0-2  .29
4-3  .34
5-3  .18
7-4  .46
5-4  .40
0-5  .60
6-4  .51
7-0  .31
7-6  .25
7-1  .21
```

Figure 20.1
A weighted undirected graph and its MST

A weighted undirected graph is a set of weighted edges. The MST is a set of edges of minimal total weight that connects the vertices (black in the edge list, thick edges in the graph drawing). In this particular graph, the weights are proportional to the distances between the vertices, but the basic algorithms that we consider are appropriate for general graphs and make no assumptions about the weights (see Figure 20.2).

descriptions and correctness proofs of some of our algorithms. We
have to consider equal weights carefully, because they are not unusual
in applications and we want to know that our algorithms operate
correctly when they are present.

Not only might there be more than one MST, but also the nomenclature does not capture precisely the concept that we are minimizing
the weight rather than the tree itself. The proper adjective to describe
a specific tree is *minimal* (one having the smallest weight). For these
reasons, many authors use more accurate terms like *minimal spanning
tree* or *minimum-weight spanning tree*. The abbreviation *MST*, which
we shall use most often, is universally understood to capture the basic
concept.

Still, to avoid confusion when describing algorithms for networks
that may have edges with equal weights, we do take care to be precise
to use the term "minimal" to refer to "an edge of minimum weight"
(among all edges in some specified set) and "maximal" to refer to "an
edge of maximum weight." That is, if edge weights are distinct, a
minimal edge is the shortest edge (and is the only minimal edge); but
if there is more than one edge of minimum weight, any one of them
might be a minimal edge.

We work exclusively with undirected graphs in this chapter. The
problem of finding a minimum-weight directed spanning tree in a digraph is different, and is more difficult.

Several classical algorithms have been developed for the MST
problem. These methods are among the oldest and most well-known
algorithms in this book. As we have seen before, the classical methods
provide a general approach, but modern algorithms and data structures can give us compact and efficient implementations. Indeed, these
implementations provide a compelling example of the effectiveness
of careful ADT design and proper choice of fundamental ADT data
structure and algorithm implementations in solving increasingly difficult algorithmic problems.

Exercises

20.1 Assume that the weights in a graph are positive. Prove that you can
rescale them by adding a constant to all of them or by multiplying them all by
a constant without affecting the MSTs, provided only that the rescaled weights
are positive.

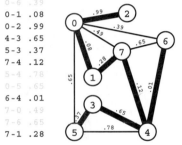

0-6	.39
0-1	.08
0-2	.99
4-3	.65
5-3	.37
7-4	.12
5-4	.78
0-5	.65
6-4	.01
7-0	.49
7-6	.65
7-1	.28

**Figure 20.2
Arbitrary weights**

*In this example, the edge weights
are arbitrary and do not relate to
the geometry of the drawn graph
representation at all. This example
also illustrates that the MST is not
necessarily unique if edge weights
may be equal: we get one MST by
including 3-4 (shown) and a different MST by including 0-5 instead
(although 7-6, which has the same
weight as those two edges, is not
in any MST).*

20.2 Show that, if edge weights are positive, a set of edges that connects all the vertices whose weights sum to a quantity no larger than the sum of the weights of any other set of edges that connects all the vertices is an MST.

20.3 Show that the property stated in Exercise 20.2 holds for graphs with negative weights, provided that there are no cycles whose edges all have non-positive weights.

○ **20.4** How would you find a *maximum* spanning tree of a weighted graph?

▷ **20.5** Show that if a graph's edges all have distinct weights, the MST is unique.

▷ **20.6** Consider the assertion that a graph has a unique MST only if its edge weights are distinct. Give a proof or a counterexample.

● **20.7** Assume that a graph has $t < V$ edges with equal weights and that all other weights are distinct. Give upper and lower bounds on the number of different MSTs that the graph might have.

20.1 Representations

In this chapter, we concentrate on weighted undirected graphs—the most natural setting for MST problems. Perhaps the simplest way to begin is to extend the basic graph representations from Chapter 17 to represent weighted graphs as follows: In the adjacency-matrix representation, the matrix can contain edge weights rather than Boolean values; in the adjacency-lists representation, we can add a field for the weights to the list elements that represent edges. This classic approach is appealing in its simplicity, but we will use a different method that is not much more complicated and will make our programs useful in more general settings. Comparative performance characteristics of the two approaches are briefly treated later in this section.

To address the issues raised when we shift from graphs where our only interest is in the presence or absence of edges to graphs where we are interested in information associated with edges, it is useful to imagine scenarios where vertices and edges are objects of unknown complexity, perhaps part of a a huge client data base that is built and maintained by some other application. For example, we might like to view streets, roads, and highways in a map data base as abstract edges with their lengths as weights, but, in the data base, a road's entry might carry a substantial amount of other information such as its name and type, a detailed description of its physical properties, how much traffic is currently using it, and so forth. Now, a client program

Program 20.1 ADT interface for graphs with weighted edges

This code defines an interface for graphs with weights and other information associated with edges. It consists of an EDGE ADT interface and a templatized GRAPH interface that may be used for any EDGE implementation. GRAPH implementations manipulate edge pointers (provided by clients with insert), not edges. The edge class also includes member functions that give information about the orientation of the edge: Either e->from(v) is true, e->v() is v and e->other(v) is e->w(); or e->from(v) is false, e->w() is v and e->other(v) is e->v().

```cpp
class EDGE
  {
    public:
      EDGE(int, int, double);
      int v() const;
      int w() const;
      double wt() const;
      bool from(int) const;
      int other(int) const;
  };
template <class Edge> class GRAPH
  {
    public:
      GRAPH(int, bool);
      ~GRAPH();
      int V() const;
      int E() const;
      bool directed() const;
      int insert(Edge *);
      int remove(Edge *);
      Edge *edge(int, int);
      class adjIterator
        {
          public:
            adjIterator(const GRAPH &, int);
            Edge *beg();
            Edge *nxt();
            bool end();
        };
  };
```

Program 20.2 Example of a graph-processing client function

This function illustrates the use of our weighted-graph interface in Program 20.1. For any implementation of the interface, edges returns a vector containing pointers to all the graph's edges. As in Chapters 17 through 19, we generally use the iterator functions only in the manner illustrated here.

```
template <class Graph, class Edge>
vector <Edge *> edges(const Graph &G)
{ int E = 0;
  vector <Edge *> a(G.E());
  for (int v = 0; v < G.V(); v++)
    {
      typename Graph::adjIterator A(G, v);
      for (Edge* e = A.beg(); !A.end(); e = A.nxt())
        if (e->from(v)) a[E++] = e;
    }
  return a;
}
```

---

could extract the information that it needs, build a graph, process it, and then interpret the results in the context of the data base, but that might be a difficult and costly process. In particular, it amounts to (at least) making a copy of the graph.

A better alternative is for the client to define an Edge data type and for our implementations to manipulate *pointers* to edges. Program 20.1 shows the details of the EDGE, GRAPH, and iterator ADTs that we use to support this approach. Clients can easily meet our minimal requirements for the EDGE data type while retaining the flexibility to define application-specific data types for use in other contexts. Our implementations can manipulate edge pointers and use the interface to extract the information they need from EDGEs without regard to how they are represented. Program 20.2 is an example of a client program that uses this interface.

For testing algorithms and basic applications, we use a class EDGE, which has two ints and a double as private data members that are initialized from constructor arguments and are the return values of the v(), w(), and wt() member functions, respectively (see

Program 20.3 Weighted-graph class (adjacency matrix)

For dense weighted graphs, we use a matrix of pointers to Edges, with a pointer to the edge v-w in row v and column w. For undirected graphs, we put another pointer to the edge in row w and column v. The null pointer indicates the absence of an edge; when we remove an edge, we remove our pointer to it. This implementation does not check for parallel edges, but clients could use edge to do so.

```
template <class Edge> class DenseGRAPH
{ int Vcnt, Ecnt; bool digraph;
  vector <vector <Edge *> > adj;
public:
  DenseGRAPH(int V, bool digraph = false) :
    adj(V), Vcnt(V), Ecnt(0), digraph(digraph)
    {
      for (int i = 0; i < V; i++)
        adj[i].assign(V, 0);
    }
  int V() const { return Vcnt; }
  int E() const { return Ecnt; }
  bool directed() const { return digraph; }
  void insert(Edge *e)
    { int v = e->v(), w = e->w();
      if (adj[v][w] == 0) Ecnt++;
      adj[v][w] = e;
      if (!digraph) adj[w][v] = e;
    }
  void remove(Edge *e)
    { int v = e->v(), w = e->w();
      if (adj[v][w] != 0) Ecnt--;
      adj[v][w] = 0;
      if (!digraph) adj[w][v] = 0;
    }
  Edge* edge(int v, int w) const
    { return adj[v][w]; }
  class adjIterator;
  friend class adjIterator;
};
```

Program 20.4 Iterator class for adjacency-matrix representation

This code is a straightforward adaptation of Program 17.8 to return edge pointers.

```
template <class Edge>
class DenseGRAPH<Edge>::adjIterator
{ const DenseGRAPH<Edge> &G;
  int i, v;
public:
  adjIterator(const DenseGRAPH<Edge> &G, int v) :
    G(G), v(v), i(0) { }
  Edge *beg()
    { i = -1; return nxt(); }
  Edge *nxt()
    {
      for (i++; i < G.V(); i++)
        if (G.edge(v, i)) return G.adj[v][i];
      return 0;
    }
  bool end() const
    { return i >= G.V(); }
};
```

Exercise 20.8). To avoid proliferation of simple types, we use edge weights of type double throughout this chapter and Chapter 21. In our examples, we use edge weights that are real numbers between 0 and 1. This decision does not conflict with various alternatives that we might need in applications, because we can explicitly or implicitly rescale the weights to fit this model (see Exercises 20.1 and 20.10). For example, if the weights are positive integers less than a known maximum value, we can divide them all by the maximum value to convert them to real numbers between 0 and 1.

If we wanted to do so, we could build a more general ADT interface and use any data type for edge weights that supports addition, subtraction, and comparisons, since we do little more with the weights than to accumulate sums and make decisions based on their values. In Chapter 22, our algorithms are concerned with comparing linear combinations of edge weights, and the running time of some algorithms depends on arithmetic properties of the weights, so we switch to integer weights to allow us to more easily analyze the algorithms.

Programs 20.3 and 20.4 implement the weighted-graph ADT of Program 20.1 with an adjacency-matrix representation. As before, inserting an edge into an undirected graph amounts to storing a pointer to it in two places in the matrix—one for each orientation of the edge. As is true of algorithms that use the adjacency-matrix representation for unweighted graphs, the running time of any algorithm that uses this representation is proportional to V^2 (to initialize the matrix) or higher.

With this representation, we test for the existence of an edge v–w by testing whether the pointer in row v and column w is null. In some situations, we could avoid such tests by using sentinel values for the weights, but we avoid the use of sentinel values in our implementations.

Program 20.5 gives the implementation details of the weighted-graph ADT that uses edge pointers for an adjacency-lists representation. A vertex-indexed vector associates each vertex with a linked list of that vertex's incident edges. Each list node contains a pointer to an edge. As with the adjacency matrix, we could, if desired, save space by putting just the destination vertex and the weight in the list nodes (leaving the source vertex implicit) at the cost of a more complicated iterator (see Exercises 20.11 and 20.14).

At this point, it is worthwhile to compare these representations with the simple representations that were mentioned at the beginning of this section (see Exercises 20.11 and 20.12). If we are building a graph from scratch, using pointers certainly requires more space. Not only do we need space for the pointers, but also we need space for the indices (vertex names), which are implicit in the simple representations. To use edge pointers in the adjacency-matrix representation, we need extra space for V^2 edge pointers and E pairs of indices. Similarly, to use edge pointers in the adjacency-list representation we need extra space for E edge pointers and E indices.

On the other hand, the use of edge pointers is likely to lead to faster code, because the compiled client code will follow one pointer to get direct access to an edge's weight, in contrast to the simple representation, where an Edge needs to be constructed and its fields accessed. If the space cost is prohibitive, using the minimal representations (and

Program 20.5 Weighted-graph class (adjacency lists)

This implementation of the interface in Program 20.1 is based on adjacency lists and is therefore appropriate for sparse weighted graphs. As with unweighted graphs, we represent each edge with a list node, but here each node contains a pointer to the edge that it represents, not just the destination vertex. The iterator class is a straightforward adaption of Program 17.10 (see Exercise 20.13).

```cpp
template <class Edge> class SparseMultiGRAPH
{ int Vcnt, Ecnt; bool digraph;
  struct node
    { Edge* e; node* next;
      node(Edge* e, node* next): e(e), next(next) {}
    };
  typedef node* link;
  vector <link> adj;
public:
  SparseMultiGRAPH(int V, bool digraph = false) :
    adj(V), Vcnt(V), Ecnt(0), digraph(digraph) { }
  int V() const { return Vcnt; }
  int E() const { return Ecnt; }
  bool directed() const { return digraph; }
  void insert(Edge *e)
    {
      adj[e->v()] = new node(e, adj[e->v()]);
      if (!digraph)
        adj[e->w()] = new node(e, adj[e->w()]);
      Ecnt++;
    }
  class adjIterator;
  friend class adjIterator;
};
```

perhaps streamlining the iterators to save time) certainly is a reasonable alternative; otherwise, the flexibility afforded by the pointers is probably worth the space.

To reduce clutter, we do use the simple representations in all of our figures. That is, rather than showing a matrix of pointers to edge

	0	1	2	3	4	5	6	7
0	*	.32	.29	*	*	.60	.51	.31
1	.32	*	*	*	*	*	*	.21
2	.29	*	*	*	*	*	*	*
3	*	*	*	*	.34	.18	*	*
4	*	*	*	.34	*	.40	.51	.46
5	.60	*	*	.18	.40	*	*	*
6	.51	*	*	*	.51	*	*	.25
7	.31	.21	*	*	.46	*	.25	*

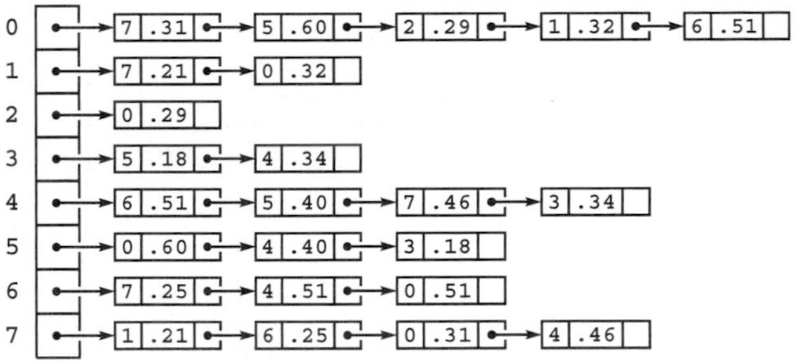

```
0 → 7 .31 → 5 .60 → 2 .29 → 1 .32 → 6 .51
1 → 7 .21 → 0 .32
2 → 0 .29
3 → 5 .18 → 4 .34
4 → 6 .51 → 5 .40 → 7 .46 → 3 .34
5 → 0 .60 → 4 .40 → 3 .18
6 → 7 .25 → 4 .51 → 0 .51
7 → 1 .21 → 6 .25 → 0 .31 → 4 .46
```

Figure 20.3
Weighted-graph representations (undirected)

The two standard representations of weighted undirected graphs include weights with each edge representation, as illustrated in the adjacency-matrix (left) and adjacency-lists (right) representation of the graph depicted in Figure 20.1. For simplicity in these figures, we show the weights in the matrix entries and list nodes; in our programs we use pointers to client edges. The adjacency matrix is symmetric and the adjacency lists contain two nodes for each edge, as in unweighted directed graphs. Nonexistent edges are represented null pointers in the matrix (indicated by asterisks in the figure) and are not present at all in the lists. Self-loops are absent in both of the representations illustrated here because MST algorithms are simpler without them; other algorithms that process weighted graphs use them (see Chapter 21).

structures that contain pairs of integers and weights, we simply show a matrix of weights, and rather than showing list nodes that contain pointers to edge structures, we show nodes that contain destination vertices. The adjacency-matrix and adjacency-lists representations of our sample graph are shown in Figure 20.3.

As with our undirected-graph implementations, we do not explicitly test for parallel edges in either implementation. Depending upon the application, we might alter the adjacency-matrix representation to keep the parallel edge of lowest or highest weight, or to effectively coalesce parallel edges to a single edge with the sum of their weights. In the adjacency-lists representation, we allow parallel edges to remain in the data structure, but we could build more powerful data structures to eliminate them using one of the rules just mentioned for adjacency matrices (see Exercise 17.49).

How should we represent the MST itself? The MST of a graph G is a subgraph of G that is also a tree, so we have numerous options. Chief among them are

- A graph
- A linked list of edges
- A vector of pointers to edges
- A vertex-indexed vector with parent links

Figure 20.4 illustrates these options for the example MST in Figure 20.1. Another alternative is to define and use an ADT for trees.

The same tree might have many different representations in any of the schemes. In what order should the edges be presented in the list-of-edges representation? Which node should be chosen as the root in the parent-link representation (see Exercise 20.21)? Generally

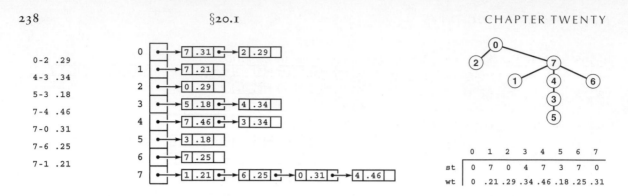

Figure 20.4
MST representations

This figure depicts various representations of the MST in Figure 20.1. The most straightforward is a list of its edges, in no particular order (left). The MST is also a sparse graph, and might be represented with adjacency lists (center). The most compact is a parent-link representation: we choose one of the vertices as the root and keep two vertex-indexed vectors, one with the parent of each vertex in the tree, the other with the weight of the edge from each vertex to its parent (right). The orientation of the tree (choice of root vertex) is arbitrary, not a property of the MST. We can convert from any one of these representations to any other in linear time.

speaking, when we run an MST algorithm, the particular MST representation that results is an artifact of the algorithm used and does not reflect any important features of the MST.

From an algorithmic point of view, the choice of MST representation is of little consequence because we can convert easily from each of these representations to any of the others. To convert from the graph representation to a vector of edges, we can use the `GRAPHedges` function of Program 20.2. To convert from the parent-link representation in a vector `st` (with weights in another vector `wt`) to a vector of pointers to edges in `mst`, we can use the loop

```
for (k = 1; k < G.V(); k++)
  mst[k] = new EDGE(k, st[k], wt[k]);
```

This code is for the typical case where the MST is rooted at 0, and it does not put the dummy edge 0-0 onto the MST edge list.

These two conversions are trivial, but how do we convert from the vector-of-edge-pointers representation to the parent-link representation? We have the basic tools to accomplish this task easily as well: We convert to the graph representation using a loop like the one just given (changed to call `insert` for each edge), then run a a DFS starting at any vertex to compute the parent-link representation of the DFS tree, in linear time.

In short, although the choice of MST representation is a matter of convenience, we package all of our algorithms in a graph-processing class `MST` that computes a private vector `mst` of pointers to edges. Depending on the needs of applications, we can implement member functions for this class to return this vector or to give client programs other information about the MST, but we do not specify further details of this interface, other than to include a show member function that calls a similar function for each edge in the MST (see Exercise 20.8).

Exercises

▷ **20.8** Write a WeightedEdge class that implements the EDGE interface of Program 20.1 and also includes a member function show that prints edges and their weights in the format used in the figures in this chapter.

▷ **20.9** Implement an io class for weighted graphs that has show, scan, and scanEZ member functions (see Program 17.4).

▷ **20.10** Build a graph ADT that uses integer weights, but keep track of the minimum and maximum weights in the graph and include an ADT function that always returns weights that are numbers between 0 and 1.

▷ **20.11** Give an interface like Program 20.1 such that clients and implementations manipulate Edges (not pointers to them).

○ **20.12** Develop an implementation of your interface from Exercise 20.11 that uses a minimal matrix-of-weights representation, where the iterator function nxt uses the information implicit in the row and column indices to create an Edge to return to the client.

20.13 Implement the iterator class for use with Program 20.5 (see Program 20.4).

○ **20.14** Develop an implementation of your interface from Exercise 20.11 that uses a minimal adjacency-lists representation, where list nodes contain the weight and the destination vertex (but not the source) and the iterator function nxt uses implicit information to create an Edge to return to the client.

▷ **20.15** Modify the sparse-random-graph generator in Program 17.12 to assign a random weight (between 0 and 1) to each edge.

▷ **20.16** Modify the dense-random-graph generator in Program 17.13 to assign a random weight (between 0 and 1) to each edge.

20.17 Write a program that generates random weighted graphs by connecting vertices arranged in a $\sqrt{V}$-by-$\sqrt{V}$ grid to their neighbors (as in Figure 19.3, but undirected) with random weights (between 0 and 1) assigned to each edge.

20.18 Write a program that generates a random complete graph that has weights chosen from a Gaussian distribution.

● **20.19** Write a program that generates V random points in the plane then builds a weighted graph by connecting each pair of points within a given distance d of one another with an edge whose weight is the distance (see Exercise 17.74). Determine how to set d so that the expected number of edges is E.

● **20.20** Find a large weighted graph online—perhaps a map with distances, telephone connections with costs, or an airline rate schedule.

20.21 Write down an 8-by-8 matrix that contains parent-link representations of all the orientations of the MST of the graph in Figure 20.1. Put the parent-link representation of the tree rooted at i in the ith row of the matrix.

▷ **20.22** Assume that a MST class constructor produces a vector-of-edge-pointers representation of an MST in mst[1] through mst[V]. Add a member function ST for clients (as in, for example, Program 18.3) such that ST(v) returns v's parent in the tree (v if it is the root).

▷ **20.23** Under the assumptions of Exercise 20.22, write a member function that returns the total weight of the MST.

○ **20.24** Suppose that a MST class constructor produces a parent-link representation of an MST in a vector st. Give code to be added to the constructor to compute a vector-of-edge-pointers representation in entries 1 through V of a private vector mst.

▷ **20.25** Define a TREE class. Then, under the assumptions of Exercise 20.22, write a member function that returns a TREE.

20.2 Underlying Principles of MST Algorithms

The MST problem is one of the most heavily studied problems that we encounter in this book. Basic approaches to solving it were invented long before the development of modern data structures and modern techniques for analyzing the performance of algorithms, at a time when finding the MST of a graph that contained, say, thousands of edges was a daunting task. As we shall see, several new MST algorithms differ from old ones essentially in their use and implementation of modern algorithms and data structures for basic tasks, which (coupled with modern computing power) makes it possible for us to compute MSTs with millions or even billions of edges.

One of the defining properties of a tree (see Section 5.4) is that adding an edge to a tree creates a unique cycle. This property is the basis for proving two fundamental properties of MSTs, which we now consider. All the algorithms that we encounter are based on one or both of these two properties.

The first property, which we refer to as the *cut property*, has to do with identifying edges that must be in an MST of a given graph. The few basic terms from graph theory that we define next make possible a concise statement of this property, which follows.

Definition 20.2 *A* **cut** *in a graph is a partition of the vertices into two disjoint sets. A* **crossing edge** *is one that connects a vertex in one set with a vertex in the other.*

We sometimes specify a cut by specifying a set of vertices, leaving implicit the assumption that the cut comprises that set and its complement. Generally, we use cuts where both sets are nonempty—otherwise there are no crossing edges.

Property 20.1 (Cut property) *Given any cut in a graph, every minimal crossing edge belongs to some MST of the graph, and every MST contains a minimal crossing edge.*

Proof: The proof is by contradiction. Suppose that e is a minimal crossing edge that is not in any MST, and let T be any MST; or suppose that T is an MST that contains no minimal crossing edge, and let e be any minimal crossing edge. In either case, T is an MST that does not contain the minimal crossing edge e. Now consider the graph formed by adding e to T. This graph has a cycle that contains e, and that cycle must contain at least one other crossing edge—say, f, which is equal or higher weight than e (since e is minimal). We can get a spanning tree of equal or lower weight by deleting f and adding e, contradicting either the minimality of T or the assumption that e is not in T. ∎

If a graph's edge weights are distinct, it has a unique MST; and the cut property says that the shortest crossing edge for every cut must be in the MST. When equal weights are present, we may have multiple minimal crossing edges. At least one of them will be in any given MST and the others may be present or absent.

Figure 20.5 illustrates several examples of this cut property. Note that there is no requirement that the minimal edge be the *only* MST edge connecting the two sets; indeed, for typical cuts there are several MST edges that connect a vertex in one set with a vertex in the other. If we could be sure that there were only one such edge, we might be able to develop divide-and-conquer algorithms based on judicious selection of the sets; but that is not the case.

We use the cut property as the basis for algorithms to find MSTs, and it also can serve as an *optimality condition* that characterizes MSTs. Specifically, the cut property implies that every edge in an MST is a minimal crossing edge for the cut defined by the vertices in the two subtrees connected by the edge.

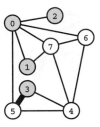

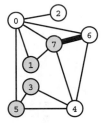

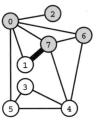

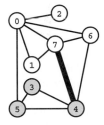

Figure 20.5
Cut property

These four examples illustrate Property 20.1. If we color one set of vertices gray and another set white, then the shortest edge connecting a gray vertex with a white one belongs to an MST.

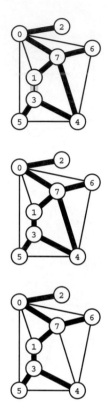

**Figure 20.6
Cycle property**

Adding the edge 1-3 *to the graph in Figure 20.1 invalidates the MST* (top). *To find the MST of the new graph, we add the new edge to the MST of the old graph, which creates a cycle* (center). *Deleting the longest edge on the cycle* (4-7) *yields the MST of the new graph* (bottom). *One way to verify that a spanning tree is minimal is to check that each edge not on the MST has the largest weight on the cycle that it forms with tree edges. For example, in the bottom graph,* 4-6 *has the largest weight on the cycle* 4-6-7-1-3-4.

The second property, which we refer to as the *cycle property*, has to do with identifying edges that do *not* have to be in a graph's MST. That is, if we ignore these edges, we can still find an MST.

Property 20.2 (Cycle property) *Given a graph G, consider the graph G′ defined by adding an edge e to G. Adding e to an MST of G and deleting a maximal edge on the resulting cycle gives an MST of G′.*

Proof: If e is longer than all the other edges on the cycle, it cannot be on an MST of G', because of Property 20.1: Removing e from any such MST would split the latter into two pieces, and e would not be the shortest edge connecting vertices in each of those two pieces, because some other edge on the cycle must do so. Otherwise, let t be a maximal edge on the cycle created by adding e to the MST of G. Removing t would split the original MST into two pieces, and edges of G connecting those pieces are no shorter than t; so e is a minimal edge in G' connecting vertices in those two pieces. The subgraphs induced by the two subsets of vertices are identical for G and G', so an MST for G' consists of e and the MSTs of those two subsets.

In particular, note that if e is maximal on the cycle, then we have shown that there exists an MST of G' that does not contain e (the MST of G). ∎

Figure 20.6 illustrates this cycle property. Note that the process of taking any spanning tree, adding an edge that creates a cycle, and then deleting a maximal edge on that cycle gives a spanning tree of weight less than or equal to the original. The new tree weight will be less than the original if and only if the added edge is shorter than some edge on the cycle.

The cycle property also serves as the basis for an optimality condition that characterizes MSTs: It implies that every edge in a graph that is not in a given MST is a maximal edge on the cycle that it forms with MST edges.

The cut property and the cycle property are the basis for the classical algorithms that we consider for the MST problem. We consider edges one at a time, using the cut property to accept them as MST edges or the cycle property to reject them as not needed. The algorithms differ in their approaches to efficiently identifying cuts and cycles.

The first approach to finding the MST that we consider in detail is to build the MST one edge at a time: Start with any vertex as a single-vertex MST, then add $V - 1$ edges to it, always taking next a minimal edge that connects a vertex on the MST to a vertex not yet on the MST. This method is known as *Prim's algorithm*; it is the subject of Section 20.3.

Property 20.3 *Prim's algorithm computes an MST of any connected graph.*

Proof: As described in detail in Section 20.2, the method is a generalized graph-search method. Implicit in the proof of Property 18.12 is the fact that the edges chosen are a spanning tree. To show that they are an MST, apply the cut property, using vertices on the MST as the first set and vertices not on the MST as the second set. ∎

Another approach to computing the MST is to apply the cycle property repeatedly: We add edges one at a time to a putative MST, deleting a maximal edge on the cycle if one is formed (see Exercises 20.33 and 20.71). This method has received less attention than the others that we consider because of the comparative difficulty of maintaining a data structure that supports efficient implementation of the "delete the longest edge on the cycle" operation.

The second approach to finding the MST that we consider in detail is to process the edges in order of their length (shortest first), adding to the MST each edge that does not form a cycle with edges previously added, stopping after $V - 1$ edges have been added. This method is known as *Kruskal's algorithm*; it is the subject of Section 20.4.

Property 20.4 *Kruskal's algorithm computes an MST of any connected graph.*

Proof: We prove by induction that the method maintains a forest of MST subtrees. If the next edge to be considered would create a cycle, it is a maximal edge on the cycle (since all others appeared before it in the sorted order), so ignoring it still leaves an MST, by the cycle property. If the next edge to be considered does not form a cycle, apply the cut property, using the cut defined by the set of vertices connected to one of the edge's vertex by MST edges (and its complement). Since the edge does not create a cycle, it is the only crossing edge, and since we consider the edges in sorted order, it is a minimal edge and therefore

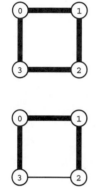

Figure 20.7
Cycles in Boruvka's algorithm

In the graph of four vertices and four edges shown here, the edges are all the same length. When we connect each vertex to a nearest neighbor, we have to make a choice between minimal edges. In the example at the top, we choose 1 from 0, 2 from 1, 3 from 2, and 0 from 3, which leads to a cycle in the putative MST. Each of the edges are in some MST, but not all are in every MST. To avoid this problem, we adopt a tie-breaking rule, as shown in the bottom: Choose the minimal edge to the vertex with the lowest index. Thus, we choose 1 from 0, 0 from 1, 1 from 2, and 0 from 3, which yields an MST. The cycle is broken because highest-numbered vertex 3 is not chosen from either of its neighbors 2 or 1, and it can choose only one of them (0).

in an MST. The basis for the induction is the V individual vertices; once we have chosen $V - 1$ edges, we have one tree (the MST). No unexamined edge is shorter than an MST edge, and all would create a cycle, so ignoring all of the rest of the edges leaves an MST, by the cycle property. ∎

The third approach to building an MST that we consider in detail is known as *Boruvka's algorithm*; it is the subject of Section 20.4. The first step is to add to the MST the edges that connect each vertex to its closest neighbor. If edge weights are distinct, this step creates a forest of MST subtrees (we prove this fact and consider a refinement that does so even when equal-weight edges are present in a moment). Then, we add to the MST the edges that connect each tree to a closest neighbor (a minimal edge connecting a vertex in one tree with a vertex in any other), and iterate the process until we are left with just one tree.

Property 20.5 *Boruvka's algorithm computes the MST of any connected graph.*

First, suppose that the edge weights are distinct. In this case, each vertex has a unique closest neighbor, the MST is unique, and we know that each edge added is an MST edge by applying the cut property (it is the shortest edge crossing the cut from a vertex to all the other vertices). Since every edge chosen is from the unique MST, there can be no cycles, each edge added merges two trees from the forest into a bigger tree, and the process continues until a single tree, the MST, remains.

If edge weights are not distinct, there may be more than one closest neighbor, and a cycle could form when we add the edges to closest neighbors (see Figure 20.7). Put another way, we might include two edges from the set of minimal crossing edges for some vertex, when only one belongs on the MST. To avoid this problem, we need an appropriate tie-breaking rule. One choice is to choose, among the minimal neighbors, the one with the lowest vertex number. Then any cycle would present a contradiction: If v is the highest-numbered vertex in the cycle, then neither neighbor of v would have led to its choice as the closest, and v would have led to the choice of only one of its lower-numbered neighbors, not both. ∎

These algorithms are all special cases of a general paradigm that is still being used by researchers seeking new MST algorithms. Specifically, we can apply *in arbitrary order* the cut property to accept an edge as an MST edge or the cycle property to reject an edge, continuing until neither can increase the number of accepted or rejected edges. At that point, any division of the graph's vertices into two sets has an MST edge connecting them (so applying the cut property cannot increase the number of MST edges), and all graph cycles have at least one non-MST edge (so applying the cycle property cannot increase the number of non-MST edges). Together, these properties imply that a complete MST has been computed.

More specifically, the three algorithms that we consider in detail can be unified with a generalized algorithm where we begin with a forest of single-vertex MST subtrees (each with no edges) and perform the step of adding to the MST a minimal edge connecting any two subtrees in the forest, continuing until $V - 1$ edges have been added and a single MST remains. By the cut property, no edge that causes a cycle need be considered for the MST, since some other edge was previously a minimal edge crossing a cut between MST subtrees containing each of its vertices. With Prim's algorithm, we grow a single tree an edge at a time; with Kruskal's and Boruvka's algorithms, we coalesce trees in a forest.

As described in this section and in the classical literature, the algorithms involve certain high-level abstract operations, such as the following:

- Find a minimal edge connecting two subtrees.
- Determine whether adding an edge would create a cycle.
- Delete the longest edge on a cycle.

Our challenge is to develop algorithms and data structures that implement these operations efficiently. Fortunately, this challenge presents us with an opportunity to put to good use basic algorithms and data structures that we developed earlier in this book.

MST algorithms have a long and colorful history that is still evolving; we discuss that history as we consider them in detail. Our evolving understanding of different methods of implementing the basic abstract operations has created some confusion surrounding the origins of the algorithms over the years. Indeed, the methods were first described in the 1920s, pre-dating the development of computers as we know them, as well as pre-dating our basic knowledge about sorting and other algorithms. As we now know, the choices of underlying algorithm and data structure can have substantial influences on performance, even when we are implementing the most basic schemes. In recent years, research on the MST problem has concentrated on such implementation issues, still using the classical schemes. For consistency and clarity, we refer to the basic approaches by the names listed here, although abstract versions of the algorithms were considered earlier, and modern implementations use algorithms and data structures invented long after these methods were first contemplated.

As yet unsolved in the design and analysis of algorithms is the quest for a linear-time MST algorithm. As we shall see, many of our implementations are linear-time in a broad variety of practical situations, but they are subject to a nonlinear worst case. The development of an algorithm that is guaranteed to be linear-time for sparse graphs is still a research goal.

Beyond our normal quest in search of the best algorithm for this fundamental problem, the study of MST algorithms underscores the importance of understanding the basic performance characteristics of fundamental algorithms. As programmers continue to use algorithms and data structures at increasingly higher levels of abstraction, situations of this sort become increasingly common. Our ADT implementations have varying performance characteristics—as we use higher-level ADTs as components when solving more yet higher-level problems, the possibilities multiply. Indeed, we often use algorithms that are based on using MSTs and similar abstractions (enabled by the efficient implementations that we consider in this chapter) to help us solve other problems at a yet higher level of abstraction.

Exercises

▷ **20.26** Label the following points in the plane 0 through 5, respectively:

$$(1, 3) \ (2, 1) \ (6, 5) \ (3, 4) \ (3, 7) \ (5, 3).$$

Taking edge lengths to be weights, give an MST of the graph defined by the edges

$$1\text{-}0 \ 3\text{-}5 \ 5\text{-}2 \ 3\text{-}4 \ 5\text{-}1 \ 0\text{-}3 \ 0\text{-}4 \ 4\text{-}2 \ 2\text{-}3.$$

20.27 Suppose that a graph has distinct edge weights. Does its shortest edge have to belong to the MST? Prove that it does or give a counterexample.

20.28 Answer Exercise 20.27 for the graph's *longest* edge.

20.29 Give a counterexample that shows why the following strategy does not necessarily find the MST: "Start with any vertex as a single-vertex MST, then add $V - 1$ edges to it, always taking next a minimal edge incident upon the vertex most recently added to the MST."

20.30 Suppose that a graph has distinct edge weights. Does a minimal edge on every cycle have to belong to the MST? Prove that it does or give a counterexample.

20.31 Given an MST for a graph G, suppose that an edge in G is deleted. Describe how to find an MST of the new graph in time proportional to the number of edges in G.

20.32 Show the MST that results when you repeatedly apply the cycle property to the graph in Figure 20.1, taking the edges in the order given.

20.33 Prove that repeated application of the cycle property gives an MST.

20.34 Describe how each of the algorithms described in this section can be adapted (if necessary) to the problem of finding a *minimal spanning forest* of a weighted graph (the union of the MSTs of its connected components).

20.3 Prim's Algorithm and Priority-First Search

Prim's algorithm is perhaps the simplest MST algorithm to implement, and it is the method of choice for dense graphs. We maintain a cut of the graph that is comprised of *tree* vertices (those chosen for the MST) and *nontree* vertices (those not yet chosen for the MST). We start by putting any vertex on the MST, then put a minimal crossing edge on the MST (which changes its nontree vertex to a tree vertex) and repeat the same operation $V - 1$ times, to put all vertices on the tree.

A brute-force implementation of Prim's algorithm follows directly from this description. To find the edge to add next to the MST, we could examine all the edges that go from a tree vertex to a nontree vertex, then pick the shortest of the edges found to put on the MST. We do not consider this implementation here because it is overly expensive (see Exercises 20.35 through 20.37). Adding a simple data structure to eliminate excessive recomputation makes the algorithm both simpler and faster.

Adding a vertex to the MST is an incremental change: To implement Prim's algorithm, we focus on the nature of that incremental change. The key is to note that our interest is in the shortest distance from each nontree vertex to the tree. When we add a vertex v to the tree, the only possible change for each nontree vertex w is that adding

Figure 20.8
Prim's MST algorithm

The first step in computing the MST with Prim's algorithm is to add 0 to the tree. Then we find all the edges that connect 0 to other vertices (which are not yet on the tree) and keep track of the shortest (top left). The edges that connect tree vertices with nontree vertices (the fringe*) are shadowed in gray and listed below each graph drawing. For simplicity in this figure, we list the fringe edges in order of their length so that the shortest is the first in the list. Different implementations of Prim's algorithm use different data structures to maintain this list and to find the minimum. The second step is to move the shortest edge 0-2 (along with the vertex that it takes us to) from the fringe to the tree (second from top, left). Third, we move 0-7 from the fringe to the tree, replace 0-1 by 7-1 and 0-6 by 7-6 on the fringe (because adding 7 to the tree brings 1 and 6 closer to the tree), and add 7-4 to the fringe (because adding 7 to the tree makes 7-4 an edge that connects a tree vertex with a nontree vertex) (third from top, left). Next, we move edge 7-1 to the tree (bottom, left). To complete the computation, we take 7-6, 7-4, 4-3, and 3-5 off the queue, updating the fringe after each insertion to reflect any shorter or new paths discovered (right, top to bottom).*

An oriented drawing of the growing MST is shown at the right of each graph drawing. The orientation is an artifact of the algorithm: We generally view the MST itself as a set of edges, unordered and unoriented.

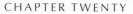

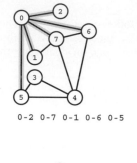

0-2 0-7 0-1 0-6 0-5

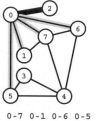

0-7 0-1 0-6 0-5

7-1 7-6 7-4 0-5

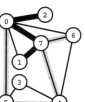

7-6 7-4 0-5

7-4 0-5

4-3 4-5

3-5

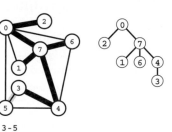

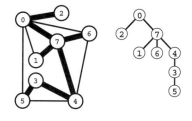

	0	1	2	3	4	5	6	7
mst	0	7-1	0-2	4-3	7-4	3-5	7-6	0-7
wt		.21	.29	.34	.46	.18	.25	.31

v brings w closer than before to the tree. In short, we do not need to check the distance from w to all tree vertices—we just need to keep track of the minimum and check whether the addition of v to the tree necessitates that we update that minimum.

To implement this idea, we need data structures that can give us the following information:

- The tree edges
- The shortest edge connecting each nontree vertex to the tree
- The length of that edge

The simplest implementation for each of these data structures is a vertex-indexed vector (we can use such a vector for the tree edges by indexing on vertices as they are added to the tree). Program 20.6 is an implementation of Prim's algorithm for dense graphs. It uses the vectors mst, fr, and wt (respectively) for these three data structures.

After adding a new edge (and vertex) to the tree, we have two tasks to accomplish:

- Check to see whether adding the new edge brought any nontree vertex closer to the tree.
- Find the next edge to add to the tree.

The implementation in Program 20.6 accomplishes both of these tasks with a single scan through the nontree vertices, updating wt[w] and fr[w] if v-w brings w closer to the tree, then updating the current minimum if wt[w] (the length of fr[w]) indicates that w is closer to the tree than any other nontree vertex with a lower index).

Property 20.6 *Using Prim's algorithm, we can find the MST of a dense graph in linear time.*

Proof: It is immediately evident from inspection of the program that the running time is proportional to V^2 and therefore is linear for dense graphs. ∎

Figure 20.8 shows an example MST construction with Prim's algorithm; Figure 20.9 shows the evolving MST for a larger example.

Program 20.6 is based on the observation that we can interleave the *find the minimum* and update operations in a single loop where we examine all the nontree edges. In a dense graph, the number of edges that we may have to examine to update the distance from the nontree vertices to the tree is proportional to V, so looking at all the nontree edges to find the one that is closest to the tree does not represent

Figure 20.9
Prim's MST algorithm

This sequence shows how the MST grows as Prim's algorithm discovers 1/4, 1/2, 3/4, and all of the edges in the MST (top to bottom). An oriented representation of the full MST is shown at the right.

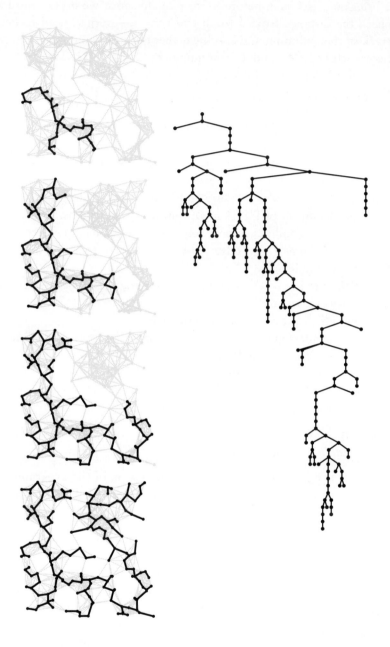

Program 20.6 Prim's MST algorithm

This implementation of Prim's algorithm is the method of choice for dense graphs and can be used for any graph representation that supports the edge existence test. The outer loop grows the MST by choosing a minimal edge crossing the cut between the vertices on the MST and vertices not on the MST. The w loop finds the minimal edge while at the same time (if w is not on the MST) maintaining the invariant that the edge fr[w] is the shortest edge (of weight wt[w]) from w to the MST.

      The result of the computation is a vector of edge pointers. The first (mst[0]) is unused; the rest (mst[1] through mst[G.V()]) comprise the MST of the connected component of the graph that contains 0.

```cpp
template <class Graph, class Edge> class MST
{ const Graph &G;
  vector<double> wt;
  vector<Edge *> fr, mst;
public:
  MST(const Graph &G) : G(G),
    mst(G.V()), wt(G.V(), G.V()), fr(G.V())
    { int min = -1;
      for (int v = 0; min != 0; v = min)
      {
        min = 0;
        for (int w = 1; w < G.V(); w++)
          if (mst[w] == 0)
            { double P; Edge* e = G.edge(v, w);
              if (e)
                if ((P = e->wt()) < wt[w])
                  { wt[w] = P; fr[w] = e; }
              if (wt[w] < wt[min]) min = w;
            }
        if (min) mst[min] = fr[min];
      }
    }
  void show()
  { for (int v = 1; v < G.V(); v++)
      if (mst[v]) mst[v]->show();}
};
```

excessive extra cost. But in a sparse graph, we can expect to use substantially fewer than V steps to perform each of these operations. The crux of the strategy that we will use to do so is to focus on the set of potential edges to be added next to the MST—a set that we call the *fringe*. The number of fringe edges is typically substantially smaller than the number of nontree edges, and we can recast our description of the algorithm as follows. Starting with a self loop to a start vertex on the fringe and an empty tree, we perform the following operation until the fringe is empty:

> *Move a minimal edge from the fringe to the tree. Visit the vertex that it leads to, and put onto the fringe any edges that lead from that vertex to an nontree vertex, replacing the longer edge when two edges on the fringe point to the same vertex.*

From this formulation, it is clear that Prim's algorithm is nothing more than a generalized graph search (see Section 18.8), where the fringe is a priority queue based on a *remove the minimum* operation (see Chapter 9). We refer to generalized graph searching with priority queues as *priority-first search (PFS)*. With edge weights for priorities, PFS implements Prim's algorithm.

This formulation encompasses a key observation that we made already in connection with implementing BFS in Section 18.7. An even simpler general approach is to simply keep on the fringe all of the edges that are incident upon tree vertices, letting the priority-queue mechanism find the shortest one and ignore longer ones (see Exercise 20.41). As we saw with BFS, this approach is unattractive because the fringe data structure becomes unnecessarily cluttered with edges that will never get to the MST. The size of the fringe could grow to be proportional to E (with whatever attendant costs having a fringe this size might involve), while the PFS approach just outlined ensures that the fringe will never have more than V entries.

As with any implementation of a general algorithm, we have a number of available approaches for interfacing with priority-queue ADTs. One approach is to use a priority queue of edges, as in our generalized graph-search implementation of Program 18.10. Program 20.7 is an implementation that is essentially equivalent to Program 18.10 but uses a vertex-based approach so that it can use an indexed priority-queue, as described in Section 9.6. (We consider a complete implementation of the specific priority-queue interface used by Program 20.7 is at the end of this chapter, in Program 20.10.) We identify the *fringe vertices*, the subset of nontree vertices that are connected by fringe edges to tree vertices, and keep the same vertex-indexed vectors mst, fr, and wt as in Program 20.6. The priority queue contains the index of each fringe vertex, and that entry gives access to the shortest edge connecting the fringe vertex with the tree and the length of that edge, through the second and third vectors.

The first call to pfs in the constructor in Program 20.7 finds the MST in the connected component that contains vertex 0, and subsequent calls find MSTs in other components, so this class actually finds minimal spanning forests in graphs that are not connected (see Exercise 20.34).

Property 20.7 *Using a PFS implementation of Prim's algorithm that uses a heap for the priority-queue implementation, we can compute an MST in time proportional to $E \lg V$.*

Proof: The algorithm directly implements the generic idea of Prim's algorithm (add next to the MST a minimal edge that connects a vertex on the MST with a vertex not on the MST). Each priority-queue operation requires less than $\lg V$ steps. Each vertex is chosen with a *remove the minimum* operation; and, in the worst case, each edge might require a *change priority* operation. ∎

Priority-first search is a proper generalization of breadth-first and depth-first search because those methods also can be derived through appropriate priority settings. For example, we can (somewhat artificially) use a variable cnt to assign a unique priority cnt++ to each vertex when we put that vertex on the priority queue. If we define P to be cnt, we get preorder numbering and DFS because newly encountered nodes have the highest priority. If we define P to be V-cnt, we get BFS because old nodes have the highest priority. These priority assignments make the priority queue operate like a stack and a queue, respectively. This equivalence is purely of academic interest since the priority-queue operations are unnecessary for DFS and BFS. Also, as discussed in Section 18.8, a formal proof of equivalence would require a precise attention to replacement rules to obtain the same sequence of vertices as result from the classical algorithms.

Program 20.7 Priority-first search

The function `pfs` is a generalized graph search that uses a priority queue for the fringe (see Section 18.8). The priority P is defined such that this class implements Prim's MST algorithm; other priority definitions give other algorithms. The main loop moves the highest-priority (lowest-weight) edge from the fringe to the tree, then checks every edge adjacent to the new tree vertex to see whether it implies changes in the fringe. Edges to vertices not on the fringe or the tree are added to the fringe; shorter edges to fringe vertices replace corresponding fringe edges.

    The `PQi` class is an indirect priority-queue interface (see Section 9.6) modified to pass a reference to the priority array to the constructor, to substitute `getmin` for `delmax`, and to substitute `lower` for `change`. Program 20.10 is an implementation of this interface.

```
template <class Graph, class Edge> class MST
{ const Graph &G;
  vector<double> wt;
  vector<Edge *> fr, mst;
  void pfs(int s)
  { PQi<double> pQ(G.V(), wt);
    pQ.insert(s);
    while (!pQ.empty())
    { int v = pQ.getmin();
      mst[v] = fr[v];
      typename Graph::adjIterator A(G, v);
      for (Edge* e = A.beg(); !A.end(); e = A.nxt())
        { double P = e->wt(); int w = e->other(v);
          if (fr[w] == 0)
            { wt[w] = P; pQ.insert(w); fr[w] = e; }
          else if (mst[w] == 0 && P < wt[w])
            { wt[w] = P; pQ.lower(w); fr[w] = e; }
        }
    }
  }
public:
  MST(Graph &G) : G(G),
    fr(G.V()), mst(G.V()), wt(G.V(), -1)
    { for (int v = 0; v < G.V(); v++)
        if (mst[v] == 0) pfs(v); }
};
```

As we shall see, PFS encompasses not just DFS, BFS, and Prim's MST algorithm but also several other classical algorithms. The various algorithms differ only in their priority functions. Thus, the running times of all these algorithms depend on the performance of the priority-queue ADT. Indeed, we are led to a general result that encompasses not just the two implementations of Prim's algorithms that we have examined in this section but also a broad class of fundamental graph-processing algorithms.

Property 20.8 *For all graphs and all priority functions, we can compute a spanning tree with PFS in linear time plus time proportional to the time required for V* **insert**, *V* **delete the minimum**, *and E* **decrease key** *operations in a priority queue of size at most V.*

Proof: The proof of Property 20.7 establishes this more general result. We have to examine all the edges in the graph; hence the "linear time" clause. The algorithm never increases the priority (it changes the priority to only a lower value); by more precisely specifying what we need from the priority-queue ADT (*decrease key*, not necessarily *change priority*), we strengthen this statement about performance. ∎

In particular, use of an unordered-array priority-queue implementation gives an optimal solution for dense graphs that has the same worst-case performance as the classical implementation of Prim's algorithm (Program 20.6). That is, Properties 20.6 and 20.7 are special cases of Property 20.8; throughout this book we shall see numerous other algorithms that essentially differ in only their choice of priority function and their priority-queue implementation.

Property 20.7 is an important general result: The time bound stated is a worst-case upper bound that guarantees performance within a factor of $\lg V$ of optimal (linear time) for a large class of graph-processing problems. Still, it is somewhat pessimistic for many of the graphs that we encounter in practice, for two reasons. First, the $\lg V$ bound for priority-queue operation holds only when the number of vertices on the fringe is proportional to V, and even then it is just an upper bound. For a real graph in a practical application, the fringe might be small (see Figures 20.10 and 20.11), and some priority-queue operations might take many fewer than $\lg V$ steps. Although noticeable, this effect is likely to account for only a small constant factor in the running time; for example, a proof that the fringe never

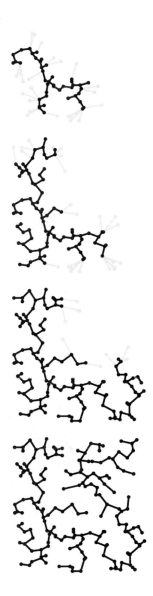

Figure 20.10
PFS implementation of Prim's MST algorithm

With PFS, Prim's algorithm processes just the vertices and edges closest to the MST (in gray).

has more than $\sqrt{V}$ vertices on it would improve the bound by only a factor of 2. More important, we generally perform many fewer than E *decrease key* operations since we do that operation only when we find an edge to a fringe node that is shorter than the current best-known edge to a fringe node. This event is relatively rare: Most edges have no effect on the priority queue (see Exercise 20.40). It is reasonable to regard PFS as an essentially linear-time algorithm unless $V \lg V$ is significantly greater than E.

The priority-queue ADT and generalized graph-searching abstractions make it easy for us to understand the relationships among various algorithms. Since these abstractions (and software mechanisms to support their use) were developed many years after the basic methods, relating the algorithms to classical descriptions of them becomes an exercise for historians. However, knowing basic facts about the history is useful when we encounter descriptions of MST algorithms in the research literature or in other texts, and understanding how these few simple abstractions tie together the work of numerous researchers over a time span of decades is persuasive evidence of their value and power. Thus, we consider briefly the origins of these algorithms here.

An MST implementation for dense graphs essentially equivalent to Program 20.6 was first presented by Prim in 1961, and, independently, by Dijkstra soon thereafter. It is usually referred to as *Prim's algorithm*, although Dijkstra's presentation was more general, so some scholars refer to the MST algorithm as a special case of Dijkstra's algorithm. But the basic idea was also presented by Jarnik in 1939, so some authors refer to the method as *Jarnik's algorithm*, thus characterizing Prim's (or Dijkstra's) role as finding an efficient implementation of the algorithm for dense graphs. As the priority-queue ADT came into use in the early 1970s, its application to finding MSTs of sparse graphs was straightforward; the fact that MSTs of sparse graphs could be computed in time proportional to $E \lg V$ became widely known without attribution to any particular researcher. Since that time, as we discuss in Section 20.6, many researchers have concentrated on finding efficient priority-queue implementations as the key to finding efficient MST algorithms for sparse graphs.

Exercises

▷ **20.35** Analyze the performance of the brute-force implementation of Prim's algorithm mentioned at the beginning of this section for a complete weighted

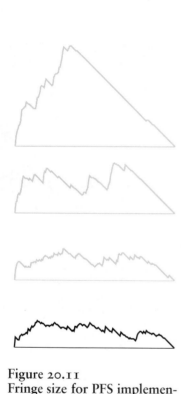

Figure 20.11
Fringe size for PFS implementation of Prim's algorithm

The plot at the bottom shows the size of the fringe as the PFS proceeds for the example in Figure 20.10. For comparison, the corresponding plots for DFS, randomized search, and BFS from Figure 18.28 are shown above in gray.

graph with V vertices. *Hint*: The following combinatorial sum might be useful: $\sum_{1 \leq k < V} k(V - k) = (V + 1)V(V - 1)/6$.

○ **20.36** Answer Exercise 20.35 for graphs in which all vertices have the same fixed degree t.

○ **20.37** Answer Exercise 20.35 for general sparse graphs that have V vertices and E edges. Since the running time depends on the weights of the edges and on the degrees of the vertices, do a worst-case analysis. Exhibit a family of graphs for which your worst-case bound is confirmed.

20.38 Show, in the style of Figure 20.8, the result of computing the MST of the network defined in Exercise 20.26 with Prim's algorithm.

• **20.39** Describe a family of graphs with V vertices and E edges for which the worst-case running time of the PFS implementation of Prim's algorithm is confirmed.

•• **20.40** Develop a reasonable generator for random graphs with V vertices and E edges such that the running time of the PFS implementation of Prim's algorithm (Program 20.7) is nonlinear.

○ **20.41** Modify Program 20.7 so that it works like Program 18.8, in that it keeps on the fringe all edges incident upon tree vertices. Run empirical studies to compare your implementation with Program 20.7, for various weighted graphs (see Exercises 20.9–14).

20.42 Derive a priority queue implementation for use by Program 20.7 from the interface defined in Program 9.12 (so any implementation of that interface could be used).

20.43 Use the STL `priority_queue` to implement the priority-queue interface that is used by Program 20.7.

20.44 Suppose that you use a priority-queue implementation that maintains a sorted list. What would be the worst-case running time for graphs with V vertices and E edges, to within a constant factor? When would this method be appropriate, if ever? Defend your answer.

○ **20.45** An MST edge whose deletion from the graph would cause the MST weight to increase is called a *critical edge*. Show how to find all critical edges in a graph in time proportional to $E \lg V$.

20.46 Run empirical studies to compare the performance of Program 20.6 to that of Program 20.7, using an unordered array implementation for the priority queue, for various weighted graphs (see Exercises 20.9–14).

• **20.47** Run empirical studies to determine the effect of using an index-heap–tournament (see Exercise 9.53) priority-queue implementation instead of Program 9.12 in Program 20.7, for various weighted graphs (see Exercises 20.9–14).

20.48 Run empirical studies to analyze tree weights (see Exercise 20.23) as a function of V, for various weighted graphs (see Exercises 20.9–14).

20.49 Run empirical studies to analyze maximum fringe size as a function of V, for various weighted graphs (see Exercises 20.9–14).

20.50 Run empirical studies to analyze tree height as a function of V, for various weighted graphs (see Exercises 20.9–14).

20.51 Run empirical studies to study the dependence of the results of Exercises 20.49 and 20.50 on the start vertex. Would it be worthwhile to use a random starting point?

• **20.52** Write a client program that does dynamic graphical animations of Prim's algorithm. Your program should produce images like Figure 20.10 (see Exercises 17.56 through 17.60). Test your program on random Euclidean neighbor graphs and on grid graphs (see Exercises 20.17 and 20.19), using as many points as you can process in a reasonable amount of time.

20.4 Kruskal's Algorithm

Prim's algorithm builds the MST one edge at a time, finding a new edge to attach to a single growing tree at each step. Kruskal's algorithm also builds the MST one edge at a time; but, by contrast, it finds an edge that connects two trees in a spreading forest of growing MST subtrees. We start with a degenerate forest of V single-vertex trees and perform the operation of combining two trees (using the shortest edge possible) until there is just one tree left: the MST.

Figure 20.12 shows a step-by-step example of the operation of Kruskal's algorithm; Figure 20.13 illustrates the algorithm's dynamic characteristics on a larger example. The disconnected forest of MST subtrees evolves gradually into a tree. Edges are added to the MST in order of their length, so the forests comprise vertices that are connected to one another by relatively short edges. At any point during the execution of the algorithm, each vertex is closer to some vertex in its subtree than to any vertex not in its subtree.

Kruskal's algorithm is simple to implement, given the basic algorithmic tools that we have considered in this book. Indeed, we can use any sort from Part 3 to sort the edges by weight and any of the connectivity algorithms from Chapter 1 to eliminate those that cause cycles! Program 20.8 is an implementation along these lines of an MST function for a graph ADT that is functionally equivalent to the other MST implementations that we consider in this chapter. The implementation does not depend on the graph representation: It calls a

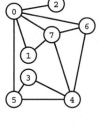

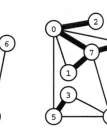

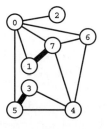

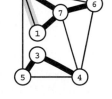

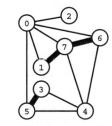

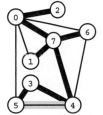

```
0-6 .51        5-3 .18
0-1 .32        7-1 .21
0-2 .29        7-6 .25
4-3 .34        0-2 .29
5-3 .18        7-0 .31
7-4 .46        0-1 .32
5-4 .40        4-3 .34
0-5 .60        5-4 .40
6-4 .51        7-4 .46
7-0 .31     *  0-6 .51
7-6 .25     *  6-4 .51
7-1 .21     *  0-5 .60
```

Figure 20.12
Kruskal's MST algorithm

Given a list of a graph's edges in arbitrary order (left edge list), *the first step in Kruskal's algorithm is to sort them by weight* (right edge list). *Then we go through the edges on the list in order of their weight, adding edges that do not create cycles to the MST. We add* 5-3 *(the shortest edge), then* 7-1, *then* 7-6 *(left), then* 0-2 *(right, top) and* 0-7 *(right, second from top). The edge with the next largest weight,* 0-1, *creates a cycle and is not included. Edges that we do not add to the MST are shown in gray on the sorted list. Then we add* 4-3 *(right, third from top). Next, we reject* 5-4 *because it causes a cycle, then we add* 7-4 *(right, bottom). Once the MST is complete, any edges with larger weights would cause cycles and be rejected (we stop when we have added* $V - 1$ *edges to the MST). These edges are marked with asterisks on the sorted list.*

Figure 20.13
Kruskal's MST algorithm

*This sequence shows 1/4, 1/2,
3/4, and the full MST as it evolves.*

`GRAPH` client to return a vector that contains the graph's edges, then computes the MST from that vector.

Note that there are two ways in which Kruskal's algorithm can terminate. If we find $V - 1$ edges, then we have a spanning tree and can stop. If we examine all the edges without finding $V - 1$ tree edges, then we have determined that the graph is not connected, precisely as we did in Chapter 1.

Analyzing the running time of Kruskal's algorithm is a simple matter because we know the running time of its constituent ADT operations.

Property 20.9 *Kruskal's algorithm computes the MST of a graph in time proportional to $E \lg E$.*

Proof: This property is a consequence of the more general observation that the running time of Program 20.8 is proportional to the cost of sorting E numbers plus the cost of E *find* and $V - 1$ *union* operations. If we use standard ADT implementations such as mergesort and weighted union-find with halving, the cost of sorting dominates. ∎

We consider the comparative performance of Kruskal's and Prim's algorithm in Section 20.6. For the moment, note that a running time proportional to $E \lg E$ is not necessarily worse than $E \lg V$, because E is at most V^2, so $\lg E$ is at most $2 \lg V$. Performance differences for specific graphs are due to what the properties of the implementations are and to whether the actual running time approaches these worst-case bounds.

In practice, we might use quicksort or a fast system sort (which is likely to be based on quicksort). Although this approach may give the usual unappealing (in theory) quadratic worst case for the sort, it is likely to lead to the fastest run time. Indeed, on the other hand, we could use a radix sort to do the sort in linear time (under certain conditions on the weights) so that the cost of the E *find* operations dominates and then adjust Property 20.9 to say that the running time of Kruskal's algorithm is within a constant factor of $E \lg^* E$ under those conditions on the weights (see Chapter 2). Recall that the function $\lg^* E$ is the number of iterations of the binary logarithm function before the result is less than 1, which is less than 5 if E is less than 2^{65536}. In other words, these adjustments make Kruskal's algorithm effectively *linear* in most practical circumstances.

Program 20.8 Kruskal's MST algorithm

This implementation uses our sorting ADT from Chapter 6 and our union-find ADT from Chapter 4 to find the MST by considering the edges in order of their weights, discarding edges that create cycles until finding $V - 1$ edges that comprise a spanning tree.

Not shown are a wrapper class `EdgePtr` that wraps pointers to Edges so sort can compare them using an overloaded `<`, as described in Section 6.8, and a version of Program 20.2 with a third template argument.

```
template <class Graph, class Edge, class EdgePtr>
class MST
{ const Graph &G;
  vector<EdgePtr> a, mst;
  UF uf;
public:
  MST(Graph &G) : G(G), uf(G.V()), mst(G.V())
  { int V = G.V(), E = G.E();
    a = edges<Graph, Edge, EdgePtr>(G);
    sort<EdgePtr>(a, 0, E-1);
    for (int i = 0, k = 1; i < E && k < V; i++)
      if (!uf.find(a[i]->v, a[i]->w))
        { uf.unite(a[i]->v, a[i]->w);
          mst[k++] = a[i]; }
  }
};
```

Typically, the cost of finding the MST with Kruskal's algorithm is even lower than the cost of processing all edges because the MST is complete well before a substantial fraction of the (long) graph edges is ever considered. We can take this fact into account to reduce the running time significantly in many practical situations by keeping edges that are longer than the longest MST edge entirely out of the sort. One easy way to accomplish this objective is to use a priority queue, with an implementation that does the *construct* operation in linear time and the *remove the minimum* operation in logarithmic time.

For example, we can achieve these performance characteristics with a standard heap implementation, using bottom-up construction (see Section 9.4). Specifically, we make the following changes to Program 20.8: First, we change the call on `sort` to a call on `pq.construct()` to build a heap in time proportional to E. Second, we change the inner loop to take the shortest edge off the priority queue with `e = pq.delmin()` and to change all references to `a[i]` to refer to `e`.

Property 20.10　*A priority-queue–based version of Kruskal's algorithm computes the MST of a graph in time proportional to* $E + X \lg V$, *where* X *is the number of graph edges not longer than the longest edge in the MST.*

Proof: See the preceding discussion, which shows the cost to be the cost of building a priority queue of size E plus the cost of running the X *delete the minimum*, X *find*, and $V - 1$ *union* operations. Note that the priority-queue–construction costs dominate (and the algorithm is linear time) unless X is greater than $E / \lg V$. ∎

We can also apply the same idea to reap similar benefits in a quicksort-based implementation. Consider what happens when we use a straight recursive quicksort, where we partition at `i`, then recursively sort the subfile to the left of `i` and the subfile to the right of `i`. We note that, by construction of the algorithm, the first `i` elements are in sorted order after completion of the first recursive call (see Program 9.2). This obvious fact leads immediately to a fast implementation of Kruskal's algorithm: If we put the check for whether the edge `a[i]` causes a cycle between the recursive calls, then we have an algorithm that, by construction, has checked the first `i` edges, in sorted order, after completion of the first recursive call! If we include a test to return when we have found `V-1` MST edges, then we have an algorithm that sorts only as many edges as we need to compute the MST, with a few extra partitioning stages involving larger elements (see Exercise 20.57). Like straight sorting implementations, this algorithm could run in quadratic time in the worst case, but we can provide a probabilistic guarantee that the worst-case running time will not come close to this limit. Also, like straight sorting implementations, this program is likely to be faster than a heap-based implementation because of its shorter inner loop.

If the graph is not connected, the partial-sort versions of Kruskal's algorithm offer no advantage because all the edges have to be considered. Even for a connected graph, the longest edge in the graph might be in the MST, so any implementation of Kruskal's method would still have to examine all the edges. For example, the graph might consist of tight clusters of vertices all connected together by short edges, with one outlier connected to one of the vertices by a long edge. Despite such anomalies, the partial-sort approach is probably worthwhile because it offers significant gain when it applies and incurs little if any extra cost.

Historical perspective is relevant and instructive here as well. Kruskal presented this algorithm in 1956, but, again, the relevant ADT implementations were not carefully studied for many years, so the performance characteristics of implementations such as the priority-queue version of Program 20.8 were not well understood until the 1970s. Other interesting historical notes are that Kruskal's paper mentioned a version of Prim's algorithm (see Exercise 20.59) and that Boruvka mentioned both approaches. Efficient implementations of Kruskal's method for sparse graphs preceded implementations of Prim's method for sparse graphs because union-find (and sort) ADTs came into use before priority-queue ADTs. Generally, as was true of implementations of Prim's algorithm, advances in the state of the art for Kruskal's algorithm are attributed primarily to advances in ADT performance. On the other hand, the applicability of the union-find abstraction to Kruskal's algorithm and the applicability of the priority-queue abstraction to Prim's algorithm have been prime motivations for many researchers to seek better implementations of those ADTs.

Exercises

▷ **20.53** Show, in the style of Figure 20.12, the result of computing the MST of the network defined in Exercise 20.26 with Kruskal's algorithm.

○ **20.54** Run empirical studies to analyze the length of the longest edge in the MST and the number of graph edges that are not longer than that one, for various weighted graphs (see Exercises 20.9–14).

● **20.55** Develop an implementation of the union-find ADT that implements *find* in constant time and *union* in time proportional to $\lg V$.

20.56 Run empirical tests to compare your ADT implementation from Exercise 20.55 to weighted union-find with halving (Program 1.4) when Kruskal's algorithm is the client, for various weighted graphs (see Exercises 20.9–14). Separate out the cost of sorting the edges so that you can study the effects of the change both on the total cost and on the part of the cost associated with the union-find ADT.

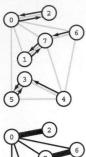

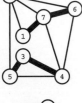

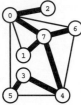

Figure 20.14
Boruvka's MST algorithm

The diagram at the top shows a directed edge from each vertex to its closest neighbor. These edges show that 0-2, 1-7, and 3-5 are each the shortest edge incident on both their vertices, 6-7 is 6's shortest edge, and 4-3 is 4's shortest edge. These edges all belong to the MST and comprise a forest of MST subtrees (center), as computed by the first phase of Boruvka's algorithm. In the second phase, the algorithm completes the MST computation (bottom) by adding the edge 0-7, which is the shortest edge incident on any of the vertices in the subtrees it connects, and the edge 4-7, which is the shortest edge incident on any of the vertices in the bottom subtree.

20.57 Develop an implementation based on the idea described in the text where we integrate Kruskal's algorithm with quicksort so as to check MST membership of each edge as soon as we know that all smaller edges have been checked.

○ **20.58** Adapt Kruskal's algorithm to implement two ADT functions that fill a client-supplied vertex-indexed vector classifying vertices into k clusters with the property that no edge of length greater than d connects two vertices in different clusters. For the first function, take k as an argument and return d; for the second, take d as an argument and return k. Test your program on random Euclidean neighbor graphs and on grid graphs (see Exercises 20.17 and 20.19) of various sizes for various values of k and d.

20.59 Develop an implementation of Prim's algorithm that is based on presorting the edges.

• **20.60** Write a client program that does dynamic graphical animations of Kruskal's algorithm (see Exercise 20.52). Test your program on random Euclidean neighbor graphs and on grid graphs (see Exercises 20.17 and 20.19), using as many points as you can process in a reasonable amount of time.

20.5 Boruvka's Algorithm

The next MST algorithm that we consider is also the oldest. Like Kruskal's algorithm, we build the MST by adding edges to a spreading forest of MST subtrees; but we do so in stages, adding several MST edges at each stage. At each stage, we find the shortest edge that connects each MST subtree with a different one, then add all such edges to the MST.

Again, our union-find ADT from Chapter 1 leads to an efficient implementation. For this problem, it is convenient to extend the interface to make the *find* operation available to clients. We use this function to associate an index with each subtree so that we can tell quickly to which subtree a given vertex belongs. With this capability, we can implement efficiently each of the necessary operations for Boruvka's algorithm.

First, we maintain a vertex-indexed vector that identifies, for each MST subtree, the nearest neighbor. Then, we perform the following operations on each edge in the graph:

• If it connects two vertices in the same tree, discard it.

• Otherwise, check the nearest-neighbor distances between the two trees the edge connects and update them if appropriate.

After this scan of all the graph edges, the nearest-neighbor vector has the information that we need to connect the subtrees. For each vertex index, we perform a *union* operation to connect it with its nearest neighbor. In the next stage, we discard all the longer edges that connect other pairs of vertices in the now-connected MST subtrees. Figures 20.14 and 20.15 illustrate this process on our sample algorithm

Program 20.9 is a direct implementation of Boruvka's algorithm. There are three major factors that make this implementation efficient:

- The cost of each *find* operation is essentially constant.
- Each stage decreases the number of MST subtrees in the forest by at least a factor of 2.
- A substantial number of edges is discarded during each stage.

It is difficult to quantify precisely all these factors, but the following bound is easy to establish.

Property 20.11 *The running time of Boruvka's algorithm for computing the MST of a graph is $O(E \lg V \lg^* E)$.*

Proof: Since the number of trees in the forest is halved at each stage, the number of stages is no larger than $\lg V$. The time for each stage is at most proportional to the cost of E *find* operations, which is less than $E \lg^* E$, or linear for practical purposes. ∎

The running time given in Property 20.11 is a conservative upper bound since it does not take into account the substantial reduction in the number of edges during each stage. The *find* operations take constant time in the early passes, and there are very few edges in the later passes. Indeed, for many graphs, the number of edges decreases exponentially with the number of vertices, and the total running time is proportional to E. For example, as illustrated in Figure 20.16, the algorithm finds the MST of our larger sample graph in just four stages.

It is possible to remove the $\lg^* E$ factor to lower the theoretical bound on the running time of Boruvka's algorithm to be proportional to $E \lg V$, by representing MST subtrees with doubly-linked lists instead of using the *union* and *find* operations. However, this improvement is sufficiently more complicated to implement and the potential performance improvement sufficiently marginal that it is not likely to be worth considering for use in practice (see Exercises 20.66 and 20.67).

	0	1	2	3	4	5	6	7
initial	0	1	2	3	4	5	6	7
stage 1	0	1	0	3	3	3	1	1
stage 2	1	1	1	1	1	1	1	1

Figure 20.15
Union-find array in Boruvka's algorithm

This figure depicts the contents of the union-find array corresponding to the example depicted in Figure 20.14. Initially, each entry contains its own index, indicating a forest of singleton vertices. After the first stage, we have three components, represented by the indices 0, 1, and 3 (the union-find trees are all flat for this tiny example). After the second stage, we have just one component, represented by 1.

Program 20.9 Boruvka's MST algorithm

This implementation of Boruvka's MST algorithm uses a version of the union-find ADT from Chapter 4 (with a single-argument `find` added to the interface) to associate indices with MST subtrees as they are built. Each phase checks all the remaining edges; those that connect disjoint subtrees are kept for the next phase. The array `a` has the edges not yet discarded and not yet in the MST. The index `N` is used to store those being saved for the next phase (the code resets `E` from `N` at the end of each phase) and the index `h` is used to access the next edge to be checked. Each component's nearest neighbor is kept in the array `b` with `find` component numbers as indices. At the end of each phase, each component is united with its nearest neighbor and the nearest-neighbor edges added to the MST.

```cpp
template <class Graph, class Edge> class MST
{ const Graph &G;
  vector<Edge *> a, b, mst;
  UF uf;
public:
  MST(const Graph &G): G(G), uf(G.V()), mst(G.V()+1)
  { a = edges<Graph, Edge>(G);
    int N, k = 1;
    for (int E = a.size(); E != 0; E = N)
    { int h, i, j;
      b.assign(G.V(), 0);
      for (h = 0, N = 0; h < E; h++)
      { Edge *e = a[h];
        i = uf.find(e->v()), j = uf.find(e->w());
        if (i == j) continue;
        if (!b[i] || e->wt() < b[i]->wt()) b[i] = e;
        if (!b[j] || e->wt() < b[j]->wt()) b[j] = e;
        a[N++] = e;
      }
      for (h = 0; h < G.V(); h++)
       if (b[h])
         if (!uf.find(i = b[h]->v(), j = b[h]->w()))
           { uf.unite(i, j); mst[k++] = b[h]; }
    }
  }
};
```

As we mentioned, Boruvka's is the oldest of the algorithms that we consider: It was originally conceived in 1926, for a power-distribution application. The method was rediscovered by Sollin in 1961; it later attracted attention as the basis for MST algorithms with efficient asymptotic performance and as the basis for parallel MST algorithms.

Exercises

▷ **20.61** Show, in the style of Figure 20.14, the result of computing the MST of the network defined in Exercise 20.26 with Boruvka's algorithm.

○ **20.62** Why does Program 20.9 do a *find* test before doing the *union* operation? *Hint*: Consider equal-length edges.

○ **20.63** Explain why b(h) could be null in the test in Program 20.9 that guards the *union* operation.

• **20.64** Describe a family of graphs with V vertices and E edges for which the number of edges that survive each stage of Boruvka's algorithm is sufficiently large that the worst-case running time is achieved.

20.65 Develop an implementation of Boruvka's algorithm that is based on a presorting of the edges.

○ **20.66** Develop an implementation of Boruvka's algorithm that uses doubly-linked circular lists to represent MST subtrees, so that subtrees can be merged and renamed in time proportional to E during each stage (and the equivalence-relations ADT is therefore not needed).

○ **20.67** Do empirical studies to compare your implementation of Boruvka's algorithm in Exercise 20.66 with the implementation in the text (Program 20.9), for various weighted graphs (see Exercises 20.9–14).

• **20.68** Do empirical studies to tabulate the number of stages and the number of edges processed per stage in Boruvka's algorithm, for various weighted graphs (see Exercises 20.9–14).

20.69 Develop an implementation of Boruvka's algorithm that constructs a new graph (one vertex for each tree in the forest) at each stage.

• **20.70** Write a client program that does dynamic graphical animations of Boruvka's algorithm (see Exercises 20.52 and 20.60). Test your program on random Euclidean neighbor graphs and on grid graphs (see Exercises 20.17 and 20.19), using as many points as you can process in a reasonable amount of time.

20.6 Comparisons and Improvements

Table 20.1 summarizes the running times of the basic MST algorithms that we have considered; Table 20.2 presents the results of an empirical

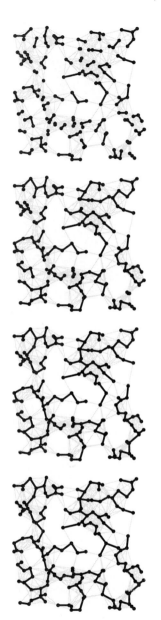

**Figure 20.16
Boruvka's MST algorithm**

The MST evolves in just four stages for this example (top to bottom).

study comparing the algorithms. From these tables, we can conclude that the adjacency-matrix implementation of Prim's algorithm is the method of choice for dense graphs, that all the other methods perform within a small constant factor of the best possible (the time that it takes to extract the edges) for graphs of intermediate density, and that Kruskal's method essentially reduces the problem to sorting for sparse graphs.

In short, we might consider the MST problem to be "solved" for practical purposes. For most graphs, the cost of finding the MST is only slightly higher than the cost of extracting the graph's edges. This rule holds except for huge graphs that are extremely sparse, but the available performance improvement over the best known algorithms even in this case is approximately a factor of 10 at best. The results in Table 20.2 are dependent on the model used to generate graphs, but they are borne out for many other graph models as well (see, for example, Exercise 20.80). Still, the theoretical results do not deny the existence of an algorithm that is guaranteed to run in linear time for all graphs; here we take a look at the extensive research on improved implementations of these methods.

First, much research has gone into developing better priority-queue implementations. The *Fibonacci heap* data structure, an extension of the binomial queue, achieves the theoretically optimal performance of taking constant time for *decrease key* operations and logarithmic time for *remove the minimum* operations, which behavior translates, by Property 20.8, to a running time proportional to $E + V \lg V$ for Prim's algorithm. Fibonacci heaps are more complicated than binomial queues and are somewhat unwieldy in practice, but some simpler priority-queue implementations have similar performance characteristics (*see reference section*).

One effective approach is to use radix methods for the priority-queue implementation. Performance of such methods is typically equivalent to that of radix sorting for Kruskal's method, or even to that of using a radix quicksort for the partial-sorting method that we discussed in Section 20.4.

Another simple early approach, proposed by D. Johnson in 1977, is one of the most effective: Implement the priority queue for Prim's algorithm with d-ary heaps, instead of with standard binary heaps (see Figure 20.17). Program 20.10 is a complete implementation of the

Table 20.1 Cost of MST algorithms

This table summarizes the cost (worst-case running time) of various MST algorithms considered in this chapter. The formulas are based on the assumptions that an MST exists (which implies that $E \geq V - 1$) and that there are X edges not longer than the longest edge in the MST (see Property 20.10). These worst-case bounds may be too conservative to be useful in predicting performance on real graphs. The algorithms run in near-linear time in a broad variety of practical situations.

algorithm	worst-case cost	comment
Prim (standard)	V^2	optimal for dense graphs
Prim (PFS, heap)	$E \lg V$	conservative upper bound
Prim (PFS, d-heap)	$E \log_d V$	linear unless extremely sparse
Kruskal	$E \lg E$	sort cost dominates
Kruskal (partial sort)	$E + X \lg V$	cost depends on longest edge
Boruvka	$E \lg V$	conservative upper bound

priority-queue interface that we have been using that is based on this method. For this priority-queue implementation, *decrease key* takes less than $\log_d V$ steps, and *remove the minimum* takes time proportional to $d \log_d V$. By Property 20.8, this behavior leads to a running time proportional to $V d \log_d V + E \log_d V$ for Prim's algorithm, which is linear for graphs that are not sparse.

Property 20.12 *Given a graph with V vertices and E edges, let d denote the density E/V. If $d < 2$, then the running time of Prim's algorithm is proportional to $V \lg V$. Otherwise, we can improve the worst-case running time by a factor of $\lg(E/V)$ by using a $\lceil E/V \rceil$-ary heap for the priority queue.*

Proof: Continuing the discussion in the previous paragraph, the number of steps is $V d \log_d V + E \log_d V$, so the running time is at most proportional to $E \log_d V = (E \lg V)/\lg d$. ∎

When E is proportional to $V^{1+\epsilon}$, Property 20.12 leads to a worst-case running time proportional to E/ϵ, and that value is linear for any constant ϵ. For example, if the number of edges is proportional to $V^{3/2}$, the cost is less than $2E$; if the number of edges is proportional to

Table 20.2 Empirical study of MST algorithms

This table shows relative timings for various algorithms for finding the MST, for random weighted graphs of various density. For low densities, Kruskal's algorithm is best because it amounts to a fast sort. For high densities, the classical implementation of Prim's algorithm is best because it does not incur list-processing overhead. For intermediate densities, the PFS implementation of Prim's algorithm runs within a small factor of the time that it takes to examine each graph edge.

E	V	C	H	J	P	K	K*	e/E	B	e/E
density 2										
20000	10000	2	22	27		9	11	1.00	14	3.3
50000	25000	8	69	84		24	31	1.00	38	3.3
100000	50000	15	169	203		49	66	1.00	89	3.8
200000	100000	30	389	478		108	142	1.00	189	3.6
density 20										
20000	1000	2	5	4	20	6	5	.20	9	4.2
50000	2500	12	12	13	130	16	15	.28	25	4.6
100000	5000	14	27	28		34	31	.30	55	4.6
200000	10000	29	61	61		73	68	.35	123	5.0
density 100										
100000	1000	14	17	17	24	30	19	.06	51	4.6
250000	2500	36	44	44	130	81	53	.05	143	5.2
500000	5000	73	93	93		181	113	.06	312	5.5
1000000	10000	151	204	198		377	218	.06	658	5.6
density $V/2.5$										
400000	1000	61	60	59	20	137	78	.02	188	4.5
2500000	2500	597	409	400	128	1056	687	.01	1472	5.5

Key:
    C extract edges only
    H Prim's algorithm (adjacency lists/indexed heap)
    J Johnson's version of Prim's algorithm (*d*-heap priority queue)
    P Prim's algorithm (adjacency-matrix representation)
    K Kruskal's algorithm
    K* Partial-sort version of Kruskal's algorithm
    B Boruvka's algorithm
    e edges examined (*union* operations)

$V^{4/3}$, the cost is less than $3E$; and if the number of edges is proportional to $V^{5/4}$, the cost is less than $4E$. For a graph with 1 million vertices, the cost is less than $6E$ unless the density is less than 10.

The temptation to minimize the bound on the worst-case running time in this way needs to be tempered with the realization that the $Vd\log_d V$ part of the cost is not likely to be avoided (for *remove the minimum*, we have to examine d successors in the heap as we sift down), but the $E\lg d$ part is not likely to be achieved (since most edges will not require a priority-queue update, as we showed in the discussion following Property 20.8).

For typical graphs such as those in the experiments in Table 20.2, decreasing d has no effect on the running time, and using a large value of d can slow down the implementation slightly. Still, the slight protection offered for worst-case performance makes the method worthwhile since it is so easy to implement. In principle, we could tune the implementation to pick the best value of d for certain types of graphs (choose the largest value that does not slow down the algorithm), but a small fixed value (such as 4, 5, or 6) will be fine except possibly for some particular huge classes of graphs that have atypical characteristics.

Using d-heaps is not effective for sparse graphs because d has to be an integer greater than or equal to 2, a condition that implies that we cannot bring the asymptotic running time lower than $V\lg V$. If the density is a small constant, then a linear-time MST algorithm would have to run in time proportional to V.

The goal of developing practical algorithms for computing the MST of sparse graphs in linear time remains elusive. A great deal of research has been done on variations of Boruvka's algorithm as the basis for nearly linear-time MST algorithms for extremely sparse graphs (*see reference section*). Such research still holds the potential to lead us eventually to a practical linear-time MST algorithm and has even shown the existence of a randomized linear time algorithm. While these algorithms are generally quite complicated, simplified versions of some of them may yet be shown to be useful in practice. In the meantime, we can use the basic algorithms that we have considered here to compute the MST in linear time in most practical situations, perhaps paying an extra factor of $\lg V$ for some sparse graphs.

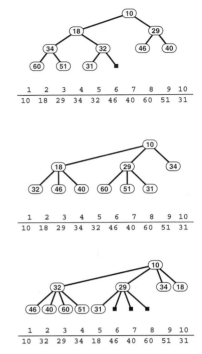

Figure 20.17
2-, 3-, and 4-ary heaps

When we store a standard binary heap-ordered complete tree in an array (top), we use implicit links to take us from a node i down the tree to its children $2i$ and $2i+1$ and up the tree to its parent $i/2$. In a 3-ary heap (center), implicit links for i are to its children $3i-1$, $3i$, and $3i+1$ and to its parent $\lfloor(i+1)/3\rfloor$; and in a 4-ary heap (bottom), implicit links for i are to its children $4i-2$, $4i-1$, $4i$, and $4i+1$ and to its parent $\lfloor(i+2)/4\rfloor$. Increasing the branching factor in an implicit heap implementation can be valuable in applications, like Prim's algorithm, that require a significant number of decrease key operations.

Program 20.10 Multiway heap PQ implementation

This class uses multiway heaps to implement the indirect priority-queue interface that we use in this book. It is based on changing Program 9.12 to have the constructor take a reference to a vector of priorities, to implement getmin and lower instead of delmax and change, and to generalize fixUp and fixDown so that they maintain a d-way heap (so *remove the minimum* takes time proportional to $d \log_d V$, but *decrease key* requires less than $\log_d V$ steps).

```cpp
template <class keyType> class PQi
{ int d, N;
  vector<int> pq, qp;
  const vector<keyType> &a;
  void exch(int i, int j)
    { int t = pq[i]; pq[i] = pq[j]; pq[j] = t;
      qp[pq[i]] = i; qp[pq[j]] = j; }
  void fixUp(int k)
    { while (k > 1 && a[pq[(k+d-2)/d]] > a[pq[k]])
        { exch(k, (k+d-2)/d); k = (k+d-2)/d; } }
  void fixDown(int k, int N)
    { int j;
      while ((j = d*(k-1)+2) <= N)
        {
          for (int i = j+1; i < j+d && i <= N; i++)
            if (a[pq[j]] > a[pq[i]]) j = i;
          if (!(a[pq[k]] > a[pq[j]])) break;
          exch(k, j); k = j;
        }
    }
public:
  PQi(int N, const vector<keyType> &a, int d = 3) :
    a(a), pq(N+1, 0), qp(N+1, 0), N(0), d(d) { }
  int empty() const { return N == 0; }
  void insert(int v)
    { pq[++N] = v; qp[v] = N; fixUp(N); }
  int getmin()
    { exch(1, N); fixDown(1, N-1); return pq[N--]; }
  void lower(int k)
    { fixUp(qp[k]); }
};
```

Exercises

∘ **20.71** [V. Vyssotsky] Develop an implementation of the algorithm discussed in Section 20.2 that builds the MST by adding edges one at a time and deleting the longest edges on the cycle formed (see Exercise 20.33). Use a parent-link representation of a forest of MST subtrees. *Hint*: Reverse pointers when traversing paths in trees.

20.72 Run empirical tests to compare the running time of your implementation in Exercise 20.71 with that of Kruskal's algorithm, for various weighted graphs (see Exercises 20.9–14). Check whether randomizing the order in which the edges are considered affects your results.

● **20.73** Describe how you would find the MST of a graph so large that only V edges can fit into main memory at once.

∘ **20.74** Develop a priority-queue implementation for which *remove the minimum* and *find the minimum* are constant-time operations, and for which *decrease key* takes time proportional to the logarithm of the priority-queue size. Compare your implementation with 4-heaps when you use Prim's algorithm to find the MST of sparse graphs, for various weighted graphs (see Exercises 20.9–14).

20.75 Run empirical studies to compare the performance of various priority-queue implementations when used in Prim's algorithm for various weighted graphs (see Exercises 20.9–14). Consider d-heaps for various values of d, binomial queues, the STL `priority_queue`, balanced trees, and any other data structure that you think might be effective.

20.76 Develop an implementation that generalizes Boruvka's algorithm to maintain a generalized queue containing the forest of MST subtrees. (Using Program 20.9 corresponds to using a FIFO queue.) Experiment with other generalized-queue implementations, for various weighted graphs (see Exercises 20.9–14).

● **20.77** Develop a generator for random connected cubic graphs (each vertex of degree 3) that have random weights on the edges. Fine-tune for this case the MST algorithms that we have discussed, then determine which is the fastest.

∘ **20.78** For $V = 10^6$, plot the ratio of the upper bound on the cost for Prim's algorithm with d-heaps to E as a function of the density d, for d in the range from 1 to 100.

∘ **20.79** Table 20.2 suggests that the standard implementation of Kruskal's algorithm is significantly faster than the partial-sort implementation for low-density graphs. Explain this phenomenon.

● **20.80** Run an empirical study, in the style of Table 20.2, for random complete graphs that have Gaussian weights (see Exercise 20.18).

20.7 Euclidean MST

Suppose that we are given N points in the plane and we want to find the shortest set of lines connecting all the points. This geometric problem is called the *Euclidean MST* problem (see Figure 20.18). One way to solve it is to build a complete graph with N vertices and $N(N-1)/2$ edges—one edge connecting each pair of vertices weighted with the distance between the corresponding points. Then, we can use Prim's algorithm to find the MST in time proportional to N^2.

This solution is generally too slow. The Euclidean problem is somewhat different from the graph problems that we have been considering because all the edges are implicitly defined. The size of the input is just proportional to N, so the solution that we have sketched is a *quadratic* algorithm for the problem. Research has proved that it is possible to do better. The geometric structure makes most of the edges in the complete graph irrelevant to the problem, and we do not need to add most of them to the graph before we construct the minimum spanning tree.

Property 20.13 *We can find the Euclidean MST of N points in time proportional to $N \log N$.*

This fact is a direct consequence of two basic facts about points in the plane that we discuss in detail in Part 7. First, a graph known as the *Delauney triangulation* contains the MST, by definition. Second, the Delauney triangulation is a planar graph whose number of edges is proportional to N. ∎

In principle, then, we could compute the Delauney triangulation in time proportional to $N \log N$, then run either Kruskal's algorithm or the priority-first search method to find the Euclidean MST, in time proportional to $N \log N$. But writing a program to compute the Delauney triangulation is a challenge for even an experienced programmer, so this approach may be overkill for this problem in practice.

Other approaches derive from the geometric algorithms that we consider in Part 7. For randomly distributed points, we can divide up the plane into squares such that each square is likely to contain about $\lg N/2$ points, as we did for the closest-point computation in Program 3.20. Then, even if we include in the graph only the edges connecting each point to the points in the neighboring squares, we

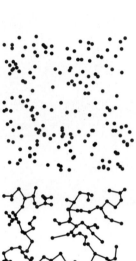

Figure 20.18
Euclidean MST

Given a set of N points in the plane (top), the Euclidean MST is the shortest set of lines connecting them together (bottom). This problem is not just a graph-processing problem, because we need to make use of global geometric information about the points to avoid having to process all N^2 implicit edges connecting the points.

are likely (but are not guaranteed) to get all the edges in the minimum spanning tree; in that case, we could use Kruskal's algorithm or the PFS implementation of Prim's algorithm to finish the job efficiently. The example that we have used in Figure 20.10, Figure 20.13, Figure 20.16 and similar figures was created in this way (see Figure 20.19). Or, we could develop a version of Prim's algorithm based on using near-neighbor algorithms to avoid updating distant vertices.

With all the possible choices that we have for approaching this problem and with the possibility of linear algorithms for the general MST problem, it is important to note that there is a simple lower bound on the best that we could do.

Property 20.14 *Finding the Euclidean MST of N points is no easier than sorting N numbers.*

Proof: Given a list of numbers to be sorted, convert the list into a list of points where the x coordinate is taken from the corresponding number of the list and the y coordinate is 0. Find the MST of that list of points. Then (as we did for Kruskal's algorithm), put the points into a graph ADT and run DFS to produce a spanning tree, starting at the point with the lowest x coordinate. That spanning tree amounts to a linked-list sort of the numbers in order; thus, we have solved the sorting problem. ∎

Precise interpretations of this lower bound are complicated because the basic operations used for the two problems (comparisons of coordinates for the sorting problem, distances for the MST problem) are different and because there is a possibility of using methods such as radix sort and grid methods. However, we may interpret the bound to mean that, as we do sorting, we should consider a Euclidean MST algorithm that uses $N \lg N$ comparisons to be optimal unless we exploit numerical properties of the coordinates, in which case we might expect to it to be linear time (*see reference section*).

It is interesting to reflect on the relationship between graph and geometric algorithms that is brought out by the Euclidean MST problem. Many of the practical problems that we might encounter could be formulated either as geometric problems or as graph problems. If the physical placement of objects is a dominating characteristic, then the geometric algorithms of Part 7 may be called for; but if interconnec-

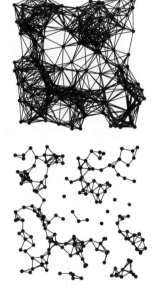

Figure 20.19
Euclidean near-neighbor graphs

One way to compute the Euclidean MST is to generate a graph with edges connecting every pair of points within a distance d, as in the graph in Figure 20.8 et al. However, this method yields too many edges if d is too large (top) and is not guaranteed to have edges connecting all the points if d is smaller than the longest edge in the MST (bottom).

tions between objects are of fundamental importance, then the graph algorithms of this section may be better.

The Euclidean MST seems to fall at the interface between these two approaches (the input involves geometry and the output involves interconnections), and the development of simple, straightforward methods for the Euclidean MST remains an elusive goal. In Chapter 21, we see a similar problem that falls at this interface, but where a Euclidean approach admits substantially faster algorithms than do the corresponding graph problems.

Exercises

▷ **20.81** Give a counterexample to show why the following method for finding the Euclidean MST does not work: "Sort the points on their x coordinates, then find the minimum spanning trees of the first half and the second half, then find the shortest edge that connects them."

○ **20.82** Develop a fast version of Prim's algorithm for computing the Euclidean MST of a uniformly distributed set of points in the plane based on ignoring distant points until the tree approaches them.

•• **20.83** Develop an algorithm that, given a set of N points in the plane, finds a set of edges of cardinality proportional to N that is certain to contain the MST and is sufficiently easy to compute that you can develop a concise and efficient implementation of your algorithm.

○ **20.84** Given a random set of N points in the unit square (uniformly distributed), empirically determine a value of d, to within two decimal places, such that the set of edges defined by all pairs of points within distance d of one another is 99 percent certain to contain the MST.

○ **20.85** Work Exercise 20.84 for points where each coordinate is drawn from a Gaussian distribution with mean 0.5 and standard deviation 0.1.

• **20.86** Describe how you would improve the performance of Kruskal's and Boruvka's algorithm for sparse Euclidean graphs.

Shortest Paths

EVERY PATH IN a weighted digraph has an associated *path weight*, the value of which is the sum of the weights of that path's edges. This essential measure allows us to formulate such problems as "find the lowest-weight path between two given vertices." These *shortest-paths problems* are the topic of this chapter. Not only are shortest-paths problems intuitive for many direct applications, but they also take us into a powerful and general realm where we seek efficient algorithms to solve general problems that can encompass a broad variety of specific applications.

Several of the algorithms that we consider in this chapter relate directly to various algorithms that we examined in Chapters 17 through 20. Our basic graph-search paradigm applies immediately, and several of the specific mechanisms that we used in Chapters 17 and 19 to address connectivity in graphs and digraphs provide the basis for us to solve shortest-paths problems.

For economy, we refer to weighted digraphs as *networks*. Figure 21.1 shows a sample network, with standard representations. We have already developed an ADT interface with adjacency-matrix and adjacency-lists class implementations for networks in Section 20.1— we just pass true as a second argument when we call the constructor so that the class keeps one representation of each edge, precisely as we did when deriving digraph representations in Chapter 19 from the undirected graph representations in Chapter 17 (see Programs 20.1 through 20.4).

As discussed at length in Chapter 20, we use pointers to abstract edges for weighted digraphs to broaden the applicability of our implementations. This approach has certain implications that are different

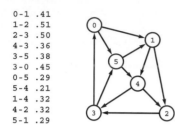

0-1	.41
1-2	.51
2-3	.50
4-3	.36
3-5	.38
3-0	.45
0-5	.29
5-4	.21
1-4	.32
4-2	.32
5-1	.29

	0	1	2	3	4	5
0	0	.41				.29
1		0	.51		.32	
2			0	.50		
3	.45			0		.38
4			.32	.36	0	
5		.29			.21	0

Adjacency lists:

0	→ 0 0	→ 5 .29	→ 1 .41
1	→ 1 0	→ 4 .32	→ 2 .51
2	→ 2 0	→ 3 .50
3	→ 3 0	→ 0 .45	→ 5 .38
4	→ 4 0	→ 2 .32	→ 3 .36
5	→ 5 0	→ 1 .29	→ 4 .21

Figure 21.1
**Sample network and represen-
tations**

*This network (weighted digraph)
is shown in four representations:
list of edges, drawing, adjacency
matrix, and adjacency lists (left
to right). As we did for MST algorithms, we show the weights in
matrix entries and in list nodes,
but use edge pointers in our programs. While we often use edge
weights that are proportional to
their lengths in the drawing (as
we did for MST algorithms), we
do not insist on this rule because
most shortest-paths algorithms handle arbitrary nonnegative weights
(negative weights do present special challenges). The adjacency
matrix is not symmetric, and the
adjacency lists contain one node
for each edge (as in unweighted
digraphs). Nonexistent edges are
represented by null pointers in the
matrix (blank in the figure) and are
not present at all in the lists. Self-
loops of length 0 are present because they simplify our implementations of shortest-paths algorithms.
They are omitted from the list of
edges at left for economy and to
indicate the typical scenario where
we add them by convention when
we create an adjacency-matrix or
adjacency-lists representation.*

for digraphs than the ones that we considered for undirected graphs in
Section 20.1 and are worth noting. First, since there is only one representation of each edge, we do not need to use the `from` function in
the edge class (see Program 20.1) when using an iterator: In a digraph,
`e->from(v)` is `true` for every edge pointer `e` feturn by an iterator for
v. Second, as we saw in Chapter 19, it is often useful when processing
a digraph to be able to work with its reverse graph, but we need a
different approach than that taken by Program 19.1, because that implementation creates edges to create the reverse, and we assume that a
graph ADT whose clients provide pointers to edges should not create
edges on its own (see Exercise 21.3).

In applications or systems for which we need all types of graphs,
it is a textbook exercise in software engineering to define a network
ADT from which ADTs for the unweighted undirected graphs of Chapters 17 and 18, the unweighted digraphs of Chapter 19, or the weighted
undirected graphs of Chapter 20 can be derived (see Exercise 21.10).

When we work with networks, it is generally convenient to keep
self-loops in all the representations. This convention allows algorithms
the flexibility to use a sentinel maximum-value weight to indicate that a
vertex cannot be reached from itself. In our examples, we use self-loops
of weight 0, although positive-weight self-loops certainly make sense
in many applications. Many applications also call for parallel edges,
perhaps with differing weights. As we mentioned in Section 20.1,
various options for ignoring or combining such edges are appropriate
in various different applications. In this chapter, for simplicity, none of
our examples use parallel edges, and we do not allow parallel edges in
the adjacency-matrix representation; we also do not check for parallel
edges or remove them in adjacency lists.

All the connectivity properties of digraphs that we considered in
Chapter 19 are relevant in networks. In that chapter, we wished to

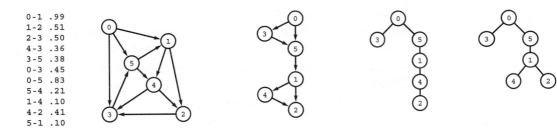

0-1 .99
1-2 .51
2-3 .50
4-3 .36
3-5 .38
0-3 .45
0-5 .83
5-4 .21
1-4 .10
4-2 .41
5-1 .10

know whether it is *possible* to get from one vertex to another; in this chapter, we take weights into consideration—we wish to find the *best* way to get from one vertex to another.

Definition 21.1   *A* **shortest path** *between two vertices s and t in a network is a directed simple path from s to t with the property that no other such path has a lower weight.*

This definition is succinct, but its brevity masks points worth examining. First, if t is not reachable from s, there is no path at all, and therefore there is no shortest path. For convenience, the algorithms that we consider often treat this case as equivalent to one in which there exists an infinite-weight path from s to t. Second, as we did for MST algorithms, we use networks where edge weights are proportional to edge lengths in examples, but the definition has no such requirement and our algorithms (other than the one in Section 21.5) do not make this assumption. Indeed, shortest-paths algorithms are at their best when they discover counterintuitive shortcuts, such as a path between two vertices that passes through several other vertices but has total weight smaller than that of a direct edge connecting those vertices. Third, there may be multiple paths of the same weight from one vertex to another; we typically are content to find one of them. Figure 21.2 shows an example with general weights that illustrates these points.

The restriction in the definition to simple paths is unnecessary in networks that contain edges that have nonnegative weight, because any cycle in a path in such a network can be removed to give a path that is no longer (and is shorter unless the cycle comprises zero-weight edges). But when we consider networks with edges that could have negative weight, the need for the restriction to simple paths is readily apparent: Otherwise, the concept of a shortest path is meaningless if there is a cycle in the network that has negative weight. For example,

**Figure 21.2
Shortest-path trees**

A shortest-path tree (SPT) defines shortest paths from the root to other vertices (see Definition 21.2). In general, different paths may have the same length, so there may be multiple SPTs defining the shortest paths from a given vertex. In the example network shown at left, all shortest paths from 0 are subgraphs of the DAG shown to the right of the network. A tree rooted at 0 spans this DAG if and only if it is an SPT for 0. The two trees at right are such trees.

suppose that the edge 3–5 in the network in Figure 21.1 were to have weight –.38, and edge 5–1 were to have weight –.31. Then, the weight of the cycle 1-4-3-5-1 would be .32 + .36 – .38 – .31 = –.01, and we could spin around that cycle to generate arbitrarily short paths. Note carefully that, as is true in this example, it is *not* necessary for all the edges on a negative-weight cycle to be of negative weight; what counts is the *sum* of the edge weights. For brevity, we use the term *negative cycle* to refer to directed cycles whose total weight is negative.

In the definition, suppose that some vertex on a path from s to t is also on a negative cycle. In this case, the existence of a (nonsimple) shortest path from s to t would be a contradiction, because we could use the cycle to construct a path that had a weight lower than any given value. To avoid this contradiction, we restrict to simple paths in the definition so that the concept of a shortest path is well defined in any network. However, we do not consider negative cycles in networks until Section 21.7, because, as we see there, they present a truly fundamental barrier to the solution of shortest-paths problems.

To find shortest paths in a weighted undirected graph, we build a network with the same vertices and with two edges (one in each direction) corresponding to each edge in the graph. There is a one-to-one correspondence between simple paths in the network and simple paths in the graph, and the costs of the paths are the same; so shortest-paths problems are equivalent. Indeed, we build precisely such a network when we build the standard adjacency-lists or adjacency-matrix representation of a weighted undirected graph (see, for example, Figure 20.3). This construction is not helpful if weights can be negative, because it gives negative cycles in the network, and we do not know how to solve shortest-paths problems in networks that have negative cycles (see Section 21.7). Otherwise, the algorithms for networks that we consider in this chapter also work for weighted undirected graphs.

In certain applications, it is convenient to have weights on vertices instead of, or in addition to, weights on edges; and we might also consider more complicated problems where both the number of edges on the path and the overall weight of the path play a role. We can handle such problems by recasting them in terms of edge-weighted networks (see, for example, Exercise 21.4) or by slightly extending the basic algorithms (see, for example, Exercise 21.52).

	0	.41	0-1	.82	0-5-4-2	.86	0-5-4-3	.50	0-5-4	.29	0-5
1.13	1-4-3-0		1	.51	1-2	.68	1-4-3	.32	1-4	1.06	1-4-3-5
.95	2-3-0	1.17	2-3-5-1		2	.50	2-3	1.09	2-3-5-4	.88	2-3-5
.45	3-0	.67	3-5-1	.91	3-5-4-2	0	3	.59	3-5-4	.38	3-5
.81	4-3-0	1.03	4-3-5-1	.32	4-2	.36	4-3	0	4	.74	4-3-5
1.02	5-4-3-0	.29	5-1	.53	5-4-2	.57	5-4-3	.21	5-4	0	5

Because the distinction is clear from the context, we do not introduce special terminology to distinguish shortest paths in weighted graphs from shortest paths in graphs that have no weights (where a path's weight is simply its number of edges—see Section 17.7). The usual nomenclature refers to (edge-weighted) networks, as used in this chapter, since the special cases presented by undirected or unweighted graphs are handled easily by algorithms that process networks.

We are interested in the same basic problems that we defined for undirected and unweighted graphs in Section 18.7. We restate them here, noting that Definition 21.1 implicitly generalizes them to take weights into account in networks.

Source–sink shortest path   Given a start vertex s and a finish vertex t, find a shortest path in the graph from s to t. We refer to the start vertex as the *source* and to the finish vertex as the *sink*, except in contexts where this usage conflicts with the definition of sources (vertices with no incoming edges) and sinks (vertices with no outgoing edges) in digraphs.

Single-source shortest paths   Given a start vertex s, find shortest paths from s to each other vertex in the graph.

All-pairs shortest paths   Find shortest paths connecting each pair of vertices in the graph. For brevity, we sometimes use the term *all shortest paths* to refer to this set of V^2 paths.

If there are multiple shortest paths connecting any given pair of vertices, we are content to find any one of them. Since paths have varying number of edges, our implementations provide member functions that allow clients to trace paths in time proportional to the paths' lengths. Any shortest path also implicitly gives us the shortest-path length, but our implementations explicitly provide lengths. In summary, to be precise, when we say "find a shortest path" in the problem statements just given, we mean "compute the shortest-path length and a way to trace a specific path in time proportional to that path's length."

**Figure 21.3
All shortest paths**

This table gives all the shortest paths in the network of Figure 21.1 and their lengths. This network is strongly connected, so there exist paths connecting each pair of vertices.

The goal of a source-sink shortest-path algorithm is to compute one of the entries in this table; the goal of a single-source shortest-paths algorithm is to compute one of the rows in this table; and the goal of an all-pairs shortest-paths algorithm is to compute the whole table. Generally, we use more compact representations, which contain essentially the same information and allow clients to trace any path in time proportional to its number of edges (see Figure 21.8).

Figure 21.3 illustrates shortest paths for the example network in Figure 21.1. In networks with V vertices, we need to specify V paths to solve the single-source problem, and to specify V^2 paths to solve the all-pairs problem. In our implementations, we use a representation more compact than these lists of paths; we first noted it in Section 18.7, and we consider it in detail in Section 21.1.

In C++ implementations, we build our algorithmic solutions to these problems into ADT implementations that allow us to build efficient client programs that can solve a variety of practical graph-processing problems. For example, as we see in Section 21.3, we implement solutions to the all-pairs shortest-paths classes as constructors within classes that support constant-time shortest-path queries. We also build classes to solve single-source problems so that clients who need to compute shortest paths from a specific vertex (or a small set of them) can avoid the expense of computing shortest paths for other vertices. Careful consideration of such issues and proper use of the algorithms that we examine can mean the difference between an efficient solution to a practical problem and a solution that is so costly that no client could afford to use it.

Shortest-paths problems arise in various guises in numerous applications. Many of the applications appeal immediately to geometric intuition, but many others involve arbitrary cost structures. As we did with minimum spanning trees (MSTs) in Chapter 20, we sometimes take advantage of geometric intuition to help develop an understanding of algorithms that solve the problems but stay cognizant that our algorithms operate properly in more general settings. In Section 21.5, we do consider specialized algorithms for Euclidean networks. More important, in Sections 21.6 and 21.7, we see that the basic algorithms are effective for numerous applications where networks represent an abstract model of the computation.

Road maps   Tables that give distances between all pairs of major cities are a prominent feature of many road maps. We presume that the map maker took the trouble to be sure that the distances are the shortest ones, but our assumption is not necessarily always valid (see, for example, Exercise 21.11). Generally, such tables are for undirected graphs that we should treat as networks with edges in both directions corresponding to each road, though we might contemplate handling one-way streets for city maps and some similar applications.

As we see in Section 21.3, it is not difficult to provide other useful information, such as a table that tells how to execute the shortest paths (see Figure 21.4). In modern applications, embedded systems provide this kind of capability in cars and transportation systems. Maps are Euclidean graphs; in Section 21.4, we examine shortest-paths algorithms that take into account the vertex position when they seek shortest paths.

Airline routes   Route maps and schedules for airlines or other transportation systems can be represented as networks for which various shortest-paths problems are of direct importance. For example, we might wish to minimize the time that it takes to fly between two cities, or to minimize the cost of the trip. Costs in such networks might involve functions of time, of money, or of other complicated resources. For example, flights between two cities typically take more time in one direction than the other because of prevailing winds. Air travelers also know that the fare is not necessarily a simple function of the distance between the cities—situations where it is cheaper to use a circuitous route (or endure a stopover) than to take a direct flight are all too common. Such complications can be handled by the basic shortest-paths algorithms that we consider in this chapter; these algorithms are designed to handle any positive costs.

The fundamental shortest-paths computations suggested by these applications only scratch the surface of the applicability of shortest-paths algorithms. In Section 21.6, we consider problems from applications areas that appear unrelated to these natural ones, in the context of a discussion of *reduction*, a formal mechanism for proving relationships among problems. We solve problems for these applications by transforming them into abstract shortest-paths problems that do not have the intuitive geometric feel of the problems just described. Indeed, some applications lead us to consider shortest-paths problems in networks with negative weights. Such problems can be far more difficult to solve than are problems where negative weights cannot occur. Shortest-paths problems for such applications not only bridge a gap between elementary algorithms and unsolved algorithmic challenges but also lead us to powerful and general problem-solving mechanisms.

As with MST algorithms in Chapter 20, we often mix the weight, cost, and distance metaphors. Again, we normally exploit the natural appeal of geometric intuition even when working in more general

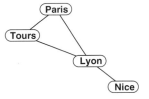

	Lyon	Nice	Paris	Tours
Lyon		200	400	420
Nice	200		600	620
Paris	400	600		120
Tours	420	620	120	

	Lyon	Nice	Paris	Tours
Lyon		Nice	Paris	Tours
Nice	Lyon		Paris	Lyon
Paris	Lyon	Lyon		Tours
Tours	Lyon	Lyon	Paris	

**Figure 21.4
Distances and paths**

Road maps typically contain distance tables like the one in the center for this tiny subset of French cities connected by highways as shown in the graph at the top. Though rarely found in maps, a table like the one at the bottom would also be useful, as it tells what signs to follow to execute the shortest path. For example, to decide how to get from Paris to Nice, we can check the table, which says to begin by following signs to Lyon.

settings with arbitrary edge weights; thus we refer to the "length" of paths and edges when we should say "weight" and to one path as "shorter" than another when we should say that it "has lower weight." We also might say that v is "closer" to s than w when we should say that "the lowest-weight directed path from s to v has weight lower than that of the lowest-weight directed path s to w," and so forth. This usage is inherent in the standard use of the term "shortest paths" and is natural even when weights are not related to distances (see Figure 21.2); however, when we expand our algorithms to handle negative weights in Section 21.6, we must abandon such usage.

This chapter is organized as follows. After introducing the basic underlying principles in Section 21.1, we introduce basic algorithms for the single-source and all-pairs shortest-paths problems in Sections 21.2 and 21.3. Then, we consider acyclic networks (or, in a clash of short-hand terms, weighted DAGs) in Section 21.4 and ways of exploiting geometric properties for the source–sink problem in Euclidean graphs in Section 21.5. We then cast off in the other direction to look at more general problems in Sections 21.6 and 21.7, where we explore shortest-paths algorithms, perhaps involving networks with negative weights, as a high-level problem-solving tool.

Exercises

▷ **21.1** Label the following points in the plane 0 through 5, respectively:

(1, 3) (2, 1) (6, 5) (3, 4) (3, 7) (5, 3).

Taking edge lengths to be weights, consider the network defined by the edges

1-0 3-5 5-2 3-4 5-1 0-3 0-4 4-2 2-3.

Draw the network and give the adjacency-lists structure that is built by Program 20.5.

21.2 Show, in the style of Figure 21.3, all shortest paths in the network defined in Exercise 21.1.

○ **21.3** Develop a network class implementation that represents the reverse of the weighted digraph defined by the edges inserted. Include a "reverse copy" constructor that takes a graph as argument and inserts all that graph's edges to build its reverse.

○ **21.4** Show that shortest-paths computations in networks with nonnegative weights on *both* vertices and edges (where the weight of a path is defined to be the sum of the weights of the vertices and the edges on the path) can be handled by building a network ADT that has weights on only the edges.

21.5 Find a large network online—perhaps a geographic database with entries for roads that connect cities or an airline or railroad schedule that contains distances or costs.

21.6 Write a random-network generator for sparse networks based on Program 17.12. To assign edge weights, define a random-edge–weight ADT and write two implementations: one that generates uniformly distributed weights, another that generates weights according to a Gaussian distribution. Write client programs to generate sparse random networks for both weight distributions with a well-chosen set of values of V and E so that you can use them to run empirical tests on graphs drawn from various distributions of edge weights.

∘ **21.7** Write a random-network generator for dense networks based on Program 17.13 and edge-weight generators as described in Exercise 21.6. Write client programs to generate random networks for both weight distributions with a well-chosen set of values of V and E so that you can use them to run empirical tests on graphs drawn from these models.

21.8 Implement a representation-independent network client function that builds a network by taking edges with weights (pairs of integers between 0 and $V - 1$ with weights between 0 and 1) from standard input.

• **21.9** Write a program that generates V random points in the plane, then builds a network with edges (in both directions) connecting all pairs of points within a given distance d of one another (see Exercise 17.74), setting each edge's weight to the distance between the two points that that edge connects. Determine how to set d so that the expected number of edges is E.

∘ **21.10** Write a base class and derived classes that implement ADTs for graphs that may be undirected or directed graphs, weighted or unweighted, and dense or sparse.

▷ **21.11** The following table from a published road map purports to give the length of the shortest routes connecting the cities. It contains an error. Correct the table. Also, add a table that shows how to execute the shortest routes, in the style of Figure 21.4.

	Providence	Westerly	New London	Norwich
Providence	±	53	54	48
Westerly	53	±	18	101
New London	54	18	±	12
Norwich	48	101	12	±

21.1 Underlying Principles

Our shortest-paths algorithms are based on a simple operation known as *relaxation*. We start a shortest-paths algorithm knowing only the network's edges and weights. As we proceed, we gather information about the shortest paths that connect various pairs of vertices. Our algorithms all update this information incrementally, making new inferences about shortest paths from the knowledge gained so far. At each step, we test whether we can find a path that is shorter than some known path. The term "relaxation" is commonly used to describe this step, which *relaxes* constraints on the shortest path. We can think of a rubber band stretched tight on a path connecting two vertices: A successful relaxation operation allows us to relax the tension on the rubber band along a shorter path.

Our algorithms are based on applying repeatedly one of two types of relaxation operations:

- *Edge relaxation:* Test whether traveling along a given edge gives a new shortest path to its destination vertex.
- *Path relaxation:* Test whether traveling through a given vertex gives a new shortest path connecting two other given vertices.

Edge relaxation is a special case of path relaxation; we consider the operations separately, however, because we use them separately (the former in single-source algorithms; the latter in all-pairs algorithms). In both cases, the prime requirement that we impose on the data structures that we use to represent the current state of our knowledge about a network's shortest paths is that we can update them easily to reflect changes implied by a relaxation operation.

First, we consider edge relaxation, which is illustrated in Figure 21.5. All the single-source shortest-paths algorithms that we consider are based on this step: Does a given edge lead us to consider a shorter path to its destination from the source?

The data structures that we need to support this operation are straightforward. First, we have the basic requirement that we need to compute the shortest-paths lengths from the source to each of the other vertices. Our convention will be to store in a vertex-indexed vector wt the lengths of the shortest known paths from the source to each vertex. Second, to record the paths themselves as we move from vertex to vertex, our convention will be the same as the one that we used for other graph-search algorithms that we examined in Chapters 18 through 20: We use a vertex-indexed vector spt to record the last edge on a shortest path from the source to the indexed vertex. These edges constitute a tree.

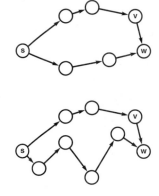

Figure 21.5
Edge relaxation

These diagrams illustrate the relaxation operation that underlies our single-source shortest-paths algorithms. We keep track of the shortest known path from the source s to each vertex and ask whether an edge v-w gives us a shorter path to w. In the top example, it does not; so we would ignore it. In the bottom example, it does; so we would update our data structures to indicate that the best known way to get to w from s is to go to v, then take v-w.

With these data structures, implementing edge relaxation is a straightforward task. In our single-source shortest-paths code, we use the following code to relax along an edge e from v to w:

```
if (wt[w] > wt[v] + e->wt())
  { wt[w] = wt[v] + e->wt(); spt[w] = e; }
```

This code fragment is both simple and descriptive; we include it in this form in our implementations, rather than defining relaxation as a higher-level abstract operation.

Definition 21.2 *Given a network and a designated vertex s, a* **shortest-paths tree (SPT)** *for s is a subnetwork containing s and all the vertices reachable from s that forms a directed tree rooted at s such that every tree path is a shortest path in the network.*

There may be multiple paths of the same length connecting a given pair of nodes, so SPTs are not necessarily unique. In general, as illustrated in Figure 21.2, if we take shortest paths from a vertex s to every vertex reachable from s in a network and from the subnetwork induced by the edges in the paths, we may get a DAG. Different shortest paths connecting pairs of nodes may each appear as a subpath in some longer path containing both nodes. Because of such effects, we generally are content to compute any SPT for a given digraph and start vertex.

Our algorithms generally initialize the entries in the wt vector with a sentinel value. That value needs to be sufficiently small that the addition in the relaxation test does not cause overflow and sufficiently large that no simple path has a larger weight. For example, if edge weights are between 0 and 1, we can use the value V. Note that we have to take extra care to check our assumptions when using sentinels in networks that could have negative weights. For example, if both vertices have the sentinel value, the relaxation code just given takes no action if e.wt is nonnegative (which is probably what we intend in most implementations), but it will change wt[w] and spt[w] if the weight is negative.

Our code always uses the *destination* vertex as the index to save the SPT edges (spt[w]->w() == w). For economy and consistency with Chapters 17 through 19, we use the notation st[w] to refer to the vertex spt[w]->v() (in the text and particularly in the figures) to emphasize that the spt vector is actually a parent-link representation of

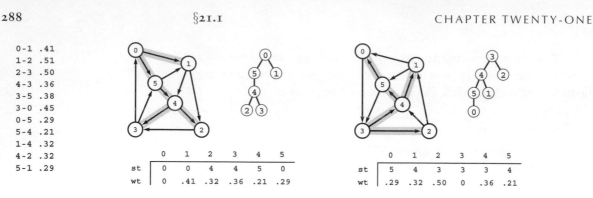

	0	1	2	3	4	5
st	0	0	4	4	5	0
wt	0	.41	.32	.36	.21	.29

	0	1	2	3	4	5
st	5	4	3	3	3	4
wt	.29	.32	.50	0	.36	.21

Figure 21.6
Shortest paths trees

The shortest paths from 0 to the other nodes in this network are 0-1, 0-5-4-2, 0-5-4-3, 0-5-4, and 0-5, respectively. These paths define a spanning tree, which is depicted in three representations (gray edges in the network drawing, oriented tree, and parent links with weights) in the center. Links in the parent-link representation (the one that we typically compute) run in the opposite direction than links in the digraph, so we sometimes work with the reverse digraph. The spanning tree defined by shortest paths from 3 to each of the other nodes in the reverse is depicted on the right. The parent-link representation of this tree gives the shortest paths from each of the other nodes to 2 in the original graph. For example, we can find the shortest path 0-5-4-3 from 0 to 3 by following the links st[0] = 5, st[5] = 4, *and* st[4] = 3.

the shortest-paths tree, as illustrated in Figure 21.6. We can compute the shortest path from s to t by traveling up the tree from t to s; when we do so, we are traversing edges in the direction opposite from their direction in the network and are visiting the vertices on the path in reverse order (t, st[t], st[st[t]], and so forth).

One way to get the edges on the path in order from source to sink from an SPT is to use a stack. For example, the following code prints a path from the source to a given vertex w:

```
stack <EDGE *> P; EDGE *e = spt[w];
while (e) { P.push(e); e = spt[e->v()]); }
if (P.empty()) cout << P.top()->v();
while (!P.empty())
    { cout << "-" << P.top()->w(); P.pop(); }
```

In a class implementation, we could use code similar to this to provide clients with a vector that contains the edges of the path.

If we simply want to print or otherwise process the edges on the path, going all the way through the path in reverse order to get to the first edge in this way may be undesirable. One approach to get around this difficulty is to work with the reverse network, as illustrated in Figure 21.6. We use reverse order and edge relaxation in single-source problems because the SPT gives a compact representation of the shortest paths from the source to all the other vertices, in a vector with just V entries.

Next, we consider path relaxation, which is the basis of some of our all-pairs algorithms: Does going through a given vertex lead us to a shorter path that connects two other given vertices? For example, suppose that, for three vertices s, x, and t, we wish to know whether it is better to go from s to x and then from x to t or to go from s to t without going through x. For straight-line connections in a Euclidean space, the triangle inequality tells us that the route through x cannot be shorter than the direct route from s to t, but for paths in a network, it could be (see Figure 21.7). To determine which, we need to know the lengths of paths from s to x, x to t, and of those from s to t (that do not include x). Then, we simply test whether or not the sum of the first two is less than the third; if it is, we update our records accordingly.

Path relaxation is appropriate for all-pairs solutions where we maintain the lengths of the shortest paths that we have encountered between all pairs of vertices. Specifically, in all-pairs–shortest-paths code of this kind, we maintain a vector of vectors d such that d[s][t] is the shortest-path length from s to t, and we also maintain a vector of vectors p such that p[s][t] is the next vertex on a shortest path from s to t. We refer to the former as the *distances* matrix and the latter as the *paths* matrix. Figure 21.8 shows the two matrices for our example network. The distances matrix is a prime objective of the computation, and we use the paths matrix because it is clearly more compact than, but carries the same information as, the full list of paths that is illustrated in Figure 21.3.

In terms of these data structures, path relaxation amounts to the following code:

```
if (d[s][t] > d[s][x] + d[x][t])
  { d[s][t] = d[s][x] + d[x][t]; p[s][t] = p[s][x]; }
```

Like edge relaxation, this code reads as a restatement of the informal description that we have given, so we use it directly in our implementations. More formally, path relaxation reflects the following.

Property 21.1 *If a vertex x is on a shortest path from s to t, then that path consists of a shortest path from s to x followed by a shortest path from x to t.*

Proof: By contradiction. We could use any shorter path from s to x or from x to t to build a shorter path from s to t. ∎

We encountered the path-relaxation operation when we discussed transitive-closure algorithms, in Section 19.3. If the edge and path weights are either 1 or infinite (that is, a path's weight is 1 only if all that path's edges have weight 1), then path relaxation is the operation that we used in Warshall's algorithm (if we have a path from s to x and a path from x to t, then we have a path from s to t). If we define a path's weight to be the number of edges on that path, then

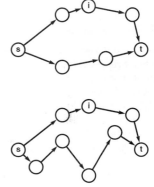

**Figure 21.7
Path relaxation**

These diagrams illustrate the relaxation operation that underlies our all-pairs shortest-paths algorithms. We keep track of the best known path between all pairs of vertices and ask whether a vertex i is evidence that the shortest known path from s to t could be improved. In the top example, it is not; in the bottom example, it is. Whenever we encounter a vertex i such that the length of the shortest known path from s to i plus the length of the shortest known path from i to t is smaller than the length of the shortest known path from s to t, then we update our data structures to indicate that we now know a shorter path from s to t (head towards i first).

```
0-1 .41
1-2 .51
2-3 .50
4-3 .36
3-5 .38
3-0 .45
0-5 .29
5-4 .21
1-4 .32
4-2 .32
5-1 .29
```

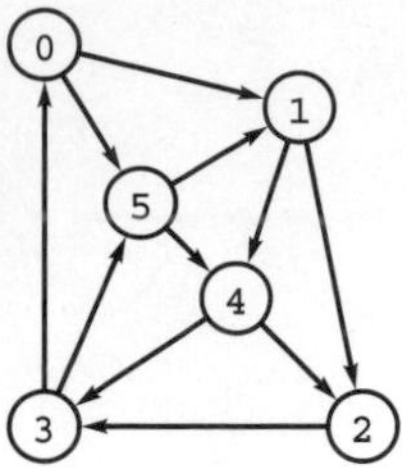

	0	1	2	3	4	5
0	0	.41	.82	.86	.50	.29
1	1.13	0	.51	.68	.32	1.06
2	.95	1.17	0	.50	1.09	.88
3	.45	.67	.91	0	.59	.38
4	.81	1.03	.32	.36	0	.74
5	1.02	.29	.53	.57	.21	0

	0	1	2	3	4	5
0	0	1	5	5	5	5
1	4	1	2	4	4	4
2	3	3	2	3	3	3
3	0	5	5	3	5	5
4	3	3	2	3	4	3
5	4	1	4	4	4	5

Figure 21.8
All shortest paths

The two matrices on the right are compact representations of all the shortest paths in the sample network on the left, containing the same information in the exhaustive list in Figure 21.3. The distances matrix on the left contains the shortest-path length: The entry in row s and column t is the length of the shortest path from s to t. The paths matrix on the right contains the information needed to execute the path: The entry in row s and column t is the next vertex on the path from s to t.

Warshall's algorithm generalizes to Floyd's algorithm for finding all shortest paths in unweighted digraphs; it further generalizes to apply to networks, as we see in Section 21.3.

From a mathematician's perspective, it is important to note that these algorithms all can be cast in a general algebraic setting that unifies and helps us to understand them. From a programmer's perspective, it is important to note that we can implement each of these algorithms using an abstract + operator (to compute path weights from edge weights) and an abstract < operator (to compute the minimum value in a set of path weights), both solely in the context of the relaxation operation (see Exercises 19.55 and 19.56).

Property 21.1 implies that a shortest path from s to t contains shortest paths from s to every other vertex along the path to t. Most shortest-paths algorithms also compute shortest paths from s to every vertex that is closer to s than to t (whether or not the vertex is on the path from s to t), although that is not a requirement (see Exercise 21.18). Solving the source–sink shortest-paths problem with such an algorithm when t is the vertex that is farthest from s is equivalent to solving the single-source shortest-paths problem for s. Conversely, we could use a solution to the single-source shortest-paths problem from s as a method for finding the vertex that is farthest from s.

The paths matrix that we use in our implementations for the all-pairs problem is also a representation of the shortest-paths trees for each of the vertices. We defined p[s][t] to be the vertex that follows s on a shortest path from s to t. It is thus the same as the vertex that precedes s on the shortest path from t to s in the reverse network. In other words, *column* t in the paths matrix of a network is a vertex-indexed vector that represents the SPT for vertex t in its reverse. Conversely, we can build the paths matrix for a network by

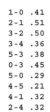

```
1-0  .41
2-1  .51
3-2  .50
3-4  .36
5-3  .38
0-3  .45
5-0  .29
4-5  .21
4-1  .32
2-4  .32
1-5  .29
```

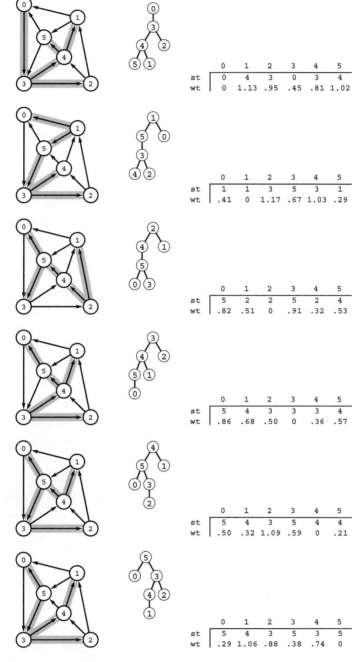

	0	1	2	3	4	5
st	0	4	3	0	3	4
wt	0	1.13	.95	.45	.81	1.02

	0	1	2	3	4	5
st	1	1	3	5	3	1
wt	.41	0	1.17	.67	1.03	.29

	0	1	2	3	4	5
st	5	2	2	5	2	4
wt	.82	.51	0	.91	.32	.53

	0	1	2	3	4	5
st	5	4	3	3	3	4
wt	.86	.68	.50	0	.36	.57

	0	1	2	3	4	5
st	5	4	3	5	4	4
wt	.50	.32	1.09	.59	0	.21

	0	1	2	3	4	5
st	5	4	3	5	3	5
wt	.29	1.06	.88	.38	.74	0

Figure 21.9
All shortest paths in a network

These diagrams depict the SPTs for each vertex in the reverse of the network in Figure 21.8 (0 to 5, top to bottom), as network subtrees (left), oriented trees (center), and parent-link representation including a vertex-indexed array for path length (right). Putting the arrays together to form path and distance matrices (where each array becomes a column) gives the solution to the all-pairs shortest-paths problem illustrated in Figure 21.8.

filling each column with the vertex-indexed vector representation of the SPT for the appropriate vertex in the reverse. This correspondence is illustrated in Figure 21.9.

In summary, relaxation gives us the basic abstract operations that we need to build our shortest paths algorithms. The primary complication is the choice of whether to provide the first or final edge on the shortest path. For example, single-source algorithms are more naturally expressed by providing the final edge on the path so that we need only a single vertex-indexed vector to reconstruct the path, since all paths lead back to the source. This choice does not present a fundamental difficulty because we can either use the reverse graph as warranted or provide member functions that hide this difference from clients. For example, we could specify a member function in the interface that returns the edges on the shortest path in a vector (see Exercises 21.15 and 21.16).

Accordingly, for simplicity, all of our implementations in this chapter include a member function dist that returns a shortest-path length and *either* a member function path that returns the first edge on a shortest path *or* a member function pathR that returns the final edge on a shortest path. For example, our single-source implementations that use edge relaxation typically implement these functions as follows:

```
Edge *pathR(int w) const { return spt[w]; }
double dist(int v) { return wt[v]; }
```

Similarly, our all-paths implementations that use path relaxation typically implement these functions as follows:

```
Edge *path(int s, int t) { return p[s][t]; }
double dist(int s, int t) { return d[s][t]; }
```

In some situations, it might be worthwhile to build interfaces that standardize on one or the other or both of these options; we choose the most natural one for the algorithm at hand.

Exercises

▷ **21.12** Draw the SPT from 0 for the network defined in Exercise 21.1 and for its reverse. Give the parent-link representation of both trees.

21.13 Consider the edges in the network defined in Exercise 21.1 to be *undirected* edges such that each edge corresponds to equal-weight edges in both directions in the network. Answer Exercise 21.12 for this corresponding network.

▷ **21.14** Change the direction of edge 0–2 in Figure 21.2. Draw two different SPTs that are rooted at 2 for this modified network.

21.15 Write a function that uses the `pathR` member function from a single-source implementation to put pointers to the edges on the path from the source v to a given vertex w in an STL `vector`.

21.16 Write a function that uses the `path` member function from an all-paths implementation to put pointers to the edges on the path from a given vertex v to another given vertex w in an STL `vector`.

21.17 Write a program that uses your function from Exercise 21.16 to print out all of the paths, in the style of Figure 21.3.

21.18 Give an example that shows how we could know that a path from s to t is shortest without knowing the length of a shorter path from s to x for some x.

21.2 Dijkstra's Algorithm

In Section 20.3, we discussed Prim's algorithm for finding the minimum spanning tree (MST) of a weighted undirected graph: We build it one edge at a time, always taking next the shortest edge that connects a vertex on the MST to a vertex not yet on the MST. We can use a nearly identical scheme to compute an SPT. We begin by putting the source on the SPT; then, we build the SPT one edge at a time, always taking next the edge that gives a shortest path from the source to a vertex not on the SPT. In other words, we add vertices to the SPT in order of their distance (through the SPT) to the start vertex. This method is known as *Dijkstra's algorithm*.

As usual, we need to make a distinction between the algorithm at the level of abstraction in this informal description and various concrete implementations (such as Program 21.1) that differ primarily in graph representation and priority-queue implementations, even though such a distinction is not always made in the literature. We shall consider other implementations and discuss their relationships with Program 21.1 after establishing that Dijkstra's algorithm correctly performs the single-source shortest-paths computation.

Property 21.2   *Dijkstra's algorithm solves the single-source shortest-paths problem in networks that have nonnegative weights.*

Proof: Given a source vertex s, we have to establish that the tree path from the root s to each vertex x in the tree computed by Dijkstra's algorithm corresponds to a shortest path in the graph from s to x. This fact follows by induction. Assuming that the subtree so far computed has the property, we need only to prove that adding a new vertex x adds a shortest path to that vertex. But all other paths to x must begin with a tree path followed by an edge to a vertex not on the tree. By construction, all such paths are longer than the one from s to x that is under consideration.

The same argument shows that Dijkstra's algorithm solves the source–sink shortest-paths problem, if we start at the source and stop when the sink comes off the priority queue. ∎

The proof breaks down if the edge weights could be negative, because it assumes that a path's length does not decrease when we add more edges to the path. In a network with negative edge weights, this assumption is not valid because *any* edge that we encounter might lead to some tree vertex and might have a sufficiently large negative weight to give a path to that vertex shorter than the tree path. We consider this defect in Section 21.7 (see Figure 21.28).

Figure 21.10 shows the evolution of an SPT for a sample graph when computed with Dijkstra's algorithm; Figure 21.11 shows an oriented drawing of a larger SPT tree. Although Dijkstra's algorithm differs from Prim's MST algorithm in only the choice of priority, SPT trees are different in character from MSTs. They are rooted at the start vertex and all edges are directed away from the root, whereas MSTs are unrooted and undirected. We sometimes represent MSTs as directed, rooted trees when we use Prim's algorithm, but such structures are still different in character from SPTs (compare the oriented drawing in Figure 20.9 with the drawing in Figure 21.11). Indeed, the nature of the SPT somewhat depends on the choice of start vertex as well, as depicted in Figure 21.12.

Dijkstra's original implementation, which is suitable for dense graphs, is precisely like Prim's MST algorithm. Specifically, we simply change the assignment of the priority P in Program 20.6 from

```
P = e->wt()
```

(the edge weight) to

```
P = wt[v] + e->wt()
```

(the distance from the source to the edge's destination). This change gives the classical implementation of Dijkstra's algorithm: We grow

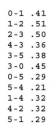

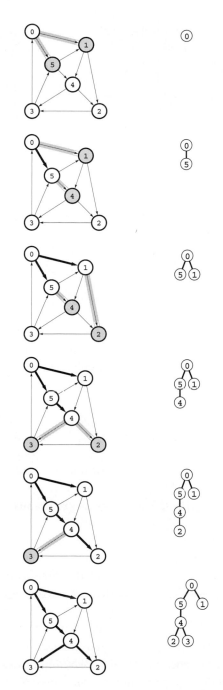

Figure 21.10
Dijkstra's algorithm

This sequence depicts the construction of a shortest-paths spanning tree rooted at vertex 0 by Dijkstra's algorithm for a sample network. Thick black edges in the network diagrams are tree edges, and thick gray edges are fringe edges. Oriented drawings of the tree as it grows are shown in the center, and a list of fringe edges is given on the right.

The first step is to add 0 to the tree and the edges leaving it, 0-1 and 0-5, to the fringe (top). Second, we move the shortest of those edges, 0-5, from the fringe to the tree and check the edges leaving it: The edge 5-4 is added to the fringe and the edge 5-1 is discarded because it is not part of a shorter path from 0 to 1 than the known path 0-1 (second from top). The priority of 5-4 on the fringe is the length of the path from 0 that it represents, 0-5-4. Third, we move 0-1 from the fringe to the tree, add 1-2 to the fringe, and discard 1-4 (third from top). Fourth, we move 5-4 from the fringe to the tree, add 4-3 to the fringe, and replace 1-2 with 4-2 because 0-5-4-2 is a shorter path than 0-1-2 (fourth from top). We keep at most one edge to any vertex on the fringe, choosing the one on the shortest path from 0. We complete the computation by moving 4-2 and then 4-3 from the fringe to the tree (bottom).

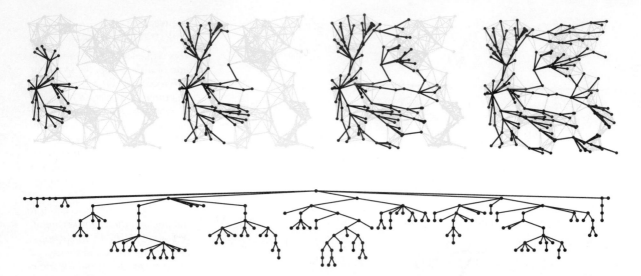

Figure 21.11
Shortest-paths spanning tree

This figure illustrates the progress of Dijkstra's algorithm in solving the single-source shortest-paths problem in a random Euclidean near-neighbor digraph (with directed edges in both directions corresponding to each line drawn), in the same style as Figures 18.13, 18.24, and 20.9. The search tree is similar in character to BFS because vertices tend to be connected to one another by short paths, but it is slightly deeper and less broad because distances lead to slightly longer paths than path lengths.

an SPT one edge at a time, each time updating the distance to the tree of all vertices adjacent to its destination while at the same time checking all the nontree vertices to find an edge to move to the tree whose destination vertex is a nontree vertex of minimal distance from the source.

Property 21.3 *With Dijkstra's algorithm, we can find any SPT in a dense network in linear time.*

Proof: As for Prim's MST algorithm, it is immediately clear, from inspection of the code of Program 20.6, that the running time is proportional to V^2, which is linear for dense graphs. ∎

For sparse graphs, we can do better, by viewing Dijkstra's algorithm as a generalized graph-searching method that differs from depth-first search (DFS), from breadth-first search (BFS), and from Prim's MST algorithm in only the rule used to add edges to the tree. As in Chapter 20, we keep edges that connect tree vertices to nontree vertices on a generalized queue called the *fringe*, use a priority queue to implement the generalized queue, and provide for updating priorities so as to encompass DFS, BFS, and Prim's algorithm in a single implementation (see Section 20.3). This priority-first search (PFS) scheme also encompasses Dijkstra's algorithm. That is, changing the assignment of P in Program 20.7 to

```
P = wt[v] + e->wt()
```

(the distance from the source to the edge's destination) gives an implementation of Dijkstra's algorithm that is suitable for sparse graphs.

Program 21.1 is an alternative PFS implementation for sparse graphs that is slightly simpler than Program 20.7 and that directly matches the informal description of Dijkstra's algorithm given at the beginning of this section. It differs from Program 20.7 in that it initializes the priority queue with all the vertices in the network and maintains the queue with the aid of a sentinel value for those vertices that are neither on the tree nor on the fringe (unseen vertices with sentinel values); in contrast, Program 20.7 keeps on the priority queue only those vertices that are reachable by a single edge from the tree. Keeping all the vertices on the queue simplifies the code but can incur a small performance penalty for some graphs (see Exercise 21.31).

The general results that we considered concerning the performance of priority-first search (PFS) in Chapter 20 give us specific information about the performance of these implementations of Dijkstra's algorithm for sparse graphs (Program 21.1 and Program 20.7, suitably modified). For reference, we restate those results in the present context. Since the proofs do not depend on the priority function, they apply without modification. They are worst-case results that apply to both programs, although Program 20.7 may be more efficient for many classes of graphs because it maintains a smaller fringe.

Property 21.4   *For all networks and all priority functions, we can compute a spanning tree with PFS in time proportional to the time required for V* **insert**, *V* **delete the minimum**, *and E* **decrease key** *operations in a priority queue of size at most V.*

Proof: This fact is immediate from the priority-queue–based implementations in Program 20.7 or Program 21.1. It represents a conservative upper bound because the size of the priority queue is often much smaller than *V*, particularly for Program 20.7. ∎

Property 21.5   *With a PFS implementation of Dijkstra's algorithm that uses a heap for the priority-queue implementation, we can compute any SPT in time proportional to E* lg *V.*

Program 21.1 Dijkstra's algorithm (priority-first search)

This class implements a single-source shortest-paths ADT with linear-time preprocessing, private data that takes space proportional to V, and constant-time member functions that give the length of the shortest path and the final vertex on the path from the source to any given vertex. The constructor is an implementation of Dijkstra's algorithm that uses a priority queue of vertices (in order of their distance from the source) to compute an SPT. The priority-queue interface is the same one used in Program 20.7 and implemented in Program 20.10.

   The constructor is also a generalized graph search that implements other PFS algorithms with other assignments to the priority P (*see text*). The statement to reassign the weight of tree vertices to 0 is needed for a general PFS implementation but not for Dijkstra's algorithm, since the priorities of the vertices added to the SPT are nondecreasing.

```
template <class Graph, class Edge> class SPT
{ const Graph &G;
  vector<double> wt;
  vector<Edge *> spt;
public:
  SPT(const Graph &G, int s) : G(G),
    spt(G.V()), wt(G.V(), G.V())
  { PQi<double> pQ(G.V(), wt);
    for (int v = 0; v < G.V(); v++) pQ.insert(v);
    wt[s] = 0.0; pQ.lower(s);
    while (!pQ.empty())
    { int v = pQ.getmin(); // wt[v] = 0.0;
      if (v != s && spt[v] == 0) return;
      typename Graph::adjIterator A(G, v);
      for (Edge* e = A.beg(); !A.end(); e = A.nxt())
        { int w = e->w();
          double P = wt[v] + e->wt();
          if (P < wt[w])
            { wt[w] = P; pQ.lower(w); spt[w] = e; }
        }
    }
  }
  Edge *pathR(int v) const { return spt[v]; }
  double dist(int v) const { return wt[v]; }
};
```

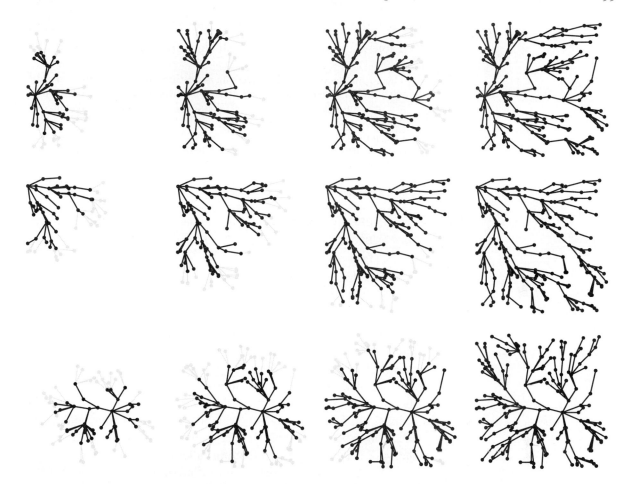

Figure 21.12
SPT examples

These three examples show growing SPTs for three different source
locations: left edge (top), upper left
corner (center), and center (bottom).

Proof: This result is a direct consequence of Property 21.4. ∎

Property 21.6 *Given a graph with V vertices and E edges, let d denote the density E/V. If $d < 2$, then the running time of Dijkstra's algorithm is proportional to $V \lg V$. Otherwise, we can improve the worst-case running time by a factor of $\lg(E/V)$, to $O(E \lg_d V)$ (which is linear if E is at least $V^{1+\epsilon}$) by using a $\lceil E/V \rceil$-ary heap for the priority queue.*

Proof: This result directly mirrors Property 20.12 and the multiway-heap priority-queue implementation discussed directly thereafter. ∎

Table 21.1 Priority-first search algorithms

These four classical graph-processing algorithms all can be implemented with PFS, a generalized priority-queue–based graph search that builds graph spanning trees one edge at a time. Details of search dynamics depend upon graph representation, priority-queue implementation, and PFS implementation; but the search trees generally characterize the various algorithms, as illustrated in the figures referenced in the fourth column.

algorithm	priority	result	Figure
DFS	reverse preorder	recursion tree	18.13
BFS	preorder	SPT (edges)	18.24
Prim	edge weight	MST	20.8
Dijkstra	path weight	SPT	21.9

Table 21.1 summarizes pertinent information about the four major PFS algorithms that we have considered. They differ in only the priority function used, but this difference leads to spanning trees that are entirely different from one another in character (as required). For the example in the figures referred to in the table (and for many other graphs), the DFS tree is tall and thin, the BFS tree is short and fat, the SPT is like the BFS tree but neither quite as short nor quite as fat, and the MST is neither short and fat nor tall and thin.

We have also considered four different implementations of PFS. The first is the classical dense-graph implementation that encompasses Dijkstra's algorithm and Prim's MST algorithm (Program 20.6); the other three are sparse-graph implementations that differ in priority-queue contents:

- Fringe edges (Program 18.10)
- Fringe vertices (Program 20.7)
- All vertices (Program 21.1)

Of these, the first is primarily of pedagogical value, the second is the most refined of the three, and the third is perhaps the simplest. This framework already describes 16 different implementations of classical graph-search algorithms—when we factor in different priority-queue implementations, the possibilities multiply further. This proliferation

---

Table 21.2 Cost of implementations of Dijkstra's algorithm

This table summarizes the cost (worst-case running time) of various implementations of Dijkstra's algorithm. With appropriate priority-queue implementations, the algorithm runs in linear time (time proportional to V^2 for dense networks, E for sparse networks), except for networks that are extremely sparse.

algorithm	worst-case cost	comment
classical	V^2	optimal for dense graphs
PFS, full heap	$E \lg V$	simplest implementation
PFS, fringe heap	$E \lg V$	conservative upper bound
PFS, d-heap	$E \lg_d V$	linear unless extremely sparse

---

of networks, algorithms, and implementations underscores the utility of the general statements about performance in Properties 21.4 through 21.6, which are also summarized in Table 21.2.

As is true of MST algorithms, actual running times of shortest-paths algorithms are likely to be lower than these worst-case time bounds suggest, primarily because most edges do not necessitate *decrease key* operations. In practice, except for the sparsest of graphs, we regard the running time as being linear.

The name *Dijkstra's algorithm* is commonly used to refer both to the abstract method of building an SPT by adding vertices in order of their distance from the source and to its implementation as the V^2 algorithm for the adjacency-matrix representation, because Dijkstra presented both in his 1959 paper (and also showed that the same approach could compute the MST). Performance improvements for sparse graphs are dependent on later improvements in ADT technology and priority-queue implementations that are not specific to the shortest-paths problem. Improved performance of Dijkstra's algorithm is one of the most important applications of that technology (*see reference section*). As with MSTs, we use terminology such as the "PFS implementation of Dijkstra's algorithm using d-heaps" to identify specific combinations.

We saw in Section 18.8 that, in unweighted undirected graphs, using preorder numbering for priorities causes the priority queue to operate as a FIFO queue and leads to a BFS. Dijkstra's algorithm gives us another realization of BFS: When all edge weights are 1, it visits vertices in order of the number of edges on the shortest path to the start vertex. The priority queue does not operate precisely as a FIFO queue would in this case, because items with equal priority do not necessarily come out in the order in which they went in.

Each of these implementations puts the edges of an SPT from vertex 0 in the vertex-indexed vector spt, with the shortest-path length to each vertex in the SPT in the vertex-indexed vector wt and provides member functions that gives clients access to this data. As usual, we can build various graph-processing functions and classes around this basic data (see Exercises 21.21 through 21.28).

Exercises

▷ **21.19** Show, in the style of Figure 21.10, the result of using Dijkstra's algorithm to compute the SPT of the network defined in Exercise 21.1 with start vertex 0.

○ **21.20** How would you find a *second* shortest path from s to t in a network?

21.21 Write a client function that uses an SPT object to find the most distant vertex from a given vertex s (the vertex whose shortest path from s is the longest).

21.22 Write a client function that uses an SPT object to compute the average of the lengths of the shortest paths from a given vertex to each of the vertices reachable from it.

21.23 Develop a class based on Program 21.1 with a path member function that returns an STL vector containing pointers to the edges on the shortest path connecting s and t in order from s to t on an STL vector.

▷ **21.24** Write a client function that uses your class from Exercise 21.23 to print the shortest paths from a given vertex to each of the other vertices in a given network.

21.25 Write a client function that uses an SPT object to find all vertices within a given distance d of a given vertex in a given network. The running time of your function should be proportional to the size of the subgraph induced by those vertices and the vertices incident on them.

21.26 Develop an algorithm for finding an edge whose removal causes maximal increase in the shortest-path length from one given vertex to another given vertex in a given network.

• **21.27** Implement a class that uses SPT objects to perform a *sensitivity analysis* on the network's edges with respect to a given pair of vertices s and t: Compute a V-by-V matrix such that, for every u and v, the entry in row u and column v is 1 if u–v is an edge in the network whose weight can be increased without the shortest-path length from s to t being increased and is 0 otherwise.

○ **21.28** Implement a class that uses SPT objects to find a shortest path connecting one given set of vertices with another given set of vertices in a given network.

21.29 Use your solution from Exercise 21.28 to implement a client function that finds a shortest path from the left edge to the right edge in a random grid network (see Exercise 20.17).

21.30 Show that an MST of an undirected graph is equivalent to a *bottleneck SPT* of the graph: For every pair of vertices v and w, it gives the path connecting them whose longest edge is as short as possible.

21.31 Run empirical studies to compare the performance of the two versions of Dijkstra's algorithm for the sparse graphs that are described in this section (Program 21.1 and Program 20.7, with suitable priority definition), for various networks (see Exercises 21.4–8). Use a standard-heap priority-queue implementation.

21.32 Run empirical studies to learn the best value of d when using a d-heap priority-queue implementation (see Program 20.10) for each of the three PFS implementations that we have discussed (Program 18.10, Program 20.7 and Program 21.1), for various networks (see Exercises 21.4–8).

• **21.33** Run empirical studies to determine the effect of using an index-heap-tournament priority-queue implementation (see Exercise 9.53) in Program 21.1, for various networks (see Exercises 21.4–8).

○ **21.34** Run empirical studies to analyze height and average path length in SPTs, for various networks (see Exercises 21.4–8).

21.35 Develop a class for the source–sink shortest-paths problem that is based on code like Program 21.1 but that initializes the priority queue with *both* the source and the sink. Doing so leads to the growth of an SPT from each vertex; your main task is to decide precisely what to do when the two SPTs collide.

• **21.36** Describe a family of graphs with V vertices and E edges for which the worst-case running time of Dijkstra's algorithm is achieved.

•• **21.37** Develop a reasonable generator for random graphs with V vertices and E edges for which the running time of the heap-based PFS implementation of Dijkstra's algorithm is superlinear.

• **21.38** Write a client program that does dynamic graphical animations of Dijkstra's algorithm. Your program should produce images like Figure 21.11 (see Exercises 17.56 through 17.60). Test your program on random Euclidean networks (see Exercise 21.9).

21.3 All-Pairs Shortest Paths

In this section, we consider two classes that solve the all-pairs shortest-paths problem. The algorithms that we implement directly generalize two basic algorithms that we considered in Section 19.3 for the transitive-closure problem. The first method is to run Dijkstra's algorithm from each vertex to get the shortest paths from that vertex to each of the others. If we implement the priority queue with a heap, the worst-case running time for this approach is proportional to $V E \lg V$, and we can improve this bound to $V E$ for many types of networks by using a d-ary heap. The second method, which allows us to solve the problem directly in time proportional to V^3, is an extension of Warshall's algorithm that is known as *Floyd's algorithm*.

Both of these classes implement an *abstract–shortest-paths* ADT interface for finding shortest distances and paths. This interface, which is shown in Program 21.2, is a generalization to weighted digraphs of the *abstract–transitive-closure* interface for connectivity queries in digraphs that we studied in Chapter 19. In both class implementations, the constructor solves the all-pairs shortest-paths problem and saves the result in private data members to support query functions that return the shortest-path length from one given vertex to another and either the first or last edge on the path. Implementing such an ADT is a primary reason to use all-pairs shortest-paths algorithms in practice.

Program 21.3 is a sample client program that uses the all–shortest-paths ADT interface to find the *weighted diameter* of a network. It checks all pairs of vertices to find the one for which the shortest-path length is longest; then, it traverses the path, edge by edge. Figure 21.13 shows the path computed by this program for our Euclidean network example.

The goal of the algorithms in this section is to support constant-time implementations of the query functions. Typically, we expect to have a huge number of such requests, so we are willing to invest substantial resources in private data members and preprocessing in the constructor to be able to answer the queries quickly. Both of the algorithms that we consider use space proportional to V^2 for the private data members.

The primary disadvantage of this general approach is that, for a huge network, we may not have so much space available (or we might

Figure 21.13
Diameter of a network

The largest entry in a network's all-shortest-paths matrix is the diameter of the network: the length of the longest of the shortest paths, depicted here for our sample Euclidean network.

Program 21.2 All-pairs shortest-paths ADT

Our solutions to the all-pairs shortest-paths problem are all classes with a constructor and two query functions: a `dist` function that returns the length of the shortest path from the first argument to the second; and one of two possible path functions, either `path`, which returns a pointer to the first edge on the shortest path, or `pathR`, which returns a pointer to the final edge on the shortest path. If there is no such path, the path function returns 0 and `dist` is undefined.

We use `path` or `pathR` as convenient for the algorithm under scrutiny; in practice, we might need to settle upon one or the other (or both) in the interface and use various transfer functions in implementations, as discussed in Section 21.1 and in the exercises at the end of this section.

```
template <class Graph, class Edge> class SPall
{
  public:
    SPall(const Graph &);
    Edge *path(int, int) const;
    Edge *pathR(int, int) const;
    double dist(int, int) const;
};
```

---

not be able to afford the requisite preprocessing time). In principle, our interface provides us with the latitude to trade off preprocessing time and space for query time. If we expect only a few queries, we can do no preprocessing and simply run a single-source algorithm for each query, but intermediate situations require more advanced algorithms (see Exercises 21.48 through 21.50). This problem generalizes one that challenged us for much of Chapter 19: the problem of supporting fast reachability queries in limited space.

The first all-pairs shortest-paths ADT function implementation that we consider solves the problem by using Dijkstra's algorithm to solve the single-source problem for each vertex. In C++, we can express the method directly, as shown in Program 21.4: We build a vector of SPT objects, one to solve the single-source problem for each vertex. This method generalizes the BFS-based method for unweighted undirected graphs that we considered in Section 17.7. It is also similar

Program 21.3 Computing the diameter of a network

This client function illustrates the use of the interface in Program 21.2. It finds the longest of the shortest paths in the given network, prints the path, and returns its weight (the diameter of the network).

```
template <class Graph, class Edge>
double diameter(Graph &G)
  { int vmax = 0, wmax = 0;
    allSP<Graph, Edge> all(G);
    for (int v = 0; v < G.V(); v++)
      for (int w = 0; w < G.V(); w++)
        if (all.path(v, w))
          if (all.dist(v, w) > all.dist(vmax, wmax))
            { vmax = v; wmax = w; }
    int v = vmax; cout << v;
    while (v != wmax)
      { v = all.path(v, wmax)->w(); cout << "-" << v; }
    return all.dist(vmax, wmax);
  }
```

to our use of a DFS that starts at each vertex to compute the transitive closure of unweighted digraphs, in Program 19.4.

Property 21.7 *With Dijkstra's algorithm, we can find all shortest paths in a network that has nonnegative weights in time proportional to $VE\log_d V$, where $d = 2$ if $E < 2V$, and $d = E/V$ otherwise.*

Proof: Immediate from Property 21.6. ∎

As are our bounds for the single-source shortest-paths and the MST problems, this bound is conservative; and a running time of VE is likely for typical graphs.

To compare this implementation with others, it is useful to study the matrices implicit in the vector-of-vectors structure of the private data members. The wt vectors form precisely the distances matrix that we considered in Section 21.1: The entry in row s and column t is the length of the shortest path from s to t. As illustrated in Figures 21.8 and 21.9, the spt vectors from the transpose of the paths matrix: The entry in row s and column t is the last entry on the shortest path from s to t.

Program 21.4 Dijkstra's algorithm for all shortest paths

This class uses Dijkstra's algorithm to build an SPT for each vertex so that it can answer pathR and dist queries for any pair of vertices.

```
#include "SPT.cc"
template <class Graph, class Edge> class allSP
{ const Graph &G;
  vector< SPT<Graph, Edge> *> A;
public:
  allSP(const Graph &G) : G(G), A(G.V())
    { for (int s = 0; s < G.V(); s++)
        A[s] = new SPT<Graph, Edge>(G, s); }
  Edge *pathR(int s, int t) const
    { return A[s]->pathR(t); }
  double dist(int s, int t) const
    { return A[s]->dist(t); }
};
```

For dense graphs, we could use an adjacency-matrix representation and avoid computing the reverse graph by implicitly transposing the matrix (interchanging the row and column indices), as in Program 19.7. Developing an implementation along these lines is an interesting programming exercise and leads to a compact implementation (see Exercise 21.43); however, a different approach, which we consider next, admits an even more compact implementation.

The method of choice for solving the all-pairs shortest-paths problem in dense graphs, which was developed by R. Floyd, is precisely the same as Warshall's method, except that instead of using the logical *or* operation to keep track of the existence of paths, it checks distances for each edge to determine whether that edge is part of a new shorter path. Indeed, as we have noted, Floyd's and Warshall's algorithms are identical in the proper abstract setting (see Sections 19.3 and 21.1).

Program 21.5 is an all-pairs shortest-paths ADT function that implements Floyd's algorithm. It explictly uses the matrices from Section 21.1 as private data members: a V-by-V vector of vectors d for the distances matrix, and another V-by-V vector of vectors p for the paths table. For every pair of vertices s and t, the constructor sets

Program 21.5 Floyd's algorithm for all shortest paths

This implementation of the interface in Program 21.2 uses Floyd's algorithm, a generalization of Warshall's algorithm (see Program 19.3) that finds the shortest paths between each pair of points instead of just testing for their existence.

   After initializing the distances and paths matrices with the graph's edges, we do a series of relaxation operations to compute the shortest paths. The algorithm is simple to implement, but verifying that it computes the shortest paths is more complicated (*see text*).

```cpp
template <class Graph, class Edge> class allSP
{ const Graph &G;
  vector <vector <Edge *> > p;
  vector <vector <double> > d;
public:
  allSP(const Graph &G) : G(G), p(G.V()), d(G.V())
    { int V = G.V();
      for (int i = 0; i < V; i++)
        { p[i].assign(V, 0); d[i].assign(V, V); }
      for (int s = 0; s < V; s++)
        for (int t = 0; t < V; t++)
          if (G.edge(s, t))
            { p[s][t] = G.edge(s, t);
              d[s][t] = G.edge(s, t)->wt(); }
      for (int s = 0; s < V; s++) d[s][s] = 0;
      for (int i = 0; i < V; i++)
        for (int s = 0; s < V; s++)
          if (p[s][i])
            for (int t = 0; t < V; t++)
              if (s != t)
                if (d[s][t] > d[s][i] + d[i][t])
                  { p[s][t] = p[s][i];
                    d[s][t] = d[s][i] + d[i][t]; }
    }
  Edge *path(int s, int t) const
    { return p[s][t]; }
  double dist(int s, int t) const
    { return d[s][t]; }
};
```

d[s][t] to the shortest-path length from s to t (to be returned by the dist member function) and p[s][t] to the index of the next vertex on the shortest path from s to t (to be returned by the path member function). The implementation is based upon the path relaxation operation that we considered in Section 21.1.

Property 21.8 *With Floyd's algorithm, we can find all shortest paths in a network in time proportional to V^3.*

Proof: The running time is immediate from inspection of the code. We prove that the algorithm is correct by induction in precisely the same way as we did for Warshall's algorithm. The ith iteration of the loop computes a shortest path from s to t in the network that does not include any vertices with indices greater than i (except possibly the endpoints s and t). Assuming this fact to be true for the ith iteration of the loop, we prove it to be true for the (i+1)st iteration of the loop. A shortest path from s to t that does not include any vertices with indices greater than i+1 is either (*i*) a path from s to t that does not include any vertices with indices greater than i, of length d[s][t], that was found on a previous iteration of the loop, by the inductive hypothesis; or (*ii*) comprising a path from s to i and a path from i to t, neither of which includes any vertices with indices greater than i, in which case the inner loop sets d[s][t]. ∎

Figure 21.14 is a detailed trace of Floyd's algorithm on our sample network. If we convert each blank entry to 0 (to indicate the absence of an edge) and convert each nonblank entry to 1 (to indicate the presence of an edge), then these matrices describe the operation of Warshall's algorithm in precisely the same manner as we did in Figure 19.15. For Floyd's algorithm, the nonblank entries indicate more than the existence of a path; they give information about the shortest known path. An entry in the distance matrix has the length of the shortest known path connecting the vertices corresponding to the given row and column; the corresponding entry in the paths matrix gives the next vertex on that path. As the matrices become filled with nonblank entries, running Warshall's algorithm amounts to just double-checking that new paths connect pairs of vertices already known to be connected by a path; in contrast, Floyd's algorithm must compare (and update if necessary) each new path to see whether the new path leads to shorter paths.

**Figure 21.14
Floyd's algorithm**

This sequence shows the construction of the all-pairs shortest-paths matrices with Floyd's algorithm. For i *from* 0 *to* 5 *(top to bottom), we consider, for all* s *and* t, *all of the paths from* s *to* t *having no intermediate vertices greater than* i *(the shaded vertices). Initially, the only such paths are the network's edges, so the distances matrix (center) is the graph's adjacency matrix and the paths matrix (right) is set with* p[s][t] = t *for each edge* s-t. *For vertex* 0 *(top), the algorithm finds that* 3-0-1 *is shorter than the sentinel value that is present because there is no edge* 3-1 *and updates the matrices accordingly. It does not do so for paths such as* 3-0-5, *which is not shorter than the known path* 3-5. *Next the algorithm considers paths through* 0 *and* 1 *(second from top) and finds the new shorter paths* 0-1-2, 0-1-4, 3-0-1-2, 3-0-1-4, *and* 5-1-2. *The third row from the top shows the updates corresponding to shorter paths through* 0, 1, *and* 2 *and so forth.*

Black numbers overstriking gray ones in the matrices indicate situations where the algorithm finds a shorter path than one it found earlier. For example, .91 *overstrikes* 1.37 *in row* 3 *and column* 2 *in the bottom diagram because the algorithm discovered that* 3-5-4-2 *is shorter than* 3-0-1-2.

	0	1	2	3	4	5
0	0	.41				.29
1		0	.51		.32	
2			0	.50		
3	.45	.86		0		.38
4			.32	.36	0	
5		.29			.21	0

	0	1	2	3	4	5
0	0	1				5
1		1	2		4	
2			2	3		
3	0	0		3		5
4			2	3	4	
5		1			4	5

	0	1	2	3	4	5
0	0	.41	.92		.73	.29
1		0	.51		.32	
2			0	.50		
3	.45	.86	1.37	0	1.18	.38
4			.32	.36	0	
5		.29	.80		.21	0

	0	1	2	3	4	5
0	0	1	1		1	5
1		1	2		4	
2			2	3		
3	0	0	0	3	0	5
4			2	3	4	
5		1	1		4	5

	0	1	2	3	4	5
0	0	.41	.92	1.42	.73	.29
1		0	.51	1.01	.32	
2			0	.50		
3	.45	.86	1.37	0	1.18	.38
4			.32	.36	0	
5		.29	.80	1.3	.21	0

	0	1	2	3	4	5
0	0	1	1	1	1	5
1		1	2	2	4	
2			2	3		
3	0	0	0	3	0	5
4			2	3	4	
5		1	1	1	4	5

	0	1	2	3	4	5
0	0	.41	.92	1.42	.73	.29
1	1.46	0	.51	1.01	.32	1.39
2	.95	1.36	0	.50	1.68	.88
3	.45	.86	1.37	0	1.18	.38
4	.81	1.22	.32	.36	0	.74
5	1.75	.29	.80	1.3	.21	0

	0	1	2	3	4	5
0	0	1	1	1	1	5
1	2	1	2	2	4	2
2	3	3	2	3	3	3
3	0	0	0	3	0	5
4	3	3	2	3	4	3
5	1	1	1	1	4	5

	0	1	2	3	4	5
0	0	.41	.92	1.09	.73	.29
1	1.13	0	.51	1.68	.32	1.06
2	.95	1.36	0	.50	1.68	.88
3	.45	.86	1.37	0	1.18	.38
4	.81	1.22	.32	.36	0	.74
5	1.02	.29	.53	.57	.21	0

	0	1	2	3	4	5
0	0	1	1	1	1	5
1	4	1	2	4	4	4
2	3	3	2	3	3	3
3	0	0	0	3	0	5
4	3	3	2	3	4	3
5	4	1	4	4	4	5

	0	1	2	3	4	5
0	0	.41	.82	1.86	.50	.29
1	1.13	0	.51	.68	.32	1.06
2	.95	1.17	0	.50	1.09	.88
3	.45	.67	1.91	0	1.59	.38
4	.81	1.03	.32	.36	0	.74
5	1.02	.29	.53	.57	.21	0

	0	1	2	3	4	5
0	0	1	5	5	5	5
1	4	1	2	4	4	4
2	3	3	2	3	3	3
3	0	5	5	3	5	5
4	3	3	2	3	4	3
5	4	1	4	4	4	5

Comparing the worst-case bounds on the running times of Dijkstra's and Floyd's algorithms, we can draw the same conclusion for these all-pairs shortest-paths algorithms as we did for the corresponding transitive-closure algorithms in Section 19.3. Running Dijkstra's algorithm on each vertex is clearly the method of choice for sparse networks, because the running time is close to VE. As density increases, Floyd's algorithm—which always takes time proportional to V^3—becomes competitive (see Exercise 21.67); it is widely used because it is so simple to implement.

A more fundamental distinction between the algorithms, which we examine in detail in Section 21.7, is that Floyd's algorithm is effective in even those networks that have negative weights (provided that there are no negative cycles). As we noted in Section 21.2, Dijkstra's method does not necessarily find shortest paths in such graphs.

The classical solutions to the all-pairs shortest-paths problem that we have described presume that we have space available to hold the distances and paths matrices. Huge sparse graphs, where we cannot afford to have any V-by-V matrices, present another set of challenging and interesting problems. As we saw in Chapter 19, it is an open problem to reduce this space cost to be proportional to V while still supporting constant-time shortest-path-length queries. We found the analogous problem to be difficult even for the simpler reachability problem (where we are satisfied with learning in constant time whether there is *any* path connecting a given pair of vertices), so we cannot expect a simple solution for the all-pairs shortest-paths problem. Indeed, the number of different shortest path lengths is, in general, proportional to V^2 even for sparse graphs. That value, in some sense, measures the amount of information that we need to process, and perhaps indicates that when we do have restrictions on space, we must expect to spend more time on each query (see Exercises 21.48 through 21.50).

Exercises

▷ **21.39** Estimate, to within a factor of 10, the largest graph (measured by its number of vertices) that your computer and programming system could handle if you were to use Floyd's algorithm to compute all its shortest paths in 10 seconds.

▷ **21.40** Estimate, to within a factor of 10, the largest graph of density 10 (measured by its number of edges) that your computer and programming system could handle if you were to use Dijkstra's algorithm to compute all its shortest paths in 10 seconds.

21.41 Show, in the style of Figure 21.9, the result of using Dijkstra's algorithm to compute all shortest paths of the network defined in Exercise 21.1.

21.42 Show, in the style of Figure 21.14, the result of using Floyd's algorithm to compute all shortest paths of the network defined in Exercise 21.1.

○ **21.43** Combine Program 20.6 and Program 21.4 to make an implementation of the all-pairs shortest-paths ADT interface (based on Dijkstra's algorithm) for dense networks that supports `path` queries but does not explicitly compute the reverse network. Do not define a separate function for the single-source solution—put the code from Program 20.6 directly in the inner loop and put results directly in private data members d and p like those in Program 21.5).

21.44 Run empirical tests, in the style of Table 20.2, to compare Dijkstra's algorithm (Program 21.4 and Exercise 21.43) and Floyd's algorithm (Program 21.5), for various networks (see Exercises 21.4–8).

21.45 Run empirical tests to determine the number of times that Floyd's and Dijkstra's algorithms update the values in the distances matrix, for various networks (see Exercises 21.4–8).

21.46 Give a matrix in which the entry in row s and column t is equal to the number of different simple directed paths connecting s and t in Figure 21.1.

21.47 Implement a class whose constructor computes the path-count matrix that is described in Exercise 21.46 so that it can provide count queries through a public member function in constant time.

21.48 Develop a class implementation of the abstract–shortest-paths ADT for sparse graphs that cuts the space cost to be proportional to V, by increasing the query time to be proportional to V.

● **21.49** Develop a class implementation of the abstract–shortest-paths ADT for sparse graphs that uses substantially less than $O(V^2)$ space but supports queries in substantially less than $O(V)$ time. *Hint*: Compute all shortest paths for a subset of the vertices.

● **21.50** Develop a class implementation of the abstract–shortest-paths ADT for sparse graphs that uses substantially less than $O(V^2)$ space and (using randomization) supports queries in constant *expected* time.

○ **21.51** Develop a class implementation of the abstract–shortest-paths ADT that takes the *lazy* approach of using Dijkstra's algorithm to build the SPT (and associated distance vector) for each vertex s the first time that the client issues a shortest-path query from s, then references the information on subsequent queries.

21.52 Modify the shortest-paths ADT and Dijkstra's algorithm to handle shortest-paths computations in networks that have weights on both vertices and edges. Do not rebuild the graph representation (the method described in Exercise 21.4); modify the code instead.

● 21.53 Build a small model of airline routes and connection times, perhaps based upon some flights that you have taken. Use your solution to Exercise 21.52 to compute the fastest way to get from one of the served destinations to another. Then test your program on real data (see Exercise 21.5).

21.4 Shortest Paths in Acyclic Networks

In Chapter 19, we found that, despite our intuition that DAGs should be easier to process than general digraphs, developing algorithms with substantially better performance for DAGs than for general digraphs is an elusive goal. For shortest-paths problems, we do have algorithms for DAGs that are simpler and faster than the priority-queue–based methods that we have considered for general digraphs. Specifically, in this section we consider algorithms for acyclic networks that

- Solve the single-source problem in linear time.
- Solve the all-pairs problem in time proportional to VE.
- Solve other problems, such as finding longest paths.

In the first two cases, we cut the logarithmic factor from the running time that is present in our best algorithms for sparse networks; in the third case, we have simple algorithms for problems that are intractable for general networks. These algorithms are all straightforward extensions to the algorithms for reachability and transitive closure in DAGs that we considered in Chapter 19.

Since there are no cycles at all, there are no negative cycles; so negative weights present no difficulty in shortest-paths problems on DAGs. Accordingly, we place no restrictions on edge-weight values throughout this section.

Next, a note about terminology: We might choose to refer to directed graphs with weights on the edges and no cycles either as *weighted DAGs* or as *acyclic networks*. We use both terms interchangeably to emphasize their equivalence and to avoid confusion when we refer to the literature, where both are widely used. It is sometimes convenient to use the former to emphasize differences from unweighted DAGs that are implied by weights and the latter to emphasize differences from general networks that are implied by acyclicity.

The four basic ideas that we applied to derive efficient algorithms for unweighted DAGs in Chapter 19 are even more effective for weighted DAGs.

- Use DFS to solve the single-source problem.
- Use a source queue to solve the single-source problem.
- Invoke either method, once for each vertex, to solve the all-pairs problem.
- Use a single DFS (with dynamic programming) to solve the all-pairs problem.

These methods solve the single-source problem in time proportional to E and the all-pairs problem in time proportional to VE. They are all effective because of topological ordering, which allows us compute shortest paths for each vertex without having to revisit any decisions. We consider one implementation for each problem in this section; we leave the others for exercises (see Exercises 21.62 through 21.65).

We begin with a slight twist. Every DAG has at least one source but could have several, so it is natural to consider the following shortest-paths problem.

Multisource shortest paths   Given a set of start vertices, find, for each other vertex w, a shortest path among the shortest paths from each start vertex to w.

This problem is essentially equivalent to the single-source shortest-paths problem. We can convert a multisource problem into a single-source problem by adding a dummy source vertex with zero-length edges to each source in the network. Conversely, we can convert a single-source problem to a multisource problem by working with the induced subnetwork defined by all the vertices and edges reachable from the source. We rarely construct such subnetworks explicitly, because our algorithms automatically process them if we treat the start vertex as though it were the only source in the network (even when it is not).

Topological sorting immediately presents a solution to the multisource shortest-paths problem and to numerous other problems. We maintain a vertex-indexed vector wt that gives the weight of the shortest known path from any source to each vertex. To solve the multisource shortest-paths problem, we initialize the wt vector to 0 for sources and a large sentinel value for all the other vertices. Then, we process the vertices in topological order. To process a vertex v, we perform a relaxation operation for each outgoing edge v-w that updates the shortest path to w if v-w gives a shorter path from a source to w (through v). This process checks all paths from any source to each vertex in the graph; the relaxation operation keeps track of the minimum-length such path, and the topological sort ensures that we process the vertices in an appropriate order.

We can implement this method directly in one of two ways. The first is to add a few lines of code to the topological sort code in Program 19.8: Just after we remove a vertex v from the source queue, we perform the indicated relaxation operation for each of its edges (see Exercise 21.56). The second is to put the vertices in topological order, then to scan through them and to perform the relaxation operations precisely as described in the previous paragraph.

These same processes (with other relaxation operations) can solve many graph-processing problems. For example, Program 21.6 is an implementation of the second approach (sort, then scan) for solving the *multisource longest-paths* problem: For each vertex in the network, what is a longest path from some source to that vertex? We interpret the wt entry associated with each vertex to be the length of the *longest* known path from any source to that vertex, initialize all of the weights to 0, and change the sense of the comparison in the relaxation operation. Figure 21.15 traces the operation of Program 21.6 on a sample acyclic network.

Property 21.9 *We can solve the multisource shortest-paths problem and the multisource longest-paths problem in acyclic networks in linear time.*

Proof: The same proof holds for longest path, shortest path, and many other path properties. To match Program 21.6, we state the proof for longest paths. We show by induction on the loop variable i that, for all vertices v = ts[j] with j < i that have been processed, wt[v] is the length of the longest path from a source to v. When v = ts[i], let t be the vertex preceding v on any path from a source to v. Since vertices in the ts vector are in topologically sorted order, t must have been processed already. By the induction hypothesis, wt[t] is the length of the longest path to t, and the relaxation step in the code checks whether that path gives a longer path to v through t. The induction hypothesis also implies that all paths to v are checked in this way as v is processed. ∎

This property is significant because it tells us that processing acyclic networks is considerably easier than processing networks that

Figure 21.15
Computing longest paths in an acyclic network

In this network, each edge has the weight associated with the vertex that it leads from, listed at the top left. Sinks have edges to a dummy vertex 10, which is not shown in the drawings. The wt *array contains the length of the longest known path to each vertex from some source, and the* st *array contains the previous vertex on the longest path. This figure illustrates the operation of Program 21.6, which picks from among the sources (the shaded nodes in each diagram) using the FIFO discipline, though any of the sources could be chosen at each step. We begin by removing 0 and checking each of its incident edges, discovering one-edge paths of length .41 to 1, 7, and 9. Next, we remove 5 and record the one-edge path from 5 to 10 (left, second from top). Next, we remove 9 and record the paths 0-9-4 and 0-9-6, of length .70 (left, third from top). We continue in this way, changing the arrays whenever we find longer paths. For example, when we remove 7 (left, second from bottom) we record paths of length .73 to 8 and 3; then, later, when we remove 6, we record longer paths (of length .91) to 8 and 3 (right, top). The point of the computation is to find the longest path to the dummy node 10. In this case, the result is the path 0-9-6-8-2, of length 1.73.*

0	.41
1	.51
2	.50
3	.36
4	.38
5	.45
6	.21
7	.32
8	.32
9	.29

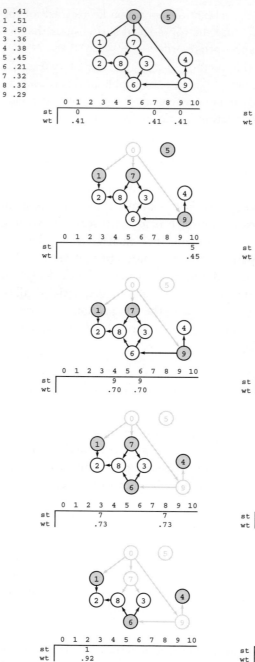

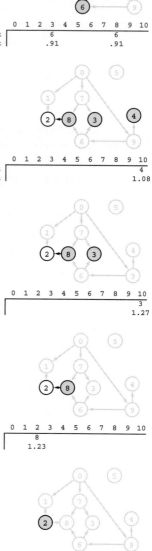

Program 21.6 Longest paths in an acyclic network

To find the *longest* paths in an acyclic network, we consider the vertices in topological order, keeping the weight of the longest known path to each vertex in a vertex-indexed vector wt by doing a relaxation step for each edge. The vector lpt defines a a spanning forest of longest paths (rooted at the sources) so that path(v) returns the last edge on the longest path to v.

```
#include "dagTS.cc"
template <class Graph, class Edge> class LPTdag
{ const Graph &G;
  vector<double> wt;
  vector<Edge *> lpt;
public:
  LPTdag(const Graph &G) : G(G),
    lpt(G.V()), wt(G.V(), 0)
  { int j, w;
    dagTS<Graph> ts(G);
    for (int v = ts[j = 0]; j < G.V(); v = ts[++j])
    { typename Graph::adjIterator A(G, v);
      for (Edge* e = A.beg(); !A.end(); e = A.nxt())
        if (wt[w = e->w()] < wt[v] + e->wt())
          { wt[w] = wt[v] + e->wt(); lpt[w] = e; }
    }
  }
  Edge *pathR(int v) const { return lpt[v]; }
  double dist(int v) const { return wt[v]; }
};
```

---

have cycles. For shortest paths, the method is faster than Dijkstra's algorithm by a factor proportional to the cost of the priority-queue operations in Dijkstra's algorithm. For longest paths, we have a linear algorithm for acyclic networks but an intractable problem for general networks. Moreover, negative weights present no special difficulty here, but they present formidable barriers for algorithms on general networks, as discussed in Section 21.7.

The method just described depends on only the fact that we process the vertices in topological order. Therefore, any topological-

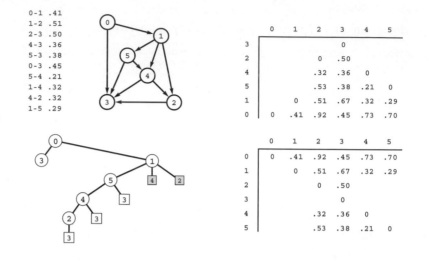

Figure 21.16
Shortest paths in an acyclic network

This diagram depicts the computation of the all-shortest-distances matrix (bottom right) for a sample weighted DAG (top left), computing each row as the last action in a recursive DFS function. Each row is computed from the rows for adjacent vertices, which appear earlier in the list, because the rows are computed in reverse topological order (postorder traversal of the DFS tree shown at the bottom left). The array on the top right shows the rows of the matrix in the order that they are computed. For example, to compute each entry in the row for 0 we add .41 to the corresponding entry in the row for 1 (to get the distance to it from 0 after taking 0-1), then add .45 to the corresponding entry in the row for 3 (to get the distance to it from 0 after taking 0-3), and take the smaller of the two. The computation is essentially the same as computing the transitive closure of a DAG (see, for example, Figure 19.23). The most significant difference between the two is that the transitive-closure algorithm could ignore down edges (such as 1-2 in this example) because they go to vertices known to be reachable, while the shortest-paths algorithm has to check whether paths associated with down edges are shorter than known paths. If we were to ignore 1-2 in this example, we would miss the shortest paths 0-1-2 and 1-2.

```
0-1 .41
1-2 .51
2-3 .50
4-3 .36
5-3 .38
0-3 .45
5-4 .21
1-4 .32
4-2 .32
1-5 .29
```

	0	1	2	3	4	5
3				0		
2			0	.50		
4			.32	.36	0	
5			.53	.38	.21	0
1		0	.51	.67	.32	.29
0	0	.41	.92	.45	.73	.70

	0	1	2	3	4	5
0	0	.41	.92	.45	.73	.70
1		0	.51	.67	.32	.29
2			0	.50		
3				0		
4			.32	.36	0	
5			.53	.38	.21	0

sorting algorithm can be adapted to solve shortest- and longest-paths problems and other problems of this type (see, for example, Exercises 21.56 and 21.62).

As we know from Chapter 19, the DAG abstraction is a general one that arises in many applications. For example, we see an application in Section 21.6 that seems unrelated to networks but that can be addressed directly with Program 21.6.

Next, we turn to the all-pairs shortest-paths problem for acyclic networks. As in Section 19.3, one method that we could use to solve this problem is to run a single-source algorithm for each vertex (see Exercise 21.65). The equally effective approach that we consider here is to use a single DFS with dynamic programming, just as we did for computing the transitive closure of DAGs in Section 19.5 (see Program 19.9). If we consider the vertices at the end of the recursive function, we are processing them in reverse topological order and can derive the shortest-path vector for each vertex from the shortest-path vectors for each adjacent vertex, simply by using each edge in a relaxation step.

Program 21.7 is an implementation along these lines. The operation of this program on a sample weighted DAG is illustrated in Figure 21.16. Beyond the generalization to include relaxation, there is one important difference between this computation and the transitive-

---

Program 21.7 All shortest paths in an acyclic network

This implementation of the interface in Program 21.2 for weighted DAGs is derived by adding appropriate relaxation operations to the dynamic-programming–based transitive-closure function in Program 19.9.

```
template <class Graph, class Edge> class allSPdag
{ const Graph &G;
  vector <vector <Edge *> > p;
  vector <vector <double> > d;
  void dfsR(int s)
  { typename Graph::adjIterator A(G, s);
    for (Edge* e = A.beg(); !A.end(); e = A.nxt())
    { int t = e->w(); double w = e->wt();
      if (d[s][t] > w)
        { d[s][t] = w; p[s][t] = e; }
      if (p[t][t] == 0) dfsR(t);
      for (int i = 0; i < G.V(); i++)
        if (p[t][i])
          if (d[s][i] > w + d[t][i])
            { d[s][i] = w + d[t][i]; p[s][i] = e; }
    }
  }
public:
  allSPdag(const Graph &G) : G(G),
    p(G.V()), d(G.V())
  { int V = G.V();
    for (int i = 0; i < V; i++)
      { p[i].assign(V, 0); d[i].assign(V, V); }
    for (int s = 0; s < V; s++)
      if (p[s][s] == 0) dfsR(s);
  }
  Edge *path(int s, int t) const
    { return p[s][t]; }
  double dist(int s, int t) const
    { return d[s][t]; }
};
```

Figure 21.17
All longest paths in an acyclic network

Our method for computing all shortest paths in acyclic networks works even if the weights are negative. Therefore, we can use it to compute *longest paths, simply by first negating all the weights, as illustrated here for the network in Figure 21.16. The longest simple path in this network is 0-1-5-4-2-3, of weight 1.73.*

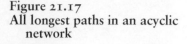

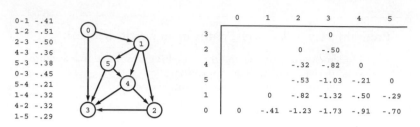

```
0-1  -.41
1-2  -.51
2-3  -.50
4-3  -.36
5-3  -.38
0-3  -.45
5-4  -.21
1-4  -.32
4-2  -.32
1-5  -.29
```

	0	1	2	3	4	5
3				0		
2			0	-.50		
4			-.32	-.82	0	
5			-.53	-1.03	-.21	0
1		0	-.82	-1.32	-.50	-.29
0	0	-.41	-1.23	-1.73	-.91	-.70

closure computation for DAGs: In Program 19.9, we had the choice of ignoring down edges in the DFS tree because they provide no new information about reachability; in Program 21.7, however, we need to consider all edges, because any edge might lead to a shorter path.

Property 21.10 *We can solve the all-pairs shortest-paths problem in acyclic networks with a single DFS in time proportional to VE.*

Proof: This fact follows immediately from the strategy of solving the single-source problem for each vertex (see Exercise 21.65). We can also establish it by induction, from Program 21.7. After the recursive calls for a vertex v, we know that we have computed all shortest paths for each vertex on v's adjacency list, so we can find shortest paths from v to each vertex by checking each of v's edges. We do V relaxation steps for each edge, for a total of VE relaxation steps. ∎

Thus, for acyclic networks, topological sorting allows us to avoid the cost of the priority queue in Dijkstra's algorithm. Like Floyd's algorithm, Program 21.7 also solves problems more general than those solved by Dijkstra's algorithm, because, unlike Dijkstra's (see Section 21.7), this algorithm works correctly even in the presence of negative edge weights. If we run the algorithm after negating all the weights in an acyclic network, it finds all *longest* paths, as depicted in Figure 21.17. Or, we can find longest paths by reversing the inequality test in the relaxation algorithm, as in Program 21.6.

The other algorithms for finding shortest paths in acyclic networks that are mentioned at the beginning of this section generalize the methods from Chapter 19 in a manner similar to the other algorithms that we have examined in this chapter. Developing implementations of them is a worthwhile way to cement your understanding of both DAGs and shortest paths (see Exercises 21.62 through 21.65). All the methods run in time proportional to VE in the worst case, with actual costs dependent on the structure of the DAG. In principle, we might do even better for certain sparse weighted DAGs (see Exercise 19.117).

Exercises

▷ **21.54** Give the solutions to the multisource shortest- and longest-paths problems for the network defined in Exercise 21.1, with the directions of edges 2–3 and 1–0 reversed.

▷ **21.55** Modify Program 21.6 such that it solves the multisource shortest-paths problem for acyclic networks.

▷ **21.56** Implement a class with the same interface as Program 21.6 that is derived from the source-queue–based topological-sorting code of Program 19.8, performing the relaxation operations for each vertex just after that vertex is removed from the source queue.

○ **21.57** Define an ADT for the relaxation operation, provide implementations, and modify Program 21.6 to use your ADT such that you can use Program 21.6 to solve the multisource shortest-paths problem, the multisource longest-paths problem, and other problems, just by changing the relaxation implementation.

21.58 Use your generic implementation from Exercise 21.57 to implement a class with member functions that return the length of the longest paths from any source to any other vertex in a DAG, the length of the shortest such path, and the number of vertices reachable via paths whose lengths fall within a given range.

● **21.59** Define properties of relaxation such that you can modify the proof of Property 21.9 to apply an abstract version of Program 21.6 (such as the one described in Exercise 21.57).

▷ **21.60** Show, in the style of Figure 21.16, the computation of the all-pairs shortest-paths matrices for the network defined in Exercise 21.54 by Program 21.7.

○ **21.61** Give an upper bound on the number of edge weights accessed by Program 21.7, as a function of basic structural properties of the network. Write a program to compute this function, and use it to estimate the accuracy of the VE bound, for various acyclic networks (add weights as appropriate to the models in Chapter 19).

○ **21.62** Write a DFS-based solution to the multisource shortest-paths problem for acyclic networks. Does your solution work correctly in the presence of negative edge weights? Explain your answer.

▷ **21.63** Extend your solution to Exercise 21.62 to provide an implementation of the all-pairs shortest-paths ADT interface for acyclic networks that builds the all-paths and all-distances matrices in time proportional to VE.

21.64 Show, in the style of Figure 21.9, the computation of all shortest paths of the network defined in Exercise 21.54 using the DFS-based method of Exercise 21.63.

▷ **21.65** Modify Program 21.6 such that it solves the single-source shortest-paths problem in acyclic networks, then use it to develop an implementation of the all-pairs shortest-paths ADT interface for acyclic networks that builds the all-paths and all-distances matrices in time proportional to VE.

○ **21.66** Work Exercise 21.61 for the DFS-based (Exercise 21.63) and for the topological-sort–based (Exercise 21.65) implementations of the all-pairs shortest-paths ADT. What inferences can you draw about the comparative costs of the three methods?

21.67 Run empirical tests, in the style of Table 20.2, to compare the three class implementations for the all-pairs shortest-paths problem described in this section (see Program 21.7, Exercise 21.63, and Exercise 21.65), for various acyclic networks (add weights as appropriate to the models in Chapter 19).

21.5 Euclidean Networks

In applications where networks model maps, our primary interest is often in finding the best route from one place to another. In this section, we examine a strategy for this problem: a fast algorithm for the source–sink shortest-path problem in *Euclidean networks*, which are networks whose vertices are points in the plane and whose edge weights are defined by the geometric distances between the points.

These networks satisfy two important properties that do not necessarily hold for general edge weights. First, the distances satisfy the triangle inequality: The distance from s to d is never greater than the distance from s to x plus the distance from x to d. Second, vertex positions give a lower bound on path length: No path from s to d will be shorter than the distance from s to d. The algorithm for the source–sink shortest-paths problem that we examine in this section takes advantage of these two properties to improve performance.

Often, Euclidean networks are also *symmetric*: Edges run in both directions. As mentioned at the beginning of the chapter, such networks arise immediately if, for example, we interpret the adjacency-matrix or adjacency-lists representation of an undirected weighted Euclidean graph (see Section 20.7) as a weighted digraph (network). When we draw an undirected Euclidean network, we assume this interpretation to avoid proliferation of arrowheads in the drawings.

The basic idea is straightforward: Priority-first search provides us with a general mechanism to search for paths in graphs. With Dijkstra's algorithm, we examine paths in order of their distance from the start vertex. This ordering ensures that, when we reach the sink, we have examined all paths in the graph that are shorter, none of which took us to the sink. But in a Euclidean graph, we have additional information: If we are looking for a path from a source s to a sink d and we encounter a third vertex v, then we know that not only do we have to take the path that we have found from s to v, but also the best that we could possibly do in traveling from v to d is first to take an edge v–w and then to find a path whose length is the straight-line distance from w to d (see Figure 21.18). With priority-first search, we can easily take into account this extra information to improve performance. We use the standard algorithm, but we use the sum of the following three quantities as the priority of each edge v–w: the length of the known path from s to v, the weight of the edge v–w, and the distance from w to t. If we always pick the edge for which this number is smallest, then, when we reach t, we are still assured that there is no shorter path in the graph from s to t. Furthermore, in typical networks we reach this conclusion after doing far less work than we would were we using Dijkstra's algorithm.

To implement this approach, we use a standard PFS implementation of Dijkstra's algorithm (Program 21.1, since Euclidean graphs are normally sparse, but also see Exercise 21.73) with two changes: First, instead of initializing wt[s] at the beginning of the search to 0.0, we set it to the quantity dist(s, d), where distance is a function that returns the distance between two vertices. Second, we define the priority P to be the function

$$(wt[v] + e{\to}wt() + distance(w, d) - distance(v, d))$$

instead of the function (wt[v] + e->wt()) that we used in Program 21.1 (recall that v and w are local variables that are set to the values e->v() and e->w(), respectively. These changes, to which we refer as the *Euclidean heuristic*, maintain the invariant that the quantity wt[v] - distance(v, d) is the length of the shortest path through the network from s to v, for every tree vertex v (and therefore wt[v] is a lower bound on the length of the shortest possible path through v from s to d). We compute wt[w] by adding to this quantity the edge weight (the distance to w) plus the distance from w to the sink d.

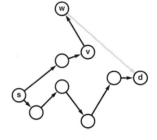

Figure 21.18
Edge relaxation (Euclidean)

In a Euclidean graph, we can take distances to the destination into account in the relaxation operation as we compute shortest paths. In this example, we could deduce that the path depicted from s to v plus v–w cannot lead to a shorter path from s to d than the one already found because the length of any such path must be at least the length of the path from s to v plus the length of v–w plus the straight-line distance from w to d, which is greater than the length of the known path from s to d. Tests like this one can significantly reduce the number of paths that we have to consider.

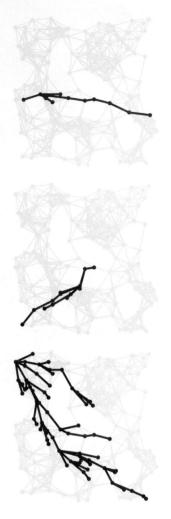

Figure 21.19
Shortest path in a Euclidean graph

When we direct the shortest-path search towards the destination vertex, we can restrict the search to vertices within a relatively small ellipse around the path, as illustrated in these three examples, which show SPT subtrees from the examples in Figure 21.12.

Property 21.11 *Priority-first search with the Euclidean heuristic solves the source–sink shortest-paths problem in Euclidean graphs.*

Proof: The proof of Property 21.2 applies: At the time that we add a vertex x to the tree, the addition of the distance from x to d to the priority does not affect the reasoning that the tree path from s to x is a shortest path in the graph from s to x, since the same quantity is added to the length of all paths to x. When d is added to the tree, we know that no other path from s to d is shorter than the tree path, because any such path must consist of a tree path followed by an edge to some vertex w that is not on the tree, followed by a path from w to d (whose length cannot be shorter than the distance from w to d); and, by construction, we know that the length of the path from s to w plus the distance from w to d is no smaller than the length of the tree path from s to d. ∎

In Section 21.6, we discuss another simple way to implement the Euclidean heuristic. First, we make a pass through the graph to change the weight of each edge: For each edge v-w, we add the quantity `distance(w, d) - distance(v, d)`. Then, we run a standard shortest-path algorithm, starting at s (with `wt[s]` initialized to `distance(s, d)`) and stopping when we reach d. This method is computationally equivalent to the method that we have described (which essentially computes the same weights on the fly) and is a specific example of a basic operation known as *reweighting* a network. Reweighting plays an essential role in solving the shortest-paths problems with negative weights; we discuss it in detail in Section 21.6.

The Euclidean heuristic affects the performance but not the correctness of Dijkstra's algorithm for the source–sink shortest-paths computation. As discussed in the proof of Property 21.2, using the standard algorithm to solve the source–sink problem amounts to building an SPT that has all vertices closer to the start than the sink d. With the Euclidean heuristic, the SPT contains just the vertices whose path from s *plus* distance to d is smaller than the length of the shortest path from s to d. We expect this tree to be substantially smaller for many applications because the heuristic prunes a substantial number of long paths. The precise savings is dependent on the structure of the graph and the geometry of the vertices. Figure 21.19 shows the operation of the Euclidean heuristic on our sample graph, where the savings are substantial. We refer to the method as a heuristic because there is no guarantee that there will be any savings at all: It could always be the case that the only path from source to sink is a long one that wanders arbitrarily far from the source before heading back to the sink (see Exercise 21.80).

Figure 21.20 illustrates the basic underlying geometry that describes the intuition behind the Euclidean heuristic: If the shortest-path length from s to d is z, then vertices examined by the algorithm fall roughly within the ellipse defined as the locus of points x for which the distance from s to x plus the distance from x to d is equal to z. For typical Euclidean graphs, we expect the number of vertices in this ellipse to be far smaller than the number of vertices in the circle of radius z that is centered at the source (those that would be examined by Dijkstra's algorithm).

Precise analysis of the savings is a difficult analytic problem and depends on models of both random point sets and random graphs (*see reference section*). For typical situations, we expect that, if the standard algorithm examines X vertices in computing a source–sink shortest path, the Euclidean heuristic will cut the cost to be proportional to $\sqrt{X}$, which leads to an expected running time proportional to V for dense graphs and proportional to $\sqrt{V}$ for sparse graphs. This example illustrates that the difficulty of developing an appropriate model or analyzing associated algorithms should not dissuade us from taking advantage of the substantial savings that are available in many applications, particularly when the implementation (add a term to the priority) is trivial.

The proof of Property 21.11 applies for *any* function that gives a lower bound on the distance from each vertex to d. Might there be other functions that will cause the algorithm to examine even fewer vertices than the Euclidean heuristic? This question has been studied in a general setting that applies to a broad class of combinatorial search algorithms. Indeed, the Euclidean heuristic is a specific instance of an algorithm called A^* (pronounced "ay-star"). This theory tells us that using the best available lower-bound function is *optimal*; stated another way, the better the bound function, the more efficient the search. In this case, the optimality of A* tells us that the Euclidean heuristic will certainly examine no more vertices than Dijkstra's algorithm (which is A* with a lower bound of 0). The analytic results just

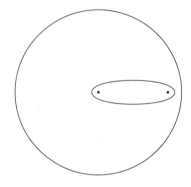

**Figure 21.20
Euclidean heuristic cost
bounds**

When we direct the shortest-path search towards the destination vertex, we can restrict the search to vertices within an ellipse around the path, as compared to the circle centered at s that is required by Dijkstra's algorithm. The radius of the circle and the shape of the ellipse are determined by the length of the shortest path.

described give more precise information for specific random network models.

We can also use properties of Euclidean networks to help build efficient implementations of the abstract–shortest-paths ADT, trading time for space more effectively than we can for general networks (see Exercises 21.48 through 21.50). Such algorithms are important in applications such as map processing, where networks are huge and sparse. For example, suppose that we want to develop a navigation system based on shortest paths for a map with millions of roads. We perhaps can store the map itself in a small onboard computer, but the distances and paths matrices are much too large to be stored (see Exercises 21.39 and 21.40); therefore, the all-paths algorithms of Section 21.3 are not effective. Dijkstra's algorithm also may not give sufficiently short response times for huge maps. Exercises 21.77 through 21.78 explore strategies whereby we can invest a reasonable amount of preprocessing and space to provide fast responses to source–sink shortest-paths queries.

Exercises

• **21.68** Find a large Euclidean graph online—perhaps a map with an underlying table of locations and distances between them, telephone connections with costs, or airline routes and rates.

21.69 Using the strategies described in Exercises 17.71 through 17.73, write programs that generate random Euclidean graphs by connecting vertices arranged in a $\sqrt{V}$-by-$\sqrt{V}$ grid.

▷ **21.70** Show that the partial SPT computed by the Euclidean heuristic is independent of the value that we use to initialize wt[s]. Explain how to compute the shortest-path lengths from the initial value.

▷ **21.71** Show, in the style of Figure 21.10, what is the result when you use the Euclidean heuristic to compute a shortest path from 0 to 6 in the network defined in Exercise 21.1.

○ **21.72** Describe what happens if the function distance(s, t), used for the Euclidean heuristic, returns the actual shortest-path length from s to t for all pairs of vertices.

21.73 Develop an class implementation for shortest paths in dense Euclidean graphs that is based upon a graph representation that supports the edge function and an implementation of Dijkstra's algorithm (Program 20.6, with an appropriate priority function).

21.74 Run empirical studies to test the effectiveness of the Euclidean shortest-path heuristic, for various Euclidean networks (see Exercises 21.9, 21.68,

21.69, and 21.80). For each graph, generate $V/10$ random pairs of vertices, and print a table that shows the average distance between the vertices, the average length of the shortest path between the vertices, the average ratio of the number of vertices examined with the Euclidean heuristic to the number of vertices examined with Dijkstra's algorithm, and the average ratio of the area of the ellipse associated with the Euclidean heuristic with the area of the circle associated with Dijkstra's algorithm.

21.75 Develop a class implementation for the source–sink shortest-paths problem in Euclidean graphs that is based on the bidirectional search described in Exercise 21.35.

∘ **21.76** Use a geometric interpretation to provide an estimate of the ratio of the number of vertices in the SPT produced by Dijkstra's algorithm for the source–sink problem to the number of vertices in the SPTs produced in the two-way version described in Exercise 21.75.

21.77 Develop a class implementation for shortest paths in Euclidean graphs that performs the following preprocessing step in the constructor: Divide the map region into a W-by-W grid, and then use Floyd's all-pairs shortest-paths algorithm to compute a W^2-by-W^2 matrix, where row i and column j contain the length of a shortest path connecting any vertex in grid square i to any vertex in grid square j. Then, use these shortest-path lengths as lower bounds to improve the Euclidean heuristic. Experiment with a few different values of W such that you expect a small constant number of vertices per grid square.

21.78 Develop an implementation of the all-pairs shortest-paths ADT for Euclidean graphs that combines the ideas in Exercises 21.75 and 21.77.

21.79 Run empirical studies to compare the effectiveness of the heuristics described in Exercises 21.75 through 21.78, for various Euclidean networks (see Exercises 21.9, 21.68, 21.69, and 21.80).

21.80 Expand your empirical studies to include Euclidean graphs that are derived by removal of all vertices and edges from a circle of radius r in the center, for $r = 0.1, 0.2, 0.3,$ and 0.4. (These graphs provide a severe test of the Euclidean heuristic.)

21.81 Give a direct implementation of Floyd's algorithm for an implementation of the network ADT for implicit Euclidean graphs defined by N points in the plane with edges that connect points within d of each other. Do not explicitly represent the graph; rather, given two vertices, compute their distance to determine whether an edge exists and, if one does, what its length is.

21.82 Develop an implementation for the scenario described in Exercise 21.81 that builds a neighbor graph and then uses Dijkstra's algorithm from each vertex (see Program 21.1).

21.83 Run empirical studies to compare the time and space needed by the algorithms in Exercises 21.81 and 21.82, for $d = 0.1, 0.2, 0.3,$ and 0.4.

• **21.84** Write a client program that does dynamic graphical animations of the Euclidean heuristic. Your program should produce images like Figure 21.19

(see Exercise 21.38). Test your program on various Euclidean networks (see Exercises 21.9, 21.68, 21.69, and 21.80).

21.6 Reduction

It turns out that shortest-paths problems—particularly the general case, where negative weights are allowed (the topic of Section 21.7)—represent a general mathematical model that we can use to solve a variety of other problems that seem unrelated to graph processing. This model is the first among several such general models that we encounter. As we move to more difficult problems and increasingly general models, one of the challenges that we face is to characterize precisely relationships among various problems. Given a new problem, we ask whether we can solve it easily by transforming it to a problem that we know how to solve. If we place restrictions on the problem, will we be able to solve it more easily? To help answer such questions, we digress briefly in this section to discuss the technical language that we use to describe these types of relationships among problems.

Definition 21.3 *We say that a problem A **reduces to** another problem B if we can use an algorithm that solves B to develop an algorithm that solves A, in a total amount of time that is, in the worst case, no more than a constant times the worst-case running time of the algorithm that solves B. We say that two problems are **equivalent** if they reduce to each other.*

We postpone until Part 8 a rigorous definition of what it means to "use" one algorithm to "develop" another. For most applications, we are content with the following simple approach. We show that A reduces to B by demonstrating that we can solve any instance of A in three steps:

- Transform it to an instance of B.
- Solve that instance of B.
- Transform the solution of B to be a solution of A.

As long as we can perform the transformations (and solve B) efficiently, we can solve A efficiently. To illustrate this proof technique, we consider two examples.

Property 21.12 *The transitive-closure problem reduces to the all-pairs shortest-paths problem with nonnegative weights.*

	0	1	2	3	4	5
0	.10	.10				.10
1		.10	.10		.10	
2			.10			
3	.10		.10	.10	.10	.10
4		.10		.10		
5		.10			.10	.10

	0	1	2	3	4	5
0	.10	.10	.20		.20	.10
1		.10	.10		.10	
2			.10			
3	.10	.20	.10	.10	.10	.10
4			.10		.10	
5		.10	.20		.10	.10

	0	1	2	3	4	5
0	1	1	1	0	1	1
1	0	1	1	0	1	0
2	0	0	1	0	0	0
3	1	1	1	1	1	1
4	0	0	1	0	1	0
5	0	1	1	0	1	1

**Figure 21.21
Transitive-closure reduction**

Given a digraph (left), *we can transform its adjacency matrix (with self-loops) into an adjacency matrix representing a network by assigning an arbitrary weight to each edge* (left matrix). *As usual, blank entries in the matrix represent a sentinel value that indicates the absence of an edge. Given the all-pairs shortest-paths-lengths matrix of that network* (center matrix), *the transitive closure of the digraph* (right matrix) *is simply the matrix formed by subsituting 0 for each sentinel and 1 for all other entries.*

Proof: We have already pointed out the direct relationship between Warshall's algorithm and Floyd's algorithm. Another way to consider that relationship, in the present context, is to imagine that we need to compute the transitive closure of digraphs using a library function that computes all shortest paths in networks. To do so, we add self-loops if they are not present in the digraph; then, we build a network directly from the adjacency matrix of the digraph, with an arbitrary weight (say 0.1) corresponding to each 1 and the sentinel weight corresponding to each 0. Then, we call the all-pairs shortest-paths function. Next, we can easily compute the transitive closure from the all-pairs shortest-paths matrix that the function computes: Given any two vertices u and v, there is a path from u to v in the digraph if and only if the length of the path from u to v in the network is nonzero (see Figure 21.21). ∎

This property is a formal statement that the transitive-closure problem is no more difficult than the all-pairs shortest-paths problem. Since we happen to know algorithms for transitive closure that are even faster than the algorithms that we know for all-pairs shortest-paths problems, this information is no surprise. Reduction is more interesting when we use it to establish a relationship between problems that we do not know how to solve, or between such problems and other problems that we can solve.

Property 21.13   *In networks with no constraints on edge weights, the longest-path and shortest-path problems (single-source or all-pairs) are equivalent.*

Proof: Given a shortest-path problem, negate all the weights. A longest path (a path with the highest weight) in the modified network is a shortest path in the original network. An identical argument shows that the shortest-path problem reduces to the longest-path problem. ∎

This proof is trivial, but this property also illustrates that care is justified in stating and proving reductions, because it is easy to take reductions for granted and thus to be misled. For example, it is decidedly *not* true that the longest-path and shortest-path problems are equivalent in networks with nonnegative weights.

At the beginning of this chapter, we outlined an argument that shows that the problem of finding shortest paths in undirected weighted graphs reduces to the problem of finding shortest paths in networks, so we can use our algorithms for networks to solve shortest-paths problems in undirected weighted graphs. Two further points about this reduction are worth contemplating in the present context. First, the converse does not hold: Knowing how to solve shortest-paths problems in undirected weighted graphs does not help us to solve them in networks. Second, we saw a flaw in the argument: If edge weights could be negative, the reduction gives networks with negative cycles, and we do not know how to find shortest paths in such networks. Even though the reduction fails, it turns out to be still possible to find shortest paths in undirected weighted graphs with no negative cycles with an unexpectedly complicated algorithm (*see reference section*). Since this problem does not reduce to the directed version, this algorithm does not help us to solve the shortest-path problem in general networks.

The concept of reduction essentially describes the process of using one ADT to implement another, as is done routinely by modern systems programmers. If two problems are equivalent, we know that if we can solve either of them efficiently, we can solve the other efficiently. We often find simple one-to-one correspondences, such as the one in Property 21.13, that show two problems to be equivalent. In this case, we have not yet discussed how to solve either problem, but it is useful to know that if we could find an efficient solution to one of them, we could use that solution to solve the other one. We saw another example in Chapter 17: When faced with the problem of determining whether or not a graph has an odd cycle, we noted that the problem is equivalent to determining whether or not the graph is two-colorable.

Reduction has two primary applications in the design and analysis of algorithms. First, it helps us to classify problems according to their difficulty at an appropriate abstract level without necessarily developing and analyzing full implementations. Second, we often do reductions to establish lower bounds on the difficulty of solving various problems, to help indicate when to stop looking for better algorithms. We have seen examples of these uses in Sections 19.3 and 20.7; we see others later in this section.

Beyond these direct practical uses, the concept of reduction also has widespread and profound implications for the theory of computation; these implications are important for us to understand as we tackle increasingly difficult problems. We discuss this topic briefly at the end of this section and consider it in full formal detail in Part 8.

The constraint that the cost of the transformations should not dominate is a natural one and often applies. In many cases, however, we might choose to use reduction even when the cost of the transformations does dominate. One of the most important uses of reduction is to provide efficient solutions to problems that might otherwise seem intractable by performing a transformation to a well-understood problem that we know how to solve efficiently. Reducing A to B, even if computing the transformations is much more expensive than is solving B, may give us a much more efficient algorithm for solving A than we could otherwise devise. There are many other possibilities. Perhaps we are interested in expected cost rather than the worst case. Perhaps we need to solve two problems B and C to solve A. Perhaps we need to solve multiple instances of B. We leave further discussion of such variations until Part 8, because all the examples that we consider before then are of the simple type just discussed.

In the particular case where we solve a problem A by simplifying another problem B, we know that A reduces to B, but not necessarily vice versa. For example, selection reduces to sorting because we can find the kth smallest element in a file by sorting the file and then indexing (or scanning) to the kth position, but this fact certainly does not imply that sorting reduces to selection. In the present context, the shortest-paths problem for weighted DAGs and the shortest-paths problem for networks with positive weights both reduce to the general shortest-paths problem. This use of reduction corresponds to the intuitive notion of one problem being more general than another. Any sorting algorithm solves any selection problem, and, if we can solve the shortest-paths problem in general networks, we certainly can use that solution for networks with various restrictions; but the converse is not necessarily true.

This use of reduction is helpful, but the concept becomes more useful when we use it to gain information about the relationships between problems in different domains. For example, consider the following problems, which seem at first blush to be far removed from graph processing. Through reduction, we can develop specific relationships between these problems and the shortest-paths problem.

Job scheduling   A large set of jobs, of varying durations, needs to be performed. We can be working on any number of jobs at a given time, but a set of precedence relationships specify, for a set of pairs of jobs, that the first must be completed before the second can be started. What is the minimum amount of time required to complete all the jobs while satisfying all the precedence constraints? Specifically, given a set of jobs (with durations) and a set of precedence constraints, schedule the jobs (find a start time for each) so as to achieve this minimum.

Figure 21.22 depicts an example instance of the job-scheduling problem. It uses a natural network representation, which we use in a moment as the basis for a reduction. This version of the problem is perhaps the simplest of literally hundreds of versions that have been studied—versions that involve other job characteristics and other constraints, such as the assignment of personnel or other resources to the jobs, other costs associated with specific jobs, deadlines, and so forth. In this context, the version that we have described is commonly called *precedence-constrained scheduling with unlimited parallelism*; we use the term *job scheduling* as shorthand.

To help us to develop an algorithm that solves the job-scheduling problem, we consider the following problem, which is widely applicable in its own right.

Difference constraints   Assign nonnegative values to a set variables x_0 through x_n that minimize the value of x_n while satisfying a set of *difference constraints* on the variables, each of which specifies that the difference between two of the variables must be greater than or equal to a given constant.

Figure 21.23 depicts an example instance of this problem. It is a purely abstract mathematical formulation that can serve as the basis for solving numerous practical problems (*see reference section*).

The difference-constraint problem is a special case of a much more general problem where we allow general linear combinations of the variables in the equations.

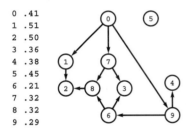

```
0 .41
1 .51
2 .50
3 .36
4 .38
5 .45
6 .21
7 .32
8 .32
9 .29
```

Figure 21.22
Job scheduling

In this network, vertices represent jobs to be completed (with weights indicating the amount of time required) and edges represent precedence relationships between them. For example, the edges from 7 to 8 and 3 mean that job 7 must be finished before job 8 or job 3 can be started. What is the minimum amount of time required to complete all the jobs?

Linear programming Assign nonnegative values to a set of variables x_0 through x_n that minimize the value of a specified linear combination of the variables, subject to a set of constraints on the variables, each of which specifies that a given linear combination of the variables must be greater than or equal to a given constant.

Linear programming is a widely used general approach to solving a broad class of optimization problems that we will not consider it in detail until Part 8. Clearly, the difference-constraints problem reduces to linear programming, as do many other problems. For the moment, our interest is in the relationships among the difference-constraints, job-scheduling, and shortest-paths problems.

Property 21.14 *The job-scheduling problem reduces to the difference-constraints problem.*

Proof: Add a dummy job and a precedence constraint for each job saying that the job must finish before the dummy job starts. Given a job-scheduling problem, define a system of difference equations where each job i corresponds to a variable x_i, and the constraint that j cannot start until i finishes corresponds to the equation $x_j \geq x_i + c_i$, where c_i is the length of job i. The solution to the difference-constraints problem gives precisely a solution to the job-scheduling problem, with the value of each variable specifying the start time of the corresponding job. ■

Figure 21.23 illustrates the system of difference equations created by this reduction for the job-scheduling problem in Figure 21.22. The practical significance of this reduction is that we can use to solve job-scheduling problems any algorithm that can solve difference-constraint problems.

It is instructive to consider whether we can use this construction in the opposite way: Given a job-scheduling algorithm, can we use it to solve difference-constraints problems? The answer to this question is that the correspondence in the proof of Property 21.14 does *not* help us to show that the difference-constraints problem reduces to the job-scheduling problem, because the systems of difference equations that we get from job-scheduling problems have a property that does not necessarily hold in every difference-constraints problem. Specifically, if two equations have the same second variable, then they have the same constant. Therefore, an algorithm for job scheduling does not

$$x_1 - x_0 \geq .41$$
$$x_7 - x_0 \geq .41$$
$$x_9 - x_0 \geq .41$$
$$x_2 - x_1 \geq .51$$
$$x_8 - x_6 \geq .21$$
$$x_3 - x_6 \geq .21$$
$$x_8 - x_7 \geq .32$$
$$x_3 - x_7 \geq .32$$
$$x_2 - x_8 \geq .32$$
$$x_4 - x_9 \geq .29$$
$$x_6 - x_9 \geq .29$$
$$x_{10} - x_2 \geq .50$$
$$x_{10} - x_3 \geq .36$$
$$x_{10} - x_4 \geq .38$$
$$x_{10} - x_5 \geq .45$$

Figure 21.23
Difference constraints

Finding an assignment of nonnegative values to the variables that minimizes the value of x_{10} subject to this set of inequalities is equivalent to the job-scheduling problem instance illustrated in Figure 21.22. For example, the equation $x_8 \geq x_7 + .32$ means that job 8 cannot start until job 7 is completed.

immediately give a direct way to solve a system of difference equations that contains two equations $x_i - x_j \geq a$ and $x_k - x_j \geq b$, where $a \neq b$. When proving reductions, we need to be aware of situations like this: A proof that A reduces to B must show that we can use an algorithm for solving B to solve *any* instance of A.

By construction, the constants in the difference-constraints problems produced by the construction in the proof of Property 21.14 are always nonnegative. This fact turns out to be significant.

Property 21.15 *The difference-constraints problem with positive constants is equivalent to the single-source longest-paths problem in an acyclic network.*

Proof: Given a system of difference equations, build a network where each variable x_i corresponds to a vertex i and each equation $x_i - x_j \geq c$ corresponds to an edge i-j of weight c. For example, assigning to each edge in the digraph of Figure 21.22 the weight of its source vertex gives the network corresponding to the set of difference equations in Figure 21.23. Add a dummy vertex to the network, with a zero-weight edge to every other vertex. If the network has a cycle, the system of difference equations has no solution (because the positive weights imply that the values of the variables corresponding to each vertex strictly decrease as we move along a path, and, therefore, a cycle would imply that some variable is less than itself), so report that fact. Otherwise, the network has no cycle, so solve the single-source longest-paths problem from the dummy vertex. There exists a longest path for every vertex because the network is acyclic (see Section 21.4). Assign to each variable the length of the longest path to the corresponding vertex in the network from the dummy vertex. For each variable, this path is evidence that its value satisfies the constraints and that no smaller value does so.

Unlike the proof of Property 21.14, this proof does extend to show that the two problems are equivalent because the construction works in both directions. We have no constraint that two equations with the same second variable in the equation must have the same constants, and no constraint that edges leaving any given vertex in the network must have the same weight. Given any acyclic network with positive weights, the same correspondence gives a system of difference constraints with positive constants whose solution directly yields a

Program 21.8 Job scheduling

This implementation reads a list of jobs with lengths followed by a list of precedence constraints from standard input, then prints on standard output a list of job starting times that satisfy the constraints. It solves the job-scheduling problem by reducing it to the longest-paths problem for acyclic networks, using Properties 21.14 and 21.15 and Program 21.6.

```
#include "GRAPHbasic.cc"
#include "GRAPHio.cc"
#include "LPTdag.cc"
typedef WeightedEdge EDGE;
typedef DenseGRAPH<EDGE> GRAPH;
int main(int argc, char *argv[])
  { int i, s, t, N = atoi(argv[1]);
    double duration[N];
    GRAPH G(N, true);
    for (int i = 0; i < N; i++)
      cin >> duration[i];
    while (cin >> s >> t)
      G.insert(new EDGE(s, t, duration[s]));
    LPTdag<GRAPH, EDGE> lpt(G);
    for (i = 0; i < N; i++)
      cout << i << " " << lpt.dist(i) << endl;
  }
```

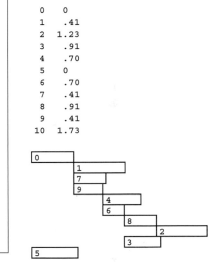

```
0    0
1    .41
2    1.23
3    .91
4    .70
5    0
6    .70
7    .41
8    .91
9    .41
10   1.73
```

**Figure 21.24
Job schedule**

This figure illustrates the solution to the job-scheduling problem of Figure 21.22, derived from the correspondence between longest paths in weighted DAGs and job schedules. The longest path lengths in the wt *array that is computed by the longest paths algorithm in Program 21.6 (see Figure 21.15) are precisely the required job start times (top, right column). We start jobs 0 and 5 at time 0, jobs 1, 7, and 9 at time* .41*, jobs 4 and 6 at time* .70*, and so forth.*

solution to the single-source longest-paths problem in the network. Details of this proof are left as an exercise (see Exercise 21.90). ∎

The network in Figure 21.22 depicts this correspondence for our sample problem, and Figure 21.15 shows the computation of the longest paths in the network, using Program 21.6 (the dummy start vertex is implicit in the implementation). The schedule that is computed in this way is shown in Figure 21.24.

Program 21.8 is an implementation that shows the application of this theory in a practical setting. It transforms any instance of the job-scheduling problem into an instance of the longest-path problem in acyclic networks, then uses Program 21.6 to solve it.

We have been implicitly assuming that a solution exists for any instance of the job-scheduling problem; however, if there is a cycle in the set of precedence constraints, then there is no way to schedule the jobs to meet them. Before looking for longest paths, we should check for this condition by checking whether the corresponding network has a cycle (see Exercise 21.100). Such a situation is typical, and a specific technical term is normally used to describe it.

Definition 21.4 *A problem instance that admits no solution is said to be* **infeasible***.*

In other words, for job-scheduling problems, the question of determining whether a job-scheduling problem instance is feasible reduces to the problem of determining whether a digraph is acyclic. As we move to ever-more-complicated problems, the question of feasibility becomes an ever-more-important (and ever-more-difficult!) part of our computational burden.

We have now considered three interrelated problems. We might have shown directly that the job-scheduling problem reduces to the single-source longest-paths problem in acyclic networks, but we have also shown that we can solve any difference-constraints problem (with positive constants) in a similar manner (see Exercise 21.94), as well as any other problem that reduces to a difference-constraints problem or a job-scheduling problem. We could, alternatively, develop an algorithm to solve the difference-constraints problem and use that algorithm to solve the other problems, but we have *not* shown that a solution to the job-scheduling problem would give us a way to solve the others.

These examples illustrate the use of reduction to broaden the applicability of proven implementations. Indeed, modern systems programming emphasizes the need to reuse software by developing new interfaces and using existing software resources to build implementations. This important process, which is sometimes referred to as *library programming*, is a practical realization of the idea of reduction.

Library programming is extremely important in practice, but it represents only part of the story of the implications of reduction. To illustrate this point, we consider the following version of the job-scheduling problem.

Job scheduling with deadlines   Allow an additional type of constraint in the job-scheduling problem, to specify that a job must begin *before* a specified amount of time has elapsed, relative to another job. (Conventional deadlines are relative to the start job.) Such constraints are commonly needed in time-critical manufacturing processes and in many other applications, and they can make the job-scheduling problem considerably more difficult to solve.

Suppose that we need to add a constraint to our example of Figures 21.22 through 21.24 that job 2 must start earlier than a certain number c of time units after job 4 starts. If c is greater than .53, then the schedule that we have computed fits the bill, since it says to start job 2 at time 1.23, which is .53 after the end time of job 4 (which starts at .70). If c is less than .53, we can shift the start time of 4 later to meet the constraint. If job 4 were a long job, this change could increase the finish time of the whole schedule. Worse, if there are other constraints on job 4, we may not be able to shift its start time. Indeed, we may find ourselves with constraints that no schedule can meet: For instance, we could not satisfy a constraint in our example that job 2 must start earlier than d time units after the start of job 6 for d less than .53 because the constraints that 2 must follow 8 and 8 must follow 6 imply that 2 must start *later* than .53 time units after the start of 6.

If we add both of the two constraints described in the previous paragraph to the example, then both of them affect the time that 4 can be scheduled, the finish time of the whole schedule, and whether a feasible schedule exists, depending on the values of c and d. Adding more constraints of this type multiplies the possibilities and turns an easy problem into a difficult one. Therefore, we are justified in seeking the approach of reducing the problem to a known problem.

Property 21.16 *The job-scheduling-with-deadlines problem reduces to the shortest-paths problem (with negative weights allowed).*

Proof: Convert precedence constraints to inequalities using the same reduction described in Property 21.14. For any deadline constraint, add an inequality $x_i - x_j \leq d_j$, or, equivalently $x_j - x_i \geq -d_j$, where d_j is a positive constant. Convert the set of inequalities to a network using the same reduction described in Property 21.15. Negate all the weights. By the same construction given in the proof of Property 21.15, any shortest-path tree rooted at 0 in the network corresponds to a schedule. ∎

This reduction takes us to the realm of shortest paths with negative weights. It says that if we can find an efficient solution to the shortest-paths problem with negative weights, then we can find an efficient solution to the job-scheduling problem with deadlines. (Again, the correspondence in the proof of Property 21.16 does *not* establish the converse (see Exercise 21.91).)

Adding deadlines to the job-scheduling problem corresponds to allowing negative constants in the difference-constraints problem and negative weights in the shortest-paths problem. (This change also requires that we modify the difference-constraints problem to properly handle the analog of negative cycles in the shortest paths problem.) These more general versions of these problems are more difficult to solve than the versions that we first considered, but they are also likely to be more useful as more general models. A plausible approach to solving all of them would seem to be to seek an efficient solution to the shortest-paths problem with negative weights.

Unfortunately, there is a fundamental difficulty with this approach, and it illustrates the other part of the story in the use of reduction to assess the relative difficulty of problems. We have been using reduction in a positive sense, to expand the applicability of solutions to general problems; but it also applies in a negative sense, to show the limits on such expansion.

The difficulty is that the general shortest-paths problem is too hard to solve. We see next how the concept of reduction helps us to make this statement with precision and conviction. In Section 17.8, we discussed a set of problems, known as the NP-hard problems, that we consider to be intractable because all known algorithms for solving them require exponential time in the worst case. We show here that the general shortest-paths problem is NP-hard.

As mentioned briefly in Section 17.8 and discussed in detail in Part 8, we generally take the fact that a problem is NP-hard to mean not just that no efficient algorithm is known that is guaranteed to solve the problem but also that we have little hope of finding one. In this context, we use the term *efficient* to refer to algorithms whose running time is bounded by some polynomial function of the size of the input, in the worst case. We assume that the discovery of an efficient algorithm to solve any NP-hard problem would be a stunning research breakthrough. The concept of NP-hardness is important in identifying problems that are difficult to solve, because it is often easy to prove that a problem is NP-hard, using the following technique.

Property 21.17 *A problem is NP-hard if there is an efficient reduction to it from any NP-hard problem.*

This property depends on the precise meaning of an *efficient reduction* from one problem A to another problem B. We defer such definitions to Part 8 (two different definitions are commonly used). For the moment, we simply use the term to cover the case where we have efficient algorithms both to transform an instance of A to an instance of B and to transform a solution of B to a solution of A.

Now, suppose that we have an efficient reduction from an NP-hard problem A to a given problem B. The proof is by contradiction: If we have an efficient algorithm for B, then we could use it to solve any instance of A in polynomial time, by reduction (transform the given instance of A to an instance of B, solve that problem, then transform the solution). But no known algorithm can make such a guarantee for A (because A is NP-hard), so the assumption that there exists a polynomial-time algorithm for B is incorrect: B is also NP-hard. ∎

This technique is extremely important because people have used it to show a huge number of problems to be NP-hard, giving us a broad variety of problems from which to choose when we want to develop a proof that a new problem is NP-hard. For example, we encountered one of the classic NP-hard problems in Section 17.7. The Hamilton-path problem, which asks whether there is a simple path containing all the vertices in a given graph, was one of the first problems shown to be NP-hard (*see reference section*). It is easy to formulate as a shortest-paths problem, so Property 21.17 implies that the shortest-paths problem itself is NP-hard:

Property 21.18 *In networks with edge weights that could be negative, shortest-paths problems are NP-hard.*

Proof: Our proof consists of reducing the Hamilton-path problem to the shortest-paths problem. That is, we show that we could use any algorithm that can find shortest paths in networks with negative edge weights to solve the Hamilton-path problem. Given an undirected graph, we build a network with edges in both directions corresponding to each edge in the graph and with all edges having weight -1. The shortest (simple) path starting at any vertex in this network is of length $1 - V$ if and only if the graph has a Hamilton path. Note that this network is replete with negative cycles. Not only does every cycle in the graph correspond to a negative cycle in the network, but also every *edge* in the graph corresponds to a cycle of weight -2 in the network.

The implication of this construction is that the shortest-paths problem is NP-hard, because if we could develop an efficient algorithm for the shortest-paths problem in networks, then we would have an efficient algorithm for the Hamilton-path problem in graphs. ∎

One response to the discovery that a given problem is NP-hard is to seek versions of that problem that we *can* solve. For shortest-paths problems, we are caught between having a host of efficient algorithms for acyclic networks or for networks in which edge weights are nonnegative and having no good solution for networks that could have cycles and negative weights. Are there other kinds of networks that we can address? That is the subject of Section 21.7. There, for example, we see that the job-scheduling-with-deadlines problem reduces to a version of the shortest-paths problem that we can solve efficiently. This situation is typical: As we address ever-more-difficult computational problems, we find ourselves working to identify the versions of those problems that we can expect to solve.

As these examples illustrate, reduction is a simple technique that is helpful in algorithm design, and we use it frequently. Either we can solve a new problem by proving that it reduces to a problem that we know how to solve, or we can prove that the new problem will be difficult by proving that a problem that we know to be difficult reduces to the problem in question.

Table 21.3 gives us a more detailed look at the various implications of reduction results among the four general problem classes that we discussed in Chapter 17. Note that there are several cases where a reduction provides no new information; for example, although selection reduces to sorting and the problem of finding longest paths in acyclic networks reduces to the problem of finding shortest paths in general networks, these facts shed no new light on the relative difficulty of the problems. In other cases, the reduction may or may not provide new information; in still other cases, the implications of a reduction are truly profound. To develop these concepts, we need a precise and formal description of reduction, as we discuss in detail in Part 8; here, we summarize informally the most important uses of reduction in practice, with examples that we have already seen.

Table 21.3 Reduction implications

This table summarizes some implications of reducing a problem A to another problem B, with examples that we have discussed in this section. The profound implications of cases 9 and 10 are so far-reaching that we generally assume that it is not possible to prove such reductions (see Part 8). Reduction is most useful in cases 1, 6, 11, and 16, to learn a new algorithm for A or prove a lower bound on B; in cases 13-15, to learn new algorithms for A; and in case 12, to learn the difficulty of B.

	A	B	$A \Rightarrow B$ implication	example
1	easy	easy	new B lower bound	sorting $\Rightarrow$ EMST
2	easy	tractable	none	TC $\Rightarrow$ APSP($+$)
3	easy	intractable	none	SSSP(DAG) $\Rightarrow$ SSSP($\pm$)
4	easy	unknown	none	
5	tractable	easy	A easy	
6	tractable	tractable	new A solution	DC($+$) $\Rightarrow$ SSSP(DAG)
7	tractable	intractable	none	
8	tractable	unknown	none	
9	intractable	easy	profound	
10	intractable	tractable	profound	
11	intractable	intractable	same as 1 or 6	SSLP($\pm$) $\Rightarrow$ SSSP($\pm$)
12	intractable	unknown	B intractable	HP $\Rightarrow$ SSSP($\pm$)
13	unknown	easy	A easy	JS $\Rightarrow$ SSSP(DAG)
14	unknown	tractable	A tractable	
15	unknown	intractable	A solvable	
16	unknown	unknown	same as 1 or 6	JSWD $\Rightarrow$ SSSP($\pm$)

Key:

EMST	Euclidean minimum spanning tree
TC	transitive closure
APSP	all-pairs shortest paths
SSSP	single-source shortest paths
SSLP	single-source longest paths
($+$)	(in networks with nonnegative weights)
($\pm$)	(in networks with weights that could be negative)
(DAG)	(in acyclic networks)
DC	difference constraints
HP	Hamilton paths
JS(WD)	job scheduling (with deadlines)

Upper bounds   If we have an efficient algorithm for a problem B and can prove that A reduces to B, then we have an efficient algorithm for A. There may exist some other better algorithm for A, but B's performance is an upper bound on the best that we can do for A. For example, our proof that job scheduling reduces to longest paths in acyclic networks makes our algorithm for the latter an efficient algorithm for the former.

Lower bounds   If we know that any algorithm for problem A has certain resource requirements and we can prove that A reduces to B, then we know that B has at least those same resource requirements, because a better algorithm for B would imply the existence of a better algorithm for A (as long as the cost of the reduction is lower than the cost of B). That is, A's performance is a lower bound on the best that we can do for B. For example, we used this technique in Section 19.3 to show that computing the transitive closure is as difficult as Boolean matrix multiplication, and we used it in Section 20.7 to show that computing the Euclidean MST is as difficult as sorting.

Intractability   In particular, we can prove a problem to be intractable by showing that an intractable problem reduces to it. For example, Property 21.18 shows that the shortest-paths problem is intractable because the Hamilton-path problem reduces to the shortest-paths problem.

Beyond these general implications, it is clear that more detailed information about the performance of specific algorithms to solve specific problems can be directly relevant to other problems that reduce to the first ones. When we find an upper bound, we can analyze the associated algorithm, run empirical studies, and so forth to determine whether it represents a better solution to the problem. When we develop a good general-purpose algorithm, we can invest in developing and testing a good implementation and then develop associated ADTs that expand its applicability.

We use reduction as a basic tool in this and the next chapter. We emphasize the general relevance of the problems that we consider, and the general applicability of the algorithms that solve them, by reducing other problems to them. It is also important to be aware of a hierarchy among increasingly general problem-formulation models. For example, linear programming is a general formulation that is important not just because many problems reduce to it but also because it is *not* known to be NP-hard. In other words, there is no known way to reduce the general shortest-paths problem (or any other NP-hard problem) to linear programming. We discuss such issues in Part 8.

Not all problems can be solved, but good general models have been devised that are suitable for broad classes of problems that we do know how to solve. Shortest paths in networks is our first example of such a model. As we move to ever-more-general problem domains, we enter the field of *operations research (OR)*, the study of mathematical methods of decision making, where developing and studying such models is central. One key challenge in OR is to find the model that is most appropriate for solving a problem and to fit the problem to the model. This activity is sometimes known as *mathematical programming* (a name given to it before the advent of computers and the new use of the word "programming"). Reduction is a modern concept that is in the same spirit as mathematical programming and is the basis for our understanding of the cost of computation in a broad variety of applications.

Exercises

▷ **21.85** Use the reduction of Property 21.12 to develop a transitive-closure implementation (with the same interface as Programs 19.3 and 19.4) that uses the all-pairs shortest-paths ADT of Section 21.3.

21.86 Show that the problem of computing the number of strong components in a digraph reduces to the all-pairs shortest-paths problem with nonnegative weights.

21.87 Give the difference-constraints and shortest-paths problems that correspond—according to the constructions of Properties 21.14 and 21.15— to the job-scheduling problem, where jobs 0 to 7 have lengths

.4 .2 .3 .4 .2 .5 .1

and constraints

5-1 4-6 6-0 3-2 6-1 6-2,

respectively.

▷ **21.88** Give a solution to the job-scheduling problem of Exercise 21.87.

○ **21.89** Suppose that the jobs in Exercise 21.87 also have the constraints that job 1 must start before job 6 ends, and job 2 must start before job 4 ends. Give the shortest-paths problem to which this problem reduces, using the construction described in the proof of Property 21.16.

21.90 Show that the all-pairs longest-paths problem in acyclic networks with positive weights reduces to the difference-constraints problem with positive constants.

▷ **21.91** Explain why the correspondence in the proof of Property 21.16 does not extend to show that the shortest-paths problem reduces to the job-scheduling-with-deadlines problem.

21.92 Extend Program 21.8 to use symbolic names instead of integers to refer to jobs (see Program 17.10).

21.93 Design an ADT interface that provides clients with the ability to pose and solve difference-constraints problems.

21.94 Write a class that implements your interface from Exercise 21.93, basing your solution to the difference-constraints problem on a reduction to the shortest-paths problem in acyclic networks.

21.95 Provide an implementation for a class that solves the single-source shortest-paths problem in acyclic networks with negative weights, which is based on a reduction to the difference-constraints problem and uses your interface from Exercise 21.93.

○ **21.96** Your solution to the shortest-paths problem in acyclic networks for Exercise 21.95 assumes the existence of an implementation that solves the difference-constraints problem. What happens if you use the implementation from Exercise 21.94, which assumes the existence of an implementation for the shortest-paths problem in acyclic networks?

○ **21.97** Prove the equivalence of any two NP-hard problems (that is, choose two problems and prove that they reduce to each other).

●● **21.98** Give an explicit construction that reduces the shortest-paths problem in networks with integer weights to the Hamilton-path problem.

● **21.99** Use reduction to implement a class that uses a network ADT that solves the single-source shortest-paths problem to solve the following problem: Given a digraph, a vertex-indexed vector of positive weights, and a start vertex v, find the paths from v to each other vertex such that the sum of the weights of the vertices on the path is minimized.

○ **21.100** Program 21.8 does not check whether the job-scheduling problem that it takes as input is feasible (has a cycle). Characterize the schedules that it prints out for infeasible problems.

21.101 Design an ADT interface that gives clients the ability to pose and solve job-scheduling problems. Write a class that implements your interface, basing your solution to the job-scheduling problem on a reduction to the shortest-paths problem in acyclic networks, as in Program 21.8.

○ **21.102** Add a function to your class from Exercise 21.101 (and provide an implementation) that prints out a longest path in the schedule. (Such a path is known as a *critical path*.)

21.103 Write a client for your interface from Exercise 21.101 that outputs a PostScript program that draws the schedule in the style of Figure 21.24 (see Section 4.3).

○ **21.104** Develop a model for generating job-scheduling problems. Use this model to test your implementations of Exercises 21.101 and 21.103 for a reasonable set of problem sizes.

21.105 Write a class that implements your interface from Exercise 21.101, basing your solution to the job-scheduling problem on a reduction to the difference-constraints problem.

○ **21.106** A PERT (performance-evaluation-review-technique) chart is a network that represents a job-scheduling problem, with *edges* representing jobs, as described in Figure 21.25. Write a class that implements your job-scheduling interface of Exercise 21.101 that is based on PERT charts.

21.107 How many vertices are there in a PERT chart for a job-scheduling problem with V jobs and E constraints?

21.108 Write programs to convert between the edge-based job-scheduling representation (PERT chart) discussed in Exercise 21.106 and the vertex-based representation used in the text (see Figure 21.22).

21.7 Negative Weights

We now turn to the challenge of coping with negative weights in shortest-paths problems. Perhaps negative edge weights seem unlikely, given our focus through most of this chapter on intuitive examples, where weights represent distances or costs; however, we also saw in Section 21.6 that negative edge weights arise in a natural way when we reduce other problems to shortest-paths problems. Negative weights are not merely a mathematical curiosity; on the contrary, they significantly extend the applicability of the shortest-paths problems as a model for solving other problems. This potential utility is our motivation to search for efficient algorithms to solve network problems that involve negative weights.

Figure 21.26 is a small example that illustrates the effects of introducing negative weights on a network's shortest paths. Perhaps the most important effect is that when negative weights are present, *low-weight shortest paths tend to have more edges than higher-weight paths*. For positive weights, our emphasis was on looking for *shortcuts*; but when negative weights are present, we seek *detours* that use as many edges with negative weights as we can find. This effect turns our intuition in seeking "short" paths into a liability in understanding the algorithms, so we need to suppress that line of intuition and consider the problem on a basic abstract level.

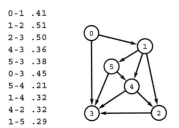

```
0-1  .41
1-2  .51
2-3  .50
4-3  .36
5-3  .38
0-3  .45
5-4  .21
1-4  .32
4-2  .32
1-5  .29
```

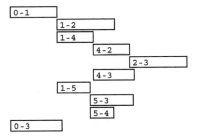

**Figure 21.25
A PERT chart**

A PERT chart is a network representation for job-scheduling problems where we represent jobs by edges. The network at the top is a representation of the job-scheduling problem depicted in Figure 21.22, where jobs 0 through 9 in Figure 21.22 are represented by edges 0–1, 1–2, 2–3, 4–3, 5–3, 0–3, 5–4, 1–4, 4–2, and 1–5, respectively, here. The critical path in the schedule is the longest path in the network.

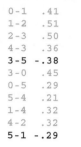

0-1	.41
1-2	.51
2-3	.50
4-3	.36
3-5	-.38
3-0	.45
0-5	.29
5-4	.21
1-4	.32
4-2	.32
5-1	-.29

	0	1	2	3	4	5
0	0	0	.51	.68	.32	.29
1	1.13	0	.51	.68	.32	.30
2	.95	-.17	0	.50	.15	.12
3	.45	-.67	-.16	0	-.35	-.38
4	.81	-.31	.20	.36	0	-.02
5	.84	-.29	.22	.39	.03	0

	0	1	2	3	4	5
0	0	5	5	5	5	5
1	4	1	2	4	4	4
2	3	3	2	3	3	3
3	0	5	5	3	5	5
4	3	3	3	3	4	3
5	1	1	1	1	1	5

Figure 21.26
A sample network with negative edges

This sample network is the same as the network depicted in Figure 21.1, except that the edges 3-5 and 5-1 are negative. Naturally, this change dramatically affects the shortest paths structure, as we can easily see by comparing the distance and path matrices at the right with their counterparts in Figure 21.9. For example, the shortest path from 0 to 1 in this network is 0-5-1, which is of length 0; and the shortest path from 2 to 1 is 2-3-5-1, which is of length -.17.

The relationship shown in the proof of Property 21.18 between shortest paths in networks and Hamilton paths in graphs ties in with our observation that finding paths of low weight (which we have been calling "short") is tantamount to finding paths with a high number of edges (which we might consider to be "long"). With negative weights, we are looking for long paths rather than short paths.

The first idea that suggests itself to remedy the situation is to find the smallest (most negative) edge weight, then to add the absolute value of that number to all the edge weights to transform the network into one with no negative weights. This naive approach does not work at all, because shortest paths in the new network bear little relation to shortest paths in the old one. For example, in the network illustrated in Figure 21.26, the shortest path from 4 to 2 is 4-3-5-1-2. If we add .38 to all the edge weights in the graph to make them all positive, the weight of this path grows from .20 to 1.74. But the weight of 4-2 grows from .32 to just .70, so that edge becomes the shortest path from 4 to 2. The more edges a path has, the more it is penalized by this transformation; that result, from the observation in the previous paragraph, is precisely the opposite of what we need. Even though this naive idea does not work, the goal of transforming the network into an equivalent one with no negative weights but the same shortest paths is worthy; at the end of the section, we consider an algorithm that achieves this goal.

Our shortest-paths algorithms to this point have all placed one of two restrictions on the shortest-paths problem so that they can offer an efficient solution: They either disallow cycles or disallow negative weights. Is there a less stringent restriction that we could impose on networks that contain both cycles and negative weights that would still lead to tractable shortest-paths problems? We touched on an answer to this question at the beginning of the chapter, when we had to add the restriction that paths be simple so that the problem would make sense if there were negative cycles. Should we perhaps restrict attention to networks that have no such cycles?

Shortest paths in networks with no negative cycles Given a network that may have negative edge weights but does not have any negative-weight cycles, solve one of the following problems: Find a shortest path connecting two given vertices (shortest-path problem), find shortest paths from a given vertex to all the other vertices (single-source problem), or find shortest paths connecting all pairs of vertices (all-pairs problem).

The proof of Property 21.18 leaves the door open for the possibility of efficient algorithms for solving this problem because it breaks down if we disallow negative cycles. To solve the Hamilton-path problem, we would need to be able to solve shortest-paths problems in networks that have huge numbers of negative cycles.

Moreover, many practical problems reduce precisely to the problem of finding shortest paths in networks that contain no negative cycles. We have already seen one such example.

Property 21.19 *The job-scheduling-with-deadlines problem reduces to the shortest-paths problem in networks that contain no negative cycles.*

Proof: The argument that we used in the proof of Property 21.15 shows that the construction in the proof of Property 21.16 leads to networks that contain no negative cycles. From the job-scheduling problem, we construct a difference-constraints problem with variables that correspond to job start times; from the difference-constraints problem, we construct a network. We negate all the weights to convert from a longest-paths problem to a shortest-paths problem—a transformation that corresponds to reversing the sense of all the inequalities. Any simple path from i to j in the network corresponds to a sequence of inequalities involving the variables. The existence of the path implies, by collapsing these inequalities, that $x_i - x_j \leq w_{ij}$, where w_{ij} is the sum of the weights on the path from i to j. A negative cycle corresponds to 0 on the left side of this inequality and a negative value on the right, so the existence of such a cycle is a contradiction. ∎

	$	P	Y	C	S
$	1.0	1.631	0.669	0.008	0.686
P	0.613	1.0	0.411	0.005	0.421
Y	1.495	2.436	1.0	0.012	1.027
C	120.5	197.4	80.82	1.0	82.91
S	1.459	2.376	0.973	0.012	1.0

	$	P	Y	C	S
$	0.0	0.489	-0.402	-4.791	-0.378
P	-0.489	0.0	-0.891	-5.278	-0.865
Y	0.402	0.89	0.0	-4.391	0.027
C	4.791	5.285	4.392	0.0	4.418
S	0.378	0.865	-0.027	-4.415	0.0

Figure 21.27
Arbitrage

The table at the top specifies conversion factors from one currency to another. For example, the second entry in the top row says that $1 buys 1.631 units of currency P. Converting $1000 to currency P and back again would yield $1000*(1.631)*(0.613) = $999, a loss of $1. But converting $1000 to currency P then to currency Y and back again yields $1000*(1.631)*(0.411)*(1.495) = $1002, a .2% arbitrage opportunity. If we take the negative of the logarithm of all the numbers in the table (bottom), *we can consider it to be the adjacency matrix for a complete network with edge weights that could be positive or negative. In this network, nodes correspond to currencies, edges to conversions, and paths to sequences of conversions. The conversion just described corresponds to the cycle $-P-Y-$ in the graph, which has weight −0.489 + 0.890 − 0.402 = −.002. The best arbitrage opportunity is the shortest cycle in the graph.*

As we noted when we first discussed the job-scheduling problem in Section 21.6, this statement implicitly assumes that our job-scheduling problems are feasible (have a solution). In practice, we would not make such an assumption, and part of our computational burden would be determining whether or not a job-scheduling-with-deadlines problem is feasible. In the construction in the proof of Property 21.19, a negative cycle in the network implies an infeasible problem, so this task corresponds to the following problem.

Negative cycle detection Does a given network have a negative cycle? If it does, find one such cycle.

On the one hand, this problem is not necessarily easy (a simple cycle-checking algorithm for digraphs does not apply); on the other hand, it is not necessarily difficult (the reduction of Property 21.16 from the Hamilton-path problem does not apply). Our first challenge will be to develop an algorithm for this task.

In the job-scheduling-with-deadlines application, negative cycles correspond to error conditions that are presumably rare, but for which we need to check. We might even develop algorithms that remove edges to break the negative cycle and iterate until there are none. In other applications, detecting negative cycles is the prime objective, as in the following example.

Arbitrage Many newspapers print tables showing conversion rates among the world's currencies (see, for example, Figure 21.27). We can view such tables as adjacency-matrix representations of complete networks. An edge s-t with weight x means that we can convert 1 unit of currency s into x units of currency t. Paths in the network specify multistep conversions. For example, if there is also an edge t-w with weight y, then the path s-t-w represents a way to convert 1 unit of currency s into xy units of currency w. We might expect xy to be equal to the weight of s-w in all cases, but such tables represent a complex dynamic system where such consistency cannot be guaranteed. If we find a case where xy is smaller than the weight of s-w, then we may be able to outsmart the system. Suppose that the weight of w-s is z and $xyz > 1$, then the cycle s-t-w-s gives a way to convert 1 unit of currency s into more than 1 units (xyz) of currency s. That is, we can make a $100(xyz - 1)$ percent profit by converting from s to t to w back to s. This situation is an example of an *arbitrage* opportunity that would allow us to make unlimited profits were it not for forces outside the model, such as limitations on the size of transactions. To convert this problem to a shortest-paths problem, we take the logarithm of all the numbers so that path weights correspond to adding edge weights instead of multiplying them, and then we take the negative to invert the comparison. Then the edge weights might be negative or positive, and a shortest path from s to t gives a best way of converting from currency s to currency t. The lowest-weight cycle is the best arbitrage opportunity, but any negative cycle is of interest.

Can we detect negative cycles in a network or find shortest paths in networks that contain no negative cycles? The existence of efficient algorithms to solve these problems does not contradict the NP-hardness of the general problem that we proved in Property 21.18, because no reduction from the Hamilton-path problem to either problem is known. Specifically, the reduction of Property 21.18 says that what we cannot do is to craft an algorithm that can guarantee to find efficiently the lowest-weight path in any given network when negative edge weights are allowed. That problem statement is too general. But we can solve the restricted versions of the problem just mentioned, albeit not as easily as we can the other restricted versions of the problem (positive weights and acyclic networks) that we studied earlier in this chapter.

In general, as we noted in Section 21.2, Dijkstra's algorithm does not work in the presence of negative weights, even when we restrict attention to networks that contain no negative cycles. Figure 21.28 illustrates this fact. The fundamental difficulty is that the algorithm depends on examining paths in increasing order of their length. The proof that the algorithm is correct (see Property 21.2) assumes that adding an edge to a path makes that path longer.

Floyd's algorithm makes no such assumption and is effective even when edge weights may be negative. If there are no negative cycles, it computes shortest paths; remarkably enough, if there are negative cycles, it detects at least one of them.

Property 21.20 *Floyd's algorithm solves the negative-cycle–detection problem and the all-pairs shortest-paths problem in networks that contain no negative cycles, in time proportional to V^3.*

Proof: The proof of Property 21.8 does not depend on whether or not edge weights are negative; however, we need to interpret the results

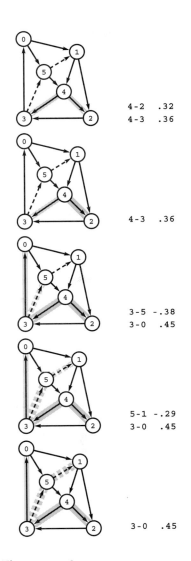

4-2 .32
4-3 .36

4-3 .36

3-5 -.38
3-0 .45

5-1 -.29
3-0 .45

3-0 .45

Figure 21.28
Failure of Dijkstra's algorithm (negative weights)

In this example, Dijkstra's algorithm decides that 4-2 is the shortest path from 4 to 2 (of length .32) and misses the shorter path 4-3-5-1-2 (of length .20).

differently when negative edge weights are present. Each entry in the matrix is evidence of the algorithm having discovered a path of that length; in particular, any negative entry on the diagonal of the distances matrix is evidence of the presence of at least one negative cycle. In the presence of negative cycles, we cannot directly infer any further information, because the paths that the algorithm implicitly tests are not necessarily simple: Some may involve one or more trips around one or more negative cycles. However, if there are no negative cycles, then the paths that are computed by the algorithm are simple, because any path with a cycle would imply the existence of a path that connects the same two points which has fewer edges and is not of higher weight (the same path with the cycle removed). ■

The proof of Property 21.20 does not give specific information about how to find a specific negative cycle from the distances and paths matrices computed by Floyd's algorithm. We leave that task for an exercise (see Exercise 21.122).

Floyd's algorithm solves the all-pairs shortest-paths problem for graphs that contain no negative cycles. Given the failure of Dijkstra's algorithm in networks that contain weights that could be negative, we could also use Floyd's algorithm to solve the the all-pairs problem for sparse networks that contain no negative cycles, in time proportional to V^3. If we have a single-source problem in such networks, then we can use this V^3 solution to the all-pairs problem that, although it amounts to overkill, is the best that we have yet seen for the single-source problem. Can we develop faster algorithms for these problems—ones that achieve the running times that we achieve with Dijkstra's algorithm when edge weights are positive ($E \lg V$ for single-source shortest paths and $VE \lg V$ for all-pairs shortest paths)? We can answer this question in the affirmative for the all-pairs problem and also can bring down the worst-case cost to VE for the single-source problem, but breaking the VE barrier for the general single-source shortest-paths problem is a longstanding open problem.

The following approach, developed by R. Bellman and L. Ford in the late 1950s, provides a simple and effective basis for attacking single-source shortest-paths problems in networks that contain no negative cycles. To compute shortest paths from a vertex s, we maintain (as usual) a vertex-indexed vector wt such that wt[t] contains the shortest-path length from s to t. We initialize wt[s] to 0 and all other

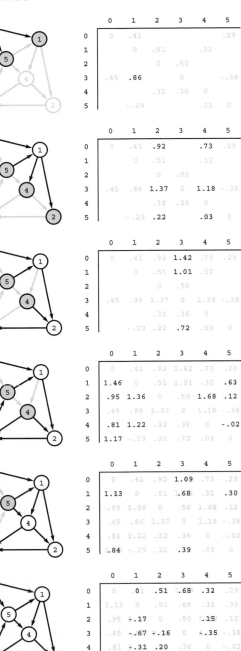

Step 1

	0	1	2	3	4	5
0	0	.41				.29
1		0	.51		.32	
2			0	.50		
3	.45	.86		0		-.38
4			.32	.36	0	
5		-.29			.21	0

	0	1	2	3	4	5
0	0	1				5
1		1	2		4	
2			2	3		
3	0	0		3		5
4			2	3	4	
5		1			4	5

Step 2

	0	1	2	3	4	5
0	0	.41	.92		.73	.29
1		0	.51		.32	
2			0	.50		
3	.45	.86	1.37	0	1.18	-.38
4			.32	.36	0	
5		-.29	.22		.03	0

	0	1	2	3	4	5
0	0	1	1		1	5
1		1	2		4	
2			2	3		
3	0	0	0	3	0	5
4			2	3	4	
5		1	1		1	5

Step 3

	0	1	2	3	4	5
0	0	.41	.92	1.42	.73	.29
1		0	.51	1.01	.32	
2			0	.50		
3	.45	.86	1.37	0	1.18	-.38
4			.32	.36	0	
5		-.29	.22	.72	.03	0

	0	1	2	3	4	5
0	0	1	1	1	1	5
1		1	2	2	4	
2			2	3		
3	0	0	0	3	0	5
4			2	3	4	
5		1	1	1	1	5

Step 4

	0	1	2	3	4	5
0	0	.41	.92	1.42	.73	.29
1	1.46	0	.51	1.01	.32	.63
2	.95	1.36	0	.50	1.68	.12
3	.45	.86	1.37	0	1.18	-.38
4	.81	1.22	.32	.36	0	-.02
5	1.17	-.29	.22	.72	.03	0

	0	1	2	3	4	5
0	0	1	1	1	1	5
1	2	1	2	2	4	2
2	3	3	2	3	3	3
3	0	0	0	3	0	5
4	3	3	2	3	4	3
5	1	1	1	1	1	5

Step 5

	0	1	2	3	4	5
0	0	.41	.92	1.09	.73	.29
1	1.13	0	.51	.68	.32	.30
2	.95	1.36	0	.50	1.68	.12
3	.45	.86	1.37	0	1.18	-.38
4	.81	1.22	.32	.36	0	-.02
5	1.84	-.29	.22	.39	.03	0

	0	1	2	3	4	5
0	0	1	1	1	1	5
1	4	1	2	4	4	4
2	3	3	2	3	3	3
3	0	0	0	3	0	5
4	3	3	2	3	4	3
5	1	1	1	1	1	5

Step 6

	0	1	2	3	4	5
0	0	.01	.51	.68	.32	.29
1	1.13	0	.51	.68	.32	.30
2	.95	-.17	0	.50	1.15	.12
3	.45	-.67	-.16	0	-.35	-.38
4	.81	-.31	.20	.36	0	-.02
5	.84	-.29	.22	.39	.03	0

	0	1	2	3	4	5
0	0	5	5	5	5	5
1	4	1	2	4	4	4
2	3	3	2	3	3	3
3	0	5	5	3	5	5
4	3	3	3	3	4	3
5	1	1	1	1	1	5

**Figure 21.29
Floyd's algorithm (negative weights)**

This sequence shows the construction of the all–shortest-paths matrices for a digraph with negative weights, using Floyd's algorithm. The first step is the same as depicted in Figure 21.14. Then the negative edge 5-1 comes into play in the second step, where the paths 5-1-2 and 5-1-4 are discovered. The algorithm involves precisely the same sequence of relaxation steps for any edge weights, but the outcome differs.

wt entries to a large sentinel value, then compute shortest paths as follows:

> Considering the network's edges in any order, relax along each edge. Make V such passes.

We use the term *Bellman–Ford algorithm* to refer to the generic method of making V passes through the edges, considering the edges in any order. Certain authors use the term to describe a more general method (see Exercise 21.130).

For example, in a graph represented with adjacency lists, we could implement the Bellman–Ford algorithm to find the shortest paths from a start vertex s by initializing the wt entries to a value larger than any path length and the spt entries to null pointers, then proceeding as follows:

```
wt[s] = 0;
for (i = 0; i < G->V(); i++)
  for (v = 0; v < G->V(); v++)
  {
    if (v != s && spt[v] == 0) continue;
    typename Graph::adjIterator A(G, v);
    for (Edge* e = A.beg(); !A.end(); e = A.nxt())
     if (wt[e->w()] > wt[v] + e->wt())
      { wt[e->w()] = wt[v] + e->wt(); st[e->w()] = e; }
  }
```

This code exhibits the simplicity of the basic method. It is not used in practice, however, because simple modifications yield implementations that are more efficient for most graphs, as we soon see.

Property 21.21 *With the Bellman–Ford algorithm, we can solve the single-source shortest-paths problem in networks that contain no negative cycles in time proportional to VE.*

Proof: We make V passes through all E edges, so the total time is proportional to VE. To show that the computation achieves the desired result, we show by induction on i that, after the ith pass, wt[v] is no greater than the length of the shortest path from s to v that contains i or fewer edges, for all vertices v. The claim is certainly true if i is 0. Assuming the claim to be true for i, there are two cases for each given vertex v: Among the paths from s to v with i+1 or fewer edges, there may or may not be a shortest path with i+1 edges. If the shortest of the paths with i+1 or fewer edges from s to v is of length i or less,

Program 21.9 Bellman–Ford algorithm

This implementation of the Bellman–Ford algorithm maintains a FIFO queue of all vertices for which relaxing along an outgoing edge could be effective. We take a vertex off the queue and relax along all of its edges. If any of them leads to a shorter path to some vertex, we put that on the queue. The sentinel value G->V separates the current batch of vertices (which changed on the last iteration) from the next batch (which change on this iteration) and allows us to stop after G->V passes.

```
SPT(Graph &G, int s) : G(G),
  spt(G.V()), wt(G.V(), G.V())
{ QUEUE<int> Q; int N = 0;
  wt[s] = 0.0;
  Q.put(s); Q.put(G.V());
  while (!Q.empty())
  { int v;
    while ((v = Q.get()) == G.V())
      { if (N++ > G.V()) return; Q.put(G.V()); }
    typename Graph::adjIterator A(G, v);
    for (Edge* e = A.beg(); !A.end(); e = A.nxt())
      { int w = e->w();
        double P = wt[v] + e->wt();
        if (P < wt[w])
          { wt[w] = P; Q.put(w); spt[w] = e; }
      }
  }
}
```

then wt[v] will not change and will remain valid. Otherwise, there is a path from s to v with i+1 edges that is shorter than any path from s to v with i or fewer edges. That path must consist of a path with i edges from s to some vertex w plus the edge w-v. By the induction hypothesis, wt[w] is an upper bound on the shortest distance from s to w, and the (i+1)st pass checks whether each edge constitutes the final edge in a new shortest path to that edge's destination. In particular, it checks the edge w-v.

After V-1 iterations, then, wt[v] is a lower bound on the length of any shortest path with V-1 or fewer edges from s to v, for all vertices

v. We can stop after V-1 iterations because any path with V or more edges must have a (positive- or zero-cost) cycle and we could find a path with V-1 or fewer edges that is the same length or shorter by removing the cycle. Since wt[v] is the length of *some* path from s to v, it is also an upper bound on the shortest-path length, and therefore must be equal to the shortest-path length.

Although we did not consider it explicitly, the same proof shows that the spt vector contains pointers to the edges in the shortest-paths tree rooted at s. ∎

For typical graphs, examining every edge on every pass is wasteful. Indeed, we can easily determine a priori that numerous edges are not going to lead to a successful relaxation in any given pass. In fact, the only edges that could lead to a change are those emanating from a vertex whose value changed on the previous pass.

Program 21.9 is a straightforward implementation where we use a FIFO queue to hold these edges so that they are the only ones examined on each pass. Figure 21.30 shows an example of this algorithm in operation.

Program 21.9 is effective for solving the single-source shortest-paths problem in networks that arise in practice, but its worst-case performance is still proportional to VE. For dense graphs, the running time is not better than for Floyd's algorithm, which finds all shortest paths, rather than just those from a single source. For sparse graphs, the implementation of the Bellman–Ford algorithm in Program 21.9 is up to a factor of V faster than Floyd's algorithm but is nearly a factor of V slower than the worst-case running time that we can achieve with Dijkstra's algorithm for networks with no negative-weight edges (see Table 19.2).

Other variations of the Bellman–Ford algorithm have been studied, some of which are faster for the single-source problem than the FIFO-queue version in Program 21.9, but all take time proportional to at least VE in the worst case (see, for example, Exercise 21.132). The basic Bellman–Ford algorithm was developed decades ago; and, despite the dramatic strides in performance that we have seen for many other graph problems, we have not yet seen algorithms with better worst-case performance for networks with negative weights.

The Bellman–Ford algorithm is also a more efficient method than Floyd's algorithm for detecting whether a network has negative cycles.

0-1	.41
1-2	.51
2-3	.50
4-3	.36
3-5	-.38
3-0	.45
0-5	.29
5-4	.21
1-4	.32
4-2	.32
5-1	-.29

	0	1	2	3	4	5
st			4	4	0	
wt			.32	.36	0	

	0	1	2	3	4	5
st	3		4	4	0	3
wt	.81		.32	.36	0	-.02

	0	1	2	3	4	5
st	3	5	4	4	0	3
wt	.81	-.31	.32	.36	0	-.02

	0	1	2	3	4	5
st	3	5	1	4	0	3
wt	.81	-.31	.20	.36	0	-.02

**Figure 21.30
Bellman-Ford algorithm (with negative weights)**

This figure shows the result of using the Bellman-Ford algorithm to find the shortest paths from vertex 4 in the network depicted in Figure Figure 21.26. The algorithm operates in passes, where we examine all edges emanating from all vertices on a FIFO queue. The contents of the queue are shown below each graph drawing, with the shaded entries representing the contents of the queue for the previous pass. When we find an edge that can reduce the length of a path from 4 to its destination, we do a relaxation operation that puts the destination vertex on the queue and the edge on the SPT. The gray edges in the graph drawings comprise the SPT after each stage, which is also shown in oriented form in the center (all edges pointing down). We begin with an empty SPT and 4 on the queue (top). In the second pass, we relax along 4-2 and 4-3, leaving 2 and 3 on the queue. In the third pass, we examine but do not relax along 2-3 and then relax along 3-0 and 3-5, leaving 0 and 5 on the queue. In the fourth pass, we relax along 5-1 and then examine but do not relax along 1-0 and 1-5, leaving 1 on the queue. In the last pass (bottom), we relax along 1-2. The algorithm initially operates like BFS, but, unlike all of our other graph search methods, it might change tree edges, as in the last step.

Property 21.22   *With the Bellman–Ford algorithm, we can solve the negative-cycle–detection problem in time proportional to* VE.

Proof: The basic induction in the proof of Property 21.21 is valid even in the presence of negative cycles. If we run a Vth iteration of the algorithm and any relaxation step succeeds, then we have found a shortest path with V edges that connects s to some vertex in the network. Any such path must have a cycle (connecting some vertex w to itself) and that cycle must be negative, by the inductive hypothesis, since the path from s to the second occurrence of w must be shorter than the path from s to the first occurrence of w for w to be included on the path the second time. The cycle will also be present in the tree; thus, we could also detect cycles by periodically checking the spt edges (see Exercise 21.134).

This argument holds for only those vertices that are in the same strongly connected component as the source s. To detect negative cycles in general, we can either compute the strongly connected components and initialize weights for one vertex in each component to 0 (see Exercise 21.126) or add a dummy vertex with edges to every other vertex (see Exercise 21.127). ■

To conclude this section, we consider the all-pairs shortest-paths problem. Can we do better than Floyd's algorithm, which runs in time proportional to V^3? Using the Bellman–Ford algorithm to solve the all-pairs problem by solving the single-source problem at each vertex exposes us to a worst-case running time that is proportional to V^2E. We do not consider this solution in more detail because there is a way to guarantee that we can solve the all-paths problem in time proportional to $VE \log V$. It is based on an idea that we considered at the beginning of this section: transforming the network into a network that has only nonnegative weights and that has the same shortest-paths structure.

In fact, we have a great deal of flexibility in transforming any network to another one with different edge weights but the same shortest paths. Suppose that a vertex-indexed vector wt contains an arbitrary assignment of weights to the vertices of a network G. With these weights, we define the operation of *reweighting* the graph as follows:

- To reweight an edge, add to that edge's weight the difference between the weights of the edge's source and destination.
- To reweight a network, reweight all of that network's edges.

For example, the following straightforward code reweights a network, using our standard conventions:

```
for (v = 0; v < G->V(); v++)
  { typename Graph::adjIterator A(G, v);
    for (Edge* e = A.beg(); !A.end(); e = A.nxt())
      e->wt() = e->wt() + wt[v] - wt[e->w()]
  }
```

This operation is a simple linear-time process that is well-defined for all networks, regardless of the weights. Remarkably, the shortest paths in the transformed network are the same as the shortest paths in the original network.

Property 21.23 *Reweighting a network does not affect its shortest paths.*

Proof: Given any two vertices s and t, reweighting changes the weight of any *path* from s to t, precisely by adding the difference between the weights of s and t. This fact is easy to prove by induction on the length of the path. The weight of *every* path from s to t is changed by the same amount when we reweight the network, long paths and short paths alike. In particular, this fact implies immediately that the shortest-path length between any two vertices in the transformed network is the same as the shortest-path length between them in the original network. ∎

Since paths between different pairs of vertices are reweighted differently, reweighting could affect questions that involve comparing shortest-path lengths (for example, computing the network's diameter). In such cases, we need to invert the reweighting after completing the shortest-paths computation but before using the result.

Reweighting is no help in networks with negative cycles: The operation does not change the weight of any cycle, so we cannot remove negative cycles by reweighting. But for networks with no negative cycles, we can seek to discover a set of vertex weights such that reweighting leads to edge weights that are nonnegative, no matter what the original edge weights. With nonnegative edge weights, we can then solve the all-pairs shortest-paths problem with the all-pairs version of Dijkstra's algorithm. For example, Figure 21.31 gives such an example for our sample network, and Figure 21.32 shows the shortest-paths computation with Dijkstra's algorithm on the transformed network with no negative edges. The following property shows that we can always find such a set of weights.

Property 21.24 *In any network with no negative cycles, pick any vertex s and assign to each vertex v a weight equal to the length of a shortest path to v from s. Reweighting the network with these vertex weights yields nonnegative edge weights for each edge that connects vertices reachable from s.*

Proof: Given any edge v–w, the weight of v is the length of a shortest path to v, and the weight of w is the length of a shortest path to w. If v–w is the final edge on a shortest path to w, then the difference between the weight of w and the weight of v is precisely the weight of v–w. In other words, reweighting the edge will give a weight of 0. If the shortest path through w does not go through v, then the weight of v plus the weight of v–w must be greater than or equal to the weight of w. In other words, reweighting the edge will give a positive weight. ■

Just as we did when we used the Bellman–Ford algorithm to detect negative cycles, we have two ways to proceed to make every edge weight nonnegative in an arbitrary network with no negative cycles. Either we can begin with a source from each strongly connected component, or we can add a dummy vertex with an edge of length 0 to every network vertex. In either case, the result is a shortest-paths spanning forest that we can use to assign weights to every vertex (weight of the path from the root to the vertex in its SPT).

For example, the weight values chosen in Figure 21.31 are precisely the lengths of shortest paths from 4, so the edges in the shortest-paths tree rooted at 4 have weight 0 in the reweighted network.

In summary, we can solve the all-pairs shortest-paths problem in networks that contain negative edge weights but no negative cycles by proceeding as follows:
- Apply the Bellman–Ford algorithm to find a shortest-paths forest in the original network.
- If the algorithm detects a negative cycle, report that fact and terminate.
- Reweight the network from the forest.
- Apply the all-pairs version of Dijkstra's algorithm to the reweighted network.

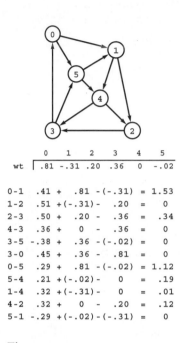

	0	1	2	3	4	5
wt	.81	-.31	.20	.36	0	-.02

```
0-1   .41 +  .81 -(-.31) = 1.53
1-2   .51 +(-.31)-  .20  =   0
2-3   .50 +  .20 -  .36  =  .34
4-3   .36 +   0  -  .36  =   0
3-5  -.38 +  .36 -(-.02) =   0
3-0   .45 +  .36 -  .81  =   0
0-5   .29 +  .81 -(-.02) = 1.12
5-4   .21 +(-.02)-   0   =  .19
1-4   .32 +(-.31)-   0   =  .01
4-2   .32 +   0  -  .20  =  .12
5-1  -.29 +(-.02)-(-.31) =   0
```

Figure 21.31
Reweighting a network

Given any assignment of weights to vertices (top), *we can reweight all of the edges in a network by adding to each edge's weight the difference of the weights of its source and destination vertices. Reweighting does not affect the shortest paths because it makes the same change to the weights of all paths connecting each pair of vertices. For example, consider the path 0–5–4–2–3: Its weight is .29 + .21 + .32 + .50 = 1.32; its weight in the reweighted network is 1.12 + .19 + .12 + .34 = 1.77; these weights differ by .45 = .81 − .36, the difference of the weights of 0 and 3; and the weights of all paths between 0 and 3 change by this same amount.*

```
1-0  1.51
2-1   0
3-2   .34
3-4   0
5-3   0
0-3   0
5-0  1.12
4-5   .23
4-1   .01
2-4   .12
1-5   0
```

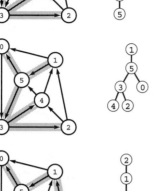

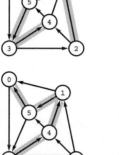

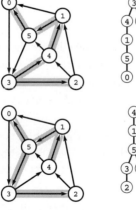

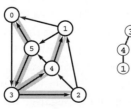

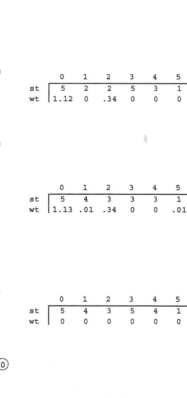

	0	1	2	3	4	5
st	0	4	3	0	3	1
wt	0	.01	.34	0	0	.01

	0	1	2	3	4	5
st	5	1	3	5	3	1
wt	.41	0	1.17	.67	1.03	.29

	0	1	2	3	4	5
st	5	2	2	5	3	1
wt	1.12	0	.34	0	0	0

	0	1	2	3	4	5
st	5	4	3	3	3	1
wt	1.13	.01	.34	0	0	.01

	0	1	2	3	4	5
st	5	4	3	5	4	1
wt	0	0	0	0	0	0

	0	1	2	3	4	5
st	5	4	3	5	3	5
wt	1.12	.01	.34	0	0	0

Figure 21.32
All shortest paths in a reweighted network

These diagrams depict the SPTs for each vertex in the reverse of the reweighted network from Figure 21.31, as could be computed with Dijkstra's algorithm to give us shortest paths in the original network in Figure Figure 21.26. The paths are the same as for the network before reweighting, so, as in Figure 21.9, the st vectors in these diagrams are the columns of the paths matrix in Figure Figure 21.26. The wt vectors in this diagram correspond to the columns in the distances matrix, but we have to undo the reweighting for each entry by subtracting the weight of the source vertex and adding the weight of the final vertex in the path (see Figure 21.31). For example, from the third row from the bottom here we can see that the shortest path from 0 to 3 is 0-5-1-4-3 in both networks, and its length is 1.13 in the reweighted network shown here. Consulting Figure 21.31, we can calculate its length in the original network by subtracting the weight of 0 and adding the weight of 3 to get the result 1.13 - .81 + .36 = .68, the entry in row 0 and column 3 of the distances matrix in Figure Figure 21.26. All shortest paths to 4 in this network are of length 0 because we used those paths for reweighting.

After this computation, the paths matrix gives shortest paths in both networks, and the distances matrix give the path lengths in the reweighted network. This series of steps is sometimes known as *Johnson's algorithm* (*see reference section*).

Property 21.25 *With Johnson's algorithm, we can solve the all-pairs shortest-paths problem in networks that contain no negative cycles in time proportional to $VE \log_d V$, where $d = 2$ if $E < 2V$, and $d = E/V$ otherwise.*

Proof: See Properties 21.22 through 21.24 and the summary in the previous paragraph. The worst-case bound on the running time is immediate from Properties 21.7 and 21.22. ∎

To implement Johnson's algorithm, we combine the implementation of Program 21.9, the reweighting code that we gave just before Property 21.23, and the all-pairs shortest-paths implementation of Dijkstra's algorithm in Program 21.4 (or, for dense graphs, Program 20.6). As noted in the proof of Property 21.22, we have to make appropriate modifications to the Bellman–Ford algorithm for networks that are not strongly connected (see Exercises 21.135 through 21.137). To complete the implementation of the all-pairs shortest-paths interface, we can either compute the true path lengths by subtracting the weight of the start vertex and adding the weight of the destination vertex (undoing the reweighting operation for the paths) when copying the two vectors into the distances and paths matrices in Dijkstra's algorithm, or we can put that computation in GRAPHdist in the ADT implementation.

For networks with no negative weights, the problem of detecting cycles is easier to solve than is the problem of computing shortest paths from a single source to all other vertices; the latter problem is easier to solve than is the problem of computing shortest paths connecting all pairs of vertices. These facts match our intuition. By contrast, the analogous facts for networks that contain negative weights are counterintuitive: The algorithms that we have discussed in this section show that, for networks that have negative weights, the best known algorithms for these three problems have similar worst-case performance characteristics. For example, it is nearly as difficult, in the worst case, to determine whether a network has a single negative cycle as it is to find all shortest paths in a network of the same size that has no negative cycles.

Exercises

▷ **21.109** Modify your random-network generators from Exercises 21.6 and 21.7 to generate weights between a and b (where a and b are both between -1 and 1), by rescaling.

▷ **21.110** Modify your random-network generators from Exercises 21.6 and 21.7 to generate negative weights by negating a fixed percentage (whose value is supplied by the client) of the edge weights.

○ **21.111** Develop client programs that use your generators from Exercises 21.109 and 21.110 to produce networks that have a large percentage of negative weights but have at most a few negative cycles, for as large a range of values of V and E as possible.

21.112 Find a currency-conversion table online or in a newspaper. Use it to build an arbitrage table. *Note*: Avoid tables that are derived (calculated) from a few values and that therefore do not give sufficiently accurate conversion information to be interesting. *Extra credit*: Make a killing in the money-exchange market!

● **21.113** Build a sequence of arbitrage tables using the source for conversion that you found for Exercise 21.112 (any source publishes different tables periodically). Find all the arbitrage opportunities that you can in the tables, and try to find patterns among them. For example, do opportunities persist day after day, or are they fixed quickly after they arise?

21.114 Develop a model for generating random arbitrage problems. Your goal is to generate tables that are as similar as possible to the tables that you used in Exercise 21.113.

21.115 Develop a model for generating random job-scheduling problems that include deadlines. Your goal is to generate nontrivial problems that are likely to be feasible.

21.116 Modify your interface and implementations from Exercise 21.101 to give clients the ability to pose and solve job-scheduling problems that include deadlines, using a reduction to the shortest-paths problem.

○ **21.117** Explain why the following argument is invalid: The shortest-paths problem reduces to the difference-constraints problem by the construction used in the proof of Property 21.15, and the difference-constraints problem reduces trivially to linear programming, so, by Property 21.17, linear programming is NP-hard.

21.118 Does the shortest-paths problem in networks with no negative cycles reduce to the job-scheduling problem with deadlines? (Are the two problems equivalent?) Prove your answer.

∘ **21.119** Find the lowest-weight cycle (best arbitrage opportunity) in the example shown in Figure 21.27.

▷ **21.120** Prove that finding the lowest-weight cycle in a network that may have negative edge weights is NP-hard.

▷ **21.121** Show that Dijkstra's algorithm does work correctly for a network in which edges that leave the source are the only edges with negative weights.

▷ **21.122** Develop a class based on Floyd's algorithm that provides clients with the capability to test networks for the existence of negative cycles.

21.123 Show, in the style of Figure 21.29, the computation of all shortest paths of the network defined in Exercise 21.1, with the weights on edges 5–1 and 4–2 negated, using Floyd's algorithm.

• **21.124** Is Floyd's algorithm optimal for complete networks (networks with V^2 edges)? Prove your answer.

21.125 Show, in the style of Figures 21.30 through 21.32, the computation of all shortest paths of the network defined in Exercise 21.1, with the weights on edges 5–1 and 4–2 negated, using the Bellman–Ford algorithm.

▷ **21.126** Develop a class based on the Bellman–Ford algorithm that provides clients with the capability to test networks for the existence of negative cycles, using the method of starting with a source in each strongly connected component.

▷ **21.127** Develop a class based on the Bellman–Ford algorithm that provides clients with the capability to test networks for the existence of negative cycles, using a dummy vertex with edges to all the network vertices.

∘ **21.128** Give a family of graphs for which Program 21.9 takes time proportional to VE to find negative cycles.

▷ **21.129** Show the schedule that is computed by Program 21.9 for the job-scheduling-with-deadlines problem in Exercise 21.89.

∘ **21.130** Prove that the following generic algorithm solves the single-source shortest-paths problem: "Relax *any* edge; continue until there are no edges that can be relaxed."

21.131 Modify the implementation of the Bellman–Ford algorithm in Program 21.9 to use a randomized queue rather than a FIFO queue. (The result of Exercise 21.130 proves that this method is correct.)

∘ **21.132** Modify the implementation of the Bellman–Ford algorithm in Program 21.9 to use a deque rather than a FIFO queue such that edges are put onto the deque according to the following rule: If the edge has previously been on the deque, put it at the beginning (as in a stack); if it is being encountered for the first time, put it at the end (as in a queue).

21.133 Run empirical studies to compare the performance of the implementations in Exercises 21.131 and 21.132 with Program 21.9, for various general networks (see Exercises 21.109 through 21.111).

○ **21.134** Modify the implementation of the Bellman–Ford algorithm in Program 21.9 to implement a function that returns the index of any vertex on any negative cycle or −1 if the network has no negative cycle. When a negative cycle is present, the function should also leave the spt vector such that following links in the vector in the normal way (starting with the return value) traces through the cycle.

○ **21.135** Modify the implementation of the Bellman–Ford algorithm in Program 21.9 to set vertex weights as required for Johnson's algorithm, using the following method. Each time that the queue empties, scan the spt vector to find a vertex whose weight is not yet set and rerun the algorithm with that vertex as source (to set the weights for all vertices in the same strong component as the new source), continuing until all strong components have been processed.

▷ **21.136** Develop an implementation of the all-pairs shortest-paths ADT interface for sparse networks (based on Johnson's algorithm) by making appropriate modifications to Programs 21.9 and 21.4.

21.137 Develop an implementation of the all-pairs shortest-paths ADT interface for dense networks (based on Johnson's algorithm) (see Exercises 21.136 and 21.43). Run empirical studies to compare your implementation with Floyd's algorithm (Program 21.5), for various general networks (see Exercises 21.109 through 21.111).

● **21.138** Add a member function to your solution to Exercise 21.137 that allows a client to decrease the cost of an edge. Return a flag that indicates whether that action creates a negative cycle. If it does not, update the paths and distances matrices to reflect any new shortest paths. Your function should take time proportional to V^2.

● **21.139** Extend your solution to Exercise 21.138 with member functions that allow clients to insert and delete edges.

● **21.140** Develop an algorithm that breaks the VE barrier for the single-source shortest-paths problem in general networks, for the special case where the weights are known to be bounded in absolute value by a constant.

21.8 Perspective

Table 21.4 summarizes the algorithms that we have discussed in this chapter and gives their worst-case performance characteristics. These algorithms are broadly applicable because, as discussed in Section 21.6, shortest-paths problems are related to a large number of other problems in a specific technical sense that directly leads to efficient algorithms for solving the entire class, or at least indicates such algorithms exist.

Table 21.4 Costs of shortest-paths algorithms

This table summarizes the cost (worst-case running time) of various shortest-paths algorithms considered in this chapter. The worst-case bounds marked as conservative may not be useful in predicting performance on real networks, particularly the Bellman–Ford algorithm, which typically runs in linear time.

weight constraint	algorithm	cost	comment
single-source			
nonnegative	Dijkstra	V^2	optimal (dense networks)
nonnegative	Dijkstra (PFS)	$E \lg V$	conservative bound
acyclic	source queue	E	optimal
no negative cycles	Bellman±Ford	VE	room for improvement?
none	open	?	NP-hard
all-pairs			
nonnegative	Floyd	V^3	same for all networks
nonnegative	Dijkstra (PFS)	$VE \lg V$	conservative bound
acyclic	DFS	VE	same for all networks
no negative cycles	Floyd	V^3	same for all networks
no negative cycles	Johnson	$VE \lg V$	conservative bound
none	open	?	NP-hard

The general problem of finding shortest paths in networks where edge weights could be negative is intractable. Shortest-paths problems are a good illustration of the fine line that often separates intractable problems from easy ones, since we have numerous algorithms to solve the various versions of the problem when we restrict the networks to have positive edge weights or to be acyclic, or even when we restrict to subproblems where there are negative edge weights but no negative cycles. Several of the algorithms are optimal or nearly so, although there are significant gaps between the best known lower bound and the best known algorithm for the single-source problem in networks that contain no negative cycles and for the all-pairs problem in networks that contain nonnegative weights.

The algorithms are all based on a small number of abstract operations and can be cast in a general setting. Specifically, the only operations that we perform on edge weights are addition and comparison: any setting in which these operations make sense can serve as the platform for shortest-paths algorithms. As we have noted, this point of view unifies our algorithms for computing the transitive closure of digraphs with our algorithms for finding shortest paths in networks. The difficulty presented by negative edge weights corresponds to a monotonicity property on these abstract operations: If we can ensure that the sum of two weights is never less than either of the weights, then we can use the algorithms in Sections 21.2 through 21.4; if we cannot make such a guarantee, we have to use the algorithms from Section 21.7. Encapsulating these considerations in an ADT is easily done and expands the utility of the algorithms.

Shortest-paths problems put us at a crossroad, between elementary graph-processing algorithms and problems that we cannot solve. They are the first of several other classes of problems with a similar character that we consider, including *network-flow problems* and *linear programming*. As in shortest paths, there is a fine line between easy and intractable problems in those areas. Not only are numerous efficient algorithms available when various restrictions are appropriate, but also there are numerous opportunities where better algorithms have yet to be invented and numerous occasions where we are faced with the certainty of NP-hard problems.

Many such problems were studied in detail as OR problems before the advent of computers or computer algorithms. Historically, OR has focused on general mathematical and algorithmic models, whereas computer science has focused on specific algorithmic solutions and basic abstractions that can both admit efficient implementations and help to build general solutions. As models from OR and basic algorithmic abstractions from computer science have both been applied to develop implementations on computers that can solve huge practical problems, the line between OR and computer science has blurred in some areas: For example, researchers in both fields seek efficient solutions to problems such as shortest-paths problems. As we address more difficult problems, we draw on classical methods from both fields of research.

CHAPTER TWENTY-TWO

Network Flow

G RAPHS, DIGRAPHS, AND networks are just mathematical abstractions, but they are useful in practice because they help us to solve numerous important problems. In this chapter, we extend the network problem-solving model to encompass a dynamic situation where we imagine material flowing through the network, with different costs attached to different routes. These extensions allow us to tackle a surprisingly broad variety of problems with a long list of applications.

We see that these problems and applications can be handled within a few natural models that we can relate to one another through reduction. There are several different ways, all of which are technically equivalent, to formulate the basic problems. To implement algorithms that solve them all, we settle on two specific problems, develop efficient algorithms to solve them, then develop algorithms that solve other problems by finding reductions to the known problems.

In real life, we do not always have the freedom of choice that this idealized scenario suggests, because not all pairs of reduction relationships between these problems have been proved, and because few optimal algorithms for solving any of the problems are known. Perhaps no efficient direct solution to a given problem has yet been invented, and perhaps no efficient reduction that directly relates a given pair of problems has yet been devised. The network-flow formulation that we cover in this chapter has been successful not only because simple reductions to it are easy to define for many problems, but also because numerous efficient algorithms for solving the basic network-flow problems have been devised.

supply	channels	cost	cap
0: 4	0-3:	2	2
1: 4	0-7:	1	3
2: 6	1-4:	5	5
distribution	2-4:	3	4
3	2-9:	1	4
4	3-5:	3	2
5	3-6:	4	1
6	4-5:	2	5
demand	4-6:	1	4
7: 7	5-7:	6	6
8: 3	5-8:	3	4
9: 4	6-9:	4	3

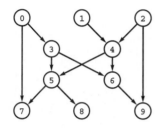

Figure 22.1
Distribution problem

In this instance of the distribution problem, we have three supply vertices (0 through 2), four distribution points (3 through 6), three demand vertices (7 through 9), and twelve channels. Each supply vertex has a rate of production; each demand vertex a rate of consumption; and each channel a maximum capacity and a cost per unit distributed. The problem is to minimize costs while distributing material through the channels (without exceeding capacity anywhere) such that the total rate of material leaving each supply vertex equals its rate of production; the total rate at which material arrives at each demand vertex equals its rate of consumption; and the total rate at which material arrives at each distribution point equals the total rate at which material leaves.

The following examples illustrate the range of problems that we can handle with network-flow models, algorithms, and implementations. They fall into general categories known as *distribution* problems, *matching* problems, and *cut* problems, each of which we examine in turn. We indicate several different related problems, rather than lay out specific details in these examples. Later in the chapter, when we undertake to develop and implement algorithms, we give rigorous descriptions of many of the problems mentioned here.

In *distribution* problems, we are concerned with moving objects from one place to another within a network. Whether we are distributing hamburger and chicken to fast-food outlets or toys and clothes to discount stores along highways throughout the country—or software to computers or bits to display screens along communications networks throughout the world—the essential problems are the same. Distribution problems typify the challenges that we face in managing a large and complex operation. Algorithms to solve them are broadly applicable and are critical in numerous applications.

Merchandise distribution   A company has factories, where goods are produced; distribution centers, where the goods are stored temporarily; and retail outlets, where the goods are sold. The company must distribute the goods from factories through distribution centers to retail outlets on a regular basis, using distribution channels that have varying capacities and unit distribution costs. Is it possible to get the goods from the warehouses to the retail outlets such that supply meets demand everywhere? What is the least-cost way to do so? Figure 22.1 illustrates a distribution problem.

Figure 22.2 illustrates the *transportation* problem, a special case of the merchandise-distribution problem where we eliminate the distribution centers and the capacities on the channels. This version is important in its own right and is significant (as we see in Section 22.7) not just because of important direct applications but also because it turns out not to be a "special case" at all—indeed, it is equivalent in difficulty to the general version of the problem.

Communications   A communications network has a set of requests to transmit messages between servers that are connected by channels (abstract wires) that are capable of transferring information at varying rates. What is the maximum rate at which information can be transferred between two specified servers in the network? If there are costs associated with the channels, what is the cheapest way to send the information at a given rate that is less than the maximum?

Traffic flow   A city government needs to formulate a plan for evacuating people from the city in an emergency. What is the minimum amount of time that it would take to evacuate the city, if we suppose that we can control traffic flow so as to realize the minimum? Traffic planners also might formulate questions like this when deciding which new roads, bridges, or tunnels might alleviate rush-hour or vacation-weekend traffic problems.

In *matching* problems, the network represents the possible ways to connect pairs of vertices, and our goal is to choose among the connections (according to a specified criterion) without including any vertex twice. In other words, the chosen set of edges defines a way to pair vertices with one another. We might be matching students to colleges, applicants to jobs, courses to available hours for a school, or members of Congress to committee assignments. In each of these situations, we might imagine a variety of criteria defining the characteristics of the matches sought.

Job placement   A job-placement service arranges interviews for a set of students with a set of companies; these interviews result in a set of job offers. Assuming that an interview followed by a job offer represents mutual interest in the student taking a job at the company, it is in everyone's best interests to maximize the number of job placements. Figure 22.3 is an example illustrating that this task can be complicated.

Minimum-distance point matching   Given two sets of N points, find the set of N line segments, each with one endpoint from each of the point sets, with minimum total length. One application of this purely geometric problem is in radar tracking systems. Each sweep of the radar gives a set of points that represent planes. We assume that the planes are kept sufficiently well spaced that solving this problem allows us to associate each plane's position on one sweep to its position on the next, thus giving us the paths of all the planes. Other data-sampling applications can be cast in this framework.

In *cut* problems, such as the one illustrated in Figure 22.4, we remove edges to cut networks into two or more pieces. Cut problems are directly related to fundamental questions of graph connectivity

supply		channels	cost
0:	3	0-6:	2
1:	4	0-7:	1
2:	6	0-8:	5
3:	3	1-6:	3
4:	2	1-5:	1
demand		2-8:	3
5:	6	2-9:	4
6:	6	3-6:	2
7:	7	3-7:	1
8:	3	4-9:	6
9:	4	4-5:	3

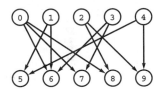

**Figure 22.2
Transportation problem**

The transportation problem is like the distribution problem, but with no channel-capacity restrictions and no distribution points. In this instance, we have five supply vertices (0 through 4), five demand vertices (5 through 9), and twelve channels. The problem is to find the lowest-cost way to distribute material through the channels such that supply exactly meets demand everywhere. Specifically, we require an assignment of weights (distribution rates) to the edges such that the sum of weights on outgoing edges equals the supply at each supply vertex; the sum of weights on ingoing edges equals the demand at each demand vertex; and the total cost (sum of weight times cost for all edges) is minimized over all such assignments.

Alice
  Adobe
  Apple
  HP
Bob
  Adobe
  Apple
  Yahoo
Carol
  HP
  IBM
  Sun
Dave
  Adobe
  Apple
Eliza
  IBM
  Sun
  Yahoo
Frank
  HP
  Sun
  Yahoo

Adobe
  Alice
  Bob
  Dave
Apple
  Alice
  Bob
  Dave
HP
  Alice
  Carol
  Frank
IBM
  Carol
  Eliza
Sun
  Carol
  Eliza
  Frank
Yahoo
  Bob
  Eliza
  Frank

Figure 22.3
Job placement

Suppose that we have six students, each needing jobs, and six companies, each needing to hire a student. These two lists (one sorted by student, the other sorted by company) give a list of job offers, which indicate mutual interest in matching students and jobs. Is there some way to match students to jobs so that every job is filled and every student gets a job? If not, what is the maximum number of jobs that can be filled?

that we first examined in Chapter 18. In this chapter, we discuss a central theorem that demonstrates a surprising connection between cut and flow problems, substantially expanding the reach of network-flow algorithms.

Network reliability A simplified model considers a telephone network as consisting of a set of wires that connect telephones through switches such that there is the possibility of a switched path through trunk lines connecting any two given telephones. What is the maximum number of trunk lines that could be cut without any pair of switches being disconnected?

Cutting supply lines A country at war moves supplies from depots to troops along an interconnected highway system. An enemy can cut off the troops from the supplies by bombing roads, with the number of bombs required to destroy a road proportional to that road's width. What is the minimum number of bombs that the enemy must drop to ensure that no troops can get supplies?

Each of the applications just cited immediately suggests numerous related questions, and there are still other related models, such as the job-scheduling problems that we considered in Chapter 21. We consider further examples throughout this chapter, yet still treat only a small fraction of the important, directly related practical problems.

The network-flow model that we consider in this chapter is important not just because it provides us with two simply stated problems to which many of the practical problems reduce but also because we have efficient algorithms for solving the two problems. This breadth of applicability has led to the development of numerous algorithms and implementations. The solutions that we consider illustrate the tension between our quest for implementations of general applicability and our quest for efficient solutions to specific problems. The study of network-flow algorithms is fascinating because it brings us tantalizingly close to compact and elegant implementations that achieve both goals.

We consider two particular problems within the network-flow model: the *maxflow* problem and the *mincost-flow* problem. We see specific relationships among these problem-solving models, the shortest-path model of Chapter 21, the linear-programming (LP) model of Part 8, and numerous specific problem models including some of those just discussed.

At first blush, many of these problems might seem to be completely different from network-flow problems. Determining a given problem's relationship to known problems is often the most important step in developing a solution to that problem. Moreover, this step is often significant because, as is usual with graph algorithms, we must understand the fine line between trivial and intractable problems before we attempt to develop implementations. The infrastructure of problems and the relationships among the problems that we consider in this chapter provides a helpful context for addressing such issues.

In the rough categorization that we began with in Chapter 17, the algorithms that we examine in this chapter demonstrate that network-flow problems are "easy," because we have straightforward implementations that are guaranteed to run in time proportional to a polynomial in the size of the network. Other implementations, although not guaranteed to run in polynomial time in the worst case, are compact and elegant and have been proved to solve a broad variety of other practical problems, such as the ones discussed here. We consider them in detail because of their utility. Researchers still seek faster algorithms, in order to enable huge applications and to save costs in critical ones. Ideal optimal algorithms that are guaranteed to be as fast as possible are yet to be discovered for network-flow problems.

On the one hand, some of the problems that we reduce to network-flow problems are known to be easier to solve with specialized algorithms. In principle, we might consider implementing and improving these specialized algorithms. Although that approach is productive in some situations, efficient algorithms for solving many of the problems (other than through reduction to network flow) are not known. Even when specialized algorithms are known, developing implementations that can outperform good network-flow codes can be a significant challenge. Moreover, researchers are still improving network-flow algorithms, and the possibility remains that a good network-flow algorithm might outperform known specialized methods for a given practical problem.

On the other hand, network-flow problems are special cases of the even more general LP problems that we discuss in Part 8. Although we could (and people often do) use an algorithm that solves LP problems to solve network-flow problems, the network-flow algorithms that we consider are simpler and more efficient than are those

Figure 22.4
Cutting supply lines

This diagram represents the roads connecting an army's supply depot at the top to the troops at the bottom. The black dots represent an enemy bombing plan that would separate troops from supplies. The enemy's goal is to minimize the cost of bombing (perhaps assuming that the cost of cutting an edge is proportional to its width), and the army's goal is to design its road network to maximize the enemy's minimum cost. The same model is useful in improving the reliability of communications networks and many other applications.

that solve LP problems. But researchers are still improving LP solvers, and the possibility remains that a good algorithm for LP problems might—when used for practical network-flow problems—outperform all the algorithms that we consider in this chapter.

The classical solutions to network-flow problems are closely related to the other graph algorithms that we have been examining, and we can write surprisingly concise programs that solve them, using the algorithmic tools we have developed. As we have seen in many other situations, good algorithms and data structures can achieve substantial reductions in running times. Development of better implementations of classical generic algorithms is still being studied, and new approaches continue to be discovered.

In Section 22.1 we consider basic properties of *flow networks*, where we interpret a network's edge weights as *capacities* and consider properties of *flows*, which are a second set of edge weights that satisfy certain natural constraints. Next, we consider the *maxflow* problem, which is to compute a flow that is best in a specific technical sense. In Sections 22.2 and 22.3, we consider two approaches to solving the maxflow problem, and examine a variety of implementations. Many of the algorithms and data structures that we have considered are directly relevant to the development of efficient solutions of the maxflow problem. We do not yet have the best possible algorithms to solve the maxflow problem, but we consider specific useful implementations. In Section 22.4, to illustrate the reach of the maxflow problem, we consider different formulations, as well as other reductions involving other problems.

Maxflow algorithms and implementations prepare us to discuss an even more important and general model known as the *mincost-flow problem*, where we assign *costs* (another set of edge weights) and define flow costs, then look for a solution to the maxflow problem that is of minimal cost. We consider a classic generic solution to the mincost-flow problem known as the *cycle-canceling* algorithm; then, in Section 22.6, we give a particular implementation of the cycle-canceling algorithm known as the *network simplex* algorithm. In Section 22.7, we discuss reductions to the mincost-flow problem that encompass, among others, all the applications that we just outlined.

Network-flow algorithms are an appropriate topic to conclude this book for several reasons. They represent a payoff on our investment in learning basic algorithmic tools such as linked lists, priority queues, and general graph-search methods. The graph-processing classes that we have studied lead immediately to compact and efficient class implementations for network-flow problems. These implementations take us to a new level of problem-solving power and are immediately useful in numerous practical applications. Furthermore, studying their applicability and understanding their limitations sets the context for our examination of better algorithms and harder problems—the undertaking of Part 8.

22.1 Flow Networks

To describe network-flow algorithms, we begin with an idealized physical model in which several of the basic concepts are intuitive. Specifically, we imagine a collection of interconnected oil pipes of varying sizes, with switches controlling the direction of flow at junctions, as in the example illustrated in Figure 22.5. We suppose further that the network has a single source (say, an oil field) and a single sink (say, a large refinery) to which all the pipes ultimately connect. At each vertex, the flowing oil reaches an equilibrium where the amount of oil flowing in is equal to the amount flowing out. We measure both flow and pipe capacity in the same units (say, gallons per second).

If every switch has the property that the total capacity of the ingoing pipes is equal to the total capacity of the outgoing pipes, then there is no problem to solve: We simply fill all pipes to full capacity. Otherwise, not all pipes are full, but oil flows through the network, controlled by switch settings at the junctions, such that the amount of oil flowing into each junction is equal to the amount of oil flowing out. But this local equilibrium at the junctions implies an equilibrium in the network as a whole: We prove in Property 22.1 that the amount of oil flowing into the sink is equal to the amount flowing out of the source. Moreover, as illustrated in Figure 22.6, the switch settings at the junctions of this amount of flow from source to sink have nontrivial effects on the flow through the network. Given these facts, we are interested in the following question: What switch settings will maximize the amount of oil flowing from source to sink?

We can model this situation directly with a network (a weighted digraph, as defined in Chapter 21) that has a single source and a single

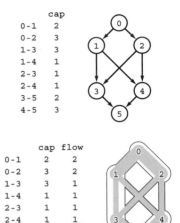

	cap
0-1	2
0-2	3
1-3	3
1-4	1
2-3	1
2-4	1
3-5	2
4-5	3

	cap	flow
0-1	2	2
0-2	3	2
1-3	3	1
1-4	1	1
2-3	1	1
2-4	1	1
3-5	2	2
4-5	3	2

Figure 22.5
Network flow

A flow network is a weighted network where we interpret edge weights as capacities (top). Our objective is to compute a second set of edge weights, bounded by the capacities, which we call the flow. The bottom drawing illustrates our conventions for drawing flow networks. Each edge's width is proportional to its capacity; the amount of flow in each edge is shaded in gray; the flow is always directed down the page from a single source at the top to a single sink at the bottom; and intersections (such as 1-4 and 2-3 in this example) do not represent vertices unless labeled as such. Except for the source and the sink, flow in is equal to flow out at every vertex: For example, vertex 2 has 2 units of flow coming in (from 0) and 2 units of flow going out (1 unit to 3 and 1 unit to 4).

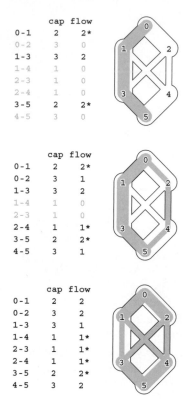

	cap	flow
0-1	2	2*
0-2	3	0
1-3	3	2
1-4	1	0
2-3	1	0
2-4	1	0
3-5	2	2*
4-5	3	0

	cap	flow
0-1	2	2*
0-2	3	1
1-3	3	2
1-4	1	0
2-3	1	0
2-4	1	1*
3-5	2	2*
4-5	3	1

	cap	flow
0-1	2	2
0-2	3	2
1-3	3	1
1-4	1	1*
2-3	1	1*
2-4	1	1*
3-5	2	2*
4-5	3	2

Figure 22.6
Controlling flow in a network

We might initialize the flow in this network by opening the switches along the path 0-1-3-5, which can handle 2 units of flow (top), and by opening switches along the path 0-2-4-5 to get another 1 unit of flow in the network (center). Asterisks indicate full edges.

Since 0-1, 2-4, and 3-5 are full, there is no direct way to get more flow from 0 to 5, but if we change the switch at 1 to redirect enough flow to fill 1-4, we open up enough capacity in 3-5 to allow us to add flow on 0-2-3-5, giving a maxflow for this network (bottom).

sink. The edges in the network correspond to the oil pipes, the vertices correspond to the junctions with switches that control how much oil goes into each outgoing edge, and the weights on the edges correspond to the capacity of the pipes. We assume that the edges are directed, specifying that oil can flow in only one direction in each pipe. Each pipe has a certain amount of flow, which is less than or equal to its capacity, and every vertex satisfies the equilibrium condition that the flow in is equal to the flow out.

This flow-network abstraction is a useful problem-solving model that applies directly to a variety of applications and indirectly to still more. We sometimes appeal to the idea of oil flowing through pipes for intuitive support of basic ideas, but our discussion applies equally well to goods moving through distribution channels and to numerous other situations.

The flow model directly applies to a distribution scenario: We interpret the flow values as rates of flow, so that a flow network describes the flow of goods in a manner precisely analogous to the flow of oil. For example, we can interpret the flow in Figure 22.5 as specifying that we should be sending two items per time unit from 0 to 1 and from 0 to 2, one item per time unit from 1 to 3 and from 1 to 4, and so forth.

Another way to interpret the flow model for a distribution scenario is to interpret flow values as amounts of goods so that a flow network describes a one-time transfer of goods. For example, we can interpret the flow in Figure 22.5 as describing the transfer of four items from 0 to 5 in the following three-step process: First, send two items from 0 to 1 and two items from 0 to 2, leaving two items at each of those vertices. Second, send one item each from 1 to 3, 1 to 4, 2 to 3, and 2 to 4, leaving two items each at 3 and 4. Third, complete the transfer by sending two items from 3 to 5 and two items from 4 to 5.

As with our use of distance in shortest-paths algorithms, we are free to abandon any physical intuition when convenient because all the definitions, properties, and algorithms that we consider are based entirely on an abstract model that does not necessarily obey physical laws. Indeed, a prime reason for our interest in the network-flow model is that it allows us to solve numerous other problems through reduction, as we see in Sections 22.4 and 22.6. Because of this broad applicability, it is worthwhile to consider precise statements of the terms and concepts that we have just informally introduced.

Definition 22.1 *We refer to a network with a designated source s and a designated sink t as an* **st-network**.

We use the modifier "designated" here to mean that s does not necessarily have to be a source (vertex with no incoming edges) and t does not necessarily have to be a sink (vertex with no outgoing edges), but that we nonetheless treat them as such, because our discussion (and our algorithms) will ignore edges directed into s and edges directed out of t. To avoid confusion, we use networks with a single source and a single sink in examples; we consider more general situations in Section 22.4. We refer to s and t as "the source" and "the sink," respectively, in the st-network because those are the roles that they play in the network. We also refer to the other vertices in the network as the *internal* vertices.

Definition 22.2 *A* **flow network** *is an st-network with positive edge weights, which we refer to as* **capacities**. *A* **flow** *in a flow network is a set of nonnegative edge weights—which we refer to as* **edge flows**—*satisfying the conditions that no edge's flow is greater than that edge's capacity and that the total flow into each internal vertex is equal to the total flow out of that vertex.*

We refer to the total flow into a vertex (the sum of the flows on its incoming edges) as the vertex's *inflow* and the total flow out of a vertex (the sum of the flows on its outgoing edges) as the vertex's *outflow*. By convention, we set the flow on edges into the source and edges out of the sink to zero, and in Property 22.1 we prove that the source's outflow is always equal to the sink's inflow, which we refer to as the network's *value*. With these definitions, the formal statement of our basic problem is straightforward.

Maximum flow Given an st-network, find a flow such that no other flow from s to t has larger value. For brevity, we refer to such a flow as a *maxflow* and the problem of finding one in a network as the *maxflow problem*. In some applications, we might be content to know just the maxflow value, but we generally want to know a flow (edge flow values) that achieves that value.

Variations on the problem immediately come to mind. Can we allow multiple sources and sinks? Should we be able to handle networks with no sources or sinks? Can we allow flow in either direction in the edges? Can we have capacity restrictions for the vertices instead of or in addition to the restrictions for the edges? As is typical with graph algorithms, separating restrictions that are trivial to handle from those that have profound implications can be a challenge. We investigate this challenge and give examples of reducing to maxflow a variety of problems that seem different in character, after we consider algorithms to solve the basic problem, in Sections 22.2 and 22.3.

The characteristic property of flows is the local equilibrium condition that inflow be equal to outflow at each internal vertex. There is no such constraint on capacities; indeed, the imbalance between total capacity of incoming edges and total capacity of outgoing edges is what characterizes the maxflow problem. The equilibrium constraint has to hold at each and every internal vertex, and it turns out that this local property determines global movement through the network, as well. Although this idea is intuitive, it needs to be proved.

Property 22.1 *Any st-flow has the property that outflow from s is equal to the inflow to t.*

Proof: (We use the term *st-flow* to mean "flow in an *st*-network.") Augment the network with an edge from a dummy vertex into s, with flow and capacity equal to the outflow from s, and with an edge from t to another dummy vertex, with flow and capacity equal to the inflow to t. Then, we can prove a more general property by induction: Inflow is equal to outflow for any *set* of vertices (not including the dummy vertices).

This property is true for any single vertex, by local equilibrium. Now, assume that it is true for a given set of vertices S and that we add a single vertex v to make the set $S' = S \cup \{v\}$. To compute inflow and outflow for S', note that each edge from v to some vertex in S reduces outflow (from v) by the same amount as it reduces inflow (to S); each edge to v from some vertex in S reduces inflow (to v) by the same amount as it reduces outflow (from S); and all other edges provide inflow or outflow for S' if and only if they do so for S or v. Thus, inflow and outflow are equal for S', and the value of the flow is equal to the sum of the values of the flows of v and S minus sum of the flows on the edges connecting v to a vertex in S (in either direction).

Applying this property to the set of all the network's vertices, we find that the source's inflow from its associated dummy vertex (which

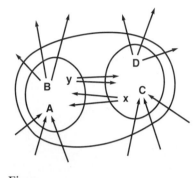

Figure 22.7
Flow equilibrium

This diagram illustrates the preservation of flow equilibrium when we merge sets of vertices. The two smaller figures represent any two disjoint sets of vertices, and the letters represent flow in sets of edges as indicated: A is the amount of flow into the set on the left from outside the set on the right, x is the amount of flow into the set on the left from the set on the right, and so forth. Now, if we have flow equilibrium in the two sets, then we must have

$$A + x = B + y$$

for the set on the left and

$$C + y = D + x$$

for the set on the right. Adding these two equations and canceling the $x + y$ terms, we conclude that

$$A + C = B + D,$$

or inflow is equal to outflow for the union of the two sets.

```
0-1  1              0-1  1
1-3  3      1-3  2   1-3  1      1-3  1
2-0  1              2-0  1
2-1  1                                   2-1  1
3-5  7      3-5  2   3-5  1      3-5  1      3-5  3
4-1  2      4-1  2
4-2  2              4-2  1      4-2  1
4-3  3                                               4-3  3
5-4  7      5-4  2   5-4  1      5-4  1      5-4  3
          1-3-5-4-1  0-1-3-5-4-2-0  1-3-5-4-2-1  3-5-4-3
```

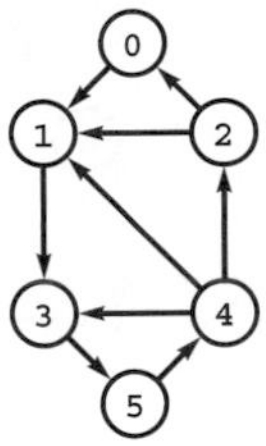

Figure 22.8
Cycle flow representation

This figure demonstrates that the circulation at left decomposes into the four cycles 1-3-5-4-1, 0-1-3-5-4-2-0, 1-3-5-4-2-1, 3-5-4-3, with weights 2, 1, 1, and 3, respectively. Each cycle's edges appear in its respective column, and summing each edge's weight from each cycle in which it appears (across its respective row) gives its weight in the circulation.

is equal to the source's outflow) is equal to the sink's outflow to its associated dummy vertex (which is equal to the sink's inflow). ∎

Corollary *The value of the flow for the union of two sets of vertices is equal to the sum of the values of the flows for the two sets minus the sum of the weights of the edges that connect a vertex in one to a vertex in the other.*

Proof: The proof just given for a set S and a vertex v still works if we replace v by a set T (which is disjoint from S) in the proof. An example of this property is illustrated in Figure 22.7. ∎

We can dispense with the dummy vertices in the proof of Property 22.1, augment any flow network with an edge from t to s with flow and capacity equal to the network's value, and know that inflow is equal to outflow for any set of nodes in the augmented network. Such a flow is called a *circulation*, and this construction demonstrates that the maxflow problem reduces to the problem of finding a circulation that maximizes the flow along a given edge. This formulation simplifies our discussion in some situations. For example, it leads to an interesting alternate representation of flows as a set of cycles, as illustrated in Figure 22.8.

Given a set of cycles and a flow value for each cycle, it is easy to compute the corresponding circulation by following through each cycle and adding the indicated flow value to each edge. The converse property is more surprising: We can find a set of cycles (with a flow value for each) that is equivalent to any given circulation.

Property 22.2 (Flow decomposition theorem) *Any circulation can be represented as flow along a set of at most E directed cycles.*

Proof: A simple algorithm establishes this result. Iterate the following process as long as there is any edge that has flow: Starting with any

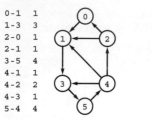

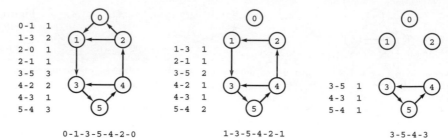

0-1-3-5-4-1   0-1-3-5-4-2-0   1-3-5-4-2-1   3-5-4-3

Figure 22.9
Cycle flow decomposition process

To decompose any circulation into a set of cycles, we iterate the following process: Follow any path until encountering a node for the second time, then find the minimum weight on the indicated cycle, then subtract that weight from each edge on the cycle and remove any edge whose weight becomes 0. For example, the first iteration is to follow the path 0-1-3-5-4-1 to find the cycle 1-3-5-4-1, then subtract 1 from the weights of each of the edges on the cycle, which causes us to remove 4-1 because its weight becomes 0. In the second iteration, we remove 0-1 and 2-0; in the third iteration, we remove 1-3, 4-2, and 2-1; and in the fourth iteration, we remove 3-5, 5-4, and 4-3.

edge that has flow, follow any edge leaving that edge's destination vertex that has flow and continue until encountering a vertex that has already been visited (a cycle has been detected). Go back around the cycle to find an edge with minimal flow; then reduce the flow on every edge in the cycle by that amount. Each iteration of this process reduces the flow on at least one edge to 0, so there are at most E cycles. ∎

Figure 22.9 illustrates the process described in the proof. For *st*-flows, applying this property to the circulation created by the addition of an edge from t to s gives the result that any *st*-flow can be represented as flow along a set of at most E directed paths, each of which is either a path from s to t or a cycle.

Corollary *Any st-network has a maxflow such that the subgraph induced by nonzero flow values is acyclic.*

Proof: Cycles that do not contain t–s do not contribute to the value of the flow, so we can change the flow to 0 along any such cycle without changing the value of the flow. ∎

Corollary *Any st-network has a maxflow that can be represented as flow along a set of at most E directed paths from s to t.*

Proof: Immediate. ∎

This representation provides a useful insight into the nature of flows that is helpful in the design and analysis of maxflow algorithms.

On the one hand, we might consider a more general formulation of the maxflow problem where we allow for multiple sources and sinks. Doing so would allow our algorithms to be used for a broader range of applications. On the other hand, we might consider special cases, such as restricting attention to acyclic networks. Doing so might make the problem easier to solve. In fact, as we see in Section 22.4, these variants are equivalent in difficulty to the version that we are considering. Therefore, in the first case, we can adapt our algorithms and implementations to the broader range of applications; in the second case, we cannot expect an easier solution. In our figures, we use acyclic networks because the examples are easier to understand when they have an implicit flow direction (down the page), but our implementations allow networks with cycles.

To implement maxflow algorithms, we use the GRAPH class of Chapter 20, but with pointers to a more sophisticated EDGE class. Instead of the single weight that we used in Chapters 20 and 21, we use pcap and pflow private data members (with cap() and flow() public member functions that return their values) for capacity and flow, respectively. Even though networks are directed graphs, our algorithms need to traverse edges in both directions, so we use the *undirected* graph representation from Chapter 20 and the member function from to distinguish u–v from v–u.

This approach allows us to separate the abstraction needed by our algorithms (edges going in both directions) from the client's concrete data structure and leaves a simple goal for our algorithms: Assign values to the flow data members in the client's edges that maximize flow through the network. Indeed, a critical component of our implementations involves a changing network abstraction that is dependent on flow values and implemented with EDGE member functions. We will consider an EDGE implementation (Program 22.2) in Section 22.2.

Since flow networks are typically sparse, we use an adjacency-lists-based GRAPH representation like the SparseMultiGRAPH implementation of Program 20.5. More important, typical flow networks may have multiple edges (of varying capacities) connecting two given vertices. This situation requires no special treatment with SparseMultiGRAPH, but with an adjacency-matrix–based representation, clients have to collapse such edges into a single edge.

In the network representations of Chapters 20 and 21, we used the convention that weights are real numbers between 0 and 1. In this chapter, we assume that the weights (capacities and flows) are all m-bit integers (between 0 and $2^m - 1$). We do so for two primary reasons. First, we frequently need to test for equality among linear combinations of weights, and doing so can be inconvenient in floating-point representations. Second, the running times of our algorithms

---

Program 22.1 Flow check and value computation

A call to flow(G, v) computes the difference between v's ingoing and outgoing flows in G. A call to flow(G, s, t) checks the network flow values from the source (s) to the sink (t), returning 0 if ingoing flow is not equal to outgoing flow at some internal node or if some flow value is negative; the flow value otherwise.

```
template <class Graph, class Edge> class check
{
 public:
  static int flow(Graph &G, int v)
    { int x = 0;
      typename Graph::adjIterator A(G, v);
      for (Edge* e = A.beg(); !A.end(); e = A.nxt())
        x += e->from(v) ? e->flow() : -e->flow();
      return x;
    }
  static bool flow(Graph &G, int s, int t)
    {
      for (int v = 0; v < G.V(); v++)
        if ((v != s) && (v != t))
          if (flow(G, v) != 0) return false;
      int sflow = flow(G, s);
      if (sflow < 0) return false;
      if (sflow + flow(G, t) != 0) return false;
      return true;
    }
};
```

---

can depend on the relative values of the weights, and the parameter $M = 2^m$ gives us a convenient way to bound weight values. For example, the ratio of the largest weight to the smallest nonzero weight is less than M. The use of integer weights is but one of many possible alternatives (see, for example, Exercise 20.8) that we could choose to address these problems.

We sometimes refer to edges as having infinite capacity, or, equivalently, as being *uncapacitated*. That might mean that we do not compare flow against capacity for such edges, or we might use a sentinel value that is guaranteed to be larger than any flow value.

Program 22.1 is an client function that checks whether a flow satisfies the equilibrium condition at every node and returns that flow's value if the flow does. Typically, we might include a call to this function as the final action of a maxflow algorithm. Despite our confidence as mathematicians in Property 22.1, our paranoia as programmers dictates that we also check that the flow out of the source is equal to the flow into the sink. It might also be prudent to check that no edge's flow exceeds that edge's capacity and that the data structures are internally consistent (see Exercise 22.12).

Exercises

▷ **22.1** Find two different maxflows in the flow network shown in Figure 22.10.

22.2 Under our assumption that capacities are positive integers less than M, what is the maximum possible flow value for any st-network with V vertices and E edges? Give two answers, depending on whether or not parallel edges are allowed.

▷ **22.3** Give an algorithm to solve the maxflow problem for the case that the network forms a tree if the sink is removed.

○ **22.4** Give a family of networks with E edges having circulations where the process described in the proof of Property 22.2 produces E cycles.

22.5 Write an EDGE class that represents capacities and flows as real numbers between 0 and 1 that are expressed with d digits to the right of the decimal point, where d is a fixed constant.

▷ **22.6** Write a program that builds a flow network by reading edges (pairs of integers between 0 and $V - 1$) with integer capacities from standard input. Assume that the capacity upper bound M is less than 2^{20}.

22.7 Extend your solution to Exercise 22.6 to use symbolic names instead of integers to refer to vertices (see Program 17.10).

○ **22.8** Find a large network online that you can use as a vehicle for testing flow algorithms on realistic data. Possibilities include transportation networks (road, rail, or air), communications networks (telephone or computer connections), or distribution networks. If capacities are not available, devise a reasonable model to add them. Write a program that uses the interface of Program 22.2 to implement flow networks from your data, perhaps using your solution to Exercise 22.7. If warranted, develop additional private functions to clean up the data, as described in Exercises 17.33–35.

22.9 Write a random-network generator for sparse networks with capacities between 0 and 2^{20}, based on Program 17.7. Use a separate class for capacities

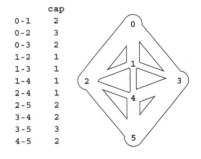

	cap
0-1	2
0-2	3
0-3	2
1-2	1
1-3	1
1-4	1
2-4	1
2-5	2
3-4	2
3-5	3
4-5	2

Figure 22.10
Flow network for exercises

This flow network is the subject of several exercises throughout the chapter.

and develop two implementations: one that generates uniformly distributed capacities and another that generates capacities according to a Gaussian distribution. Implement client programs that generate random networks for both weight distributions with a well-chosen set values of V and E, so that you can use them to run empirical tests on graphs drawn from various distributions of edge weights.

22.10 Write a random-network generator for dense networks with capacities between 0 and 2^{20}, based on Program 17.8 and edge-capacity generators as described in Exercise 22.9. Write client programs to generate random networks for both weight distributions with a well-chosen set values of V and E, so that you can use them to run empirical tests on graphs drawn from these models.

• **22.11** Write a program that generates V random points in the plane, then builds a flow network with edges (in both directions) connecting all pairs of points within a given distance d of each other (see Program 3.20), setting each edge's capacity using one of the random models described in Exercise 22.9. Determine how to set d so that the expected number of edges is E.

▷ **22.12** Modify Program 22.1 to also check that flow is less than capacity for all edges.

▷ **22.13** Find all the maxflows in the network depicted in Figure 22.11. Give cycle representations for each of them.

22.14 Write a function that reads values and cycles (one per line, in the format illustrated in Figure 22.8) and builds a network having the corresponding flow.

22.15 Write a client function that finds the cycle representation of a network's flow using the method described in the proof of Property 22.2 and prints values and cycles (one per line, in the format illustrated in Figure 22.8).

○ **22.16** Write a function that removes cycles from a network's *st*-flow.

○ **22.17** Write a program that assigns integer flows to each edge in any given digraph that contains no sinks and no sources such that the digraph is a flow network that is a circulation.

○ **22.18** Suppose that a flow represents goods to be transferred by trucks between cities, with the flow on edge u–v representing the amount to be taken from city u to v in a given day. Write a client function that prints out daily orders for truckers, telling them how much and where to pick up and how much and where to drop off. Assume that there are no limits on the supply of truckers and that nothing leaves a given distribution point until everything has arrived.

22.2 Augmenting-Path Maxflow Algorithms

An effective approach to solving maxflow problems was developed by L. R. Ford and D. R. Fulkerson in 1962. It is a generic method for

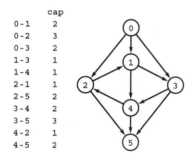

```
      cap
0-1    2
0-2    3
0-3    2
1-3    1
1-4    1
2-1    1
2-5    2
3-4    2
3-5    3
4-2    1
4-5    2
```

Figure 22.11
Flow network with cycle

This flow network is like the one depicted in Figure 22.10, but with the direction of two of the edges reversed, so there are two cycles. It is also the subject of several exercises throughout the chapter.

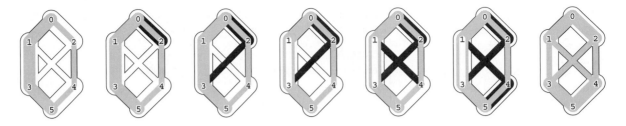

Figure 22.12
Augmenting flow along a path

This sequence shows the process of increasing flow in a network along a path of forward and backward edges. Starting with the flow depicted at the left and reading from left to right, we increase the flow in 0-2 and then 2-3 (additional flow is shown in black). Then we decrease the flow in 1-3 (shown in white) and divert it to 1-4 and then 4-5, resulting in the flow at the right.

increasing flows incrementally along paths from source to sink that serves as the basis for a family of algorithms. It is known as the *Ford–Fulkerson method* in the classical literature; the more descriptive term *augmenting-path method* is also widely used.

Consider any directed path (not necessarily a simple one) from source to sink through an *st*-network. Let x be the minimum of the unused capacities of the edges on the path. We can increase the network's flow value by at least x, by increasing the flow in all edges on the path by that amount. Iterating this action, we get a first attempt at computing flow in a network: Find another path, increase the flow along that path, and continue until all paths from source to sink have at least one full edge (so that we can no longer increase flow in this way). This algorithm will compute the maxflow in some cases, but will fall short in other cases. Figure 22.6 illustrates a case where it fails.

To improve the algorithm such that it always finds a maxflow, we consider a more general way to increase the flow, along any path from source to sink through the network's underlying undirected graph. The edges on any such path are either *forward* edges, which go with the flow (when we traverse the path from source to sink, we traverse the edge from its source vertex to its destination vertex) or *backward* edges, which go against the flow (when we traverse the path from source to sink, we traverse the edge from its destination vertex to its source vertex). Now, for any path with no full forward edges and no empty backward edges, we can increase the amount of flow in the network by increasing flow in forward edges and *decreasing* flow in backward edges. The amount by which the flow can be increased is limited by the minimum of the unused capacities in the forward edges and the flows in the backward edges. Figure 22.12 depicts an example. In the new flow, at least one of the forward edges along the

**Figure 22.13
Augmenting-path sequences**

In these three examples, we augment a flow along different sequences of augmenting paths until no augmenting path can be found. The flow that results in each case is a maximum flow. The key classical theorem in the theory of network flows states that we get a maximum flow in any network, no matter what sequence of paths we use (see Property 22.5).

path becomes full or at least one of the backward edges along the path becomes empty.

The process just sketched is the basis for the classical Ford–Fulkerson maxflow algorithm (augmenting-path method). We summarize it as follows:

Start with zero flow everywhere. Increase the flow along any path from source to sink with no full forward edges or empty backward edges, continuing until there are no such paths in the network.

Remarkably, this method always finds a maxflow, *no matter how* we choose the paths. Like the MST method discussed in Section 20.1 and the Bellman–Ford shortest-paths method discussed in Section 21.7, it is a generic algorithm that is useful because it establishes the correctness of a whole family of more specific algorithms. We are free to use any method whatever to choose the path.

Figure 22.13 illustrates several different sequences of augmenting paths that all lead to a maxflow for a sample network. Later in this section, we examine several algorithms that compute sequences of augmenting paths, all of which lead to a maxflow. The algorithms differ in the number of augmenting paths they compute, the lengths of the paths, and the costs of finding each path, but they all implement the Ford–Fulkerson algorithm and find a maxflow.

To show that any flow computed by any implementation of the Ford–Fulkerson algorithm indeed has maximal value, we show that this fact is equivalent to a key fact known as the *maxflow–mincut theorem*. Understanding this theorem is a crucial step in understanding network-flow algorithms. As suggested by its name, the theorem is based on a direct relationship between flows and *cuts* in networks, so we begin by defining terms that relate to cuts.

Recall from Section 20.1 that a *cut* in a graph is a partition of the vertices into two disjoint sets, and a *crossing edge* is an edge that connects a vertex in one set to a vertex in the other set. For flow networks, we refine these definitions as follows (see Figure 22.14).

Definition 22.3 *An st-cut is a cut that places vertex s in one of its sets and vertex t in the other.*

Each crossing edge corresponding to an st-cut is either an st-edge that goes from a vertex in the set containing s to a vertex in the set containing t, or a ts-edge that goes in the other direction. We sometimes refer to the set of crossing edges as a **cut set**. The **capacity** of an st-cut in a flow network is the sum of the capacities of that cut's st-edges, and the **flow across** an st-cut is the difference between the sum of the flows in that cut's st-edges and the sum of the flows in that cut's ts-edges.

Removing a cut set divides a connected graph into two connected components, leaving no path connecting any vertex in one to any vertex in the other. Removing all the edges in an st-cut of a network leaves no path connecting s to t in the underlying undirected graph, but adding any one of them back could create such a path.

Cuts are the appropriate abstraction for the application mentioned at the beginning of the chapter where a flow network describes the movement of supplies from a depot to the troops of an army. To cut off supplies completely and in the most economical manner, an enemy might solve the following problem.

Minimum cut   Given an st-network, find an st-cut such that the capacity of no other cut is smaller. For brevity, we refer to such a cut as a *mincut*, and to the problem of finding one in a network as the *mincut problem*.

The mincut problem is a generalization of the connectivity problems that we discussed briefly in Section 18.6. We analyze specific relationships in detail in Section 22.4.

The statement of the mincut problem includes no mention of flows, and these definitions might seem to digress from our discussion of the augmenting-path algorithm. On the surface, computing a mincut (a set of edges) seems easier than computing a maxflow (an assignment of weights to all the edges). On the contrary, the key fact of this chapter is that the maxflow and mincut problems are intimately related. The augmenting-path method itself, in conjunction with two facts about flows and cuts, provides a proof.

Property 22.3   *For any st-flow, the flow across each st-cut is equal to the value of the flow.*

Proof: This property is an immediate consequence of the generalization of Property 22.1 that we discussed in the associated proof (see Figure 22.7). Add an edge t-s with flow equal to the value of the flow such that inflow is equal to outflow for any set of vertices. Then, for any st-cut where C_s is the vertex set containing s and C_t is the vertex set containing t, the inflow to C_s is the inflow to s (the value of the flow) plus the sum of the flows in the backward edges across the cut; and the outflow from C_s is the sum of the flows in the forward edges across the cut. Setting these two quantities equal establishes the desired result. ∎

Property 22.4   *No st-flow's value can exceed the capacity of any st-cut.*

Proof: The flow across a cut certainly cannot exceed that cut's capacity, so this result is immediate from Property 22.3. ∎

In other words, cuts represent bottlenecks in networks. In our military application, an enemy that is not able to cut off army troops

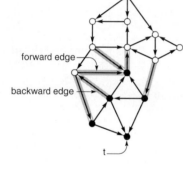

**Figure 22.14
st-cut terminology**

An st-network has one source s and one sink t. An st-cut is a partition of the vertices into a set containing s (white) and another set containing t (black). The edges that connect a vertex in one set with a vertex in the other (highlighted in gray) are known as a cut set. A forward edge goes from a vertex in the set containing s to a vertex in the set containing t; a backward edge goes the other way. There are four forward edges and two backward edges in the cut set shown here.

forward edge

backward edge

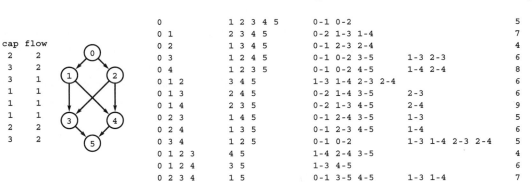

s-set	t-set	forward	backward	cap
0	1 2 3 4 5	0-1 0-2		5
0 1	2 3 4 5	0-2 1-3 1-4		7
0 2	1 3 4 5	0-1 2-3 2-4		4
0 3	1 2 4 5	0-1 0-2 3-5	1-3 2-3	6
0 4	1 2 3 5	0-1 0-2 4-5	1-4 2-4	8
0 1 2	3 4 5	1-3 1-4 2-3 2-4		6
0 1 3	2 4 5	0-2 1-4 3-5	2-3	6
0 1 4	2 3 5	0-2 1-3 4-5	2-4	9
0 2 3	1 4 5	0-1 2-4 3-5	1-3	5
0 2 4	1 3 5	0-1 2-3 4-5	1-4	6
0 3 4	1 2 5	0-1 0-2	1-3 1-4 2-3 2-4	5
0 1 2 3	4 5	1-4 2-4 3-5		4
0 1 2 4	3 5	1-3 4-5		6
0 2 3 4	1 5	0-1 3-5 4-5	1-3 1-4	7
0 1 2 3 4	5	3-5 4-5		5

Figure 22.15
All *st*-cuts

*This list gives, for all the st-cuts of the network at left, the vertices in the set containing **s**, the vertices in the set containing **t**, forward edges, backward edges, and capacity (sum of capacities of the forward edges). For any flow, the flow across all the cuts (flow in forward edges minus flow in backward edges) is the same. For example, for the flow in the network at left, the flow across the cut separating 0 1 3 and 2 4 5 is 2 + 1 + 2 (the flow in 0-2, 1-4, and 3-5, respectively) minus 1 (the flow in 2-3), or 4. This calculation also results in the value 4 for every other cut in the network, and the flow is a maximum flow because its value is equal to the capacity of the minimum cut (see Property 22.5). There are two minimum cuts in this network.*

completely from their supplies could still be sure that supply flow is restricted to at most the capacity of any given cut. We certainly might imagine that the cost of making a cut is proportional to its capacity in this application, thus motivating the invading army to find a solution to the mincut problem. More important, these facts also imply, in particular, that no flow can have value higher than the capacity of any minimum cut.

Property 22.5 (Maxflow–mincut theorem) *The maximum value among all st-flows in a network is equal to the minimum capacity among all st-cuts.*

Proof: It suffices to exhibit a flow and a cut such that the value of the flow is equal to the capacity of the cut. The flow has to be a maxflow because no other flow value can exceed the capacity of the cut and the cut has to be a minimum cut because no other cut capacity can be lower than the value of the flow (by Property 22.4). The Ford–Fulkerson algorithm gives precisely such a flow and cut: When the algorithm terminates, identify the first full forward or empty backward edge on every path from s to t in the graph. Let C_s be the set of all vertices that can be reached from s with an undirected path that does not contain a full forward or empty backward edge, and let C_t be the remaining vertices. Then, t must be in C_t, so (C_s, C_t) is an *st*-cut, whose cut set consists entirely of full forward or empty backward edges. The flow across this cut is equal to the cut's capacity (since forward edges are full and the backward edges are empty) and also to the value of the network flow (by Property 22.3). ∎

This proof also establishes explicitly that the Ford–Fulkerson algorithm finds a maxflow. No matter what method we choose to find an augmenting path, and no matter what paths we find, we always end up with a cut whose flow is equal to its capacity, and therefore also is equal to the value of the network's flow, which therefore must be a maxflow.

Another implication of the correctness of the Ford–Fulkerson algorithm is that, for any flow network with integer capacities, there exists a maxflow solution where the flows are all integers. Each augmenting path increases the flow by a positive integer (the minimum of the unused capacities in the forward edges and the flows in the backward edges, all of which are always positive integers). This fact justifies our decision to restrict our attention to integer capacities and flows. It is possible to design a maxflow with noninteger flows, even when capacities are all integers (see Exercise 22.23), but we do not need to consider such flows. This restriction is important: Generalizing to allow capacities and flows that are real numbers can lead to unpleasant anomalous situations. For example, the Ford–Fulkerson algorithm might lead to an infinite sequence of augmenting paths that does not even converge to the maxflow value (*see reference section*).

The generic Ford–Fulkerson algorithm does not specify any particular method for finding an augmenting path. Perhaps the most natural way to proceed is to use the generalized graph-search strategy of Section 18.8. To this end, we begin with the following definition.

Definition 22.4 *Given a flow network and a flow, the* **residual network** *for the flow has the same vertices as the original and one or two edges in the residual network for each edge in the original, defined as follows: For each edge* v–w *in the original, let* f *be the flow and* c *the capacity. If* f *is positive, include an edge* w–v *in the residual with capacity* f; *and if* f *is less than* c, *include an edge* v–w *in the residual with capacity* c–f.

If v–w is empty (f is equal to 0), there is a single corresponding edge v–w with capacity c in the residual; if v–w is full (f is equal to c), there is a single corresponding edge w–v with capacity f in the residual; and if v–w is neither empty nor full, both v–w and w–v are in the residual with their respective capacities.

Program 22.2 defines the EDGE class that we use to implement the residual network abstraction with class function members. With such

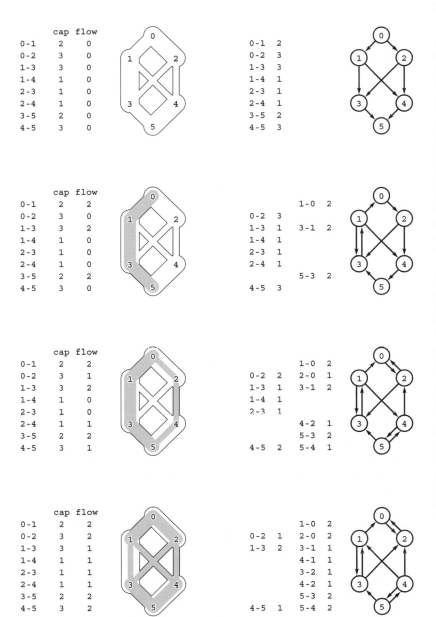

Figure 22.16
Residual networks (augmenting paths)

Finding augmenting paths in a flow network is equivalent to finding directed paths in the residual network that is defined by the flow. For each edge in the flow network, we create an edge in each direction in the residual network: one in the direction of the flow with weight equal to the unused capacity, and one in the opposite direction with weight equal to the flow. We do not include edges of weight 0 in either case. Initially (top), the residual network is the same as the flow network with weights equal to capacities. When we augment along the path 0-1-3-5 (second from top), we fill edges 0-1 and 3-5 to capacity so that they switch direction in the residual network, we reduce the weight of 1-3 to correspond to the remaining flow, and we add the edge 3-1 of weight 2. Similarly, when we augment along the path 0-2-4-5, we fill 2-4 to capacity so that it switches direction, and we have edges in either direction between 0 and 2 and between 4 and 5 to represent flow and unused capacity. After we augment along 0-2-3-1-4-5 (bottom), no directed paths from source to sink remain in the residual network, so there are no augmenting paths.

Program 22.2 Flow-network edges

To implement flow networks, we use the *undirected* GRAPH class from Chapter 20 to manipulate pointers to edges that implement this interface. The edges are *directed*, but the member functions implement the residual network abstraction, which encompasses both orientations of each edge (*see text*).

```
class EDGE
{ int pv, pw, pcap, pflow;
public:
  EDGE(int v, int w, int cap) :
      pv(v), pw(w), pcap(cap), pflow(0) { }
  int v() const { return pv; }
  int w() const { return pw; }
  int cap() const { return pcap; }
  int flow() const { return pflow; }
  bool from (int v) const
    { return pv == v; }
  int other(int v) const
    { return from(v) ? pw : pv; }
  int capRto(int v) const
    { return from(v) ? pflow : pcap - pflow; }
  void addflowRto(int v, int d)
    { pflow += from(v) ? -d : d; }
};
```

---

an implementation, we continue to work exclusively with pointers to client edges. Our algorithms work with the residual network, but they are actually examining capacities and changing flow (through edge pointers) in the client's edges. The member functions from and Plotherl allow us to process edges in either orientation: e.other(v) returns the endpoint of e that is not v. The member functions capRto and addflowRto implement the residual network: If e is a pointer to an edge v-w with capacity c and flow f, then e->capRto(w) is c-f and e->capRto(v) is f; e->addflowRto(w, d) adds d to the flow; and e->addflowRto(v, d) subtracts d from the flow.

Residual networks allow us to use any generalized graph search (see Section 18.8) to find an augmenting path, since any path from

Program 22.3 Augmenting-paths maxflow implementation

This class implements the generic augmenting-paths (Ford–Fulkerson)
maxflow algorithm. It uses PFS to find a path from source to sink in
the residual network (see Program 22.4), then adds as much flow as
possible to that path, repeating the process until there is no such path.
Constructing an object of this class sets the flow values in the given
network's edges such that the flow from source to sink is maximal.

The st vector holds the PFS spanning tree, with st[v] containing
a pointer to the edge that connects v to its parent. The ST function
returns the parent of its argument vertex. The augment function uses ST
to traverse the path to find its capacity and then augment flow.

```
template <class Graph, class Edge> class MAXFLOW
{ const Graph &G;
  int s, t;
  vector<int> wt;
  vector<Edge *> st;
  int ST(int v) const { return st[v]->other(v); }
  void augment(int s, int t)
    { int d = st[t]->capRto(t);
      for (int v = ST(t); v != s; v = ST(v))
        if (st[v]->capRto(v) < d)
          d = st[v]->capRto(v);
      st[t]->addflowRto(t, d);
      for (int v = ST(t); v != s; v = ST(v))
        st[v]->addflowRto(v, d);
    }
  bool pfs();
public:
  MAXFLOW(const Graph &G, int s, int t) : G(G),
    s(s), t(t), st(G.V()), wt(G.V())
  { while (pfs()) augment(s, t); }
};
```

source to sink in the residual network corresponds directly to an augmenting path in the original network. Increasing the flow along the
path implies making changes in the residual network: For example, at
least one edge on the path becomes full or empty, so at least one edge in
the residual network changes direction or disappears (but our use of an

Program 22.4 PFS for augmenting-paths implementation

This priority-first search implementation is derived from the one that we used for Dijkstra's algorithm (Program 21.1) by changing it to use integer weights, to process edges in the residual network, and to stop when it reaches the sink or return `false` if there is no path from source to sink. The given definition of the priority P leads to the maximum-capacity augmenting path (negative values are kept on the priority queue so as to adhere to the interface of Program 20.10); other definitions of P yield various different maxflow algorithms.

```
template <class Graph, class Edge>
bool MAXFLOW<Graph, Edge>::pfs()
  { PQi<int> pQ(G.V(), wt);
    for (int v = 0; v < G.V(); v++)
      { wt[v] = 0; st[v] = 0; pQ.insert(v); }
    wt[s] = -M; pQ.lower(s);
    while (!pQ.empty())
    { int v = pQ.getmin(); wt[v] = -M;
      if (v == t || (v != s && st[v] == 0)) break;
      typename Graph::adjIterator A(G, v);
      for (Edge* e = A.beg(); !A.end(); e = A.nxt())
        { int w = e->other(v);
          int cap = e->capRto(w);
          int P = cap < -wt[v] ? cap : -wt[v];
          if (cap > 0 && -P < wt[w])
            { wt[w] = -P; pQ.lower(w); st[w] = e; }
        }
    }
    return st[t] != 0;
  }
```

abstract residual network means that we just check for positive capacity and do not need to actually insert and delete edges). Figure 22.16 shows a sequence of augmenting paths and the corresponding residual networks for an example.

Program 22.3 is a priority-queue–based implementation that encompasses all these possibilities, using the slightly modified version of our PFS graph-search implementation from Program 21.1 that is shown in Program 22.4. This implementation allows us to choose among several different classical implementations of the Ford–Fulkerson algorithm, simply by setting priorities so as to implement various data structures for the fringe.

As discussed in Section 21.2, using a priority queue to implement a stack, queue, or randomized queue for the fringe data structure incurs an extra factor of $\lg V$ in the cost of fringe operations. Since we could avoid this cost by using a generalized-queue ADT in an implementation like Program 18.10 with direct implementations, we assume when analyzing the algorithms that the costs of fringe operations are constant in these cases. By using the single implementation in Program 22.3, we emphasize the direct relationships amoung various Ford–Fulkerson implementations.

Although it is general, Program 22.3 does not encompass all implementations of the Ford–Fulkerson algorithm (see, for example, Exercises 22.36 and 22.38). Researchers continue to develop new ways to implement the algorithm. But the family of algorithms encompassed by Program 22.3 is widely used, gives us a basis for understanding computation of maxflows, and introduces us to straightforward implementations that perform well on practical networks.

As we soon see, these basic algorithmic tools get us simple (and useful, for many applications) solutions to the network-flow problem. A complete analysis establishing which specific method is best is a complex task, however, because their running times depend on

- The number of augmenting paths needed to find a maxflow
- The time needed to find each augmenting path

These quantities can vary widely, depending on the network being processed and on the graph-search strategy (fringe data structure).

Perhaps the simplest Ford–Fulkerson implementation uses the *shortest* augmenting path (as measured by the number of edges on the path, not flow or capacity). This method was suggested by Edmonds and Karp in 1972. To implement it, we use a queue for the fringe, either by using the value of an increasing counter for P or by using a queue ADT instead of a priority-queue ADT in Program 22.3. In this case, the search for an augmenting path amounts to breadth-first search (BFS) in the residual network, precisely as described in Sections 18.8 and 21.2. Figure 22.17 shows this implementation of the Ford–Fulkerson method in operation on a sample network. For brevity, we refer to this method as the *shortest-augmenting-path* maxflow algorithm. As is evident

Figure 22.17
Shortest augmenting paths

This sequence illustrates how the shortest-augmenting-path implementation of the Ford–Fulkerson method finds a maximum flow in a sample network. Path lengths increase as the algorithm progresses: The first four paths in the top row are of length 3; the last path in the top row and all of the paths in the second row are of length 4; the first two paths in the bottom row are of length 5; and the process finishes with two paths of length 7 that each have a backward edge.

from the figure, the lengths of the augmenting paths form a non-decreasing sequence. Our analysis of this method, in Property 22.7, proves that this property is characteristic.

Another Ford–Fulkerson implementation suggested by Edmonds and Karp is the following: *Augment along the path that increases the flow by the largest amount.* The priority value P that is used in Program 22.3 implements this method. This priority makes the algorithm choose edges from the fringe to give the maximum amount of flow that can be pushed through a forward edge or diverted from a backward edge. For brevity, we refer to this method as the *maximum-capacity-augmenting-path* maxflow algorithm. Figure 22.18 illustrates the algorithm on the same flow network as that in Figure 22.17.

These are but two examples (ones we can analyze!) of Ford–Fulkerson implementations. At the end of this section, we consider others. Before doing so, we consider the task of analyzing augmenting-path methods in order to learn their properties and, ultimately, to decide which one will have the best performance.

Figure 22.18
Maximum-capacity augmenting paths

This sequence illustrates how the maximum-capacity–augmenting-path implementation of the Ford–Fulkerson method finds a maxflow in a sample network. Path capacities decrease as the algorithm progresses, but their lengths may increase or decrease. The method needs only nine augmenting paths to compute the same maxflow as the one depicted in Figure 22.17.

In trying to choose among the family of algorithms represented by Program 22.3, we are in a familiar situation. Should we focus on worst-case performance guarantees, or do those represent a mathematical fiction that may not relate to networks that we encounter in practice? This question is particularly relevant in this context, because the classical worst-case performance bounds that we can establish are much higher than the actual performance results that we see for typical graphs.

Many factors further complicate the situation. For example, the worst-case running time for several versions depends not just on V and E, but also on the values of the edge capacities in the network. Developing a maxflow algorithm with fast guaranteed performance has been a tantalizing problem for several decades, and numerous methods have been proposed. Evaluating all these methods for all the types of networks that are likely to be encountered in practice, with sufficient precision to allow us to choose among them, is not as clear-cut as is the same task for other situations that we have studied, such as typical practical applications of sorting or searching algorithms.

Keeping these difficulties in mind, we now consider the classical results about the worst-case performance of the Ford–Fulkerson method: One general bound and two specific bounds, one for each of the two augmenting-path algorithms that we have examined. These results serve more to give us insight into characteristics of the algorithms than to allow us to predict performance to a sufficient degree of ac-

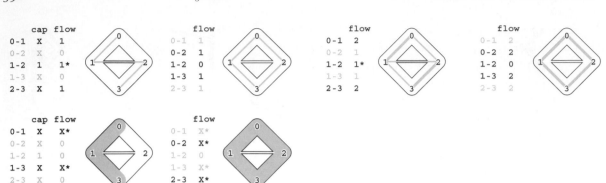

Figure 22.19
Two scenarios for the Ford–Fulkerson algorithm

This network illustrates that the number of iterations used by the Ford–Fulkerson algorithm depends on the capacities of the edges in the network and the sequence of paths chosen by the implementation. It consists of four edges of capacity X and one of capacity 1. The scenario depicted at the top shows that an implementation that alternates between using 0-1-2-3 and 0-2-1-3 as augmenting paths (for example, one that prefers long paths) would require X pairs of iterations like the two pairs shown, each pair incrementing the total flow by 2. The scenario depicted at the bottom shows that an implementation that chooses 0-1-3 and then 0-2-3 as augmenting paths (for example, one that prefers short paths) finds the maximum flow in just two iterations.

If edge capacities are, say, 32-bit integers, the scenario depicted at the top would be billions of times slower than the scenario depicted the bottom.

curacy for meaningful comparison. We discuss empirical comparisons of the methods at the end of the section.

Property 22.6 *Let M be the maximum edge capacity in the network. The number of augmenting paths needed by any implementation of the Ford–Fulkerson algorithm is at most equal to VM.*

Proof: Any cut has at most V edges, of capacity M, for a total capacity of VM. Every augmenting path increases the flow through every cut by at least 1, so the algorithm must terminate after VM passes, since all cuts must be filled to capacity after that many augmentations. ∎

As discussed below, such a bound is of little use in typical situations because M can be a very large number. Worse, it is easy to describe situations where the number of iterations is proportional to the maximum edge capacity. For example, suppose that we use a *longest* augmenting-path algorithm (perhaps based on the intuition that the longer the path, the more flow we put on the network's edges). Since we are counting iterations, we ignore, for the moment, the cost of computing such a path. The (classical) example shown in Figure 22.19 shows a network for which the number of iterations of a longest augmenting-path algorithm is equal to the maximum edge capacity. This example tells us that we must undertake a more detailed scrutiny to know whether other specific implementations use substantially fewer iterations than are indicated by Property 22.6.

For sparse networks and networks with small integer capacities, Property 22.6 does give an upper bound on the running time of any Ford–Fulkerson implementation that is useful.

Corollary *The time required to find a maxflow is* $O(VEM)$, *which is* $O(V^2M)$ *for sparse networks.*

Proof: Immediate from the basic result that generalized graph search is linear in the size of the graph representation (Property 18.12). As mentioned, we need an extra $\lg V$ factor if we are using a priority-queue fringe implementation. ∎

The proof actually establishes that the factor of M can be replaced by the ratio between the largest and smallest nonzero capacities in the network (see Exercise 22.25). When this ratio is low, the bound tells us that any Ford–Fulkerson implementation will find a maxflow in time proportional to the time required to (for example) solve the all-shortest-paths problem, in the worst case. There are many situations where the capacities are indeed low and the factor of M is of no concern. We will see an example in Section 22.4.

When M is large, the VEM worst-case bound is high; but it is pessimistic, as we obtained it by multiplying together worst-case bounds that derive from contrived examples. Actual costs on practical networks are typically much lower.

From a theoretical standpoint, our first goal is to discover, using the rough subjective categorizations of Section 17.8, whether or not the maximum-flow problem for networks with large integer weights is tractable (solvable by a polynomial-time algorithm). The bounds just derived do *not* resolve this question, because the maximum weight $M = 2^m$ could grow exponentially with V and E. From a practical standpoint, we seek better performance guarantees. To pick a typical practical example, suppose that we use 32-bit integers ($m = 32$) to represent edge weights. In a graph with hundreds of vertices and thousands of edges, the corollary to Property 22.6 says that we might have to perform hundreds of trillions of operations in an augmenting-path algorithm. If we are dealing with millions of vertices, this point is moot, not only because we will not have weights as large $2^{1000000}$, but also because V^3 and VE are so large as to make the bound meaningless. We are interested both in finding a polynomial bound to resolve the tractability question and in finding better bounds that are relevant for situations that we might encounter in practice.

Property 22.6 is general: It applies to any Ford–Fulkerson implementation at all. The generic nature of the algorithm leaves us with a substantial amount of flexibility to consider a number of simple implementations in seeking to improve performance. We expect that specific implementations might be subject to better worst-case bounds. Indeed, that is one of our primary reasons for considering them in the first place! Now, as we have seen, implementing and using a large class of these implementations is trivial: We just substitute different generalized-queue implementations or priority definitions in Program 22.3. Analyzing differences in worst-case behavior is more challenging, as indicated by the classical results that we consider next for the two basic augmenting-path implementations that we have considered.

First, we analyze the shortest-augmenting-path algorithm. This method is not subject to the problem illustrated in Figure 22.19. Indeed, we can use it to replace the factor of M in the worst-case running time with $VE/2$, thus establishing that the network-flow problem is tractable. We might even classify it as being easy (solvable in polynomial time on practical cases by a simple, if clever, implementation).

Property 22.7 *The number of augmenting paths needed in the shortest-augmenting-path implementation of the Ford–Fulkerson algorithm is at most $VE/2$.*

Proof: First, as is apparent from the example in Figure 22.17, no augmenting path is shorter than a previous one. To establish this fact, we show by contradiction that a stronger property holds: No augmenting path can decrease the length of the shortest path from the source s to any vertex in the residual network. Suppose that some augmenting path does so, and that v is the first such vertex on the path. There are two cases to consider: Either no vertex on the new shorter path from s to v appears anywhere on the augmenting path or some vertex w on the new shorter path from s to v appears somewhere between v and t on the augmenting path. Both situations contradict the minimality of the augmenting path.

Now, by construction, every augmenting path has at least one *critical edge*: an edge that is deleted from the residual network because it corresponds either to a forward edge that becomes filled to capacity or a backward edge that is emptied. Suppose that an edge u–v is a critical edge for an augmenting path P of length d. The next augmenting path for which it is a critical edge has to be of length at least d+2, because that path has to go from s to v, then along v–u, then from u to t. The first segment is of length at least 1 greater than the distance from s to u in P, and the final segment is of length at least 1 greater than the distance from v to t in P, so the path is of length at least 2 greater than P.

Since augmenting paths are of length at most V, these facts imply that each edge can be the critical edge on at most $V/2$ augmenting paths, so the total number of augmenting paths is at most $EV/2$. ∎

Corollary *The time required to find a maxflow in a sparse network is $O(V^3)$.*

Proof: The time required to find an augmenting path is $O(E)$, so the total time is $O(VE^2)$. The stated bound follows immediately. ∎

The quantity V^3 is sufficiently high that it does not provide a guarantee of good performance on huge networks. But that fact should not preclude us from using the algorithm on a huge network, because it is a worst-case performance result that may not be useful for predicting performance in a practical application. For example, as just mentioned, the maximum capacity M (or the maximum ratio between capacities) might be much less than V, so the corollary to Property 22.6 would provide a better bound. Indeed, in the best case, the number of augmenting paths needed by the Ford–Fulkerson method is the smaller of the outdegree of s or the indegree of t, which again might be far smaller than V. Given this range between best- and worst-case performance, comparing augmenting-path algorithms solely on the basis of worst-case bounds is not wise.

Still, other implementations that are nearly as simple as the shortest-augmenting-path method might admit better bounds or be preferred in practice (or both). For example, the maximum-augmenting-path algorithm used far fewer paths to find a maxflow than did the shortest-augmenting-path algorithm in the example illustrated in Figures 22.17 and 22.18. We now turn to the worst-case analysis of that algorithm.

First, just as for Prim's algorithm and for Dijkstra's algorithm (see Sections 20.6 and 21.2), we can implement the priority queue such that the algorithm takes time proportional to V^2 (for dense graphs) or $(E + V) \log V$ (for sparse graphs) per iteration in the worst case, although these estimates are pessimistic because the algorithm stops

Figure 22.20
Stack-based augmenting-path search

This illustrates the result of using a stack for the generalized queue in our implementation of the Ford–Fulkerson method, so that the path search operates like DFS. In this case, the method does about as well as BFS, but its somewhat erratic behavior is rather sensitive to the network representation and has not been analyzed.

when it reaches the sink. We also have seen that we can do slightly better with advanced data structures. The more important and more challenging question is how many augmenting paths are needed.

Property 22.8 *The number of augmenting paths needed in the maximal-augmenting-path implementation of the Ford–Fulkerson algorithm is at most $2E \lg M$.*

Proof: Given a network, let F be its maxflow value. Let v be the value of the flow at some point during the algorithm as we begin to look for an augmenting path. Applying Property 22.2 to the residual network, we can decompose the flow into at most E directed paths that sum to $F - v$, so the flow in at least one of the paths is at least $(F - v)/E$. Now, either we find the maxflow sometime before doing another $2E$ augmenting paths or the value of the augmenting path after that sequence of $2E$ paths is less than $(F - v)/2E$, which is less than one-half of the value of the maximum before that sequence of $2E$ paths. That is, in the worst case, we need a sequence of $2E$ paths to

decrease the path value by a factor of 2. The first path value is at most M, which we need to decrease by a factor of 2 at most $\lg M$ times, so we have a total of at most $\lg M$ sequences of $2E$ paths. ■

Corollary *The time required to find a maxflow in a sparse network is $O(V^2 \lg M \lg V)$.*

Proof: Immediate from the use of a heap-based priority-queue implementation, as for Properties 20.7 and 21.5. ■

For values of M and V that are typically encountered in practice, this bound is significantly lower than the $O(V^3)$ bound of the corollary to Property 22.7. In many practical situations, the maximum-augmenting-path algorithm uses significantly fewer iterations than does the shortest-augmenting-path algorithm, at the cost of a slightly higher bound on the work to find each path.

There are many other variations to consider, as reflected by the extensive literature on maxflow algorithms. Algorithms with better worst-case bounds continue to be discovered, and no nontrivial lower bound has been proved—that is, the possibility of a simple linear-time algorithm remains. Although they are important from a theoretical standpoint, many of the algorithms are primarily designed to lower the worst-case bounds for dense graphs, so they do not offer substantially better performance than the maximum-augmenting-path algorithm for the kinds of sparse networks that we encounter in practice. Still, there remain many options to explore in pursuit of better practical maxflow

Figure 22.21
Randomized augmenting-path search

This sequence the result of using a randomized queue for the fringe data structure in the augmenting-path search in the Ford–Fulkerson method. In this example, we happen upon the short high-capacity path and therefore need relatively few augmenting paths. While predicting the performance characteristics of this method is a challenging task, it performs well in many situations.

algorithms. We briefly consider two more augmenting-path algorithms next; in Section 22.3, we consider another family of algorithms.

One easy augmenting-path algorithm is to use the value of a decreasing counter for P or a stack implementation for the generalized queue in Program 22.3, making the search for augmenting paths like depth-first search. Figure 22.20 shows the flow computed for our small example by this algorithm. The intuition is that the method is fast, is easy to implement, and appears to put flow throughout the network. As we will see, its performance varies remarkably, from extremely poor on some networks to reasonable on others.

Another alternative is to use a randomized-queue implementation for the generalized queue so that the search for augmenting paths is a randomized search. Figure 22.21 shows the flow computed for our small example by this algorithm. This method is also fast and easy to implement; in addition, as we noted in Section 18.8, it may embody good features of both breadth-first and depth-first search. Randomization is a powerful tool in algorithm design, and this problem represents a reasonable situation in which to consider using it.

We conclude this section by looking more closely at the methods that we have examined in order to see the difficulty of comparing them or attempting to predict performance for practical applications.

As a start in understanding the quantitative differences that we might expect, we use two flow-network models that are based on the Euclidean graph model that we have been using to compare other graph algorithms. Both models use a graph drawn from V points in the plane with random coordinates between 0 and 1 with edges connecting any two points within a fixed distance of each other. They differ in the assignment of capacities to the edges.

The first model simply assigns the same constant value to each capacity. As discussed in Section 22.4, this type of network-flow problem is known to be easier than the general problem. For our Euclidean graphs, flows are limited by the outdegree of the source and the indegree of the sink, so the algorithms each need only a few augmenting paths. But the paths differ substantially for the various algorithms, as we soon see.

The second model assigns random weights from some fixed range of values to the capacities. This model generates the type of networks that people typically envision when thinking about the problem, and

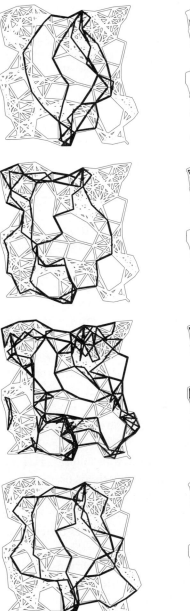
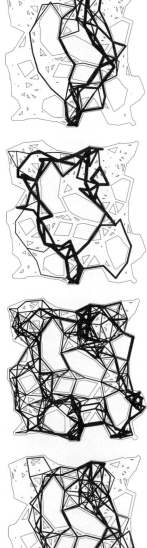

Figure 22.22
Random flow networks

This figure depicts maxflow computations on our random Euclidean graph, with two different capacity models. On the left, all edges are assigned unit capacities; on the right, edges are assigned random capacities. The source is near the middle at the top and the sink near the middle at the bottom. Illustrated top to bottom are the flows computed by the shortest-path, maximum-capacity, stack-based, and randomized algorithms, respectively. Since the vertices are not of high degree and the capacities are small integers, there are many different flows that achieve the maximum for these examples.

The indegree of the sink is 6, so all the algorithms find the flow in the unit-capacity model on the left with six augmenting paths.

The methods find augmenting paths that differ dramatically in character for the random-weight model on the right. In particular, the stack-based method finds long paths of low weight and even produces a flow with a disconnected cycle.

Table 22.1 Empirical study of augmenting-path algorithms

This table shows performance parameters for various augmenting-path network-flow algorithms for our sample Euclidean neighbor network (with random capacities with maxflow value 286) and with unit capacities (with maxflow value 6). The maximum-capacity algorithm outperforms the others for both types of networks. The random search algorithm finds augmenting paths that are not much longer than the shortest, and examines fewer nodes. The stack-based algorithm peforms very well for random weights but, though it has very long paths, is competetive for unit weights.

	paths	mean length	total edges
random capacity 1-50			
shortest	37	10.8	76394
maximum capacity	7	19.3	15660
depth-Ærst	286	123.5	631392
random	35	12.8	58016
capacity 1			
shortest	6	10.5	13877
maximum capacity	6	14.7	10736
depth-Ærst	6	110.8	12291
random	6	12.2	11223

the performance of the various algorithms on such networks is certainly instructive.

Both of these models are illustrated in Figure 22.22, along with the flows that are computed by the four methods on the two networks. Perhaps the most noticeable characteristic of these examples is that the flows themselves are different in character. All have the same value, but the networks have many maxflows, and the different algorithms make different choices when computing them. This situation is typical in practice. We might try to impose other conditions on the flows that we want to compute, but such changes to the problem can make it more difficult. The mincost-flow problem that we consider in Sections 22.5 through 22.7 is one way to formalize such situations.

Table 22.1 gives more detailed quantitative results for use of the four methods to compute the flows in Figure 22.22. An augmenting-

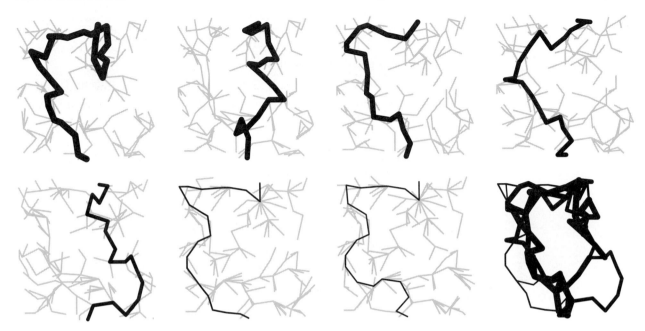

path algorithm's performance depends not just on the number of augmenting paths but also on the lengths of such paths and on the cost of finding them. In particular, the running time is proportional to the number of edges examined in the inner loop of Program 22.3. As usual, this number might vary widely, even for a given graph, depending on properties of the representation; but we can still characterize different algorithms. For example, Figures 22.23 and 22.24 show the search trees for the maximum-capacity and shortest-path algorithms, respectively. These examples help support the general conclusion that the shortest-path method expends more effort to find augmenting paths with less flow than the maximum-capacity algorithm, thus helping to explain why the latter is preferred.

Perhaps the most important lesson that we can learn from studying particular networks in detail in this way is that the gap between the upper bounds of Properties 22.6 through 22.8 and the actual number of augmenting paths that the algorithms need for a given application might be enormous. For example, the flow network illustrated in Figure 22.23 has 177 vertices and 2000 edges of capacity less than 100, so the value of the quantity $2E \lg M$ in Property 22.8 is more than 25,000; but the maximum-capacity algorithm finds the maxflow

Figure 22.23
Maximum-capacity augmenting paths (larger example)

This figure depicts the augmenting paths computed by the maximum-capacity algorithm for the Euclidean network with random weights that is shown in Figure 22.22, along with the edges in the graph-search spanning tree (in gray). The resulting flow is shown at the bottom right.

with only seven augmenting paths. Similarly, the value of the quantity $VE/2$ in Property 22.7 for this network is 177,000, but the shortest-path algorithm needs only 37 paths.

As we have already indicated, the relatively low node degree and the locality of the connections partially explain these differences between theoretical and actual performance in this case. We can prove more accurate performance bounds that account for such details; but such disparities are the rule, not the exception, in flow-network models and in practical networks. On the one hand, we might take these results to indicate that these networks are not sufficiently general to represent the networks that we encounter in practice; on the other hand, perhaps the worst-case analysis is more removed from practice than these kinds of networks.

Large gaps like this certainly provide strong motivation for researchers seeking to lower the worst-case bounds. There are many other possible implementations of augmenting-path algorithms to consider that might lead to better worst-case performance or better practical performance than the methods that we have considered (see Exercises 22.56 through 22.60). Numerous methods that are more sophisticated and have been shown to have improved worst-case performance can be found in the research literature (*see reference section*).

Another important complication follows when we consider the numerous other problems that reduce to the maxflow problem. When such reductions apply, the flow networks that result may have some special structure that some particular algorithm may be able to exploit for improved performance. For example, in Section 22.8 we will examine a reduction that gives flow networks with unit capacities on all edges.

Even when we restrict attention just to augmenting-path algorithms, we see that the study of maxflow algorithms is both an art and a science. The art lies in picking the strategy that is most effective for a given practical situation; the science lies in understanding the essential nature of the problem. Are there new data structures and algorithms that can solve the maxflow problem in linear time, or can we prove that none exist? In Section 22.3, we see that no augmenting-path algorithm can have linear worst-case performance, and we examine a different generic family of algorithms that might.

Figure 22.24
Shortest augmenting paths (larger example)

This figure depicts the augmenting paths computed by the shortest-paths algorithm for the Euclidean network with random weights that is shown in Figure 22.22, along with the edges in the graph-search spanning tree (in gray). In this case, this algorithm is much slower than the maximum-capacity algorithm depicted in Figure 22.23 both because it requires a large number of augmenting paths (the paths shown are just the first 12 out of a total of 37) and because the spanning trees are larger (usually containing nearly all of the vertices).

Exercises

22.19 Show, in the style of Figure 22.13, as many different sequences of augmenting paths as you can find for the flow network shown in Figure 22.10.

22.20 Show, in the style of Figure 22.15, all the cuts for the flow network shown in Figure 22.10, their cut sets, and their capacities.

▷ **22.21** Find a minimum cut in the flow network shown in Figure 22.11.

○ **22.22** Suppose that capacities are in equilibrium in a flow network (for every internal node, the total capacity of incoming edges is equal to the total capacity of outgoing edges). Does the Ford–Fulkerson algorithm ever use a backward edge? Prove that it does or give a counterexample.

22.23 Give a maxflow for the flow network shown in Figure 22.5 with at least one flow that is not an integer.

▷ **22.24** Develop an implementation of the Ford–Fulkerson algorithm that uses a generalized queue instead of a priority queue (see Section 18.8).

▷ **22.25** Prove that the number of augmenting paths needed by any implementation of the Ford–Fulkerson algorithm is no more than V times the smallest integer larger than the ratio of the largest edge capacity to the smallest edge capacity.

22.26 Prove a linear-time *lower bound* for the maxflow problem: Show that, for any values of V and E, any maxflow algorithm might have to examine every edge in some network with V vertices and E edges.

▷ **22.27** Give a network like Figure 22.19 for which the shortest-augmenting-path algorithm has the worst-case behavior that is illustrated.

22.28 Give an adjacency-lists representation of the network in Figure 22.19 for which our implementation of the stack-based search (Program 22.3, using a stack for the generalized queue) has the worst-case behavior that is illustrated.

22.29 Show, in the style of Figure 22.16, the flow and residual networks after each augmenting path when we use the shortest-augmenting-path algorithm to find a maxflow in the flow network shown in Figure 22.10. Also include the graph-search trees for each augmenting path. When more than one path is possible, show the one that is chosen by the implementations given in this section.

22.30 Do Exercise 22.29 for the maximum-capacity–augmenting-path algorithm.

22.31 Do Exercise 22.29 for the stack-based–augmenting-path algorithm.

○ **22.32** Exhibit a family of networks for which the maximum-augmenting-path algorithm needs $2E \lg M$ augmenting paths.

• **22.33** Can you arrange the edges such that our implementations take time proportional to E to find each path in your example in Exercise 22.32? If necessary, modify your example to achieve this goal. Describe the adjacency-lists representation that is constructed for your example. Explain how the worst case is achieved.

22.34 Run empirical studies to determine the number of augmenting paths and the ratio of the running time to V for each of the four algorithms described in this section, for various networks (see Exercises 22.7–12).

22.35 Develop and test an implementation of the augmenting-path method that uses the source–sink shortest-path heuristic for Euclidean networks of Section 21.5.

22.36 Develop and test an implementation of the augmenting-path method that is based on alternately growing search trees rooted at the source and at the sink (see Exercises 21.35 and 21.75).

• **22.37** The implementation of Program 22.3 stops the graph search when it finds the first augmenting path from source to sink, augments, then starts the search all over again. Alternatively, it could go on with the search and find another path, continuing until all vertices have been marked. Develop and test this second approach.

22.38 Develop and test implementations of the augmenting-path method that use paths that are not simple.

▷ **22.39** Give a sequence of simple augmenting paths that produces a flow with a cycle in the network depicted in Figure 22.11.

○ **22.40** Give an example showing that not all maxflows can be the result of starting with an empty network and augmenting along a sequence of simple paths from source to sink.

22.41 [Gabow] Develop a maxflow implementation that uses $m = \lg M$ phases, where the ith phase solves the maxflow problem using the leading i bits of the capacities. Start with zero flow everywhere; then, after the first phase, initialize the flow by doubling the flow found during the previous phase. Run empirical studies for various networks (see Exercises 22.7–12) to compare this implementation to the basic methods.

• **22.42** Prove that the running time of the algorithm described in Exercise 22.41 is $O(VE \lg M)$.

22.43 Experiment with hybrid methods that use one augmenting-path method at the beginning, then switch to a different augmenting path to finish up (part of your task is to decide what are appropriate criteria for when to switch). Run empirical studies for various networks (see Exercises 22.7–12) to compare these to the basic methods, studying methods that perform better than others in more detail.

22.44 Experiment with hybrid methods that alternate between two or more different augmenting-path methods. Run empirical studies for various networks (see Exercises 22.7–12) to compare these to the basic methods, studying variations that perform better than others in more detail.

○ **22.45** Experiment with hybrid methods that choose randomly among two or more different augmenting-path methods. Run empirical studies for various networks (see Exercises 22.7–12) to compare these to the basic methods, studying variations that perform better than others in more detail.

○ **22.46** Write a flow-network client function that, given an integer c, finds an edge for which increasing the capacity of that edge by c increases the maxflow by the maximum amount. Your function may assume that the client has already computed a maximum flow with MAXFLOW.

•• **22.47** Suppose that you are given a mincut for a network. Does this information make it easier to compute a maxflow? Develop an algorithm that uses a given mincut to speed up substantially the search for maximum-capacity augmenting paths.

• **22.48** Write a client program that does dynamic graphical animations of augmenting-path algorithms. Your program should produce images like Figure 22.17 and the other figures in this section (see Exercises 17.55–59). Test your implementation for the Euclidean networks among Exercises 22.7–12.

22.3 Preflow-Push Maxflow Algorithms

In this section, we consider another approach to solving the maxflow problem. Using a generic method known as the *preflow-push* method, we incrementally move flow along the outgoing edges of vertices that have more inflow than outflow. The preflow-push approach was developed by A. Goldberg and R. E. Tarjan in 1986 on the basis of various earlier algorithms. It is widely used because of its simplicity, flexibility, and efficiency.

As defined in Section 22.1, a flow must satisfy the equilibrium conditions that the outflow from the source is equal to the inflow to the sink and that inflow is equal to the outflow at each of the internal nodes. We refer to such a flow as a *feasible* flow. An augmenting-path algorithm always maintains a feasible flow: It increases the flow along augmenting paths until a maxflow is achieved. By contrast, the preflow-push algorithms that we consider in this section maintain maxflows that are not feasible because some vertices have more inflow than outflow: They push flow through such vertices until a feasible flow is achieved (no such vertices remain).

Definition 22.5 *In a flow network, a* **preflow** *is a set of positive edge flows satisfying the conditions that the flow on each edge is no greater than that edge's capacity and that inflow is no smaller than outflow*

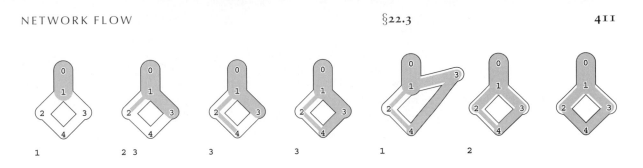

Figure 22.25
Preflow-push example

In the preflow-push algorithm, we maintain a list of the active nodes that have more incoming than outgoing flow (shown below each network). One version of the algorithm is a loop that chooses an active node from the list and pushes flow along outgoing edges until it is no longer active, perhaps creating other active nodes in the process. In this example, we push flow along 0-1, which makes 1 active. Next, we push flow along 1-2 and 1-3, which makes 1 inactive but 2 and 3 both active. Then, we push flow along 2-4, which makes 2 inactive. But 3-4 does not have sufficient capacity for us to push flow along it to make 3 inactive, so we also push flow back along 3-1 to do so, which makes 1 active. Then we can push the flow along 1-2 and then 2-4, which makes all nodes inactive and leaves a maxflow.

*for every internal vertex. An **active** vertex is an internal vertex whose inflow is larger than its outflow (by convention, the source and sink are never active).*

We refer to the difference between an active vertex's inflow and outflow as that vertex's *excess*. To change the set of active vertices, we choose one and *push* its excess along an outgoing edge, or, if there is insufficient capacity to do so, push the excess back along an incoming edge. If the push equalizes the vertex's inflow and outflow, the vertex becomes inactive; the flow pushed to another vertex may activate that vertex. The preflow-push method provides a systematic way to push excess out of active vertices repeatedly so that the process terminates in a maxflow, with no active vertices. We keep active vertices on a generalized queue. As for the augmenting-path method, this decision gives a generic algorithm that encompasses a whole family of more specific algorithms.

Figure 22.25 is a small example that illustrates the basic operations used in preflow-push algorithms, in terms of the metaphor that we have been using, where we imagine that flow can go only down the page. Either we push excess flow out of an active vertex down an outgoing edge or we imagine that the vertex temporarily moves up so we can push excess flow back down an incoming edge.

Figure 22.26 is an example that illustrates why the preflow-push approach might be preferred to the augmenting-paths approach. In this network, any augmenting-path method successively puts a tiny amount of flow through a long path over and over again, slowly filling up the edges on the path until finally the maxflow is reached. By contrast, the preflow-push method fills up the edges on the long path as it traverses that path for the first time, then distributes that flow directly to the sink without traversing the long path again.

As we did in augmenting-path algorithms, we use the residual network (see Definition 22.4) to keep track of the edges that we might push flow through. Every edge in the residual network represents a potential place to push flow. If a residual-network edge is in the same direction as the corresponding edge in the flow network, we increase the flow; if it is in the opposite direction, we decrease the flow. If the increase fills the edge or the decrease empties the edge, the corresponding edge disappears from the residual network. For preflow-push algorithms, we use an additional mechanism to help decide which of the edges in the residual network can help us to eliminate active vertices.

Definition 22.6 *A* **height function** *for a given flow in a flow network is a set of nonnegative vertex weights* $h(0) \ldots h(V-1)$ *such that* $h(t) = 0$ *for the sink* t *and* $h(u) \leq h(v) + 1$ *for every edge* u–v *in the residual network for the flow. An* **eligible edge** *is an edge* u–v *in the residual network with* $h(u) = h(v) + 1$.

A trivial height function, for which there are no eligible edges, is $h(0) = h(1) = \ldots = h(V-1) = 0$. If we set $h(s) = 1$, then any edge that emanates from the source and has flow corresponds to an eligible edge in the residual network.

We define a more interesting height function by assigning to each vertex the latter's shortest-path distance to the sink (its distance to the root in any BFS tree for the reverse of the network rooted at t, as illustrated in Figure 22.27). This height function is valid because $h(t) = 0$, and, for any pair of vertices u and v connected by an edge u–v, any shortest path to t starting with u–v is of length $h(v) + 1$; so the shortest-path length from u to t, or $h(u)$, must be less than or equal to that value. This function plays a special role because it puts each vertex at the maximum possible height. Working backward, we see that t has to be at height 0; the only vertices that could be at height 1 are those with an edge directed to t in the residual network; the only vertices that could be at height 2 are those that have edges directed to vertices that could be at height 1, and so forth.

Property 22.9 *For any flow and associated height function, a vertex's height is no larger than the length of the shortest path from that vertex to the sink in the residual network.*

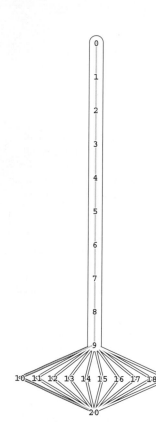

Figure 22.26
**Bad case for the Ford–
   Fulkerson algorithm**

This network represents a family of networks with V vertices for which any augmenting-path algorithm requires V/2 paths of length V/2 (since every augmenting path has to include the long vertical path), for a total running time proportional to V^2. Preflow-push algorithms find maxflows in such networks in linear time.

Proof: For any given vertex u, let d be the shortest-path length from u to t, and let $u = u_1, u_2, \ldots, u_d = t$ be a shortest path. Then

$$h(u) = h(u_1) \leq h(u_2) + 1$$
$$\leq h(u_3) + 2$$
$$\vdots$$
$$\leq h(u_d) + d = h(t) + d = d$$

∎

The intuition behind height functions is the following: When an active node's height is less than the height of the source, it is possible that there is some way to push flow from that node down to the sink; when an active node's height exceeds the height of the source, we know that that node's excess needs to be pushed back to the source. To establish this latter fact, we reorient our view of Property 22.9, where we thought about the length of the shortest path to the sink as an upper bound on the height; instead, we think of the height as a lower bound on the shortest-path length:

Corollary *If a vertex's height is greater than V, then there is no path from that vertex to the sink in the residual network.*

Proof: If there is a path from the vertex to the sink, the implication of Property 22.9 would be that the path's length is greater than V, but that cannot be true because the network has only V vertices. ∎

Now that we understand these basic mechanisms, the generic preflow-push algorithm is simple to describe. We start with any height function and assign zero flow to all edges except those connected to the source, which we fill to capacity. Then, we repeat the following step until no active vertices remain:

> *Choose an active vertex. Push flow through some eligible edge leaving that vertex (if any). If there are no such edges, increment the vertex's height.*

We do not specify what the initial height function is, how to choose the active vertex, how to choose the eligible edge, or how much flow to push. We refer to this generic method as the *edge-based* preflow-push algorithm.

The algorithm depends on the height function to identify eligible edges. We also use the height function both to prove that the algorithm

	0	1	2	3	4	5
h	3	2	2	1	1	0

**Figure 22.27
Initial height function**

The tree at the right is a BFS tree rooted at 5 for the reverse of our sample network (left). The vertex-indexed array h *gives the distance from each vertex to the root and is a valid height function: For every edge* u-v *in the network,* h[u] *is less than or equal to* h[v]+1.

computes a maxflow and to analyze performance. Therefore, it is critical to ensure that the height function remains valid throughout the execution of the algorithm.

Property 22.10 *The edge-based–preflow-push algorithm preserves the validity of the height function.*

Proof: We increment $h(u)$ only if there are no edges u-v with $h(u) = h(v)+1$. That is, $h(u) < h(v)+1$ for all edges u-v before incrementing $h(u)$, so $h(u) \leq h(v) + 1$ afterward. For any incoming edges w-u, incrementing $h(u)$ certainly preserves the inequality $h(w) \leq h(u) + 1$. Incrementing $h(u)$ does not affect inequalities corresponding to any other edge, and we never increment $h(t)$ (or $h(s)$). Together, these observations imply the stated result. ∎

All the excess flow emanates from the source. Informally, the generic preflow-push algorithm tries to push the excess flow to the sink; if it cannot do so, it eventually pushes the excess flow back to the source. It behaves in this manner because nodes with excess always stay connected to the source in the residual network.

Property 22.11 *While the preflow-push algorithm is in execution on a flow network, there exists a (directed) path in that flow network's residual network from each active vertex to the source, and there are no (directed) paths from source to sink in the residual network.*

Proof: By induction. Initially, the only flow is in the edges leaving the source, which are filled to capacity, so the destination vertices of those edges are the only active vertices. Since the edges are filled to capacity, there is an edge in the residual network from each of those vertices to the source and there are no edges in the residual network leaving the source. Thus, the stated property holds for the initial flow.

The source is reachable from every active vertex because the only way to add to the set of active vertices is to push flow from an active vertex down an eligible edge. This operation leaves an edge in the residual network from the receiving vertex back to the active vertex, from which the source is reachable, by the inductive hypothesis.

Initially, no other nodes are reachable from the source in the residual network. The first time that another node u becomes reachable from the source is when flow is pushed back along u-s (thus causing s-u to be added to the residual network). But this can happen only when $h(u)$ is greater than $h(s)$, which can happen only after $h(u)$ has been incremented, because there are no edges in the residual network to vertices with lower height. The same argument shows that all nodes reachable from the source have greater height. But the sink's height is always 0, so it cannot be reachable from the source. ∎

Corollary *During the preflow-push algorithm, vertex heights are always less than $2V$.*

Proof: We need to consider only active vertices, since the height of each inactive vertex is either the same as or 1 greater than it was the last time that the vertex was active. By the same argument as in the proof of Property 22.9, the path from a given active vertex to the source implies that that vertex's height is at most $V - 2$ greater than the height of the source (t cannot be on the path). The height of the source never changes, and it is initially no greater than V. Thus, active vertices are of height at most $2V - 2$, and no vertex has height $2V$ or greater. ∎

The generic preflow-push algorithm is simple to state and implement. Less clear, perhaps, is why it computes a maxflow. The height function is the key to establishing that it does so.

Property 22.12 *The preflow-push algorithm computes a maxflow.*

Proof: First, we have to show that the algorithm terminates. There must come a point where there are no active vertices. Once we push all the excess flow out of a vertex, that vertex cannot become active again until some of that flow is pushed back; and that pushback can happen only if the height of the vertex is increased. If we have a sequence of active vertices of unbounded length, some vertex has to appear an unbounded number of times; and it can do so only if its height grows without bound, contradicting the corollary to Property 22.9.

When there are no active vertices, the flow is feasible. Since, by Property 22.11, there is also no path from source to sink in the residual network, the flow is a maxflow, by the same argument as that in the proof of Property 22.5. ∎

It is possible to refine the proof that the algorithm terminates to give an $O(V^2 E)$ bound on its worst-case running time. We leave the details to exercises (see Exercises 22.66 through 22.67), in favor of the simpler proof in Property 22.13, which applies to a less general version of the algorithm. Specifically, the implementations that we consider are based on the following more specialized instructions for the iteration:

> *Choose an active vertex. Increase the flow along an eligible edge leaving that vertex (filling it if possible), continuing until the vertex becomes inactive or no eligible edges remain. In the latter case, increment the vertex's height.*

That is, once we have chosen a vertex, we push out of it as much flow as possible. If we get to the point that the vertex still has excess flow but no eligible edges remain, we increment the vertex's height. We refer to this generic method as the *vertex-based* preflow-push algorithm. It is a special case of the edge-based generic algorithm, where we keep choosing the same active vertex until it becomes inactive or we have used up all the eligible edges leaving it. The correctness proof in Property 22.12 applies to any implementation of the edge-based generic algorithm, so it immediately implies that the vertex-based algorithm computes a maxflow.

Program 22.5 is an implementation of the vertex-based generic algorithm that uses a generalized queue for the active vertices. It is a direct implementation of the method just described and represents a family of algorithms that differ only in their initial height function (see, for example, Exercise 22.52) and in their generalized-queue ADT implementation. This implementation assumes that the generalized queue disallows duplicate vertices; alternatively, we could add code to Program 22.5 to avoid enqueueing duplicates (see Exercises 22.61 and 22.62).

Perhaps the simplest data structure to use for active vertices is a FIFO queue. Figure 22.28 shows the operation of the algorithm on a sample network. As illustrated in the figure, it is convenient to break up the sequence of active vertices chosen into a sequence of *phases*, where a phase is defined to be the contents of the queue after all the vertices that were on the queue in the previous phase have been processed. Doing so helps us to bound the total running time of the algorithm.

Property 22.13 *The worst-case running time of the FIFO queue implementation of the preflow-push algorithm is proportional to $V^2 E$.*

Proof: We bound the number of phases using a *potential function*. This argument is a simple example of a powerful technique in the

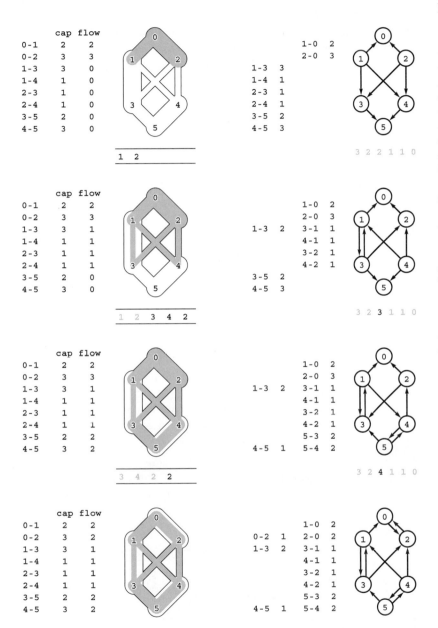

**Figure 22.28
Residual networks (FIFO
preflow-push)**

This figure shows the flow networks (left) and the residual networks (right) for each phase of the FIFO preflow-push algorithm operating on our sample network. Queue contents are shown below the flow networks and distance labels below the residual networks. In the initial phase, we push flow through 0-1 and 0-2, thus making 1 and 2 active. In the second phase, we push flow from these two vertices to 3 and 4, which makes them active and 1 inactive (2 remains active and its distance label is incremented). In the third phase, we push flow through 3 and 4 to 5, which makes them inactive (2 still remains active and its distance label is again incremented). In the fourth phase, 2 is the only active node, and the edge 2-0 is admissible because of the distance-label increments, and one unit of flow is pushed back along 2-0 to complete the computation.

Program 22.5 Preflow-push maxflow implementation

This implementation of the generic vertex-based–preflow-push maxflow algorithm uses a generalized queue that disallows duplicates for active nodes. The wt vector contains each vertex's excess flow and therefore implicitly defines the set of active vertices. By convention, s is initially active but never goes back on the queue and t is never active. The main loop chooses an active vertex v, then pushes flow through each of its eligible edges (adding vertices that receive the flow to the active list, if necessary), until either v becomes inactive or all its edges have been considered. In the latter case, v's height is incremented and it goes back onto the queue.

```
template <class Graph, class Edge> class MAXFLOW
{ const Graph &G;
  int s, t;
  vector<int> h, wt;
  void initheights();
public:
  MAXFLOW(const Graph &G, int s, int t) : G(G),
    s(s), t(t), h(G.V()), wt(G.V(), 0)
  { initheights();
    GQ gQ(G.V());
    gQ.put(s); wt[t] = -(wt[s] = M*G.V());
    while (!gQ.empty())
    { int v = gQ.get();
      typename Graph::adjIterator A(G, v);
      for (Edge* e = A.beg(); !A.end(); e = A.nxt())
        { int w = e->other(v);
          int cap = e->capRto(w);
          int P = cap < wt[v] ? cap : wt[v];
          if (P > 0 && v == s || h[v] == h[w]+1)
            { e->addflowRto(w, P);
              wt[v] -= P; wt[w] += P;
              if ((w != s) && (w != t)) gQ.put(w); }
        }
      if (v != s && v != t && wt[v] > 0)
        { h[v]++; gQ.put(v); }
    }
  }
};
```

analysis of algorithms and data structures that we examine in more detail in Part 8.

Define the quantity ϕ to be 0 if there are no active vertices and to be the maximum height of the active vertices otherwise, then consider the effect of each phase on the value of ϕ. Let $h_0(s)$ be the initial height of the source. At the beginning, $\phi = h_0(s)$; at the end, $\phi = 0$.

First, we note that the number of phases where the height of some vertex increases is no more than $2V^2 - h_0(s)$, since each of the V vertex heights can be increased to a value of at most $2V$, by the corollary to Property 22.11. Since ϕ can increase only if the height of some vertex increases, the number of phases where ϕ increases is no more than $2V^2 - h_0(s)$.

If, however, no vertex's height is incremented during a phase, then ϕ must decrease by at least 1, since the effect of the phase was to push all excess flow from each active vertex to vertices that have smaller height.

Together, these facts imply that the number of phases must be less than $4V^2$: The value of ϕ is $h_0(s)$ at the beginning and can be incremented at most $2V^2 - h_0(s)$ times and therefore can be decremented at most $2V^2$ times. The worst case for each phase is that all vertices are on the queue and all of their edges are examined, leading to the stated bound on the total running time.

This bound is tight. Figure 22.29 illustrates a family of flow networks for which the number of phases used by the preflow-push algorithm is proportional to V^2. ∎

Because our implementations maintain an implicit representation of the residual network, they examine edges leaving a vertex even when those edges are not in the residual network (to test whether or not they are there). It is possible to show that we can reduce the bound in Property 22.13 from V^2E to V^3 for an implementation that eliminates this cost by maintaining an explicit representation of the residual network. Although the theoretical bound is the lowest that we have seen for the maxflow problem, this change may not be worth the trouble, particularly for the sparse graphs that we see in practice (see Exercises 22.63 through 22.65).

Again, these worst-case bounds tend to be pessimistic and thus not necessarily useful for predicting performance on real networks (though the gap is not as excessive as we found for augmenting-path

Figure 22.29
FIFO preflow-push worst case

This network represents a family of networks with V vertices such that the total running time of the preflow-push algorithm is proportional to V^2. It consists of unit-capacity edges emanating from the source (vertex 0) and horizontal edges of capacity $v - 2$ running from left to right towards the sink (vertex 10). In the initial phase of the preflow-push algorithm (top), we push one unit of flow out each edge from the source, making all the vertices active except the source and the sink. In a standard adjacency-lists representation, they appear on the FIFO queue of active vertices in reverse order, as shown below the network. In the second phase (center), we push one unit of flow from 9 to 10, making 9 inactive (temporarily); then we push one unit of flow from 8 to 9, making 8 inactive (temporarily) and making 9 active; then we push one unit of flow from 7 to 8, making 7 inactive (temporarily) and making 8 active; and so forth. Only 1 is left inactive. In the third phase (bottom), we go through a similar process to make 2 inactive, and the same process continues for $V - 2$ phases.

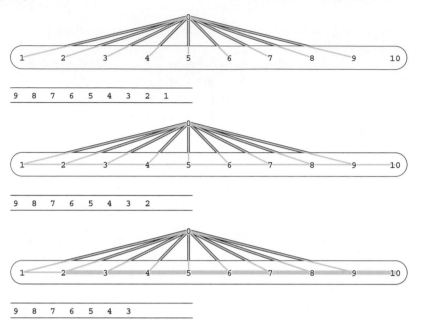

algorithms). For example, the FIFO algorithm finds the flow in the network illustrated in Figure 22.30 in 15 phases, whereas the bound in the proof of Property 22.13 says only that it must do so in fewer than 182.

To improve performance, we might try using a stack, a randomized queue, or any other generalized queue in Program 22.5. One approach that has proved to do well in practice is to implement the generalized queue such that GQget returns the highest active vertex. We refer to this method as the *highest-vertex–preflow-push* maxflow algorithm. We can implement this strategy with a priority queue, although it is also possible to take advantage of the particular properties of heights to implement the generalized-queue operations in constant time. A worst-case time bound of $V^2\sqrt{E}$ (which is $V^{5/2}$ for sparse graphs) has been proved for this algorithm (*see reference section*); as usual, this bound is pessimistic. Many other preflow-push variants have been proposed, several of which reduce the worst-case time bound to be close to VE (*see reference section*).

Table 22.2 shows performance results for preflow-push algorithms corresponding to those for augmenting-path algorithms in Ta-

Figure 22.30
Preflow-push algorithm
(FIFO)

*This sequence illustrates how
the FIFO implementation of the
preflow-push method finds a maximum flow in a sample network. It
proceeds in phases: First it pushes
as much flow as it can from the
source along the edges leaving the
source (top left). Then, it pushes
flow from each of those nodes,
continuing until all nodes are in
equilibrium.*

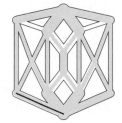

Table 22.2 Empirical study of preflow-push algorithms

This table shows performance parameters (number of vertices expanded and number of adjacency-list nodes touched) for various preflow-push network-flow algorithms for our sample Euclidean neighbor network (with random capacities with maxflow value 286) and with unit capacities (with maxflow value 6). Differences among the methods are minimal for both types of networks. For random capacities, the number of edges examined is about the same as for the random augmenting-path algorithm (see Table 22.1). For unit capacities, the augmenting-path algorithms examine substantially fewer edges for these networks.

	vertices	edges
random capacity 1-50		
shortest	2450	57746
depth-Ærst	2476	58258
random	2363	55470
capacity 1		
shortest	1192	28356
depth-Ærst	1234	29040
random	1390	33018

ble 22.1, for the two network models discussed in Section 22.2. These experiments show much less performance variation for the various preflow-push methods than we observed for augmenting-path methods.

There are many options to explore in developing preflow-push implementations. We have already discussed three major choices:

- Edge-based versus vertex-based generic algorithm
- Generalized queue implementation
- Initial assignment of heights

There are several other possibilities to consider and many options to try for each, leading to a multitude of different algorithms to study (see, for example, Exercises 22.56 through 22.60). The dependence of an algorithm's performance on characteristics of the input network further multiplies the possibilities.

The two generic algorithms that we have discussed (augmenting-path and preflow-push) are among the most important from an extensive research literature on maxflow algorithms. The quest for better maxflow algorithms is still a potentially fruitful area for further research. Researchers are motivated to develop and study new algorithms and implementations by the reality of faster algorithms for practical problems and by the possibility that a simple linear algorithm exists for the maxflow problem. Until one is discovered, we can work confidently with the algorithms and implementations that we have discussed; numerous studies have shown them to be effective for a broad range of practical maxflow problems.

Exercises

▷ **22.49** Describe the operation of the preflow-push algorithm in a network whose capacities are in equilibrium.

22.50 Use the concepts described in this section (height functions, eligible edges, and pushing of flow through edges) to describe augmenting-path maxflow algorithms.

22.51 Show, in the style of Figure 22.28, the flow and residual networks after each phase when you use the FIFO preflow-push algorithm to find a maxflow in the flow network shown in Figure 22.10.

▷ **22.52** Implement the `initheights()` function for Program 22.5, using breadth-first search from the sink.

22.53 Do Exercise 22.51 for the highest-vertex–preflow-push algorithm.

○ **22.54** Modify Program 22.5 to implement the highest-vertex–preflow-push algorithm, by implementing the generalized queue as a priority queue. Run empirical tests so that you can add a line to Table 22.2 for this variant of the algorithm.

22.55 Plot the number of active vertices and the number of vertices and edges in the residual network as the FIFO preflow-push algorithm proceeds, for specific instances of various networks (see Exercises 22.7–12).

○ **22.56** Implement the generic edge-based–preflow-push algorithm, using a generalized queue of eligible edges. Run empirical studies for various networks (see Exercises 22.7–12) to compare these to the basic methods, studying generalized-queue implementations that perform better than others in more detail.

22.57 Modify Program 22.5 to recalculate the vertex heights periodically to be shortest-path lengths to the sink in the residual network.

○ **22.58** Evaluate the idea of pushing excess flow out of vertices by spreading it evenly among the outgoing edges, rather than perhaps filling some and leaving others empty.

22.59 Run empirical tests to determine whether the shortest-paths computation for the initial height function is justified in Program 22.5 by comparing its performance as given for various networks (see Exercises 22.7–12)with its performance when the vertex heights are just initialized to zero.

○ **22.60** Experiment with hybrid methods involving combinations of the ideas above. Run empirical studies for various networks (see Exercises 22.7–12) to compare these to the basic methods, studying variations that perform better than others in more detail.

22.61 Modify the implementation of Program 22.5 such that it explicitly disallows duplicate vertices on the generalized queue. Run empirical tests for various networks (see Exercises 22.7–12) to determine the effect of your modification on actual running times.

22.62 What effect does allowing duplicate vertices on the generalized queue have on the worst-case running-time bound of Property 22.13?

22.63 Modify the implementation of Program 22.5 to maintain an explicit representation of the residual network.

○ **22.64** Sharpen the bound in Property 22.13 to $O(V^3)$ for the implementation of Exercise 22.63. *Hint*: Prove separate bounds on the number of pushes that correspond to deletion of edges in the residual network and on the number of pushes that do not result in full or empty edges.

22.65 Run empirical studies for various networks (see Exercises 22.7–12) to determine the effect of using an explicit representation of the residual network (see Exercise 22.63) on actual running times.

22.66 For the edge-based generic preflow-push algorithm, prove that the number of pushes that correspond to deleting an edge in the residual network is less than $2VE$. Assume that the implementation keeps an explicit representation of the residual network.

• **22.67** For the edge-based generic preflow-push algorithm, prove that the number of pushes that do not correspond to deleting an edge in the residual network is less than $4V^2(V + E)$. *Hint*: Use the sum of the heights of the active vertices as a potential function.

• **22.68** Run empirical studies to determine the actual number of edges examined and the ratio of the running time to V for several versions of the preflow-push algorithm for various networks (see Exercises 22.7–12). Consider various algorithms described in the text and in the previous exercises, and concentrate on those that perform the best on huge sparse networks. Compare your results with your result from Exercise 22.34.

• **22.69** Write a client program that does dynamic graphical animations of preflow-push algorithms. Your program should produce images like Figure 22.30 and the other figures in this section (see Exercise 22.48). Test your implementation for the Euclidean networks among Exercises 22.7–12.

22.4 Maxflow Reductions

In this section, we consider a number of reductions to the maxflow problem in order to demonstrate that the maxflow algorithms of Sections 22.2 and 22.3 are important in a broad context. We can remove various restrictions on the network and solve other flow problems; we can solve other network- and graph-processing problems; and we can solve problems that are not network problems at all. This section is devoted to examples of such uses—to establish maxflow as a general problem-solving model.

We also consider relationships between the maxflow problem and problems that are more difficult so as to set the context for considering those problems later on. In particular, we note that the maxflow problem is a special case of the mincost-flow problem that is the subject of Sections 22.5 and 22.6, and we describe how to formulate maxflow problems as LP problems, which we will address in Part 8. Mincost flow and LP represent problem-solving models that are more general than the maxflow model. Although we normally can solve maxflow problems more easily with the specialized algorithms of Sections 22.2 and 22.3 than with algorithms that solve these more general problems, it is important to be cognizant of the relationships among problem-solving models as we progress to more powerful ones.

We use the term *standard maxflow problem* to refer to the version of the problem that we have been considering (maxflow in edge-capacitated *st*-networks). This usage is solely for easy reference in this section. Indeed, we begin by considering reductions that show the restrictions in the standard problem to be essentially immaterial, because several other flow problems reduce to or are equivalent to the standard problem. We could adopt any of the equivalent problems as the "standard" problem. A simple example of such a problem, already noted as a consequence of Property 22.1, is that of finding a circulation in a network that maximizes the flow in a specified edge. Next, we consider other ways to pose the problem, in each case noting its relationship to the standard problem.

Maxflow in general networks Find the flow in a network that maximizes the total outflow from its sources (and therefore the total inflow to its sinks). By convention, define the flow to be zero if there are no sources or no sinks.

	cap
0-3	2
0-6	3
1-3	3
1-4	1
2-4	1
2-5	1
3-5	2
4-6	3

	cap
0-3	2
0-6	3
1-3	3
1-4	1
2-4	1
2-5	1
3-5	2
4-6	3
7-0	5
7-1	4
7-2	2
5-8	3
6-8	6

Figure 22.31
Reduction from multiple sources and sinks

The network at the top has three sources (0, 1, and 2) and two sinks (5 and 6). To find a flow that maximizes the total flow out of the sources and into the sinks, we find a maxflow in the st-network illustrated at the bottom. This network is a copy of the original network, with the addition of a new source 7 and a new sink 8. There is an edge from 7 to each original-network source with capacity equal to the sum of the capacities of that source's outgoing edges, and an edge from each original-network sink to 8 with capacity equal to the sum of the capacities of that sink's incoming edges.

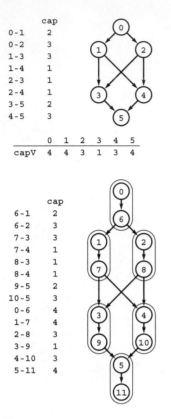

	cap
0-1	2
0-2	3
1-3	3
1-4	1
2-3	1
2-4	1
3-5	2
4-5	3

	0	1	2	3	4	5
capV	4	4	3	1	3	4

	cap
6-1	2
6-2	3
7-3	3
7-4	1
8-3	1
8-4	1
9-5	2
10-5	3
0-6	4
1-7	4
2-8	3
3-9	1
4-10	3
5-11	4

Figure 22.32
Removing vertex capacities

To solve the problem of finding a maxflow in the network at the top such that flow through each vertex does not exceed the capacity bound given in the vertex-indexed array capV, *we build the standard network at the bottom: Associate a new vertex u* (where u* denotes u+V) with each vertex u, add an edge u-u* whose capacity is the capacity of u, and include an edge u*-v for each edge u-v. Each u-u* pair is encircled in the diagram. Any flow in the bottom network corresponds directly to a flow in the top network that satisfies the vertex-capacity constraints.*

Property 22.14 *The maxflow problem for general networks is equivalent to the maxflow problem for st-networks.*

Proof: A maxflow algorithm for general networks will clearly work for *st*-networks, so we just need to establish that the general problem reduces to the *st*-network problem. To do so, first find the sources and sinks (using, for example, the method that we used to initialize the queue in Program 19.8), and return zero if there are none of either. Then, add a dummy source vertex s and edges from s to each source in the network (with each such edge's capacity set to that edge's destination vertex's outflow) and a dummy sink vertex t and edges from each sink in the network to t (with each such edge's capacity set to that edge's source vertex's inflow) Figure 22.31 illustrates this reduction. Any maxflow in the *st*-network corresponds directly to a maxflow in the original network. ∎

Vertex-capacity constraints Given a flow network, find a maxflow satisfying additional constraints specifying that the flow through each vertex must not exceed some fixed capacity.

Property 22.15 *The maxflow problem for flow networks with capacity constraints on vertices is equivalent to the standard maxflow problem.*

Proof: Again, we could use any algorithm that solves the capacity-constraint problem to solve a standard problem (by setting capacity constraints at each vertex to be larger than its inflow or outflow), so we need only to show a reduction to the standard problem. Given a flow network with capacity constraints, construct a standard flow network with two vertices u and u* corresponding to each original vertex u, with all incoming edges to the original vertex going to u, all outgoing edges coming from u*, and an edge u-u* of capacity equal to the vertex capacity. This construction is illustrated in Figure 22.32. The flows in the edges of the form u*-v in any maxflow for the transformed network give a maxflow for the original network that must satisfy the vertex-capacity constraints because of the edges of the form u-u*. ∎

Allowing multiple sinks and sources or adding capacity constraints seem to generalize the maxflow problem; the interest of Properties 22.14 and 22.15 is that these problems are actually no more difficult than the standard problem. Next, we consider a version of the problem that might seem to be easier to solve.

Acyclic networks   Find a maxflow in an acyclic network. Does the presence of cycles in a flow network make more difficult the task of computing a maxflow?

We have seen many examples of digraph-processing problems that are much more difficult to solve in the presence of cycles. Perhaps the most prominent example is the shortest-paths problem in weighted digraphs with edge weights that could be negative (see Section 21.7), which is simple to solve in linear time if there are no cycles but NP-complete if cycles are allowed. But the maxflow problem, remarkably, is no easier for acyclic networks.

Property 22.16   *The maxflow problem for acyclic networks is equivalent to the standard maxflow problem.*

Proof: Again, we need only to show that the standard problem reduces to the acyclic problem. Given any network with V vertices and E edges, we construct a network with $2V + 2$ vertices and $E + 3V$ edges that is not just acyclic but has a simple structure.

Let u* denote u+V, and build a bipartite digraph consisting of two vertices u and u* corresponding to each vertex u in the original network and one edge u-v* corresponding to each edge u-v in the original network with the same capacity. Now, add to the bipartite digraph a source s and a sink t and, for each vertex u in the original graph, an edge s-u and an edge u*-t, both of capacity equal to the sum of the capacities of u's outgoing edges in the original network. Also, let X be the sum of the capacities of the edges in the original network, and add edges from u to u*, with capacity $X + 1$. This construction is illustrated in Figure 22.33.

To show that any maxflow in the original network corresponds to a maxflow in the transformed network, we consider cuts rather than flows. Given any st-cut of size c in the original network, we show how to construct an st-cut of size $c + X$ in the transformed network; and, given any minimal st-cut of size $c + X$ in the transformed network, we show how to construct an st-cut of size c in the original network. Thus, given a minimal cut in the transformed network, the corresponding cut in the original network is minimal. Moreover, our construction gives a flow whose value is equal to the minimal-cut capacity, so it is a maxflow.

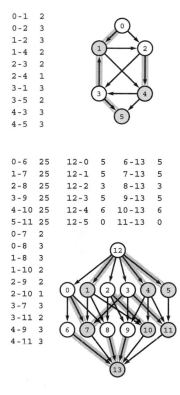

0-1	2
0-2	3
1-2	3
1-4	2
2-3	2
2-4	1
3-1	3
3-5	2
4-3	3
4-5	3

0-6	25	12-0	5	6-13	5
1-7	25	12-1	5	7-13	5
2-8	25	12-2	3	8-13	3
3-9	25	12-3	5	9-13	5
4-10	25	12-4	6	10-13	6
5-11	25	12-5	0	11-13	0
0-7	2				
0-8	3				
1-8	3				
1-10	2				
2-9	2				
2-10	1				
3-7	3				
3-11	2				
4-9	3				
4-11	3				

Figure 22.33
Reduction to acyclic network

Each vertex u *in the top network corresponds to two vertices* u *and* u* *(where* u* *denotes* u+V*) in the bottom network and each edge* u-v *in the top network corresponds to an edge* u-v* *in the bottom network. Additionally, the bottom network has uncapacitated edges* u-u*, *a source* s *with an edge to each unstarred vertex, and a sink* t *with an edge from each starred vertex. The shaded and unshaded vertices (and edges which connect shaded to unshaded) illustrate the direct relationship among cuts in the two networks (*see text*).*

Given any cut of the original network that separates the source from the sink, let S be the source's vertex set and T the sink's vertex set. Construct a cut of the transformed network by putting vertices in S in a set with s and vertices in T in a set with t and putting u and u* on the same side of the cut for all u, as illustrated in Figure 22.33. For every u, either s–u or P|u*-t| is in the cut set, and u–v* is in the cut set if and only if u–v is in the cut set of the original network; so the total capacity of the cut is equal to the capacity of the cut in the original network plus X.

Given any minimal st-cut of the transformed network, let S^* be s's vertex set and T^* t's vertex set. Our goal is to construct a cut of the same capacity with u and u* both in the same cut vertex set for all u so that the correspondence of the previous paragraph gives a cut in the original network, completing the proof. First, if u is in S^* and u* in T^*, then u–u* must be a crossing edge, which is a contradiction: u–u* cannot be in any minimal cut, because a cut consisting of all the edges corresponding to the edges in the original graph is of lower cost. Second, if u is in T^* and u* is in S^*, then s–u must be in the cut, because that is the only edge connecting s to u. But we can create a cut of equal cost by substituting all the edges directed out of u for s–u, moving u to S^*.

Given any flow in the transformed network of value $c + X$, we simply assign the same flow value to each corresponding edge in the original network to get a flow with value c. The cut transformation at the end of the previous paragraph does not affect this assignment, because it manipulates edges with flow value zero. ■

The result of the reduction not only is an acyclic network, but also has a simple bipartite structure. The reduction says that we could, if we wished, adopt these simpler networks, rather than general networks, as our standard. It would seem that perhaps this special structure would lead to faster maxflow algorithms. But the reduction shows that we could use any algorithm that we found for these special acyclic networks to solve maxflow problems in general networks, at only modest extra cost. Indeed, the classical maxflow algorithms exploit the flexibility of the general network model: Both the augmenting-path and preflow-push approaches that we have considered use the concept of a residual network, which involves introducing cycles into the network.

When we have a maxflow problem for an acyclic network, we typically use the standard algorithm for general networks to solve it.

The construction of Property 22.16 is elaborate, and it illustrates that reduction proofs can require care, if not ingenuity. Such proofs are important because not all versions of the maxflow problem are equivalent to the standard problem, and we need to know the extent of the applicability of our algorithms. Researchers continue to explore this topic because reductions relating various natural problems have not yet been established, as illustrated by the following example.

Maxflow in undirected networks   An undirected flow network is a weighted graph with integer edge weights that we interpret to be capacities. A circulation in such a network is an assignment of weights and directions to the edges satisfying the conditions that the flow on each edge is no greater than that edge's capacity and that the total flow into each vertex is equal to the total flow out of that vertex. The undirected maxflow problem is to find a circulation that maximizes the flow in specified direction in a specified edge (that is, from some vertex s to some other vertex t). This problem perhaps corresponds more naturally than the standard problem to our liquid-flowing-through-pipes model: It corresponds to allowing liquid to flow through a pipe in either direction.

Property 22.17   *The maxflow problem for undirected st-networks reduces to the maxflow problem for st-networks.*

Proof: Given an undirected network, construct a directed network with the same vertices and two directed edges corresponding to each edge, one in each direction, both with the capacity of the undirected edge. Any flow in the original network certainly corresponds to a flow with the same value in the transformed network. The converse is also true: If u-v has flow f and v-u flow g in the undirected network, then we can put the flow $f - g$ in u-v in the directed network if $f \geq g$; $g - f$ in v-u otherwise. Thus, any maxflow in the directed network is a maxflow in the undirected network: The construction gives a flow, and any flow with a higher value in the directed network would correspond to some flow with a higher value in the undirected network; but no such flow exists. ∎

This proof does not establish that the problem for undirected networks is equivalent to the standard problem. That is, it leaves open

	cap
0-1	2
0-2	3
1-3	3
1-4	1
2-3	1
2-4	1
3-5	2
4-5	3

	cap
0-1	2
1-0	2
0-2	3
2-0	3
1-3	3
3-1	3
1-4	1
4-1	1
2-3	1
3-2	1
2-4	1
4-2	1
3-5	2
5-3	2
4-5	3
5-4	3

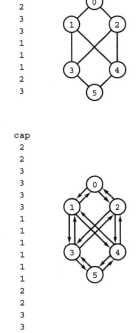

Figure 22.34
Reduction from undirected networks

To solve a maxflow problem in an undirected network, we can consider it to be a directed network with edges in each direction. Note that the residual network for such a network has four edges corresponding to each edge in the undirected network.

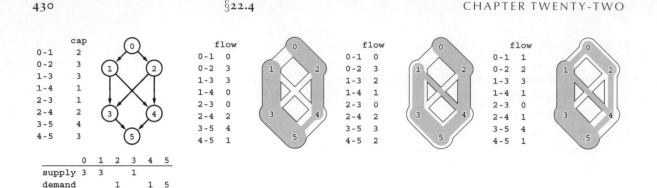

Figure 22.35
Feasible flow

In a feasible-flow problem, we specify supply and demand constraints at the vertices in addition to the capacity constraints on the edges. We seek any flow for which outflow equals supply plus inflow at supply vertices and inflow equals outflow plus demand at demand vertices. Three solutions to the feasible-flow problem at left are shown on the right.

the possibility that finding maxflows in undirected networks is easier than finding maxflows in standard networks (see Exercise 22.81).

In summary, we can handle networks with multiple sinks and sources, undirected networks, networks with capacity constraints on vertices, and many other types of networks (see, for example, Exercise 22.79) with the maxflow algorithms for *st*-networks in the previous two sections. In fact, Property 22.16 says that we could solve all these problems with even an algorithm that works for only acyclic networks.

Next, we consider a problem that is not an explicit maxflow problem but that we can reduce to the maxflow problem and therefore solve with maxflow algorithms. It is one way to formalize a basic version of the merchandise-distribution problem described at the beginning of this chapter.

Feasible flow Suppose that a weight is assigned to each vertex in a flow network, and is to be interpreted as supply (if positive) or demand (if negative), with the sum of the vertex weights equal to zero. Define a flow to be *feasible* if the difference between each vertex's outflow and inflow is equal to that vertex's weight (supply if positive and demand if negative). Given such a network, determine whether or not a feasible flow exists. Figure 22.35 illustrates a feasible-flow problem.

Supply vertices correspond to warehouses in the merchandise-distribution problem; demand vertices correspond to retail outlets; and edges correspond to roads on the trucking routes. The feasible-flow problem answers the basic question of whether it is possible to find a way to ship the goods such that supply meets demand everywhere.

Program 22.6 Feasible flow via reduction to maxflow

This class solves the feasible-flow problem by reduction to maxflow, using the construction illustrated in Figure 22.36. The constructor takes as argument a network and a vertex-indexed vector sd such that sd[i] represents, if it is positive, the supply at vertex i and, if it is negative, the demand at vertex i.

As indicated in Figure 22.36, the constructor makes a new graph with the same edges but with two extra vertices s and t, with edges from s to the supply nodes and from the demand nodes to t Then it finds a maxflow and checks whether all the extra edges are filled to capacity.

```
#include "MAXFLOW.cc"
template <class Graph, class Edge> class FEASIBLE
{ const Graph &G;
  void freeedges(const Graph &F, int v)
   { typename Graph::adjIterator A(F, v);
     for (EDGE* e = A.beg(); !A.end(); e = A.nxt())
       delete e;
   }
public:
  FEASIBLE(const Graph &G, vector<int> sd) : G(G)
  {
    Graph F(G.V()+2);
    for (int v = 0; v < G.V(); v++)
    {
      typename Graph::adjIterator A(G, v);
      for (EDGE* e = A.beg(); !A.end(); e = A.nxt())
        F.insert(e);
    }
    int s = G.V(), t = G.V()+1;
    for (int i = 0; i < G.V(); i++)
      if (sd[i] >= 0)
        F.insert(new EDGE(s, i, sd[i]));
      else
        F.insert(new EDGE(i, t, -sd[i]));
    MAXFLOW<Graph, Edge>(F, s, t);
    freeedges(F, s); freeedges(F, t);
  }
};
```

Property 22.18   *The feasible-flow problem reduces to the maxflow problem.*

Proof: Given a feasible-flow problem, construct a network with the same vertices and edges but with no weights on the vertices. Instead, add a source vertex s that has an edge to each supply vertex with weight equal to that vertex's supply and a sink vertex t that has an edge from each demand vertex with weight equal to the negation of that vertex's demand (so that the edge weight is positive). Solve the maxflow problem on this network. The original network has a feasible flow if and only if all the edges out of the source and all the edges into the sink are filled to capacity in this flow. Figure 22.36 illustrates an example of this reduction. ∎

Developing classes that implement reductions of the type that we have been considering can be a challenging software-engineering task, primarily because the objects that we are manipulating are represented with complicated data structures. To reduce another problem to a standard maxflow problem, should we create a new network? Some of the problems require extra data, such as vertex capacities or supply and demand, so creating a standard network without these data might be justified. Our use of edge pointers plays a critical role here: If we copy a network's edges and then compute a maxflow, what are we to do with the result? Transferring the computed flow (a weight on each edge) from one network to another when both are represented with adjacency lists is not a trivial computation. With edge pointers, the new network has copies of pointers, not edges, so we can transfer flow assignments right through to the client's network. Program 22.6 is an implementation that illustrates some of these considerations in a class for solving feasible-flow problems using the reduction of Property 22.16.

A canonical example of a flow problem that we cannot handle with the maxflow model, and that is the subject of Sections 22.5 and 22.6, is an extension of the feasible-flow problem. We add a second set of edge weights that we interpret as costs, define flow costs in terms of these weights, and ask for a feasible flow of minimal cost. This model formalizes the general merchandise-distribution problem. We are interested not just in whether it is possible to move the goods but also in what is the lowest-cost way to move them.

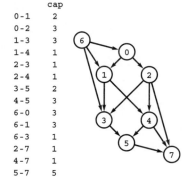

```
      cap
0-1    2
0-2    3
1-3    3
1-4    1
2-3    1
2-4    1
3-5    2
4-5    3
6-0    3
6-1    3
6-3    1
2-7    1
4-7    1
5-7    5
```

Figure 22.36
Reduction from feasible flow

This network is a standard network constructed from the feasible-flow problem in Figure 22.35 by adding edges from a new source vertex to the supply vertices (each with capacity equal to the amount of the supply) and edges to a new sink vertex from the demand vertices (each with capacity equal to the amount of the demand). The network in Figure 22.35 has a feasible flow if and only if this network has a flow (a maxflow) that fills all the edges from the sink and all the edges to the source.

All the problems that we have considered so far in this section have the same basic goal (computing a flow in a flow network), so it is perhaps not surprising that we can handle them with a flow-network problem-solving model. As we saw with the maxflow–mincut theorem, we can use maxflow algorithms to solve graph-processing problems that seem to have little to do with flows. We now turn to examples of this kind.

Maximum-cardinality bipartite matching Given a bipartite graph, find a set of edges of maximum cardinality such that each vertex is connected to at most one other vertex.

For brevity, we refer to this problem simply as the *bipartite-matching* problem except in contexts where we need to distinguish it from similar problems. It formalizes the job-placement problem discussed at the beginning of this chapter. Vertices correspond to individuals and employers; edges correspond to a "mutual interest in the job" relation. A solution to the bipartite-matching problem maximizes total employment. Figure 22.37 illustrates the bipartite graph that models the example problem in Figure 22.3.

It is an instructive exercise to think about finding a direct solution to the bipartite-matching problem, without using the graph model. For example, the problem amounts to the following combinatorial puzzle: "Find the largest subset of a set of pairs of integers (drawn from disjoint sets) with the property that no two pairs have the same integer." The example depicted in Figure 22.37 corresponds to solving this puzzle on the pairs 0-6, 0-7, 0-8, 1-6, and so forth. The problem seems straightforward at first, but, as was true of the Hamilton-path problem that we considered in Section 17.7 (and many other problems), a naive approach that chooses pairs in some systematic way until finding a contradiction might require exponential time. That is, there are far too many subsets of the pairs for us to try all possibilities; a solution to the problem must be clever enough to examine only a few of them. Solving specific matching puzzles like the one just given or developing algorithms that can solve efficiently any such puzzle are nontrivial tasks that help to demonstrate the power and utility of the network-flow model, which provides a reasonable way to do bipartite matching.

Property 22.19 *The bipartite-matching problem reduces to the maxflow problem.*

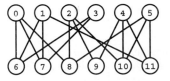

**Figure 22.37
Bipartite matching**

This instance of the bipartite-matching problem formalizes the job-placement example depicted in Figure 22.3. Finding the best way to match the students to the jobs in that example is equivalent to finding the maximum number of vertex-disjoint edges in this bipartite graph.

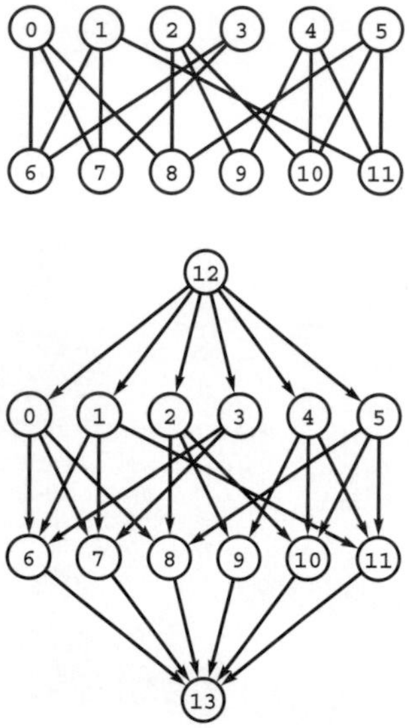

Figure 22.38
Reduction from bipartite matching

To find a maximum matching in a bipartite graph (top), we construct an st-network (bottom) by directing all the edges from the top row to the bottom row, adding a new source with edges to each vertex on the top row, adding a new sink with edges to each vertex on the bottom row, and assigning capacity 1 to all edges. In any flow, at most one outgoing edge from each vertex on the top row can be filled and at most one incoming edge to each vertex on the bottom row can be filled, so a solution to the maxflow problem on this network gives a maximum matching for the bipartite graph.

Proof: Given a bipartite-matching problem, construct an instance of the maxflow problem by directing all edges from one set to the other, adding a source vertex with edges directed to all the members of one set in the bipartite graph, and adding a sink vertex with edge directed from all the members of the other set. To make the resulting digraph a network, assign each edge capacity 1. Figure 22.38 illustrates this construction.

Now, any solution to the maxflow problem for this network provides a solution to the corresponding bipartite-matching problem. The matching corresponds exactly to those edges between vertices in the two sets that are filled to capacity by the maxflow algorithm. First, the network flow always gives a legal matching: Since each vertex has an edge of capacity one either coming in (from the sink) or going out (to the source), at most one unit of flow can go through each vertex, implying in turn that each vertex will be included at most once in the matching. Second, no matching can have more edges, since any such matching would lead directly to a better flow than that produced by the maxflow algorithm. ∎

For example, in Figure 22.38, an augmenting-path maxflow algorithm might use the paths s-0-6-t, s-1-7-t, s-2-8-t, s-4-9-t, s-5-10-t, and s-3-6-0-7-1-11-t to compute the matching 0-7, 1-11, 2-8, 3-6, 4-9, and 5-10. Thus, there is a way to match all the students to jobs in Figure 22.3.

Program 22.7 is a client program that reads a bipartite-matching problem from standard input and uses the reduction described in this proof to solve it. What is the running time of this program for huge networks? Certainly, the running time depends on the maxflow algorithm and implementation that we use. Also, we need to take into account that the networks that we build have a special structure (unit-capacity bipartite flow networks)—not only do the running times of the various maxflow algorithms that we have considered not necessarily approach their worst-case bounds, but also we can substantially reduce the bounds. For example, the first bound that we considered, for the generic augmenting-path algorithm, provides a quick answer.

Corollary *The time required to find a maximum-cardinality matching in a bipartite graph is $O(VE)$.*

Proof: Immediate from Property 22.6. ∎

Program 22.7 Bipartite matching via reduction to maxflow

This client reads a bipartite matching problem with $V + V$ vertices and E edges from standard input, then constructs a flow network corresponding to the bipartite matching problem, finds the maximum flow in the network, and uses the solution to print a maximum bipartite matching.

```
#include "GRAPHbasic.cc"
#include "MAXFLOW.cc"
int main(int argc, char *argv[])
{ int s, t, N = atoi(argv[1]);
  GRAPH<EDGE> G(2*N+2);
  for (int i = 0; i < N; i++)
    G.insert(new EDGE(2*N, i, 1));
  while (cin >> s >> t)
    G.insert(new EDGE(s, t, 1));
  for (int i = N; i < 2*N; i++)
    G.insert(new EDGE(i, 2*N+1, 1));
  MAXFLOW<GRAPH<EDGE>, EDGE>(G, 2*N, 2*N+1);
  for (int i = 0; i < N; i++)
    {
      GRAPH<EDGE>::adjIterator A(G, i);
      for (EDGE* e = A.beg(); !A.end(); e = A.nxt())
        if (e->flow() == 1 &&  e->from(i))
        cout << e->v() << "-" << e->w() << endl;
    }

}
```

The operation of augmenting-path algorithms on unit-capacity bipartite networks is simple to describe. Each augmenting path fills one edge from the source and one edge into the sink. These edges are never used as back edges, so there are at most V augmenting paths. The VE upper bound holds for any algorithm that finds augmenting paths in time proportional to E.

Table 22.3 shows performance results for solving random bipartite-matching problems using various augmenting-path algorithms. It is clear from this table that actual running times for this problem are closer to the VE worst case than to the optimal (linear)

Table 22.3 Empirical study for bipartite matching

This table shows performance parameters (number of vertices expanded and number of adjacency-list nodes touched) when various augmenting-path maxflow algorithms are used to compute a maximum bipartite matching for graphs with 2000 pairs of vertices and 500 edges (top) and 4000 edges (bottom). For this problem, depth-first search is the most effective method.

	vertices	edges
500 edges, match cardinality 347		
shortest	1071	945599
maximum capacity	1067	868407
depth-Ærst	1073	477601
random	1073	644070
4000 edges, match cardinality 971		
shortest	3483	8280585
maximum capacity	6857	6573560
depth-Ærst	34109	1266146
random	3569	4310656

---

time. It is possible, with judicious choice and tuning of the maxflow implementation, to speed up this method by a factor of $\sqrt{V}$ (see Exercises 22.91 and 22.92).

This problem is representative of a situation that we face more frequently as we examine new problems and more general problem-solving models, demonstrating the effectiveness of reduction as a practical problem-solving tool. If we can find a reduction to a known general model such as the maxflow problem, we generally view that as a major step toward developing a practical solution, because it at least indicates not only that the problem is tractable, but also that we have numerous efficient algorithms for solving the problem. In many situations, it is reasonable to use an existing maxflow class to solve the problem and move on to the next problem. If performance remains a critical issue, we can study the relative performance of various maxflow algorithms or implementations, or we can use their behavior as the starting point to develop a better, special-purpose algorithm.

The general problem-solving model provides both an upper bound that we can choose either to live with or to strive to improve, and a host of implementations that have proved effective on a variety of other problems.

Next, we discuss problems relating to connectivity in graphs. Before considering the use of maxflow algorithms to solve connectivity problems, we examine the use of the maxflow–mincut theorem to take care of a piece of unfinished business from Chapter 18: The proofs of the basic theorems relating to paths and cuts in undirected graphs. These proofs are further testimony to the fundamental importance of the maxflow–mincut theorem.

Property 22.20 (Menger's Theorem) *The minimum number of edges whose removal disconnects two vertices in a digraph is equal to the maximum number of edge-disjoint paths between the two vertices.*

Proof: Given a digraph, define a flow network with the same vertices and edges with all edge capacities defined to be 1. By Property 22.2, we can represent any st-flow as a set of edge-disjoint paths from s to t, with the number of such paths equal to the value of the flow. The capacity of any st-cut is equal to that cut's cardinality. Given these facts, the maxflow–mincut theorem implies the stated result. ■

The corresponding results for undirected graphs, and for vertex connectivity for digraphs and for undirected graphs, involve reductions similar to those considered here and are left for exercises (see Exercises 22.94 through 22.96).

Now we turn to algorithmic implications of the direct connection between flows and connectivity that is established by the maxflow–mincut theorem. Property 22.5 is perhaps the most important algorithmic implication (the mincut problem reduces to the maxflow problem), but the converse is *not* known to be true (see Exercise 22.47). Intuitively, it seems as though knowing a mincut should make easier the task of finding a maxflow, but no one has been able to demonstrate how. This basic example highlights the need to proceed with care when working with reductions among problems.

Still, we can also use maxflow algorithms to handle numerous connectivity problems. For example, they help solve the first nontrivial graph-processing problems that we encountered, in Chapter 18.

Edge connectivity   What is the minimum number of edges that need to be removed to separate a given graph into two pieces? Find a set of edges of minimal cardinality that does this separation.

Vertex connectivity   What is the minimum number of vertices that need to be removed to separate a given graph into two pieces? Find a set of vertices of minimal cardinality that does this separation.

These problems also are relevant for digraphs, so there are a total of four problems to consider. As with Menger's theorem, we consider one of them in detail (edge connectivity in undirected graphs) and leave the others for exercises.

Property 22.21   *The time required to determine the edge connectivity of an undirected graph is $O(E^2)$.*

Proof: We can compute the minimum size of any cut that separates two given vertices by computing the maxflow in the st-network formed from the graph by assigning unit capacity to each edge. The edge connectivity is equal to the minimum of these values over all pairs of vertices.

We do not need to do the computation for all pairs of vertices, however. Let s* be a vertex of minimal degree in the graph. Note that the degree of s* can be no greater than $2E/V$. Consider any minimum cut of the graph. By definition, the number of edges in the cut set is equal to the graph's edge connectivity. The vertex s* appears in one of the cut's vertex sets, and the other set must have some vertex t, so the size of any minimal cut separating s* and t must be equal to the graph's edge connectivity. Therefore, if we solve V-1 maxflow problems (using s* as the source and each other vertex as the sink), the minimum flow value found is the edge connectivity of the network.

Now, any augmenting-path maxflow algorithm with s* as the source uses at most $2E/V$ paths; so, if we use any method that takes at most E steps to find an augmenting path, we have a total of at most $(V - 1)(2E/V)E$ steps to find the edge connectivity and that implies the stated result. ∎

This method, unlike all the other examples of this section, is not a direct reduction of one problem to another, but it does give a practical algorithm for computing edge connectivity. Again, with a careful maxflow implementation tuned to this specific problem, we can improve performance—it is possible to solve the problem in time proportional to VE (*see reference section*). The proof of Property 22.21 is an example of the more general concept of *efficient* (polynomial-time) reductions that we first encountered in Section 21.7 and that plays an essential role in the theory of algorithms discussed in Part 8. Such a reduction both proves the problem to be tractable and provides an algorithm for solving it—significant first steps in coping with a new combinatorial problem.

We conclude this section by considering a strictly mathematical formulation of the maxflow problem, using linear programming (LP) (see Section 21.6). This exercise is useful because it helps us to see relationships to other problems that can be so formulated.

The formulation is straightforward: We consider a system of inequalities that involve one variable corresponding to each edge, two inequalities corresponding to each edge, and one equation corresponding to each vertex. The value of the variable is the edge flow, the inequalities specify that the edge flow must be between 0 and the edge's capacity, and the equations specify that the total flow on the edges that go into each vertex must be equal to the total flow on the edges that go out of that vertex.

Figure 22.39 illustrates an example of this construction. Any maxflow problem can be cast as a LP problem in this way. LP is a versatile approach to solving combinatorial problems, and a great number of the problems that we study can be formulated as linear programs. The fact that maxflow problems are easier to solve than LP problems may be explained by the fact that the constraints in the LP formulation of maxflow problems have a specific structure not necessarily found in all LP problems.

Even though the LP problem is much more difficult in general than are specific problems such as the maxflow problem, there are powerful algorithms that can solve LP problems efficiently. The worst-case running time of these algorithms certainly exceeds the worst-case running of the specific algorithms that we have been considering, but an immense amount of practical experience over the past several decades has shown them to be effective for solving problems of the type that arise in practice.

The construction illustrated in Figure 22.39 indicates a proof that the maxflow problem reduces to the LP problem, unless we insist

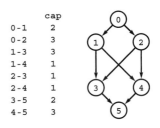

	cap
0-1	2
0-2	3
1-3	3
1-4	1
2-3	1
2-4	1
3-5	2
4-5	3

Maximize x_{50}
subject to the constraints

$$x_{01} \leq 2$$
$$x_{02} \leq 3$$
$$x_{13} \leq 3$$
$$x_{14} \leq 1$$
$$x_{23} \leq 1$$
$$x_{24} \leq 1$$
$$x_{35} \leq 2$$
$$x_{45} \leq 3$$
$$x_{50} = x_{01} + x_{02}$$
$$x_{01} = x_{13} + x_{14}$$
$$x_{02} = x_{23} + x_{24}$$
$$x_{13} + x_{23} = x_{35}$$
$$x_{14} + x_{24} = x_{45}$$
$$x_{35} + x_{45} = x_{50}$$

Figure 22.39
LP formulation of a maxflow problem

This linear program is equivalent to the maxflow problem for the sample network of Figure 22.5. There is one inequality for each edge (which specifies that flow cannot exceed capacity) and one equality for each vertex (which specifies that flow in must equal flow out). We use a dummy edge from sink to source to capture the flow in the network, as described in the discussion following Property 22.2.

that flow values be integers. When we examine LP in detail in Part 8, we describe a way to overcome the difficulty that the LP formulation does not carry the constraint that the results have integer values.

This context gives us a precise mathematical framework that we can use to address ever more general problems and to create ever more powerful algorithms to solve those problems. The maxflow problem is easy to solve and also is versatile in its own right, as indicated by the examples in this section. Next, we examine a harder problem (still easier than LP) that encompasses a still-wider class of practical problems. We discuss ramifications of building solutions to these increasingly general problem-solving models at the end of this chapter, setting the stage for a full treatment in Part 8.

Exercises

▷ **22.70** Define a class for finding a circulation with maximal flow in a specified edge. Provide an implementation that uses MAXFLOW.

22.71 Define a class for finding a maxflow in a network with no constraint on the number of sources or sinks. Provide an implementation that uses MAXFLOW.

22.72 Define a class for finding a maxflow in an undirected network. Provide an implementation that uses MAXFLOW.

22.73 Define a class for finding a maxflow in a network with capacity constraints on vertices. Provide an implementation that uses MAXFLOW.

▷ **22.74** Develop a class for feasible-flow problems that includes member functions allowing clients to set supply–demand values and to check that flow values are properly related at each vertex.

22.75 Do Exercise 22.18 for the case that each distribution point has limited capacity (that is, there is a limit on the amount of goods that can be stored there at any given time).

▷ **22.76** Show that the maxflow problem reduces to the feasible-flow problem (so that the two problems are therefore equivalent).

22.77 Find a feasible flow for the flow network shown in Figure 22.10, given the additional constraints that 0, 2, and 3 are supply vertices with weight 4, and that 1, 4, and 5 are supply vertices with weights 1, 3, and 5, respectively.

○ **22.78** Write a program that takes as input a sports league's schedule and current standings and determines whether a given team is eliminated. Assume that there are no ties. *Hint*: Reduce to a feasible-flow problem with one source node that has a supply value equal to the total number of games remaining to play in the season, sink nodes that correspond to each pair of teams having a demand value equal to the number of remaining games between that pair, and distribution nodes that correspond to each team. Edges should connect the supply node to each team's distribution node (of capacity equal to the number of games that team would have to win to beat X if X were to win all its remaining games), and there should be an (uncapacitated) edge connecting each team's distribution node to each of the demand nodes involving that team.

● **22.79** Prove that the maxflow problem for networks with lower bounds on edges reduces to the standard maxflow problem.

▷ **22.80** Prove that, for networks with lower bounds on edges, the problem of finding a *minimal* flow (that respects the bounds) reduces to the maxflow problem (see Exercise 22.79).

●●● **22.81** Prove that the maxflow problem for *st*-networks reduces to the maxflow problem for undirected networks, or find a maxflow algorithm for undirected networks that has a worst-case running time substantially better than those of the algorithms in Sections 22.2 and 22.3.

▷ **22.82** Find all the matchings with five edges for the bipartite graph in Figure 22.37.

22.83 Extend Program 22.7 to use symbolic names instead of integers to refer to vertices (see Program 17.10).

○ **22.84** Prove that the bipartite-matching problem is equivalent to the problem of finding maxflows in networks where all edges are of unit capacity.

22.85 We might interpret the example in Figure 22.3 as describing student preferences for jobs and employer preferences for students, the two of which may not be mutual. Does the reduction described in the text apply to the *directed* bipartite-matching problem that results from this interpretation, where edges in the bipartite graph are directed (in either direction) from one set to the other? Prove that it does or provide a counterexample.

○ **22.86** Construct a family of bipartite-matching problems where the average length of the augmenting paths used by any augmenting-path algorithm to solve the corresponding maxflow problem is proportional to E.

22.87 Show, in the style of Figure 22.28, the operation of the FIFO preflow-push network-flow algorithm on the bipartite-matching network shown in Figure 22.38.

○ **22.88** Extend Table 22.3 to include various preflow-push algorithms.

● **22.89** Suppose that the two sets in a bipartite-matching problem are of size S and T, with $S \ll T$. Give as sharp a bound as you can for the worst-case running time to solve this problem, for the reduction of Property 22.19 and the maximal-augmenting-path implementation of the Ford–Fulkerson algorithm (see Property 22.8).

● **22.90** Exercise 22.89 for the FIFO-queue implementation of the preflow-push algorithm (see Property 22.13).

22.91 Extend Table 22.3 to include implementations that use the all-augmenting-paths approach described in Exercise 22.37.

•• **22.92** Prove that the running time of the method described in Exercise 22.91 is $O(\sqrt{V}E)$ for BFS.

○ **22.93** Do empirical studies to plot the expected number of edges in a maximal matching in random bipartite graphs with $V + V$ vertices and E edges, for a reasonable set of values for V and sufficient values of E to plot a smooth curve that goes from zero to V.

○ **22.94** Prove Menger's theorem (Property 22.20) for undirected graphs.

• **22.95** Prove that the minimum number of vertices whose removal disconnects two vertices in a digraph is equal to the maximum number of vertex-disjoint paths between the two vertices. *Hint*: Use a vertex-splitting transformation, similar to the one illustrated in Figure 22.32.

• **22.96** Extend your proof for Exercise 22.95 to apply to undirected graphs.

22.97 Implement an edge-connectivity class for the graph ADT of Chapter 17 whose constructor uses the algorithm described in this section to support a public member function that returns the graph's connectivity.

22.98 Extend your solution to Exercise 22.97 to put in a user-supplied vector a minimal set of edges that separates the graph. How big a vector should the user expect?

• **22.99** Develop an algorithm for computing the edge connectivity of digraphs (the minimal number of edges whose removal leaves a digraph that is not strongly connected). Implement a class based on your algorithm for the digraph ADT of Chapter 19.

• **22.100** Develop algorithms based on your solutions to Exercises 22.95 and 22.96 for computing the vertex connectivity of digraphs and undirected graphs. Implement classes based on your algorithms for the digraph ADT of Chapter 19 and the graph ADT of Chapter 17, respectively (see Exercises 22.97 and 22.98).

22.101 Describe how to find the vertex connectivity of a digraph by solving $V \lg V$ unit-capacity maxflow problems. *Hint*: Use Menger's theorem and binary search.

○ **22.102** Run empirical studies based on your solution to Exercise 22.97 to determine edge connectivity of various graphs (see Exercises 17.63–76).

▷ **22.103** Give an LP formulation for the problem of finding a maxflow in the flow network shown in Figure 22.10.

○ **22.104** Formulate as an LP problem the bipartite-matching problem in Figure 22.37.

22.5 Mincost Flows

It is not unusual for there to be numerous solutions to a given maxflow problem. This fact leads to the question of whether we might wish to impose some additional criteria for choosing one of them. For example, there are clearly many solutions to the unit-capacity flow problems shown in Figure 22.22; perhaps we would prefer the one that uses the fewest edges or the one with the shortest paths, or perhaps we would like to know whether there exists one comprising disjoint paths. Such problems are more difficult than the standard maxflow problem; they fall into a more general model known as the *mincost-flow problem*, which is the subject of this section.

As with the maxflow problem, there are numerous equivalent ways to pose the mincost-flow problem. We consider one standard formulation in detail in this section, then consider various reductions in Section 22.7.

Specifically, we use the *mincost-maxflow* model: We define an edge type that includes integer costs, use the edge costs to define a flow cost in a natural way, then ask for a maximal flow of minimal cost. As we learn, not only do we have efficient and effective algorithms for this problem, but also the problem-solving model is of broad applicability.

Definition 22.8 *The* **flow cost** *of an edge in a flow network with edge costs is the product of that edge's flow and cost. The* **cost** *of a flow is the sum of the flow costs of that flow's edges.*

We continue to assume that capacities are positive integers less than M. We also assume edge costs to be nonnegative integers less than C. (Disallowing negative costs is primarily a matter of convenience, as discussed in Section 22.7.) As before, we assign names to these upper-bound values because the running times of some algorithms depend on the latter. With these basic assumptions, the problem that we wish to solve is trivial to define.

Mincost maxflow Given a flow network with edge costs, find a maxflow such that no other maxflow has lower cost.

Figure 22.40 illustrates different maxflows in a flow network with costs, including a mincost maxflow. Certainly, the computational burden of minimizing cost is no less challenging than the burden of maximizing flow with which we were concerned in Sections 22.2

Figure 22.40
Maxflows in flow networks with costs

These flows all have the same (maximal) value, but their costs (the sum of the products of edge flows and edge costs) differ. The maxflow in the center has minimal cost (no maxflow has lower cost).

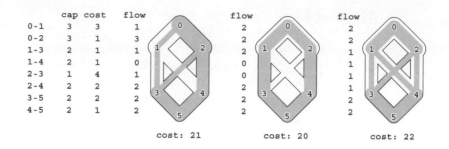

	cap	cost	flow	flow	flow
0-1	3	3	1	2	2
0-2	3	1	3	2	2
1-3	2	1	1	2	1
1-4	2	1	0	0	1
2-3	1	4	1	0	1
2-4	2	2	2	2	1
3-5	2	2	2	2	2
4-5	2	1	2	2	2

cost: 21   cost: 20   cost: 22

and 22.3. Indeed, costs add an extra dimension that presents significant new challenges. Even so, we can shoulder this burden with a generic algorithm that is similar to the augmenting-path algorithm for the maxflow problem.

Numerous other problems reduce to or are equivalent to the mincost-maxflow problem. For example, the following formulation is of interest because it encompasses the merchandise-distribution problem that we considered at the beginning of the chapter.

Mincost feasible flow Recall that we define a flow in a network with vertex weights (supply if positive, demand if negative) to be *feasible* if the sum of the vertex weights is negative and the difference between each vertex's outflow and inflow. Given such a network, find a feasible flow of minimal cost.

To describe the network model for the mincost–feasible-flow problem, we use the term *distribution network* for brevity to mean "capacitated flow network with edge costs and supply or demand weights on vertices."

In the merchandise-distribution application, supply vertices correspond to warehouses, demand vertices to retail outlets, edges to trucking routes, supply or demand values to the amount of material to be shipped or received, and edge capacities to the number and capacity of the trucks available for the various routes. A natural way to interpret each edge's cost is as the cost of moving a unit of flow through that edge (the cost of sending a unit of material in a truck along the corresponding route). Given a flow, an edge's flow cost is the part of the cost of moving the flow through the network that we can attribute to that edge. Given an amount of material that is to be shipped along a given edge, we can compute the cost of shipping it by multiplying the cost per unit by the amount. Doing this computation for each edge

---

Program 22.8 Computing flow cost

This function, which might be added to Program 22.1, returns the cost of a network's flow. It sums cost times flow for all positive-capacity edges, allowing for uncapacitated edges to be used as dummy edges.

```
static int cost(Graph &G)
{ int x = 0;
  for (int v = 0; v < G.V(); v++)
    {
      typename Graph::adjIterator A(G, v);
      for (Edge* e = A.beg(); !A.end(); e = A.nxt())
        if (e->from(v) && e->costRto(e->w()) < C)
          x += e->flow()*e->costRto(e->w());
    }
  return x;
}
```

---

and adding the results together gives us the total shipping cost, which we would like to minimize.

Property 22.22 *The mincost–feasible-flow problem and the mincost-maxflow problems are equivalent.*

Proof: Immediate, by the same correspondence as Property 22.18 (see also Exercise 22.76). ∎

Because of this equivalence and because the mincost–feasible-flow problem directly models merchandise-distribution problems and many other applications, we use the term *mincost flow* to refer to both problems in contexts where we could refer to either. We consider other reductions in Section 22.7.

To implement edge costs in flow networks, we add an integer pcost private data member to the EDGE class from Section 22.1 and a member function cost() to return its value to clients. Program 22.8 is a client function that computes the cost of a flow in a graph built with pointers to such edges. As when we work with maxflows, it is also prudent to implement a function to check that inflow and outflow values are properly related at each vertex and that the data structures are consistent (see Exercise 22.12).

The first step in developing algorithms to solve the mincost-flow problem is to extend the definition of residual networks to include costs on the edges.

Definition 22.9   *Given a flow in a flow network with edge costs, the* **residual network** *for the flow has the same vertices as the original and one or two edges in the residual network for each edge in the original, defined as follows: For each edge* u-v *in the original, let* f *be the flow,* c *the capacity, and* x *the cost. If* f *is positive, include an edge* v-u *in the residual with capacity* f *and cost* -x*; if* f *is less than* c*, include an edge* u-v *in the residual with capacity* c-f *and cost* x*.*

This definition is nearly identical to Definition 22.4, but the difference is crucial. Edges in the residual network that represent backward edges have *negative* cost. To implement this convention, we use the following member function in the edge class:

```
int costRto(int v)
  { return from(v) ? -pcost : pcost; }
```

Traversing backward edges corresponds to removing flow in the corresponding edge in the original network, so the cost has to be reduced accordingly. *Because of the negative edge costs, these networks can have negative-cost cycles.* The concept of negative cycles, which seemed artificial when we first considered it in the context of shortest-paths algorithms, plays a critical role in mincost-flow algorithms, as we now see. We consider two algorithms, both based on the following optimality condition.

Property 22.23   *A* maxflow *is a* **mincost maxflow** *if and only if its residual network contains no negative-cost (directed) cycle.*

Proof: Suppose that we have a mincost maxflow whose residual network has a negative-cost cycle. Let x be the capacity of a minimal-capacity edge in the cycle. Augment the flow by adding x to edges in the flow corresponding to positive-cost edges in the residual network (forward edges) and subtracting x from edges corresponding to negative-cost edges in the residual network (backward edges). These changes do not affect the difference between inflow and outflow at any vertex, so the flow remains a maxflow, but they change the network's cost by x times the cost of the cycle, which is negative, thereby contradicting the assertion that the cost of the original flow was minimal.

NETWORK FLOW §22.5 447

To prove the converse, suppose that we have a maxflow $\mathcal{F}$ with no negative-cost cycles whose cost is not minimal, and consider any mincost maxflow $\mathcal{M}$. By an argument identical to the flow-decomposition theorem (Property 22.2), we can find at most E directed cycles such that adding those cycles to the flow $\mathcal{F}$ gives the flow $\mathcal{M}$. But, since $\mathcal{F}$ has no negative cycles, this operation cannot lower the cost of $\mathcal{F}$, a contradiction. In other words, we should be able to convert $\mathcal{F}$ to $\mathcal{M}$ by augmenting along cycles, but we cannot do so because we have no negative-cost cycles to use to lower the flow cost. ∎

This property leads immediately to a simple generic algorithm for solving the mincost-flow problem, called the *cycle-canceling* algorithm.

Find a maxflow. Augment the flow along any negative-cost cycle in the residual network, continuing until none remain.

This method brings together machinery that we have developed over this chapter and the previous one to provide effective algorithms for solving the wide class of problems that fit into the mincost-flow model. Like several other generic methods that we have seen, it admits several different implementations, since the methods for finding the initial maxflow and for finding the negative-cost cycles are not specified. Figure 22.41 shows an example mincost-maxflow computation that uses cycle canceling.

Since we have already developed algorithms for computing a maxflow and for finding negative cycles, we immediately have the implementation of the cycle-canceling algorithm given in Program 22.9. We use any maxflow implementation to find the initial maxflow and the Bellman–Ford algorithm to find negative cycles (see Exercise 22.108). To these two implementations, we need to add only a loop to augment flow along the cycles.

We can eliminate the initial maxflow computation in the cycle-canceling algorithm by adding a dummy edge from source to sink and assigning to it a cost that is higher than the cost of any source–sink path in the network (for example, VC) and a flow that is higher than the maxflow (for example, higher than the source's outflow). With this initial setup, cycle canceling moves as much flow as possible out of the dummy edge, so the resulting flow is a maxflow. A mincost-flow computation using this technique is illustrated in Figure 22.42. In the figure, we use an initial flow equal to the maxflow to make plain that the algorithm is simply computing another flow of the same value but

Figure 22.41
Residual networks (cycle canceling)

Each of the flows depicted here is a maxflow for the flow network depicted at the top, but only the one at the bottom is a mincost maxflow. To find it, we start with any maxflow and augment flow around negative cycles. The initial maxflow (second from top) has a cost of 22, which is not a mincost maxflow because the residual network (shown at right) has three negative cycles. In this example, we augment along 4-1-0-2-4 to get a maxflow of cost 21 (third from top), which still has one negative cycle. Augmenting along that cycle gives a mincost flow (bottom). Note that augmenting along 3-2-4-1-3 in the first step would have brought us to the mincost flow in one step.

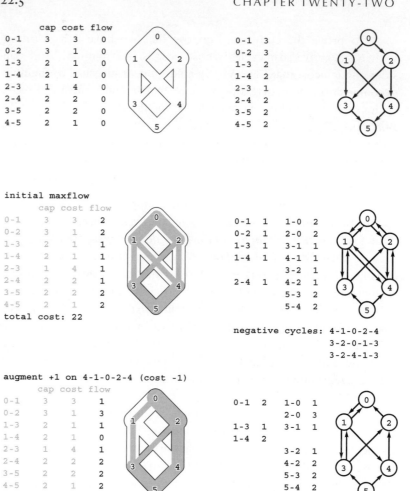

	cap	cost	flow
0-1	3	3	0
0-2	3	1	0
1-3	2	1	0
1-4	2	1	0
2-3	1	4	0
2-4	2	2	0
3-5	2	2	0
4-5	2	1	0

0-1	3
0-2	3
1-3	2
1-4	2
2-3	1
2-4	2
3-5	2
4-5	2

initial maxflow

	cap	cost	flow
0-1	3	3	2
0-2	3	1	2
1-3	2	1	1
1-4	2	1	1
2-3	1	4	1
2-4	2	2	1
3-5	2	2	2
4-5	2	1	2

total cost: 22

0-1	1	1-0	2
0-2	1	2-0	2
1-3	1	3-1	1
1-4	1	4-1	1
		3-2	1
2-4	1	4-2	1
		5-3	2
		5-4	2

negative cycles: 4-1-0-2-4
3-2-0-1-3
3-2-4-1-3

augment +1 on 4-1-0-2-4 (cost -1)

	cap	cost	flow
0-1	3	3	1
0-2	3	1	3
1-3	2	1	1
1-4	2	1	0
2-3	1	4	1
2-4	2	2	2
3-5	2	2	2
4-5	2	1	2

total cost: 21

0-1	2	1-0	1
		2-0	3
1-3	1	3-1	1
1-4	2		
		3-2	1
		4-2	2
		5-3	2
		5-4	2

negative cycle: 3-2-0-1-3

augment +1 on 3-2-0-1-3 (cost -1)

	cap	cost	flow
0-1	3	3	2
0-2	3	1	2
1-3	2	1	2
1-4	2	1	0
2-3	1	4	0
2-4	2	2	2
3-5	2	2	2
4-5	2	1	2

total cost: 20

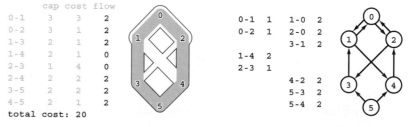

0-1	1	1-0	2
0-2	1	2-0	2
		3-1	2
1-4	2		
2-3	1		
		4-2	2
		5-3	2
		5-4	2

Program 22.9 Cycle canceling

This class solves the mincost-maxflow problem by canceling negative-cost cycles. It uses MAXFLOW to find a maxflow and a private member function negcyc (see Exercise 22.108) to find negative cycles. While a negative cycle exists, this code finds one, computes the maximum amount of flow to push through it, and does so. The augment function is the same as in Program 22.3, which was coded (with some foresight!) to work properly when the path is a cycle.

```
template <class Graph, class Edge> class MINCOST
{ const Graph &G;
  int s, t;
  vector<int> wt;
  vector <Edge *> st;
  int ST(int v) const;
  void augment(int, int);
  int negcyc(int);
  int negcyc();
public:
  MINCOST(const Graph &G, int s, int t) : G(G),
    s(s), t(t), st(G.V()), wt(G.V())
  { MAXFLOW<Graph, Edge>(G, s, t);
    for (int x = negcyc(); x != -1; x = negcyc())
      { augment(x, x); }
  }
};
```

---

lower cost (in general, we do not know the flow value, so there is some flow left in the dummy edge at the end, which we ignore). As is evident from the figure, some augmenting cycles include the dummy edge and increase flow in the network; others do not include the dummy edge and reduce cost. Eventually, we reach a maxflow; at that point, all the augmenting cycles reduce cost without changing the value of the flow, as when we started with a maxflow.

Technically, using a dummy-flow initialization is neither more nor less generic than using a maxflow initialization for cycle canceling. The former does encompass all augmenting-path maxflow algorithms, but not all maxflows can be computed with an augmenting-path algo-

Figure 22.42
Cycle canceling without initial maxflow

This sequence illustrates the computation of a mincost maxflow from an initially empty flow with the cycle-canceling algorithm by using a dummy edge from sink to source in the residual network with infinite capacity and infinite negative cost. The dummy edge makes any augmenting path from 0 to 5 a negative cycle (but we ignore it when augmenting and computing the cost of the flow). Augmenting along such a path increases the flow, as in augmenting-path algorithms (top three rows). When there are no cycles involving the dummy edge, there are no paths from source to sink in the residual network, so we have a maxflow (third from top). At that point, augmenting along a negative cycle decreases the cost without changing the flow value (bottom). In this example, we compute a maxflow, then decrease its cost; but that need not be the case. For example, the algorithm might have augmented along the negative cycle 1-4-5-3-1 instead of 0-1-4-5-0 in the second step. Since every augmentation either increases the flow or reduces the cost, we always wind up with a mincost maxflow.

augment +2 on 0-1-3-5-0 (cost +6)

	cap	cost	flow
0-1	3	3	2
0-2	3	1	0
1-3	2	1	2
1-4	2	1	0
2-3	1	4	0
2-4	2	2	0
3-5	2	2	2
4-5	2	1	0
5-0	*	*	

total cost: 12

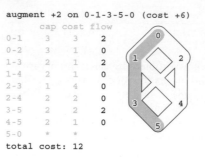

0-1	1	1-0	2
0-2	3		
		3-1	2
1-4	2		
2-3	1		
2-4	2		
		5-3	2
4-5	2		
5-0	*		

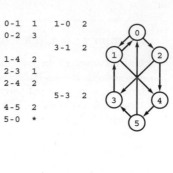

augment +1 on 0-1-4-5-0 (cost +5)

	cap	cost	flow
0-1	3	3	3
0-2	3	1	0
1-3	2	1	2
1-4	2	1	1
2-3	1	4	0
2-4	2	2	0
3-5	2	2	2
4-5	2	1	1
5-0	*	*	

total cost: 17

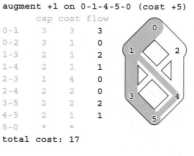

		1-0	3
0-2	3		
		3-1	2
1-4	1	4-1	1
2-3	1		
2-4	2		
		5-3	2
4-5	1	5-4	1
5-0	*		

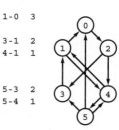

augment +1 on 0-2-4-5-0 (cost +4)

	cap	cost	flow
0-1	3	3	3
0-2	3	1	1
1-3	2	1	2
1-4	2	1	1
2-3	1	4	0
2-4	2	2	1
3-5	2	2	2
4-5	2	1	2
5-0	*	*	

total cost: 21

		1-0	3
0-2	2	2-0	1
		3-1	2
1-4	1	4-1	1
2-3	1		
2-4	1	4-2	1
		5-3	2
		5-4	2
5-0	*		

augment +1 on 4-1-0-2-4 (cost -1)

	cap	cost	flow
0-1	3	3	2
0-2	3	1	2
1-3	2	1	2
1-4	2	1	0
2-3	1	4	0
2-4	2	2	2
3-5	2	2	2
4-5	2	1	2
5-0	*	*	

total cost: 20

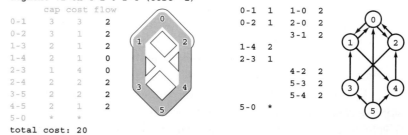

0-1	1	1-0	2
0-2	1	2-0	2
		3-1	2
1-4	2		
2-3	1		
		4-2	2
		5-3	2
		5-4	2
5-0	*		

rithm (see Exercise 22.40). On the one hand, by using this technique, we may be giving up the benefits of a sophisticated maxflow algorithm; on the other hand, we may be better off reducing costs during the process of building a maxflow. In practice, dummy-flow initialization is widely used because it is so simple to implement.

As for maxflows, the existence of this generic algorithm guarantees that every mincost-flow problem (with capacities and costs that are integers) has a solution where flows are all integers; and the algorithm computes such a solution (see Exercise 22.107). Given this fact, it is easy to establish an upper bound on the amount of time that any cycle-canceling algorithm will require.

Property 22.24 *The number of augmenting cycles needed in the generic cycle-canceling algorithm is less than ECM.*

Proof: In the worst case, each edge in the initial maxflow has capacity M, cost C, and is filled. Each cycle reduces this cost by at least 1. ∎

Corollary *The time required to solve the mincost-flow problem in a sparse network is $O(V^3CM)$.*

Proof: Immediate by multiplying the worst-case number of augmenting cycles by the worst-case cost of the Bellman–Ford algorithm for finding them (see Property 21.22). ∎

Like that of augmenting-path methods, this running time is extremely pessimistic, as it assumes not only that we have a worst-case situation where we need to use a huge number of cycles to minimize cost, but also that we have another worst-case situation where we have to examine a huge number of edges to find each cycle. In many practical situations, we use relatively few cycles that are relatively easy to find, and the cycle-canceling algorithm is effective.

It is possible to develop a strategy that finds negative-cost cycles and ensures that the number of negative-cost cycles used is less than VE (*see reference section*). This result is significant because it establishes the fact that the mincost-flow problem is tractable (as are all the problems that reduce to it). However, practitioners typically use implementations that admit a bad worst case (in theory) but use substantially fewer iterations on the problems that arise in practice than predicted by the worst-case bounds.

The mincost-flow problem represents the most general problem-solving model that we have yet examined, so it is perhaps surprising that we can solve it with such a simple implementation. Because of the importance of the model, numerous other implementations of the cycle-canceling method and numerous other different methods have been developed and studied in detail. Program 22.9 is a remarkably simple and effective starting point, but it suffers from two defects that can potentially lead to poor performance. First, each time that we seek a negative cycle, we start from scratch. Can we save intermediate information during the search for one negative cycle that can help us find the next? Second, Program 22.9 just takes the first negative cycle that the Bellman–Ford algorithm finds. Can we direct the search towards negative cycles with particular properties? In Section 22.6, we consider an improved implementation, still generic, that represents a response to both of these questions.

Exercises

22.105 Expand your class for feasible flows from Exercise 22.74 to include costs. Use MINCOST to solves the mincost–feasible-flow problem.

▷ **22.106** Given a flow network whose edges are not all maximal capacity and cost, give an upper bound better than ECM on the cost of a maxflow.

22.107 Prove that, if all capacities and costs are integers, then the mincost-flow problem has a solution where all flow values are integers.

22.108 Implement the negcyc() function for Program 22.9, using the Bellman-Ford algorithm (see Exercise 21.134).

▷ **22.109** Modify Program 22.9 to initialize with flow in a dummy edge instead of computing a flow.

○ **22.110** Give all possible sequences of augmenting cycles that might have been depicted in Figure 22.41.

○ **22.111** Give all possible sequences of augmenting cycles that might have been depicted in Figure 22.42.

22.112 Show, in the style of Figure 22.41, the flow and residual networks after each augmentation when you use the cycle-canceling implementation of Program 22.9 to find a mincost flow in the flow network shown in Figure 22.10, with cost 2 assigned to 0–2 and 0–3; cost 3 assigned to 2–5 and 3–5; cost 4 assigned to 1–4; and cost 1 assigned to all of the other edges. Assume that the maxflow is computed with the shortest-augmenting-path algorithm.

22.113 Answer Exercise 22.112, but assume that the program is modified to start with a maxflow in a dummy edge from source to sink, as in Figure 22.42.

22.114 Extend your solutions to Exercises 22.6 and 22.7 to handle costs in flow networks.

22.115 Extend your solutions to Exercises 22.9 through 22.11 to include costs in the networks. Take each edge's cost to be roughly proportional to the Euclidean distance between the vertices that the edge connects.

22.6 Network Simplex Algorithm

The running time of the cycle-canceling algorithm is based on not just the number of negative-cost cycles that the algorithm uses to reduce the flow cost but also the time that the algorithm uses to find each of the cycles. In this section, we consider a basic approach that both dramatically decreases the cost of identifying negative cycles and admits methods for reducing the number of iterations. This implementation of the cycle-canceling algorithm is known as the *network simplex* algorithm. It is based on maintaining a tree data structure and reweighting costs such that negative cycles can be identified quickly.

To describe the network simplex algorithm, we begin by noting that, with respect to any flow, each network edge u–v is in one of three states (see Figure 22.43):

- *Empty*, so flow can be pushed from only u to v
- *Full*, so flow can be pushed from only v to u
- *Partial* (neither empty nor full), so flow can pushed either way

This classification is familiar from our use of residual networks throughout this chapter. If u–v is an empty edge, then u–v is in the residual network, but v–u is not; if u–v is a full edge, then v–u is in the residual network, but u–v is not; if u–v is a partial edge, then both u–v and v–u are in the residual network.

Definition 22.10 *Given a maxflow with no cycle of partial edges, a* **feasible spanning tree** *for the maxflow is any spanning tree of the network that contains all the flow's partial edges.*

In this context, we ignore edge directions in the spanning tree. That is, any set of $V - 1$ directed edges that connects the network's V vertices (ignoring edge directions) constitutes a spanning tree, and a spanning tree is feasible if all nontree edges are either full or empty.

The first step in the network simplex algorithm is to build a spanning tree. One way to build it is to compute a maxflow, to break

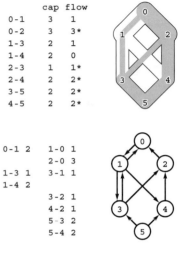

	cap	flow
0-1	3	1
0-2	3	3*
1-3	2	1
1-4	2	0
2-3	1	1*
2-4	2	2*
3-5	2	2*
4-5	2	2*

0-1	2	1-0	1
		2-0	3
1-3	1	3-1	1
1-4	2		
		3-2	1
		4-2	1
		5-3	2
		5-4	2

Figure 22.43
Edge classification

With respect to any flow, every edge is either empty, full, or partial (neither empty nor full). In this flow, edge 1–4 is empty; edges 0–2, 2–3, 2–4, 3–5, and 4–5 are full; and edges 0–1 and 1–3 are partial. Our conventions in figures give two ways to identify an edge's state: In the flow column, 0 entries are empty edges; starred entries are full edges; and entries that are neither 0 nor starred are partial edges. In the residual network (bottom), empty edges appear only in the left column; full edges appear only in the right column; and partial edges appear in both columns.

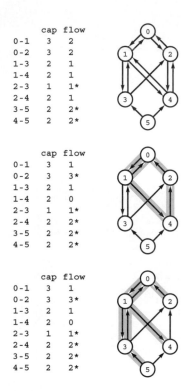

cap	flow
0-1	3	2
0-2	3	2
1-3	2	1
1-4	2	1
2-3	1	1*
2-4	2	1
3-5	2	2*
4-5	2	2*

cap	flow
0-1	3	1
0-2	3	3*
1-3	2	1
1-4	2	0
2-3	1	1*
2-4	2	2*
3-5	2	2*
4-5	2	2*

cap	flow
0-1	3	1
0-2	3	3*
1-3	2	1
1-4	2	0
2-3	1	1*
2-4	2	2*
3-5	2	2*
4-5	2	2*

Figure 22.44
Maxflow spanning tree

Given any maxflow (top), we can construct a maxflow that has a spanning tree such that no nontree edges are partial by the two-step process illustrated in this example. First, we break cycles of partial edges; in this case, we break the cycle 0-2-4-1-0 by pushing 1 unit of flow along it. We can always fill or empty at least one edge in this way; in this case, we empty 1-4 and fill both 0-2 and 2-4 (center). Second, we add empty or full edges to the set of partial edges to make a spanning tree; in this case, we add 0-2, 1-4 and 3-5 (bottom).

cycles of partial edges by augmenting along each cycle to fill or empty one of its edges, then to add full or empty edges to the remaining partial edges to make a spanning tree. An example of this process is illustrated in Figure 22.44. Another option is to start with the maxflow in a dummy edge from source to sink. Then, this edge is the only possible partial edge, and we can build a spanning tree for the flow with any graph search. An example of such a spanning tree is illustrated in Figure 22.45.

Now, adding any nontree edge to a spanning tree creates a cycle. The basic mechanism behind the network simplex algorithm is a set of vertex weights that allows immediate identification of the edges that, when added to the tree, create negative-cost cycles in the residual network. We refer to these vertex weights as *potentials* and use the notation $\phi(v)$ to refer to the potential associated with v. Depending on context, we refer to potentials as a function defined on the vertices, or as a set of integer weights with the implicit assumption that one is assigned to each vertex, or as a vertex-indexed vector (since we always store them that way in implementations).

Definition 22.11 *Given a flow in a flow network with edge costs, let $c(u, v)$ denote the cost of u-v in the flow's residual network. For any potential function ϕ, the* **reduced cost** *of an edge u-v in the residual network with respect to ϕ, which we denote by $c^*(u, v)$, is defined to be the value $c(u, v) - (\phi(u) - \phi(v))$.*

In other words, the reduced cost of every edge is the difference between that edge's actual cost and the difference of the potentials of the edge's vertices. In the merchandise distribution application, we can see the intuition behind node potentials: If we interpret the potential $\phi(u)$ as the cost of buying a unit of material at node u, the full cost $c^*(u, v) + \phi(u) - \phi(v)$ is the cost of buying at u, shipping to v and selling at v.

We maintain a vertex-indexed vector phi for the vertex potentials and compute the reduced cost of an edge v-w by subtracting from the edge's cost the value (phi[v] - phi[w]). That is, there is no need to store the reduced edge costs anywhere, because it is so easy to compute them.

In the network simplex algorithm, we use feasible spanning trees to define vertex potentials such that reduced edge costs with respect to those potentials give direct information about negative-cost cycles.

Specifically, we maintain a feasible spanning tree throughout the execution of the algorithm, and we set the values of the vertex potentials such that all tree edges have reduced cost zero.

Property 22.25 *We say that a set of vertex potentials is **valid** with respect to a spanning tree if all tree edges have zero reduced cost. All valid vertex potentials for any given spanning tree imply the same reduced costs for each network edge.*

Proof: Given two different potential functions ϕ and ϕ' that are both valid with respect to a given spanning tree, we show that they differ by an additive constant: That $\phi(u) = \phi'(u) + \Delta$ for all u and some constant Δ. Then, $\phi(u) - \phi(v) = \phi'(u) - \phi'(v)$ for all u and v, implying that all reduced costs are the same for the two potential functions.

For any two vertices u and v that are connected by a tree edge, we must have $\phi(v) = \phi(u) - c(u, v)$, by the following argument. If u-v is a tree edge, then $\phi(v)$ must be equal to $\phi(u) - c(u, v)$ to make the reduced cost $c(u, v) - \phi(u) + \phi(v)$ equal to zero; if v-u is a tree edge, then $\phi(v)$ must be equal to $\phi(u) + c(v, u) = \phi(u) - c(u, v)$ to make the reduced cost $c(v, u) - \phi(v) + \phi(u)$ equal to zero. The same argument holds for ϕ', so we must also have $\phi'(v) = \phi'(u) - c(u, v)$.

Subtracting, we find that $\phi(v) - \phi'(v) = \phi(u) - \phi'(u)$ for any u and v connected by a tree edge. Denoting this difference by Δ for any vertex and applying the equality along the edges of any search tree of the spanning tree immediately gives the desired result that $\phi(u) = \phi'(u) + \Delta$ for all u. ∎

Another way to imagine the process of defining a set of valid vertex potentials is that we start by fixing one value, then compute the values for all vertices connected to that vertex by tree edges, then compute them for all vertices connected to those vertices, and so forth. No matter where we start the process, the potential difference between any two vertices is the same, determined by the structure of the tree. Figure 22.46 depicts an example. We consider the details of the task of computing potentials after we examine the relationship between reduced costs on nontree edges and negative-cost cycles.

Property 22.26 *We say that a nontree edge is **eligible** if the cycle that it creates with tree edges is a negative-cost cycle in the residual network. An edge is eligible if and only if it is a full edge with positive reduced cost or an empty edge with negative reduced cost.*

	cap	cost	flow
0-1	3	3	0
0-2	3	1	0
1-3	2	1	0
1-4	2	1	0
2-3	1	4	0
2-4	2	2	0
3-5	2	2	0
4-5	2	1	0
0-5	6	9	4

Figure 22.45
Spanning tree for dummy maxflow

If we start with flow on a dummy edge from source to sink, then that is the only possible partial edge, so we can use any spanning tree of the remaining nodes to build a spanning tree for the flow. In the example, the edges 0–5, 0–1, 0–2, 1–3, and 1–4 comprise a spanning tree for the initial maxflow. All of the nontree edges are empty.

Figure 22.46
Vertex potentials

Vertex potentials are determined by the structure of the spanning tree and by an initial assignment of a potential value to any vertex. At left is a set of edges that comprise a spanning tree of the ten vertices 0 through 9. In the center is a representation of that tree with 5 at the root, vertices connected to 5 one level lower, and so forth. When we assign the root the potential value 0, there is a unique assignment of potentials to the other nodes that make the difference between the potentials of each edge's vertices equal to its cost. At right is a different representation of the same tree with 0 at the root. The potentials that we get by assigning 0 the value 0 differ from those in the center by a constant offset. All our computations use the difference between two potentials: This difference is the same for any pair of potentials no matter what vertex we start with (and no matter what value we assign it), so our choice of starting vertex and value is immaterial.

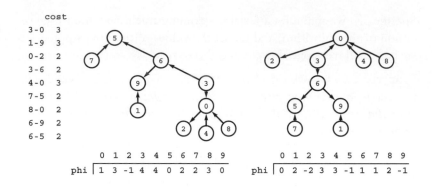

Proof: Suppose that the edge u–v creates the cycle t1-t2-t3-...-td-t1 with tree edges t1-t2, t2-t3, ..., where v is t1 and u is td. The reduced cost definitions of each edge imply the following:

$$c(u, v) = c^*(u, v) + \phi(u) - \phi(t_1)$$
$$c(t_1, t_2) = \phi(t_1) - \phi(t_2)$$
$$c(t_2, t_3) = \phi(t_2) - \phi(t_3)$$
$$\vdots$$
$$c(t_{d-1}, u) = \phi(t_{d-1}) - \phi(u)$$

The left-hand side of the sum of these equations gives the total cost of the cycle, and the right-hand side collapses to $c^*(u, v)$. In other words, the edge's reduced cost gives the cycle cost, so only the edges described can give a negative-cost cycle ∎

Property 22.27 *If we have a flow and a feasible spanning tree with no eligible edges, the flow is a mincost flow.*

Proof: If there are no eligible edges, then there are no negative-cost cycles in the residual network, so the optimality condition of Property 22.23 implies that the flow is a mincost flow. ∎

An equivalent statement is that if we have a flow and a set of vertex potentials such that reduced costs of tree edges are all zero, full nontree edges are all nonnegative, and empty nontree edges are all nonpositive, then the flow is a mincost flow.

If we have eligible edges, we can choose one and augment along the cycle that it creates with tree edges to get a lower-cost flow. As we did with the cycle-canceling implementation in Section 22.5, we go through the cycle to find the maximum amount of flow that we can push, then go through the cycle again to push that amount, which fills or empties at least one edge. If that is the eligible edge that we used to create the cycle, it becomes ineligible (its reduced cost stays the same, but it switches from full to empty or empty to full). Otherwise, it becomes partial. By adding it to the tree and removing a full edge or an empty edge from the cycle, we maintain the invariant that no nontree edges are partial and that the tree is a feasible spanning tree. Again, we consider the mechanics of this computation later in this section.

In summary, feasible spanning trees give us vertex potentials, which give us reduced costs, which give us eligible edges, which give us negative-cost cycles. Augmenting along a negative-cost cycle reduces the flow cost and also implies changes in the tree structure. Changes in the tree structure imply changes in the vertex potentials; changes in the vertex potentials imply changes in reduced edge costs; and changes in reduced costs imply changes in the set of eligible edges. After making all these changes, we can pick another eligible edge and start the process again. This generic implementation of the cycle-canceling algorithm for solving the mincost-flow problem is called the *network simplex* algorithm.

> *Build a feasible spanning tree and maintain vertex potentials such that all tree vertices have zero reduced cost. Add an eligible edge to the tree, augment the flow along the cycle that it makes with tree edges, and remove from the tree an edge that is filled or emptied, continuing until no eligible edges remain.*

This implementation is a generic one because the initial choice of spanning tree, the method of maintaining vertex potentials, and the method of choosing eligible edges are not specified. The strategy for choosing eligible edges determines the number of iterations, which trades off against the differing costs of implementing various strategies and recalculating the vertex potentials.

Property 22.28 *If the generic network simplex algorithm terminates, it computes a mincost flow.*

Proof : If the algorithm terminates, it does so because there are no negative-cost cycles in the residual network, so by Property 22.23 the maxflow is of mincost. ∎

The condition that the algorithm might not terminate derives from the possibility that augmenting along a cycle might fill or empty multiple edges, thus leaving edges in the tree through which no flow can be pushed. If we cannot push flow, we cannot reduce the cost, and we could get caught in an infinite loop adding and removing edges to make a fixed sequence of spanning trees. Several ways to avoid this problem have been devised; we discuss them later in this section after we look in more detail at implementations.

The first choice that we face in developing an implementation of the network simplex algorithm is what representation to use for the spanning tree. We have three primary computational tasks that involve the tree:

- Computing the vertex potentials
- Augmenting along the cycle (and identifying an empty or a full edge on it)
- Inserting a new edge and removing an edge on the cycle formed

Each of these tasks is an interesting exercise in data structure and algorithm design. There are several data structures and numerous algorithms that we might consider, with varied performance characteristics. We begin by considering perhaps the simplest available data structure—which we first encountered in Chapter 1(!)—the parent-link tree representation. After we examine algorithms and implementations that are based on the parent-link representation for the tasks just listed and describe their use in the context of the network simplex algorithm, we discuss alternative data structures and algorithms.

As we did in several other implementations in this chapter, beginning with the augmenting-path maxflow implementation, we keep links into the network representation, rather than simple indices in the tree representation, to allow us to have access to the flow values that need to be changed without losing access to the vertex name.

Program 22.10 is an implementation that assigns vertex potentials in time proportional to V. It is based on the following idea, also illustrated in Figure 22.47. We start with any vertex and recursively compute the potentials of its ancestors, following parent links up to the root, to which, by convention, we assign potential 0. Then, we

---

Program 22.10 Vertex potential calculation

The recursive function `phiR` follows parent links up the tree until finding one whose potential is valid (by convention the potential of the root is always valid), then computes potentials for vertices on the path on the way back down as the last actions of the recursive invocations. It marks each vertex whose potential it computes by setting its mark entry to the current value of `valid`.

```
int phiR(int v)
  {
    if (mark[v] == valid) return phi[v];
    phi[v] = phiR(ST(v)) - st[v]->costRto(v);
    mark[v] = valid;
    return phi[v];
  }
```

---

pick another vertex and use parent links to compute recursively the potentials of its ancestors. The recursion terminates when we reach an ancestor whose potential is known; then, on the way out of the recursion, we travel back down the path, computing each node's potential from its parent. We continue this process until we have computed all potential values. Once we have traveled along a path, we do not revisit any of its edges, so this process runs in time proportional to V.

Given two nodes in a tree, their *least common ancestor (LCA)* is the root of the smallest subtree that contains them both. The cycle that we form by adding an edge connecting two nodes consists of that edge plus the edges on the two paths from the two nodes to their LCA. The augmenting cycle formed by adding v-w goes through v-w to w, up the tree to the LCA of v and w (say r), then down the tree to v, so we have to consider edges in opposite orientation in the two paths.

As before, we augment along the cycle by traversing the paths once to find the maximum amount of flow that we can push through their edges then traversing the two paths again, pushing flow through them. We do not need to consider edges in order around the cycle; it suffices to consider them all (in either direction). Accordingly, we can simply follow paths from each of the two nodes to their LCA. To augment along the cycle formed by the addition of v-w, we push flow from v to w; from v along the path to the LCA r; and from w along

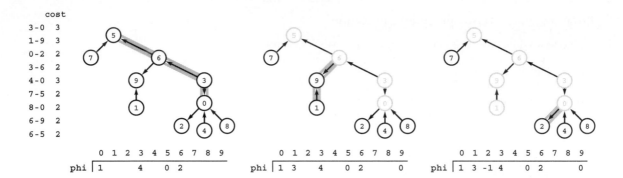

Figure 22.47
Computing potentials through parent links

We start at 0, follow the path to the root, set pt[5] *to 0, then work down the path, first setting 6 to make* pt[6] − pt[5] *equal to the cost of 6-5, then setting* p[3] *to make* p[3] − p[6] *equal to the cost of 3-6, and so forth* (left). *Then we start at 1 and follow parent links until hitting a vertex whose potential is known (6 in this case) and work down the path to compute potentials on 9 and 1 (center). When we start at 2, we can compute its potential from its parent* (right)*; when we start at 3, we see that its potential is already known, and so forth. In this example, when we try each vertex after 1, we either find that its potential is already done or we can compute the value from its parent. We never retrace an edge, no matter what the tree structure, so the total running time is linear.*

the path to r, but in reverse direction for each edge. Program 22.11 is an implementation of this idea, in the form of a function that augments a cycle and also returns an edge that is emptied or filled by the augmentation.

The implementation in Program 22.11 uses a simple technique to avoid paying the cost of initializing all the marks each time that we call it. We maintain the marks as global variables, initialized to zero. Each time that we seek an LCA, we increment a global counter and mark vertices by setting their corresponding entry in a vertex-indexed vector to that counter. After initialization, this technique allows us to perform the computation in time proportional to the length of the cycle. In typical problems, we might augment along a large number of small cycles, so the time saved can be substantial. As we learn, the same technique is useful in saving time in other parts of the implementation.

Our third tree-manipulation task is to substitute an edge u-v for another edge in the cycle that it creates with tree edges. Program 22.12 is an implementation of a function that accomplishes this task for the parent-link representation. Again, the LCA of u and v is important, because the edge to be removed is either on the path from u to the LCA or on the path from v to the LCA. Removing an edge detaches all its descendants from the tree, but we can repair the damage by reversing the links between u-v and the removed edge, as illustrated in Figure 22.48.

These three implementations support the basic operations underlying the network simplex algorithm: We can choose an eligible edge by examining reduced costs and flows; we can use the parent-link representation of the spanning tree to augment along the negative cycle

Program 22.11 Augmenting along a cycle

To find the least common ancestor of two vertices, we mark nodes while moving up the tree from them in synchrony. The LCA is the root if it is the only marked node seen; otherwise the LCA is the first marked node seen that is not the root. To augment, we use a function similar to the one in Program 22.3 that preserves tree paths in st and returns an edge that was emptied or filled by the augmentation (*see text*).

```
int lca(int v, int w)
  { mark[v] = ++valid; mark[w] = valid;
    while (v != w)
      {
        if (v != t) v = ST(v);
        if (v != t && mark[v] == valid) return v;
        mark[v] = valid;
        if (w != t) w = ST(w);
        if (w != t && mark[w] == valid) return w;
        mark[w] = valid;
      }
    return v;
  }
Edge *augment(Edge *x)
  { int v = x->v(), w = x->w(); int r = lca(v, w);
    int d = x->capRto(w);
    for (int u = w; u != r; u = ST(u))
      if (st[u]->capRto(ST(u)) < d)
        d = st[u]->capRto(ST(u));
    for (int u = v; u != r; u = ST(u))
      if (st[u]->capRto(u) < d)
        d = st[u]->capRto(u);
    x->addflowRto(w, d); Edge* e = x;
    for (int u = w; u != r; u = ST(u))
      { st[u]->addflowRto(ST(u), d);
        if (st[u]->capRto(ST(u)) == 0) e = st[u]; }
    for (int u = v; u != r; u = ST(u))
      { st[u]->addflowRto(u, d);
        if (st[u]->capRto(u) == 0) e = st[u]; }
    return e;
  }
```

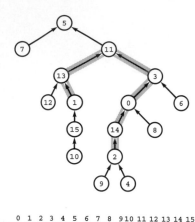

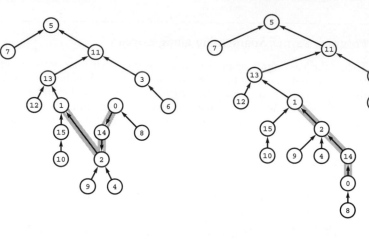

	0	1	2	3	4	5	6	7	8	9	10	11	12	13	14	15
ST	3	13	14	11	2	5	3	5	0	2	15	5	13	11	0	1

	0	1	2	3	4	5	6	7	8	9	10	11	12	13	14	15
ST	14	13	1	11	2	5	3	5	0	2	15	5	13	11	2	1

Figure 22.48
Spanning tree substitution

This example illustrates the basic tree-manipulation operation in the network simplex algorithm for the parent-link representation. At left is a sample tree with links all pointing upwards, as indicated by the parent-link structure ST. *(In our code, the function* ST *computes the parent of the given vertex from the edge pointer in the vertex-indexed vector* st.) *Adding the edge 1-2 creates a cycle with the paths from 1 and 2 to their LCA, 11. If we then delete one of those edges, say 0-3, the structure remains a tree. To update the parent-link array to reflect the change, we switch the directions of all the links from 2 up to 3 (center). The tree at right is the same tree with node positions changed so that links all point up, as indicated by the parent-link array that represents the tree (bottom right).*

formed with tree edges and the chosen eligible edge; and we can update the tree and recalculate potentials. These operations are illustrated for an example flow network in Figures 22.49 and 22.50.

Figure 22.49 illustrates initialization of the data structures using a dummy edge with the maxflow on it, as in Figure 22.42. Shown there are an initial feasible spanning tree with its parent-link representation, the corresponding vertex potentials, the reduced costs for the nontree edges, and the initial set of eligible edges. Also, rather than computing the maxflow value in the implementation, we use the outflow from the source, which is guaranteed to be no less than the maxflow value; we use the maxflow value here to make the operation of the algorithm easier to trace.

Figure 22.50 illustrates the changes in the data structures for each of a sequence of eligible edges and augmentations around negative-cost cycles. The sequence does not reflect any particular method for choosing eligible edges; it represents the choices that make the augmenting paths the same as depicted in Figure 22.42. These figures show all vertex potentials and all reduced costs after each cycle augmentation, even though many of these numbers are implicitly defined and are not necessarily computed explicitly by typical implementations. The purpose of these two figures is to illustrate the overall progress of the algorithm and the state of the data structures as the algorithm moves

---

Program 22.12 Spanning tree substitution

The function update adds an edge to the spanning tree and removes
an edge on the cycle thus created. The edge to be removed is on the
path from one of the two vertices on the edge added to their LCA. This
implementation uses the function onpath to find the edge removed and
the function reverse to reverse the edges on the path between it and
the edge added.

```
bool onpath(int a, int b, int c)
  {
    for (int i = a; i != c; i = ST(i))
      if (i == b) return true;
    return false;
  }
void reverse(int u, int x)
  { Edge *e = st[u];
    for (int i = ST(u); i != x; i = ST(i))
      { Edge *y = st[i]; st[i] = e; e = y; }
  }
void update(Edge *w, Edge *y)
  { int u = y->w(), v = y->v(), x = w->w();
    if (st[x] != w) x = w->v();
    int r = lca(u, v);
    if (onpath(u, x, r))
      { reverse(u, x); st[u] = y; return; }
    if (onpath(v, x, r))
      { reverse(v, x); st[v] = y; return; }
  }
```

---

from one feasible spanning tree to another simply by adding an eligible
edge and removing a tree edge on the cycle that is formed.

One critical fact that is illustrated in the example in Figure 22.50
is that the algorithm might not even terminate, because full or empty
edges on the spanning tree can stop us from pushing flow along the
negative cycle that we identify. That is, we can identify an eligible edge
and the negative cycle that it makes with spanning tree edges, but the
maximum amount of flow that we can push along the cycle may be
0. In this case, we still substitute the eligible edge for an edge on the

Figure 22.49
Network simplex initialization

To initialize the data structures for the network simplex algorithm, we start with zero flow on all edges (left), then add a dummy edge 0–5 from source to sink with flow no less than the maxflow value (for clarity, we use a value equal to the maxflow value here). The cost value 9 for the dummy edge is greater than the cost of any cycle in the network; in the implementation, we use the value CV. The dummy edge is not shown in the flow network, but it is included in the residual network (center).

We initialize the spanning tree with the sink at the root, the source as its only child, and a search tree of the graph induced by the remaining nodes in the residual network. The implementation uses the parent-edge representation of the tree in the array st and the related parent-vertex function ST; our figures depict this representation and two others: the rooted representation shown on the right and the set of shaded edges in the residual network.

The vertex potentials are in the pt array and are computed from the tree structure so as to make the difference of a tree edge's vertex potentials equal to its cost.

The column labeled costR in the center gives the reduced costs for nontree edges, which are computed for each edge by adding the difference of its vertex potentials to its cost. Reduced costs for tree edges are zero and left blank. Empty edges with negative reduced cost and full edges with positive reduced cost (eligible edges) are marked with asterisks.

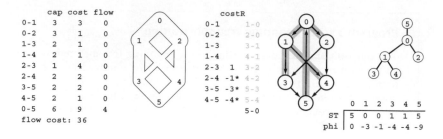

	cap	cost	flow
0-1	3	3	0
0-2	3	1	0
1-3	2	1	0
1-4	2	1	0
2-3	1	4	0
2-4	2	2	0
3-5	2	2	0
4-5	2	1	0
0-5	6	9	4

flow cost: 36

costR
0-1		1-0
0-2		2-0
1-3		3-1
1-4		4-1
2-3	1	3-2
2-4	-1*	4-2
3-5	-3*	5-3
4-5	-4*	5-4
		5-0

	0	1	2	3	4	5
ST	5	0	0	1	1	5
phi	0	-3	-1	-4	-4	-9

cycle, but we make no progress in reducing the cost of the flow. To ensure that the algorithm terminates we need to prove that we cannot end up in an endless sequence of zero-flow augmentations.

If there is more than one full or empty edge on the augmenting cycle, the substitution algorithm in Program 22.12 always deletes from the tree the one closest to the LCA of the eligible edge's two vertices. Fortunately, it has been shown that this particular strategy for choosing the edge to remove from the cycle suffices to ensure that the algorithm terminates (*see reference section*).

The final important choice that we face in developing an implementation of the network simplex algorithm is a strategy for identifying eligible edges and choosing one to add to the tree. Should we maintain a data structure containing eligible edges? If so, how sophisticated a data structure is appropriate? The answer to these questions depends somewhat on the application and the dynamics of solving particular instances of the problem. If the total number of eligible edges is small, then it is worthwhile to maintain a separate data structure; if most edges are eligible most of the time, it is not. Maintaining a separate data structure could spare us the expense of searching for eligible edges, but also could require costly update computations. What criteria should we use to pick from among the eligible edges? Again, there are many that we might adopt. We consider examples in our implementations, then discuss alternatives. For example, Program 22.13 illustrates a function that finds an eligible edge of minimal reduced cost: No other edge gives a cycle for which augmenting along the cycle would lead to a greater reduction in the total cost.

Program 22.14 is a full implementation of the network simplex algorithm that uses the strategy of choosing the eligible edge giving a negative cycle whose cost is highest in absolute value. The implemen-

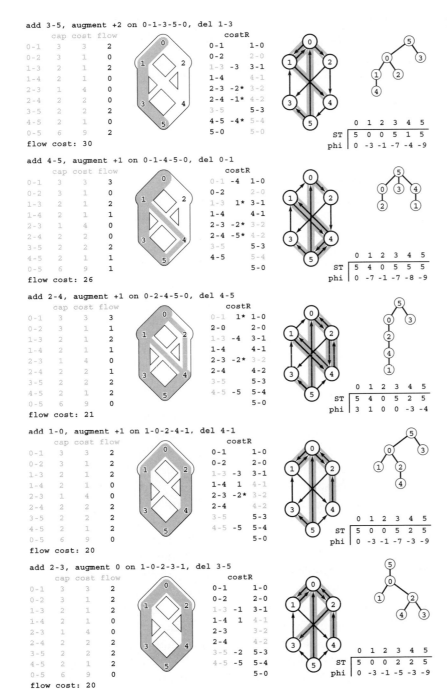

```
add 3-5, augment +2 on 0-1-3-5-0, del 1-3
      cap cost flow                    costR
0-1    3    3    2            0-1        1-0
0-2    3    1    0            0-2        2-0
1-3    2    1    2            1-3  -3    3-1
1-4    2    1    0            1-4        4-1
2-3    1    4    0            2-3  -2*   3-2
2-4    2    2    0            2-4  -1*   4-2
3-5    2    2    2            3-5        5-3
4-5    2    1    0            4-5  -4*   5-4
0-5    6    3    2            5-0        5-0
flow cost: 30
```

	0	1	2	3	4	5
ST	5	0	0	5	1	5
phi	0	-3	-1	-7	-4	-9

```
add 4-5, augment +1 on 0-1-4-5-0, del 0-1
      cap cost flow                    costR
0-1    3    3    3            0-1  -4    1-0
0-2    3    1    0            0-2        2-0
1-3    2    1    2            1-3   1*   3-1
1-4    2    1    1            1-4        4-1
2-3    1    4    0            2-3  -2*   3-2
2-4    2    2    0            2-4  -5*   4-2
3-5    2    2    2            3-5        5-3
4-5    2    1    1            4-5        5-4
0-5    6    9    1                       5-0
flow cost: 26
```

	0	1	2	3	4	5
ST	5	4	0	5	5	5
phi	0	-7	-1	-7	-8	-9

```
add 2-4, augment +1 on 0-2-4-5-0, del 4-5
      cap cost flow                    costR
0-1    3    3    3            0-1   1*   1-0
0-2    3    1    1            0-2        2-0
1-3    2    1    2            1-3  -4    3-1
1-4    2    1    1            1-4        4-1
2-3    1    4    0            2-3  -2*   3-2
2-4    2    2    1            2-4        4-2
3-5    2    2    2            3-5        5-3
4-5    2    1    2            4-5  -5    5-4
0-5    6    9    0                       5-0
flow cost: 21
```

	0	1	2	3	4	5
ST	5	4	0	5	2	5
phi	3	1	0	0	-3	-4

```
add 1-0, augment +1 on 1-0-2-4-1, del 4-1
      cap cost flow                    costR
0-1    3    3    2            0-1        1-0
0-2    3    1    2            0-2        2-0
1-3    2    1    2            1-3  -3    3-1
1-4    2    1    0            1-4   1    4-1
2-3    1    4    0            2-3  -2*   3-2
2-4    2    2    2            2-4        4-2
3-5    2    2    2            3-5        5-3
4-5    2    1    2            4-5  -5    5-4
0-5    6    9    0                       5-0
flow cost: 20
```

	0	1	2	3	4	5
ST	5	0	0	5	2	5
phi	0	-3	-1	-7	-3	-9

```
add 2-3, augment 0 on 1-0-2-3-1, del 3-5
      cap cost flow                    costR
0-1    3    3    2            0-1        1-0
0-2    3    1    2            0-2        2-0
1-3    2    1    2            1-3  -1    3-1
1-4    2    1    0            1-4   1    4-1
2-3    1    4    0            2-3        3-2
2-4    2    2    2            2-4        4-2
3-5    2    2    2            3-5  -2    5-3
4-5    2    1    2            4-5  -5    5-4
0-5    6    9    0                       5-0
flow cost: 20
```

	0	1	2	3	4	5
ST	5	0	0	2	2	5
phi	0	-3	-1	-5	-3	-9

Figure 22.50
Residual networks and spanning trees (network simplex)

Each row in this figure corresponds to an iteration of the network simplex algorithm following the initialization depicted in Figure 22.49: On each iteration, it chooses an eligible edge, augments along a cycle, and updates the data structures as follows: First, the flow is augmented, including implied changes in the residual network. Second, the tree structure ST is changed by adding an eligible edge and deleting an edge on the cycle that it makes with tree edges. Third, the table of potentials phi is updated to reflect the changes in the tree structure. Fourth, the reduced costs of the nontree edges (column marked costR in the center) are updated to reflect the potential changes, and these values used to identify empty edges with negative reduced cost and full edges with positive reduced costs as eligible edges (marked with asterisks on reduced costs). Implementations need not actually make all these computations (they only need to compute potential changes and reduced costs sufficient to identify an eligible edge), but we include all the numbers here to provide a full illustration of the algorithm.

The final augmentation for this example is degenerate. It does not increase the flow, but it leaves no eligible edges, which guarantees that the flow is a mincost maxflow.

Program 22.13 Eligible edge search

This function finds the eligible edge of lowest reduced cost. It is a straightforward implementation that that traverses all the edges in the network.

```
int costR(Edge *e, int v)
  { int R = e->cost() + phi[e->w()] - phi[e->v()];
    return  e->from(v) ? R : -R; }
Edge *besteligible()
{ Edge *x = 0;
  for (int v = 0, min = C*G.V(); v < G.V(); v++)
    {
      typename Graph::adjIterator A(G, v);
      for (Edge* e = A.beg(); !A.end(); e = A.nxt())
        if (e->capRto(e->other(v)) > 0)
          if (e->capRto(v) == 0)
            if (costR(e, v) < min)
              { x = e; min = costR(e, v); }
    }
  return x;
}
```

tation uses the tree-manipulation functions and the eligible-edge search of Programs 22.10 through 22.13, but the comments that we made regarding our first cycle-canceling implementation (Program 22.9) apply: It is remarkable that such a simple piece of code is sufficiently powerful to provide useful solutions in the context of a general problem-solving model with the reach of the mincost-flow problem.

The worst-case performance bound for Program 22.14 is at least a factor of V lower than that for the cycle-canceling implementation in Program 22.9, because the time per iteration is just E (to find the eligible edge) rather than VE (to find a negative cycle). Although we might suspect that using the maximum augmentation will result in fewer augmentations than just taking the first negative cycle provided by the Bellman–Ford algorithm, that suspicion has not been proved valid. Specific bounds on the number of augmenting cycles used are difficult to develop, and, as usual, these bounds are far higher than the numbers that we see in practice. As mentioned earlier, there are

Program 22.14 Network simplex (basic implementation)

This class uses the network simplex algorithm to solve the mincost flow problem. It uses a standard DFS function dfsR an initial tree (see Exercise 22.117), then it enters a loop where it uses the functions in Programs 22.10 through 22.13 to compute all the vertex potentials, examine all the edges to find the one that creates the lowest-cost negative cycle, and augment along that cycle.

```
template <class Graph, class Edge> class MINCOST
{ const Graph &G; int s, t; int valid;
  vector<Edge *> st; vector<int> mark, phi;
  void dfsR(Edge);
  int ST(int);
  int phiR(int);
  int lca(int, int);  Edge *augment(Edge *);
  bool onpath(int, int, int);
  void reverse(int, int);
  void update(Edge *, Edge *);
  int costR(Edge *, int); Edge *besteligible();
public:
  MINCOST(Graph &G, int s, int t) : G(G), s(s), t(t)
    st(G.V()), mark(G.V(), -1), phi(G.V())
    {
    Edge *z = new EDGE(s, t, M*G.V(), C*G.V());
    G.insert(z);
    z->addflowto(t, z->cap());
    dfsR(z);
    for (valid = 1; ; valid++ )
      {
        phi[t] = z->costRto(s); mark[t] = valid;
        for (int v = 0; v < G.V(); v++)
          if (v != t) phi[v] = phiR(v);
        Edge *x = besteligible();
        if (costR(x, x->v()) == 0) break;
        update(augment(x), x);
      }
    G.remove(z); delete z;
  }
```

theoretical results demonstrating that certain strategies can guarantee that the number of augmenting cycles is bounded by a polynomial in the number of edges, but practical implementations typically admit an exponential worst case.

In light of these considerations, there are many options to consider in pursuit of improved performance. For example, Program 22.15 is another implementation of the network simplex algorithm. The straightforward implementation in Program 22.14 always takes time proportional to V to revalidate the tree potentials and always takes time proportional to E to find the eligible edge with the largest reduced cost. The implementation in Program 22.15 is designed to eliminate both of these costs in typical networks.

First, even if choosing the maximum edge leads to the fewest number of iterations, expending the effort of examining every edge to find the maximum edge may not be worthwhile. We could do numerous augmentations along short cycles in the time that it takes to scan all the edges. Accordingly, it is worthwhile to consider the strategy of using *any* eligible edge, rather than taking the time to find a particular one. In the worst case, we might have to examine all the edges or a substantial fraction of them to find an eligible edge, but we typically expect to need to examine relatively few edges to find an eligible one. One approach is to start from the beginning each time; another is to pick a random starting point (see Exercise 22.126). This use of randomness also makes an artificially long sequence of augmenting paths unlikely.

Second, we adopt a *lazy* approach to computing potentials. Rather than compute all the potentials in the vertex-indexed vector phi, then refer to them when we need them, we call the function phiR to get each potential value; it travels up the tree to find a valid potential, then computes the necessary potentials on that path. To implement this approach, we simply change the function that defines the cost to use the function call phiR(u), instead of the array access phi[u]. In the worst case, we calculate all the potentials in the same way as before; but if we examine only a few eligible edges, then we calculate only those potentials that we need to identify them.

Such changes do not affect the worst-case performance of the algorithm, but they certainly speed it up in practical applications. Several other ideas for improving the performance of the network

---

Program 22.15 Network simplex (improved implementation)

Replacing references to phi by calls to phiR in the function R and replacing the for loop in the constructor in Program 22.14 by this code gives a network simplex implementation that saves time on each iteration by calculating potentials only when needed, and by taking the first eligible edge that it finds.

```
int old = 0;
for (valid = 1; valid != old; )
  {
    old = valid;
    for (int v = 0; v < G.V(); v++)
    {
      typename Graph::adjIterator A(G, v);
      for (Edge* e = A.beg(); !A.end(); e = A.nxt())
        if (e->capRto(e->other(v)) > 0)
          if (e->capRto(v) == 0)
            { update(augment(e), e); valid++; }
    }
  }
```

---

simplex algorithm are explored in the exercises (see Exercises 22.126 through 22.130); those represent only a small sample of the ones that have been proposed.

As we have emphasized throughout this book, the task of analyzing and comparing graph algorithms is complex. With the network simplex algorithm, the task is further complicated by the variety of different implementation approaches and the broad array of types of applications that we might encounter (see Section 22.5). Which implementation is best? Should we compare implementations based on the worst-case performance bounds that we can prove? How accurately can we quantify performance differences of various implementations, for specific applications. Should we use multiple implementations, each tailored to specific applications?

Readers are encouraged to gain computational experience with various network simplex implementations and to address some of these questions by running empirical studies of the kind that we have emphasized throughout this book. When seeking to solve mincost flow problems, we are faced with the familiar fundamental challenges, but the experience that we have gained in tackling increasingly difficult problems throughout this book provides ample background to develop efficient implementations that can effectively solve a broad variety of important practical problems. Some such studies are described in the exercises at the end of this and the next section, but these exercises should be viewed as a starting point. Each reader can craft a new empirical study that sheds light on some particular implementation/application pair of interest.

The potential to improve performance dramatically for critical applications through proper deployment of classic data structures and algorithms (or development of new ones) for basic tasks makes the study of network-simplex implementations a fruitful research area, and there is a large literature on network simplex implementations. In the past, progress in this research has been crucial, because it helps reduce the huge cost of solving network simplex problems. People tend to rely on carefully crafted libraries to attack these problems, and that is still appropriate in many situations. However, it is difficult for such libraries to keep up with recent research and to adapt to the variety of problems that arise in new applications. With the speed and size of modern computers, accessible implementations like Programs 22.12 and 22.13 can be starting points for the development of effective problem-solving tools for numerous applications.

Exercises

▷ **22.116** Give a maxflow with associated feasible spanning tree for the flow network shown in Figure 22.10.

▷ **22.117** Implement the `dfsR` function for Program 22.14.

○ **22.118** Implement a function that removes cycles of partial edges from a given network's flow and builds a feasible spanning tree for the resulting flow, as illustrated in Figure 22.44. Package your function so that it could be used to build the initial tree in Program 22.14 or Program 22.15.

22.119 In the example in Figure 22.46, show the effect of reversing the direction of the edge connecting 6 and 5 on the potential tables.

○ **22.120** Construct a flow network and exhibit a sequence of augmenting edges such that the generic network simplex algorithm does not terminate.

▷ **22.121** Show, in the style of Figure 22.47, the process of computing potentials for the tree rooted at 0 in Figure 22.46.

22.122 Show, in the style of Figure 22.50, the process of computing a min-cost maxflow in the flow network shown in Figure 22.10, starting with the basic maxflow and associated basic spanning tree that you found in Exercise 22.116.

○ **22.123** Suppose that all nontree edges are empty. Write a function that computes the flows in the tree edges, putting the flow in the edge connecting v and its parent in the tree in the vth entry of a vector flow.

○ **22.124** Do Exercise 22.123 for the case where some nontree edges may be full.

22.125 Use Program 22.12 as the basis for an MST algorithm. Run empirical tests comparing your implementation with the three basic MST algorithms described in Chapter 20 (see Exercise 20.66).

22.126 Describe how to modify Program 22.15 such that it starts the scan for an eligible edge at a random edge rather than at the beginning each time.

22.127 Modify your solution to Exercise 22.126 such that each time it searches for an eligible edge it starts where it left off in the previous search.

22.128 Modify the private member functions in this section to maintain a triply linked tree structure that includes each node's parent, leftmost child, and right sibling (see Section 5.4). Your functions to augment along a cycle and substitute an eligible edge for a tree edge should take time proportional to the length of the augmenting cycle, and your function to compute potentials should take time proportional to the size of the smaller of the two subtrees created when the tree edge is deleted.

○ **22.129** Modify the private member functions in this section to maintain, in addition to basic parent-edge tree vector, two other vertex-indexed vectors: one containing each vertex's distance to the root, the other containing each vertex's successor in a DFS. Your functions to augment along a cycle and substitute an eligible edge for a tree edge should take time proportional to the length of the augmenting cycle, and your function to compute potentials should take time proportional to the size of the smaller of the two subtrees created when the tree edge is deleted.

● **22.130** Explore the idea of maintaining a generalized queue of eligible edges. Consider various generalized-queue implementations and various improvements to avoid excessive edge-cost calculations, such as restricting attention to a subset of the eligible edges so as to limit the size of the queue or possibly allowing some ineligible edges to remain on the queue.

● **22.131** Run empirical studies to determine the number of iterations, the number of vertex potentials calculated, and the ratio of the running time to E for several versions of the network simplex algorithm, for various networks (see Exercises 22.7–12). Consider various algorithms described in the text and in the previous exercises, and concentrate on those that perform the best on huge sparse networks.

• **22.132** Write a client program that does dynamic graphical animations of network simplex algorithms. Your program should produce images like those in Figure 22.50 and the other figures in this section (see Exercise 22.48). Test your implementation for the Euclidean networks among Exercises 22.7–12.

22.7 Mincost-Flow Reductions

Mincost flow is a general problem-solving model that can encompass a variety of useful practical problems. In this section, we substantiate this claim by proving specific reductions from a variety of problems to mincost flow.

The mincost-flow problem is obviously more general than the maxflow problem, since any mincost maxflow is an acceptable solution to the maxflow problem. Specifically, if we assign to the dummy edge a cost 1 and to all other edges a cost 0 in the construction of Figure 22.42, any mincost maxflow minimizes the flow in the dummy edge and therefore maximizes the flow in the original network. Therefore, all the problems discussed in Section 22.4 that reduce to the maxflow problem also reduce to the mincost-flow problem. This set of problems includes bipartite matching, feasible flow, and mincut, among numerous others.

More interesting, we can examine properties of our algorithms for the mincost-flow problem to develop new generic algorithms for the maxflow problem. We have already noted that the generic cycle-canceling algorithm for the mincost-maxflow problem gives a generic augmenting-path algorithm for the maxflow problem. In particular, this approach leads to an implementation that finds augmenting paths without having to search the network (see Exercises 22.133 and 22.134). On the other hand, the algorithm might produce zero-flow augmenting paths, so its performance characteristics are difficult to evaluate (*see reference section*).

The mincost-flow problem is also more general than the shortest-paths problem, by the following simple reduction.

Property 22.29 *The single-source–shortest-paths problem (in networks with no negative cycles) reduces to the mincost–feasible-flow problem.*

Proof: Given a single-source–shortest-paths problem (a network and a source vertex s), build a flow network with the same vertices, edges, and edge costs; and give each edge unlimited capacity. Add a new

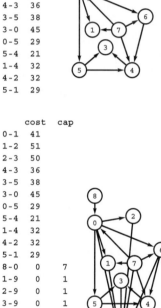

	cost	cap
0-1	41	
1-2	51	
2-3	50	
4-3	36	
3-5	38	
3-0	45	
0-5	29	
5-4	21	
1-4	32	
4-2	32	
5-1	29	
8-0	0	7
1-9	0	1
2-9	0	1
3-9	0	1
4-9	0	1
5-9	0	1
6-9	0	1
7-9	0	1

0-1　41
1-2　51
2-3　50
4-3　36
3-5　38
3-0　45
0-5　29
5-4　21
1-4　32
4-2　32
5-1　29

Figure 22.51
Reduction from shortest paths

Finding a single-source–shortest-paths tree in the network at the top is equivalent to solving the mincost-maxflow problem in the flow network at the bottom.

source vertex with an edge to s that has cost zero and capacity V-1 and a new sink vertex with edges from each of the other vertices with costs zero and capacities 1. This construction is illustrated in Figure 22.51.

Solve the mincost–feasible-flow problem on this network. If necessary, remove cycles in the solution to produce a spanning-tree solution. This spanning tree corresponds directly to a shortest-paths spanning tree of the original network. Detailed proof of this fact is left as an exercise (see Exercise 22.138). ∎

Thus, all the problems discussed in Section 21.6 that reduce to the single-source–shortest-paths problem also reduce to the mincost-flow problem. This set of problems includes job scheduling with deadlines and difference constraints, among numerous others.

As we found when studying maxflow problems, it is worthwhile to consider the details of the operation of the network simplex algorithm when solving a shortest-paths problem using the reduction of Property 22.29. In this case, the algorithm maintains a spanning tree rooted at the source, much like the search-based algorithms that we considered in Chapter 21, but the node potentials and reduced costs provide increased flexibility in developing methods to choose the next edge to add to the tree.

We do not generally exploit the fact that the mincost-flow problem is a proper generalization of both the maxflow and the shortest-paths problems, because we have specialized algorithms with better performance guarantees for both problems. If such implementations are not available, however, a good implementation of the network simplex algorithm is likely to produce quick solutions to particular instances of both problems. Of course, we must avoid reduction loops when using or building network-processing systems that take advantage of such reductions. For example, the cycle-canceling implementation in Program 22.9 uses both maxflow and shortest paths to solve the mincost-flow problem (see Exercise 21.96).

Next, we consider equivalent network models. First, we show that assuming that costs are nonnegative is not restrictive, as we can transform networks with negative costs into networks without them.

Property 22.30 *In mincost-flow problems, we can assume, without loss of generality, that edge costs are nonnegative.*

Proof: We prove this fact for feasible mincost flows in distribution networks. The same result is true for mincost maxflows because of the equivalence of the two problems proved in Property 22.22 (see Exercises 22.143 and 22.144).

Given a distribution network, we replace any edge u–v that has cost $x < 0$ and capacity c by an edge v–u of the same capacity that has cost $-x$ (a positive number). Furthermore, we can decrement the supply-demand value of u by c and increment the supply-demand value of v by c. This operation corresponds to pushing c units of flow from u to v and adjusting the network accordingly.

For negative-cost edges, if a solution to the mincost-flow problem for the transformed network puts flow f in the edge v–u, we put flow $c - f$ in u–v in the original network; for positive-cost edges, the transformed network has the same flow as in the original. This flow assignment preserves the supply or demand constraint at all the vertices.

The flow in v–u in the transformed network contributes fx to the cost and the flow in u–v in the original network contributes $-cx + fx$ to the cost. The first term in this expression does not depend on the flow, so the cost of any flow in the transformed network is equal to the cost of the corresponding flow in the original network plus the sum of the products of the capacities and costs of all the negative-cost edges (which is a negative quantity). Any minimal-cost flow in the transformed network is therefore a minimal-cost flow in the original network. ■

This reduction shows that we can restrict attention to positive costs, but we generally do not bother to do so in practice because our implementations in Sections 22.5 and 22.6 work exclusively with residual networks and handle negative costs with no difficulty. It is important to have *some* lower bound on costs in some contexts, but that bound does not need to be zero (see Exercise 22.145).

Next, we show, as we did for the maxflow problem, that we could, if we wanted, restrict attention to acyclic networks. Moreover, we can also assume that edges are uncapacitated (there is no upper bound on the amount of flow in the edges). Combining these two variations leads to the following classic formulation of the mincost-flow problem.

Transportation   Solve the mincost-flow problem for a bipartite distribution network where all edges are directed from a supply vertex to a demand vertex and have unlimited capacity. As discussed at the beginning of this chapter (see Figure 22.2), the usual way to think of this problem is as modeling the distribution of goods from warehouses (supply vertices) to retail outlets (demand vertices) along distribution channels (edges) at a certain cost per unit amount of goods.

Property 22.31   *The transportation problem is equivalent to the mincost-flow problem.*

Proof: Given a transportation problem, we can solve it by assigning a capacity for each edge higher than the supply or demand values of the vertices that it connects and solving the resulting mincost–feasible-flow problem on the resulting distribution network. Therefore, we need only to establish a reduction from the standard problem to the transportation problem.

For variety, we describe a new transformation, which is linear only for sparse networks. A construction similar to the one that we used in the proof of Property 22.16 establishes the result for nonsparse networks (see Exercise 22.148).

Given a standard distribution network with V vertices and E edges, build a transportation network with V supply vertices, E demand vertices and $2E$ edges, as follows. For each vertex in the original network, include a vertex in the bipartite network with supply or demand value set to the original value plus the sum of the capacities of the outgoing edges; and for each edge u–v in the original network with capacity c, include a vertex in the bipartite network with supply or demand value –c (we use the notation [u–v] to refer to this vertex). For each edge u–v in the original network, include two edges in the bipartite network: one from u to [u–v] with the same cost, and one from v to [u–v] with cost 0.

The following one-to-one correspondence preserves costs between flows in the two networks: An edge u–v has flow value f in the original network if and only if edge u–[u–v] has flow value f, and edge v–[u–v] has flow value c–f in the bipartite network (those two flows must sum to c because of the supply–demand constraint at vertex [u–v]. Thus, any mincost flow in one network corresponds to a mincost flow in the other. ∎

Since we have not considered direct algorithms for solving the transportation problem, this reduction is of academic interest only. To use it, we would have to convert the resulting problem back to a (different) mincost-flow problem, using the simple reduction mentioned at the beginning of the proof of Property 22.31. Perhaps such networks admit more efficient solutions in practice; perhaps they do not. The point of studying the equivalence between the transportation problem and the mincost-flow problem is to understand that removing capacities and restricting attention to bipartite networks would seem to simplify the mincost-flow problem substantially; however, that is not the case.

We need to consider another classical problem in this context. It generalizes the bipartite-matching problem that is discussed in detail in Section 22.4. Like that problem, it is deceptively simple.

Assignment   Given a weighted bipartite graph, find a set of edges of minimum total weight such that each vertex is connected to exactly one other vertex.

For example, we might generalize our job-placement problem to include a way for each company to quantify its desire for each applicant (say by assigning an integer to each applicant, with lower integers going to the better applicants) and for each applicant to quantify his or her desire for each company. Then, a solution to the assignment problem would provide a reasonable way to take these relative preferences into account.

Property 22.32   *The assignment problem reduces to the mincost-flow problem.*

Proof: This result can be established via a simple reduction to the transportation problem. Given an assignment problem, construct a transportation problem with the same vertices and edges, with all vertices in one of the sets designated as supply vertices with value 1 and all vertices in the other set designated as demand vertices with value 1. Assign capacity 1 to each edge, and assign a cost corresponding to that edge's weight in the assignment problem. Any solution to this instance of the transportation problem is simply a set of edges of minimal total cost that each connect a supply vertex to a demand vertex and therefore corresponds directly to a solution to the original assignment problem.

Reducing this instance of the transportation problem to the mincost-maxflow problem gives a construction that is essentially equivalent to the construction that we used to reduce the bipartite-matching problem to the maxflow problem (see Exercise 22.158). ■

This relationship is *not* known to be an equivalence. There is no known way to reduce a general mincost-flow problem to the assignment problem. Indeed, like the single-source–shortest-paths problem and the maxflow problem, the assignment problem seems to be easier than the mincost-flow problem in the sense that algorithms that solve it are known that have better asymptotic performance than the best known algorithms for the mincost-flow problem. Still, the network simplex algorithm is sufficiently well refined that a good implementation of it is a reasonable choice for solving assignment problems. Moreover, as with maxflow and shortest paths, we can tailor the network simplex algorithm to get improved performance for the assignment problem (*see reference section*).

Our next reduction to the mincost-flow problem brings us back to a basic problem related to paths in graphs like the ones that we first considered in Section 17.7. As in the Euler-path problem, we want a path that includes all the edges in a graph. Recognizing that not all graphs have such a path, we relax the restriction that edges must appear only once.

Mail carrier Given a network (weighted digraph), find a cyclic path of minimal weight that includes each edge at least once (see Figure 22.52). Recall that our basic definitions in Chapter 17 make the distinction between cyclic paths (which may revisit vertices and edges) and cycles (which consist of distinct vertices, except the first and the final, which are the same).

The solution to this problem would describe the best route for a mail carrier (who has to cover all the streets on her route) to follow. A solution to this problem might also describe the route that a snowplow should take during a snowstorm, and there are many similar applications.

The mail carrier's problem is an extension of the Euler-tour problem that we discussed in Section 17.7: The solution to Exercise 17.92 is a simple test for whether a digraph has an Euler tour, and Program 17.14 is an effective way to find an Euler tour for such digraphs. That tour solves the mail carrier's problem because it includes each edge exactly once—no path could have lower weight. The problem becomes more difficult when indegrees and outdegrees are not necessarily equal. In the general case, some edges must be traversed more than once: The problem is to minimize the total weight of all the multiply traversed edges.

Property 22.33 *The mail carrier's problem reduces to the mincost-flow problem.*

Proof: Given an instance of the mail carrier's problem (a weighted digraph), define a distribution network on the same vertices and edges, with all the vertex supply or demand values set to 0, edge costs set to the weights of the corresponding edge, and no upper bounds on edge capacities, but all edge capacities constrained to be greater than 1. We interpret a flow value f in an edge u–v as saying that the mail carrier needs to traverse u–v a total of f times.

Find a mincost flow for this network by using the transformation of Exercise 22.146 to remove the lower bound on edge capacities. The flow-decomposition theorem says that we can express the flow as a set of cycles, so we can build a cyclic path from this flow in the same way that we built an Euler tour in an Eulerian graph: We traverse any cycle, taking a detour to traverse another cycle whenever we encounter a node that is on another cycle. ■

A careful look at the mail carrier's problem illustrates yet again the fine line between trivial and intractable in graph algorithms. Suppose that we consider the two-way version of the problem where the network is undirected, and the mail carrier must travel in both directions along each edge. Then, as we noted in Section 18.5, depth-first search (or any graph search) will provide an immediate solution. If, however, it suffices to traverse each undirected edge in either direction, then a solution is significantly more difficult to formulate than is the simple reduction to mincost flow that we just examined, but the problem is still tractable. If some edges are directed and others undirected, the problem becomes NP-hard (*see reference section*).

These are only a few of the scores of practical problems that have been formulated as mincost-flow problems. The mincost-flow problem is even more versatile than the maxflow problem or shortest-paths problems, and the network simplex algorithm effectively solves all problems encompassed by the model.

As we did when we studied maxflow, we can examine how any mincost-flow problem can be cast as an LP problem, as illustrated in

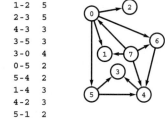

0-1	4
1-2	5
2-3	5
4-3	3
3-5	3
3-0	4
0-5	2
5-4	2
1-4	3
4-2	3
5-1	2

Figure 22.52
Mail carrier's problem

Finding the shortest path that includes each edge at least once is a challenge even for this small network, but the problem can be solved efficiently through reduction to the mincost-flow problem.

Figure 22.53. The formulation is a straightforward extension of the maxflow formulation: We add equations that set a dummy variable to be equal to the cost of the flow, then set the objective so as to minimize that variable. LP models allow addition of arbitrary (linear) constraints. Some constraints may lead to problems that still may be equivalent to mincost-flow problems, but others do not. That is, many problems do not reduce to mincost-flow problems: In particular, LP encompasses a much broader set of problems. The mincost-flow problem is a next step toward that general problem-solving model, which we consider in Part 8.

There are other models that are even more general than the LP model; but LP has the additional virtue that, while LP problems are in general more difficult than mincost-flow problems, effective and efficient algorithms have been invented to solve them. Indeed, perhaps the most important such algorithm is known as the *simplex* method: The network simplex method is a specialized version of the simplex method that applies to the subset of LP problems that correspond to mincost-flow problems, and understanding the network simplex algorithm is a helpful first step in understanding the simplex algorithm.

Exercises

○ **22.133** Show that, when the network simplex algorithm is computing a maxflow, the spanning tree is the union of t-s, a tree containing s and a tree containing t.

22.134 Develop a maxflow implementation based on Exercise 22.133. Choose an eligible edge at random.

22.135 Show, in the style of Figure 22.50, the process of computing a maxflow in the flow network shown in Figure 22.10 using the reduction described in the text and the network simplex implementation of Program 22.14.

22.136 Show, in the style of Figure 22.50, the process of finding shortest paths from 0 in the flow network shown in Figure 22.10 using the reduction described in the text and the network simplex implementation of Program 22.14.

○ **22.137** Prove that all edges in the spanning tree described in the proof of Property 22.29 are on paths directed from the source to leaves.

○ **22.138** Prove that the spanning tree described in the proof of Property 22.29 corresponds to a shortest-paths tree in the original network.

22.139 Suppose that you use the network simplex algorithm to solve a problem created by a reduction from the single-source–shortest-paths problem as

	cap	cost
0-1	2	3
0-2	3	1
1-3	3	1
1-4	1	1
2-3	1	4
2-4	1	2
3-5	2	2
4-5	3	1
0-5	*	9

Maximize $-c$
subject to the constraints
$$x_{01} \leq 2$$
$$x_{02} \leq 3$$
$$x_{13} \leq 3$$
$$x_{14} \leq 1$$
$$x_{23} \leq 1$$
$$x_{24} \leq 1$$
$$x_{35} \leq 2$$
$$x_{45} \leq 3$$
$$x_{50} = x_{01} + x_{02}$$
$$x_{01} = x_{13} + x_{14}$$
$$x_{02} = x_{23} + x_{24}$$
$$x_{13} + x_{23} = x_{35}$$
$$x_{14} + x_{24} = x_{45}$$
$$x_{35} + x_{45} = x_{50}$$

Figure 22.53
LP formulation of a mincost-maxflow problem

This linear program is equivalent to the mincost-maxflow problem for the sample network of Figure 22.40. The edge equalities and vertex inequalities are the same as in Figure 22.39, but the objective is different. The variable c represents the total cost, which is a linear combination of the other variables. In this case,
$c = -9x_{50} + 3x_{01} + x_{02} + x_{13} + x_{14} + 4x_{23} + 2x_{24} + 2x_{35} + x_{45}.$

described in the proof of Property 22.29. (*i*) Prove that the algorithm never uses a zero-cost augmenting path. (*ii*) Show that the edge that leaves the cycle is always the parent of the destination vertex of the edge that is added to the cycle. (*iii*) As a consequence of Exercise 22.138, the network simplex algorithm does not need to maintain edge flows. Provide a full implementation that takes advantage of this observation. Choose the new tree edge at random.

22.140 Suppose that we assign a positive cost to each edge in a network. Prove that the problem of finding a single-source–shortest-paths tree of minimal cost reduces to the mincost-maxflow problem.

22.141 Suppose that we modify the job-scheduling-with-deadlines problem in Section 21.6 to stipulate that jobs can miss their deadlines, but that they incur a fixed positive cost if they do. Show that this modified problem reduces to the mincost-maxflow problem.

22.142 Implement a class that finds mincost maxflows in distribution networks with negative costs. Use your solution to Exercise 22.105 (which assumes that costs are all nonnegative).

○ **22.143** Suppose that the costs of 0–2 and 1–3 in Figure 22.40 are –1, instead of 1. Show how to find a mincost maxflow by transforming the network to a network with positive costs and finding a mincost maxflow of the new network.

22.144 Implement a class that finds mincost maxflows in networks with negative costs. Use MINCOST (which assumes that costs are all nonnegative).

○ **22.145** Do the implementations in Sections 22.5 and 22.6 depend in a fundamental way on costs being nonnegative? If they do, explain how; if they do not, explain what fixes (if any) are required to make them work properly for networks with negative costs, or explain why no such fixes are possible.

22.146 Extend your feasible-flow ADT from Exercise 22.74 to include lower bounds on the capacities of edges. Implement a class that computes a mincost maxflow that respects these bounds (if one exists).

22.147 Give the result of using the reduction in the text to reduce the flow network described in Exercise 22.112 to the transportation problem.

○ **22.148** Show that the mincost-maxflow problem reduces to the transportation problem with just V extra vertices and edges by using a construction similar to the one used in the proof of Property 22.16.

▷ **22.149** Implement a class for the transportation problem that is based on the simple reduction to the mincost-flow problem given in the proof of Property 22.30.

○ **22.150** Develop a class implementation for the mincost-flow problem that is based on the reduction to the transportation problem described in the proof of Property 22.31.

○ **22.151** Develop a class implementation for the mincost-flow problem that is based on the reduction to the transportation problem described in Exercise 22.148.

22.152 Write a program to generate random instances of the transportation problem, then use them as the basis for empirical tests on various algorithms and implementations to solve that problem.

22.153 Find a large instance of the transportation problem online.

22.154 Run empirical studies to compare the two different methods of reducing arbitrary mincost-flow problems to the transportation problem that are discussed in the proof of Property 22.31.

22.155 Write a program to generate random instances of the assignment problem, then use them as the basis for empirical tests on various algorithms and implementations to solve that problem.

22.156 Find a large instance of the assignment problem online.

22.157 The job-placement problem described in the text favors the employers (their total weights are maximized). Formulate a version of the problem such that applicants also express their wishes. Explain how to solve your version.

22.158 Do empirical studies to compare the performance of the two network simplex implementations in Section 22.6 for solving random instances of the assignment problem (see Exercise 22.155) with V vertices and E edges, for a reasonable set of values for V and E.

22.159 The mail carrier's problem clearly has no solution for networks that are not strongly connected (the mail carrier can visit only those vertices that are in the strong component where she starts), but that fact is not mentioned in the reduction of Property 22.33. What happens when we use the reduction on a network that is not strongly connected?

22.160 Run empirical studies for various weighted graphs (see Exercises 21.4–8) to determine average length of the mail carrier's path.

22.161 Give a direct proof that the single-source–shortest-paths problem reduces to the assignment problem.

22.162 Describe how to formulate an arbitrary assignment problem as an LP problem.

○ **22.163** Do Exercise 22.18 for the case where the cost value associated with each edge is −1 (so you minimize unused space in the trucks).

○ **22.164** Devise a cost model for Exercise 22.18 such that the solution is a maxflow that takes a minimal number of days.

22.8 Perspective

Our study of graph algorithms appropriately culminates in the study
of network-flow algorithms for four reasons. First, the network-flow
model validates the practical utility of the graph abstraction in countless applications. Second, the maxflow and mincost-flow algorithms
that we have examined are natural extensions of graph algorithms that
we studied for simpler problems. Third, the implementations exemplify the important role of fundamental algorithms and data structures
in achieving good performance. Fourth, the maxflow and mincost-flow
models illustrate the utility of the approach of developing increasingly
general problem-solving models and using them to solve broad classes
of problems. Our ability to develop efficient algorithms that solve
these problems leaves the door open for us to develop more general
models and to seek algorithms that solve those problems.

Before considering these issues in further detail, we develop further context by listing important problems that we have *not* covered in
this chapter, even though they are closely related to familiar problems.

Maximum matching   In a graph with edge weights, find a subset of edges in which no vertex appears more than once and whose
total weight is such that no other such set of edges has a higher total
weight. We can reduce the *maximum-cardinality matching* problem
in unweighted graphs immediately to this problem, by setting all edge
weights to 1.

The assignment problem and maximum-cardinality bipartite-
matching problems reduce to maximum matching for general graphs.
On the other hand, maximum matching does not reduce to mincost
flow, so the algorithms that we have considered do not apply. The
problem is tractable, although the computational burden of solving
it for huge graphs remains significant. Treating the many techniques
that have been tried for matching on general graphs would fill an entire
volume: The problem is one of those studied most extensively in graph
theory. We have drawn the line in this book at mincost flow, but we
revisit maximum matching in Part 8.

Multicommodity flow   Suppose that we need to compute a
second flow such that the sum of an edge's two flows is limited by
that edge's capacity, both flows are in equilibrium, and the total cost is
minimized. This change models the presence of two different types of
material in the merchandise-distribution problem; for example, should

we put more hamburger or more potatoes in the truck bound for the fast-food restaurant? This change also makes the problem much more difficult and requires more advanced algorithms than those considered here; for example, no analogue to the maxflow–mincut theorem is known to hold for the general case. Formulating the problem as an LP problem is a straightforward extension of the example shown in Figure 22.53, so the problem is tractable (because LP is tractable).

Convex and nonlinear costs   The simple cost functions that we have been considering are linear combinations of variables, and our algorithms for solving them depend in an essential way on the simple mathematical structure underlying these functions. Many applications call for more complicated functions. For example, when we minimize distances, we are led to sums of squares of costs. Such problems cannot be formulated as LP problems, so they require problem-solving models that are even more powerful. Many such problems are not tractable.

Scheduling   We have presented a few scheduling problems as examples. They are barely representative of the hundreds of different scheduling problems that have been posed. The research literature is replete with the study of relationships among these problems and the development of algorithms and implementations to solve the problems (*see reference section*). Indeed, we might have chosen to use scheduling rather than network-flow algorithms to develop the idea for defining general problem-solving models and implementing reductions to solve particular problems (the same might be said of matching). Many scheduling problems reduce to the mincost-flow model.

The scope of combinatorial computing is vast indeed, and the study of problems of this sort is certain to occupy researchers for many years to come. We revisit many of these problems in Part 8, in the context of coping with intractability.

We have presented only a fraction of the studied algorithms that solve maxflow and mincost-flow problems. As indicated in the exercises throughout this chapter, combining the many options available for different parts of various generic algorithms leads to a large number of different algorithms. Algorithms and data structures for basic computational tasks play a significant role in the efficacy of many of these approaches; indeed, some of the important general-purpose algorithms that we have studied were developed in the quest for efficient implementations of network-flow algorithms. This topic is still being studied by many researchers. The development of better algorithms for network-flow problems certainly depends on intelligent use of basic algorithms and data structures.

The broad reach of network-flow algorithms and our extensive use of reductions to extend this reach makes this section an appropriate place to consider some implications of the concept of reduction. For a large class of combinatorial algorithms, these problems represent a watershed in our studies of algorithms, where we stand between the study of efficient algorithms for particular problems and the study of general problem-solving models. There are important forces pulling in both directions.

We are drawn to develop as general a model as possible, because the more general the model, the more problems it encompasses, thereby increasing the usefulness of an efficient algorithm that can solve any problem that reduces to the model. Developing such an algorithm may be a significant, if not impossible, challenge. Even if we do not have an algorithm that is guaranteed to be reasonably efficient, we typically have good algorithms that perform well for specific classes of problems that are of interest. Specific analytic results are often elusive, but we often have persuasive empirical evidence. Indeed, practitioners typically will try the most general model available (or one that has a well-developed solution package) and will look no further if the model works in reasonable time. However, we certainly should strive to avoid using overly general models that lead us to spend excessive amounts of time solving problems for which more specialized models can be effective.

We are also drawn to seek better algorithms for important specific problems, particularly for huge problems or huge numbers of instances of smaller problems where computational resources are a critical bottleneck. As we have seen for numerous examples throughout this book and in Parts 1 through 4, we often can find a clever algorithm that can reduce resource costs by factors of hundreds or thousands or more, which is extremely significant if we are measuring costs in hours or dollars. The general outlook described in Chapter 2, which we have used successfully in so many domains, remains extremely valuable in such situations, and we can look forward to the development of clever algorithms throughout the spectrum of graph algorithms and combinatorial algorithms. Perhaps the most important drawback to depending too heavily on a specialized algorithm is that often a small change to the model will invalidate the algorithm. When we use an overly general model and an algorithm that gets our problem solved, we are less vulnerable to this defect.

Software libraries that encompass many of the algorithms that we have addressed may be found in many programming environments. Such libraries certainly are important resources to consider for specific problems. However, libraries may be difficult to use, obsolete, or poorly matched to the problem at hand. Experienced programmers know the importance of considering the trade-off between taking advantage of a library resource and becoming overly dependent on that resource (if not subject to premature obsolescence). Some of the implementations that we have considered are efficient, simple to develop, and broad in scope. Adapting and tuning such implementations to address problems at hand can be the proper approach in many situations.

The tension between theoretical studies that are restricted to what we can prove and empirical studies that are relevant to only the problems at hand becomes ever more pronounced as the difficulty of the problems that we address increases. The theory provides the guidance that we need to gain a foothold on the problem, and practical experience provides the guidance that we need to develop implementations. Moreover, experience with practical problems suggests new directions for the theory, perpetuating the cycle that expands the class of practical problems that we can solve.

Ultimately, whichever approach we pursue, the goal is the same: We want a broad spectrum of problem-solving models, effective algorithms for solving problems within those models, and efficient implementations of those algorithms that can handle practical problems. The development of increasingly general problem-solving models (such as the shortest paths, maxflow, and mincost-flow problems), the increasingly powerful generic algorithms (such as the Bellman–Ford algorithm for the shortest-paths problem, the augmenting-path algorithm for the maxflow problem, and the network simplex algorithm for the mincost-maxflow problem) brought us a long way towards the goal. Much of this work was done in the 1950s and 1960s. The subsequent emergence of fundamental data structures (Parts 1 through 4) and of algorithms that provide effective implementations of these generic methods (this book) has been an essential force leading to our current ability to solve such a large class of huge problems.

References for Part Five

The algorithms textbooks listed below cover most of the basic graph-processing algorithms in Chapters 17 through 21. These books are basic references that give careful treatments of fundamental and advanced graph algorithms, with extensive references to the recent literature. The book by Even and the monograph by Tarjan are devoted to thorough coverage of many of the same topics that we have discussed. Tarjan's original paper on the application of depth-first search to solve strong connectivity and other problems merits further study. The source-queue topological sort implementation in Chapter 19 is from Knuth's book. Original references for some of the other specific algorithms that we have covered are listed below.

The algorithms for minimum spanning trees in dense graphs in Chapter 20 are quite old, but the original papers by Dijkstra, Prim, and Kruskal still make interesting reading. The survey by Graham and Hell provides a thorough and entertaining history of the problem. The paper by Chazelle is the state of the art in the quest for a linear MST algorithm.

The book by Ahuja, Magnanti, and Orlin is a comprehensive treatment of network-flow algorithms (and shortest-paths algorithms). Further information on nearly every topic covered in Chapters 21 and 22 may be found in that book. Another source for further material is the classic book by Papadimitriou and Steiglitz. Though most of that book is about much more advanced topics, it carefully treats many of the algorithms that we have discussed. Both books have extensive and detailed information about source material from the research literature. The classic work by Ford and Fulkerson is still worthy of study, as it introduced many of the fundamental concepts.

We have briefly introduced numerous advanced topics from (the yet to be published) Part 8, including reducibility, intractability, and linear programming, among several others. This reference list is focused on the material that we cover in detail and cannot do justice to these advanced topics. The algorithms texts treat many of them, and the book by Papadimitriou and Steiglitz provides a thorough introduction. There are numerous other books and a vast research literature on these topics.

R. K. Ahuja, T. L. Magnanti, and J. B. Orlin, *Network Flows: Theory, Algorithms, and Applications*, Prentice Hall, 1993.

B. Chazelle, "A minimum spanning tree algorithm with inverse-Ackermann type complexity," *Journal of the ACM*, **47** (2000).

T. H. Cormen, C. L. Leiserson, and R. L. Rivest, *Introduction to Algorithms*, MIT Press and McGraw-Hill, 1990.

E. W. Dijkstra, "A note on two problems in connexion with graphs," *Numerische Mathematik*, **1** (1959).

P. Erdös and A. Renyi, "On the evolution of random graphs," *Magyar Tud. Akad. Mat. Kutato Int Kozl*, **5** (1960).

S. Even, *Graph Algorithms*, Computer Science Press, 1979.

L. R. Ford and D. R. Fulkerson, *Flows in Networks*, Princeton University Press, 1962.

H. N. Gabow, "Path-based depth-first search for strong and biconnected components," *Information Processing Letters*, **74** (2000).

R. L. Graham and P. Hell, "On the history of the minimum spanning tree problem," *Annals of the History of Computing*, **7** (1985).

D. B. Johnson, "Efficient shortest path algorithms," Journal of the ACM, **24** (1977).

D. E. Knuth, *The Art of Computer Programming. Volume 1: Fundamental Algorithms*, third edition, Addison-Wesley, 1997.

J. R. Kruskal Jr., "On the shortest spanning subtree of a graph and the traveling salesman problem," *Proceedings AMS*, **7**, 1 (1956).

K. Mehlhorn, *Data Structures and Algorithms 2: NP-Completeness and Graph Algorithms*, Springer-Verlag, 1984.

C. H. Papadimitriou and K. Steiglitz, *Combinatorial Optimization: Algorithms and Complexity*, Prentice-Hall, 1982.

R. C. Prim, "Shortest connection networks and some generalizations," *Bell System Technical Journal*, **36** (1957).

R. E. Tarjan, "Depth-first search and linear graph algorithms," *SIAM Journal on Computing*, **1**, 2 (1972).

R. E. Tarjan, *Data Structures and Network Algorithms*, Society for Industrial and Applied Mathematics, Philadelphia, PA, 1983.

Index

ALGORITHMS

Essential Volumes for Every Programmer's Library

Robert Sedgewick has thoroughly rewritten his long popular work to provide current and comprehensive coverage of the most important algorithms and data structures. His substantially expanded *Third Edition* now comprises three volumes, with implementations in key programming languages.

Parts 1–4. The first volume published covers basic algorithms and data structures, with implementations available in C or C++.

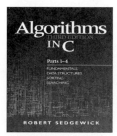

**Algorithms in C,
Third Edition, Parts 1–4**
*Fundamentals, Data Structures,
Sorting, Searching*

ISBN 0-201-31452-5
© 1998
Paperback

**Algorithms in C++,
Third Edition, Parts 1–4**
*Fundamentals, Data Structures,
Sorting, Searching*

ISBN 0-201-35088-2
© 1999
Paperback

Part 5. The second volume published focuses on graph algorithms, with implementations available in C or C++.

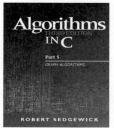

**Algorithms in C,
Third Edition, Part 5**
Graph Algorithms

ISBN 0-201-31663-3
© 2002
Paperback

**Algorithms in C++,
Third Edition, Part 5**
Graph Algorithms

ISBN 0-201-36118-3
© 2002
Paperback

Parts 6–8. A future third volume will cover strings, geometry, and a variety of other advanced topics.

Coming Next

A Java version of the first volume
will be available early in 2002.

**Algorithms in Java,
Third Edition, Parts 1–4**
*Fundamentals, Data Structures,
Sorting, Searching*

ISBN 0-201-36120-5
Coming in 2002
Paperback

Bundles

The first two volumes are now available in a single package. Instructors should contact their local Addison-Wesley representative for details.

http://www.awl.com/cseng/

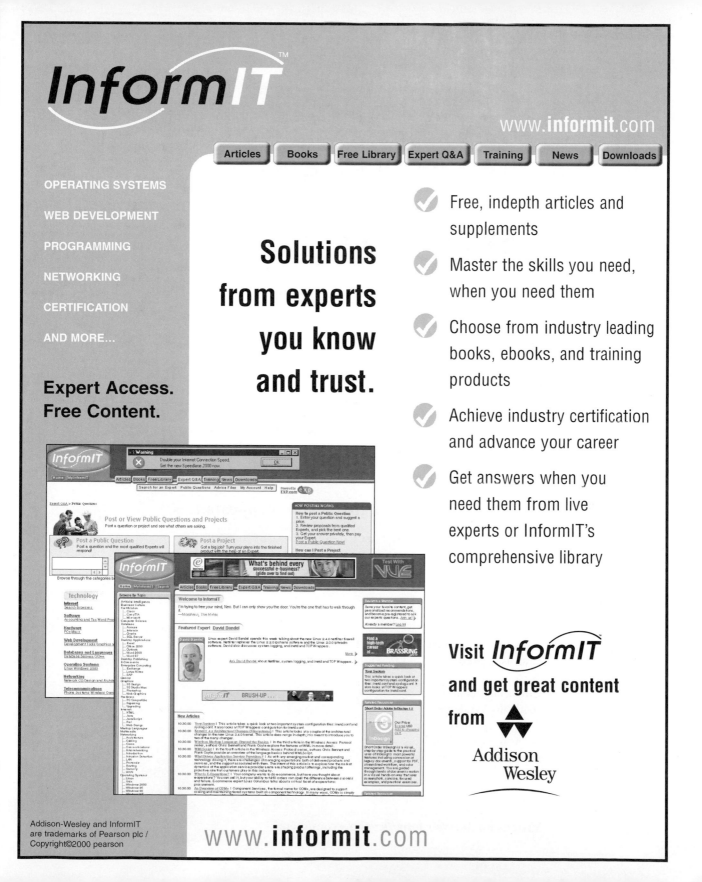

Register
Your Book
at www.aw.com/cseng/register

You may be eligible to receive:
- Advance notice of forthcoming editions of the book
- Related book recommendations
- Chapter excerpts and supplements of forthcoming titles
- Information about special contests and promotions throughout the year
- Notices and reminders about author appearances, tradeshows, and online chats with special guests

Contact us

If you are interested in writing a book or reviewing manuscripts prior to publication, please write to us at:

Editorial Department
Addison-Wesley Professional
75 Arlington Street, Suite 300
Boston, MA 02116 USA
Email: AWPro@aw.com

Addison-Wesley

Visit us on the Web: http://www.aw.com/cseng

Cost Control in Building Design

Cost Control
in Building Design

An interactive learning text

Roger Flanagan
Department of Construction Management & Engineering
The University of Reading

and

Brian Tate
Department of Land and Construction Management
University of Portsmouth

b

Blackwell
Science

692.5/FLA

11398407

© 1997 by
Blackwell Science Ltd
Editorial Offices:
Osney Mead, Oxford OX2 0EL
25 John Street, London WC1N 2BL
23 Ainslie Place, Edinburgh EH3 6AJ
350 Main Street, Malden
  MA 02148 5018, USA
54 University Street, Carlton
  Victoria 3053, Australia

Other Editorial Offices:

Blackwell Wissenschafts-Verlag GmbH
  Kurfürstendamm 57
  10707 Berlin, Germany

Zehetnergasse 6
A-1140 Wien
Austria

First published 1997

Set in 10/13 Zapf
by DP Photosetting, Aylesbury, Bucks
Printed and bound in Great Britain by
Hartnolls Ltd, Bodmin, Cornwall

DISTRIBUTORS

Marston Book Services Ltd
PO Box 269
Abingdon
Oxon OX14 4YN
(*Orders:* Tel: 01235 465500
         Fax: 01235 465555)

USA
  Blackwell Science, Inc.
  Commerce Place
  350 Main Street
  Malden, MA 02148 5018
  (*Orders:* Tel: 800 759 6102
           617 388 8250
    Fax: 617 388 8255)

Canada
  Copp Clark Professional
  200 Adelaide Street, West, 3rd Floor
  Toronto, Ontario M5H 1W7
  (*Orders:* Tel: 416 597-1616
           800 815 9417
    Fax: 416 597 1617)

Australia
  Blackwell Science Pty Ltd
  54 University Street
  Carlton, Victoria 3053
  (*Orders:* Tel: 03 9347 0300
           Fax: 03 9347 5001)

A catalogue record for this title is available from the
British Library

ISBN 0-632-04028-9

Library of Congress
Cataloging-in-Publication Data
is available

This publication contains material from *Research and Development Building Management Handbook
4: Cost Control in Building Design – A Programmed Text* which was written by the Programme
Division of International Tutor Machines Ltd in conjunction with the Directorate of Building
Management, Ministry of Public Buildings & Works. © Crown copyright 1968. Reproduced
with the permission of the Controller of Her Majesty's Stationery Office.

The RIBA Outline Plan of Work is reproduced with the permission of the copyright holder.
© RIBA Publishing.

Contents

Preface

The importance of cost control in the construction industry does not have to be justified. Clients want projects to be built within budget, on time, and to their required standard. Contractors and specialist contractors want to build a facility to meet the clients' needs within the tender figure, but also ensures they make a reasonable profit. Cost control is at the heart of the management of the construction process.

This book is notable for two reasons. Firstly, it explores all the issues that affect cost control on a construction project. Secondly, the contents are presented in the form of a 'programmed text'. It uses as its starting point the HMSO programmed text on cost control in building design produced in the 1960s. Over the past 30 years a great deal has changed in the construction industry. There are now severe pressures to reduce the cost of projects and to build faster. Cost cannot simply be monitored, it must be managed and controlled. That requires a good understanding of cost planning from the concept stage right through to completion.

There is a great deal for the student and young professional to learn. The purpose of this book is to develop the ideas of cost control from first principles and to take them forward into practice.

Programmed learning has shown its potential in many spheres. The main advantages are that individuals can go at the pace that is best for them. The material is presented in a readily understandable form which can be followed at any convenient time and is not restricted to a set of lectures or talks.

The material in the book is equally applicable to any project in the international construction market place. Cost control and cost planning are as appropriate to projects being built in the developing world as they are in the developed world. This book uses examples from the British construction industry, but is not restricted to simply British thinking.

The book is divided into two parts, the first part deals with the principles of cost control. The second part deals with the techniques of cost control. Worked examples are used throughout to guide the reader from first principles to the most up-to-date thinking in the area of cost control and management.

Part 1

The Principles of Cost Control

1 The Importance of Control over Expenditure

This chapter *is not* in programmed form.

The construction industry and the environment in which it operates have changed significantly – the process of change now seems to be never ending and hectic. There have been:

- ❑ new approaches to buying design and construction
- ❑ fragmentation of the industry with the increase in specialist trade contracting
- ❑ the demise of direct employment and the growth of labour-only and fixed-term contracts
- ❑ fee competition for consultancy services
- ❑ the introduction of partnering
- ❑ more conflict and less trust
- ❑ clients wanting more value for money.

The boom–bust business cycles mean that the industry lurches from over-supply of resources to under supply. Against this background, contractors and consultants have to cope with the ever-increasing pressures for faster construction to a higher quality at a lower cost. Information technology has also made an impact with computer aided design (CAD) and electronic data interchange of information.

However, what has not changed is the importance of effective cost control. Costs should not be simply monitored, they need to be controlled and managed from the early design stage through to project completion. Some CAD systems give cost information, but they cannot control costs, that requires specialist human knowledge.

Clients want:

- ❑ certainty of price
- ❑ projects constructed within budget

3

❏ completion on time
❏ the best quality possible for the price
❏ value for money
❏ no surprises.

Contractors and consultants want:

❏ a reasonable return for the risks they take
❏ payment on time
❏ clients who do not keep changing their minds
❏ satisfied clients
❏ repeat business.

The aims of clients and contractors are not in conflict; they are complementary.

Four pressures

In this chapter we examine how change has come about by reference to four pressures:

1 *Society is having to cope with rapid technological and sociological change at a pace never seen before. Managing risk, avoiding unpleasant surprises ensuring value for money and speeding up the overall project delivery time is important for clients.*

'Time is money' said Samuel Johnson, and it is still true today. Speed of design and construction have become very important. The traditional route to getting something built was to fully design the project, produce a bill of quantities, obtain tenders, award the contract to the lowest bidder. The system is tried and tested and is still largely used today. The failing is that the project is often only half or three-quarters designed when it goes to tender. The shortcoming is not the fault of the design team, it is simply that pressures cause the project to get to the construction phase as quickly as possible.

Procurement systems which overlap the design and construction phase have become accepted practice for larger projects. Management contracting, construction management, and various other agency fee arrangements adopt this approach. Here cost control is exercised via a cost plan based on work packages where both design and production costs jointly come under scrutiny.

Design and build, sometimes called package deal and turnkey approaches, can also be used by clients where they want single-point responsibility. However, even here clients will demand early cost advice and budget control from their professional advisers, before finally passing the risk for cost control to the contractor. The degree and method of cost control exercised by consultants will depend on the type of design and build used.

For some, the traditional approach is more appropriate, where design consultants produce a completed or near complete design prior to start on site. This will entail a fairly lengthy design stage and consideration needs to be given to controlling costs over this stage.

One way or another, both in the commercial and non-commercial world, time is important to many clients. Where design is separated from the production stage, clients are less willing to tolerate the delay caused by redesigning buildings when tenders are too high. We therefore need a technique for producing designs for buildings which can be built within the expenditure limits.

When the risk of cost control is passed to the contractor, as with most forms of design and build contracts, then the contractor will develop suitable cost control strategies. Although much of the design might be complete prior to start on site, nevertheless the design still has a certain amount of flexibility built into it. Thus design and production costs are brought together under the control of the contractor. Given this situation it is likely that the contractor will use cost control procedures which look at resource costs. Resource costing is a subject in its own right which is only briefly discussed later.

2 *The second pressure is that construction projects are more complex. This has been brought about, in part, by the requirements of clients who know what they want to achieve. In brief, clients' requirements are becoming more complicated and more demanding.*

Wherever you look, buildings and project schemes are becoming more complex. Take as an example a typical modern shopping centre located in the heart of a city, with all shopping units housed under one roof, providing covered malls, integrated parking facilities, and goods storage, but separating the means of goods delivery. Consider the control of the internal environment, fire safety, security control systems, and the trading requirements with point of sale computer systems. This is very different to constructing the one-off shop in the village street. Similarly, think of a hospital project where 50% of the cost is in the environmental engineering services.

Much of the complexity comes about because of the environmental engineering services element. More thought is given to the internal environment. For example, atria are now commonly incorporated into building designs. Another example is the increased use of information technology which has meant that buildings designed no more than 20 years ago are technologically obsolete.

This increasing technical complexity of construction means that there are many more opportunities for the cost of a project to get out of hand. We therefore need an effective system for the strict control of costs from inception to completion of a project and then onwards throughout the life of the facility. Throughout this programme we will be discussing control of costs. Unless otherwise stated, 'cost' shall mean 'cost to the client'.

3 *The third pressure stems from the increased number of groups who have interests in a project.*

Undertaking a construction project is a complex process which involves many bodies and organisations. Effective co-ordination between the various parties is crucial for successful completion of both design and construction. In general, these parties are frequently referred to as the 'client', the 'design team' and the 'construction group'.

The 'client' can be an owner-occupier, a pension fund, an insurance company, a development company, a retail organisation, a large industrial corporation, a privatised utility, a housing association, or a government department. The full list is extensive. Some build for profit (office blocks), some as a factor of production (factories, oil rigs), some to fulfil a social need (old people's homes, schools), and some to enjoy the use of the facility (churches, housing). Most importantly, the word 'client' (referred to as the owner or promoter in many countries) is a catch-all term that hides a multitude of interests and needs. All clients are different in their expectations, and the design and construction team must recognise this. However, in every case the management of the cost will be high on their agenda.

Client group
The client group will frequently comprise a range of members including:

- ❏ technical advisers
- ❏ legal advisers
- ❏ financial advisers
- ❏ property advisers
- ❏ maintenance engineers
- ❏ project managers
- ❏ manufacturing/process experts.

Design team
Design teams will frequently comprise:

- ❏ architects
- ❏ structural engineers
- ❏ quantity surveyors/cost consultants
- ❏ project managers
- ❏ acoustics engineers
- ❏ interior designers
- ❏ landscape architects
- ❏ hydraulics engineers
- ❏ mechanical electrical engineers.

Construction group
The construction group will include:

- ❏ the general contractor
- ❏ specialist contractors
- ❏ specialist suppliers
- ❏ component manufacturers
- ❏ sub-contractors
- ❏ utility companies including gas, electricity, water, telephone
- ❏ building materials suppliers.

Other groups

Other groups who may have an interest in the construction process include:

- central government
- local authorities (planning, highways and building control)
- labour unions
- heritage/conservation groups.

The funding of construction projects has become very complex. For example, on the Channel Tunnel project there were 220 financial institutions involved. On a commercial development project built to lease to tenants there could be many funding bodies, ranging from the developer to, not least, the final occupier or tenant. A project might have an international flavour with overseas banks involved, or there might be a grant from the European Union or similar body.

There are few projects in the world where the design team has been told not to worry about the cost!

Public sector organisations are subject to audit and public scrutiny of their accounts; value for money and accountability are high on their priority list. In the private sector, a public company must act in the best interests of the shareholders, while a privately owned company will always be seeking to optimise expenditure. In every case, whenever an organisation gets involved in a construction project, the overriding objective will be to manage the cost within budget.

Actual building expenditure must accord closely to estimated expenditure. The cost consultants are usually instructed to forecast and budget the cost of a building at the very early concept stage before drawings and specifications are available, and they are often required to keep to their first estimate. Clients are increasingly resorting to litigation when things go wrong.

4 *The fourth pressure stems from modern practice in design, where new ideas, techniques, materials and components are used.*

Methods of construction or, perhaps more accurately, of assembly have advanced. Improvements in site plant and equipment, both large and small, have transformed the site processes. Architectural ideas have changed and designs have progressed, so much so that at times there is no precedent or data base from previous projects upon which to base estimates.

This increasing range of choice in materials, types of building and architectural developments in design styles can have a tendency to make one-off initial cost estimates unreliable so that the final account is seldom equal to this first estimate. Under such conditions continuous cost control is required.

Where continuous cost control has not been exercised, then it is quite likely that tenders received will exceed a client's budget limit. In such a situation the usual response is to look for savings within the specification. At this late stage, such action usually has undesirable implications for the architect's carefully thought-out design. Accordingly, unless effective techniques are put into place from the outset, it might not be possible to achieve a balanced design and thus ensure value for money.

The cost planning framework

Cost planning is a system of relating the design of buildings to their cost, so that, while taking full account of quality, utility and appearance, the cost is planned to be within the economic limit of expenditure. Cost planning procedures are applied in an attempt to reduce the amount of resources (and therefore cost) incurred during each stage of the development process, including design, construction, operation and maintenance, and subsequent replacement.

Although effective execution of the development process will demand an integrated approach to cost planning, this book focuses solely on the design process. Design cost planning is particularly crucial as decisions made during the early stages of the development process carry more far-reaching economic consequences than the relatively limited decisions which can be made later in the process, as illustrated by Fig. 1.1.

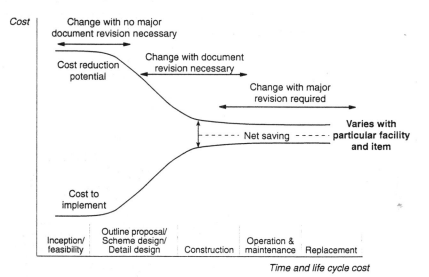

Fig. 1.1 Impact on cost of incorporating a corrective change or a better idea

Figure 1.1 shows the typical life cycle of a project from concept through to operation and occupation. The cost reduction potential curve illustrates that the most significant cost reductions are achieved during the design and development stages of the project. During these stages large cost savings can be achieved as the design is flexible enough to incorporate relatively significant changes. Once the project has reached the construction stage, the potential for achieving cost reductions is significantly lower. Additionally, any cost reduction associated with this curve will have a resultant cost of implementation. The 'cost to implement' curve must be viewed against the 'cost reduction' curve in order to assess the net saving to the total project cost.

During the later stages of the project life cycle the net saving potential will diminish as the two curves converge. In fact, some changes will not be implemented as the net effect on total cost is nil or negative.

Figure 1.1 also illustrates that any changes to the project will require alterations to documentation (drawings, specifications, bills of quantities, schedules, etc.). During the early stages of the project design, changes are unlikely to result in significant document revisions, particularly prior to the production of detailed drawings. More documentation will be produced and the potential for disruption is increased during subsequent stages of the project's life cycle.

Chapter 1 – Summary

In this chapter we have identified four main pressures which make it more difficult, and consequently even more important, to control building costs for clients.

It is equally important that if cost control is directly related to capital costs with little regard for aesthetic qualities or life cycle costs, then the buildings which result will suffer. Under these circumstances clients will not be best served or receive real value for their investment.

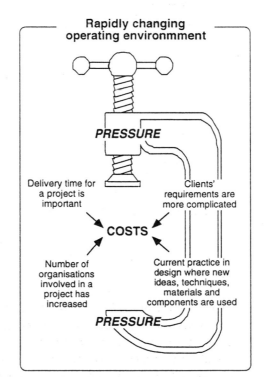

Turn to page 11 ⟩

2 The Purpose of Cost Control

This chapter *is* in programmed form and you must follow the page directions exactly.

Turn to page 12 ⟶

from page 11

As you work through this chapter (and the other programmed chapters) you will find it useful to have at hand a notebook and a pen or pencil.

Write down the number of each page to which you are directed, *before* you read the page. In this way, you will be able to follow your route through the programme, or find your place again easily after a break.

Also make sure you write down your answer to every question. Where a choice of answers is given, write down your choice *before* proceeding to the next page.

Feel free to make any notes from the programme as you work through it.

Turn to page 13

from page 12 In Chapter 1, you read why there was a need for cost control. This need is due to *four* main pressures:

Four

pressures

(1) The delivery time for a project is important.
(2) Client's requirements are more complicated.
(3) The number of organisations involved in a project has increased.
(4) Current practice in design, where new ideas, techniques, materials and components are used.

Now that we have established the need for a cost control system, we must ask ourselves what the system should do; that is, what is the purpose of this system? Let us see how you view this problem of cost control.

Write down what you consider to be the purpose of a cost control system.

Compare your answer with the four possible answers shown below, and then turn to the appropriate page. Pick the answer which corresponds most closely to yours.

To give the client good value for money. *Turn to page 20*

Value for money	*Value for money does not simply mean the lowest initial capital cost. There has to be a balance between quality, fitness for purpose, initial capital cost, and the life cycle cost over the life of the element. The life cycle cost means expenditure on the running costs including maintenance, fuel, cleaning, and replacement.*

To achieve the required balance of expenditure between the various parts of the building. *Turn to page 18*

Balance of expenditure	*Balance of expenditure between the various parts of the building means ensuring that the cost is distributed across the elements to meet the client's and designer's requirements. For example, it may not be appropriate to spend an excessive amount on the finishings with the result that the roof specification and cost has to be minimised.*

To keep expenditure within the amount allowed by the client. *Turn to page 16*

All of the above three. *Turn to page 14*

⊃ *from page 13* You chose: **All of the above three.**

You are perfectly correct.

There are *three* purposes of having a cost control system:

(1) Giving the client good value for money.

(2) Achieving the required balance of expenditure between the various parts of the building.

(3) Keeping expenditure within the amount allowed by the client.

> **Important**.
> Remember these as they will be used throughout the text.

This programme will be concerned mainly with the third purpose – keeping expenditure within the amount allowed by the client – although in achieving this third purpose, the other two purposes can also be satisfied.

This means that the final account to the client *should not* excceed the first estimate.

Turn to page 19 ⊃

This means that the final account to the client *can* exceed the first estimate.

Turn to page 17 ⊃

Turn to the page corresponding to the statement which you consider to be correct.

from pages 16, 18, 20

There are *three* purposes of having a cost control system.

This programme will be concerned mainly with the third purpose – keeping expenditure within the amount allowed by the client – although in achieving this third purpose, the other two purposes can also be satisfied.

This means that the final account to the client *should not* exceed the first estimate. *Turn to page 19*

This means that the final account to the client *can* exceed the first estimate. *Turn to page 17*

Turn to the page corresponding to the statement which you consider to be correct.

Some terminology:

Estimate	*The estimated cost based upon information that is available ranging from brief to detailed design information. A contractor estimates the cost of a project and submits a tender, which is a contractual offer.*
Forecast price prediction	*Term sometimes used in practice to represent an estimate.*
Budget	*The amount established for the project which should not be exceeded.*
First estimate	*Term we have used already which is the client's first estimate and is often used to establish the budget.*
Final account	*The cost of the project upon completion.*

⟩ *from page 13* You chose:

To keep expenditure within the amount allowed by the client.

You are only partly correct, as

To give the client good value for money

and

To achieve the required balance of expenditure between the various parts of the building

are also important.

How many purposes of cost control are there?

Write down your answer.

Turn to page 15 ⟩

⊃ *from pages*
  14, 15

You are incorrect.

When a client accepts a first estimate, the first estimate becomes the 'amount allowed by the client'. In a straightforward project, therefore, the final cost of the building should *not* exceed the first estimate.

The only possible exception to this is when the client orders additional work after the first estimate has been accepted.

The final account may of course be *less* than the first estimate, but this is a very rare occurrence!

Suppose a client is presented with an account for £1 000 000 when the estimate was £800 000. Has the main purpose been fulfilled?

Write down your answer.

Turn to page 21 ⊃

⊃ *from page 13* You chose: **To achieve the required balance of expenditure between the various parts of the building.**

Balance of expenditure	*Balance of expenditure between the various parts of the building means ensuring that the cost is distributed across the elements to meet the client's and designer's requirements. For example, it may not be appropriate to spend an excessive amount on the finishings with the result that the roof specification and cost has to be minimised.*

You are only partly correct, as

To give the client good value for money

and

To keep expenditure within the amount allowed by the client

are also important.

How many purposes of cost control are there?

Write down your answer.

Turn to page 15 ⊃

from pages 14, 15

You are correct.

When a client accepts a first estimate, the first estimate then becomes the 'amount allowed by the client', in effect the budget for the construction cost. As long as the client does not order any additional work after he has accepted the first estimate, the final account should not exceed the first estimate.

If a client is presented with an account for £1 000 000 when the estimate was £800 000, has the main purpose been fulfilled?

Write down your answer.

> • *The total cost. Bear in mind that the total cost for the project will include the land cost, the design team fees, legal expenses, construction cost, taxation costs, planning and building control fees, and the cost of the interest charges on any debt capital used to finance the project. Hence, while the construction cost may be £2 000 000, the total cost of the project to the client may well be £4 500 000.* •

Turn to page 21

⤵ *from page 13* You chose: **To give the client good value for money.**

Value for money	*Value for money does not simply mean the lowest initial capital cost. There has to be a balance between quality, fitness for purpose, initial capital cost, and the life cycle cost over the life of the element. The life cycle cost means expenditure on the running costs including maintenance, fuel, cleaning and replacement.*

You are only partly correct, as

To achieve the required balance of expenditure between the various parts of the building

and

To keep expenditure within the amount allowed by the client

are also important.

How many purposes of cost control are there?

Write down your answer.

Turn to page 15 ⤵

⊃ *from page 21*

You said: **The design team *would* keep their first estimate within this amount.**

You are correct.

If the design team did not do this, then the client would have to reject their design as there would not be sufficient finance for building.

We have been discussing one way in which the first estimate is formulated: the client stipulates the desired cost limit and the design team examines the feasibility of keeping the first estimate within this amount.

The other possibility is that the client may give the design team a detailed description of the building he requires and asks the design team to submit an estimate.

Provided that the client accepts this estimate, will he expect the final cost to exceed this?

Write down your answer.

Turn to page 25 ⊃

⟩ *from pages 17, 19*

No, the main purpose has not been fulfilled.

Let us consider how the design team decides on a first estimate for a project. Basically, there are two possibilities.

One possibility is that the client can stipulate the maximum amount that can be spent on the project.

What would happen then?

The design team *would* keep their first estimate within this amount

Turn to page 22 ⟩

The design team *would not* keep their first estimate within this amount.

Turn to page 24 ⟩

⊃ *from page 24*   **No.**

If the client did accept, they would be unable to pay the extra £80 000. In these circumstances, the client must either amend the brief or abandon the project.

We have been discussing one way in which the first estimate is formulated: the client stipulates the desired cost limit and the design team examines the feasibility of keeping the first estimate within this amount.

The other possibility is that the client may give the design team a detailed description of the required building and ask the design team to submit an estimate.

Provided that the client accepts the estimate, will he expect the final cost to exceed this?

Write down your answer.

Turn to page 25 ⊃

from page 21

You said: **The design team *would not* keep their first estimate within this amount.**

You are wrong.

If the client only had £800 000 to spend, there would be no point in the design team making the estimate greater than £800 000, as this represents the maximum the client could spend on the building. The client would therefore not have accepted the estimate.

If the estimate is justifiably greater than £800 000 – that is, the building the client wants just cannot be built for £800 000 – then it is up to the design team to persuade the client either to be prepared to spend more or amend the brief to the design team.

Could the client then accept an estimate of £880 000, if the maximum funds for building are £800 000?

Write down your answer.

Experienced and inexperienced clients	*It is important that the clients realise what they are getting for their investment. Clients range from organisations that have an ongoing development programme, such as a department store chain or a hospital trust, to those that build once in their lives. The first type of client is experienced and understands the industry, the latter group is inexperienced and will not fully understand what will be provided.*

Turn to page 23

↪ *from pages 22, 23*

No.

Provided the brief is not altered, he will expect the final account, on completion of the building, not to exceed the first estimate.

We have been discussing the possibilities of:

(a) the client stipulating a maximum cost, and

(b) the client giving a detailed brief to the design team to work out the cost.

Most projects, of course, lie somewhere between these two extremes.

Now, write down the purpose of cost control with which this programme will be concerned.

Turn to page 27 ↪

from page 28

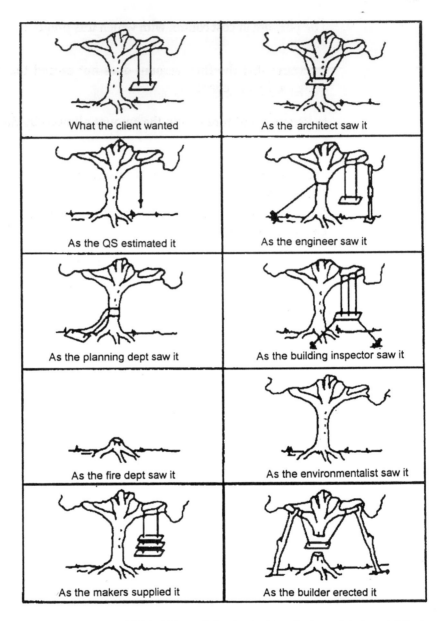

What the client wanted	As the architect saw it
As the QS estimated it	As the engineer saw it
As the planning dept saw it	As the building inspector saw it
As the fire dept saw it	As the environmentalist saw it
As the makers supplied it	As the builder erected it

(Original idea and sketches by Dave Taylor and Anthony Walker)

Turn to page 29

from page 25 You should have written:

The purpose of cost control with which this programme is concerned is:

**to ensure that the final account does not exceed the first estimate accepted by the client
and
to keep expenditure within the amount allowed by the client**

This forms the objective of the cost control procedures which will be discussed in this programme.

These procedures are designed to control the effects of the four pressures mentioned in Chapter 1.

Turn to page 28

⊃ *from page 27* ## Chapter 2 – Summary

The Three Purposes of Cost Control

(1) To give the client good value for money.
(2) To achieve the required balance of expenditure between the various parts of the building.
(3) To keep expenditure within the amount allowed by the client.

This programme is mainly concerned with the third purpose, that is, keeping expenditure within the amount allowed by the client. Thus tenders received should not exceed the amount allowed by the client. In achieving this purpose, however, the other two purposes can also be satisfied.

The ultimate aim is to ensure that the final account does not exceed the first estimate.

In this programme we only go as far as discussing cost control procedures during the design stages.

These procedures are designed to control the effects of the four pressures mentioned in Chapter 1.

Communication	*Clear, concise and accurate communications are essential to ensure that all participants in the process understand what is required. The illustration on page 26 shows vividly what can go wrong.*

Turn to page 26 ⊃

3 The Principles of Cost Control

This chapter *is* in programmed form and you must follow the page directions exactly.

Turn to page 30

from page 29 In the last chapter, you learned that there are three purposes of a cost control system, and that we shall be most concerned in this programme with the third purpose – that is, keeping expenditure within the amount allowed by the client.

In this programme, we shall concentrate on the design stage prior to operations on site. We will assume that the architect is responsible for leading the design team, although this is not essential as, for example, overall management could fall to an independent project manager. We are following, in principle, the RIBA *Outline Plan of Work*, and we will make reference to that document in subsequent chapters. Furthermore, we shall only deal with the processes as far as the Tender Stage. Cost control practices during construction are dealt with in other texts.

In this chapter, we will consider the nature of this system; that is, the principles of a cost control system at the design stage.

Analysis of any control system, more often than not, highlights the fact that there are three basic principles:

The Three Basic Principles

Principle One

There must be a frame of reference or set of conditions which must be adhered to.

Principle Two

There must be a method of checking or a feed-back system.

Principle Three

There must be a means of remedial action.

> **Important.**
> Remember these as they will be used throughout the text.

Let us now consider these principles in the context of a cost control system.

How will a cost control system incorporate these three basic principles?

Turn to page 31

from page 30 Remember, the three basic principles of a control system are:

Principle One
There must be a frame of reference or set of conditions which must be adhered to.

Principle Two
There must be a method of checking or a feed-back system.

Principle Three
There must be a means of remedial action.

Now let us apply these principles to a cost control system in building.

Principle One (having a frame of reference) consists of *two* stages:

(1) Establishing a realistic first estimate.
(2) Planning how this estimate should be spent among the parts of the building.

Should the realistic first estimate be within the amount allowed by the client?

Write down your answer.

The first estimate *The first estimate is often the figure that clients remember most. It sets the budget. It can sometimes be based on information that is a best guess.*

Turn to page 33

from pages
35, 37

The first principle of a cost control system consists of *two* stages:

(1) Establishing a realistic first estimate.
(2) Planning how this estimate should be spent among the elements or parts of the building.

Is there a cost target for each element or work package?

Write down your answer.

A realistic first estimate   *Note the term 'realistic'. Three words need to be defined: accuracy, reliability, realistic. Consider two people shooting at the targets shown in A and B below:*

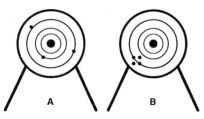

A had one shot on the bullseye and the other three are all over the target, whereas B's shots are all clustered in one place. B's shots are more considered and possibly reliable but they are not accurate as they missed the bullseye. When estimating it may be necessary to keep checking that the target is the bullseye.

A realistic estimate means that it is neither over-optimistic nor too pessimistic.

Turn to page 39

from page 31

Yes.

One of the purposes of a cost control system is to keep expenditure within the amount allowed by the client.

When the client has accepted the realistic first estimate, this sum is considered as the cost limit for the project. By **cost limit**, we mean the cost agreed between client and design team as the amount beyond which the project may not be pursued.

The second part of **principle one**, establishing how the estimate is to be spent among the parts of the building, entails splitting the cost limit into a number of smaller cost limits, one for each part of the building.

Will the sum of the small cost limits – usually known as 'cost targets' – equal the cost limit of the building project?

Yes.

Turn to page 35

No.

Turn to page 37

⟩ *from page 39* **Yes.**

According to the definition, a roof is an element. Opinion differs as to what should constitute a full list of elements, but we will not indulge in this discussion here. In this book we shall use standard elements as in the BCIS (Building Cost Information Service) *Detailed Cost Analyses*.

List of elements

1	SUBSTRUCTURE		5	SERVICES
2	SUPERSTRUCTURE		5A	Sanitary appliances
2A	Frame		5B	Services equipment
2B	Upper floors		5C	Disposal installations
2C	Roof		5D	Water installations
2D	Stairs		5E	Heat source
2E	External walls		5F	Space heating and air treatment
2F	Windows and external doors		5G	Ventilating systems
2G	Internal walls and partitions		5H	Electrical installations
2H	Internal doors		5I	Gas installations
3	INTERNAL FINISHES		5J	Lift and conveyor installations
3A	Wall finishes		5K	Protective installations
3B	Floor finishes		5L	Communications installations
3C	Ceiling finishes		5M	Special installations
4	FITTINGS		5N	Builder's work in connection
			5O	Builder's profit & attendance
			6	EXTERNAL WORKS
			6A	Site works
			6B	Drainage
			6C	External services
			6D	Minor building works
			7	PRELIMINARIES

Note (1) Group elements shown in upper-case letters (BCIS uses these for *concise cost analyses*).

(2) Numbering of elements follows BCIS format.

Into how many cost targets will a cost limit be split?

Write down your answer.

Turn to page 36 ⟩

from page 33

You said **Yes.**

You are correct.

The sum of the cost tar[g]

The first principle of a co[n]
consists of two stages.

Write down the two st[ages]

from page 34

In the case of the B[
detailed element[
plus targets f[
33 cost ta[
for C[
or[

Managin[
eleme[
wi[

Turn to page 32

...IS list of elements, there are 7 group elements and 30 ...s. You will need cost targets for the 30 detailed elements, ...or SUBSTRUCTURE, FITTINGS, and PRELIMINARIES, making ...rgets. In addition, most tender documents will often include a sum ...ONTINGENCIES (for unforeseen work encountered during site ...erations) which should be included with the cost targets. So:

There are a possible 34 cost targets.

More often than not several elements will have a 'nil' value, e.g. upper floors, stairs and lift installations, in a single-storey building.

Having established a realistic first estimate or cost limit, and having planned how to distribute this estimate among the elements, we have incorporated **Principle One** of a cost control system.

We must next incorporate **Principle Two**. To do this, we must detect and measure departures from targets and thereby check that the estimate is being spent as originally established. This is called **cost checking**.

Principle Three consists of taking any necessary remedial action.
Remedial action may mean re-designing the element, changing the specification, or seeking an alternative solution.

When should this remedial action be taken?

Write down your answer.

...g cost by ...nts is used ...ely throughout the world. For example, the USA, Australia, Canada and South Africa all have their own list of elemental categories.

Turn to page 38

from page 33 You said **No.**

You are incorrect.

If we take the overall cost limit, and split it into smaller sums of money, then adding together these smaller cost targets must give the overall cost limit.

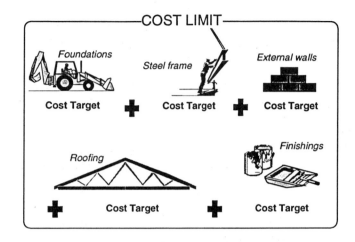

The first principle of a control system, when applied to a cost control system, consists of two stages.

Write down the two stages.

Turn to page 32

⊃ *from page 36* The remedial action should be taken immediately, before the design process moves on too far.

The remedial action ensures that expenditure is contained within the amount agreed between the client and the design team, that is, the cost limit.

Occasionally, suitable remedial action is impossible, and additional finances must be obtained to complete the project. For example, the ground conditions may not be what was envisaged and a detailed site investigation may show that the foundations will need to be deeper and larger, thus incurring additional expenditure.

Who will supply the additional funds?

Write down your answer.

A note of realism *The design process is iterative, which means that the design develops as more things are discovered about the project. For example, at the early stage of design the architect may have specified a pitched roof and the outline of the roof shape. By the stage of working drawings everything will be known about the tile type, location of gutters, lap of tiles, etc. Hence, assumptions have to be made at the early stages.*

Architects and engineers do not design in elements that would not be realistic. It is the task of the cost controller to identify the elements from the drawings.

Turn to page 40 ⊃

from page 32 **There *is* a cost target for each element or work package.**

Element	*An element is often defined as: a major component common to most buildings which usually fulfils the same function, or functions, irrespective of its construction or specification.*

As we have mentioned previously, you do not have to use elements for the cost control of management contracts which uses work packages in order to establish how the estimate should be spent among the parts of the project. Work packages relate to the trades or skills for the contract package award, for example, the joinery works might be one work package. However, for the purposes of managing the cost at the design stage, there is still the need to focus on elements.

From here on, we will ignore work packages and only concern ourselves with **elements** as defined above.

Do you think a roof is an element?

Yes/No.

Turn to page 34

from page 38 The client will generally be asked to supply the necessary additional finance. This implies that the initial estimate was incorrect and could be an embarrassment to the design team. But the presentation to the client of a carefully completed and detailed budget is the most convincing argument available as to the necessity for additional finance.

> • *Do not confuse a **budget** with **finance**. A **budget** is a financial limit. The **finance** for a project may come from a wide range of sources such as a loan from a bank, building society or insurance company, a government grant, or retained earnings.* •

Turn to page 41

from page 40 **Chapter 3 – Summary**

Cost control systems are based on *three* principles:

Principle One
There must be a frame of reference.

Principle Two
There must be a method of checking.

Principle Three
There must be a means of remedial action.

Having a frame of reference in a cost control system (Principle One) consists of *two* stages:

(1) Establishing a realistic first estimate.
(2) Planning how this estimate should be spent among the elements or parts of the building.

Turn to page 42

from page 41

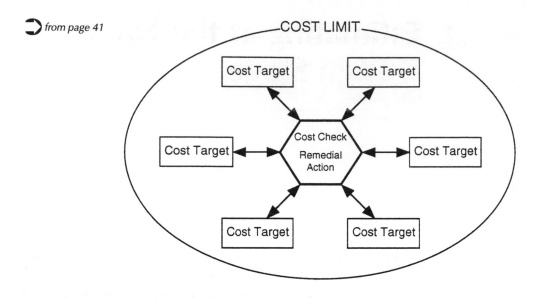

The cost limit is established and split into cost targets   **Principle One**

These targets are checked as the design progresses.   **Principle Two**

Remedial action is taken if necessary.   **Principle Three**

Turn to page 43

4 Estimating at the Early Design Stage

This chapter *is not* in programmed form.

Traditional estimating techniques originated in mid-Victorian times. The techniques were designed to help the builder to calculate the tender for a project. They were not used to help a design team to prepare an estimate for a client at an early stage in building design.

During this period, general conditions such as less complex uses for buildings, lower standards of comfort and fewer amenities and little or no state control of building, led to the development of two estimating methods.

The first of these, **approximate quantities**, entailing the measurement of all the work in a proposed building, stems from a contractor being concerned solely with the price of labour, materials, plant, overheads and profit and not with the function or use of a construction project.

The second method, **single rate estimating**, such as the 'superficial floor area' method and 'cubing', evolved as clients began to demand estimates at an early stage before detailed drawings and specifications were available. The 'cube' method has been superseded by the 'superficial floor area' method (also referred to as the 'm^2' method). Single rate estimating methods, to be effective, must be used to compare costs of buildings of similar type, construction and finishes, built on similar sites under similar conditions.

Both of these estimating techniques are important and are still the methods most frequently employed today.

Providing one or two cost estimates during the design process is not sufficient. What is required is a technique of cost control. Neither of the two popular methods of estimating exercises any control over costs, as neither fulfils all three purposes of cost control, as stated in Chapter 2:

❑ to give the client good value for money;
❑ to achieve the required balance of expenditure between the various parts of the building;
❑ to keep expenditure within the amount allowed by the client;

nor incorporates all **three** principles of cost control, as stated in Chapter 3: there must be a:

❑ frame of reference, establishing a realistic first estimate and planning how the estimate should be distributed among the elements;
❑ method of checking or feed-back;
❑ means of remedial action.

We will now examine traditional practices in the light of the third purpose of cost control – to keep expenditure within the amount allowed by the client – and also in the light of the principles of cost control.

Let us begin by looking at the various stages in the design process. The nomenclature we shall use in this programme is the RIBA *Outline Plan of Work*. On the next page is a condensed form of that plan together with a brief description of each stage.

Outline plan of work

Usual terminology	Stage	Purpose of work/decision to be reached	Tasks to be done
Briefing	**A** **Inception**	To prepare general outline of requirements and plan future action.	Set up client organisation for briefing. Consider requirements, appoint architect.
	B **Feasibility**	To provide the client with an appraisal and recommendation in order that he may determine the form in which the project is to proceed, ensuring that it is feasible, functionally and technically, and financially viable.	Carry out studies of user requirements, site conditions, planning, design, cost, etc., as necessary to reach decisions.
Sketch plans	**C** **Outline proposals**	To determine general approach to layout, design and construction in order to obtain authoritative approval of the client on the outline proposals and accompanying report.	Develop the brief further. Carry out studies on user requirements, technical problems, planning, design and costs, as necessary to reach decisions.
	D **Scheme design**	To complete the brief and decide on particular proposals, including planning arrangement appearance, constructional method, outline specification, and cost, and to obtain all approvals.	Final development of the brief, full design of the project by the architect, preliminary design by the engineers, preparation of cost plan and full explanatory report. Submission of proposals for all approvals.
		Brief should not be modified after this point.	
Working drawings	**E** **Detail design**	To obtain final decision on every matter related to design, specification, construction and cost.	Full design of every part and component of the building by collaboration of all concerned. Complete cost checking of design.
		Any further change in location, size, shape, or cost after this time will result in abortive work.	
	F **Production information**	To prepare production information and make final detailed decisions to carry out work.	Preparation of final production information, i.e. drawings, schedules and specifications.
	G **Bills of Quantities**	To prepare and complete all information and arrangements for obtaining tender.	Preparation of Bills of Quantities and tender documentation.
	H **Tender action**	Action as recommended in NJCC *Code of Procedure for Single Stage Selective Tendering.*	Action as recommended in NJCC *Code of Procedure for Single Stage Selective Tendering.*

It is important to be aware that there is a range of project activities spanning the life of a construction project from its inception through to completion. The RIBA Plan of Work represents a suggested set of procedures for architects during each stage of the construction project. It also embodies activities necessary for the provision of effective cost control. The outline plan of work describes the range of activities carried out up until tendering of the project, commonly referred to as the **design process**. Subsequent stages include project planning, operations on site, project completion and feed-back. The following brief description of the RIBA plan of work provides an insight into the roles of participants throughout the design process.

A **Inception**.   Relates to the client's initial decision to build. During this stage the client will consider the outline requirements and appoint an architect and other members of the design team.

B **Feasibility**.   During this stage the design team will attempt to establish the client's requirements in more detail. This involves the consideration of functional, technical and financial issues. Basic cost information is required in order to establish the overall viability of the project.

C **Outline proposals**.   Having established the overall viability of the project, this stage determines an overall sketch design with regard to layout and construction. Alternative design forms and construction methods will be considered. The cost implications of differing design solutions will be evaluated. The outline cost plan will be prepared during this stage.

D **Scheme design**.   Major issues affecting design, planning, construction method and specification will be considered at this stage. Sketch plans will cover most of the major elements of the building including structural framework, environmental engineering services and internal finishings. As the design evolves, the elements must be checked and, if necessary, earlier cost estimates revised. More accurate cost targets will be defined for all the major building elements.

E **Detail design**.   During this stage all issues relating to design, specification, construction and cost are resolved. Drawings are prepared for all the building components. Cost advice will continue to be given about differing construction methods, materials and layouts. Detailed consideration should be given to the impact of maintenance and running costs associated with alternative design solutions.

F **Production information**.   All final working drawings are now prepared and project schedules and specifications are finalised. Cost checks will be made to ensure that the design conforms to the cost plan.

Chapter Four – Summary

There are *two* traditional estimating procedures in common usage:

1 **Approximate quantities** Pricing composite items based on materials and labour.

2 **Single rate estimating** (e.g. superficial area method). Comparing with similar buildings.

Both are *unsatisfactory* unless incorporated into and used in conjunction with cost control techniques.

Problems are likely to arise where estimates are prepared without implementing a proper cost control system. Traditional estimates are only prepared and considered at the following stages:

Stage	What is done	Method used	Reason for being unsatisfactory
B **Feasibility**	First estimate prepared	Approximate quantities *or* single rate estimating (e.g. m^2 method)	First part of Principle One violated (i.e. first estimate cannot be realistic)
D **Scheme design**	Firm estimate prepared	Approximate quantities *or* single rate estimating (e.g. m^2 method)	Second part of Principle One violated (i.e. cost targets have not been planned)
H **Tender action**	Differences between tender price and first estimate explained	Pricing full Bill of Quantities	The objective of keeping the tender price within the first estimate is not achieved

In addition, as costs are not considered at the detail design stage, Principles Two and Three are violated.

The Three

Basic

Principles

Principle One
There must be a frame of reference or set of conditions which must be adhered to.

Principle Two
There must be a method of checking or a feed-back system.

Principle Three
There must be a means of remedial action.

Turn to page 49

5 Cost Control during Inception, Feasibility and Outline Proposals

> This chapter *is not* in programmed form.

This chapter covers three stages of the RIBA *Outline Plan of Work*:

A Inception

B Feasibility

C Outline Proposals

In the remainder of Part 1, we will explain how the three principles of cost control are incorporated into a full cost control system. This will be appropriate for situations in which an architect is responsible for leading the client and design team. The cost control system and the information it generates follows the design process as described by the RIBA *Outline Plan of Work*. However it must be remembered that the plan of work represents an outline method of working only. It is a model and therefore will need to be modified to suit different design teams.

As stated previously, what follows will not be entirely appropriate for alternative procurement approaches, in particular, where the relationship between architect and builder and the timing of the design stage to construction phase is radically altered. However, the principles of cost control will still apply and can be adapted to suit alternative approaches.

We now consider how the three principles are incorporated into a full cost control system. The techniques as outlined will be described in more detail in Part 2 of the programme.

(As you read this chapter, you will find it useful to refer occasionally to the RIBA *Outline Plan of Work*.)

A **Inception**   Inception is the first stage of the client's initial decision to build. The design team is not yet appointed so no cost control procedures are carried out. At the inception stage the client organisation is set up for briefing. The client considers his requirements for the building and appoints a designer.

The brief   *Preparing a detailed and comprehensive brief is very important. The brief states precisely what the client wants. For example, with an airport bulding, it might be the proposed number of passengers to be handled or the number of aircraft movements to be coped with. A brief can be from a few pages up to a very comprehensive document. The design team must interpret the brief to decide the type of project to be designed.*

B **Feasibility**   The second stage is the feasibility stage, where the design team provides appraisals and recommendations regarding the form in which the project is to proceed.

An effective cost control system must then be set up, incorporating the three principles of cost control. The first principle to be incorporated into the system is Principle One, establishing a realistic first estimate, and deciding how to allocate this estimate among the elements.

Two approaches to setting a realistic first estimate can be considered. Firstly, the design team may be required to produce an estimate which defines the cost limit for the project. Alternatively, the design team may have to confirm that a building can be completed within the cost limit set by the client. In practice, an approach between these two extremes is usually adopted.

The information provided by the client will vary from project to project. However, whatever the approach, the function of the building is known, usually from the outset, and the location and description of the site is also available. The main factors for consideration are:

- ❏ area (the floor area of the building)
- ❏ quality (the standard of accommodation to be provided)
- ❏ shape and aesthetic features
- ❏ the constraints imposed by the planning authority on the site
- ❏ the delivery time for the project (when the client wants occupation)
- ❏ the balance between initial capital cost and the long-term costs
- ❏ cost (the likely costs).

There are other factors which can come into consideration, but for ease of demonstration, these are ignored here.

How the cost control system works

Step 1 *When a project is completed, the final account is analysed into elemental categories giving a cost per square metre for the overall project and the elemental categories. This is called a cost analysis.*

Step 2 *The cost analyses are stored in files and on computer for future reference. Remember, there is a time dimension for the analyses to be considered as demonstrated below.*

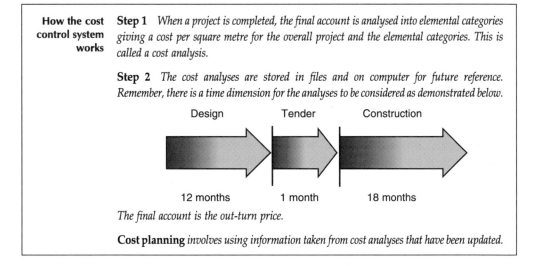

The final account is the out-turn price.

Cost planning *involves using information taken from cost analyses that have been updated.*

When either confirming or setting a realistic first estimate, consideration needs to be given to what is possible and probable. This can be done by a method of **interpolation**.

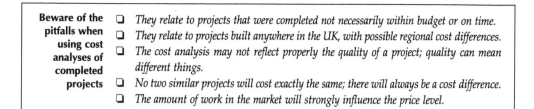

Beware of the pitfalls when using cost analyses of completed projects	❑ *They relate to projects that were completed not necessarily within budget or on time.* ❑ *They relate to projects built anywhere in the UK, with possible regional cost differences.* ❑ *The cost analysis may not reflect properly the quality of a project; quality can mean different things.* ❑ *No two similar projects will cost exactly the same; there will always be a cost difference.* ❑ *The amount of work in the market will strongly influence the price level.*

Interpolation method

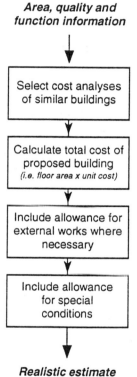

The **interpolation method** is where cost analyses of buildings of the same type are studied. This method permits the differing sizes and standards which exist between buildings to be examined and taken into account when considering costs.

The total cost of each building is generally expressed in a common unit such as cost per square metre of floor area. Thus, the total cost of the building is the cost per square metre multiplied by the total area of the floor space.

An example of part of a typical range might be:

- ❏ Cost of building A (quality X, floor space $5\,000\,\text{m}^2$) is £800 per m^2 of floor area.
- ❏ Cost of building B (quality Y, floor space $5500\,\text{m}^2$) is £1000 per m^2 of floor area.

Special care needs to be taken with **external works** as published analyses may exclude costs associated with site works, drainage, external services and separate minor buildings. Consideration must also be given to any *special conditions* such as site problems, access, etc.

From a range of costs of similar buildings an appropriate **cost limit** can be made. In calculating the cost limit, consideration needs to be given to differences in area, quality and function and adjustments made for external works and any special conditions. This technique will be described in greater detail in Part 2 of this programme.

C Outline proposals The outline proposals stage is where there is still insufficient information for cost targets to be prepared for each elemental category. Nevertheless, the cost limit is established in broad terms.

Cost allocations are typically made among the major elemental groups. For example, the cost of substructures (i.e. foundations), superstructure (including internal finishes and fittings), and plumbing, mechanical and electrical services. These are calculated using a refined version of the interpolation method requiring consideration of the cost allocations of similar buildings. Such information is published, for example, by the Building Cost Information Service (BCIS), technical journals and elsewhere. Again an appropriate sum for external works and an allowance for any special conditions also needs to be included.

These allocations are adjusted to account for significant differences in the design of the buildings and for market conditions. These broad cost allocations are set out in an **outline cost plan**.

In certain situations it may be prudent to report cost information as a range of costs. This will allow the preparation of a firm estimate to be deferred until completion of the outline design. However, as we have seen, the client is usually presented with a realistic first estimate (or a confirmation of his own cost limit) at the feasibility stage.

During the outline proposal stage a variety of general design solutions will be considered. These will be modified as necessary before a general approach is agreed. Cost studies of alternative design solutions may be required and advice given on economic aspects of each solution. Although major design decisions will be taken during this stage, the project design is still far from complete.

At the end of the outline proposal stage the cost limit is confirmed. The client is given an outline cost plan with the broad cost allocations for the major parts of the building. (These matters will be explained more fully in Part 2.)

It is important to be clear about the basis of any estimate particularly when reporting figures to the client. The design team will be concerned with estimating likely tender costs, however, the client may be more concerned about his *total costs* which include, for example, professional fees, land cost and any taxes payable, such as value added tax. For this reason, make sure your report is in an appropriate format and lists all inclusions and exclusions. As far as we are concerned, our main point of reference will be the estimation of tender costs.

Chapter 5 – Summary

An appropriate system of cost control *does* incorporate the three principles of cost control. The system is set up at the **feasibility** stage, where the realistic first estimate is prepared.

At the **outline proposals** stage, broad allocations of cost are made among the major portions of the building. To do this, it may be helpful to consult various information sources, including in-house records.

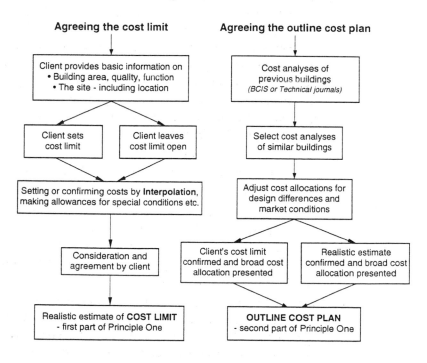

Principle One

Having a frame of reference in a cost control system consists of two stages:

- ❏ Establishing a realistic first estimate.
- ❏ Planning how this estimate should be spent among the elements of the building.

Turn to page 57 ⟩

6 Cost Control during Scheme Design

This chapter *is* in programmed form and you must follow the page directions exactly.

This chapter covers the next stage in the RIBA *Outline Plan of Work*:

D Scheme Design

Turn to page 58 ⟹

from page 57

The previous chapter described how the cost control system is set up at the **feasibility** stage and is developed at the **outline proposals** stage.

What is the next design stage?

Write down your answer.

Turn to page 60

from pages 66, 68

You said **Yes.**

You are incorrect.

The cost plan and the traditional estimate have little in common, save that they are sometimes prepared in the same way. They differ on three major points.

Let us look at these differences in detail:

1 A traditional estimate is a prediction of the cost of a specific design. The cost plan is a statement of how the design team proposes to distribute the available money among the elements of the building. This allows firm decisions regarding design detail and specification to be postponed until a later stage (i.e. during the detail design stage).

Is the cost plan specific for a particular design?

Write down your answer.

Turn to page 64

from page 58 The next stage is the **Scheme design** stage.

The brief is completed and the design developed. It should take account of the requirements of the planners, the appearance, construction method, outline specification and cost. At this stage all necessary approvals are obtained, such as approvals from local planning authorities, and approval that the drawings and specifications are in compliance with the Building Regulations and fire codes.

During the scheme design stage, sketch plans are produced and the **cost plan** is formulated. (This is sometimes referred to as the **detailed cost plan** – we will continue to refer to it as the cost plan.) During this stage comparative cost studies may be required.

The **cost plan** is a statement of how the design team proposes to distribute the available money among the elements of the building.

Notice the distinction between the outline cost plan prepared during outline proposals and the cost plan produced during scheme design:

❏ The **outline cost plan** is a statement of how the design team proposes to distribute the available money among the *major* portions of the building (i.e. substructure, superstructure, internal finishes, fittings, plumbing, mechanical and electrical services, external works, preliminaries, and contingencies).
❏ The **cost plan** comprises all the appropriate elements (i.e. drawn from the 34 cost targets as outlined in Chapter 3).

An example of an outline cost plan is given on page 253, and a cost plan is given on page 281.

In preparing the cost plan a cost target is set for each element.

What should the sum of the cost targets equal?

Write down your answer.

Turn to page 62

from pages 66, 68

You said **No.**

Correct.

Although the cost plan and the traditional estimate are sometimes prepared in the same way, they do not have the same function. They differ on three major points.

Let us look at these differences in detail.

1 The first major difference is that a traditional estimate is a prediction of the cost of a specific design.

The cost plan is a statement of how the design team proposes to distribute the available money among the elements of the building. This allows firm decisions regarding design detail and specification to be postponed until a later stage (i.e. during the detail design stage).

Is the cost plan specific for a particular design?

Write down your answer.

Turn to page 64

from page 60

We might expect the sum of the cost targets to equal the cost limit. However, at this stage, it is advisable to make an allowance for fluctuations in price level and unexpected changes in design between scheme design and receipt of tender. This is known as price and design risk. This allowance is very important as unexpected rises in wages, materials or components, together with possible design difficulties, sometimes make it impossible to keep the final cost of each element within its cost target.

Therefore, in general, the sum of the cost targets plus the price and design risk allowance will equal the cost limit.

During the scheme design stage sketch plans are produced concurrently with the detailed cost plan. These sketch plans will be more detailed than in earlier stages, showing the locations of all walls, windows, doors, partitions, staircases, wash basins, etc.

Should these sketches be produced with the cost limit and outline cost plan in mind?

No.

Turn to page 68

Yes.

Turn to page 66

from page 64 The two principles are:

Principle One
There must be a frame of reference (set up at the Scheme design stage).

Principle Two
There must be a method of checking (set up at the Detail design stage).

3 The third major difference is that the traditional estimate in no way helps the design team to detail the design within a cost framework.

Cost plan allowances are independent of a specific design. The cost plan remains valid until a satisfactory design solution is obtained or until the design team decides to amend the allowance.

In addition, the cost plan is valid for any detailed design provided the design team does not alter the chosen standards of quality and is prepared to modify any details which exceed the cost targets.

With a cost plan the design team (can/can not) change the allotment of money between elements within the overall cost limit.

Write down your answer.

Turn to page 65

from pages
59, 61

No. A cost plan *is not* specific for a particular design.

As we have said, there are *three* major differences between the cost plan and the traditional estimate.

2 The second major difference is that once the estimate is prepared, it is seldom referred to until the time comes to compare it with the lowest bid for the work.

The cost plan is used continuously throughout the **Detail design** stage as a method of checking that the detail design is contained within the cost limit. The cost plan is therefore a frame of reference. This frame of reference is set up at the **Scheme design** stage.

Write down the two principles of a cost control process which are incorporated when a cost plan is used.

Turn to page 63

from page 63 The design team **can** change the allotment of money between elements within the overall cost limit. (This will be explained fully in Chapter 7.)

The cost plan differs from the traditional estimate in *three* major ways:

(1) The cost plan is not specific for a particular design.
(2) The cost plan is referred to continuously throughout the design process.
(3) The cost plan helps the design team to detail the design within a structured cost framework.

Do you think the production of a cost plan is a joint enterprise by the whole design team?

Yes/No.

Write down your answer.

Turn to page 67

from page 62 **Yes.**

You are correct.

The outline cost plan must be used as it states how the design team proposes to distribute the available money on the major elements of the building.

In preparing the cost plan, we must bear in mind that only total areas and numbers are known, together with an indication of quality. At this stage the design team is not prepared to enter into detailed consideration of the specification. Items such as the types of doors and windows will not be specified in detail at the scheme design stage. We must acknowledge this situation in preparing the cost plan and understand what is required of the cost plan.

The cost plan is often prepared using similar techniques to those used in preparing the traditional estimate.

Will the cost plan serve the same function as the traditional estimate?

Yes. *Turn to page 59*

No. *Turn to page 61*

⊃ *from page 65* **Yes.**

All members of the design team must participate in the formulation of the cost plan and have to be committed to it. Every time a line is put on a drawing there is a cost incurred. While some members of the design team may feel the cost limit for their particular design responsibility is too low, they must accept the limit or argue the

> **Remember, the cost limit is made up of a number of cost targets – one target per element.**

case with the team and the client on the need to raise the limit or take a sum from one of the other elements.

The nature of the construction project may require specialist consultants to give advice. For instance, in the design of a concert hall there is the need for acoustics expertise to advise on sound.

Specialist consultants (should/should not) co-operate in the formulation of the cost plan.

Write down your answer.

Turn to page 71 ⊃

↪ *from page 62* **No.**

You are incorrect.

Sketch plans must be produced with the cost limit and outline cost plan in mind. The outline cost plan is a statement of how the design team proposes to distribute the available money on the major portions of the building.

In preparing the cost plan we must bear in mind that, only total superficial areas and the general layout are known, together with an indication of quality. At this stage the design team will not be in a position to enter into detailed consideration of the specification. Items such as the types of doors and windows will not be specified in detail at the scheme design stage. We must acknowledge this situation in preparing the cost plan and understand what is required of the cost plan.

The cost plan is often prepared using similar techniques to those used in preparing the traditional estimate.

Will the cost plan serve the same function as the traditional estimate?

Yes. *Turn to page 59* ↪

No. *Turn to page 61* ↪

⊃ *from page 71* **Yes.**

When consultants have been properly involved in setting targets, the design team can justifiably expect construction costs to fall within these targets.

In the USA, if the lowest tender is not within a certain percentage (usually 10%) of the estimate given to the client, then the design team must modify the design to meet the budget – they will not be reimbursed for the time spent on the exercise. It would not be unreasonable for a UK client to expect the same service.

During the scheme design stage the design team finalises the scheme design and produces statements of quality standards and functional requirements for each element which are translated into a cost target.

Is this process of translation carried out under traditional estimating practices?

Yes/No.

Write down your answer.

Turn to page 70 ⊃

⊃ *from page 69* **No.**

This process represents increased responsibility to ensure the cost targets for each element are realistic and reflect the specification and quality required.

Turn to page 72 ⊃

from page 67 Specialist consultants **should** co-operate in the formulation of the cost plan.

It would be unreasonable to expect specialist consultants to accept a cost target within their area of responsibility unless they had consented to that target during the formulation of the cost plan.

Should the design team expect attainment of cost targets concerning specialist consultants?

Yes/No.

Write down your answer.

Turn to page 69

⊃ *from page 70* **Chapter 6 – Summary**

At the **scheme design** stage, the **cost plan** (i.e. detailed cost plan) is formulated, often in a similar way to the traditional estimate. Thereby, Principle One (having a frame of reference) is incorporated. Sketch plans are prepared with the cost plan in mind.

The **cost plan** is simply a statement of how the design team proposes to distribute the available money on the elements of the building.

The cost plan differs from the traditional estimate in *three* ways:

(1) The cost plan is not specific for a particular design.
(2) The cost plan is referred to continuously throughout the design process.
(3) The cost plan helps the design team to detail the design within a structured cost framework.

The cost plan is, in addition, a joint enterprise by the whole design team including the specialist consultants.

The design team's decisions on each element are translated into cost targets, whose sum, together with the design and price risk allowance, equals the cost limit.

Turn to page 73 ⊃

7 Cost Control during Detail Design

> This chapter *is* in programmed form and you must follow the page directions exactly.

This chapter covers the fifth stage of the RIBA *Outline Plan of Work*:

E Detail Design

Turn to page 75

from page 77 **The design team must be informed of the cost for each element.**

The estimated cost of each fully designed element is compared with the corresponding cost target expressed in the cost plan.

This is a cost check for each element.

What principle of the cost control system has thus been incorporated?

Write down your answer.

Turn to page 76

from page 73

Up until now, we have been *planning* what should be done with the money available for a project. During *detail design* we take action; at this stage final decisions must be made on every matter related to design, specification, construction and cost. Every part and component of the building must be fully designed and all designs must be completely **cost checked**. Remedial action must be taken if necessary.

What cost control principle must therefore be incorporated into the process at this stage?

Write down your answer.

Turn to page 77

from page 74 **Principle Two (there must be a method of checking).**

If cost checking is not done, then all previous work is wasted and useless.

What principle of the cost control system has still to be incorporated?

Write down the principle.

Turn to page 78

⊃ *from page 75* **Principle Two (there must be a method of checking) and Principle Three (there must be a means of remedial action) must be incorporated.**

Detailed designs are prepared for each element of the building. In many countries, including the UK, the design team must also ensure that the design complies with the construction safety legislation. All designs must be complete, materials and components selected and construction problems must be solved before work may safely proceed to the next stage of design – *Production information.*

Production information means that there is sufficient detail for the contractor and specialist contractors to build the project. The contractor needs reinforcement schedules, door and ironmongery schedules, and window schedules. The specialist contractors will often prepare their shop drawings from the design information. For example, a joinery shop needs details about how every piece of timber will be cut and assembled.

In reality, a project cannot be 100% designed prior to work starting on site because information is missing. Computer aided design (CAD) systems have helped, but they can only provide information that is input.

However, the drawings prepared by the design team do not have to be polished working drawings for use on the site. Dimensioned sketches and notes in whatever form are sufficient, provided all design solutions are complete.

Since detailed designs and specifications are available, the most accurate and appropriate estimating technique is the approximate quantities method. The approximate quantities are measured for each element and priced. Prices for some specialist work may be provided by specialist contractors. For instance, the lift manufacturer may provide the price for the lift installation with due allowance being made for the builder's work.

These estimates are then checked against the corresponding cost targets in the cost plan.

Who should then be informed of the cost for each element?

Write down your answer.

Turn to page 74 ⊃

⊃ *from page 76* **Principle Three (there must be a means of remedial action).**

This remedial action must take place within the time and budget allowance so that the objective of keeping expenditure within the amount allowed by the client is achieved.

Once again if this is not done, all previous work is wasted.

Let us consider the situation where cost checking reveals that remedial action is necessary. Two courses of remedial action are possible.

1 If the cost of the element design is greater than a *realistic* cost target, the element design should be changed so that it is within the cost target.

If the anticipated cost of the electrical installations is £120 000, and the cost target was £100 000, what would be the recommendation to the design team?

Write down your answer.

Turn to page 80 ⊃

from page 80 **No.**

The overall cost limit should *not* be altered. This is the whole point of cost planning – keeping expenditure within the amount allowed by the client. The cost plan can be changed at this stage as long as the cost limit is not altered.

Of course, if the cost of the element design is just within the cost target then the cost limit will not be exceeded.

Do you think any action should be taken in this case?

Yes/No.

Turn to page 81

from page 78 **It would probably be recommended that the element design should be changed so that it is within the cost target.**

For example, wiring and lighting layouts could be re-examined for economies.

Let us now look at the second course of remedial action.

2 If the cost check of the element design shows that the cost target is *unrealistic*, cost targets should be adjusted throughout the cost plan, thereby releasing surplus funds from other elements.

In doing this will the overall cost limit be altered?

Yes/No.

Turn to page 79

⊃ *from page 79* **Yes.**

The design team must be informed, preferably in writing.

If the cost of the element design is just within the cost target, the design is confirmed in writing as being suitable for the preparation of production drawings.

If the cost is significantly within target, then surplus funds may be released for other elements.

Each element is treated in turn this way and any necessary action is taken and completed. Certain elements are more cost significant or are more likely to give trouble than others, so the cost checks on these elements are completed first. This will be explained more fully in Part 2.

If remedial action produced a building of low quality, would the design team be justified in continuing without consulting the client?

Yes/No.

Turn to page 83 ⊃

⊃ *from page 83* **The cost limit may be overspent, therefore the main purpose of cost control may not be achieved.**

The final cost check is therefore an important part of the cost control procedure at the **detail design** stage.

If this final check confirms that all is well, the project will proceed to production information, bills of quantities, tender. Not all projects will use a bill of quantities, but they will all require a schedule of materials, labour and plant.

These processes will *not* be dealt with in this programme.

Turn to page 84 ⊃

⊃ *from page 81* **No.**

In cases where remedial action would produce a building of low quality, the design team should ask the clients if they wish to release additional funds.

In this *undesirable situation*, the cost plan is a powerful tool with which to argue the case for more funds.

Once all element designs have been cost checked, a final overall cost check is carried out. The aim must be to ensure nothing has been overlooked.

What may happen if a final cost check is not performed and, as a result, one or two of the elements have been overlooked?

Write down your answer.

Turn to page 82 ⊃

⊃ *from page 82* **Chapter 7 – Summary**

At the detail design stage, **Principle Two** (there must be a method of checking) and **Principle Three** (there must be a means of remedial action) are incorporated into the cost control system.

Flow of design team work at **detail design** stage:

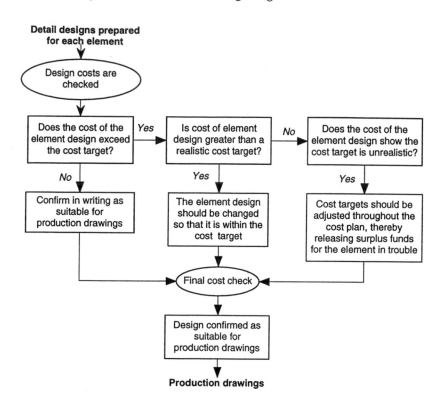

You have now completed Part 1 of this programme.

To revise this part of the programme before going on to Part 2, answer the questions on page 85.

You can find out how well you have learned the material in Part 1 by comparing your answers with the answers given on pages 86 and 87.

Part 1 Test

1 Why is the control of building costs just as important now but more difficult than in the 1980s?

2 How many purposes has a cost control system?

3 State the fundamental purpose of a cost control system through which the other purposes can be achieved.

4 What are the three basic principles of a cost control system?

5 Define in your own words:

- ❏ cost limit
- ❏ cost check
- ❏ cost target
- ❏ element
- ❏ cost plan.

6 At which stage in the design process is:

(a) a cost control system set up?
(b) the cost plan prepared?

7 What basic information about a project does a client usually give to the design team when asking them to prepare a first estimate?

8 In how many ways does the cost plan differ from the traditional estimate? (List the differences.)

9 Write down the cost control principle (or principles) incorporated at the **detail design** stage.

10 Draw a rough diagram to show the flow of design team work at the **detail design** stage.

Answers overleaf ⊃

Answers to Part 1 Test

Marks

1 Client's requirements are more complicated. (1)
Number of organisations involved in a project has increased. (1)
Delivery time for a project is important. (1)
Current practice in design where new ideas, techniques,
materials and components are used. (2)

5

2 Three. (1)

1

3 Keeping expenditure within the amount allowed by the
client *or* (3)
Ensuring the final account does not exceed the first estimate. **3**

4 **Principle One**: Having a frame of reference
or establishing a realistic first estimate and planning how the
estimate should be spent among the elements. (3)
Principle Two: Having a method of checking. (2)
Principle Three: Having a means of remedial action. (2)

7

5 The **cost limit** is the cost of a project to the client, beyond
which the project may not be pursued. (2)
A **cost check** is performed by comparing the approximate
quantities estimate of a completely designed element with
its cost target in the cost plan. (2)
A **cost target** is the allowance made for an individual
element at the scheme design stage. (2)
An **element** of a building is a major component common
to most buildings which usually fulfils the same function
or functions irrespective of its construction or specification. (3)
The **cost plan** is a statement of how the design team wishes
to spend the available money on the elements of the building. (3)

12

6 (a) Feasibility. (1)
(b) Scheme design. (1)
Note: An outline cost plan is prepared during **outline proposals**. **2**

Turn to page 87

⊃ *from page 86*   *Marks*

7 Area, quality, function (any order).   (3)

                                                                     3

8 (1) The cost plan is not specific for a particular design.   (3)
   (2) The cost plan is referred to continuously throughout
       the design process.   (2)
   (3) The cost plan helps the design team to detail the design
       within a structured cost framework.   (2)
   In addition the cost is a joint enterprise by the whole design
   team including the specialist consultant members.   (1)

                                                                     8

9 **Principle Two** (there must be a method of checking).   (1)
   Principle Three (there must be a means of remedial action). (1)

                                                                     2

10

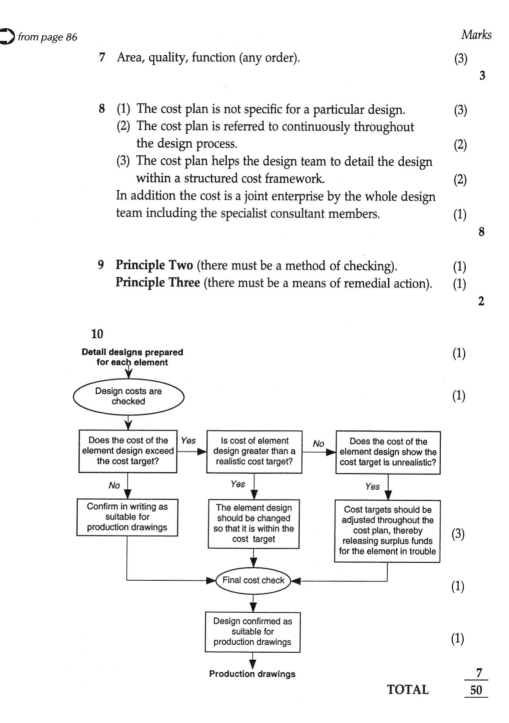

Detail designs prepared for each element   (1)

Design costs are checked   (1)

Does the cost of the element design exceed the cost target? — *Yes* → Is cost of element design greater than a realistic cost target? — *No* → Does the cost of the element design show the cost target is unrealistic?

No ↓   *Yes* ↓   *Yes* ↓

Confirm in writing as suitable for production drawings

The element design should be changed so that it is within the cost target

Cost targets should be adjusted throughout the cost plan, thereby releasing surplus funds for the element in trouble   (3)

Final cost check   (1)

Design confirmed as suitable for production drawings   (1)

Production drawings

                                                  TOTAL   <u>7</u>
                                                              <u>50</u>

Part 2

The Techniques of Cost Control

Introduction

In Part 1, you learned the purpose and the principles of cost control. In Part 2, you will learn some of the techniques which are used to control building costs during the design process.

We must make it clear that the costs discussed throughout this part of the book are initial *capital* costs and that we make no attempt to consider full life cycle costs (the running costs including maintenance, repair, cleaning, energy, insurances, etc.). In practice, capital, maintenance, and operating costs must all be considered in any comprehensive system of economic appraisal. However, such considerations are outside the scope of this programme.*

There is another facet of the cost–design interaction which is outside the scope of this programme. Building is usually undertaken for a financial or social return. It is often necessary to measure the benefits which the building or facility will give. In complex cases, this may be done by preparing a cost benefit analysis. This technique considers both tangible and intangible costs and benefits. For example, a cost benefit study was carried out for the Jubilee Line extension to Docklands to take account of the benefits to individuals and to London's economy as a whole.

No matter what economic appraisal techniques are employed, it will be necessary to prepare estimates of initial capital cost and to control the development of a design within the agreed cost estimate. Capital cost planning can, therefore, be used either on its own or supplemented by the more refined techniques outlined above.

Turn to page 91

* For further reading on this subject, see *Life Cycle Costing for Construction* and/or *Life Cycle Costing: Theory and Practice*, both by R. Flanagan and G. Norman.

8 Essential Constituents of Elemental Cost Analysis

This chapter *is* in programmed form and you must follow the page directions exactly.

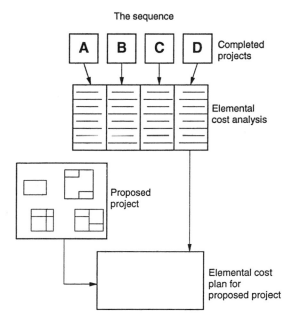

The sequence

Turn to page 92

⊃ *from page 91* An elemental cost analysis provides a meaningful yardstick for clients and the design team about the cost of similar projects. For example, by examining the cost of the roof, external walls, windows and external doors we can get an indication of how much it costs to enclose a building and keep out the weather.

Examining cost analyses

Examination of only one cost analysis yields useful information. However, because of the variations between buildings, it is obviously essential to be able to compare the cost analysis of several different buildings of the same type. This allows a wider appreciation of the distribution of costs.

What is needed is a uniform method of analysis and measurement for all analysis. The method of analysis described here is that used by the Building Cost Information Service (BCIS) of the Royal Institution of Chartered Surveyors (RICS).

Principles, instructions and definitions of this method are set out in the *Standard Form of Cost Analysis (SFCA)*, published by the RICS. Originally, three levels of information were published, namely, *concise*, *detailed* and *amplified* forms of cost analysis. Currently, only two levels, *concise* and *detailed* cost analyses, exist. This leaves a void for users of these cost analyses and many organisations seek to rectify this deficiency by collecting and keeping more detailed in-house records. See, for example, the amplified details recorded under 'specification and design notes' as shown in Appendix A.

Before discussing the essential constituents of an elemental cost analysis, let us summarise the general purpose of this form of analysis and briefly discuss a few of its specialised uses.

Turn to page 93 ⊃

from page 92 The purpose of any cost analysis is to reveal the distribution of the costs of a building among its elements *in terms which are meaningful to both designers and clients*. This allows the costs of two or more buildings to be compared.

As you can see from this statement, elemental cost analysis can obviously be used in several ways. We now discuss four of the simplest uses, under the headings of:

- ❑ appreciation
- ❑ judgement
- ❑ belated remedial action
- ❑ planning.

Appreciation

As mentioned before, one cost analysis can be used to give clients and designers an appreciation of how the costs of the elements compare with one another and with the total cost of the building.

Judgement

This appreciation can then be used in judging which elements have disproportionate cost when considered in relation to the efficiency and quality which they contribute to a building. Hence ideas as to how costs could have been allocated to obtain a more balanced design can be developed.

How can a cost analysis help the design team when a tender is found to be greater than the first estimate?

Write down your answer.

Turn to page 95

⊃ *from page 98*
Cost

The building costs analysed in an elemental cost analysis could be either the costs to the contractor or the costs to the client (i.e. the contractor's 'prices'). As the basic purpose and use of elemental cost analysis are all

for the benefit of the design professions and the client rather than the contractors, it is obviously the client's costs that are analysed.

The actual costs which a client has paid for a completed building can be obtained from the final account prepared on project completion – an accountant often refers to this as the out-turn cost. The priced bill of quantities submitted as a tender by a contractor will usually contain a number of provisional or prime cost sums which may not be exactly the same as the final cost of the items they represent.

Do you think the costs analysed should be those on the tender or those on the final account?

Cost and price   *There is often a debate about cost and price. The contractor incurs costs in constructing the project to which are added overheads and profit; the client is then charged a price for the work. We accept this definition, but for the purpose of clarity in this book, the term **cost** has been used throughout.*

*There is nothing scientific about costs. Any organisation will use the standard approach of **labour** + **materials** + **plant and equipment** + **overheads** + **profit** to arrive at a charge. The profit allowance reflects a number of factors, such as what the market will bear at that point in time.*

Tender. *Turn to page 99* ⊃

Final account. *Turn to page 102* ⊃

from page 93 If a tender is found to be greater than the first estimate, a cost analysis of the tender would show which of the elements gave rise to disproportionate costs. A rather belated substitute for cost planning could then be performed. These elements could then be re-designed in an attempt to bring the cost down. This use can be summarised as follows.

Belated remedial action

Cost analysis can be used to reveal the sources of over-expenditure during 'inquests' on receipt of tender, and thus allow belated remedial action to be taken.

What obvious use of cost analysis (that is, obvious in the context of this programme) has not yet been mentioned?

Write down your answer.

Turn to page 100

from pages 99, 102 **(a) The costs analysed are the client's costs on the tender.**

Elements

Elemental cost analysis seeks to relate costs to those functions of buildings which are common to all buildings (i.e. functions like 'keeping out the weather' rather than 'teaching children' or 'making beer barrels').

> Cost
> Elements
> Yardstick

Why is a 'trade-by-trade' or a 'common arrangement by work sections' analysis, as can be used in priced bills of quantities, unsuitable for relating costs to function?

Write down your answer.

Turn to page 103

⊃ *from page 100*

Any analysis is performed to increase our understanding of how a *whole* is made up of constituent parts.

When deciding on a method for analysing a whole project, the essential constituents need to be determined. In our case these would be:

(a)   which characteristic is to be analysed,
(b)   the sub-units which are to be considered,
(c)   the most useful way of expressing the results.

The purpose of elemental cost analysis determines that **cost** is the characteristic to be analysed. **Elements** (i.e. functional components) are the sub-units of buildings which should be considered. Since part of the purpose is to allow comparisons of the costs of two or more buildings, the best method of expressing the result will be in terms of a common **yardstick**. This allows comparison of the costs of buildings of different sizes to be made without making repeated reference to the sizes of the buildings.

Write down three words which summarise the essential constituents of elemental cost analysis.

Turn to page 98 ⊃

from page 97 The essential constituents of elemental cost analysis are:

- ❏ **Cost**   the characteristic to be analysed,
- ❏ **Elements**   the sub-units used,
- ❏ **Yardstick**   the most useful way of expressing the results.

Cost
Elements
Yardstick

The remainder of this chapter is devoted to a discussion of each of these essential constituents.

Turn to page 94

from page 94 You chose: **tender.**

You are correct.

But the argument presented on page 94 would lead the uninitiated to judge that the costs analysed should be those on the final account.

If you would like to read the argument which we have given for the analysing costs on tenders instead of those on the final account, turn to page 102 now.

If you are already convinced that it is better to analyse costs on tenders, choose from the following list the most accurate description of the costs analysed in elemental cost analyses:

(a) **The costs analysed are the client's costs on the tender.**
(b) **The costs analysed are the contractor's costs on the final account.**
(c) **The costs analysed are the client's costs on the final account.**

Write down your answer.

Turn to page 96

⊃ *from page 95* **Planning**

Cost analyses may be used as cost information during the design of future building projects.

Some of these uses are so closely related that you may well argue that they should not be considered separately: we beg to differ! The first two are useful to clients and designers during the synthesis of their appreciation of how costs are related to function and design – both 'passive' uses. The other two are useful in helping to control costs – 'active' uses.

Thus the general purpose of elemental cost analysis and the four uses mentioned in this chapter can be summarised as follows:

Purpose *The purpose of elemental cost analysis is to reveal the distribution of the cost of a project between its elements in terms which are useful to both designers and clients and, by so doing, to allow the costs of two or more buildings to be compared in a meaningful way.*

Uses *Cost analysis can be used to:*

(a) *enable clients and designers to appreciate how cost is distributed among the functional components of a building (**appreciation**);*

(b) *enable clients and designers to develop ideas as to how costs could have been allocated to obtain a more balanced design (**judgement**);*

(c) *allow remedial action to be taken on receipt of high tenders, by revealing the sources of over-expenditure (**belated remedial action**);*

(d) *help with the cost planning of future building projects (**planning**).*

Turn to page 97 ⊃

➲ *from page*
103

You chose **(b)**.

You are correct.

An 'element' may be thought of as simply a *building* functional component such as roof, windows and external doors, external walls, etc. (The term element does not describe a *user's* functional unit such as a classroom, a gymnasium, a hotel bedroom, a hospital ward, etc.)

In Part 1, an element was defined as

'a major component common to most buildings which usually fulfils the same function, irrespective of its design, specification or construction.'

This definition is worth remembering for practical purposes although not all of the elements in current use are accurately described by this definition.

The elements we shall use in this programme are those used by the Building Cost Information Service (BCIS) in their *Detailed Cost Analyses*.

Study the detailed cost analysis given in Appendix A and write down any of those elements which you consider are *not* accurately described by the definition given above.

Turn to page 104 ➲

⊃ *from page 94* You chose: **final account.**

You are incorrect.

From the preceding argument, it would certainly *appear* that the costs on the final account should be analysed in preference to those on the accepted tender.

In practice, the costs on priced bills of quantities submitted on tender are analysed. The reason for this apparently irrational choice is that costs on final accounts are not significantly different from those on tenders. Therefore, costs on tenders are analysed because they are available much earlier. This, of course, has the disadvantages that the provisional or prime cost sums on the tender may not be exactly the same as the final cost of the items. Nevertheless, the advantage of tender costs being up-to-date is generally considered to outweigh these disadvantages.

Choose from the following list the most accurate description of the costs analysed in elemental cost analyses:

(a) **The costs analysed are the client's costs on the tender.**

(b) **The costs analysed are the contractor's costs on the final account.**

(c) **The costs analysed are the client's costs on the final account.**

Write down your answer.

Turn to page 96 ⊃

◗ *from page 96* Analysis of the costs incurred by each trade is *unsuitable for relating costs to function* because many elements include work executed by several trades. Additionally, any one trade may work on a number of elements. For example, a bricklayer may work on external walls, internal partitions, and external works. Similarly, common arrangement by work sections do not relate to functions (i.e. elements).

Because of this, the purpose of elemental cost analysis cannot always be achieved by using priced bills of quantities in their original form. A separate analysis has to be produced by gathering together the costs of each element, which are usually spread over several pages and under separate headings in a bill of quantities.

Furthermore, a bill of quantities may not necessarily have been used. Converting from the bill into elements can be a major exercise. Some organisations have produced elemental bills to overcome this, but they are unpopular with contractors because they price in trades or work packages.

Which of the following is a list of building elements?

(a) **Classrooms, gymnasium, a hotel bedroom**   *Turn to page 105* ◗

(b) **Roof, windows and external doors, external walls**   *Turn to page 101* ◗

from pages 101, 105

'Preliminaries' and 'contingencies' are certainly not components of completed buildings. Note, however, that they could be regarded as fulfilling the same functions during the design and construction of different buildings!

A useful characteristic of elements is that they tend to be self-explanatory to all concerned, including clients. However, when preparing or using an analysis, items included in each element must be clearly identified. Unfortunately, there is no room in this programme to include a full specification of the items which should be included in each element.

The problems of delineation, however, are relatively minor and you will be able to understand everything in this programme without having a full specification available.

Write down our definition of a building 'element'.

Turn to page 106

from page 103

You chose **(a)**.

You are incorrect.

Classrooms, gymnasiums, and bedrooms are all *user's* functional units rather than *building* functional components (i.e. elements). Roof, windows and external doors, external walls and stairs are all considered as elements by most authorities.

In Part 1, an **element** was defined as:

'a major component common to most buildings which usually fulfils the same function, or functions, irrespective of its design, specification or construction'.

This definition is worth remembering for practical purposes, although not *all* of the elements in current use are accurately described by this definition.

The elements we shall use in this programme are those used by the Building Cost Information Service (BCIS) in their *Detailed Cost Analyses*.

Study the detailed cost analysis given in Appendix A and write down any of those elements which you consider are *not* accurately described by the definition given above.

Turn to page 104

↩ *from page 104*

A building 'elemental category' or 'element' may be defined as 'a major component common to most buildings which fulfils the same function, or functions, irrespective of its design, specification or construction'.

Thus, for example, 'roof' is an element regardless of the fact that we may be considering a tiled pitched roof or an asphalt flat roof.

Yardstick

It follows from the general purpose of elemental cost analysis that we must have a method of expressing costs which will allow sensible comparisons between buildings *of different sizes and uses*. It is obviously futile to try to compare the costs of buildings directly without first expressing them in a way which takes account of the differences in size or capacity.

> Cost
> Elements
> Yardstick

Costs of any one type of school can usefully be considered in relation to the number of pupil-places provided and, 'cost per place' is a useful yardstick to use when comparing the costs of schools of different sizes. 'Cost per place' is an example of what BCIS calls a 'functional unit cost'. Note that the word 'functional' in this context refers to the use to which the whole building is put. Other examples of functional unit cost are 'cost per m^2 of usable floor area' for office buildings, 'cost per bed' for hospitals, 'cost per seat' for theatres, etc.

Expressing costs as 'functional unit cost' is, however, *not* used as the standard method of expressing the results of elemental cost analyses.

Write down one good reason for this.

Turn to page 108 ↪

⟲ *from page 113*

(b) £40.50 per m² is incorrect.

£40.50 per m² is the cost of the upper floors per m² of *upper floors*. You were asked to calculate the cost of the upper floors per m² of 'floor area', which in this context always means *gross floor area*.

The example is repeated below. When you have calculated the correct answer, turn to page 115.

Example

In a building of gross floor area 1700 m², the upper floors have an area of 800 m² and cost £32 400. Calculate the cost of the upper floors per m² of floor area, correct to two decimal places.

Turn to page 115 ⟲

⊃ *from page 106*

'Functional unit costs' are not used as the standard method of expressing elemental cost analysis because they would not allow comparisons of the costs of buildings which have different uses (e.g. schools, sports centres, office blocks).

Furthermore, even when comparing similar buildings such as schools, functional units tend to cloud important issues concerning quality, quantity and other factors.

A perfect cost yardstick would allow meaningful comparisons to be made between buildings of similar type, design, quality, date of tender, etc. and, at the same time, also allow comparisons with buildings of different use classifications.

The costs of buildings will obviously increase as the volume enclosed by the building increases and gross floor area increases. So both 'cost per cubic metre' and 'cost per metre^2' are worth considering for use as the standard yardstick.

Are clients (and designers) more likely to think of buildings in terms of volume or floor area?

(a) **Volume.**

Turn to page 109 ⊃

(b) **Floor area.**

Turn to page 111 ⊃

⮑ *from page*
108

You chose **(a).**

You are incorrect.

As long as each room is of usable height, the height of each storey is not generally as important to clients as the gross floor area. Clients are therefore more likely to think in terms of floor area rather than in terms of volume.

In addition, costs are not affected as much by an increase in the height of each storey as they are by an increase in superficial area. In other words, costs have a closer relationship to floor area than to volume. Because of this, design teams also think in terms of floor area.

'Cost per m^2 of gross floor area' (often expressed as '£ per m^2 gfa') is, therefore, the most realistic yardstick to use for comparing costs. The costs in costs analyses are therefore expressed as 'cost per m^2 of gross floor area'.

By referring to Appendix A, write down the *units* used for our yardstick of cost.

Turn to page 113 ⮑

from page 115

$$\text{Cost of upper floors per m}^2 \text{ of floor area} = \frac{\text{cost of upper floors (£)}}{\text{gross floor area (m}^2)}$$

$$= \frac{£32\,400}{1700\,\text{m}^2}$$

$$= £19.06 \text{ per m}^2$$
(to two decimal places)

Note the distinction between this and 'cost of upper floors per m^2 of *upper floors*', which would be found by evaluating:

$$\frac{\text{cost of upper floors (£)}}{\text{area of upper floors (m}^2)}$$

Return to page 115

⊃ *from page 108*

You chose **(b).**

You are correct.

Clients and designers are more likely to think of buildings in terms of floor area than in terms of volume. As long as each room is of usable height, the height of each storey is not generally as important to clients as the floor area.

In addition, costs are nearer to being proportional to floor area than to volume, because costs are not affected as much by an increase in the height of each storey as they are by an increase in floor area.

'Costs per m^2 of gross floor area' ('£ per m^2 gfa') is, therefore, the most realistic yardstick to use for comparing costs. This is the method used for expressing the results of elemental cost analyses. You may also see, elsewhere, this expressed as 'costs per m^2 of gross *internal* floor area'.

By referring to Appendix A, write down the *units* used for our yardstick of cost.

Turn to page 113 ⊃

⟳ *from page*
113

(a) The total cost of the building is expressed as cost per m^2 of gross floor area by calculating

$$\frac{\text{total cost of building (£)}}{\text{gross floor area of building (m}^2)}$$

In Appendix A,

$$\text{total cost per m}^2 \text{ of gross floor area} = \frac{£1\,153\,793}{1408\,\text{m}^2}$$

$$= £819.46 \text{ per m}^2$$
$$\text{of gross floor area}$$

(b) The cost of each element per m^2 of gross floor area is found by calculating

$$\frac{\text{cost of element (£)}}{\text{gross floor area of building (m}^2)}$$

In Appendix A,

$$\text{cost of external walls per m}^2 \text{gfa} = \frac{£27\,069}{1408\,\text{m}^2}$$

$$= £19.23 \text{ per m}^2 \text{ of gross floor area}$$

Return to page 113 ⟳

from pages 109, 111 **All the costs per m² of gross floor area are expressed in £, correct to two decimal places.**

If you would like to see how the costs in column 4 in Appendix A are calculated, turn to page 112.

Note that the cost of each element is divided by the *gross* floor area of the building, (*and not just the floor area appropriate to the element*). This is especially easy to forget when dealing with elements such as '2B: Upper floors'.

The 'gross floor area' is always the *total* area of *enclosed* floor space. No deductions are made for partitions, stairwells, corridors, cupboards, etc. Measurements are taken to the internal face of the enclosing walls (i.e. external walls). The definition given by the *Standard Form of Cost Analysis* is:

Gross floor area

(1) Total of all enclosed spaces fulfilling the functional requirements of the building measured to the internal structural face of the enclosing walls.

(2) Includes area occupied by partitions, columns, chimney breasts, internal structural or party walls, stairwells, lift wells, and the like.

(3) Includes lift, plant, tank rooms and the like above main roof slab.

(4) Sloping surfaces such as staircases, galleries, tiered terraces and the like should be measured flat on plan.

Note:

(a) Excludes any spaces fulfilling the functional requirements of the building which are not enclosed spaces e.g. open ground floors, open covered ways and the like. These should be shown separately.

(b) Excludes private balconies and private verandas which should be shown separately.

Example
In a building with a gross floor area of 1700 m², the upper floors have an area of 800 m² and cost £32 400. Calculate the cost of the upper floors per m² of floor area, correct to two decimal places.

Which answer is correct?

(a) **£19.06 per m²** *Turn to page 115*

(b) **£40.50 per m²** *Turn to page 107*

from page 115

Some clients who deal with buildings of identical function, find 'functional unit cost' is a useful method of comparison. Hence, the cost of the actual building per functional unit is given in cost analyses for such purposes.

Type of building	Functional unit cost
School	Cost per pupil place
Hotel	Cost per bedroom
Hospital ward	Cost per bed space
Office	Cost per m^2 usable floor area. (Usable floor area is that area fulfilling the main functional requirement of the building and excludes for example all circulation areas. In a commercial context it usually equates to that area used for the calculation of rent.)

Revision

As revision for this chapter, we would like you to think carefully about the distinctions between the *purpose* of elemental cost analysis (i.e. the general reason for such an analysis being performed), the nature of the analysis (i.e. how you would describe it to someone else), and the specialised *uses* to which analyses may be put.

(a) **Compose and write down the definition of elemental cost analysis which you would use to explain it to someone who had never come across the term.**

(b) **Write down the purpose of elemental cost analysis.**

Turn to page 116

from pages 107, 113

(a) £19.06 per m² is the correct answer.

(If you would like to check your working, turn to page 110.)

'Cost per m² of gross floor area' is not a *perfect* cost yardstick. The costs of buildings are not *exactly* proportional to floor area – even for buildings which differ only in size. Costs per m² of floor area should be used with discretion. We know there will be differences in shape, height, ground conditions, external works and a host of other things, but we still need something as a basis for considering projects. As we will discuss in the next chapter, variations in quantity, quality and price level cause differences in cost per m² of gross floor area.

Nevertheless, cost per m² of gross floor area relate costs to client's principal requirement and also go a long way towards eliminating variations in cost due to differences in the size of buildings.

Throughout the world everybody uses the cost per m² as the method of communicating cost.

The following extract is from a typical cost analysis:

Functional unit	Rate
1325 m² usable floor area	£827.08

Why do you think this 'functional unit cost' has been included?

Write down your answer.

Turn to page 114

from page 114

Chapter 8 – Summary

(a) Elemental cost analysis is the analysis of the costs to clients which are given on tenders, to determine the probable cost of each element of a building.

(b) The purpose of elemental cost analysis is to show the distribution of the costs of a building among its elements in meaningful terms to both clients and design teams and, by so doing, to allow the cost of two or more buildings to be compared.

It is unlikely that your choice of words will be exactly as the above: this does not matter, as long as the meaning is the same.

(c) Write down the uses of elemental cost analysis mentioned in this chapter.

Turn to page 117

from page 116

(c)   The uses of elemental cost analysis as discussed in this chapter are:

Appreciation
Elemental cost analysis can be used to enable clients and designers to appreciate how cost is distributed among the elements of a building.

Judgement
Elemental cost analysis can be used to enable clients and designers to develop ideas as to how costs could have been allocated to obtain a more balanced distribution of cost for the design.

Belated remedial action
Elemental cost analysis can be used to allow remedial action to be taken on receipt of tenders above the budget, by revealing the sources of over-expenditure.

Planning
Elemental cost analysis can be used to help with the cost planning of future construction projects.

(d)   List the three essential constituents of elemental cost analysis.

(e)   Why are elements employed in the analysis of building costs?

(f)   Why is a yardstick used in elemental cost analysis?

(g)   What yardstick of cost is usually employed?

Write down your answers.

Turn to page 118

⊃ *from page*
117

(d) **The three essential constituents of elemental cost analysis are:**

- ❏ **cost**
- ❏ **elements**
- ❏ **yardstick.**

(e) **Elements are used as the sub-units of analysis so that costs can be related to those functions of buildings which are common to all types of buildings.**

(f) **A yardstick is used in elemental cost analysis so that costs of buildings of different sizes can be compared without explicitly considering the sizes of the buildings.**

(g) **'Cost per m^2 of gross floor area' is used as the yardstick of cost.**

Turn to page 119 ⊃

9 Factors Affecting Element Costs

This chapter *is* in programmed form and you must follow the page directions exactly.

Turn to page 120 ⟩

⊃ *from page 119*

So far we have only mentioned one of the factors which affects the costs of elements: the size of the building. Expressing the cost of each element as 'cost per m² of gross floor area' allows naive, but nevertheless useful, comparisons of the costs of buildings of different size. However, such comparisons, can only *isolate* the differences in costs per m². They cannot *account* for these differences.

For a complete understanding of costs, all of the factors affecting element costs should obviously be studied so that adjustments can be made to account for the effect of each of the factors.

Before we consider in detail how this is done, see if you can postulate one or more possible reasons for the difference between the element costs in the following example.

Example

In the building analysed in Appendix A, internal doors cost £5.87 per m² of gross floor area (element 2H).

If analysis of another building gave a figure of £9.34 per m², what possible reasons for this difference can you think of?

Write down your answers.

Turn to page 122 ⊃

⟳ *from page 128*

(a) **Wherever possible, analyses include element unit quantities in order to provide a measure of the amounts of each element in different buildings. When comparing buildings, we can judge how much of the variations in element costs is due to differences in the amounts of each element.**

(b) **Since element unit rates are relatively unaffected by variations in Quantity, they isolate the differences in cost due to Quality and Price level.**

If, however, there is a very large increase in the Quantity of an element, the element unit rate would probably decrease because cheaper rates are usually obtained for large quantities. Economies associated with large quantities affect all resources. For example, labour rates can become more competitive with the use of more efficient gang sizes, continuity of work, repetition and learning curves, etc. Savings in material costs are possible with discounts for bulk buying, use of full loads rather than half loads, etc. Mechanical plant can be used to advantage and methods of working can also show savings in element unit rates.

Therefore, when using the analyses in cost control, selected projects should be reasonably compatible both with regard to type and size. These points are considered again in later chapters.

Turn to page 131 ⟳

from page 120

There are several possible reasons, the most probable are:

(a) **There may be a larger number (*quantity*) of internal doors per m² of gross floor area in the second building.**

(b) **The doors of the second building may be of better *quality* than those in the first.**

(c) **The tender for the second building may have been prepared a few years after the tender for the first, and the increase in cost may be at least partly due to an increase in the general market *price level*.**

It is, of course, highly likely that the increase is due to a combination of these three major factors and some others.

A large amount of time and effort could obviously be spent trying to analyse each of the factors affecting element costs. In practice however, it is found that most of the difference between the costs of any one element in different buildings can usually be accounted for by considering just three major factors:

Factor 1 Quantity.

Factor 2 Quality.

Factor 3 Price level.

> **Important.**
> Remember these as they will be used throughout the text.

When the actual adjustments are made, *price level* is normally taken first, followed by *quantity*, and then *quality*. However, this order has been changed on the following pages in order to make the explanations clearer.

To determine the effect of these factors on the cost of each element, an elemental cost analysis must obviously contain a specification of the quantity and quality of each element together with the date of tender and other information relating to price level.

Turn to page 127

⤵ *from page 126*

Example

The total cost of the internal walls and partitions for building A is £80 000 and for building B is £480 000. Let us assume that all of the difference between these costs for the two buildings is due to Quantity.

Then, comparison of the costs of this element per m² of gross floor area will eliminate the difference in costs due to the differing sizes of the two buildings, but it will not eliminate the differences in costs due to the difference in density of that element in the two buildings.

	A	B	Ratio A/B
Total cost of 'internal walls and partitions'	£80 000	£480 000	1/6
Gross floor area (m²)	1000	3000	1/3
Cost per m² of gross floor area	£80	£160	1/2

In other words, using this comparison eliminates the difference in costs due to the size of the buildings; and thus any remaining difference in cost must be due to a difference in density of the element (remember we are assuming Quality and Price level do not affect cost). Further investigation will confirm this.

	A	B	Ratio A/B
Area of 'internal walls and partitions'	2000 m²	12 000 m²	1/6
Density*	2	4	1/2

$$^{*}\text{Density} = \frac{\text{area of internal walls and partitions}}{\text{gross floor area}}$$

The ratio of total costs is the same as the ratio of areas of internal walls and partitions because all of the difference between the element costs is due to Quantity. Eliminating the 1 to 3 difference in floor areas by expressing the costs as 'costs per m² of gross floor area' brings the ratio down to 1 to 2. In this case, all of this remaining difference should be due to the variation in the 'densities' of internal walls and partitions: this is confirmed by the ratio of densities, which also turns out to be 1 to 2.

In most cases, however, the ratio of 'costs per m² of gross floor area' would not be the same as the ratio of the 'densities' because the costs per m² would also reflect variations in Quality and Price level.

What way of expressing costs will isolate the difference in cost due to the combined effect of Quality and Price level?

Write down your answer.

Turn to page 130 ⤵

from page *127*

In Appendix A, the Quantity of wall finishes is 904 m².

In practice the measurements currently used as element unit quantities (as recommended in the *Standard Form of Cost Analysis*) are satisfactory for most elements. Thus, comparison of the Quantity of an element in two buildings gives a reliable indication of how costs are affected by this factor.

When comparing the costs of two or more buildings, valuable knowledge will remain hidden if only the total Quantities of each element are compared, for example, the knowledge of how much of a change in element unit quantity is due to a difference in the size of the buildings and how much is due to a difference in the density of the element in the buildings remains undisclosed.

For instance, it may be tempting to say, 'The element – "internal walls and partitions" – is more expensive because there are more internal walls and partitions'. This does not really tell us very much: there may be more internal walls and partitions because one building is larger than the other, or because one contains a higher proportion of small rooms, or both.

It is therefore useful to analyse Quantity into two factors: the Quantity due to the building size, and the Quantity due to density of the element. The first of these can obviously be assessed by comparing the gross floor areas.

How can the relative 'densities' of internal walls and partitions in two buildings be assessed?

Write down your answer.

Turn to page 126

from page 130

Element	Element unit rate
2B Upper floors	£32.14 per m^2
2H Internal doors	£131.27 per m^2
5D Water installations	£480.73 per draw-off point

When analyses are being used, it is obviously vital that confusion never occurs between 'cost of element per m^2 of gross floor area' and 'element unit rate'. Confusion is most likely with elements such as internal doors, when the latter becomes 'cost of internal doors per m^2 of internal doors' and the former is 'cost of internal doors per m^2 of gross floor area'. Both are expressed in £ per m^2.

To help to avoid this confusion, we shall always refer to

$$\frac{\text{cost of element}}{\text{gross floor area}} \quad \text{as} \quad \textbf{cost of element per m}^2 \textbf{ of gross floor area}$$

and

$$\frac{\text{cost of element}}{\text{quantity of element}} \quad \text{as} \quad \textbf{element unit rate}.$$

> **Important.**
> Remember these as they will be used throughout the text.

Example
Write down clearly labelled values, for both of the measures of cost mentioned above, for upper floors (element 2B) in Appendix A.

Turn to page 128

from page 124

The relative 'densities' of internal walls and partitions can be assessed by comparing the values of the ratio

Quantity of internal walls and partitions
$$\frac{\text{Quantity of internal walls and partitions}}{\text{gross floor area}}$$

in the two buildings.

Detailed analyses include details of 'specification and design notes'. However, there is a tendency for insufficient information to be given and as a consequence these ratios are rarely included. Nevertheless, there is no reason why individual organisations should not collect and record this information for their own in-house cost analyses.

These ratios, as well as being useful when considering how Quantity has affected the costs of an element in two or more buildings, can also be used during the design of a new project. For instance, comparison of the window-to-floor ratios for alternative design solutions *for a given floor area* will help to give a quick appreciation of the relative economy of the alternative design solutions.

As we have already discussed on page 124, it is often useful to consider how the total effect of Quantity can be attributed to the difference between the sizes of the buildings and the difference between the densities of the element in the buildings. This can be done either by comparing the gross floor areas and the densities, as we have seen, or by eliminating the effects of each factor in turn.

Expressing costs as 'costs per m^2 of gross floor area' eliminates (for our purposes) the difference in costs due to the size of the buildings, but it is still misleading, for we are ignoring the effects of different 'densities'. If Quality and Price level do not affect costs, then, comparison of the costs of the element per m^2 of gross floor area will *not* eliminate the difference in costs due to the difference in density of that element in the two buildings.

Turn to page 123

⊃ *from page 122*

We will now discuss each of the major factors in turn.

Factor 1 Quantity

The 'quantity' of an element is the 'amount' of the element in the building. It is determined by the client's requirements of floor area, span, loading, etc., and by the architect's design solutions to these requirements.

As the total cost of an element obviously depends on the quantity of the element, some measure of the quantity should be given in an analysis so that the variations in costs due to changes in quantity can be assessed.

For many elements, finding a suitable unit of measurement to reflect quantity within the building presents few problems. Thus, for different buildings which have identical quality and price levels but varying quantities of an element, straightforward comparisons and useful conclusions might be made. However, in practice this ideal 'measure of quantity' has not yet been found for all elements. It is, perhaps, too much to hope that even with further study, a number, area, or ratio will be found which will provide a simple index of the relative size of each element. This is particularly evident with environmental engineering services elements.

The term **Element Unit Quantities** (often abbreviated to EUQ) is commonly used to describe these simple measures of quantity. In places within the text we have simply referred to **Quantities** (with a capital Q), rather than using the term 'Element Unit Quantities'.

Write down the Element Unit Quantity of wall finishes given in Appendix A, (element 3A).

Turn to page 124 ⊃

from page 125

Cost of upper floors per m² of gross floor area = £16.07
Element unit rate for upper floors   = £32.14 per m²

Note   The first of these is £16.07 per m² of *gross* floor area and the second is £32.14 per m² of *upper floors only*.

Element unit rates will be used during the preparation of the cost plan in later chapters.

Why are

(a)   **element unit quantities, and**
(b)   **element unit rates given in cost analyses?**

Write down your answer.

Turn to page 121

from page
131

There is one aspect of 'quantity' which we have not yet considered.

Even when the element unit quantities for a given element are the same, a difference in the quantities of the items *within* the element may cause a difference in the cost of an element. For instance, $90\,m^2$ of glazed doors and $10\,m^2$ of flush doors would probably be more expensive than $10\,m^2$ of glazed doors and $90\,m^2$ of flush doors. However, both examples when totalled have an element unit quantity of $100\,m^2$.

In cost analyses, where is information given about the quantities of various items within each element? (See Appendix A.)

Write down your answer.

Turn to page 132

⊃ *from page 123*

Expressing costs as a ratio of cost of element to quantity of element will highlight the difference in cost due to the combined effect of Quality and Price level. This ratio is called the 'element unit rate'.

This method takes account of the quantity of an element as shown below:

$$\frac{\text{cost per m}^2 \text{ of gross floor area}}{\text{density}}$$

Expressed in full gives:

$$\frac{\text{cost of element}}{\text{gross floor area}} \times \frac{\text{gross floor area}}{\text{quantity of element}}$$

which, when simplified, gives:

$$\frac{\text{cost of element}}{\text{quantity of element}}$$

This ratio (for our purposes) should have an approximately constant value for any one element if none of the *other factors* affecting costs varies from building to building *except* the Quantity of the element. (Remember we have decided that the major factors under consideration are: Quantity, Quality and Price level.)

In Appendix A, the 'element unit rates' are given in column 6.

Example

As you can see in Appendix A, the Quantity of '2C: Roof' is measured in m^2, so the element unit rate is £71.66 per m^2.

By referring to Appendix A, write down the element unit rates, including units, for:

❑ **2B   Upper floors**
❑ **2H   Internal doors**
❑ **5D   Water installations.**

Turn to page 125 ⊃

from page
121

Summary of Quantity

The cost–element unit quantities relationship can be considered either in two stages or in one stage, as shown below.

(a)

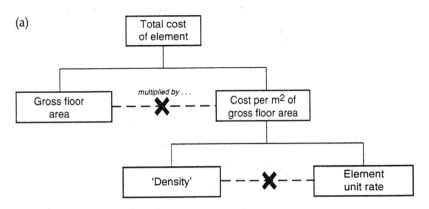

where density is element unit quantity divided by gross floor area, and cost per m^2 of gross floor area relates to the cost of the particular element being considered.

(b)

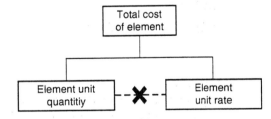

Comparison of element unit quantities gives a measure of how much of the variation in element costs between buildings is due to differences in the amount of the element.

Element unit rates isolate the differences in cost due to Quality and Price level. For these reasons use of element unit quantities and element unit rates gives a more refined answer.

Turn to page 129

from page 129

With a detailed analysis, the only place to include such information is within the 'Specification and design notes'.

Where various forms of construction or many different finishes are contained within one element, further breakdown should be given. It is suggested that the net areas and costs of the key types of construction (or finishes) should be given separately in the 'Specification and design notes' section. Indeed, it would be prudent to record the total costs, if these are significant, which must include all the costs of items pertaining to that construction.

In practice, differences in cost due to differences in the quantities of items within an element are often considered as being due to **'Quality'**.

We shall now go on to consider **Quality** and **Price level**.

Turn to page 133

⊃ *from page 132*

Factor 2 Quality

Changes in Quality obviously affect the costs of elements. However, the relationship between Quality and cost is far more complex than Quantity and cost.

What does 'Quality' mean? There is quality of design, quality of materials, quality of workmanship, quality of performance, quality of service provided to the client. Hence the idea of quality has several facets.

Perhaps easiest to understand is the quality reflected in choice of materials, for example, the type of facing bricks, the choice of finishes, etc. This is very much a question of specification. However, exact details can be hidden where simple element unit quantities do not disclose the make-up of items within the element. Much of the foregoing might relate to aesthetic qualities. Performance requirements must also be considered. As examples, consider the wearing characteristics of floor finishes, or, U-values for roofs, or then again it might be the level of engineering services required by the client. Again these design solutions would normally be reflected in specification notes.

Quality of workmanship is even harder to establish. Part of it would be specified within the detailed contract documentation (not available with a cost analysis), and part of it would be implied in the expectations of certain clients or for certain building types.

Some organisations have tried to rank 'quality' on a scale of 1 to 10. However, no simple or universal quality index has, as yet, been devised for any element. The extent of changes in cost due to variations in quality can be isolated by an experienced cost consultant from cost analyses or bills of quantities of the buildings under consideration. For example, adjusting for the variation in cost between softwood and aluminium windows can be done from knowledge of market prices. Making allowances for different levels of engineering service requirements would be more difficult and often more cost significant. In practice, because of the make-up and complexity of design, much reliance is placed on professional judgement.

What part of a detailed analysis would have to be inspected to isolate the information necessary to assess how Quality had affected costs?

Write down your answer.

Turn to page 138 ⊃

from page 137

You chose: **Ignore any differences in price level.**

You are incorrect.

This would be rather a rash approach. Tender price levels can vary quite dramatically over time and it is worth while making adjustments for these variations.

Although increases in prices are experienced most frequently, a fall in price level can also occur. This was the situation in the UK between 1989 and 1992, during a period of recession in the construction industry. At this time tender prices decreased despite increasing costs of labour, materials and plant. Contractors and specialist contractors had to price work very competitively to win projects.

Look at Fig. 9.1 which shows the cost indexes for both the UK and the USA between 1985 and 1996.

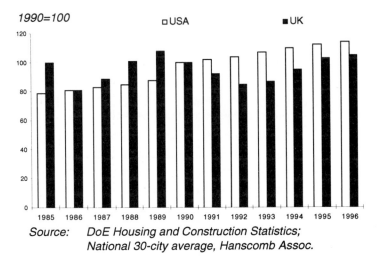

Fig. 9.1 US and UK construction cost indexes

Source: DoE Housing and Construction Statistics; National 30-city average, Hanscomb Assoc.

Also, not to be ignored are the other important factors which affect Price level:

❏ difference in individual contractor's price levels relative to the general market price level (due to differences in allowances for overheads, profits, etc.);
❏ difference in regional trends, and localised variables;
❏ difference in tendering arrangements (including selection of contractors), contract conditions, contract period, weather conditions, site conditions, etc.

It is true that differences in cost due to the *other* Price level factors are usually smaller than those due to a change in the general market price level, but nevertheless an attempt should be made to allow for them.

Return to page 137

⊃ *from page*
138

Factor 3 Price level

Consider the hypothetical situation of two buildings which have been built from *exactly* the same detailed design. Any differences between the tender costs of these two buildings can obviously not be attributed to differences in Quantity and Quality. In this case the differences between the costs (i.e. total cost *and* cost of each element) are due to a difference in the **Price level**.

By 'Price level', we mean the price level of a project *relative* to general tender price levels at a specific date, and not *absolute* prices, which are, of course, primarily dependent on specification.

Price level includes several factors, all of which affect costs.

Write down at least three of the most important of the factors which collectively affect Price level by considering the hypothetical situation outlined above.

Turn to page 140 ⊃

from page
137

You chose: **Construct and use an index which reflects changes in general tender price levels to clients.**

You are correct.

It is changes in tender levels to clients which are important and not changes in contractors' costs. Tender price levels can vary quite dramatically over time and it is worth while making adjustments for these variations.

Although increases in prices are experienced most frequently, a fall in price level can also happen, as was the case from 1989 to 1992 in the UK. This occurred even though contractors were experiencing increasing costs of labour, materials and plant. (See Fig. 9.1 on page 134.)

You have no need to construct your own index as BCIS monitors movements in price levels and publishes several price indices, including a Tender Price Index (TPI). However as the construction of the index relies on data received of live projects, the index will always lag behind the current date. Forecast figures are therefore needed to relate to the current date and future dates.

Also not to be ignored are the other important factors which affect Price level:

- ❏ difference in individual contractor's price levels relative to the general market price level (due to differences in allowances for overheads, profits, etc.);
- ❏ difference in regional trends, and localised variables;
- ❏ difference in tendering arrangements (including selection of contractors), contract conditions, contract period, weather conditions, site conditions, etc.

It is true that differences in cost due to the *other* Price level factors are usually smaller than those due to a change in the general market price level reflecting different tender dates, but nevertheless an attempt should be made to allow for them. In the UK the BCIS publish a range of price adjustment factors which allow tender prices to be modified with respect to location, contract size and procurement route. Professional judgement is required when assessing and making any adjustments for the remaining factors listed above.

For a more detailed description of:

BCIS tender price indices

Turn to page 141 ⊃

Other price adjustment factors

Turn to page 144 ⊃

If you would prefer to omit these sections at this stage, *Turn to page 146* ⊃

⟩ *from pages 134, 139, 140*

To help in the assessing, the influence of (a) tender dates and (b) contractors' price levels, any analysis should provide the following information:

- ❏ The *date of tender* so that the effects of any differences in the general market price level between two tender dates can be found by using an appropriate tender price index;
- ❏ The *location* for each project. By use of published location factors, projects in different locations can be brought to a comparable base;
- ❏ A comment on *market conditions* pertaining at the time of bidding.

In addition, site conditions, tendering arrangements and contract conditions should all be specified on the front page of analyses, but it is left to the cost consultant using professional expertise and judgement to gauge their overall effect on costs.

Assume you wish to use the cost information included in a cost analysis of a project where the date of tender is three years previous to today's date.

Can you suggest a reasonable way of allowing for differences in Price level which have occurred over this time period?

Ignore any differences in Price level. *Turn to page 134* ⟩

Construct and use an index which reflects changes in general tender price levels to clients. *Turn to page 136* ⟩

Construct and use an index which reflects changes in contractors' costs due to increases in labour, materials, and plant charges. *Turn to page 139* ⟩

from page 133

The quality of each element can be assessed from the 'Specification and design notes' in the detailed analysis (Appendix A).

Another aspect of Quality is the value provided by the specification of an element. That is, the 'worth' of the element. If this aspect of Quality is not considered by the design team, the client may be involved in unnecessary expense. For instance, hand-made special joinery may be specified whereas standard joinery from a manufacturer's catalogue may equally suffice. The decision would need to be made whether the client is prepared to pay extra for the individuality of the joinery.

For this reason, a judgement of Quality based upon 'worth' might be more illuminating than a straightforward comparison of specifications.

Methods of allowing for differences in Quality based upon both these concepts will be demonstrated during the preparation of the cost plan in later chapters.

We shall now go on to discuss **Price level**.

Turn to page 135

⟲ *from page 137*

You chose: **Construct and use an index which reflects changes in contractors' costs due to increases in labour, materials, and plant charges.**

You are incorrect.

It is prices to clients, as reflected in tenders received, which are important and not changes to contractors' costs due to increases in labour, materials, and plant charges.

Return to page 137 ⟲

from page 135

The most important factors which affect Price level are:

(a) differences in general tender price level due to difference in tender date, reflecting inflation in labour and material rates;

(b) difference in contractors' price levels relative to the general tender price level due to differences in allowances for overheads, profits, etc. when the market is low – then the contractors will be prepared to price more competitively to win work;

(c) difference in regional trends, and localised variables;

(d) difference in tendering arrangements (including selection of contractors for tender lists), contract conditions, contract period, weather conditions, site conditions, etc.

Cost analyses must include as much relevant information as possible to enable the influence of each of these factors on costs to be assessed.

Examine Appendix A, then write down the information which BCIS *Detailed Cost Analyses* **give to help assess the influence of factors (a) and (b) above.**

Turn to page 137

⊃ *from page*
136

BCIS tender price indices

What is a tender price index?

The purpose of a price index is to measure changes in price levels from one time period to another. Indices are published around the world. For the UK, tender price indices are published quarterly by the Building Cost Information Service (BCIS). These measure contractors' price levels for accepted tenders (i.e. cost to the client). All index figures are based on a given base date (expressed at a level of 100). Any changes in cost are related to this figure and can be used to calculate a percentage change over base year tender price levels.

The BCIS tender price index series is a statistical series which is based on a technique of sampling prices from the construction industry. Quarterly index figures use an analysis of projects with a contract sum in excess of £50000. The average contract value of projects analysed is approximately £1 million.

How is it compiled?

Index calculations are based on the analysis of bills of quantities for about eighty projects. Each bill of quantities is re-priced using a standard base schedule of rates. The resulting *base* tender figure is compared with the actual tender figure in order to produce a *project index*. Published tender prices indices represent an average of all project indices included in the analysis. Individual project index figures are also adjusted in order to remove tendering differences due to project size, location and procurement route.

Types of index

Tender price indices (TPI) are produced in a variety of different formats. The most commonly used index is the all-in TPI. This covers new building work in the UK and reflects all sectors of the construction industry (public, private and housing). The index is based on a random sample of schemes and represents the general trends of tender prices across all sectors (see Fig. 9.2).

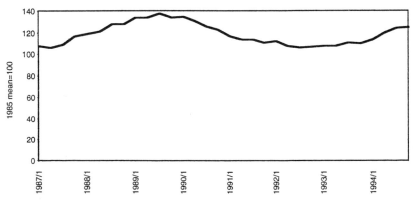

Fig. 9.2 All-in TPI

Turn to page 142 ⊃

from page 141

The adjustment of tender prices to allow for time variations is carried out by applying the following formula:

$$A = \frac{(B - C) \times 100}{C}$$

where A = percentage change,
        B = index at date required, and
        C = index at date applicable to analysed prices.

Thus, the percentage change required to update a tender price, calculated during the first quarter of 1994 to an anticipated date of tender in the last quarter of 1994, can be expressed as:

$B = 126$ (index at last quarter 1994)
$C = 114$ (index at first quarter 1994)

$$A = \frac{(126 - 114) \times 100}{114} = 10.5\%$$

In other words, general tender prices rose by 10.5% during 1994.

Individual tender price indices are also produced for sub-sets of the 'all-in TPI'. These cover a variety of different types of construction projects and regions. The following categories are defined by the BCIS:

Public sector TPI   This covers non-housing schemes for public sector clients including central and local government, health trusts, opted-out schools, etc. Some schemes for private sector clients are also included where funded from the public sector.

Housing TPI   Based on a sample of housing schemes. The majority of schemes relate to social housing.

Private sector TPI   Includes non-housing schemes for private sector clients. Some schemes for public sector clients are included where funded by the private sector.

Private commercial TPI   A sub-set of the *private sector TPI* covering offices, shops, entertainment, garages, schools and colleges, agriculture, transport and health.

Private industrial TPI   A sub-set of the *private sector TPI* including factories and warehouses.

Turn to page 143

from page 142

Refurbishment TPI Based on a specially collected sample of schemes of work dealing with conversion and refurbishment throughout the UK and covering all sectors both public and private and including housing.

Housing refurbishment TPI A sub-set of the *refurbishment TPI* which covers housing schemes only.

Non-housing refurbishment TPI A sub-set of the *refurbishment TPI* excluding housing schemes.

Frequently, the sample size for a given category may be relatively small. In such cases the resulting index may be volatile. The BCIS recommends that these indices should not be used automatically for indexing of tender prices. Rather, they should be used to monitor any major divergence from general tender price movements (the all-in TPI). Figure 9.3 illustrates the difference between the all-in TPI and the private industrial TPI.

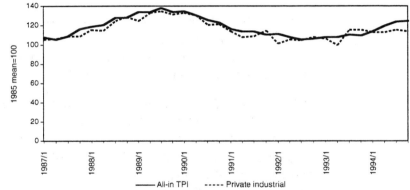

Fig. 9.3 TPI – all-in and private industrial

It can be seen that in the first quarter of 1992 the all-in TPI index was 112, whereas the private industrial index was 102. When considering projects relating to private industrial work, it may seem prudent to apply an index of 102.

However, in this situation the private industrial TPI *may* be unrepresentative of the true tender price level as the sample size used includes only a small number of projects. Thus, the all-in TPI *may* be more representative of likely tender prices due to the larger sample size. This illustrates the need for professional judgement when applying indices.

Turn to page 144

from page 143

In addition to producing historical tender price indices, forecast indices of likely future price levels are also published. These allow costs to be projected to a future tender date. Such forecasts are based on a range of published assumptions and economic indicators. Again, professional judgement will be required in assessing the likely accuracy of these indices.

Turn to page 172 for a brief discussion on the difference between a TPI and a cost index. (Make sure that you return to this page after reading the differences.)

from page 136

Other price adjustment factors

Location

The costs of a building are affected by a number of localised variables which give rise to a unique tender. These include local market conditions such as supply and demand for labour and materials, workload, taxation and grants. These variables are sufficiently volatile that not even identical buildings built at the same time within 10 kilometres of each other, obtain identical tenders.

In order to quantify the effects of location on tender prices for the UK, the BCIS publishes adjustment factors relating to Standard Statistical Regions, counties and local authority districts. The regions chosen are administrative areas and are not significant cost boundaries as far as the building industry is concerned.

While there will be small regional differences in the cost of materials due to transportation costs, the main influence is on the cost of labour. A lot of work in a particular region will increase the cost of the labour on a project.

Contract sum

Adjustment factors are also produced which allow the general relationship between tender prices and overall contract size to be incorporated into the analysis. The principle being that economies of scale are effective on larger projects, thus reducing the unit costs. There is also the principle of the learning curve effect where labour becomes more efficient when repetitive tasks are undertaken. For example, on high-rise buildings with repeat floors, the costs will reflect the repetition and efficiency.

Procurement route

Some variation in tender price can be expected due to differing forms of procurement. Adjustment factors are provided for competitive, negotiated and serial contracts.

Turn to page 145

⊃ *from page*
144

Price adjustment factors relate the impact of a given variable to the national average, for example, the cost implication of tender prices in Bristol compared with the national average for tender prices. Adjustment of tender price indices is carried out by simple multiplication, for example:

Index for first quarter 1995 = 126

Adjustment factors   Location factor (Woking) = 1.10
Procurement factor (negotiation) = 1.12
Contract size factor (£4 724 000) = 0.90

$$\text{Adjusted TPI} = 126 \times 1.10 \times 1.12 \times 0.90$$
$$= 139.71$$

This adjusted TPI can now be used in any adjustment calculations. An example of this will be given in Chapter 10.

The statistical reliability of the price adjustment factors is dependent on two factors – the number of projects included in the sample and the variability of the factors. An average factor based on a small number of widely varying figures is likely to be less reliable than one based on a large number of closely grouped figures.

The difference between 126 and 139.71 is significant. Hence, care has to be taken when applying such adjustments to a cost plan. We keep referring to professional skill and judgement; in such a situation there is no substitute.

Turn to page 146 ⊃

from pages
136, 145

Summary of Quality and Price level

An elemental cost analysis consists of an element-by-element allocation of costs.

The total cost of the building is expressed as 'cost per m^2 of gross floor area.' The cost of the building can also be expressed as a 'functional unit cost' (e.g. cost per m^2 of usable floor area, or cost per bed space, etc.).

The cost of each element is shown as 'cost per m^2 of gross floor area'. In addition, an 'element unit rate' is calculated for many, but not all, elements.

Sufficient details and specification notes are given of the factors which affect costs (Quantity, Quality, and Price level) allowing appropriate adjustments to be made.

Adjustments for Quantity have been considered in the previous section. Here we have been looking at the necessary adjustments for Quality and Price level and we saw that:

(a) For any one element, the element unit rates must be adjusted to account for variations due to Quality. Information necessary for this task can be gained by examining the **'specification and design notes'** for that element.

(b) Adjustments to account for variations due to Price level are also necessary and can be made by comparing the respective **tender dates**, **locations**, **site conditions**, and **contract conditions** given on the front page of the analyses. A **tender price index** and **location index** (such as those published by the BCIS) can then be used for part of the adjustments, but professional judgement is also required.

Turn to page 149

⊃ *from page* 149 The answer is **preliminaries and contingencies.**

Preliminaries and Contingencies

This chapter has been looking at factors affecting elemental costs, but as yet little has been said about **preliminaries and contingencies.** By referring to the analysis in Appendix A, you will see that a breakdown of the contract sum is given. Here the total for measured work is isolated from fixed sums such as provisional, prime cost and contingency sums. The total for preliminaries is also identified separately. This is the only place where the contingencies sum is declared (analysis of *element costs* excludes contingencies). The *Standard Form of Cost Analysis* recommends that both preliminaries and contingencies should each be expressed as a percentage of the remainder of the contract sum.

Preliminaries

These are items required to construct the project, which the contractor will price. They include such items as the cost of the site management team, scaffolding, site offices, toilets, canteen, first aid, insurances for the works, temporary protection, plant and equipment not specific to one task (such as dumper trucks, hoist and craneage), keeping roads clear of mud, removal of site debris, water and power for the works, temporary lighting, site telephones, cleaning the works, hoardings, safety requirements, and other general items specific to the contract conditions.

Contingencies

A contingency sum is included to cover unforeseen items and eventualities which occur during the construction of the project. It can vary in amount dependent upon the project size and type.

How are preliminaries priced by contractors?

The contractor's prices are based upon resources over time. In the case of a crane, the contractor will allow for the cost of bringing it to site, its erection, the weekly hire rate, the cost of the driver and the banksman, the fuel and insurances, the maintenance charge, the dismantling cost and the removal from site. The length of time the crane is required is crucial. From this information the weekly or daily rate will be calculated and the overall rate included in the preliminaries. The contractor has to ensure that, should the project be delayed and an extension of time granted, the additional cost incurred will be reimbursed. Similarly, the cost of the site management team, which may include a site manager, general foreman, site engineer, site quantity surveyor, safety officer and general labour, will all be priced according to the length of time they are on site.

Turn to page 148 ⊃

from page 147

Under normal circumstances a contractor will consider the preliminaries and price only the items which have a cost consequence. Problems arise as there are a variety of methods for including these prices into the bills of quantities. These options are:

(a) to include each price against the appropriate item in the preliminaries section; or

(b) to show no individual priced items, but give a total only for the preliminaries section; or

(c) to spread prices attributable to preliminaries items evenly or unevenly throughout the measured rates in the bills of quantities; or

(d) to use various combinations of the above approaches.

This presents initial problems for the analysis of this element, and also later when comparisons are made with other projects. As far as the analysis is concerned, one way of overcoming the problem is to apportion any identifiable preliminary costs evenly throughout the other elements (see analysis in Appendix A, for example).

What other major problem exists with the analysis of the 'preliminaries' section?

Write down your answer.

Turn to page 150

from page 146

From our discussions, it can be seen that it will be possible to alter and extend the diagrams on page 131. *'Element unit rate'* must now become *'adjusted element unit rate'* as shown below:

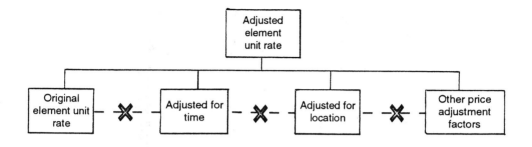

All the above adjustments may be modified after applying professional judgement.

There now remain two important factors which we have not mentioned yet.

Do you know what they are?

Write down your answer.

Turn to page 147

⟳ *from page 148*

A problem exists when trying to decide on suitable Quantities for this element.

We have talked about identifying one simple measure for each element, an **element unit quantity** (see page 127). Ideally this should provide a simple index of the relative size of each element. With preliminaries, it is generally accepted that this is best achieved by expressing preliminaries as a percentage of the remainder of the contract sum. In practice this is the normal approach, however research has shown that this is not a very satisfactory method. We will return to this subject again in later chapters when considering cost planning techniques.

Chapters 8 and 9 have briefly outlined how elemental cost analyses are set out. They have shown that analyses allow informed judgements to be made about the relative value for money offered by different buildings. This demands an understanding of costs and the factors which affect costs.

It is a short step from comparing the costs of buildings to using cost analyses to plan expenditure for future buildings, as shown in the following chapters.

Turn to page 151 ⟳

10 Cost Planning during Feasibility, Outline Proposals, and Scheme Design

This chapter *is* in programmed form and you must follow the page directions exactly.

This chapter deals with the first three stages in the RIBA *Outline Plan of Works*:

A Feasibility

B Outline Proposals

C Scheme Design

Turn to page 152

⟩ *from page*
151

Before considering the cost planning techniques used during Feasibility, Outline Proposals, and Scheme Design, let us revise what you learned during Part 1 of this programme. (*Note:* We have not included 'inception' as this does not involve cost planning.)

Which of the following statements correctly identifies a principle (or principles) of cost control common to all three stages of design mentioned above?

(1) There must be a frame of reference.
(2) There must be a method of checking.
(3) There must be a means of remedial action.
(4) There must be a frame of reference and a method of checking.

Write down your answer.

Turn to page 154 ⟩

⊃ *from page 156*

The relationship between available information and the design and cost decisions made during each design stage is as shown below.

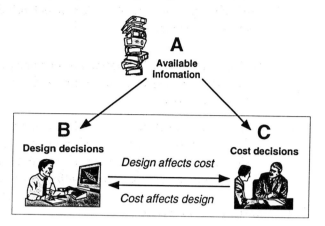

Study the table given on page 155 and the chart in Appendix B on page 320.

What items comprise A, B, and C at each of the design stages?

Write down your answer.

(If you find yourself getting lost while you are reading the remainder of the book, refer back to this short section, pages 152–156, to remind yourself of how the design process and cost planning techniques come together.)

Turn to page 155 ⊃

⟳ *from page*
152

Based on the elementary view of cost control given in Part 1, the expected answer is 'There must be a frame of reference'. It is the *only* principle incorporated in all of the three stages of design mentioned, i.e. feasibility, outline proposals, *and* scheme design.

Principle	Stage
there must be a frame of reference	feasibility, outline proposals, scheme design
there must be a method of checking	detail design
there must be a means of remedial action	detail design

The feasibility, outline proposals and scheme design stages are all concerned with *planning* both the design and the cost of the construction. The detail design stage is the crucial stage in *controlling* the cost of the design. Remedial action follows cost checking and also takes place during the detail design stage.

In one sense, however, you are correct if you said that there must be a method of checking during outline proposals and scheme design. Control would be lost if there was no way of checking that the cost limit had not been exceeded during the preparation of both the outline cost plan and the detailed cost plan.

In other words, there must be a 'method of checking' (and a 'means of remedial action') during the preparation of the 'frame of reference'.

Turn to page 156 ⟫

from page 153

	Feasibility	**Outline Proposals**	**Scheme Design**
A *Information available at the beginning of the stage*	Initial brief Space requirement Functiona! use of project Quality expectations Site location and planning constraints	General brief Planning policy Feasibility report *(including the agreed estimate)* Design criteria showing shape, overall layout and general arrangement	Detailed brief Outline design Outline cost plan

used for

	Feasibility	**Outline Proposals**	**Scheme Design**
B *Design report at the end of the stage comprises . .*	Statement of technical feasibility	Architectural, structural and engineering service concepts Outline design drawings	Brief specification Scheme design drawings

and

	Feasibility	**Outline Proposals**	**Scheme Design**
C *The cost report which comprises . . .*	First estimate	Outline cost plan	Detailed cost plan

Turn to page 157

⊃ *from page 154*

The 'frame of reference' used for cost control is prepared during the feasibility, outline proposals, and scheme design stages; both cost checking and remedial action (if necessary) take place during the detail design stage.

As you learned previously, the preparation of the frame of reference consists of:

❑ establishing a realistic first estimate (during feasibility), and
❑ planning how this estimate should be spent among the various parts of the building (during outline proposals and scheme design).

This planning is carried out during two stages:

(1) **Outline proposals** A cost target is prepared for *each major group of elements;*

(2) **Scheme design** A cost target is prepared for *each element.*

It should become obvious as you read through the remainder of the book that:

❑ the cost decisions made during feasibility are based on the client's functional requirements rather than on a particular design solution,
❑ the decisions made always take account of the limited nature of the information upon which they are based,
❑ the decisions are always made in such a way as to impose minimal restriction on the range of possible design solutions later on.

Turn to page 153 ⊃

⊃ *from page 155* # Section A

Cost planning during feasibility

Section A
Cost planning during feasibility (page 157)

Section B
Cost planning during outline proposals (page 187)

Section C
Cost planning during scheme design (page 202)

Turn to page 158 ⊃

⊃ *from page*
  157
Design teams are usually required to produce a first estimate at the feasibility stage *long* before any drawings have been prepared or any specification decided. Because of this, traditional estimates based on approximate quantities are necessarily approximate, and are not to be relied upon.

The term
'approximate' *It is unfortunate that the term* **approximate** *has become accepted terminology. The approximation reflects the lack of detailed information available about the project in the early stages. Even during the scheme design and the detail design stages the approximate quantities approach is still used. Only when design information is firm will the term be dropped.*

Despite this fact, clients expect to be able to make the decision to proceed, modify and proceed, or abandon the project at the end of the feasibility stage. After all, *feasibility* means just that.

Thus, clients need to have relevant and reliable cost information together with confidence in the design team's ability to manage costs. This will reduce the risk of difficulties later in the design process.

Design teams must therefore adopt techniques for making first estimates more reliable. These techniques must obviously be based on all the available information at this stage.

What information is usually available at the feasibility stage?

Sketch plans. *Turn to page 160* ⊃

Initial brief. *Turn to page 163* ⊃

Both of these. *Turn to page 160* ⊃

from page 163

The initial brief will contain usually only outline description of:

(a)   the use to which the building is to be put (e.g. hotel, school, office),

(b)   the usable floor area required (additions will thus have to be made to allow for circulation areas, etc.),

(c)   an indication of the quality required (e.g. for a proposed hotel whether it is to be 'one star' or 'four star') – reference is sometimes made to similar existing buildings,

(d)   details of the site.

We now consider the **interpolation method** of preparing a first estimate.

Under this method, costs of other buildings are studied, bearing in mind the space and standards provided by these buildings. Therefore, information on suitable projects needs to be assembled and studied. Efficient organisations will make use of computers to store their cost data files (BCIS is a good example). The chief advantage of such an approach is that large quantities of data can be stored and rapidly manipulated, which allows a wider range of cost studies to be considered than might be the case with manual methods. Various characteristics of the data need to be referred to when selecting appropriate cost studies for use.

For selection purposes, while all the items are important, which of the following criteria do you consider to be the *most* important?

(a)   **Only the costs of buildings of approximately the same gross floor area as the proposed building.** *Turn to page 164* ⊃

(b)   **Only the costs of buildings where the site conditions are nearly the same as the proposed building.** *Turn to page 161* ⊃

(c)   **Only the costs of buildings of the same general use (i.e. the same type of building) as the proposed building.** *Turn to page 165* ⊃

from page 158

You chose either **Sketch plans** or **Both of these.**

You are incorrect.

Sketch plans are not usually produced until the outline proposals stage (see Appendix B), *unless the client provides sketch plans or the architect starts drawings before the economic feasibility has been considered.*

We suggest that reliable estimates can be prepared when the only available information about a new project is the initial brief. Not everyone will agree with this proposition. We admit that there will be cases where the design process must be taken to a more advanced stage before a reliable estimate can be given. However, this should not occur very often. If you would like to see how we suggest that such an estimate should be prepared, turn to page 229.

When you have read through the preparation of the first estimate given between pages 229 and 242, turn back to this page.

Is the initial brief usually available at the beginning of the feasibility stage?

Write down your answer.

Turn to page 163

⟩ *from page 159*

You are incorrect. This is not the most important criterion.

Even *major* differences in site conditions can usually be allowed for more easily than the fundamental differences between two types of building such as schools and factories. Approximate quantities could be used, for instance, to make allowance for differences in site conditions.

Do you consider it more important to isolate analyses of buildings of the same type or analyses of buildings of approximately the same gross floor area as the proposed building?

Buildings of the same type. *Turn to page 165* ⟩

Buildings of approximately the same gross floor area. *Turn to page 164* ⟩

from page 164

Notice that the wall-to-floor area ratio and the cost of walls per m² of gross floor area only decreases by a factor of *10* whereas the gross floor area has increased by a factor of *100*.

The example on page 164 is rather impractical as, generally speaking, only buildings such as warehouses would be built 50 metres square. It would, therefore, be more realistic to consider how a single-storey building of length 500 metres and width 5 metres compares with building A. You might say that this also is an unrealistic size. Nevertheless, we will use it for our example. Thus, compared to building A, building B comprises:

Description	
Plan area	500 × 5 m
Gross floor area	2500 m²
External wall area	3030 m²
Wall-to-floor area ratio	1 : 21
Total cost of walls	£757 500
Cost of walls per m² of gross floor area	£303

Hence, while the increase in floor area is the same as for building B (i.e. by a factor of 100), the wall-to-floor area ratio and cost of walls, per m² of gross floor area, have in this example approximately halved when compared with building A.

This is why we say on page 164 that only *very* large differences in gross floor area (e.g. by a factor of 10 or more*) will not be catered for by considering costs per m² of gross floor area.

You should have selected 'Buildings of the same type', as being the most important criterion.

Turn to page 165

* This is given as an example and should not be taken as a general rule, as it will vary with every building type and size.

from pages 158, 160
You chose **Initial brief** or wrote down **Yes.**

You are correct.

The initial brief is the only information available at this stage (see page 155).

To appreciate the limited nature of information contained in the initial brief, consider the following.

Initial brief for the office block discussed in Chapter 11

Space	A lettable area of at least 1850 m² and maximum permissible car parking. The parking provision is considered to be essential due to the congested city centre site, poor parking facilities and inadequate public transport. The tenants are likely to be professional services, such as accounting and insurances.
Planning permission	Preliminary enquiries to the planning authority indicate that an office block three storeys high would be permitted and that the stated amount of lettable area should be achievable as it is within the plot ratio.
Use	The premises will be offered for leasing as good quality office accommodation at a rental which is in the upper market range.
Quality	An above average commercial quality is appropriate to this prime location site and will command a suitable return. Raised floors and suspended ceilings will need to be incorporated into the new design in order to accommodate IT systems. An attractive façade is considered essential.
Site	The site has been acquired and a site plan is available. (It has not been included here as it is reasonably straightforward.) It shows that the terrace houses previously occupying the site have been cleared and the foundations grubbed up. Ground conditions in the area are good.

How would you summarise the types of information that are usually contained in an initial brief?

Write down your answer.

Turn to page 159

*from pages
159, 161,
165, 166*

You are incorrect. This is not the most important criterion.

Differences in gross floor area can usually be allowed for by considering costs per m^2 of gross floor area. Only *very* large differences in gross floor area (e.g. by a factor of 10 or more*) will not be catered for by this method. Where a difference in floor areas does occur between two buildings it is necessary to take account of the decrease in the wall-to-floor area ratio which will result.

This gives rise to a decrease in the costs of external walls, windows, etc., per m^2 of floor area.

Example

	Analysed building A	Analysed building B
Dimensions		
plan area height	5m × 3m 5m	50m × 3m 50m
gross floor area	25 m²	2500 m²
external wall area	60 m²	600 m²
Wall to floor ratio		
$\dfrac{\text{wall area}}{\text{gross floor area}}$	2.4	0.24
Assume element unit rates for external walls are:	£250 per m²	£250 per m²
Total cost of walls	£15 000	£150 000
Cost of walls per m² of gross floor area	£600	£60

Note that the £150 000 and the £60 per m^2 gross floor area for the proposed building could be calculated if the information for building A, listed above, was given, so even *large* differences in gross floor area can be allowed for.

Turn to page 162

* This is given purely as an example and should not be taken as a general rule, as it will vary with building type and size.

⟳ *from pages 159, 161, 162*

You are correct. 'Buildings of the same type' is the most important criterion.

Only buildings of the same general functional use should be examined. Any variation in site conditions can be allowed for relatively easily, while variations in floor area can be adjusted by considering costs per m^2 of gross floor area. Only *very* large differences in gross floor area (e.g. perhaps by a factor of 10 or more) will not be catered for by this method. (If you wish, see page 164 for a discussion of this.)

At this stage it is important to assemble a range of costs for the particular building type required. This can be done by referring to cost analyses contained in office records, or from the BCIS, or from analyses published in the technical press.

For example, the range of costs for office blocks, used in Chapter 11 (pages 230–1) is typical of information published by BCIS. The details are presented in the form of a histogram and costs are expressed in £ per m^2 of gfa. From such information it is possible to gain *some idea* of the correct cost range. However, accuracy can be improved and more details concerning quality can be considered if detailed cost analyses are used.

Research has indicated that it is a mistake to reduce the number of cost analyses used too far. For example, you would be ill advised to use just one analysed project. Even given the use of computers, too many analyses can also present problems of a practical nature. A sensible approach suggests that the use of between 4 and 10 analysed projects is a suitable compromise. (It should be emphasised here that it is dangerous to take one element from one analysis and a second element from another analysis.)

The estimate is prepared by interpolating on the range of costs of buildings of the same use, rather than simply choosing one of the costs unaltered.

Interpolation on the range takes place in four stages:

(1) choosing the most suitable number of cost analyses (say between 4 and 10);
(2) isolating the major differences between the buildings analysed and the proposed building;
(3) making allowances for these differences, and
(4) then applying the interpolation using professional judgement combined with simple statistical procedures, such as measures of central tendency, measures of dispersion, etc.

Which of the following items of information from a brief is it most important to bear in mind when making the *final* choice from the most suitable cost analyses?

Space. *Turn to page 166* ⟳

Use. *Turn to page 167* ⟳

Quality. *Turn to page 169* ⟳

from pages 165, 167

You are incorrect.

Small variations in gross floor area can be allowed for by considering costs per m^2 of gross floor area. The cost consequences of very large differences in gross floor area may need further consideration. (On page 164, it would be possible to calculate the figure of £150 000 (or £60 per m^2 of gross floor area) if all other information was available.)

Since it is more difficult to allow for differences in *use* or *quality*, by choosing *space* you have chosen the least important of the criteria!

When initially selecting suitable analyses for the preparation of a first estimate, choice will centre on buildings of the same type (and use) as the proposed building.

We asked you to identify the most important item with regard to making the final choice. You should have selected 'Quality'.

Return to page 165

from page 165

You are incorrect.

When initially selecting suitable analyses for the preparation of a first estimate, choice will centre on buildings of the same type (and use) as the proposed building. We asked you to identify the *most important item* with regard to making the *final* choice, so choose again:

	Most important item
Selection of range of costs	of similar *use*
Final choice from the range	of similar...

Which is the correct word to complete the table above?

Space.

Turn to page 166

Quality.

Turn to page 169

⊃ *from page*
169

Remember, *all* information available should be used during the preparation of the first estimate. Valuable information is often contained in the main part of the cost analysis.

The major differences which are likely to come to light are:

(a) difference between the date of tender of the analysed building and the date of preparation of the first estimate (Price level);

(b) a difference in location (Price level);

(c) a difference in the gross floor area (Quantity);

(d) items in the analysed building which will not be required in the new project (mainly Quantity but perhaps Quality also);

(e) items which are missing from the analysed building but which will probably be needed in the proposed building (mainly Quantity but perhaps Quality also);

(f) significantly different requirements in the preliminaries and contingencies elements, e.g. temporary roads or temporary works.

Notice that the statement of Quality in an initial brief is usually vague. In fact, relatively small differences in quality which remain after choosing any cost analyses cannot be allowed for until outline proposals or later.

It is highly likely that the costs contained within all the chosen analyses will reflect different tender dates and locations. Major gains towards comparability can often be made if price level is considered first. Therefore, adjustments will be required to bring the price level of the analyses in line with the requirements of the new project.

Write down a *brief* statement of how to allow for the difference in the general tender price level between the dates of tender of the buildings analyses and the date of preparation of the first estimate.

Turn to page 172 ⊃

⟲ *from pages
165, 166,
167*

You are correct.

The usual final procedure is to select the cost analyses of buildings which approximate most closely to the **quality** desired by the client.

Thus the choice of cost analyses is made in two stages:

Stage 1	A range of cost analyses is assembled of the same *type* of building as the proposed building.
Stage 2	This range is examined to find between 4 and 10 buildings whose *quality* approximates most closely to that required by the client.

For many organisations the first stage is a normal on-going exercise of data collection, analysis, classification and storage. Where in-house data is lacking, then other sources, such as the BCIS, can be used as a supplement.

The efficiency of the second stage will depend partially on whether manual or computer-assisted methods are used. The quality and extent of the data sources, together with the approach and time available, will influence the suitability and number of analyses finally chosen.

When enough suitable analyses have been selected, then the differences between the chosen analyses and the proposed building are isolated. Allowances are made for these differences. The estimate for the proposed building is completed using this adjusted cost information and professional judgement.

When isolating the major differences between the chosen analyses and the proposed building, what should be studied?

(a) **The brief of the proposed building and the information contained on *page 1* of each BCIS analysis (or its equivalent).**

(b) **The brief of the proposed building and *all* the information contained in each BCIS analysis (or its equivalent).**

(If necessary, refer to the analysis in Appendix A.)

Turn to page 168 ⟲

from page 176

So far we have considered the selection of a narrow range (between 4 and 10) of suitable analyses.

We then discussed adjustments to these analyses to take account for differences in time and location.

These analyses will reflect buildings of varying size and we must now examine how these differences are allowed for. From Chapter 8, you will remember that the common yardstick is the cost per m^2 of gross floor area. This rate is used to compare the costs of buildings of different gross floor areas.

An overall cost per m^2 of gross floor area is selected from the range of cost analyses. This will be determined by interpolation using professional judgement, aided perhaps by simple statistical measures (e.g. measures of central tendency and measures of dispersion).

Our selected cost per m^2 of gross floor area is simply multiplied by the gross floor area required in the proposed building. Complications can arise when other allowances are necessary. This will be discussed in the next few pages.

One complication occurs if there is a *very* large difference between the size of the project and any cost analysis. It may be necessary to allow for the cost effects of a reduction in the wall-to-floor area ratio which usually accompanies a large increase in gross floor area (as discussed on page 164).

We now turn our attention to adjustments for major differences between the analysed buildings and the proposed building.

Turn to page 177

from page 177

You are incorrect.

You are wrong on *two* counts:

- ❑ you suggest subtracting a 1992 price from a 1995 price – this would obviously give a meaningless cost;
- ❑ you suggest subtracting a lump sum appropriate to a building of one gross floor area from a lump sum appropriate to a building of a different gross floor area (the two areas are $1408 \, m^2$ and $2250 \, m^2$).

To make this deduction from the updated total cost of the proposed building, the £14 040 would first have to be updated

$$£14\,040 \times \frac{128}{106}$$

and converted to a cost appropriate to the proposed building

$$£14\,040 \times \frac{128}{106} \times \frac{2250}{1408}$$

Return to page 177 and choose again

from page
168

Any difference in general tender price level and the date of preparing the first estimate is allowed for *by using an appropriate index* (see Chapter 9).

It is important to distinguish between the various types of indices which are available. Two of the most common are 'factor cost indices' and a 'tender price indices'.

- ❏ A **factor cost index** is an input index that measures changes over time in resource costs such as labour, material, and plant (i.e. costs incurred by contractors).
- ❏ A **tender price index (TPI)** is an output index that measures changes in tender price (i.e. the price a client has to pay for its building).

A 'tender price index' is therefore more appropriate for our purposes here.

Both indices can move independently. In the early 1990s, building costs continued to rise gradually while tender prices were falling. This trend was a reflection of the severe recession and lack of orders for new work affecting the building industry.

This shows that although contractors were paying higher prices for materials and equipment, they were absorbing the higher costs by increases in productivity or by lower profit margins.

In the worked example in Chapter 11, the date of tender in the analysis is September 1992 and the first estimate for the 'proposed building' is dated June 1995.

Example

Date	Tender price index	Factor cost index
September 1992	106	146
June 1995	128	162

When this first estimate is being prepared, how should the costs from the analysis be updated to allow for the increase in the general tender price level which has occurred?

Write down your answer.

Turn to page 174

⊃ *from page*
177

You are correct.

Of the three possibilities, this is the only completely correct one. You may, of course, prefer to subtract £14 040 from the total cost of the analysed building, convert the result to a cost per m^2 of gross floor area of the analysed building, then update. The arithmetic is equally complex in both cases, so it does not really matter which one is used.

The main points to notice about deductions are:

(a)   they should either be made before updating any costs, or after updating *all* costs; whichever method is used care must be exercised to ensure that costs are compatible;

(b)   they should be made before the total cost per m^2 of gross floor area is multiplied by the gross floor area of the proposed building.

We shall now discuss the slightly more complicated problem of allowing for items in a proposed building which have not been included in the analysed building.

Turn to page 178 ⊃

from page 172

From the indices on page 172,

$$\text{building costs in June 1995} = \text{costs in September 1992} \times \frac{128}{106}$$

(remember, by 'building costs' we mean costs to the client i.e. the builder's 'prices').

Costs from the analysis may therefore be updated to June 1995 by multiplying by the factor

$$\frac{128}{106}$$

(This ratio can be converted and shown as an Adjustment Factor (AF). Thus here, the AF would be 1.21.)

Notice that updating will always involve multiplying by

$$\frac{\text{the index at the later date}}{\text{the index at the earlier date}}$$

This adjustment can also be expressed as a percentage:

$$\frac{128 - 106}{106} \times 100 = 20.75\%$$

For updating purposes it is easier and quicker to use the ratio method rather than calculating and making any adjustments via a percentage.

When the price level has been rising, will this ratio of indices be greater or less than 1?

Write down your answer.

Turn to page 176

from page 178

Allowing for additions becomes more complicated when:

- ❏ it is impossible to obtain a realistic cost per m² of gross floor area for an additional item;
- ❏ when it is not known exactly how much (what quantity) of the additional item will be required.

Example

From Appendix A we find that the carpet tiles for the floor finishes were supplied by the client. The cost of supplying carpet tiles has to be added to the first estimate prepared in Chapter 11.

Which of the following methods do you prefer?

(a) Find a current cost per m² of gross floor area for the supply of carpet tiles from a manufacturer's catalogue and multiply it by an assumed area of carpet tiles required for the proposed building.

Turn to page 182

(b) Multiply a current rate for the supply of carpet tiles by the area of carpet tiles in the building analysed. Divide this by the gross floor area in the analysis and add the result to the updated cost per m² of gross floor area. Finally, multiply this rate by the gross floor area of the new project.

Turn to page 180

from page 174

When the price level has been rising, the index will have increased, so the ratio of indices will be *greater* than 1.

Updating for time is not the only item which needs to be considered. Other factors include location, selection of contractor, form of contract, type of construction, etc.

Of these items, location is perhaps the next in order of importance. Any location adjustment is relatively straightforward as any difference in price level due to location can be allowed for *by using an appropriate factor index*, which is adjusted in much the same way as that for the time allowance.

Example

Location	BCIS location factors (September 1995)
Analysis – *Reading*	1.00
New project – *Portsmouth*	0.94

This means that, on average,

$$\frac{\text{new project location}}{\text{analysis location}} = \frac{0.94}{1.00}$$

Costs from the analysis should therefore be adjusted for the new location by multiplying by this ratio.

(This ratio can be converted and shown as an Adjustment Factor (*AF*). Thus here, the *AF* would be 0.94. Furthermore the time and location adjustments can be combined to give a single adjustment factor.)

Turn to page 170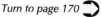

from page 170

The following example from Chapter 11 illustrates the method of deduction of items in a cost analysis which are not required in a proposed building.

Example

The cost of demountable office partitioning is included in the analysis (Appendix A), whereas in the new project this will be the tenant's responsibility. This means that deductions will have to be made for the partitioning. Let us consider this deduction. From the 'Specification and design notes' of Appendix A, we find that the cost of the demountable partitioning was £14 040.

Which of the following methods could be used for making the deduction?

(a) **Multiply the updated total cost per m² of the building analysed by the gross floor area of the proposed building, then subtract £14 040.**

Turn to page 171

(b) **Convert £14 040 to a cost per m² of gross floor area of the building analysed, subtract this from the total cost per m² of gross floor area of the analysed building, update the result, and finally, multiply this rate by the gfa of the proposed building.**

Turn to page 173

(c) **Convert £14 040 to a cost per m² of gross floor area of the building analysed, then subtract the result from the updated total cost per m² of gross floor area of the building analysed, and finally, multiply this rate by the gfa of the proposed building.**

Turn to page 179

from page 173

Allowance for additional items can be made if an appropriate cost per m^2 of gross floor area is obtained from another cost study or analysis. This need only be updated (and adjusted for location, etc., if necessary), and then multiplied by the gross floor area of the proposed building.

Example

Let us assume that a fire protection sprinkler system is required for the new project but no such provision is found in any of the selected cost analyses.

It is ascertained from other cost studies and from specialist installers that an allowance of £14.00 per m^2 should be adequate for a sprinkler system in the proposed office block. This is added to the total allowance per m^2 for the proposed building.

Notice that, a reasonably reliable allowance can be made even though the *exact specification (size and quality)* of the item has not been decided.

Write down a simple description of a situation in which it would be more difficult to make an allowance for an additional item.

Turn to page 175

⊃ *from page 177*

You are wrong in principle because the £14 040 is never updated.

This is because the total cost per m^2 of gross floor area of the analysed building is updated before the cost of partitions is subtracted. However, the figure obtained by this method would not be far wrong.

A more realistic figure would be obtained if the subtraction was performed either before updating any costs or after updating both the total cost and the cost of the demountable partitions.

Turn back to page 177 ⊃

from pages 175, 182

You have chosen the best and most likely method. However, even this method is not likely to be very accurate but it will give a more realistic answer than guessing the specific area of carpet tiles which will be required in the new project.

In case you are not sure how this allowance would be made, here are the details:

(1) The current cost of carpet tiles per m^2 of gross floor area in the building analysed would be

$$\frac{\text{(current rate for supply of carpet tiles)} \times \text{(area of carpet tiles in building analysed)}}{\text{total floor area of building analysed}}$$

(2) This figure would then be added to the updated total cost per m^2 of gross floor area, and finally it would be multiplied by the gross floor area of the new project.

(This assumes that the proportion of the gross floor area covered by carpet tiles in the proposed building will be the same as in the building analysed.)

If you would like to read through a summary of the sources of cost information most commonly used for making allowances for additional items in new projects,

Turn to page 181

If you prefer to continue,

Turn to page 184

from page 180

Reference to other analyses

The costs and quality of the required item are compared in several cost analyses. An appropriate cost per m^2 of gross floor area is then chosen for the proposed building.

Use of published or private cost studies

Regular articles can be found in all the technical journals. Also, various trade associations publish cost studies from time to time. Other sources are the BCIS and government departments.

Reference to published price books

Due to trade discounts, reference to catalogues is never as good as telephoning suppliers direct. In practice, reference to published price books is used quite frequently, but it has its dangers. One problem is the vast difference in prices found in different price books for supposedly similar items.

Approximate quantities

The approximate quantities approach should be avoided wherever possible for the reasons discussed in Part 1. However, it is sometimes necessary to develop hypothetical design solutions for particular items, measure approximate quantities, and price the items. This method had to be used in Chapter 11 for the car parking and the external works.

Estimates of prices and rates from contractors and specialist contractors

For a specialist item, such as a sprinkler system, it would be advisable to contact a specialist installer to discuss the specification, the installation requirements and to obtain guide prices. Specialist contractors will frequently provide such prices and, while they will not accept any liability for the prices given, their aim is to secure work by providing such a service.

Turn to page 184

from page 175

It is very unlikely that there will be sufficient information available during feasibility to give an assumed area of carpet tiles required for the proposed building.

It would be more realistic to use the limited information which is available: namely, the proportion of the gross floor area which is covered by carpet tiles in the building analysed. The only way that this information could be used is, of course, to assume that the proportion of the gross floor area covered by carpet tiles in the new project will be the same as in the building analysed.

To see how this allowance is made ...

Turn to page 180

⊃ *from page*
184

Copy down the following description of the interpolation method, then fill in the blanks in your copy.

When you have done this, compare your description with the one on page 185.

Preparation of first estimate by the interpolation method

(1) A range of ____ _____ of the same ____ of building as the proposed building is assembled.

(2) This range is examined to find the ____ _____ (say between 4 and 10) whose _____ approximates most closely to that desired by the client.

(3) Adjustments for both ____ and _____ are made to bring all cost analyses to a current cost base appropriate for the location of the new project.

(4) The initial brief of the proposed building and ___ of the information given in the cost analyses are studied in order to _____ the ____ _____ between the proposed and existing buildings.

(5) An initial estimate of _____ ____ is calculated from the analyses, using the gross floor area of the new project, and then

(6) _____ are made for each of the ____ _____ (including, of course, site works, drainage and external works).

(7) The first estimate is built-up using _____ _____ aided perhaps by simple statistical measures, depending on how many cost analyses are to be considered.

(8) An addition is made for _____ .

(9) Next, an allocation is included for _____ which is intended to deal with unforeseen events or circumstances which might arise during the construction stage.

(10) Finally, an allowance is made as a reserve against price and design risk. It is intended that the allowance for price risk should offset rises between the general tender price level at the date of _____ of the ____ _____ and the _____ price level on the tender, whereas the design risk allowance is intended to provide a buffer against _____ ____ _____ which may only come to light later in the design process.

Turn to page 185 ⊃

from pages 180, 181

We are essentially considering design. However, attention should be paid to client instructions before reporting any estimate. What was asked for? There can be several options. For example, construction costs at proposed tender date; construction costs at completion; total budget of construction costs, including professional fees and value added tax on both construction costs and fees; etc. Be sure to address clients' requirements and to clarify any reported figures, stating clearly both inclusions in and exclusions from the estimate.

With this in mind, remember that when all the major differences between the buildings analysed and the proposed building have been allowed for, this first estimate is still not complete. Firstly **preliminaries** should be considered. It needs to be established whether any allowance has been included for preliminaries within the figures derived from the previous cost analyses. If not, an addition should be included at this point.

Contingencies are usually excluded from cost analyses. An allowance for this sum now needs to be inserted. The contingency sum is intended to cover those unforeseen events which have a tendency to arise during the construction phase of a project. Although this has little relevance to the design stages, contingencies must be included now for client budget purposes. In Chapter 11 we have allowed 1.5%; this percentage, we judge, reflects the type of project and the risks involved.

Next, consideration should be given to the likely increase in general tender price level which might be anticipated between the *feasibility* stage and the *receipt of tender* for the new building. This can usually be done by reference to a tender price index forecast (or similar forecast figures). It has to be stressed that these only forecast general trends and are not infallible. Professional judgement, including knowledge of local conditions, needs to be applied when interpreting any forecast figures. In Chapter 11, we judge the *reserve against price rises* is 5% of the remainder of the first estimate. A 'price risk' allowance is also included in the outline cost plan at outline proposals and the detailed cost plan at scheme design. The size of the allowance is calculated afresh at each stage using the latest information available.

Finally, to accommodate some flexibility in the design process, an allowance for design risk can be contemplated. Some clients and design teams hold the view that a separate allowance should not be added for design risk. Rather they see that a design risk allowance is included in the feasibility estimate. Under these circumstances, the reserve for design risk would need to be identified, and shown separately, during production of the outline cost plan. In Chapter 11, we have chosen to indicate an allowance for design risk at feasibility stage.

Without defining *how* allowances are made, write a short account of the basic steps in preparing a first estimate by interpolation.

(Refer back to pages 165 and 169 if necessary.)

Turn to page 183

*from page
183*

Summary – Preparation of first estimate by 'interpolation'

(1)   A range of **cost analyses** of the same **type** of building as the proposed building is assembled.

(2)   This range is examined to find the **cost analyses** (say between 4 and 10) whose **quality** approximates most closely to that desired by the client.

(3)   Adjustments for both **time** and **location** are made to bring all cost analyses to a current cost base appropriate for the location of the new project.

(4)   The initial brief of the proposed building and **all** of the information given in the cost analyses are studied in order to **isolate** the **major differences** between the proposed and existing buildings.

(5)   An initial estimate of **building costs** is calculated from the analyses, using the gross floor area of the new project, and then

(6)   **Allowances** are made for each of the **major differences** (including, of course, site works, drainage and external works).

(7)   The first estimate is built-up using **professional judgement** aided perhaps by simple statistical measures, depending on how many cost analyses are to be considered.

(8)   An addition is made for **preliminaries**.

(9)   Next, an allocation is included for **contingencies** which is intended to deal with unforeseen events or circumstances which might arise during the construction stage.

(10)   Finally, an allowance is made as a reserve against price and design risk. It is intended that the allowance for price risk should offset rises between the general tender price level at the date of **preparation** of the **first estimate** and the **contractor's** price level on the tender, whereas the design risk allowance is intended to provide a buffer against **unforeseen design difficulties** which may only come to light later in the design process.

(This preparation is shown graphically on the next page.)

The first estimate will form part of the design team's report on the feasibility of the project as a whole. If the client accepts this first estimate this will be regarded as the **cost limit** for the project.

In most cases the first estimate can be given as a lump sum. However, there will be situations **where the brief is insufficiently developed** or technical difficulties are so great that a firm estimate cannot be given until after the completion of an outline design. Here, the design team may decide that the best approach at feasibility stage is to provide the client with the **cost range** within which they are confident of producing a design.

Turn to page 186

from page 185

Preparation of first estimate by the interpolation method

① Assemble cost analyses
  of similar type

② Select analyses of appropriate *Usually between 4 and 10*
  quality

③ Adjust for time and location   *Between date of analyses
                                  and date of estimate*

④ Isolate major differences   *Between brief and information
                                  given in analyses*

⑤ Calculate initial estimates   *Known gross floor area and
                                  interpolated cost/m² gross floor area*

⑥ Include allowances for major   *Including site works, drainage
  differences   and external works*

⑦ Add preliminaries

⑧ Make allowance for
  contingencies

⑨ Include reserve against price   *Between date of estimate and
                                  date of tender*

⑩ Add design risk allowance   *Covers unforeseen circumstances*

┌─────────────────────┐
│ **First estimate** │   *Define all the assumptions that
└─────────────────────┘   have been made*

If you would like to read through an example of a first estimate being prepared by 'interpolation', read pages 228 to 242, then return to this page.

If you will have to stop soon, stop now. The next section of this chapter deals with cost planning during outline proposals.

Turn to page 187

⟲ *from page* 186 # Section B

Cost planning during outline proposals

Section A
Cost planning during feasibility (page 157)

▶

Section B
Cost planning during outline proposals (page 187)

▶

Section C
Cost planning during scheme design (page 202)

To be effective, cost planning should be performed in steps of increasing detail which correspond with the increasing and associated information detail of the design.

If major cost differences between the buildings analysed and the new project are not assessed as soon as they become apparent, 'cost control' will not be as effective as it could be. (In general, the cost analyses chosen at feasibility are also used for cost planning at outline proposals and scheme design.)

What information is usually available at the beginning of outline proposals which would not usually be available at the beginning of the feasibility stage?

Design criteria.

Turn to page 194 ⟳

Outline design.

Turn to page 191 ⟳

Both of these.

Turn to page 195 ⟳

from pages 192, 194

You are incorrect.

This would be a waste of time. It might indicate whether or not the cost limit would be exceeded when more reliable cost targets were prepared during scheme design, but it would be impractical to take remedial action on the basis of cost targets which nobody was taking very seriously.

Remember, cost decisions should be as detailed as the available information allows, and no more. The objective at outline proposals is to allocate the available money to the various parts of the proposed building, without making any design assumptions which may be impossible to maintain at a later stage.

Reconsider your answer to the question: how is an outline cost plan prepared?

Choose one of the following answers.

Cost targets are prepared for each major group of elements.
Turn to page 197

Allowances are made for each of the major differences, and tabulated.
Turn to page 192

⊃ *from page*
194

Design criteria for office block

Site

(1) *Site information and ground conditions*

  (a) Levels. Site plans would normally be available at this stage indicating relevant site features and including a grid of levels or the site contours.
  (b) Soil. Clay and gravel, site investigation has been conducted.
  (c) Bearing capacity. $200\,kN/m^2$.
  (d) Water table. None encountered.
  (e) Depth of bearing strata. For three-storey block – 1.25 metres.
  (f) General. Site cleared of old terrace houses without basements. Foundations grubbed up under a separate demolition contract.
  (g) Utilities. Main drainage available, water main in road adjoining the site. Electricity supply available. No undergound utilities likely to cause difficulty.

General requirements

(2) *The building*
The building has to conform to the provisions of the Building Regulations. In particular, the structure and protected shafts shall be of 1.5 hours fire resistance. Doors to protected shafts shall be of 1 hour fire resistance.

(3) *Working conditions*
Temperature, ventilation, lighting, sanitary conveniences, etc. shall comply with the latest requirements of current legislation.

Turn to page 190 ⊃

from page 189

Structure

(4) *Frame*

Storey height for all floors	3.5 m
Span	approximately 15 m
Fire resistance	1 hour

(5) *Upper floors*

Imposed load	5 kN/m^2
Fire resistance	1 hour

(6) *Roof*

Imposed load	0.75 kN/m^2

(7) *Internal doors*

Doors to protected shafts	1 hour fire resistance

Environmental engineering services

(8) *Heating and ventilation*

Air-conditioning using four-pipe fan coil comfort cooling system.

No. of air changes per hour	3
Temperature	22°C (dry bulb)
	50% RH

(9) *Electrics*

Lighting standard	500 lux

(10) *Other services*

All normal services to typical commercial standards including:

- ❏ hot and cold water supply
- ❏ fire services
- ❏ small power
- ❏ provision for communications
- ❏ lightning protection
- ❏ lifts
- ❏ drainage, etc.

Return to page 194

↻ *from page 187*

You are incorrect. The outline design is prepared *during* the outline proposals stage.

Are the design criteria usually available at the beginning of outline proposals?

Write down your answer.

Turn to page 194 ↻

from pages 188, 194

You are incorrect.

Major differences are certainly isolated and allowed for. However, this only allows for confirmation or amendment of the cost limit.

The objective of cost planning in outline proposals is usually to start allocating the available money to the various parts of the proposed building.

Reconsider your answer to the question: how is an outline cost plan prepared? Choose one of the following answers.

Cost targets are prepared for each element on the assumption that the inaccuracies in the unreliable ones will cancel each other out.

Turn to page 188

Cost targets are prepared for each major group of elements.

Turn to page 197

from page
196

Each target cost is established by interpolation from the cost and information contained in the cost analyses (bearing in mind the requirements of the new project). Major differences, between the new project and the cost analyses must be allowed for and included within the appropriate group element cost targets.

The build-up of the outline cost plan is carried out systematically, starting with the substructure and finishing with the preliminaries. An allowance needs to be included for contingencies in order to accommodate costs associated with unforeseen events or circumstances which may or may not occur during the construction stage of the project.

Finally the price and design risk is reworked and added to the outline cost plan.

The total of the new project is arrived at by multiplying the cost per m^2 of gross floor area by the gross floor area of the new project.

During the preparation of the outline cost plan, the various allowances should obviously be made with an eye on the cost limit.

Minor juggling of figures and reworking of calculations may be necessary to arrive at the final figure to be reported to the client.

When the outline cost plan has been completed, it is sent with the outline design for the client's approval. Obviously the outline cost plan is completed by the end of the outline proposals stage.

When is the outline cost plan started: before, during, or after the preparation of the outline design?

Write down your answer.

Turn to page 198

from pages 187, 190, 191, 195

Yes. Design criteria are usually available at the beginning of outline proposals.

If you would like to see design criteria for the worked example in Chapter 11, turn to page 189.

The other information which is usually available at the beginning of outline proposals is:

(1) the general brief;
(2) the local authority planning policy;
(3) the feasibility report (including the first estimate, which has been approved by the client by this time).

The increased amount of information makes it possible to isolate several differences between the buildings analysed and the new project which cannot be spotted at feasibility. However, there is still not enough data for reliable cost targets to be prepared for each element. Instead, an 'outline cost plan' is prepared at this stage.

Write a brief description of how an outline cost plan is prepared, then choose the answer which corresponds most closely with yours.

(a) **Cost targets are prepared for each element on the assumption that the inaccuracies in the unreliable ones will cancel each other out.**   *Turn to page 188*

(b) **Cost targets are prepared for each major group of elements.**   *Turn to page 197*

(c) **Allowances are made for each of the major differences, and tabulated.**   *Turn to page 192*

⟲ *from page 187*

You are incorrect. The outline design is prepared *during* the outline proposals stage.

Are the design criteria usually available at the beginning of outline proposals?

Write down your answer.

Turn to page 194 ⟳

from page
199

The first step is to gather together again the 4 to 10 cost analyses used for the feasibility stage. It is possible that new data will have become available during the interval but more often than not the data source does not change.

The adjustments for time must be carried out again to update all of the cost analyses to the current date. The current index used at feasibility stage may no longer be appropriate.

The next step in preparing the cost target for a group of elements is to again 'isolate the differences'. This is done by comparing the specifications of the elements in the analyses with what is known about elements in the new project.

These differences can be allowed for by the methods already described when making adjustments during the preparation of the first estimate or by methods used for the preparation of cost targets for individual elements. This will be illustrated in Chapter 11. All that need concern us here is that the allowances are more detailed than those made during the feasibility stage and less detailed than those made during scheme design. The reason for this, of course, is that the information on which allowances are based becomes increasingly detailed as the design process proceeds.

The quantities of the various elements are not usually known at this stage. Differences in the sizes of the buildings are usually allowed for by considering the cost of the group of elements per m^2 of gross floor area.

How would the cost targets for each group be obtained from this information?

Write down your answer.

Turn to page 193

↪ from pages
188, 192,
194

You are correct. Cost targets are prepared for each major group of elements.

There is an important distinction between an outline cost plan and a tabulation of allowances for the major differences which become apparent at outline proposals. With the outline cost plan, a cost target is prepared for each major group of elements. (The 'groups of elements' considered in the worked example in Chapter 11 are those identified in cost analyses i.e. substructures, superstructures, finishes, fittings, services, external works, preliminaries and contingencies.) This has the advantage that it forces the design team to think clearly at this early stage about the broad allocation of expenditure to the major parts of the building.

Before preparing an outline cost plan, the reserve against price and design risk should be considered again. This is the allowance made for unforeseen design difficulties which may only come to light later in the design process and price rises occurring between the preparation of the outline cost plan and the receipt of tenders.

If a cost limit has been set at the feasibility stage, it is advisable to reconsider the reserve against the price and design risk; this should be carried out before group cost targets are prepared. This is done to identify clearly the sum that has been estimated at the feasibility stage as appropriate for distribution among the group elements, thus providing guidance when calculating cost targets for each group element. Any minor inaccuracies and discrepancies between the outline cost plan and the cost limit are then usually accounted for by recalculating and adjusting the price and design risk allowance.

Learning Resource
Centre

Turn to page 199 ↪

from page 193

Ideally designing and costing should be done at the same time. Moreover, there should be considerable interplay between the two, as indicated on page 153, in order to maintain strict control over costs (i.e. with every cost decision being allowed to affect the corresponding design decision, and vice versa).

We realise that this is an ideal approach which might not happen in practice, but it is always better to aim higher than one really expects to achieve.

For the purposes of demonstration in Chapter 11, it has been necessary to assume that the outline design has been completed before the outline cost plan is started. We have done this only to eliminate complicated descriptions of the timing and the complex decision-making of a properly conducted outline proposals stage.

Briefly describe the cost allocations and allowances that are included in an outline cost plan, and give brief details of how they are prepared.

(Refer back to pages 196 and 193 if necessary.)

Turn to page 200

from page 197

Because time has moved on, the allowance now made for price rises may well differ from the corresponding allowance included in the feasibility estimate. If you would like to see the 'price and design risk' allowance from the worked example in Chapter 11, turn to page 242.

We will now consider how the cost targets are prepared for each group of elements. (The 'groups of elements' considered in the worked example in Chapter 11 are those identified in cost analyses i.e. substructures, super-structures, finishes, fittings, services, external works, preliminaries and con-tingencies.) When discussing cost planning during the feasibility stage, we stated that research has indicated that it is a mistake to focus on one cost analysis; we suggested using between 4 and 10 analysed projects. Those same analyses should, wherever possible, be used to prepare cost targets for each group of elements.

What will be the first step in the preparation of a cost target for a group of elements?

Write down your answer.

Turn to page 196

from page 198

Summary – Cost planning during outline proposals

(1) An allowance is made for 'price and design risk' by assessing the cost of unforeseen design difficulties and possible price rises between the preparation of the outline cost plan and the receipt of tender.

(2) Cost targets are prepared for each group of elements. Major differences between the buildings analysed and the new project must be estimated and included in the appropriate group of element target costs. The group elements must include a target cost for preliminaries.

The major differences are allowed for by comparing all the information available for both the new project and the cost analyses.

(3) An allowance is made for contingencies based on assessment of the risk of unforeseen events or circumstances which might arise during the construction stage. This specifically recognises that the construction stage has specific risks. For example, even though the site investigation has shown the expected ground conditions, there may be 'soft spots' or rock encountered on part of the site which will require more money to be spent.

Turn to page 201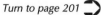

↻ *from page 200*

A *major discrepancy* may occur between the outline cost plan and the cost limit. Here, it is best for the *client and the design team to make a* **joint** *decision* as to whether it is better to juggle with the allowances or to accept the outline cost plan as a more realistic total. If this results in the cost limit being raised rather than lowered, at least the client has played an active part in the decision and has been afforded the opportunity of abandoning the project before incurring major expenditure.

When the client accepts the outline cost plan, the design team is committed to producing a scheme design within the cost shown on the outline cost plan.

We shall now discuss the cost planning techniques used during the scheme design stage.

Turn to page 202 ↻

from page 201

Section C

Cost planning during scheme design

Section A
Cost planning during feasibility (page 157)

Section B
Cost planning during outline proposals (page 187)

Section C
Cost planning during scheme design (page 202)

Turn to page 203

⟳ *from page 202*

It is best to start preparing the detailed cost plan as early as possible during this stage. Cost targets prepared early on can be checked after the scheme design drawings have been completed. The main data source available to help in preparing the cost targets will be the same 4 to 10 cost analyses used previously. As far as details of the new project are concerned, the information now available includes:

(1) the complete brief;
(2) the outline design (including drawings);
(3) the outline cost plan;
(4) all the information available at the beginning of outline proposals.

The cost plan is finalised at the end of the scheme design stage, by which time all of the scheme design drawings will also be available.

Before considering each element individually, the reserve against price and design risk is reconsidered. As at the outline proposals stage, the object is to give guidance. Subtracting this reserve from the cost shown on the outline cost plan leaves the balance available for cost targets for individual elements. Once cost targets have been set, the price and design risk reserve will be recalculated, bearing in mind the cost limit.

In general, would you expect the allowance for 'price and design risk' at scheme design to be the same size as the one made during outline proposals?

Write down your answer.

Turn to page 207 ⟳

from page 205

Differences in quantity and quality will vary from element to element. Differences in price level are more likely to affect all elements equally. Therefore, it is worth considering the allowances made for price level before we go any further.

With a computer system, price level adjustments can be handled speedily and almost automatically. Often, the only information required is the tender date, the location of the buildings analysed, and the current date and location of the proposed project. It is important, however, to understand what is involved and thus further consideration will now be given to price level adjustments.

The factors listed under 'price level' in Chapter 9 were:

(a) differences in general tender price level due to difference in tender dates;

(b) differences in contractors' price levels relative to the general tender price level (due to differences in allowances for overheads, profits, etc.);

(c) differences in regional trends, and localised variables;

(d) differences in tendering arrangements (including selection of contractors for tendering lists), contract conditions, contract period, weather conditions, site conditions, etc.

Factor (a) is the most important and probably the easiest to adjust.

Consider the changes in general tender price level between the date of tender of the buildings analysed and the proposed *receipt of tender of the new project*.

Can these be allowed for accurately by using the relevant values of a tender price level index?

Yes/No.

Write down your answer.

Turn to page 208

⊃ *from page*
207

The three factors affecting element costs are:

Factor 1 Quantity.
Factor 2 Quality.
Factor 3 Price level.

Each elemental cost target should be prepared by isolating differences in each factor between the project analysed and the new project.

The task is similar to that carried out at outline proposals stage. However, there is more information to handle as each element, rather than a group of elements, is considered.

Not all of the selected cost analyses will contain similar or suitable design details. Thus some cost items will be inappropriate when considered on an element-by-element basis, which is not a problem if the data source is wide enough to allow a selective choice to be made.

Computer systems greatly aid the process when a lot of information needs to be investigated and manipulated.

Turn to page 204 ⊃

⊃ *from page 208*

(1) **Past to present. The differences between the general tender price levels at the dates of tender of the buildings analysed and at the date of preparation of the cost plan are allowed for by using an appropriate index to update each element in turn.**

(2) **Present to future. The difference between the general tender price level at the date of preparation of the cost plan and the contractor's price level at the proposed tender date is allowed for in the 'price risk'.**

A diagram illustrates this:

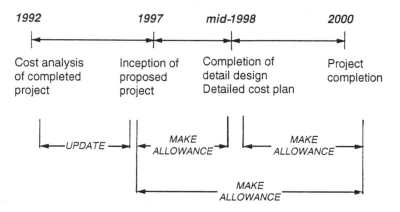

The difference in general tender price level is not the only 'price level' factor which is considered during the preparation of individual cost targets. As well as *updating* the price levels of the buildings analysed, these prices are also adjusted for *location*, using a location index.

Any of the other significant 'price level' factors should be considered and adjusted at this stage.

Obviously all the factors affecting element costs should be considered when an elemental cost target is being prepared for each element. Write down these factors.

Turn to page 209 ⊃

⊃ *from page 203*

The price and design risk reserve at scheme design will usually be slightly less than at outline proposals. The design has advanced considerably since the preparation of the outline cost plan. Therefore, the 'design risk' part of the allowance can be decreased safely. Time will also have moved on and the index previously used should be checked to see if it still holds good. Any movement will be reflected in that part of the reserve dealing with price risk.

The order in which the elements are considered will vary from project to project. One general rule is that preliminaries should be considered before any of the other elements. One reason for this is that preliminaries and contingencies can be spread over other elements instead of being considered as separate elements. The design team should decide as early as possible which method they intend adopting, as the outcome will have an appreciable effect on the level of pricing of all the other elements. The commonest practice, and the approach we adopt, is to consider preliminaries as a separate element.

Another reason for considering preliminaries first is that the contractor's profits on the other elements are sometimes included in preliminaries. It is obviously necessary to find out if this has been done in the cost analyses before considering the other elements. It is also more convenient to deal with contingencies at this time.

The order in which other elements are considered will usually be dictated by the order in which the scheme design drawings are produced. In Chapter 11 we have assumed that the scheme design drawings are available before the cost plan is started. Therefore, we have considered the elements in numerical order, apart from preliminaries and contingencies.

Turn to page 205 ⊃

➲ *from page 204*

No.

The general tender price level index at the date of tender of the new project is only a forecast. Updating on the basis of this index may not be necessarily, so accurate.

Instead of relying on this future value of the index, we use the index at the date of preparation of the cost plan. This means that the cost targets incorporate realistic allowances for general tender price level changes up to the date of preparation of the cost plan.

The change in the general tender price level between the date of preparation of the cost plan and receipt of tender is allowed for in a lump sum. This includes an allowance for possible differences between the contractor's price level and the general tender price level at the date of tender.

This lump sum is incorporated in the 'price risk' allowance.

Thus, the difference between the general tender price levels for the buildings analysed and the contractor's actual price level for the new project is allowed for in two stages.

Write down brief descriptions of these two stages.

Turn to page 206 ➲

↻ *from page 206*

There are three factors affecting element costs. These are allowed for in each of the methods used to prepare cost targets.

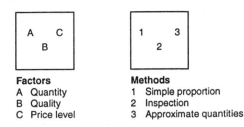

Factors
A Quantity
B Quality
C Price level

Methods
1 Simple proportion
2 Inspection
3 Approximate quantities

Simple proportion is preferred to the other two methods because a simple proportionate adjustment to an element cost automatically includes allowances for everything needed for the element in the type of building being considered.

When using approximate quantities it is easy to overlook details which will only be considered during the detail design stage. Nevertheless, this method sometimes has to be used, especially when a new requirement is under consideration.

Inspection is usually reserved for elements for which no effective measure of Quantity has been devised. These include fittings and furnishings or builder's work in connection with engineering services. Often the elements are not cost significant. In general, this should not be a criterion, as simple proportion takes very little time to complete provided there are satisfactory measures of element unit quantity.

Each of these techniques is now considered in detail, starting with 'simple proportion'.

Turn to page 210 ↻

⊃ *from page*
209

Simple proportion

This technique is called 'simple proportion' because it assumes that the cost of an element is directly proportional to the Quantity of the element.

1	Simple proportion
2	Inspection
3	Approximate quantities

Assuming that the cost of an element is directly proportional to its Quantity, then we can say:

$$\frac{\text{cost of element in new project}}{\text{quantity of element in new project}} = \frac{\text{cost of element in building analysed}}{\text{quantity of element in building analysed}}$$

We can now use this expression to calculate the cost of the element in the new building.

Example

Building analysed:	gross floor area 5862 m^2
Element:	internal walls and partitions
Total cost of element:	£323 270
Element unit quantity:	5142 m^2

Proposed project:	gross floor area 6000 m^2
Element:	internal walls and partitions
Element unit quantity:	5500 m^2

$$\text{Cost of element in new project} = \frac{£323\,270}{5142\,\text{m}^2} \times 5500\,\text{m}^2$$

$$= £345\,777$$

This is the same as saying that:

element unit rate in new project = element unit rate in analysis

However, we are getting ahead of ourselves because we said that there were three factors that affect cost targets.

What are the three factors that affect cost targets?

Write down your answer.

Turn to page 212 ⊃

⊃ *from page 212*

2 *Adjust for Quantity*

This section started by discussing the adjustment for Quantity. We noted that it is done simply by multiplying the appropriate element unit rate by the Quantity of the element in the proposed project.

This figure is then reduced to cost per m^2 of gross floor area.

Thus, returning to the example on page 210, we have:

$$\frac{£345\,777}{6000\,\text{m}^2} = £57.63 \text{ per m}^2 \text{ of gross floor area}$$

The simple proportion method should be the commonest approach employed but its use is not unlimited.

Write brief descriptions of two circumstances when the simple proportion method cannot be used for preparing a cost target.

Turn to page 213 ⊃

from page 210

The preparation of a cost target takes place in three stages to account for the three factors affecting costs:

Factor 1   Adjust for Price level.
Factor 2   Adjust for Quantity.
Factor 3   Adjust for Quality.

(We have reversed the order here to follow common practice, which is to adjust for price level first.)

1 *Adjust for Price level*

The differing tender dates and various locations of projects analysed will usually mean that 'adjusting for price' is essential. The assumption is that the method of simple proportion is not invalidated by these adjustments. Consider first adjusting for differing tender dates.

In terms of simple proportion this can be stated as:

$$\frac{\text{current element cost}}{\text{current index}} = \frac{\text{element cost in analysis}}{\text{index at analysis tender date}}$$

In more conventional terms, the adjustment required can be shown as:

$$\begin{array}{ccccc} \text{Element} & & & & \\ \text{cost in} & \boldsymbol{\times} & \text{'Updating'} & \boldsymbol{\times} & \text{'Location'} \\ \text{analysis} & & \text{index} & & \text{index} \end{array}$$

The adjustments for price and location are reasonably straightforward and should be **completed first**. This ensures that current prices applicable to the project location are used at each stage of the preparation of a target cost.

Turn to page 211

⤷ *from page 211*

Simple proportion cannot be used when

(a) there is no effective measure of Quantity for the element (i.e. no element unit quantity/rate exists), or

(b) it is not yet known what Quantity of the element will be required in the new project.

In these cases the possibility of using 'inspection' and/or 'approximate quantities' would be explored. (Both are explained later.)

3 *Adjust for Quality*

This is usually the least straightforward of the three adjustments. During scheme design the quality of each element cannot be specified with any certainty. It is not until the detail design stage that the precise specification is known. At the scheme design stage it is necessary to ensure that the cost target for each element is neither too generous nor too small for the *general* quality of the materials which the design team intends to adopt. It might seem rather difficult to determine the cost of the 'general quality' before action is given to consider the details of specification of each element. When the simple proportion method is used, however, the design team do not have to start from scratch when they try to fix a cost to their vague notions of the quality which they intend to specify in the detail design stage.

Write a brief description of why this is so.

Turn to page 215 ⤷

from page 215

Rather than decide by inspection on a percentage increase or decrease to allow for a change in quality, approximate quantities are often used. That is, the detailed design of an analysed building is altered for an element in the cost analysis which does not seem to be of a suitable quality for the new project. Approximate quantities are measured from this design, and priced in the traditional way. The change in cost is then expressed as a percentage of the total element cost in the analysis. This percentage is added to (or deducted from) the figure obtained by adjusting for Price and Quantity.

(Note: This method does not commit the design team to using this specification for the part of the element concerned, but simply to selecting one of a similar general quality.)

You may have noticed that variations in the quantities of individual items *within* each element under 'adjust for Quantity' have not been discussed. This is considered under adjustment for quality and is best explained by an example.

Example

Changing the specification of the floor finishes of a building from 10% granolithic and 90% wood block to 90% granolithic and 10% wood block will obviously change the quality of an element. However, this will not necessarily affect the element unit quantity of the floor finishes.

This is exactly the kind of change in specification which could be handled by the 'inspection' or 'approximate quantities' methods.

Throughout this programme the term 'quality of an element' is used to mean both the quality of the materials and the relative proportions of the various qualities of specification within the element.

Turn to page 216

⊃ *from page 213*

Adjusting the cost of an element for Price and Quantity gives the current cost if exactly the same detailed specification is used. By examining the specification in the cost analyses, the design team can usually spot any elements which differ in quality from those they envisage using in the new project. That is, it is easier to spot differences and make realistic allowances for them, than it would be to fix a cost to partially-formed ideas about the new project on their own.

The adjustments made for a change in the quality of an element are often expressed as percentage additions to (or deductions from) the costs obtained after adjusting for Price and Quantity.

Example: Element 2D   Stairs

The building analysed has steel tubular balustrades with PVC sheathed handrails. The design team decide that they would like to have a better quality of handrail and balustrade in the new project. Bearing in mind their cost limit and the requirements of the other elements, the design team decide to increase the allowance for the element by 15%. During the detail design stage the exact type of balustrade will be determined.

The figure obtained from the cost analysis after adjusting for Price and Quantity is: £54 366.

The cost target is therefore:

$$£54\,366 + 15\% = £62\,521$$

Turn to page 214 ⊃

from page 214

While preparing a cost plan, there is a need to ensure that the cost targets are reasonable. The obvious way to do this is to compare the cost targets with the costs of corresponding elements within other analyses. Comparing total costs, such as £31 837 and £45 081 for upper floors, is not very informative. The costs per m² of floor area or the element unit rates are more meaningful and so they will be used for this purpose.

However, bear in mind that costs per m² of gross floor area reflect differences in density, i.e.

$$\frac{\text{element unit quantity}}{\text{gross floor area}}$$

as well as Quality and Price level, whereas element unit rates do not reflect all these differences. (See Chapter 9 page 126 for a discussion on this point.)

For this reason, it is recommended that both the total target costs and the target costs per m² of gross floor area should be entered in the cost plan summary. This approach has the added advantage of expressing costs in a way which allows comparisons of costs both within one building and between buildings of different sizes.

Before moving on to the next method of adjustment (inspection), complete the following:

Write down the names and a brief description of the three adjustments made during the preparation of a cost target by simple proportions.

Turn to page 217

⟲ *from page* *216*

Summary – Adjustments made during simple proportion method

The adjustment is done in three stages:

Stage 1   *Adjust for Price.* The selected element unit rate from the cost analysis is updated and adjusted for location.

Stage 2   *Adjust for Quantity.* The adjusted element unit rate is then multiplied by the Quantity of the element for the proposed project. This is reduced to a cost per m^2 of gross floor area by dividing it by the gross floor area of the proposed building.

Stage 3   *Adjust for Quality.* Differences in either the quality of materials or the relative proportions of the various qualities of specification within the element are allowed for by adjusting the target cost and cost per m^2 gross floor area obtained above.

The total target cost and the target cost per m^2 of gross floor area are entered in the cost plan summary.

(*Note:* The Price and Quantity adjustments are usually done before the Quality adjustment because:

(a) they always have to be made, and tend to have more effect on the figure than the Quality adjustment,

(b) the quality of the element is easier to change later in the design process than the Quantity of the element.)

Turn to page 218 ⟳

from page 217

2 Inspection

This consists of assembling a range of costs ($£/m^2$ gfa) of corresponding elements in previous projects. From this a suitable cost target can be chosen.

(If you would like to see an example of this technique, turn to page 219.)

1	Simple proportion
2	Inspection
3	Approximate quantities

When is 'inspection' used? Choose the best criterion from those listed below.

(a) When simple proportion cannot be used (as discussed on page 213) and the cost involved does not justify the time required for measuring approximate quantities.

(b) When simple proportion cannot be used and the final specification of the element is likely to be similar to the specifications of the element in other projects whose cost analyses are available.

(c) When measures of Quantity are not available and considerable time would be required for measurement of approximate quantities, and the quality standard of the element in question is not unusual.

(d) When the cost involved does not justify the time required for either simple proportion or approximate quantities.

Write down your answer: (a), (b), (c), or (d).

Turn to page 220

⟩ *from page 218*

Example from Chapter 11 using 'inspection'

5C   *Disposal installations*

This is not a major element in this project which is best decided by inspection. (Approximate quantities could also be used if the cost involved justified the time required for measurement.)

The engineering services in our project are located in close proximity to staircase areas. Thus reasonably short horizontal pipe runs can be expected. We need to remember that storey heights reflect the incorporation of suspended ceilings and raised floors in our design. These points need to be considered when inspecting similar cost analyses and other data sources.

The costs of disposal installations in existing offices are as follows:

Building	Tender date	Prelims	Cost of disposal installations ($£/m^2$ gfa)
Two-storey offices, *Winchester*	Mar. 1991	10.27%	3.50
Four-storey offices, *Manchester*	Feb. 1993	7.66%	4.86
Two-storey offices, *Slough*	Jan. 1993	8.79%	4.01
Two-storey offices, *Reading*	Sept. 1992	9.50%	3.89

Making approximate adjustments for the differences in the preliminaries percentages and the tender dates of these projects, we decide to adopt an allowance of £4.75 per m^2 for the element which includes builder's work to pipe ducts.

Total element allowance = £4.75 x 2246 = £10 669

	Total	Cost per m^2 gfa
Cost target for disposal installations	£10 669	£4.75

Return to page 218 ⟩

from page 218

Both (a) and (b) are relevant.

(c) is the best criterion as it comprises (a) and (b).

(b) is relevant because we prefer to use only approximate quantities when an element in the proposed building is going to be unlike its counterpart in any other buildings whose cost analyses are available.

(d) is a non-starter: simple proportion takes very little time and should always be used when satisfactory measures of element unit quantity are available.

We now go on to consider the technique of 'approximate quantities'.

Turn to page 221

from page 220

Approximate quantities

Under the method of 'approximate quantities' a relatively detailed specification is prepared for the element in question. Approximate quantities are then measured from this specification and priced in the traditional way.

1	Simple proportion
2	Inspections
3	Approximate quantities

(If you would like to see an example of this technique, turn to page 222.)

It should be noted that:

(a)   the specification prepared for this technique is not as detailed as that prepared during the detail design stage,

(b)   when using approximate quantities it is easy to overlook details which will only be considered during the detail design stage,

(c)   only the major or most cost-significant items in any element are measured and priced; the costs associated with sundry items must be included with the rates or alternatively they may be included by adding an overall percentage at the end,

(d)   the design team is not committed to finally using the specification prepared for approximate quantities, but simply to using one of a similar general quality.

Write a brief description of the one situation in which approximate quantities should, theoretically, be used in preference to the other two techniques.

Turn to page 223

from page
221

Example from Chapter 11 using 'approximate quantities'

2G: *Internal walls and partitions*

The building analysed had demountable partitions. Most of the partitioning is left as a tenant's responsibility in our project. In addition, our standards are somewhat different and we also have the effect of increased storey heights to take into account. We therefore decide to use the approximate quantities technique.

73 m² of 100 mm blockwork partition @ £21.00 per m²	£1533
255 m² of 200 mm blockwork partition @ £32.00 per m²	£8160
77 m² of 112.5 mm common brick internal walls @ £23.00 per m²	£1771
18 WC cubicles @ £330 each	£5940
	£17 404

$$\text{Reduce to cost per m}^2 \text{ of gross floor area:} \quad \frac{£17\,404}{2246\,\text{m}^2} = £7.75/\text{m}^2$$

	Total	Cost per m² gfa
Cost target for internal walls and partitions	**£17 404**	**£7.75**

Return to page 221

⟳ *from page 221*

Theoretically, approximate quantities should only be used when an element in the proposed building is markedly different from its counterpart in all the other building analyses.

However, in practice approximate quantities can be used for all elements without destroying the usefulness of the cost plan. Using approximate quantities throughout would not violate the principles of cost control. Nevertheless, the cost plan will be prepared more quickly and cheaply, and may well be more realistic if the other two techniques are used.

Write down the names and brief descriptions of the three techniques which can be used for deciding on the cost target for an element.

Turn to page 224 ⟳

from page 223

Summary – Methods of preparing cost targets for elements

1 Simple proportion

The element cost selected from a range of cost analyses chosen at feasibility is adjusted by proportion.

2 Inspection

A target cost per m^2 of gross floor area is chosen from a cost range obtained from a selection of suitable analyses and/or cost studies.

3 Approximate quantities

A provisional specification of the required quality is prepared for the element and priced by approximate quantities.

(*Note:* No matter which technique is used, the resulting cost target should be regarded as a reasonable allowance within which the element may be designed during the detail design stage. The design team should never feel obliged to use exactly the same specification upon which the cost target is based.)

Turn to page 225

from page 224

Each of these methods of preparing cost targets takes into account all the factors which affect element costs.

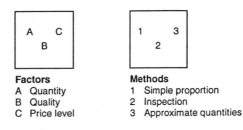

Factors
A   Quantity
B   Quality
C   Price level

Methods
1   Simple proportion
2   Inspection
3   Approximate quantities

When all the cost targets have been entered in the cost plan summary, their total must be compared with the cost limit and remedial action should be taken if necessary.

It might seem that the preparation of a cost plan takes rather a long time. In practice, it can take less time than you have spent reading this chapter!

Chapter 11 is devoted entirely to an example of cost planning from feasibility to scheme design. This has been inserted before Chapter 12 to give you a fuller appreciation of the 'planning' part of cost control before going on to consider the control of costs during the detail design stage.

Turn to page 227

11 Cost Example from Feasibility to Scheme Design

This chapter *is not* in programmed form.

This chapter is a step-by-step example of how the cost plan develops as more design information becomes available. It starts with the first estimate at the feasibility stage which we have called FS at the top of the page to help guide you through the chapter.

It moves on to the outline cost plan at the outline proposal stage – marked OP at the top of the page.

The last example is the detailed cost plan at the scheme design stage (marked SD at the top of the page). Remember the detailed cost plan is finalised at the end of the scheme design.

The example in this chapter illustrates the cost planning of an office block from the preparation of the first estimate at the feasibility stage to the detailed cost plan at the scheme design stage.

In order to keep this exercise within manageable limits we have selected just one analysis rather than a range of analyses as recommended.

The example is presented in the form of a running commentary by the design team during each of the three design stages involved. When you read a phrase like 'We decide to allow £1000', imagine yourself swept back in time to the date quoted at the beginning of that particular stage of the design.

The relevant dates are:

First estimate	June 1995
Outline cost plan	September 1995
Detailed cost plan	November 1995
Proposed tender date	September 1996

FS

Feasibility stage (June 1995)

The information available at this stage is normally very limited and, in this instance, includes:

(1) Initial brief identifying the use to which the building is to be put, the floor area required, and an indication of the desired quality.
(2) Town planning policy.
(3) Details of the site.

In addition the following data will be used:

❑ The histogram of average building prices; new office buildings generally.
❑ The detailed cost analysis of the office block, given in Appendix A.
❑ Access to indices, for adjusting price level (not included here).

The above information and data has been assembled before we start to prepare our Feasibility stage estimate.

Initial brief for proposed office premises*

Space	A lettable area of at least 1850 m² and maximum permissible car parking. The parking provision is considered to be essential due to the congested city centre site, poor parking facilities and inadequate public transport. The tenants are likely to be professional services such as accounting and insurances.
Planning permission	Preliminary enquiries to the planning authority indicate that an office block three storeys high would be permitted and that the stated amount of lettable area should be achievable as it is within the plot ratio.
Use	The premises will be offered for leasing as good-quality office accommodation at a rental which is in the upper market range.
Quality	An above-average commercial quality is appropriate to this prime location site and will command a suitable return. Raised floors and suspended ceilings will need to be incorporated into the new design in order to accommodate IT systems. An attractive façade is considered essential.
Site	The site has been acquired and a site plan is available. (It has not been included here as it is reasonably straightforward.) It shows that the terrace houses previously occupying the site have been cleared and the foundations grubbed up. Ground conditions in the area are good.

* Remember, this is the *only* information available at this stage

FS

Estimate

We must prepare our feasibility stage estimate so that the client can decide whether or not to go ahead with the project. This follows examination of the client's initial brief, an inspection of the site and local conditions, and agreement of quality standards between the design team and the client.

It is possible to gain an idea of the cost range by examining analyses of past projects for the same type of building. This information may be obtained from in-house records, or from published information. An information service, such as BCIS, publishes a wide range of suitable cost information. The histogram in Fig. 11.1 shows the cost range for office buildings, which has been updated to the 4th quarter 1995. The costs are for the building works and exclude external works, drainage, external services, professional fees and VAT. The mode is £550–£600 per m^2 gfa.

Experience and knowledge is needed to interpret these cost ranges. For example, higher quality finishes and fittings to the ground floor reception, or enhanced finishes and services for restaurants and computer suites may all increase the overall cost per m^2 gfa. Similarly, allowance must be made for the cost of any demolition and enabling works and the costs of site investigation, planning and Building Regulations approvals and work to adjoining properties.

Remember, costs will vary according to location, quality, and size of development.

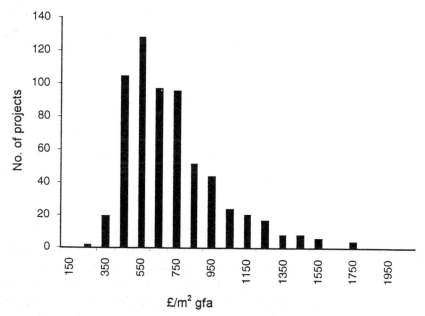

Fig. 11.1 Cost range for office buildings

FS

From this distribution, it appears that we should expect our estimate to be in the range £450 to £850 per m^2, which is fairly wide. This range is influenced by many factors including the exact quality desired (note that these prices do not include any allowance for external works). Since this histogram tells us nothing about the specific characteristics or quality of the buildings concerned, we must treat this type of study with caution. In fact some m^2 prices have been recorded well above £850.

It is, therefore, preferable to work from detailed cost analyses which provide some information about the buildings analysed. Ideally a small number (between 4 and 10) of similar analyses should be selected. This will permit adjustments to be made for items where our brief or quality standards depart from those of the cost analyses. We should obviously select analyses which are reasonably close to both our functional requirements and our standards of quality.

To keep this exercise within manageable limits we have selected just one analysis (given in Appendix A) which is in our opinion suitable with regard to architectural style and quality. Ideally, in order to provide a good match for the new project, this cost analysis should have been a three-storey rather than a two-storey construction. Also the storey heights of the chosen analysis appear to be too low for our new project, nevertheless, this does allow us to consider some important design variables and their implications for project costs. The analysis has, therefore, been accepted for our purposes.

Before considering the major differences between the building analysed and our project, we need to estimate the total floor area which will be required for our project. From studies of other office blocks, it appears reasonable to allow 20% of the lettable floor area for the additional area required for services and circulation space.

Lettable floor area required $= 1850\,\text{m}^2$

Add
Allowance for circulation space
(i.e. corridors, toilets, stairwells, lift wells, etc.),

$$1850 \times 20\% \qquad \underline{370\,\text{m}^2}$$
$$\underline{2220\,\text{m}^2}$$
$$\text{say} \quad 2250\,\text{m}^2$$

We will assume a gross floor area of 2250 m^2 for our project. Until the preparation of scheme design drawings, what is required now is a suitable all-inclusive rate to calculate our feasibility estimate. From our chosen analysis, the cost per m^2 gfa (at September 1992) for the building sub-total is £612.22 per m^2. Total cost (less contingencies) is £819.46 per m^2. We cannot use these figures without first making some necessary adjustments for Price level, Quantity and Quality.

FS

It is important to remember that at this stage we have very little information either in the form of specification and design notes or as drawn information. Bearing this in mind we shall look at the adjustments.

Adjustment for Price level

This is the adjustment for the factors listed in Chapters 9 and 10. Of these, time and location are the most important.

Adjustment for time:

Index at the analysis date   106 (September 1992)

Index at preparation of   128 (June 1995)
first estimate

> **Remember.** The index has been updated to the time the estimate is being prepared – not to project completion.

Adjustment for location:

Location factor for building   1.00 (Reading)
analysed

Location factor for the   0.94 (Portsmouth)
proposed building

The adjustment for time and location may be combined into one Adjustment Factor (*AF*) thus,

$$AF = \frac{128}{106} \times \frac{0.94}{1.00} = 1.1351 \quad \text{say} \quad \mathbf{1.14}$$

These adjustments have been calculated as a normal routine approach, accepting without question published indices and factors. It should not be forgotten that this approach should be combined with professional judgement to reflect personal knowledge of local conditions and current trends. For our example the other factors previously discussed under 'price level' do not apply.

Adjustment for Quantity and Quality

To a large extent, size differences between the office block analysis and the new project will be catered for by considering the cost per m^2 gfa. In addition we must make adjustments where major differences in the quantity or quality of an element can be found. At this stage, when considering quantity we must be alert to changes in *densities* (as discussed in Chapter 9) as this is most important when considering costs in terms of £/m^2 per gfa. Similarly, when examining quality, some thought should be given to the *mix of individual items* within an element (as discussed in Chapter 10, Section C). Given the limited information available, there is little to be gained by presenting the first estimate in an elemental format.

Inspection reveals a number of items in the analysis for which adjustments are required.

FS

1 Office partitions

The cost analysis includes demountable partitioning for office areas (see Appendix A). In the new project, apart from WC cubicles, this will be the tenant's responsibility. The reduction is as follows:

Demountable partitioning = £14 040

$$\frac{£14\,040}{1408\,m^2} = £9.97 \text{ per } m^2 \text{ gfa}$$

(1408 m^2 is the gross floor area of the building analysed.)

Update and adjust for location

$$£9.97 \times 1.14 = £11.37 \text{ per } m^2 \text{ gfa}$$

Floor finishes and suspended ceilings

The cost analysis shows that the carpet tiles were supplied under a separate contract and this supply cost is not included in the analysis (see Appendix A). Thus we must make the adjustment to the 'fix only' price for carpet tiles. We take the area of 1040 m^2 (the quantity shown in the analysis for carpet tiles). We decide, after looking through manufacturers' catalogues, upon a current rate of £13 per m^2 as an appropriate price for the supply of carpet tiles. We can calculate an appropriate addition per m^2 gfa for this adjustment.

$$\frac{1040\,m^2 \times £13}{1408\,m^2} = £9.60 \text{ per } m^2 \text{ gfa}$$

With regard to ceiling finishes, the cost analysis shows that plasterboard and skim coat on timber framing has been taken throughout the building analysed. For the proposed project, acoustic tiles in a suspended metal grid is required for the office areas. Plasterboard and skim will be retained for toilet areas.

We find a current price for suspended ceilings to our specification of £29.54 per m^2. The analysis shows the area of ceiling finish to be 1380 m^2. From this we calculate the price per m^2 gfa as follows:

$$\frac{1380\,m^2 \times £29.54}{1408\,m^2} = £28.95 \text{ per } m^2 \text{ gfa}$$

To calculate the extra cost we must deduct from this figure the cost (after updating and adjusting for location) included in the analysis for the plasterboard and skim finish (i.e. £14.07 × 1.14). Thus £28.95 − (£14.07 × 1.14) gives an extra cost of £12.91. This will be slightly on the high side, since suspended ceilings have now been allowed everywhere (including toilet areas). The additional cost is considered too small to worry about at this stage.

FS

3 Lifts

The cost analysis shows that there were no lifts in the analysed building (5J: Lift installations). The design team take the early decision that the building will be three storeys high. Although not absolutely essential, it has been decided that two lift cars will be installed in the new project. We must therefore allow for this element.

The design team give us their early impressions regarding specifications of the lifts. This includes type of lift, car size, finishes, travel speeds control system, position of lift motors, and the like. Armed with this information we seek the advice of a lift manufacturer and installer. Thus, it is established that a reasonable total cost will be £60 000. This is a current estimate as applicable to our new three-storey project and nothing will be gained by relating this figure back to our cost analysis. We still need a rate per m^2 gfa, so we use the 2250 m^2, i.e. the gross floor area of the new project.

$$\frac{£60\,000}{2250\,\text{m}^2} = £26.67 \text{ per m}^2 \text{ gfa}$$

By inspection of previous projects, we assess the builder's work in connection with the lifts at:

£3200   or   £1.42 per m^2 gfa

4 Cost implications of three-storey building and increased storey height

In order to provide the best cost comparison our cost analyses should have been of three-storey buildings with appropriate storey heights for our new project. However, we are suggesting that we were unable to find suitable analyses. Therefore, we must now consider the cost implications that this might have for our feasibility estimate.

Very clearly, there will be implications for the densities of some elements and, by implication, the associated costs per m^2 gfa. For example, in our cost analysis, the ratio of upper floors to gross floor area is:

$$\frac{704}{1408} \quad \text{i.e. } 1:2$$

If an additional upper floor were to be added to the analysed building, gfa would increase by 704 m^2 giving a revised gfa of 2112 m^2 (1408 m^2 + 704 m^2). This would thus affect the density of this element and the ratio would change to:

$$\frac{1408}{2112} \quad \text{i.e. } 2:3 \quad (1:1.5)$$

Accordingly, the costs per m^2 gfa for this element would increase. In very approximate terms, with the addition of a third floor, the new element total cost would be doubled to £45 258. Then, using the new and increased gfa of 2112 m^2, the cost per m^2 gfa would equate to £21.43. (If you wish to review this topic, refer back to Chapter 9 where this concept was first introduced.)

FS

Following on from this, as each element is inspected in turn, we should find that some costs per m² gfa will increase while others will decrease.

We now intend to consider the cost implications of the three-storey building and increased storey height. As there are likely to be implications for most of the superstructure, we need to examine all the elements in this group. Remember, the information at this stage is limited and we therefore have to make adjustments to the analysis, rather than rely on measuring element quantities for the proposed project.

In order to simplify the process, all adjustments are made before any price level changes are carried out. The adjustment for price level is applied, at the end of this section (once only).

(a) Substructures

We ascertain from the structural engineer that the addition of the third storey and increased storey heights will have little effect on the foundation design as described in the cost analysis. Therefore we believe that a similar solution to that of the cost analysis may well suffice. However, the cost per m² gfa of substructures will now fall, as the ratio between gfa and the element unit quantities for substructures increases.

Cost per m² gfa in analysis $= £32.13\,\text{m}^2$

Element unit rate in analysis $= £64.27\,\text{m}^2$

Revised gfa if analysis were for three storeys $= 2112\,\text{m}^2$

New cost per m² gfa:

$$\frac{704 \times £64.27}{2112\,\text{m}^2} = £21.42\,\text{m}^2$$

Reduction to the analysis rate is

$$£32.13 - £21.42 = £10.71 \text{ per m}^2 \text{ gfa}$$

(b) Frame

On first inspection it might be considered that increases in the cost of the frame will be adequately dealt with by the increased gross floor area of the new project. To a large extent this is correct. However, additional costs due to extra storey height have not been allowed for. We will make allowances for this in a rather crude way by increasing the cost per m² gfa in proportion to the differing storey heights.

FS

Storey height of analysed building = 2.75 m
Proposed storey height of project = 3.5 m (average)

The increase in storey height is 750 mm. This affects the costs of the columns. In fact, a quick approximate estimate, based upon the assumptions of 400 mm × 400 mm concrete columns on a three-metre grid, indicates minimal extra cost. However, the cost in the analysis of £32.22 m² gfa appears low when compared with other analyses. An appropriate range seems to be £40.00 to £65.00. We therefore decide to increase this element cost up to the low end of our range by adding 25%.

Cost per m² gfa in analysis = £32.22

25% × £32.22 = £8.06

Addition to analysis rate = £8.06 per m² gfa

(c) Upper floors

Similar arguments to those applied to substructures are also applicable to upper floors. However, this time the cost per m² gfa will increase.

Cost per m² gfa in analysis = £16.07 m²
Element unit rate in analysis = £32.14 m²
Revised rate per m² if analysis were for three storeys
i.e. two upper floors (704 × 2) = 1408 m²

Converting to cost per m² gfa gives

$$\frac{1408 \times £32.14}{2112\,m^2} = £21.43\,m^2\ gfa$$

Addition to analysis rate is

£21.43 − £16.07 = £5.36 per m² gfa

(d) Roof

Adding a storey to the analysed building means that the same roof area is now covering an additional floor. Thus, reductions in the cost per m² gfa will be achieved.

Total cost in analysis = £64 491

Converting to cost per m² gfa:

$$\frac{£64\,491}{2112\,m^2} = £30.54\ per\ m^2\ gfa$$

Reduction to analysis rate is

£45.80 − £30.54 = £15.26 per m² gfa

FS

(e)   Stairs

The stair requirements for the new project could be very similar to the provisions described in the analysis. The major difference being the additional travel from first to second floor. This will roughly double the quantities and cost contained in the analysis. Thus,

$$£15\,758 \times 2 = £31\,516$$

Also to be considered is an allowance to cover the increased storey height. We will adopt the same crude approach as we did for the frame and add 25% to our total cost of this element.

$$125\% \times £31\,516 = £39\,395$$

Converting to cost per m^2 gfa:

$$\frac{£39\,395}{2112\,\text{m}^2} = £18.65$$

Addition to analysis rate is

$$£18.65 - £11.19 = £7.46 \text{ per m}^2 \text{ gfa}$$

(f)   External walls, and (g) Windows and external doors

We decide to take these two elements together as there are several factors common to both elements. The ratio of external wall to windows in the analysis is about 40 : 60. With the new project it is suggested that this ratio will be reversed with the external envelope composed of 85% external walls and 15% windows. With traditional brick construction, it is quite normal for the element unit rate of windows to be three to four times higher than those for external walls depending on the specification. Curtain walling, which is normally considered as part of the external wall element, is also relatively expensive. We would therefore expect to see a big reduction per m^2 gfa overall for these two elements when they are considered together as one. This will be so, even after allowing for the increased storey height.

Taking the analysis, total the two element quantities, increase by 25% (increase in storey height) and then split in the ratio of 15% windows : 85% walls. Thus

$$(531 + 304) \times 125\% = 1044\,\text{m}^2 \qquad 157 : 887$$

Then (using ratio):

External walls	$887\,\text{m}^2 \times £89.04 = £78\,978$
Windows and doors	$157\,\text{m}^2 \times £324.96 = £51\,019$

Thus, cost per m^2 gfa for the two elements:

in analysis $£19.23 + £122.55 = £141.78$ per m^2 gfa

FS

when revised $\dfrac{£78\,978 + £51\,019}{1408\,\text{m}^2} = £92.33$ per m^2 gfa

Reduction to the analysis rate for these two combined elements is in the region of £141.78 – £92.33 = £49.45 per m^2 gfa

The reductions are possibly even larger than are suggested by these calculations. This is because the element unit rate for curtain walling has been used rather than a rate for windows, and this looks high. However, with the lack of information at this stage, we will accept this figure.

(h)   Internal walls and partitions
We have already made adjustments for the demountable partitions. With these omitted from this element, the cost per m^2 gfa is as follows:

$\dfrac{£26\,295 - £14\,040}{1408\,\text{m}^2} = £8.70$ per m^2 gfa

At this stage, we can only assume the densities will be the same and thus solely allow for the increase in the storey height. We propose doing this as before by adding 25% to our rate. Therefore 25% addition is

25% × £8.70 = £2.18 per m^2 gfa

(i)   Internal doors
We chose to make no change.

(j)   Internal finishes
Floor finishes and ceiling finishes have already been adjusted so we need only to consider wall finishes. The change in the ratio of external wall area to window area will result in an increase to the area of wall finishes. Internal walls and partitions are unaffected by this change. To make allowance for this increase we propose to increase the cost in the analysis by 50%. The rate per m^2 gfa in the analysis is £13.44, therefore a 50% addition is £6.72, which is to be added to the analysis.

(k)   Fittings
No adjustment required.

(l)   Services
With increased storey heights, we will make the following assumptions:

- ❏ increases in vertical pipe runs,
- ❏ no increases in horizontal pipe runs,
- ❏ possibly a slight increase in the number of pipe fittings,
- ❏ certainly no increases in other fittings and fixtures (where much of the cost will be concentrated).

FS

To allow for this we will add an arbitrary 5% to the cost analysis rate per m^2 gfa:

$£227.80 \times 5\% = £11.39$ per m^2 gfa

We can now summarise the adjustments that we have made in connection with adding a third storey and increasing storey heights.

Element	£ per m^2
(a) Substructures	−10.71
(b) Frame	+8.06
(c) Upper floors	+5.36
(d) Roof	−15.26
(e) Stairs	+7.46
(f) External walls (g) Windows and external doors	−49.45
(h) Internal walls and partitions	+2.18
(i) Internal doors	n/c
(j) Internal finishes	+6.72
(k) Fittings	n/c
(l) Services	+11.39

The cost implications of a three-storey building with increased storey height = −£34.25 per m^2 gfa

In order to ensure that we deal with all adjustments in the same way, we must now adjust for price level to reflect current prices.

$−£34.25 \times 1.14 = −£39.05$ per m^2 gfa

FS

We summarise the total cost of the office portion of our project (excluding external works, preliminaries, and contingencies):

		£ per m^2 gfa
Net cost from cost analysis		612.22
(i.e building sub-total excluding preliminaries and contingencies)		
Update and adjust for location	612.22 × 1.14 =	697.93
(as we are dealing with costs current at date of estimate)		
Less Office partitions	11.37	686.56
Add Floor finishes	9.60	
Ceiling finishes	12.91	
Lift installation	26.67	
Builders work in connection with lifts	1.42	
Less Cost implications of 3-storey construction, etc.	–39.05	
		£698.11

Multiply by gross floor area: £698.11 × 2250 m^2 = £1 570 747.50

Net cost of office portion = £1 570 750

It is worth comparing our cost of £698.11 per m^2 gfa (excluding preliminaries) with the histogram at the beginning of this section (Fig. 11.1). Early information suggests that the new project will be above the average quoted.

To complete our estimate, we now consider the following factors:

- ❏ External works. (This includes allowances for hard and soft landscaping, any work to road car parking and paved areas, fencing, work to site boundaries, and drains and sewer work. Water, electric, gas and sewerage charges include the cost of connection to the mains plus an assessment of distribution costs from the mains.)
- ❏ Preliminaries.
- ❏ Contingencies (i.e. a reserve against unforeseen items that occur during construction on site).
- ❏ Reserve against 'price and design risk (i.e. a reserve against possible price increases between the preparation of the estimate and the date of the tender).

After preparing approximate quantities, we decide that £180 000 is a suitable allowance for external works (the main consideration here has been car parking spaces).

FS

Allowing for preliminaries as a percentage of the project cost is not ideal. Further research and analysis of contractors' tenders and pricing methods is required. One approach would be to use cost significant items to build up an allowance for the cost plan. In most cases, this would involve no more than 10 or 12 cost significant items. However, for the sake of expediency we will continue to adopt the common method of inserting a percentage for this element. (Refer to any text in estimating to see how the preliminaries price is built up.)

After inspecting the figures included in the cost analysis for preliminaries and contingencies, we decide to increase both percentages slightly. Thus for preliminaries and contingencies we allow approximately 10% and 1.5% of the remainder of our estimate for these two items.

For the design risk at this early stage we decide to include 2.5%.

Now we need to consider price risk and insert a reserve against price rises which can occur between the date of producing this estimate at feasibility stage (June 1995) and the date for receipt of tenders (September 1996).

There are various forecasts of future cost trends available which would be consulted. Tender price forecasts should always be combined with professional judgement. The adjustment can then be applied as a percentage adjustment or as an adjustment factor, much in the same way as explained already. We have carried out the adjustment with a percentage addition.

FS

Summary – Feasibility stage estimate

	£	£
Office portion	1 570 750	
External works	180 000	
		1 750 750
Add		
Preliminaries (10%)	175 075	
Contingencies (1.5%)	26 261	
		1 952 086
Add		
Reserve against unforeseen design eventualities (2.5%)	48 802	
Reserve against price rises from June 1995 to September 1996 (approx. 5%)	97 604	
Total		**£2 098 492**

This estimate would probably be rounded off to say **£2 100 000** and then incorporated into the feasibility report presented to the client.

However, at feasibility stage, cost consultants do not always like reporting a single figure because design information is extremely limited. In this situation, one of the following two courses of action is usually taken:

(1) Where the client has set a cost limit, the report would confirm whether or not the project could be constructed within that limit.

(2) Where no cost limit has been set, a cost range might be reported together with some broad indication of quality.

(**Note:** *If you jumped to page 228 from Chapter 10, return to Chapter 10 after you have read this page; if not, continue to page 243.*)

We will assume that the client instructs the design team to proceed with outline proposals after he has considered the feasibility report.

The cost limit for the project is established at **£2 100 000** which relates to the proposed tender date of September 1996.

OP

Outline proposals stage (September 1995)

Preparation of outline cost plan

The information available at this stage includes:

(1) Feasibility report, including the first estimate. (A cost limit has been established.)
(2) General brief and design criteria. (The design criteria are included here.)
(3) Town planning policy.
(4) Outline design drawings. In reality these would emerge during this stage but we have assumed that they are available for the production of the outline cost plan. These drawings have not been included here but we assume that they are similar to the scheme design drawings in Appendix B. In reality these would be less detailed and there would be much more uncertainty concerning measurements and dimensions. In this regard, you will have to accept the measurements presented in Table 11.1 and within the text.

The data used to estimate cost targets for the outline cost plan will be the same as at feasibility stage and are summarised below.

Table 11.1 Measures of quantity for the outline cost plan

Gross floor area	$2250\,m^2$
Area of ground floor slab	$750\,m^2$
Area of upper floors	$1500\,m^2$
Area of roof (sloping area)	$950\,m^2$
Area of external walls (including windows and doors)	$1550\,m^2$

The gross floor area of our outline design (as measured from the outline design drawing) is approximately $2250\,m^2$. This gives us a total cost per m^2 gfa of

$$\frac{£2\,100\,000}{2250\,m^2} = £933.33 \text{ per } m^2 \text{ gfa}$$

Reserve for price and design risk

Before preparing our outline cost plan we should consider again our reserve against price and design risk.

At the feasibility stage, we allowed £146 406 representing a total of 7.5% of our estimated sum.

OP

Our office block is seen as being a relatively straightforward project. Therefore, we decide that the allowance of 2.5% is a large enough margin for any unforeseen eventualities in the development of the design and thus leave this percentage unaltered.

We must now consider how prices are expected to move between the preparation of this outline cost plan (September 1995) and the receipt of tenders (September 1996). This is done by reference to appropriate forecasts. Following this approach, we decide to allow 4.5% to cover against the likely tender price rises over this period. Together this gives us a revised total design and price risk allowance of 7%.

Thus there will be little change on the figures produced for the first estimate. The total sum was:

£146 406   i.e. £65.07 per m^2 gfa

It will be helpful to keep this figure in mind when estimating cost targets for element groups. The actual price and design risk allowance will be calculated when the summary of the outline cost plan is produced. What has to be remembered is the cost limit which has now been set.

We prepare our outline cost plan by comparing the design criteria (as given on the next two pages) and the outline design drawing (similar to the scheme design drawings shown in Appendix B) with the cost analysis (Appendix A), making appropriate adjustments where necessary for major differences.

(*Note:* We clearly indicated at the feasibility stage a separate allowance for design risk; however, a sum of money for design risk is often not shown separately until the outline design stage simply because of the lack of definition in the earlier stage both in design detail and the estimating approach. Where this latter approach is adopted, then, the allowance for design risk should not be an addition to the estimate prepared at feasibility stage, but rather a reserve which is drawn from that total. The opposite is true for price risk as an allowance for this is usually calculated and shown separately from the outset.)

OP   Design criteria for office block

Site

(1)   Site information and ground conditions
- (a)   Levels. Site plans would normally be available at this stage indicating relevant site features and indicating a grid of levels or the site contours.
- (b)   Soil. Clay and gravel.
- (c)   Bearing capacity. 200 kN/m^2.
- (d)   Water table. None encountered
- (e)   Depth of bearing strata. For three-storey block – 1.25 metres.
- (f)   General. Site cleared of old terrace houses without basements. Foundations grubbed up under a separate demolition contract.

General requirements

(2)   The building
The building shall conform to the provisions of the current Building Regulations. In particular, the structure and protected shafts shall be of 1.5 hour fire resistance. Doors to protected shafts shall be of 1 hour fire resistance.

(3)   Working conditions
Temperature, ventilation, lighting, sanitary conveniences, etc. shall comply with the latest requirements of current legislation.

Structure

(4)   Frame

Storey height for all floors	3.5 m
Span	approximately 15 m
Fire resistance	1 hour

(5)   Upper floors

Imposed load	5 kN/m^2
Fire resistance	1 hour

(6)   Roof

Imposed load	0.75 kN/m^2

(7)   Internal doors

Doors to protected shafts	1 hour fire resistance

OP

Environmental engineeering services

(8)   Heating and ventilation

Air-conditioning using four-pipe fan coil comfort cooling system.

No. of air changes per hour   3

Temperature   22°C (dry bulb)

50% RH

(9)   Electrics

Lighting standard   500 lux

(10)   Other services

All normal services to typical commercial standards including:

- ❏ hot and cold water supply
- ❏ fire services
- ❏ small power
- ❏ provision for communications
- ❏ lightning protection
- ❏ lifts
- ❏ drainage, etc.

Substructure (i.e. work below lowest floor finish)

The engineer advises that there is no significant soil problem, so a similar solution to that of the cost analysis may well suffice. It is assumed that the loads imposed by an additional storey plus the increased storey height will not alter the foundation design described in the cost analysis. There is a small addition for foundations under the lifts, but this is not a major cost. The existing foundations have already been grubbed up and no major problems are envisaged here. On reflection and after comparison with other projects, we decide the rate in the cost analysis is acceptable.

We therefore update the element unit rate from the cost analysis (i.e. £64.27 m^2) making the adjustment for location and applying the revised rate to our outline design; this is done by reference to suitable indices.

OP

Adjustment Factor (AF)

Index at analysis tender date	= 106
Index at preparation of outline cost plan	= 130

(*Note:* The index changed from 128 to 130 between June 1995 and September 1995.)

Location factor for Reading (analysed building)	= 1.00
Location factor for Portsmouth (new project)	= 0.94

$$AF = \frac{130}{106} \times \frac{0.94}{1.00} = 1.15283 \quad \text{say} \quad 1.15$$

Update element unit rate and adjust it for location:

$£64.27 \times 1.15 = £73.91$ per m^2

Area of ground floor slab measured from the outline design drawing $= 750 \, \text{m}^2$.

Allowance for substructure $= 750 \, \text{m}^2$ ground floor slab @ £73.91 per m^2

Cost per m^2 gfa:

$$\frac{750 \times £73.91}{2250 \, \text{m}^2} = £24.64 \, \text{per m}^2$$

Superstructure

We shall now examine the elements individually. The major impact will be due to the additional storey and increased storey height.

(a) Frame

The cost analysis indicates a traditional steel frame to accommodate steel decking and lightweight in situ concrete upper floors. The costs of fire protective casing to central and exposed columns have been included in this element. Also included in this element are the costs of isolated beams located in the plant room. We will probably continue to use the same type of frame design as that employed in the cost analysis.

The cost included in the analysis is £32.22 per m^2. On initial inspection this rate appears low. In any event, it should be increased in line with the differences indicated at the feasibility stage. The main differences, as already identified, are the additional storey, an increase in the gross floor area, plus the increase in storey height. The total cost for the frame needs to be increased accordingly. Examining frame costs on other project analyses shows this element cost to be in the range of £40.00–£70.00 per m^2 gross floor area. (*Note:* These are current costs.) Some cost variability can be attributed to the type of protection used and whether this cost has been included here or recorded under 5K. Protective installations.

OP

After a further detailed inspection of our data source we identify the most appropriate analyses. From these we settle upon a cost of £60.00.

Gross floor area = $2250\,\text{m}^2$
Cost of element frame = $2250 \times £60.00$ = £135 000
Cost per m^2 gfa = £60.00

(b) Upper floors

The cost analysis is for a two-storey building and our outline design is for three storeys. We must obviously allow for the additional upper floor. In addition the cost analysis describes a composite upper floor construction combining steel decking with a lightweight concrete topping. It is quite possible that our design team will select a different solution, but at this stage we do not believe the costs will be very different. (We will check this at detail design stage when more details are available.)

Update element unit rate and adjust it for location:

$£32.14 \times 1.15\ (AF) = £36.96$ per m^2

(For calculation of Adjustment Factor (*AF*), see page 247.)

Calculate element cost from the outline design drawing:

Allowance for upper floors = $1500\,\text{m}^2$ a £36.96 per m^2 = £55 440

Cost per m^2 gfa:

$$\frac{£55\,440}{2250\,\text{m}^2} = £24.64 \text{ per } \text{m}^2 \text{ gfa}$$

(c) Roof

We have assumed the design and specification will be similar. Adding an additional storey will reduce the cost of the roof when expressed in terms of £ per m^2 gfa.

Update element unit rate and adjust it for location:

$£71.66 \times 1.15\ (AF) = £82.41$ per m^2

Calculate element cost from the outline design drawing (measured as sloping area of roof):

Area of roof = $950\,\text{m}^2$

Allowance for roof = $950\,\text{m}^2$ @ £82.41 per m^2 = £78 290

Cost per m^2 gfa:

$$\frac{£78\,290}{2250\,\text{m}^2} = £34.80 \text{ per } \text{m}^2 \text{ gfa}$$

OP

(d) Stairs

The analysis shows two internal staircases constructed in concrete and two external escape staircases in galvanised steel, spiral pattern. The same requirements with regard to number and construction will suit the new project as can be seen from the outline design. However, what is different is the extra overall height made necessary by the additional floor and the increase in storey height.

From the outline design drawings we estimate that the rise of the staircase from ground to second floor is 7.00 m. This compares with 2.75 m (ground to first floor) in the analysed building. We will now use this information as a crude factor to adjust the total cost of the element. At this stage we see no need to isolate the costs associated with the two types of staircase design.

From the analysis, total cost of element $=$ £15 758

$$\text{New total for element} = £15\,758 \times \frac{7}{2.75} = £40\,111$$

Update this element total cost and adjust it for location:

£40 111 × 1.15 *(AF)* = £46 128

Reduce to cost per m^2 gfa:

$$\frac{£46\,128}{2250\,\text{m}^2} = £20.50 \text{ per m}^2 \text{ gfa}$$

(e) External walls

The external envelope of the analysed project has a greater area of windows than our new project. Although the quality of the brickwork is very similar, there are fewer straight runs and more intricate work around column casings. Due to these characteristics we assess the element unit rate in the analysis to be slightly on the high side. Therefore we have made additional reference to other analyses; and selected a current rate appropriate to the location of £80.00.

We measure the external wall area on our project from the outline design drawings by assuming a distribution of 85% solid wall and 15% windows and doors; this gives us an external wall area of 1318 m^2.

Element unit cost:

1318 m^2 @ £80.00 = £105 440

Cost per m^2 gfa:

$$\frac{£105\,440}{2250\,\text{m}^2} = £46.86 \text{ per m}^2 \text{ gfa}$$

OP

(f) Windows and external doors

Glazing style differs significantly between the analysis and the new project. Other analyses are used to select a rate appropriate to the outline design. The design team indicate that a target cost for above-average components should be allowed. Accordingly, we selected a current rate appropriate to the location of £330.00.

Following on from our calculations of external walls, the window and door area is assessed at $232\,\text{m}^2$ by assuming 15% windows and doors.

Element unit cost:

$$232\,\text{m}^2\,@\,£330.00 = £76\,560$$

Cost per m^2 gfa:

$$\frac{76\,560}{2250\,\text{m}^2} = £34.03 \text{ per m}^2 \text{ gfa}$$

(g) Internal walls and partitions

It was difficult to measure the element unit quantities. After some consideration, we decided to adopt the quality and proportional quantity in the analysed building after allowing for the demountable partitioning to the office areas which is not required. (Again at this stage we have made allowance for the increases in internal wall heights due to the increase in storey height.) We calculate what the total cost per m^2 gfa would have been for internal walls and partitions in the analysed building if it had not provided demountable office partitions, adjust for increased height, then update to obtain a realistic cost per m^2 for our project.

Total cost of internal walls and partitions in cost analysis $= £26\,295$

Less

$$\text{Demountable partitions} = \underline{£14\,040}$$
$$\overline{£12\,255}$$
$$£12\,255 \times 125\% = £15\,319$$
$$\frac{£15\,319}{1408\,\text{m}^2 \text{ (gfa in analysis)}} = £10.88\,\text{per m}^2$$

Update and adjust for location:

$$£10.88 \times 1.15 \; (AF) = £12.51 \text{ per m}^2 \text{ gfa}$$

(h) Internal doors

We decide that we can adopt the quality and proportional quantity in the analysed building.

$$\text{Cost per m}^2 \text{ gfa} = £5.87$$

Update and adjust for location:

$$£5.87 \times 1.15 \; (AF) = £6.75 \text{ per m}^2 \text{ gfa}$$

OP

We must now add these eight allowances to obtain our allowance for the superstructure.

Element	£ per m^2
(a) Frame	60.00
(b) Upper floors	24.64
(c) Roof	34.80
(d) Stairs	20.50
(e) External walls	46.86
(f) Windows and external doors	34.03
(g) Internal walls and partitions	12.51
(h) Internal doors	6.75
Total allowance for superstructure	**240.09 per m^2**

Internal finishes

The choices and standards of internal finishes for the analysed building are set out in the specification and design notes. Apart from one or two exceptions, these are quite suitable for the new project. So we will accept the analysis figure after adjusting for the supply of carpet tiles and allowing for an increase in the quantity of wall finishes and quality of the ceiling finishes. After checking the current rates again there is no reason to change the allowances made during the feasibility stage. So we will add £9.60 per m^2 gfa for the carpet tiles, and £12.91 per m^2 gfa for upgrading the ceiling finishes. We use the same approach as at feasibility stage to allow for the change in the ratio of windows to external walls. Thus, we add £6.72 for the increased quantities of wall finishes.

From the analysis,

		£ per m^2
Current cost of internal finishes = £73.43 × 1.15 (AF)	=	84.44
Increased quantity of wall finishes = £6.72 × 1.15 (AF)	=	7.73

Add allowance (all at current rates) for:

Supply of carpet tiles	=	9.60
Suspended ceiling finishes		12.91
		£114.68 per m^2

Fittings

We require very few fittings in our project since these will be mainly the tenants' responsibility. After inspection, we decide to keep the same rate of £7.24 per m^2 gfa as in the analysis.

Update and adjust for location:

£7.24 × 1.15 = **£8.33 per m^2**

OP

Services

At feasibility stage we based our estimate for services on the figure contained in the cost analysis. We added 5% to the rate as an allowance for the extra vertical pipe runs associated with the increase in storey height. In addition we also included the costs for the lift installations together with the extra builders' work in connection with the lifts.

No other design decisions have been made during outline proposals which make the feasibility allowances for these items invalid (see pages 234 and 238). We will use the same allowances here.

From the analysis,

	£ per m^2
Cost of services	= 227.80

Add:

Extra vertical pipe runs	11.39
	239.19
$AF \times 1.15$	= 275.07
Allowance for lift installation	= 26.67
Builder's work in connection with lifts	= 1.42
	£303.16 per m^2

External works

From our original assessment used at the feasibility stage, we decide that the allowance for external works can remain unaltered. (We are obviously ignoring any slight increase, which may have occurred since we prepared this first estimate.)

$$\frac{£180\,000}{2250\,\text{m}^2} = £80.00\,\text{per m}^2$$

Preliminaries and contingencies

After due consideration, we decide that we can allow for preliminaries and contingencies at the same rates as we chose at feasibility (i.e. 10% and 1.5% of the remainder of the outline cost plan).

OP

Summary – Outline cost plan

	£ per m^2	
Substructure	24.64	
Superstructure	240.09	
Internal finishes	114.68	
Fittings	8.33	
Services	303.16	
External works	80.00	770.90

Add		
Preliminaries (10%)		77.09
Contingencies (1.5%)		11.56
		859.55

Add		
Reserve against unforeseen design eventualities (2.5%)		21.49
Reserve against price rises from September 1995		
to September 1996 (4.5%)		38.68
Total		**£919.72 per m^2**

£919.72 × 2250 m^2 = £2 069 370.00

(as at anticipated tender date of September 1996)

The design team note how close it is to the feasibility stage estimate of £2 100 000, and accordingly report no change to the client, confirming that the cost limit still holds good.

SD Scheme design stage (November 1995)

It is assumed that the client accepted the first estimate between feasibility and outline proposals: we therefore regard our first estimate (£2 100 000) as being the cost limit for the project. During the outline proposals stage, we prepared our outline cost plan showing the major cost allocations and confirmed that the cost limit was reasonable.

We will now prepare our detailed cost plan. This will show how we propose to distribute expenditure among all the elements of the project. It should be remembered that this cost plan is a reflection of the client's needs and the design team's choice of standards and specification. Another client or a different design team might produce a very different cost plan.

Another design team may choose to differ from us in the choice of method for preparing cost targets for each element. Consultants may prefer to use approximate quantities or inspection where we use simple proportion, and vice versa. This is not a matter of great importance, as long as we achieve our objective of producing a cost plan which allocates the available money in such a way that the design team's wishes are satisfied. That is, sufficient money is allocated to each element to enable the desired standards to be achieved.

The information available at this stage includes:

(1) Report produced at the end of the outline proposals stage, together with the outline cost plan.
(2) Design criteria and complete brief (not included here but assumed).
(3) Scheme design drawings included in Appendix B. In reality these drawings would be produced during this period and more information than included here would be available.
(4) The measures of quantity (element unit quantity) calculated from these drawings (see next page).
(5) A record of all the decisions made to date between client and design team.

Although difficult to convey in book form such as this, you should be aware that design and project information increases as the design develops. Thus the measured quantities can be reasonably accurate, although not yet to the stage of detailed measurement. The figures are therefore a reflection of this increase in information.

We shall adopt the same procedure as at the outline proposals stage and assume that the design information produced during scheme design has all been assembled before we start to prepare the cost plan.

SD

Table 11.2 Measurement of quantity for the detailed cost plan

Gross floor area	2246 m^2
Area of ground floor slab	749 m^2
Area of upper floors	1498 m^2
Area of roof (sloping area)	957 m^2
No. of flights of stairs (internal stairs)	12
No. of external fire escape stairs	2
Area of external walls	1328 m^2
Area of windows	213 m^2
Area of external doors	12 m^2
Number of single internal doors	30
Number of double internal doors	6
Area of floor finishes	1994 m^2
Area of ceiling finishes	1983 m^2
No. of sanitary fittings	62

To save space, the table includes only the 'quantities' required for the elements whose cost targets are prepared by simple proportion

Reserve for price and design risk

Our first action in allocating the cost limit is to reconsider the reserve against price and design risk.

Perhaps the most important of these is the probability that prices will rise between the preparation of the cost plan and receipt of tender. We review our prediction made at outline proposals stage (September 1995). This was based on the published indices, particularly the Tender Price Index (TPI) and forecast, modified by our professional judgement. Less than three months have passed since we last looked at this and no change has been noted. We will therefore maintain our allowance of 4.5% for tender price rises, that is, from November 1995 to September 1996.

We now turn our attention to the design risk element. The design has advanced since the outline cost plan was prepared and several of the major questions then outstanding have now been settled. However, important design questions are still outstanding which will be addressed during the detailed design stage. As a result, we decide that the allowance of 2.5% included at outline proposal stage should remain. Thus,

total reserve for price and design risk = 7%

The allowance included at the outline proposals stage was £60.17 per m^2 of gfa. This figure can be used as a guide when allocating costs between elements. The actual amounts we will include for price and design risk can be calculated later on our summary sheet.

We will now consider preliminaries and contingencies. When we have made allowances for these two important elements, we can consider the remainder of the elements in the normal order as indicated by our analysis (Appendix A).

Element 7   Preliminaries (including insurances)

The likely duration of the project and specific requirements for site staff, site accommodation, mechanical plant (particularly cranes), insurances, and the like should be considered at this point. Preliminaries in the analysed building when expressed as a percentage of remainder of contract sum (less contingencies) is 9.5%. We decide that the building analysed and our project are reasonably similar and consider that it is not necessary to make any alterations to the percentage allowed at the feasibility stage.

Following from this we assume that, since the percentage in the analysis appears reasonable, it is likely that none of the costs usually included in preliminaries have been distributed among the other elements. Similarly, after inspection of the analysis, we conclude that the contractor's profit has been spread evenly throughout the tender and is not loaded unevenly upon one or more elements. Therefore, if we adopt a similar percentage we can operate directly on all the other element costs in the analysis, safe in the assumption that they include profits, but exclude all the costs which properly belong to preliminaries.

Because of this, we will adopt the same allowance used in the outline cost plan (i.e. 10% or £77.09 per m^2).

Total allowance for preliminaries $= £77.09 \times 2246 = £173\,144$

	Total	Cost per m^2 gfa
Cost target for preliminaries	**£173 144**	£77.09

(*Note:* As we have used a percentage to calculate this element, we can anticipate that this cost target may change slightly when we calculate our final summary sheet.)

Contingencies

It is also convenient to consider contingencies at this point. In view of the straightforward nature of this project and this site, we recommend (and the client accepts) the allowance which we made during outline proposals (i.e. £11.56 per m^2).

Total allowance for contingencies $= £11.56 \times 2246 = £25\,964$
Round off to say $£26\,000$

Cost per m^2 will therefore be

$$\frac{£26\,000}{2246} = £11.58$$

	Total	Cost per m^2 gfa
Cost target for contingencies	**£26 000**	**£11.58**

Element 1   Substructures

A comparison of the quantities and the design criteria for the analysed building and our project reveals the following significant differences:

- ❏ our project is three storeys high whereas the other was only two storeys;
- ❏ both buildings have structural steel frames, although the new project also has a significant amount of traditional brick external walling, built off a strip foundation;
- ❏ the number of column bases is greater in our proposed project than that given in the analysis
- ❏ the ground conditions for the analysed building were more difficult than for our project.

The structural engineer is of the opinion that, given the amount of external walling and when the different ground conditions are taken into account, economies could be incorporated into the design of the frame. We are satisfied that these economies will offset, to some degree, the increased number of column bases. It seems likely that the design costs for the two projects will be very similar. We decide, therefore, to deal with this element by simple proportions rather than resorting to approximate quantities.

Adjustment for Price
Adjustment Factor (*AF*)
Index at analysis tender date   106
Index at preparation of cost plan   130
Location factor for Reading (analysed building)   1.00
Location factor for Portsmouth (new project)   0.94

$$AF = \frac{130}{106} \times \frac{0.94}{1.00} = 1.15283 \quad \text{say} \quad 1.15 \quad \text{(as before)}$$

Update element unit rate and adjust it for location:

$£64.27 \times 1.15 = £73.91 \text{ per m}^2$

Adjustment for Quantity
Current element unit rate $= £73.91 \text{ per m}^2$
Quantity (from scheme design drawings) $= 749 \text{ m}^2$

$$749 \times £73.91 = £55\,359$$

Reduce to the common yardstick of cost per m² gfa:

$$\frac{£55\,359}{2246 \text{ m}^2} = £24.65 \text{ per m}^2$$

(*Note:* The index for November 1995 (date of this detailed cost plan) has not changed from the index of September 1995 (date of outline proposal stage), indicating that tender prices have remained relatively stable over this period.)

Adjustment for Quality

We will make no adjustment for quality because of our assumption that the additional column bases will be offset by the saving that should result from improved ground conditions.

(*Note:* This assumption must be confirmed early in the cost checking process. At this point in time we are confident that any possible increases in price can be covered by the design risk reserves. If the differences between the analysis and the project had been more complex, we would have prepared this cost target by approximate quantities.)

	Total	Cost per m^2 gfa
Cost target for substructures	£55 359*	£24.65*

* Small discrepancies will appear due to the approximations made in conversions to cost per m^2 of gfa (i.e. £24.65 × 2246 m^2 = £55 364). These are ignored here and on the summary when preparing the cost plan.

Element 2A Frame

The analysed project has a traditional steel frame, supporting lightweight suspended floors on steel decking. The frame for our design is also traditional, but we have an extra floor and the storey heights are increased to accommodate suspended ceilings and raised floors. Also, as identified under substructure, there is a large increase in the number of columns. In addition it is thought likely that the specification for the upper floors will be changed to precast pre-stressed composite floors with in situ concrete topping (allowed for in the upper floors element).

These changes rule out adjustment by simple proportion and the nature of our frame rules out inspection, so we use approximate quantities. We show below the summary only, as the detailed dimensions are too lengthy to include here.

Summary
Fabricated structural steel framing (Grade 50C)

	Amount	Cost per unit	Total
Columns including connections	84 t	£900	£75 600
Beams including connections	18 t	£1000	£18 000
Roof trusses	13 t	£1250	£16 250
Bases, including wedges and anchorage	38	£250	£9 500
Erection	122 t	£150	£18 300
Treatment	122 t	£85	£10 370
			£148 020
Sundries 5%			£7 401
Total			£155 421

Reduce to cost per m^2 gfa:

$$\frac{£155\,421}{2246\,m^2} = £69.20\,per\,m^2$$

(*Note:* Another element requiring confirmation early in the cost checking process.)

	Total	Cost per m^2 gfa
Cost target for frame	**£155 421**	**£69.20**

Element 2B Upper floors

As explained when discussing the frame, the design of the analysed building and our new building are not alike.

The dissimilarity rules out simple proportion and the nature of the task rules out inspection, so again we use approximate quantities. This gives us a sum of £67 410. (The details of the calculations are too lengthy to include here.)

Cost per m^2 gfa:

$$\frac{£67\,410}{2246\,m^2} = £30.01\,per\,m^2$$

	Total	Cost per m^2 gfa
Cost target for upper floors	**£67 410**	**£30.01**

(*Note:* Our estimated cost targets for the last two elements, frame and upper floors, have increased significantly from the allowances made at outline proposals stage. If these increases are not balanced out by the estimated costs of the following elements then our cost limit will be exceeded. This will then entail a major review by the design team before reporting any findings to the client.)

Element 2C Roof

There appears to be many similarities between our new project and the analysed building, so we decide to use the simple proportion method to prepare our cost target.

Adjustment for Price

Element unit rate from analysis $= £71.66$ per m^2
Current element unit rate including adjusting for location, i.e.

$$£71.66 \text{ per m}^2 \times 1.15 = £82.41 \text{ per m}^2$$

Adjustment for Quantity

Quantity (from drawings) $= 957 \text{ m}^2$
Total element cost is 957 m^2 @ £82.41 per m^2 $= £78\,866$

Cost per m^2 gfa:

$$\frac{£78\,866}{2246 \text{ m}^2} = £35.11 \text{ per m}^2$$

Adjustment for Quality

The structural steelwork in the roof has been included with element 2A (frame). This was also the approach adopted for the cost analysis. With regard to quality we need therefore to consider the coverings. The design team confirm that artificial slates, as used in the analysed building, are an adequate solution.

Therefore, we do not need to make any adjustments for quality.

	Total	Cost per m^2 gfa
Cost target for roof	£78 866	£35.11

Element 2D   Stairs

No major change in design is envisaged, so we should obviously investigate the possibility of using simple proportion. No element unit rate is given in the analysis (see Appendix A). However, very often it is possible to use the reasonable assumption that the cost of a staircase is proportional to the number of flights (provided they are of the same size and quality).

The concrete staircase in the analysed building has two flights per staircase per floor plus a half landing (a total of four flights for the building). In the new project there are three flights per floor with two quarter space landings (a total of twelve flights for the building). Bearing in mind the additional storey height, this appears reasonable and suggests the flights on average might be of a reasonably similar size. We cannot apply the same approach for the escape stairs but the overall proportions do not seem too dissimilar. We therefore decide to make our adjustment based on number of flights and applied to the total element costs as if staircases were of a similar pattern and all constructed in concrete.

Adjustment for Price
Update element total cost and adjust for location:

$$£15\,758 \times 1.15 = £18\,122$$

Adjustment for Quantity
In the ratio of 12 : 4 (as explained above)

$$£18\,122 \times \frac{12}{4} = £54\,366$$

Cost per m² gfa:

$$\frac{£54\,366}{2246\,\text{m}^2} = £24.21 \text{ per m}^2$$

Adjust for Quality

The design team have indicated that they would prefer a better quality handrail and balustrade. We could attempt to evaluate such improvements by deciding on a particular specification for the balustrade (e.g. stainless steel and plate glass) and price this by approximate quantities. Alternatively, we could decide to increase the allowance for stairs by a certain percentage and to explore during the detail design stage exactly what detailed specification of balustrade we can afford. We will use this latter method. Bearing in mind the cost limit and the requirement of other elements, we decide to increase the allowance by 15% to improve the standard.

Former allowance $= £54366$

Add increase of 15%:

$115\% \times £54366 = £62521$

Cost per m^2 gfa:

$$\frac{£62521}{2246\,\text{m}^2} = £27.84\,\text{per m}^2$$

	Total	Cost per m^2 gfa
Cost target for stairs	**£62 521**	**£27.84**

Element 2E   External walls

The elements 2E (external walls) and 2F (windows and external doors) are examined together. This reveals that the quantities shown in the analysis are very different to our new project. The differences are mainly due to increases in the storey heights and changes in the ratio of windows to walling. Changes in specification are also noticeable. Double glazed units are likely to be used for windows in the new project. Although brickwork in the new project is generally less intricate, brick arches have now been used as a design feature over all ground floor window and door openings.

Therefore, it is apparent that adjustment by proportion is not an appropriate technique: we shall resort to approximate quantities based upon an assumed specification for both these elements. We shall assume that a reasonably high quality external facing brick will be required and therefore allow a prime cost of £525 per 1000 in our rate build up. In all other respects the external wall details will be of a normal standard for this type of project (blockwork inner skins and insulated cavities). The area of external walls as measured from drawings is $1328\,m^2$.

In summary, the approximate quantities calculations are as follows:

$1328\,m^2$ of external walls @ £77.50 = £102 920

Cost per m^2 gfa:

$$\frac{£102\,920}{2246\,m^2} = £45.82\,per\,m^2$$

	Total	Cost per m^2 gfa
Cost target for external walls	**£102 920**	**£45.82**

Element 2F Windows and external doors

As previously decided, we will use approximate quantities to adjust this element. (The details of the calculations are too lengthy to include here.)

Summary of the approximate quantities calculations are:

213 m^2 of windows and external doors @ £325 = £69 225

Reduce to cost per m^2 gfa:

$$\frac{£69\,225}{2246\,m^2} = £30.82\,per\,m^2$$

	Total	Cost per m^2 gfa
Cost target for windows and external doors	£69 225	£30.82

Element 2G   Internal walls and partitions

The building analysed included costs for demountable partitions. In our project most of the partitioning is left as the tenant's responsibility. In addition, our standards are somewhat different and the increased storey heights must be taken into account: we therefore decide to use the approximate quantities technique.

73 m² of 100 mm blockwork partition @ £21.00	=	£1533
255 m² of 200 mm blockwork partition @ £32.00	=	£8160
77 m² of 112.5 mm common brick internal walls @ £23.00	=	£1771
18 WC cubicles @ £330	=	£5940
		£17 404

Cost per m² gfa:

$$\frac{£17\,404}{2246\,\text{m}^2} = £7.75 \text{ per m}^2$$

	Total	Cost per m² gfa
Cost target for internal walls and partitions	**£17 404**	**£7.75**

Element 2H Internal doors

The offices in the building analysed were fitted with similar specification flush doors. However, the proportion of single to double flush doors will be different to our project. Because of this, we cannot adopt the element unit rate from the analysis. However, since we envisage that similar types of door will be used, we can adopt the all-in unit rates (see Appendix A) for the flush doors.

Adjustment for Price
All-in unit rates from analysis are:
flush doors, including perimeter treatments, e.g. lintels, linings/frames, ironmongery, decorations, etc.

    single doors   = £240 each
    double doors   = £395 each

Updated all-in unit rates, adjusted AF

    single doors   £240 × 1.15 = £276 each
    double doors   £395 × 1.15 = £454 each

Adjustment for Quantity
The number of single and double doors, measured from the scheme design drawings, are

    single doors = 30 nr
    double doors = 6 nr

    cost of single doors = £276 × 30 = £8 280
    cost of double doors = £454 × 6   = $\underline{£2\,724}$
                                         £11 004

Cost per m^2 gfa:

$$\frac{£11\,004}{2246\,\text{m}^2} = £4.90\,\text{per m}^2$$

Adjustment for Quality
Both the fire resistance standards of the internal doors and the quality of the doors and linings in the analysis are satisfactory for our project, so no adjustment is made for quality.

	Total	Cost per m^2 gfa
Cost target for internal doors	£11 004	£4.90

Element 3A   Wall finishes

We decide that it is best to use approximate quantities based upon an assumed specification of plastered walls, with glazed tiles in the lavatory areas.

1689 m² of plaster and emulsion paint @ £15.00   = £25 335
220 m² of plaster and fabric wall covering @ £27.00   = £5 940
242 m² of glazed tiling @ £55.00   = £13 310
                                                         £44 585

Cost per m² gfa:

$$\frac{£44\,585}{2246\,m^2} = £19.85 \text{ per } m^2$$

	Total	Cost per m² gfa
Cost target for wall finishes	**£44 585**	**£19.85**

(*Note:* This does not commit us to final use of this specification, but simply to using one of a similar general quality. At this stage, we are making a reasonable allowance within which wall finishes of the desired quality can be designed during the detail design stage.)

Element 3B   Floor finishes

Office floors in the analysed building are raised access with carpet tiles. The quality of the existing access floor is considered appropriate for our design. There must be an allowance for the carpet tiles, which in the analysed building were supplied free of charge from the client. The design team have indicated that a carpet tile of medium quality would be appropriate (current costs are about £13.00 per m^2); we find the rate used for the feasibility estimate still holds good.

We can use simple proportion for this element. However, remember that the carpet tiles do not cover the whole floor area. Therefore, we cannot just add the £13.00 per m^2 to the updated element unit rate. Instead we shall calculate what the total element cost would be if a building of exactly the same design as the analysed building were to be built now, with carpet tiles supplied and laid as floor finishes. From this we can find the element unit rate for the hypothetical building to use for our project. This approach assumes that our area of access floors with carpeted floor finish will be the same proportion of the total floor finishes areas as in the analysed building.

Adjustment for Price

Total element cost in analysis	£64 650
Updated element cost, adjusted for location £64 650 × 1.15	£74 348

Adjustment for Quality

Area covered by carpet in analysis is 1040 m^2, add for supply @ £13.00 per m^2	£13 520
Current cost of the element as specified in the analysis, plus supply of carpet	£87 868

Adjustment for Quantity

Total area of floor finishes in analysis   = 1301 m^2
Total area of floor finishes in our project = 1994 m^2

$$\text{Our total element cost} = \frac{£87\,868 \times 1994}{1301} = £134\,672$$

Cost per m^2 gfa:

$$\frac{£134\,672}{2246\,\text{m}^2} = £59.96 \text{ per m}^2$$

	Total	Cost per m^2 gfa
Cost target for floor finishes	**£134 672**	**£59.96**

Element 3C   Ceiling finishes

Plasterboard and skim coat on timber framing has been used throughout the analysed building. For the proposed project, acoustic tiles in a suspended metal grid are required for the office areas. Plasterboard and skim will be used for toilet areas.

Preliminary studies indicate that we can expect to obtain a high quality suspended ceiling for £34.30 per m^2. An appropriate rate for plasterboard and skim on softwood framing would be £16.78 per m^2. These rates are slightly higher than those considered at feasibility stage.

Area of ceiling finishes (from drawings) is
1888 m^2 suspended ceiling @ £34.30   = £64 758
95 m^2 plasterboard and skim @ £16.78 = £1 594
                                           £66 352

Cost per m^2 gfa:

$$\frac{£66\,352}{2246\,m^2} = £29.54 \text{ per } m^2$$

	Total	Cost per m^2 gfa
Cost target for ceiling finishes	**£66 352**	**£29.54**

Element 4A   Fittings and furnishings

This is not a major element of the project. Therefore the technique of inspection is used, for which we obtain a selection of suitable cost analyses to give us a range of element costs. This range is studied in conjunction with available information before making a final choice. We know that all the office fittings will be supplied by the tenant, so no provision need be made for these. However, it is prudent to make a small allowance for minor items, such as shelving, pinboards, mirrors, handicap toilet grab rails, signs, and perhaps louvre blinds, as was the case with the analysed building. After studying our range of costs we decide that a sum of £20 000 will be allowed for fittings.

Cost per m^2 gfa:

$$\frac{£20\,000}{2246\,m^2} = £8.90 \text{ per } m^2$$

	Total	Cost per m^2 gfa
Cost target for fittings and furnishings	£20 000	£8.90

Element 5A   Sanitary appliances

This element may be handled by any of the three techniques, but we shall use approximate quantities.

18 no. low level WCs @ £230	=	£4140
12 no. suspended urinals @ £200	=	£2400
26 no. lavatory basins @ £180	=	£4680
6 no. cleaners' sinks @ £220	=	£1320
Short connections and overflows	=	£1820
		£14 360

Reduce to cost per m^2:

$$\frac{£14\,360}{2246\,\text{m}^2} = £6.39 \text{ per m}^2$$

	Total	Cost per m^2 gfa
Cost target for sanitary appliances	**£14 360**	**£6.39**

Note: It is interesting to compare the target cost of £14 360 with the sum obtained by simple proportion, making the Quantity and Price adjustments, (and ignoring any Quality adjustment), using element unit quantities based on the number of fittings in the analysis and in the new project:

Update element cost and adjust it for location:

£8110 × 1.15 (*AF*) = £9327

Adjustment for Quantity

$$\frac{£9327 \times 62}{38} = £15\,218$$

The outcome is obviously dependent on there being some relationship between the number of fittings required per m^2 of floor space, the type and the quality. Fundamentally it comes down to considering possible relationships between the planning parameters and occupants' requirements. For instance, office floor space will vary from between say 6 m^2 per person and 20 m^2 per person, depending on whether the design is for a high-density open-plan layout or a low-density cellular layout.

Element 5C   Disposal installations

An unimportant element in this project which is best decided by inspection. (Approximate quantities could also be used if the money involved justifies the time required for measurement.)

The environmental services in our project are located in close proximity around staircase areas, thus reasonably short horizontal pipe runs can be expected. We need to remember that increased storey heights reflect the incorporation of suspended ceilings and raised floors in our design. These points must be considered when inspecting similar cost analyses and other data sources.

The costs of disposal installations in existing offices are as follows:

Building	Tender date	Preliminaries (%)	Cost of disposal installations ($£/m^2$ gfa)
2-storey offices *Winchester*	March 1991	10.27	3.50
4-storey offices *Manchester*	February 1993	7.66	4.86
2-storey offices *Slough*	January 1993	8.79	4.01
2-storey offices *Reading*	September 1992	9.5	3.89

Making approximate adjustments for the differences in the preliminaries percentages and the tender dates of these projects, we decide to adopt an allowance of £4.75 per m^2 for the element which includes for builder's work to pipe ducts.

Total element allowance = £4.75 × 2246 m^2 = £10 669

	Total	Cost per m^2 gfa
Cost target for disposal installations	£10 669	£4.75

Element 5D   Water installations

Mains supply, cold-water services and hot-water services must all be considered with this element. The mains supply from point of entry up to storage tanks in the roof space will be similar to that in the cost analysis (apart from vertical pipe runs). For cold and hot services the main differences between our project and the analysed building will be in the distribution runs. These are governed by the number and location of draw-off points. For hot water provision we will assume local water heaters, similar to those provided in the analysed building.

Following on from the discussion concerning sanitary appliances (element 5A), it can be seen that the ratio of draw-off points to gross floor area is not dissimilar in the analysis and our project. However, we know that due to the change in storey heights the lengths of vertical pipe runs must increase. So we will provisionally adopt the figure given in the analysis for the cost of this element per m^2 gfa, increasing it slightly to cover the extra pipework. We will adopt an allowance of £20.50 per m^2.

Update the rate and adjust it for location
= £20.50 × 1.15 (AF) = £23.58 per m^2

We decide to check that £23.58 per m^2 is a reasonable figure for our project by inspecting several other analyses. We encounter difficulties when we do this for in many analyses this element has been grouped together with several others and no detailed breakdown is available. However, our in-house data sources confirm that our proposed rate per m^2 can be taken as an average figure for office blocks.

Total allowance for element = £23.58 × 2246 m^2 = £52 961

	Total	Cost per m^2 gfa
Cost target for water installations	**£52 961**	**£23.58**

Element 5E   Heat source, Element 5F   Space heating and air treatment

We decide to take these two elements together. The heating and ventilation engineers provide us with an estimate based on the available early design information and the likely heat requirements. This is done by using a combination of approximate quantities and inspection. The engineers estimate the total cost for these two elements at £345 000. This equates to £153.61 per m^2 gfa.

Since the requirements of the new project are similar to the analysed building, we compare this figure with that shown in the analysis. The updated rate in the analysis is £151.17 per m^2 (£131.45 × 1.15). Accordingly we are reassured and adopt their estimate.

	Total	Cost per m^2 gfa
Cost target for heat source and space heating and air treatment	**£345 000**	**£153.61**

(*Note:* There would be considerable discussion between the consulting engineer and the cost consultant regarding the formulation of the budget for the element, however an estimate is required. Until the design has been well developed, it is difficult for the engineer to complete the design for the services. It is beyond the scope of this book to deal with this in detail, but we suggest that once you have grasped the fundamental principles of cost planning that you read up further on this topic.)

Element 5H   Electrical installations

The information technology revolution, the advent of sophisticated micro-electronic controls for equipment and the need for more electrical power in a building, has meant an increase in the importance of the electrical installation. Finding suitable measures of quantity for all the elements in group 5 can be difficult. Electrical installations is no exception. For example, expressing the costs of this element in terms of cost per m^2 gfa, will not be entirely satisfactory. One method using approximate quantities is to measure the number of outlet points and then apply a rate per point. These rates will change depending on the design and it is usual to state the type of cables and conduits, indicating whether exposed or concealed. This approach has been quite successful with the smaller installations, particularly residential, but less successful with the larger schemes and other building types. We are therefore frequently forced to rely upon inspection for the selection of a cost target. Fortunately cost data exist and can be used to create a range upon which to base our decision.

After discussions with the electrical services engineers we establish that the lighting standard of the building analysed provides suitable levels of illumination for office accommodation. In addition, the provision of power points also appears to match our own requirements. There is a good case for simply updating the cost analysis figure of £57.33 per m^2 gfa. However, before we do this we will add 5% to the rate to give a modest increase to cover extra runs due to increased storey height. Thus

£57.33 × 105% = £60.20

Update the rate and adjust it for location = £60.20 × 1.15 (AF) = £69.23

Total element cost = £69.23 × 2246 m^2 = £155 491

	Total	Cost per m^2 gfa
Cost target for electrical installations	**£155 491**	**£69.23**

Element 5J Lift installations

There is no lift in the building analysed but for our project the design team, in discussions with the client, have decided that lifts are essential.

This kind of requirement is best met by an enquiry to lift manufacturers and installers. As a result we choose an allowance of £65 000. This is slightly higher than the rate used for the feasibility estimate but the design team have indicated that they wish to raise the specification for the lift cars.

Reduce to cost per m^2:

$$\frac{£65\,000}{2246\,m^2} = £28.94 \text{ per } m^2$$

	Total	Cost per m^2 gfa
Cost target for lift installations	£65 000	£28.94

Element 5K Protective installations

The requirements are for fire-fighting installations and lightning installations which are best decided by inspection.

We decide on an element allowance of £3.50.

Total element allowance = £3.50 × 2246 m^2 = £7861

	Total	Cost per m^2 gfa
Cost target for protective installations	£7861	£3.50

Element 5L Communication installations,
Element 5M Special installations

The tenant will be dealing with all items under these elements including security alarms and all installations in connection with information technology. Therefore no allowance is required.

Element 5N Builder's work in connection with services,
Element 5O Builder's profit and attendance on services

A difficult cost target to assess, but best decided by inspection. A number of analyses indicate that the rate included in our analysis is a reasonable sum, but it does not include the work in connection with the lift installation.

We decide to use the figure in the analysis, update it and include the addition for lifts. When we do this we arrive at a rate of £13.21 (£11.79 + £1.42).

Total allowance for element = £13.21 × 2246 m^2 = £29 670

	Total	Cost per m^2 gfa
Cost target for builder's work in connection with services and builder's profit and attendance on services	£29 670	£13.21

Element 6A   Site works

Approximate quantities suggest that an allowance of £118 000 would be realistic. We have not included all the calculation for this element, but it would not be wise to use any other method than measurement.

Reduce to cost per m^2:

$$\frac{£118\,000}{2246\,m^2} = £52.54 \text{ per } m^2$$

	Total	Cost per m^2 gfa
Cost target for site works	£118 000	£52.54

Element 6B   Drainage

Note that this element includes all drainage works outside the building up to and including disposal point, which means connection to the sewer in the public highway.

Adjustment via simple proportion and inspection is rarely appropriate for this element. Therefore, approximate quantities have been used and indicate an allowance of £56 000, following a discussion with the water company who is responsible for the main drainage beyond the site boundary. They have given an approximate depth of the sewer in the road. Some surface-water drainage may be via soakways within the boundary of the site.

Cost per m^2:

$$\frac{£56\,000}{2246\,m^2} = £24.93 \text{ per } m^2$$

	Total	Cost per m^2 gfa
Cost target for drainage	£56 000	£24.93

Element 6C   External services

Approximate quantities suggest that an allowance of £16 000 would be realistic.

Cost per m^2:

$$\frac{£16\,000}{2246\,m^2} = £7.12 \text{ per } m^2$$

	Total	Cost per m^2 gfa
Cost target for external services	£16 000	£7.12

Comment on preparation of cost plan

There are many differences between our new project and the chosen cost analysis. Therefore, we have had to use approximate quantities to set cost targets for many elements. This was done in full awareness of our previous discussion which stated that adjustment by simple proportion is preferred. Remember, using simple proportion automatically includes allowances for everything one needs for the element in the particular type of building considered. When using approximate quantities, on the other hand, extra care is required for it is easy to overlook details which will only be considered during the detail design stage.

Detailed cost plan

Summary

		Allowance	
Element		Total cost of element (£)	Cost per m² (£)
1	Substructures	55 359	24.65
2A	Frame	155 421	69.20
2B	Upper floors	67 410	30.01
2C	Roof	78 866	35.11
2D	Stairs	62 521	27.84
2E	External walls	102 920	45.82
2F	Windows and external doors	69 225	30.82
2G	Internal walls and partitions	17 404	7.75
2H	Internal doors	11 004	4.90
3A	Wall finishes	44 585	19.85
3B	Floor finishes	134 672	59.96
3C	Ceiling finishes	66 352	29.54
4A	Fittings and furnishings	20 000	8.90
5A	Sanitary appliances	14 360	6.39
5C	Disposal installations	10 669	4.75
5D	Water installations	52 961	23.58
5E	Heat source }	345 000	153.61
5F	Space heating and air treatment }		
5H	Electrical installations	155 491	69.23
5J	Lift installations	65 000	28.94
5K	Protective installations	7 861	3.50
5N	Builder's work – services }		
5O	Builder's profit and attendance on } services	29 670	13.21
6A	Site works	118 000	52.54
6B	Drainage	56 000	24.93
6C	External services	16 000	7.12
	Sub-total	**1 756 751**	**782.15**
Add	Preliminaries (10%)	175 675	78.22
Add	Contingencies (1.5% approx.)	26 000	11.58
	Sub-total	**1 958 426**	**871.95**
Add	Reserve against unforeseen design eventualities (2.5%)	48 961	21.80
	Reserve against price rises, November 1995 to September 1996 (4.5%)	88 129	39.24
	Grand total	**2 095 516**	**932.99**

As a rough check on our arithmetic,

$$£932.99 \times 2246\,m^2 = £2\,095\,496$$

This is close enough to £2 095 516 for us to rest assured that the discrepancy is due to the approximations made in the conversions to costs per m^2 during the preparation of the cost plan, as noted under element 1, substructures (page 258).

Chapter 11 – Summary

Our feasibility stage estimating, based simply on a statement of office requirements plus quality standards, car parking areas and site conditions, was £2 100 000.

At this stage, our cost plan is based on an expanded brief and the additional information as shown on the scheme design drawings. Changes are apparent in individual element totals but, overall, our cost plan total is more or less the same as our feasibility estimate. This indicates that we should be able to obtain a tender within the cost limit of £2 100 000.

Both the client and the design team have achieved the standards they require without undue restriction. There is no need to consider upgrading any of the allowances in the cost plan. If we suspected that some of the cost targets were too low, we could obviously make additions of up to £4484 at this stage. Further adjustments could be considered via trade-offs between elements, or early use of the design risk reserve.

The design team would, in these circumstances, confirm to the client that the feasibility stage estimate holds good and would go ahead with detailed design in the expectation of receiving a tender at the cost plan figure.

When the cost plan figure exceeds the feasibility and outline proposals stages estimates, the design team must examine the cost plan for all reasonable economies. Only when this has failed will they consider approaching the client for additional funds.

12 Cost Control during Detail Design Stage

This chapter *is* in programmed form and you must follow the page directions exactly.

Turn to page 284 ⟹

⊃ *from page 283*

The previous stages have all been concerned with *planning* both the design and the cost of the design. The detail design stage is the crucial stage in *controlling* the cost of the detailed design. At the end of this stage, the design team should have completed the detail design of the buildings, in accordance with both the scheme design drawings and the cost plan.

The principles of cost control during detail design were considered in Part 1. Here is a recap of those principles which are incorporated during this stage.

During the detail design stage there must be a method of checking and there must be a means of remedial action. That is, the detailed design of each element should be cost checked as soon as it is completed and remedial action should be taken if necessary.

Cost checking an element consists of estimating the probable cost of the element's detail design. It is generally accepted that the most accurate method of estimating is by approximate quantities based upon a detailed specification. Now that the full specification is available for each element, this accepted traditional technique can be used with confidence.

What prices should generally be used during cost checking?

    (a) **Prices appropriate to the date of preparation of the first estimate.**

    (b) **Prices appropriate to the date of preparation of the cost plan.**

    (c) **Prices appropriate to the date of cost checking.**

    (d) **Prices appropriate to the date of tender of the proposed building.**

Write down an answer from (a) to (d) above.

Turn to page 286 ⊃

from page 289

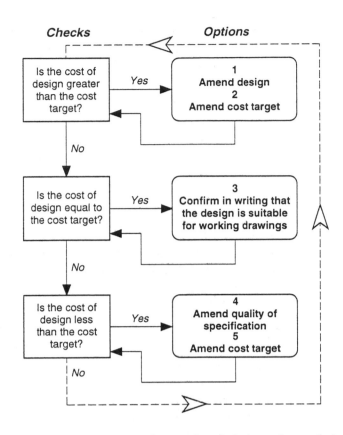

Checks   **Options**

Is the cost of design greater than the cost target?   *Yes* →

1 Amend design
2 Amend cost target

No

Is the cost of design equal to the cost target?   *Yes* →

3 Confirm in writing that the design is suitable for working drawings

No

Is the cost of design less than the cost target?   *Yes* →

4 Amend quality of specification
5 Amend cost target

No

Fig. 12.1

If the outline design and cost plan produced during scheme design are adhered to closely action '3' in Fig. 12.1 should follow the cost checking of most of the elements during detail design.

The usefulness of the cost plan depends for a large part on the cost targets being realistic. Cost targets should therefore only be altered as a last resort, after every alternative design solution for an element has been investigated and rejected as unsuitable. Nevertheless, cost targets may have to be altered as users' requirements become better understood.

If the cost target for an element has to be raised, what else should be done?

Write down your answer.

Turn to page 291

⊃ *from page* 284

(c) Prices appropriate to the date of cost checking.

These are certainly the most appropriate prices to use. They will give accurate cost checks provided you remember to update the element target costs from the cost plan which can be done by using an appropriate cost index.

If you chose

(b) Prices appropriate to the date of preparation of the cost plan.

You are not incorrect, for the prices employed in cost checking would then be appropriate to the date of preparation of the cost plan. However, in this case you would need to convert current costs back to the date of the cost plan. The reason for this is that the approximate quantities estimated from the detail design can only be compared directly with the cost target from the cost plan if the same price level is assumed for both.

Answers **(a)** and **(d)** are both inappropriate for reasons connected with price level and allowance made for design risk.

Write down the possible courses of remedial action which can be taken when cost checking shows that a cost target has been exceeded.

Turn to page 289 ⊃

from page 290

Preliminaries, contingencies, and price and design risk, but they must not be ignored.

These allowances cannot be checked in the same way as the others, but they should nevertheless be considered during detail design.

Preliminaries and contingencies can obviously be reviewed as the detailed design progresses, and any necessary changes made.

The price risk part of the price and design risk allowance would have to be changed if an unexpected change in any of the price level factors occurred during the detail design stage. The design risk part of this allowance is used to supply extra money to any of the elements which may run into trouble during the cost checking process.

When all the elements have been designed and all the allowances checked once, what should be done before leaving the detail design stage?

Write down your answer.

Turn to page 292

from page
291

(a) Would be done if any of the previously designed elements were running into trouble at the cost checking stage. If the cost of the design of the other elements were all nearly equal to their cost targets, this action may disturb the balanced design allowed for in the cost plan.

On the other hand, if there are many elements still to be designed and cost checked it may be a good idea to hold on to the savings as an extra 'design risk' allowance.

(b) In fact, all three actions would be 'correct' in different situations, but amending the design is probably the most frequent action taken.

The reason for this is that a cost plan attempts to achieve a balanced design; so increasing the quality of the specification of the element is more likely to give the client good value for money than 'returning' the savings to the client or distributing them among the other elements.

(c) If the design team is happy with the quality of the detail design, it would decide to 'return' the savings to the client.

However, being realistic, most design teams would not choose to do this, unless the detail design of elements is well advanced.

Summarise the basic cycle of operations which should occur during the detail design stage.

Turn to page 290

from page 286

There are two possible courses of remedial action:

> (1) **the design of the element can be altered in an attempt to bring its cost within the cost target, or,**
>
> (2) **as a last resort, the cost target for the element can be raised.**

The design team has the responsibility of ensuring a response to each cost check. There are three possible scenarios:

> (a) the cost of the design can be greater than the cost target,
> (b) the cost of the design can be equal to the cost target,
> (c) the cost of the design can be less than the cost target.

Bearing this in mind, write down brief descriptions of *all* the possible courses of action which may follow the cost check of an element.

Turn to page 285

from page 288

The basic cycle of operations during the detail design stage is:

(1) **Design.**
(2) **Approximate quantities estimate.**
(3) **Comparison with cost target.**
(4) **Decision and action.**

This cycle of operations is repeated until all the elements have been designed and cost checked.

Which of the allowances in a cost plan cannot be checked in this way?

Write down your answer.
(If necessary, refer to page 281 to see the detailed cost plan.)

Turn to page 287

⊃ *from page*
285

In order to avoid exceeding the cost limit, cost targets should be adjusted throughout the cost plan to release surplus funds for the element in trouble.

This highlights another disadvantage of altering a cost target: even if the overall cost limit is not exceeded, the distribution of the available money over the various parts of the building will have to be changed. The result of this may be reduced value for money compared with that envisaged during the preceding stages of the design process.

If the estimated cost of the detailed design of an element turns out to be significantly less than the cost target, what would be the most likely course of action?

(a) **The cost targets for the other elements should be amended to absorb the surplus funds.**

(b) **The quality of the specification of the element should be increased to bring the cost up to the cost target.**

(c) **The probable savings should be notified to the client.**

Write down your answer.

Turn to page 288 ⊃

⟲ *from page 287*

A final cost check is performed to make sure that nothing has been overlooked.

Notice that the drawings prepared during detail design need not be polished working drawings. These can simply be dimensioned sketches, provided that they contain all the information needed for accurate production drawings which will be prepared before other tender documents (including bills of quantities). Ideally, working drawings should not be prepared for any element until after the final cost check at the end of the detail design stage. It would be unwise to go to the expense of preparing working drawings for a design which may subsequently be changed.

We will now consider two of the refinements to the simplified account of cost checking.

Turn to page 293 ⟲

from page 292

The two refinements which we will consider are:

(1) the order in which the elements should be designed and cost checked so as to avoid unnecessary re-designing and re-checking,

(2) the best way to perform cost checking when the detail design is not produced one element at a time.

(1) The order in which elements should be designed

An itemised plan of work and timetable needs to be drawn up at the beginning of the detail design stage. This should set out the intended order in which the elements will be designed. This ensures that time spent during design is as productive as possible.

To draw up an effective cost plan, consideration must be given to the interactive nature of the design and cost planning processes. Imagine the implications where an element such as the frame is found to exceed its target cost, having been designed and cost checked too late in the programme.

There are three characteristics which would make it important to design an element early in the detail design stage. Do you know what they are?

Write down your thoughts.

Turn to page 296

from page 295

(2) The best way to perform cost checking when the detail design is not produced one element at a time

Suppose all the superstructure elements were designed concurrently and completed at the same time. If all the elements were then cost checked, it is possible that one of the important ones, such as the frame, may have over-shot its cost target. In this situation all of the superstructure elements may have to be re-designed.

Which of the following ways of dealing with this situation would you adopt?

(a) Always design element-by-element, and plan the order as previously discussed.

(b) Go ahead and re-design all the superstructure elements, hoping that the same situation did not happen too often.

(c) Cost check each element several times during the design of the group by costing the designed part of the element and adding an allowance for the part not yet designed.

Consider your answer.

Turn to page 299

from page *296*

Due to the importance of controlling the order in which elements are designed and cost checked, target dates should be set for:

(a) completion of each element's detail design;
(b) completion of each element's cost check;
(c) completion of the action following each cost check.

A lot of information will be circulating among the design team throughout the design process. This will be especially true if remedial action is necessary when any of the elements are cost checked. To avoid confusion between original and amended versions of any item, all cost checks, decisions, and alterations should be clearly communicated.

We will now go on to consider the second point mentioned on page 293.

Turn to page 294

from page 293

The three characteristics which make it desirable to design an element early in the detail design stage are:

(1) **Unreliable cost target.**
(2) **Large cost target (cost-significant element).**
(3) **A design which affects the design of other elements.**

The relative importance of these three characteristics varies from project to project. In general, the second one is less important than the other two (except when it is combined with one of the others).

In addition, the elements which exhibit each of these characteristics will also vary from project to project.

Turn to page 295

from pages 298, 299

The complications which we have discussed in the last few pages obviously make it essential to have a well-prepared plan of work for the detail design stage. Effective and frequent communication between members of the design team will be required.

Although the detail design stage is the crucial stage for 'cost control during building design', the techniques used are well-established and do not require as much discussion as those used during earlier stages.

A brief summary of the detail design cost control which we have discussed is given on page 300.

If you would like to write your own summary of this chapter, do so now, and compare it with ours.

Turn to page 300

from page 299

Although it may seem rather drawn out, the best solution is to cost check each complicated element several times during its detail design.

Example

Suppose elements A, B, C, and D were being designed concurrently. The first cost check could be performed when approximately a quarter of each element had been designed.

It is easy to prepare an approximate quantities estimate for the designed part of each element. The only slight difficulty arises when allocating allowances for parts of the elements not yet designed. The estimate plus the allowance for each element is then compared with the corresponding cost target, and action is taken.

This process is more involved (and possibly less accurate) than designing and checking one element at a time. Nevertheless it gives valuable information to the design team in time for the designs to be changed without undue trouble.

Turn to page 297

from page 294

(c) **Cost check each element several times during the design of the group by costing the designed part of the element and adding an allowance for the part not yet designed.**

Although it may be drawn out, the best solution is to cost check each complicated element several times during its detail design.

Answers **(a)** and **(b)** are both inappropriate.

In theory, **(a)** would be the easiest way of avoiding the problem. However, design teams do not design element-by-element; that is not the way the design process works. We must accept that there are often many practical difficulties which make it impossible to produce the detail design of a building in this 'ideal' way.

On the face of it, **(b)** seems to be the easy way out. In practice, however, design teams would find themselves having to do a lot of unnecessary work to regain control over costs if they adopted this method.

The only efficient way of maintaining control is to check at frequent intervals that the frame of reference is being adhered to.

If you would like to see further comment on
this point,   *Turn to page 298* ⊃

If you would prefer to continue,   *Turn to page 297* ⊃

⊃ *from page*
297

Summary – Cost control during detail design stage

(1) The latest stage at which each element must be cost checked is as soon as its design is completed.

(2) If several elements are designed concurrently, they should all be cost checked several times during their design.

(3) Whatever the result of a cost check, action must be taken.

(4) There should be a carefully prepared plan of work for the detail design stage.

(5) There should be frequent communications between the members of the design team.

(6) All communications should be recorded and dated.

You have now completed Part 2 of this programme.

To revise this part of the programme, answer the questions on page 301. The answers are given on pages 302–304.

Turn to page 301 ⊃

Part 2 Test

1 What is an elemental cost analysis?

2 Briefly describe four uses of elemental cost analyses.

3 What yardstick of cost is used in cost analyses?

4 List the major factors which affect the costs of elements, and discuss each of them briefly.

5 Define 'element unit rate', and give an example.

6 Explain how a first estimate is prepared by the interpolation method.

7 (a) Describe the cost allocations and allowances which are included in an outline cost plan.

    (b) Explain how they are prepared.

8 How does the cost planning performed during outline proposals differ from the cost planning during (a) feasibility, and (b) scheme design?

9 Name and describe three methods of preparing the cost target for an element.

10 Prepare a cost target for internal doors on the basis of the following information:
    Element unit rate in the analysis   = £145 per m^2
    Price level index at analysis tender date = 110
    'Current' price level index   = 120
    Total floor area of proposed building   = 2500 m^2
    Area of external doors in new project   = 112 m^2
    It is decided to deduct 10% to allow for a reduction in the quality of the external doors in the new project.

11 Describe the possible events which may follow the cost checking of an element.

12 Imagine a project with a cost limit of £750.00 per m^2. When half of the elements have been cost checked, the cost of the design is running at £11 per m^2 greater than the sum of the cost targets concerned. The cost check of the next element shows that it is £15 per m^2 over its cost target. What should be done?

13 List the considerations which should be borne in mind when deciding the order in which the detailed designs of the elements should be produced and checked.

Answers overleaf ⬅

301

Answers to Part 2 Test

Marks

1 An elemental cost analysis is the analysis of the client's costs (1)
on a tender to determine the cost of each element of (2)
a building.   **3**

2 *Appreciation:* to enable clients and designers to appreciate
how cost is distributed among the elements of a building. (1)
Judgement: to enable clients and designers to develop ideas (1)
as to how cost could have been allocated to obtain a
more balanced design. (1)
Belated remedial action: to allow remedial action to be taken on
receipt of high tenders by revealing the sources of
over-expenditure. (1)
Planning: to help with the cost planning of future projects. (1)
                                                                                                    5

3 Cost per m^2 of gross floor area.   **2**

4 *Quantity:* the amount of each element in the building; (1)
this is affected by both floor area and the 'density' of each
element. (1)
Quality: the quality of the materials used for an element (1)
and the relative proportions of the various qualities of
specification within the element. (1)
Price level: this covers general market price level, contractor's (1)
price level, site conditions, contract conditions, etc. (1)
                                                                                                    6

5 Element unit rate $= \dfrac{\text{cost of element}}{\text{quantity of element}}$ (2)

e.g. element unit rate for internal doors = £131.27 per m^2. (1)
                                                                                                    3

6 (a) A range of cost analyses of the same *type* of building
as the proposed building is assembled. (1)
(b) The cost analyses of the buildings whose *quality* (1)
approximates most closely to that desired by the client (1)
are selected from this range, (between 4 and 10). They
are then adjusted for time and location. (1)

Turn to page 303 ➲

Marks

(c) The major differences between the chosen analyses and   (1)
the new project are *isolated* by comparing the initial brief
of the proposed building with all of the information
given in the analyses.   (1)

(d) Allowances are made for each of these differences   (1)
(including floor area, site works, etc.).   (1)

(e) Additions are made for preliminaries and contingencies.   (1)
Then a reserve against design risk is included.   (1)

(f) An allowance is made as a reserve against price rises
between the preparation of the first estimate and the
contractor's actual price level on the tender.   (1)

11

7 (a) An allowance is made for 'price and design risk'   (1)
by assessing the cost of unforeseen design difficulties and (1)
possible price rises between the preparation of the outline
cost plan and the receipt of tender.   (1)

(b) Cost targets are prepared for each group of elements by
allowing for the major differences between the buildings   (1)
analysed and the new project, then updating to the date   (1)
of preparation of the outline cost plan. (The major   (1)
differences are allowed for by comparing all the
information available for both the new project and the
cost analyses.)

6

8 The differences which are isolated and allowed for are more
detailed than in feasibility, but less detailed than in scheme   (1)
design. The available money is allocated to the various parts   (1)
of the building during outline proposals, whereas no   (1)
allocation takes place at feasibility: this allocation is not as   (1)
detailed as in scheme design.

4

9 *Simple proportion:* The element cost selected from the cost   (1)
analyses chosen at feasibility is adjusted by proportion   (1)
for Price, Quantity, and Quality.   (1)
Inspection: The target cost per m^2 of floor is chosen from a   (1)
range obtained from a selection of suitable cost analyses   (2)
and/or cost studies.   (1)
Approximate quantities: A provisional specification of the
required quality is prepared for the element. Measurement   (2)
and pricing then proceeds using the approximate quantities   (2)
technique.   **11**

Turn to page 304 ⟩

Marks

10 *Adjustment for Price*

$$\text{'Current' element unit rate} = \frac{120}{110} \times £145.00 \text{ per m}^2$$

$$= £158.18 \text{ per m}^2 \qquad (2)$$

Adjustment for Quantity

$$112 \text{ m}^2 \times £158.18 = £17\,716 \qquad (2)$$

$$\text{Reduce to cost per m}^2 = \frac{£17\,716.16}{2500 \text{ m}^2} = £7.09 \text{ per m}^2 \qquad (2)$$

Adjustment for Quality

$$90\% \text{ of } £17\,716 = £15\,944$$

$$90\% \text{ of } £7.09 \text{ per m}^2 = £6.38 \text{ per m}^2 \qquad (3)$$

	Total	Cost per m^2
Cost target for internal doors	£15 944	£6.38

9

11 (a) If the cost of the design equals the cost target, the design
is confirmed in writing as being suitable for working
drawings. (2)

(b) If the cost of the design exceeds the cost target, the
design can be changed or, if this is impossible, the cost
target can be increased by borrowing from the other (2)
elements (1)

(c) If the cost of the design is less than the cost target,
the quality of the design can be increased, (1)
the savings can be distributed among the other elements, (1)
or the savings can be left as a saving for the client. (1)

8

12 Re-design, if possible, to come within cost target. **2**

13 (a) How much the design of the element affects the design
of other elements. (2)

(b) How unreliable the cost target is known to be (2)

(c) How large the cost target is relative to the others. (1)

5

TOTAL   **75**

Appendix A

Detailed Cost Analysis and Element Costs

BCIS On-line Analysis No. xxx

CI/SfB 320
Offices

DETAILED COST ANALYSIS

BCIS Code: A-2-1408

Job Title:	Office Units, Red Knights
Location:	Reading, Berkshire
Client:	Unipol Properties Ltd.
Date for receipt:	10 September 1992

Date of tender: September 1992

INFORMATION ON TOTAL PROJECT

Project details:

2 storey office block with self contained units on 2 floors with plant rooms in the roof voids together with external works including car parking, fencing, landscaping, services and drainage.

Site conditions:

Level demolition site with bad ground conditions but above water table. Unrestricted working space and access. Contaminated ground, approximately 400 mm excavate and removed. All excavated material removed to licensed tip.

Market conditions:

Generally competitive overall but not keen. Lowest tender not accepted due to unacceptable qualification.

Project tender price index   106 (base: 1985 BCIS Index Base)

	Competitive Tender List
Tender documentation:	Bill of Quantities
Selection of contractor:	Selected competition
Number of tenders:	
issued	6
received	6

£989,000 *
£1,167,043
£1,592,203
£1,901,202
£2,118,457

| Type of contract: | JCT private contract 1980 edition |
| Cost fluctuations: | Firm |

Contract period	
stipulated by client	9 months
offered by builder	9 months
agreed	9 months

ANALYSIS OF SINGLE BUILDING

Accommodation and design features:

2 storey office building with 2 self contained units on 2 floors with plant rooms in the roof voids. Concrete stanchion bases and ground slab.

Steel frame. Lightweight reinforced concrete upper floors on steel decking. Steel and timber roof with fibre cement slates. Facing brick/block cavity walls. Specialist curtain walls and external windows. Plasterboard ceilings and raised access floors. Air conditioning, electric installations, lightning protection.

Areas:

Basement floors	-
Ground floor	704 m^2
Upper floors	704 m^2
Gross floor area	1,408 m^2
Usable floor area	1,195 m^2
Circulation area	75 m^2
Ancillary area	74 m^2
Internal divisions	64 m^2
Gross floor area	1,408 m^2
Floor space not enclosed	3,872 m^3
Internal cube	835 m^2
Wall to floor ratio	0.59

Functional units

1,195 m^2 usable floor area

Percentage of gross floor area
2 storey construction 100%

Storey heights:
Average below ground floor   -
at ground floor   2.75 m
above ground floor   2.75 m

BRIEF COST INFORMATION

TOTAL CONTRACT

Measured work	845,192
Provisional sums	58,500
Prime cost sums	150,000
Preliminaries	100,101
Contingencies	13,250
Contract sum	£1,167,043

* Lowest tender not accepted, see MC text

being 9.5% of remainder of contract sums (less contingencies)

Element costs CI/SfB 320 Offices

Gross internal floor area: 1408 m² Date of tender: 10 September 1992

Element	Preliminaries shown separately		Element unit quantity	Element unit rate	Preliminaries apportioned	
	Total cost of element (£)	Cost per m² (£)			Total cost of element (£)	Cost per m² (£)
1 SUBSTRUCTURES	45,243	32.13	704 m²	64.27	49,541	35.19
2A Frame	45,366	32.22	1408 m²	32.22	49,676	35.28
2B Upper floors	22,629	16.07	704 m²	32.14	24,779	17.60
2C Roof	64,491	45.80	900 m²	71.66	70,618	50.15
2D Stairs	15,758	11.19			17,255	12.25
2E External walls	27,069	19.23	304 m²	89.04	29,641	21.05
2F Windows and external doors	172,555	122.55	531 m²	324.96	188,948	134.20
2G Internal walls and partitions	26,295	18.68			28,793	20.45
2H Internal doors	8,270	5.87	63 m²	131.27	9,056	6.43
SUPERSTRUCTURES	382,433	271.61			418,764	297.42
3A Wall finishes	18,930	13.44	904 m²	20.94	20,728	14.72
3B Floor finishes	64,650	45.92	1301 m²	49.69	70,792	50.28
3C Ceiling finishes	19,814	14.07	1380 m²	14.36	21,696	15.41
INTERNAL FINISHES	103,394	73.43			113,216	80.41
4A Fittings and furnishings	10,195	7.24			11,164	7.93
5A Sanitary appliances	8,110	5.76			8,880	6.31
5B Services equipment						
5C Disposal installations	5,477	3.89			5,997	4.26
5D Water installations	26,921	19.12	56 nr. draw off points	480.73	29,478	20.94

5E	Heat source				
5F	Space heating & air treatment	185,081	131.45	202,664	143.94
5G	Ventilating systems				
5H	Electrical installations	80,721	57.33	88,389	62.78
5I	Gas installations				
5J	Lift installations				
5K	Protective installations				
5L	Communications installations				
5M	Special installations				
5N	Builder's work in connection	14,432	10.25	15,803	11.22
5O	Builder's profit & attendance				
	SERVICES	320,742	227.80	351,212	249.44
	BUILDING SUB-TOTAL	862,007	612.22	943,898	670.38
6A	Site works	141,532	100.52	154,978	110.07
6B	Drainage	41,816	29.70	45,789	32.52
6C	External services	8,337	5.92	9,129	6.48
6D	Minor building works				
	EXTERNAL WORKS	191,685	136.14	209,895	149.07
7	Preliminaries	100,101	71.09		
	TOTAL (less contingencies)	1,153,793	819.46	1,153,793	819.46

CI/SfB: 320
Offices
September 1992

	Specification and design notes		Unit quantity	All-in unit rate	Cost (£)
1	SUBSTRUCTURES	Total			45,243
	Plain concrete Grade 25 in stanchion bases, and strip foundations Reinforced concrete Grade 30 in beds 150-300 mm thick		704 m²	64.27	
2A	Frame	Total			45,366
	Traditional steel frame, galvanised 'Z' roof purlins, beams for plant rooms in roof space Fire protective coating to first floor beams, fire protective casings to exposed columns				
2B	Upper floors	Total			22,629
	Lightweight concrete reinforced with fabric on proprietary ribbed steel decking. Reinforced in situ concrete floors to plant rooms Concrete casing to steel beams.				
2C	Roof	Total			64,491
	Artificial slates on battens on insulated metal decking over roof purlins to sloping roof.				
2D	Stairs	Total			15,758
	Main staircase of concrete with carpet finish to treads and risers, tubular steel open balustrades, PVC sheathed handrails.		2 Nr	4,253	8,506
	External escape stairs, galvanised steel spiral pattern.		2 Nr	3,626	7,252
2E	External walls	Total			27,069
	Decorative brick casing to steel columns forming piers between window bays.		107 m²	108.98	11,661
	Bricked face hollow walls up to window sill level to both floors.		197 m²	78.21	15,408

			Quantity	Rate	Total
2F	Windows and external doors	Total			172,555
	Colour coated aluminium framed curtain walling with top-hung opening lights, tinted sealed double glazing units.		507 m²	329.49	167,052
	Fire escape door, loading doors and pair of main entrance doors to each unit.		24 m²	229.29	5,503
2G	Internal walls and partitions	Total			26,295
	100 mm Blockwork division walls		162 m²	19.80	3,208
	200 mm Blockwork division walls		116 m²	30.12	3,494
	One-brick walls		123 m²	45.15	5,553
	Demountable partitions		112 m²	125.36	14,040
2H	Internal doors	Total			8,270
	Teak veneered flush doors, generally half or one-hour fire resistance, stained hardwood frames, linings and architraves		18 sgles	240	4,320
	Satin anodised aluminium ironmongery		10 dbles	395	3,950
3A	Wall finishes	Total			18,930
	Two-coat plaster to block walls		720 m²	14.20	10,224
	Ceramic tiles full height toilet areas and splashbacks in kitchens		184 m²	47.32	8,706
3B	Floor finishes	Total			64,650
	Office areas: Pedestal access floors, hardwood skirtings. Stain and matt finish to skirtings. Lay only carpet tiles (supplied by client).		1,040 m²	55.51	57,730
	Toilets and other areas: cement and sand screed, vinyl tiles and coved skirting.		261 m²	26.51	6,920
3C	Ceiling finishes	Total			19,814
	Plasterboard and skim coat on timber framing. Emulsion paint.		1,380 m²	14.36	

4A	Fittings and furnishings	**Total**			10,195
	Sundry fittings in entrance lobbies, including pinboards etc.				1,400
	Melamine faced chipboard vanitory tops in toilets				1,600
	Melamine faced chipboard duct cladding				795
	Grab rails etc. in disabled toilets				1,200
	Louvre blinds				5,200
5A	Sanitary appliances	**Total**			8,110
	Urinals		6 Nr	171	1,026
	Wash hand basins		14 Nr	171	2,394
	WC suites		14 Nr	190	2,660
	Cleaners' sinks		4 Nr	210	840
	Short connections to services)				
	PVC overflows. Sundries)				1,190
5C	Disposal installations	**Total**			5,477
	PVC waste pipes and soil and ventilation pipes				
5D	Water installations	**Total**			26,921
	Mains supply				
	Cold water service		56 draw off points		
	Hot water by electric water heaters			375.38	21,021
5E	Heat source	**Total**			
	Included in element 5F and 5D				
5F	Space heating & air treatment	**Total**			185,081
	Four-pipe fan coil comfort cooling system				
	Toilet extract ventilation				
5G	Ventilating systems	**Total**			
	Included in element 5F.				

5H	Electrical installations	**Total**	80,721
	Office and general lighting. Emergency and external lighting. Fire alarms. Office and general power supplies. Lightning protection.		
5N	Builder's work in connection	**Total**	14,432
	Normal builder's work in connection with service installations.		
6A	Site works	**Total**	141,532
	Macadam-surfaced car parking area. PCC block paving to pedestrian access. Landscaping.		
6B	Drainage	**Total**	41,816
	Soil and surface water drainage systems in plastic or glazed clay ware pipes and fittings; granular beds and surrounds. Precast concrete and brick manholes.		
6C	External services	**Total**	8,337
	Builder's work only for water and electrical services (no cost allowed for service connection/supplies by local utilities authorities). Builder's work for telephone and lightning protection.		
7	Preliminaries	**Total**	100,101
	9.5% of remainder of Contract Sum (exc. Contingencies).		

Proposed two-storey office block – ground floor plan

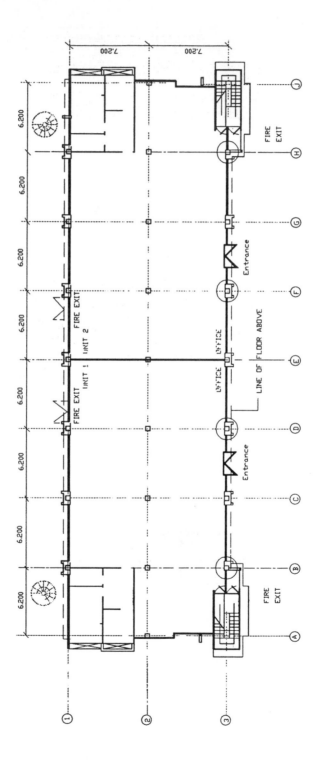

Proposed two-storey office block – elevations

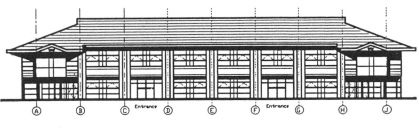

Front Elevation

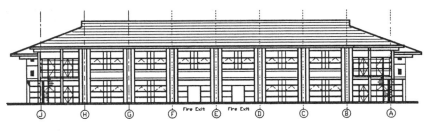

Rear Elevation

Side Elevation (handed)

Appendix B

Plans and Elevations for Proposed Office Block and Design Process Terminology

Proposed three-storey office block – ground floor plan

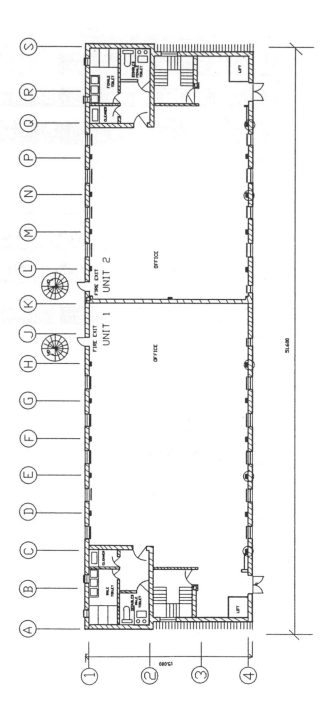

Proposed three-storey office block – elevations

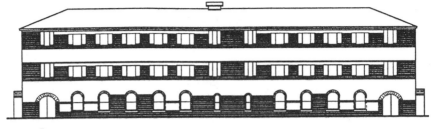

Front

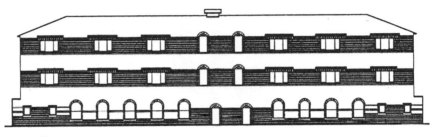

Rear

Side

Design process terminology

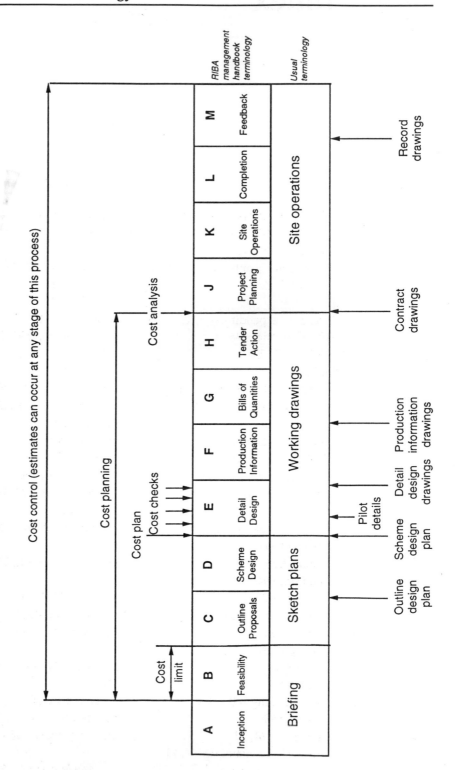

Index